Contents

REPAIRS & OVERHAUL

Advanced driving

Many people see the words 'advanced driving' and believe that it won't interest them or that it is a style of driving beyond their own abilities. Nothing could be further from the truth. Advanced driving is straightforward safe, sensible driving - the sort of driving we should all do every time we get behind the wheel.

An average of 10 people are killed every day on UK roads and 870 more are injured, some seriously. Lives are ruined daily, usually because somebody did something stupid. Something like 95% of all accidents are due to human error, mostly driver failure. Sometimes we make genuine mistakes - everyone does. Sometimes we have lapses of concentration. Sometimes we deliberately take risks.

For many people, the process of 'learning to drive' doesn't go much further than learning how to pass the driving test because of a common belief that good drivers are made by 'experience'.

Learning to drive by 'experience' teaches three driving skills:

☐ Quick reactions. (Whoops, that was close!)
☐ Good handling skills. (Horn, swerve, brake, horn).
☐ Reliance on vehicle technology. (Great stuff this ABS, stop in no distance even in the wet...)

Drivers whose skills are 'experience based' generally have a lot of near misses and the odd accident. The results can be seen every day in our courts and our hospital casualty departments.

Advanced drivers have learnt to control the risks by controlling the position and speed of their vehicle. They avoid accidents and near misses, even if the drivers around them make mistakes.

The key skills of advanced driving are **concentration,** effective all-round **observation, anticipation** and **planning.** When **good vehicle handling** is added to

these skills, all driving situations can be approached and negotiated in a safe, methodical way, leaving nothing to chance.

Concentration means applying your mind to safe driving, completely excluding anything that's not relevant. Driving is usually the most dangerous activity that most of us undertake in our daily routines. It deserves our full attention.

Observation means not just looking, but seeing and seeking out the information found in the driving environment.

Anticipation means asking yourself what is happening, what you can reasonably expect to happen and what could happen unexpectedly. (One of the commonest words used in compiling accident reports is 'suddenly'.)

Planning is the link between seeing something and taking the appropriate action. For many drivers, planning is the missing link.

If you want to become a safer and more skilful driver and you want to enjoy your driving more, contact the Institute of Advanced Motorists at www.iam.org.uk, phone 0208 996 9600, or write to IAM House, 510 Chiswick High Road, London W4 5RG for an information pack.

Working on your car can be dangerous. This page shows just some of the potential risks and hazards, with the aim of creating a safety-conscious attitude.

General hazards

Scalding

• Don't remove the radiator or expansion tank cap while the engine is hot.
• Engine oil, automatic transmission fluid or power steering fluid may also be dangerously hot if the engine has recently been running.

Burning

• Beware of burns from the exhaust system and from any part of the engine. Brake discs and drums can also be extremely hot immediately after use.

Crushing

• When working under or near a raters vehicle, always supplement the jack with axle stands, or use drive-on ramps. *Never venture under a car which is only supported by a jack.*

• Take care if loosening or tightening high-torque nuts when the vehicle is on stands. Initial loosening and final tightening should be done with the wheels on the ground.

Fire

• Fuel is highly flammable; fuel vapour is explosive.
• Don't let fuel spill onto a hot engine.
• Do not smoke or allow naked lights (including pilot lights) anywhere near a vehicle being worked on. Also beware of creating sparks (electrically or by use of tools).
• Fuel vapour is heavier than air, so don't work on the fuel system with the vehicle over an inspection pit.
• Another cause of fire is an electrical overload or short-circuit. Take care when repairing or modifying the vehicle wiring.
• Keep a fire extinguisher handy, of a type suitable for use on fuel and electrical fires.

Electric shock

• Ignition HT voltage can be dangerous, especially to people with heart problems or a pacemaker. Don't work on or near the ignition system with the engine running or the ignition switched on.

• Mains voltage is also dangerous. Make sure that any mains-operated equipment is correctly earthed. Mains power points should be protected by a residual current device (RCD) circuit breaker.

Fume or gas intoxication

• Exhaust fumes are poisonous; they often contain carbon monoxide, which is rapidly fatal if inhaled. Never run the engine in a confined space such as a garage with the doors shut.
• Fuel vapour is also poisonous, as are the vapours from some cleaning solvents and paint thinners.

Poisonous or irritant substances

• Avoid skin contact with battery acid and with any fuel, fluid or lubricant, especially antifreeze, brake hydraulic fluid and Diesel fuel. Don't syphon them by mouth. If such a substance is swallowed or gets into the eyes, seek medical advice.
• Prolonged contact with used engine oil can cause skin cancer. Wear gloves or use a barrier cream if necessary. Change out of oil-soaked clothes and do not keep oily rags in your pocket.
• Air conditioning refrigerant forms a poisonous gas if exposed to a naked flame (including a cigarette). It can also cause skin burns on contact.

Asbestos

• Asbestos dust can cause cancer if inhaled or swallowed. Asbestos may be found in gaskets and in brake and clutch linings. When dealing with such components it is safest to assume that they contain asbestos.

Special hazards

Hydrofluoric acid

• This extremely corrosive acid is formed when certain types of synthetic rubber, found in some O-rings, oil seals, fuel hoses etc, are exposed to temperatures above 400°C. The rubber changes into a charred or sticky substance containing the acid. *Once formed, the acid remains dangerous for years. If it gets onto the skin, it may be necessary to amputate the limb concerned.*
• When dealing with a vehicle which has suffered a fire, or with components salvaged from such a vehicle, wear protective gloves and discard them after use.

The battery

• Batteries contain sulphuric acid, which attacks clothing, eyes and skin. Take care when topping-up or carrying the battery.
• The hydrogen gas given off by the battery is highly explosive. Never cause a spark or allow a naked light nearby. Be careful when connecting and disconnecting battery chargers or jump leads.

Air bags

• Air bags can cause injury if they go off accidentally. Take care when removing the steering wheel and/or facia. Special storage instructions may apply.

Diesel injection equipment

• Diesel injection pumps supply fuel at very high pressure. Take care when working on the fuel injectors and fuel pipes.

⚠️ *Warning: Never expose the hands, face or any other part of the body to injector spray; the fuel can penetrate the skin with potentially fatal results.*

Remember...

DO

• Do use eye protection when using power tools, and when working under the vehicle.

• Do wear gloves or use barrier cream to protect your hands when necessary.

• Do get someone to check periodically that all is well when working alone on the vehicle.

• Do keep loose clothing and long hair well out of the way of moving mechanical parts.

• Do remove rings, wristwatch etc, before working on the vehicle – especially the electrical system.

• Do ensure that any lifting or jacking equipment has a safe working load rating adequate for the job.

DON'T

• Don't attempt to lift a heavy component which may be beyond your capability – get assistance.

• Don't rush to finish a job, or take unverified short cuts.

• Don't use ill-fitting tools which may slip and cause injury.

• Don't leave tools or parts lying around where someone can trip over them. Mop up oil and fuel spills at once.

• Don't allow children or pets to play in or near a vehicle being worked on.

Land Rover Freelander 1.8 litre 3-door Softback

The Land Rover Freelander was launched in the UK in October 1997. Available as a 3- or 5-door Softback or Hardback, as well as a 5-door Station Wagon, with a choice of 1.8 litre petrol or 2.0 litre direct injection diesel engines. Although fashionably styled, the Freelander has high ground clearance, permanent four-wheel-drive, power assisted steering, and fully independent suspension front and rear, making it a capable off-road performer, as well as exceeding current standards of on-road performance for this type of vehicle. Safety levels are further enhanced by features such as Hill Descent Control (HDC), Traction control, ABS, integral rollover cage (3-door), dual front airbags, and seatbelt pretensioners.

In June 2000, the Freelander underwent a 'facelift' which involved changes to the external and internal appearance of the vehicle. To coincide with the redesign, the existing L-Series diesel engine was replaced by the TD4 2.0 litre diesel engine of BMW origin, and an automatic transmission option (5-speed with Steptronic control) was available for the first time. ABS became standard fitment. All models are available with an immobiliser, alarm, remote central locking and air conditioning.

For the home mechanic, the Land Rover Freelander is a straightforward vehicle to maintain and most of the items requiring frequent attention are easily accessible.

Your Land Rover Freelander manual

The aim of this Manual is to help you get the best value from your vehicle. It can do so in several ways. It can help you decide what work must be done (even should you choose to get it done by a garage). It will also provide information on routine maintenance and servicing, and give a logical course of action and diagnosis when random faults occur. However, it is hoped that you will use the manual by tackling the work yourself. On simpler jobs it may even be quicker than booking the car into a garage and going there twice, to leave and collect it. Perhaps most important, a lot of money can be saved by avoiding the costs a garage must charge to cover its labour and overheads.

The manual has drawings and descriptions to show the function of the various components so that their layout can be understood. Tasks are described and photographed in a clear step-by-step sequence. The illustrations are numbered by the Section number and paragraph number to which they relate – if there is more than one illustration per paragraph, the sequence is denoted alphabetically.

References to the 'left' or 'right' of the vehicle are in the sense of a person in the driver's seat, facing forwards.

Acknowledgements

Thanks are due to Draper Tools, who provided some of the workshop tools, and to all those people at Sparkford who helped in the production of this manual.

We take great pride in the accuracy of information given in this manual, but vehicle manufacturers make alterations and design changes during the production run of a particular vehicle of which they do not inform us. No liability can be accepted by the authors or publishers for loss, damage or injury caused by any errors in, or omissions from, the information given.

Land Rover Freelander 2.0 litre 5-door Station Wagon

The following pages are intended to help in dealing with common roadside emergencies and breakdowns. You will find more detailed fault finding information at the back of the manual, and repair information in the main chapters.

If your car won't start and the starter motor doesn't turn

- ☐ If it's a model with automatic transmission, make sure the selector is in P or N.
- ☐ Open the bonnet and make sure that the battery terminals are clean and tight.
- ☐ Switch on the headlights and try to start the engine. If the headlights go very dim when you're trying to start, the battery is probably flat. Get out of trouble by jump starting (see next page) using a friend's car.

If your car won't start even though the starter motor turns as normal

- ☐ Is there fuel in the tank?
- ☐ Is there moisture on electrical components under the bonnet? Switch off the ignition, then wipe off any obvious dampness with a dry cloth. Spray a water-repellent aerosol product (WD-40 or equivalent) on ignition and fuel system electrical connectors like those shown in the photos. (Note that diesel engines don't usually suffer from damp).

A Check the condition and security of the battery connections

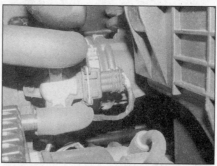

B Check the fuel injection system wiring is secure

C Check the ignition coil wiring is secure

D Check that the HT leads are securely connected to the spark plugs on petrol engines. To do this, remove the engine top cover, and spark plug cover first

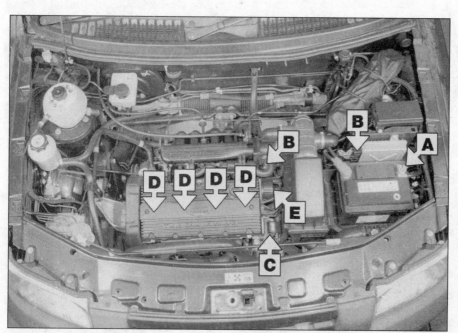

Check that electrical connections are secure (with the ignition switched off) and spray them with a water-dispersant spray like WD-40 if you suspect a problem due to damp

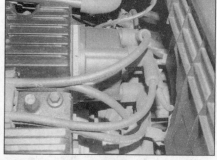

E Check that the HT leads are securely connected to the distributor cap on petrol models (where fitted)

Jump starting

When jump-starting a car using a booster battery, observe the following precautions:

✔ Before connecting the booster battery, make sure that the ignition is switched off.

✔ Ensure that all electrical equipment (lights, heater, wipers, etc) is switched off.

✔ Take note of any special precautions printed on the battery case.

✔ Make sure that the booster battery is the same voltage as the discharged one in the vehicle.

✔ If the battery is being jump-started from the battery in another vehicle, the two vehicles MUST NOT TOUCH each other.

✔ Make sure that the transmission is in neutral (or PARK, in the case of automatic transmission).

 HAYNES HiNT *Jump starting will get you out of trouble, but you must correct whatever made the battery go flat in the first place. There are three possibilities:*

1 The battery has been drained by repeated attempts to start, or by leaving the lights on.

2 The charging system is not working properly (alternator drivebelt slack or broken, alternator wiring fault or alternator itself faulty).

3 The battery itself is at fault (electrolyte low, or battery worn out).

1 Connect one end of the red jump lead to the positive (+) terminal of the flat battery

2 Connect the other end of the red lead to the positive (+) terminal of the booster battery.

3 Connect one end of the black jump lead to the negative (-) terminal of the booster battery

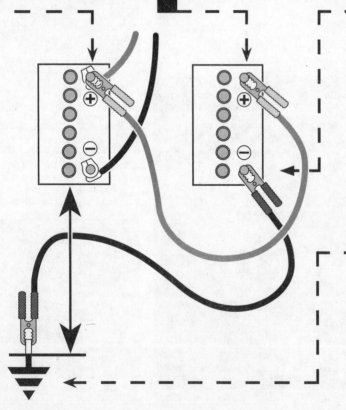

4 Connect the other end of the black jump lead to a bolt or bracket on the engine block, well away from the battery, on the vehicle to be started.

5 Make sure that the jump leads will not come into contact with the fan, drive-belts or other moving parts of the engine.

6 Start the engine using the booster battery and run it at idle speed. Switch on the lights, rear window demister and heater blower motor, then disconnect the jump leads in the reverse order of connection. Turn off the lights etc.

Wheel changing

⚠️ *Warning: Do not change a wheel in a situation where you risk being hit by other traffic. On busy roads, try to stop in a lay-by or a gateway. Be wary of passing traffic while changing the wheel – it is easy to become distracted by the job in hand.*

Preparation

- ☐ When a puncture occurs, stop as soon as it is safe to do so.
- ☐ Park on firm level ground, if possible, and well out of the way of other traffic.
- ☐ Use hazard warning lights if necessary.

- ☐ If you have one, use a warning triangle to alert other drivers of your presence.
- ☐ Apply the handbrake and engage first or reverse gear (or Park on models with automatic transmission).

- ☐ Chock the wheel diagonally opposite the one being removed using the chock provided in the tool kit.
- ☐ If the ground is soft, use a flat piece of wood to spread the load under the jack.

Changing the wheel

1 The spare wheel is fitted to a bracket on the rear door. The vehicle jack, wheel nut brace, and wheel chock are located in the left-hand rear corner of the engine compartment on models up to 2001 model year, and in the rear loadspace lockable stowage box.

2 Using the wheel nut brace, unscrew the retaining nuts and remove the spare wheel from the bracket. On models with alloy wheels, remove the locking wheel nut cover with the special tool provided.

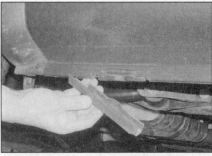

3 Use the flat wedge end of the wheel nut brace to prise off the appropriate jacking point cover.

4 Before raising the vehicle, prise off the wheel nut cover (where fitted), and use the wheel nut brace to slacken each of the wheel nuts half a turn.

5 Position the jack with the base directly under the jacking point. Turn the jack handle clockwise until the head of the jack fits snugly around the centre of the jacking point.

6 Turn the handle to raise the vehicle until the wheel is clear of the ground. If the tyre is flat make sure that the vehicle is raised sufficiently to allow the spare wheel to be fitted.

Finally . . .

- ☐ Remove the wheel chocks.
- ☐ Stow the jack and tools in the correct locations in the vehicle.
- ☐ Check the tyre pressure on the wheel just fitted. If it is low, or if you don't have a pressure gauge with you, drive slowly to the nearest garage and inflate the tyre to the correct pressure.
- ☐ Have the damaged tyre or wheel repaired as soon as possible.
- ☐ Have the wheel nuts tightened to the specified torque at the earliest opportunity.

7 Remove the nuts and lift the wheel from the vehicle. Place it beneath the sill as a precaution against the jack failing. Fit the spare wheel and tighten the nuts moderately with the wheel brace.

8 Lower the vehicle to the ground and tighten the wheel nuts in a diagonal sequence. Refit the jacking point trim, and wheel nut cover where fitted.

Identifying leaks

Puddles on the garage floor or drive, or obvious wetness under the bonnet or underneath the car, suggest a leak that needs investigating. It can sometimes be difficult to decide where the leak is coming from, especially if the engine bay is very dirty already. Leaking oil or fluid can also be blown rearwards by the passage of air under the car, giving a false impression of where the problem lies.

 Warning: Most automotive oils and fluids are poisonous. Wash them off skin, and change out of contaminated clothing, without delay.

 The smell of a fluid leaking from the car may provide a clue to what's leaking. Some fluids are distinctively coloured. It may help to clean the car carefully and to park it over some clean paper overnight as an aid to locating the source of the leak.
Remember that some leaks may only occur while the engine is running.

Sump oil

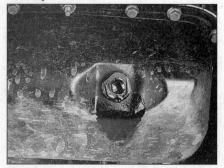

Engine oil may leak from the drain plug...

Oil from filter

...or from the base of the oil filter.

Gearbox oil

Gearbox oil can leak from the seals at the inboard ends of the driveshafts.

Antifreeze

Leaking antifreeze often leaves a crystalline deposit like this.

Brake fluid

A leak occurring at a wheel is almost certainly brake fluid.

Power steering fluid

Power steering fluid may leak from the pipe connectors on the steering rack.

Towing

When all else fails, you may find yourself having to get a tow home – or of course you may be helping somebody else. Long-distance recovery should only be done by a garage or breakdown service. For shorter distances, DIY towing using another vehicle is easy enough, but observe the following points:

☐ Lashing eyes are provided at the front and rear of the vehicle as a means of securing the vehicle onto a break-down truck.

☐ Towing eyes are provided front and rear.

Land Rover state that the front eye must only be used to tow the vehicle on all four wheels, and the rear eye as a means of towing another vehicle.

☐ The towing distance should not exceed 50 miles, and the towing speed should be limited to 30 mph.

☐ If it is necessary to tow the vehicle on two wheels (suspended from a recovery vehicle), then it is essential that the propshaft is completely removed (see Chapter 8)..

Front towing eye

Introduction

There are some very simple checks which need only take a few minutes to carry out, but which could save you a lot of inconvenience and expense.

These *Weekly checks* require no great skill or special tools, and the small amount of time they take to perform could prove to be very well spent, for example:

☐ Keeping an eye on tyre condition and pressures, will not only help to stop them wearing out prematurely, but could also save your life.

☐ Many breakdowns are caused by electrical problems. Battery-related faults are particularly common, and a quick check on a regular basis will often prevent the majority of these.

☐ If your vehicle develops a brake fluid leak, the first time you might know about it is when your brakes don't work properly. Checking the level regularly will give advance warning of this kind of problem.

☐ If the oil or coolant levels run low, the cost of repairing any engine damage will be far greater than fixing the leak, for example.

Underbonnet check points

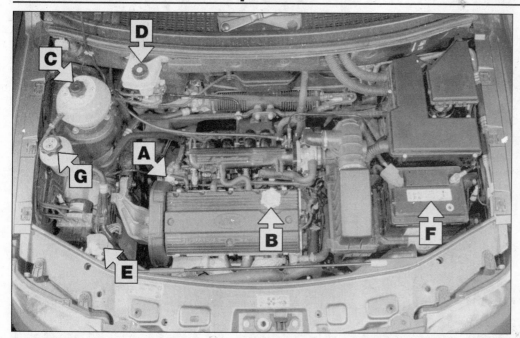

◀ **1.8 litre petrol**

A *Engine oil level dipstick*

B *Engine oil filler cap*

C *Coolant expansion tank*

D *Brake fluid reservoir*

E *Screen washer fluid reservoir*

F *Battery*

G *Power steering fluid reservoir*

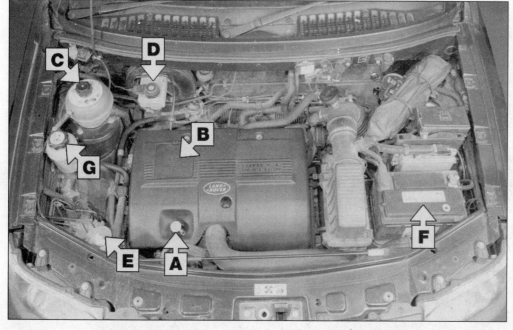

◀ **2.0 litre L-Series diesel**

A *Engine oil level dipstick*

B *Engine oil filler cap*

C *Coolant expansion tank*

D *Brake fluid reservoir*

E *Screen washer fluid reservoir*

F *Battery*

G *Power steering fluid reservoir*

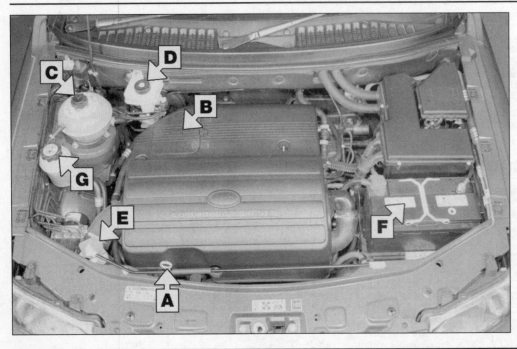

A *Engine oil level dipstick*
B *Engine oil filler cap*
C *Coolant expansion tank*
D *Brake fluid reservoir*
E *Screen washer fluid reservoir*
F *Battery*
G *Power steering fluid reservoir*

Engine oil level

Before you start

✔ Make sure that the vehicle is on level ground.
✔ Check the oil level before the vehicle is driven, or at least 5 minutes after the engine has been switched off.

HAYNES HiNT *If the oil is checked immediately after driving the vehicle, some of the oil will remain in the upper engine components, resulting in an inaccurate reading on the dipstick.*

The correct oil

Modern engines place great demands on their oil. It is very important that the correct oil for your vehicle is used (see *Lubricants and fluids*).

Vehicle care

● If you have to add oil frequently, you should check whether you have any oil leaks. Place some clean paper under the vehicle overnight, and check for stains in the morning. If there are no leaks, then the engine may be burning oil.
● Always maintain the level between the upper and lower dipstick marks (see photo 3). If the level is too low, severe engine damage may occur. Oil seal failure may result if the engine is overfilled by adding too much oil.

1 The dipstick is located on the right-hand rear of the engine on 1.8 litre petrol models. On all diesel models it is located on the right-hand front of the engine. It is brightly coloured for ease of location. See *Underbonnet check points* for the exact location of the dipstick.

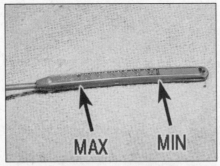
3 Note the oil level on the end of the dipstick, which should be between the upper MAX mark and the lower MIN mark. Approximately 1.0 litre of oil will raise the level from the lower mark to the upper mark.

2 Withdraw the dipstick. Using a clean rag or paper towel, wipe all the oil from the dipstick. Insert the clean dipstick into the tube as far as it will go, then withdraw it again.

4 Oil is added through the filler cap on top of the engine. Rotate the cap through a quarter-turn anti-clockwise and withdraw it. Top-up the level. A funnel may help to reduce spillage. Add the oil slowly, checking the level on the dipstick often. Do not overfill.

Coolant level

Vehicle Care

● With a sealed-type cooling system, adding coolant should not be necessary on a regular basis. If frequent topping-up is required, it is likely there is a leak. Check the radiator, all hoses and joint faces for signs of staining or wetness, and rectify as necessary.

● It is important that antifreeze is used in the cooling system all year round, not just during the winter months. Don't top up with water alone, as the antifreeze will become diluted.

1 The coolant level varies with the temperature of the engine. When the engine is cold, the coolant level should be on the MAX mark on the side of the expansion tank located in the right-hand rear corner of the engine compartment. When the engine is hot, the level will rise slightly.

2 If topping-up is necessary, wait until the engine is cold, then slowly unscrew the expansion tank filler cap anti-clockwise, to release any pressure in the system, and remove it.

3 Add a mixture of water and antifreeze through the expansion tank filler neck, until the coolant is up to the MAX level mark. Refit the cap, turning it clockwise as far as it will go until it is secure.

Brake fluid level

Before you start

✔ Make sure that the vehicle is on level ground.
✔ Cleanliness is of great importance when dealing with the braking system, so take care to clean around the reservoir cap before topping-up. Use only clean brake fluid.
✔ The fluid level in the reservoir will drop slightly as the brake pads wear down, but the fluid level must never be allowed to drop below the MIN mark.

Safety first!

● If the reservoir requires repeated topping-up, this is an indication of a fluid leak somewhere in the system, which should be investigated immediately.

● If a leak is suspected, the vehicle should not be driven until the braking system has been checked. Never take any risks where brakes are concerned.

1 The brake master cylinder and fluid reservoir are mounted on the vacuum servo unit in the engine compartment on the right-hand side of the bulkhead. The MAX and MIN level marks are indicated on the side of the reservoir and the fluid level should be maintained between these marks at all times.

2 If topping-up is necessary, wipe the area around the filler cap with a clean rag before removing the cap. It's a good idea to inspect the reservoir. The fluid should be changed if dirt is visible.

3 Carefully add fluid, avoiding spilling it on surrounding paintwork. Use only the specified hydraulic fluid; mixing different types of fluid can cause damage to the system and/or a loss of braking effectiveness. After filling to the correct level, refit the cap securely. Wipe off any spilt fluid.

Tyre condition and pressure

 Warning: Land Rover state that if new tyres are to be fitted, ensure they are fitted to the rear axle only or both front and rear axles. New tyres should not be fitted to the front axle only.

It is very important that tyres are in good condition, and at the correct pressure - having a tyre failure at any speed is highly dangerous. Tyre wear is influenced by driving style - harsh braking and acceleration, or fast cornering, will all produce more rapid tyre wear. As a general rule, the front tyres wear out faster than the rears. Interchanging the tyres from front to rear ("rotating" the tyres) may result in more even wear. However, if this is completely effective, you may have the expense of replacing all four tyres at once!

Remove any nails or stones embedded in the tread before they penetrate the tyre to cause deflation. If removal of a nail does reveal that the tyre has been punctured, refit the nail so that its point of penetration is marked. Then immediately change the wheel, and have the tyre repaired by a tyre dealer.

Regularly check the tyres for damage in the form of cuts or bulges, especially in the sidewalls. Periodically remove the wheels, and clean any dirt or mud from the inside and outside surfaces. Examine the wheel rims for signs of rusting, corrosion or other damage. Light alloy wheels are easily damaged by "kerbing" whilst parking; steel wheels may also become dented or buckled. A new wheel is very often the only way to overcome severe damage.

New tyres should be balanced when they are fitted, but it may become necessary to re-balance them as they wear, or if the balance weights fitted to the wheel rim should fall off. Unbalanced tyres will wear more quickly, as will the steering and suspension components. Wheel imbalance is normally signified by vibration, particularly at a certain speed (typically around 50 mph). If this vibration is felt only through the steering, then it is likely that just the front wheels need balancing. If, however, the vibration is felt through the whole car, the rear wheels could be out of balance. Wheel balancing should be carried out by a tyre dealer or garage.

1 Tread Depth - visual check
The original tyres have tread wear safety bands (B), which will appear when the tread depth reaches approximately 1.6 mm. The band positions are indicated by a triangular mark on the tyre sidewall (A).

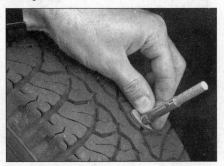

2 Tread Depth - manual check
Alternatively, tread wear can be monitored with a simple, inexpensive device known as a tread depth indicator gauge.

3 Tyre Pressure Check
Check the tyre pressures regularly with the tyres cold. Do not adjust the tyre pressures immediately after the vehicle has been used, or an inaccurate setting will result.

Tyre tread wear patterns

Shoulder Wear

Underinflation (wear on both sides)
Under-inflation will cause overheating of the tyre, because the tyre will flex too much, and the tread will not sit correctly on the road surface. This will cause a loss of grip and excessive wear, not to mention the danger of sudden tyre failure due to heat build-up.
Check and adjust pressures
Incorrect wheel camber (wear on one side)
Repair or renew suspension parts
Hard cornering
Reduce speed!

Centre Wear

Overinflation
Over-inflation will cause rapid wear of the centre part of the tyre tread, coupled with reduced grip, harsher ride, and the danger of shock damage occurring in the tyre casing.
Check and adjust pressures

If you sometimes have to inflate your car's tyres to the higher pressures specified for maximum load or sustained high speed, don't forget to reduce the pressures to normal afterwards.

Uneven Wear

Front tyres may wear unevenly as a result of wheel misalignment. Most tyre dealers and garages can check and adjust the wheel alignment (or "tracking") for a modest charge.
Incorrect camber or castor
Repair or renew suspension parts
Malfunctioning suspension
Repair or renew suspension parts
Unbalanced wheel
Balance tyres
Incorrect toe setting
Adjust front wheel alignment
Note: *The feathered edge of the tread which typifies toe wear is best checked by feel.*

Screen washer fluid level

● Screenwash additives not only keep the windscreen clean during bad weather, they also prevent the washer system freezing in cold weather – which is when you are likely to need it most. Don't top-up using plain water, as the screenwash will become diluted, and will freeze in cold weather.

⚠ **Warning: On no account use engine coolant antifreeze in the screen washer system – this may damage the paintwork.**

1 The reservoir for the windscreen and rear window (where applicable) washer systems is located in the front right-hand corner of the engine compartment. If topping up is necessary, open the cap.

2 When topping-up the reservoir a screenwash additive should be added in the quantities recommended on the bottle.

Battery

Caution: Before carrying out any work on the vehicle battery, read the precautions given in 'Safety first!' at the start of this manual.

✔ Make sure that the battery tray is in good condition, and that the clamp is tight. Corrosion on the tray, retaining clamp and the battery itself can be removed with a solution of water and baking soda. Thoroughly rinse all cleaned areas with water. Any metal parts damaged by corrosion should be covered with a zinc-based primer, then painted.
✔ Periodically (approximately every three months), check the charge condition of the battery as described in Chapter 5A.
✔ If the battery is flat, and you need to jump start your vehicle, see *Roadside Repairs*.

1 The battery is located on the front left-hand side of the engine compartment. The exterior of the battery should be inspected periodically for damage such as a cracked case or cover.

2 Check the tightness of the battery cable clamps to ensure good electrical connections. You should not be able to move them. Also check each cable for cracks and frayed conductors.

HAYNES HINT

Battery corrosion can be kept to a minimum by applying a layer of petroleum jelly to the clamps and terminals after they are reconnected.

3 If corrosion (white, fluffy deposits) is evident, remove the cables from the battery terminals, clean them with a small wire brush, then refit them. Automotive stores sell a tool for cleaning the battery post . . .

4 . . . as well as the battery cable clamps.

Electrical systems

✔ Check all external lights and the horn. Refer to the appropriate Sections of Chapter 12 for details if any of the circuits are found to be inoperative.

✔ Visually check all accessible wiring connectors, harnesses and retaining clips for security, and for signs of chafing or damage.

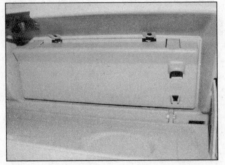

1 If a single indicator light, brake light or headlight has failed, it is likely that a bulb has blown and will need to be renewed. Refer to Chapter 12 for details. If both brake lights have failed, it is possible that the stop-light switch operated by the brake pedal has failed. Refer to Chapter 9 for details.

2 If more than one indicator light or headlight has failed, it is likely that either a fuse has blown or that there is a fault in the circuit (see Chapter 12). The main fusebox is located behind the driver's storage compartment located in the facia beneath the steering wheel. To access the fusebox located beneath the steering wheel, first open the storage compartment then depress the two catches and remove the fusebox cover.

3 To renew a blown fuse, pull it out directly from the fusebox. Fit a new fuse of the same rating, available from car accessory shops. It is important that you find the reason that the fuse blew (see Electrical fault finding in Chapter 12).

Note: *A further fusebox is located in the rear left-hand corner of the engine compartment for engine related fuses. On models with ABS and/or diesel engine models, additional fuses for the ABS and glow plugs are located on the left-hand side of the engine compartment.*

Wiper blades

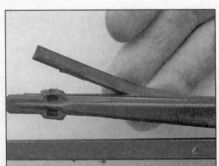

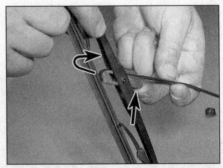

1 Check the condition of the wiper blades. If they are cracked or show any signs of deterioration, or if the glass swept area is smeared, renew them. For maximum clarity of vision, wiper blades should be renewed annually, as a matter of course.

2 To remove a wiper blade, pull the arm fully away from the glass until it locks. Swivel the blade through 90°, then depress the locking tab with a screwdriver or your fingers. Slide the wiper blade out of the hooked end of the arm, then feed the arm through the hole in the blade. When fitting the new blade, make sure that the blade locks securely into the arm, and that the blade is orientated correctly.

Lubricants and fluids

Engine

Petrol . . . . 10W/40 Multigrade engine oil to specification ACEA A2

Diesel . . . . 10W/40 or 15W/40 Multigrade engine oil to specification ACEA A3 and ACEA B3

Cooling system

Models up to June 2000 model year . . . . Antifreeze to specification BS 6580 and BS 5117. Ethylene-glycol based with non-phosphate corrosion inhibitors, containing no methanol. Mixture 50% by volume

Models June 2000-on . . . . Ethylene-glycol based antifreeze, containing no methanol with only Organic Acid Technology (OAT) corrosion inhibitors

Gearbox

Manual gearbox . . . . Texaco MTF 94 or Burmah oil MTF 1067. For topping-up **only** use 10W/40 oil to specification ACEA A2

Automatic transmission . . . . Texaco N402

Intermediate reduction drive unit . . . . Texaco S5 75W/90 to specification API GL5

Final drive . . . . Texaco Multigear 80W/90 ETL 7441 to specification API GL5

Braking system . . . . Hydraulic fluid to DOT 4

Power steering system . . . . For topping-up, use automatic transmission fluid (ATF) to Dexron IID or III specification

General greasing . . . . Multi-purpose lithium-based grease to NLGI consistency No 2

Tyre pressures (cold) – bar (psi)

Note: *Pressures apply to original-equipment tyres, and may vary if any other make or type of tyre is fitted; check with the tyre manufacturer or supplier for correct pressures if necessary.*

	Front	Rear
All models up to 2001 model year	1.8 (26)	1.8 (26)
All models 2001-on:		
Up to 4 passengers and luggage	1.8 (26)	1.8 (26)
Full load & towing	2.1 (30)	2.1 (30)

Chapter 1 Part A:
Routine maintenance and servicing – petrol models

Contents

Degrees of difficulty

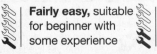

Easy, suitable for novice with little experience	**Fairly easy,** suitable for beginner with some experience	**Fairly difficult,** suitable for competent DIY mechanic	**Difficult,** suitable for experienced DIY mechanic	**Very difficult,** suitable for expert DIY or professional

Lubricants and fluids. . . . .   Refer to *Weekly checks* on page 0•17

Capacities

Engine oil
Including oil filter*. . . . . 4.5 litres
Difference between MIN and MAX on dipstick (approximate) . . . . 1.0 litre
*Capacities shown are for refilling after draining, if the engine is being filled from dry add a further 0.3 litre

Cooling system
Including reservoir . . . . 5.5 litres
Gearbox* . . . . 2.0 litres
*Capacity shown is for refilling after draining, if the gearbox is being filled from dry add a further 0.2 litre

Intermediate reduction drive unit . . . . 1.1 litres

Final drive . . . . 0.83 litres

Washer fluid reservoir . . . . 4.0 litres

Fuel tank . . . . 59 litres

Power steering system . . . . 0.34 litres

Engine
Alternator drivebelt deflection :
    All models not fitted with air conditioning (10 kg force) . . . . 6 to 8 mm
    Up to 2001 model year with air conditioning (10 kg force). . . . . 9 to 10 mm
    From 2001 model year with air conditioning . . . . Automatic

Cooling system
Antifreeze mixture:
    50% antifreeze . . . . Protection down to -37°C
    55% antifreeze . . . . Protection down to -45°C
Note: *Refer to antifreeze manufacturer for latest recommendations.*

Ignition system
Spark plugs:
    Type . . . . Unipart GSP 66527
    Electrode gap* . . . . 1.0 mm ± 0.05 mm
* The spark plug gap quoted is that recommended by Land Rover for their specified plug listed above. If spark plugs of any other type are to be fitted, refer to their manufacturer's recommendations.

Brakes
Friction material minimum thickness:
    Front brake pads . . . . 3.0 mm
    Rear brake shoes . . . . 2.0 mm

Torque wrench settings

Torque wrench settings	Nm	lbf ft
Alternator bolts.	25	18
Auxiliary drivebelt tensioner retaining bolt	25	18
Engine sump drain plug	28	21
Final drive oil plug	27	20
Ignition coil screws.	8	6
Intermediate reduction drive unit oil filler/level plug.	35	26
Manual gearbox drain plug.	35	26
Manual gearbox oil filler/level plug.	35	26
Roadwheel nuts	115	85
Spark plugs	27	20

Maintenance schedule

The maintenance intervals in this manual are provided with the assumption that you, not the dealer, will be carrying out the work. These are the minimum maintenance intervals recommended by us for vehicles driven daily. If you wish to keep your vehicle in peak condition at all times, you may wish to perform some of these procedures more often. We encourage frequent maintenance, because it enhances the efficiency, performance and resale value of your vehicle.

If the vehicle is driven in dusty areas, used

to tow a trailer, or driven frequently at slow speeds (idling in traffic) or on short journeys, more frequent maintenance intervals are recommended.

When the vehicle is new, it should be serviced by a dealer service department (or other workshop recognised by the vehicle manufacturer as providing the same standard of service) in order to preserve the warranty. The vehicle manufacturer may reject warranty claims if you are unable to prove that servicing has been carried out as and when specified, using only original equipment parts or parts certified to be of equivalent quality.

Every 250 miles (400 km) or weekly

☐ Refer to Weekly Checks

Every 6000 miles or 6 months, whichever comes first

☐ Renew the engine oil and filter (Section 3)

Note: *Land Rover recommend that the engine oil and filter are changed every 12 000 miles or 12 months. However, oil and filter changes are good for the engine and we recommend that the oil and filter are renewed more frequently, especially if the vehicle is used on a lot of short journeys.*

Every 12 000 miles or 12 months, whichever comes first

☐ Check the body and underbody for corrosion protection (Section 4)
☐ Check the power steering fluid level (Section 5)
☐ Check the manual gearbox oil level (Section 6)
☐ Check all components, pipes and hoses for fluid leaks (Section 7)
☐ Check the intermediate reduction drive unit oil level (Section 9)
☐ Check the final drive oil level (Section 8)
☐ Check the condition and tension of the auxiliary drivebelts (Section 10)
☐ Check the condition of the exhaust system and heat shields (Section 11)
☐ Check the front brake pads and discs for wear (Section 12)
☐ Check the brake pipes and hoses (Section 13)
☐ Check the steering and suspension components for condition and security (Section 14)
☐ Remove the roadwheels, and apply anti-seize compound (Section 15)
☐ Check the condition of the driveshafts and gaiters (Section 16)
☐ Check the operation and adjustment of the handbrake (Section 17)
☐ Lubricate all door locks and hinges, door stops, bonnet lock and release, and tailgate lock and hinges (Section 18)
☐ Check the operation of all electrical systems (Section 19)
☐ Check the seat belts and airbag (Section 20)
☐ Exhaust emission test (Section 21)
☐ Check the roadwheel speed sensor electrical harness – ABS models (Section 22)
☐ Renew the pollen filter (Section 23)
☐ Carry out a road test (Section 24)

Every 24 000 miles or 2 years, whichever comes first

☐ Renew the air filter element (Section 25)
☐ Check the rear brake shoes and drums for wear (Section 26)
☐ Check the front brake calipers and rear wheel cylinders (Section 27)
☐ Renew the handset batteries (Section 28)

Every 36 000 miles or 3 years, whichever comes first

☐ Renew the coolant/antifreeze (Section 29)
☐ Renew the brake fluid (Section 30)

Every 72 000 miles or 6 years, whichever comes first

☐ Renew the spark plugs and check the ignition system components (Section 31)
☐ Renew the timing belt (Section 32)

Every 96 000 miles or 8 years, whichever comes first

☐ Renew the auxiliary drivebelt (Section 33)

Every 120 000 miles

☐ Renew the fuel filter element (Section 34)

Every 10 years, regardless of mileage

☐ Renew the airbag module – vehicles up to 2002 model year (Section 35)
☐ Renew the seat belt pretensioners – vehicles up to 2002 model year (Section 36)

Every 15 years, regardless of mileage

☐ Renew the airbag module – 2002 model year-on (Section 35)
☐ Renew the seat belt pretensioners – 2002 model year-on (Section 36)

Underbonnet view of a pre-2001 model year model

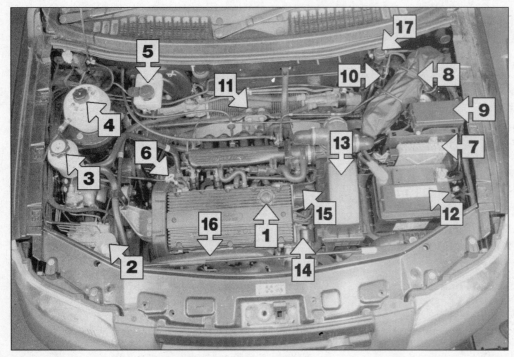

1 Engine oil filler cap
2 Washer fluid reservoir
3 Power steering fluid reservoir
4 Cooling system expansion tank
5 Brake fluid reservoir
6 Engine oil level dipstick
7 Engine management ECM
8 Toolkit/vehicle jack
9 Engine compartment fusebox
10 Charcoal canister (fuel evaporative system)
11 Steering rack
12 Battery
13 Air cleaner
14 Ignition coil
15 Distributor
16 Radiator top hose
17 Inertia fuel cut-off switch

Under bonnet view of a post-2001 model year model

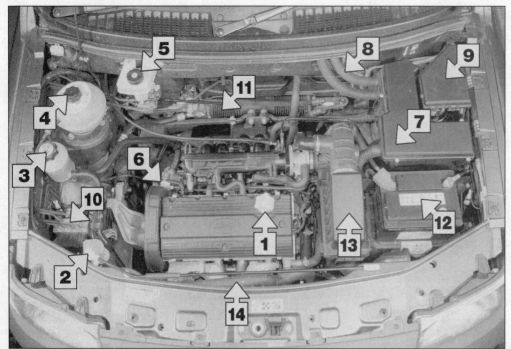

1 Engine oil filler cap
2 Washer fluid reservoir
3 Power steering fluid reservoir
4 Cooling system expansion tank
5 Brake fluid reservoir
6 Engine oil level dipstick
7 Engine management ECM
8 ECM compartment cooling hoses
9 Engine compartment fusebox
10 ABS unit
11 Steering rack
12 Battery
13 Air cleaner
14 Radiator top hose

Front underbody view

1 Driveshaft
2 Front suspension lower arm
3 Front anti-roll bar
4 Propshaft
5 Exhaust system flexible joint
6 Front brake caliper
7 Gearchange rod
8 Intermediate reduction drive unit
9 Manual transmission
10 Engine oil sump drain plug
11 Oil filter
12 Radiator bottom hose
13 Exhaust system front downpipe

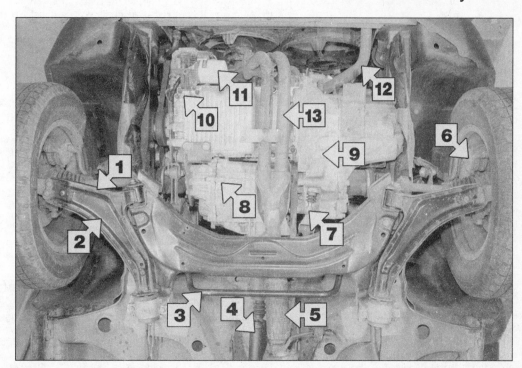

Rear underbody view

1 Transverse link
2 Driveshaft
3 Trailing link
4 Handbrake cables
5 Charcoal canister (fuel evaporative system) – post-2001 model year only
6 Fuel tank
7 Propshaft
8 Final drive unit
9 Exhaust pipe
10 Fuel filler hose
11 Rear silencer box

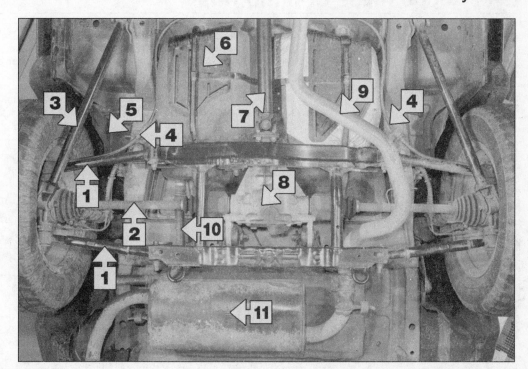

1 General information

This Chapter is designed to help the home mechanic maintain his/her vehicle for safety, economy, long life and peak performance.

The Chapter contains a master maintenance schedule, followed by Sections dealing specifically with each task in the schedule. Visual checks, adjustments, component renewal and other helpful items are included. Refer to the accompanying illustrations of the engine compartment and the underside of the vehicle for the locations of various components.

Servicing your vehicle in accordance with the mileage/time maintenance schedule and the following Sections will provide a planned maintenance programme, which should result in a long and reliable service life. This is a comprehensive plan, so maintaining some items but not others at the specified service intervals will not produce the same results.

As you service your vehicle, you will discover that many of the procedures can – and should – be grouped together, because of the particular procedure being performed, or because of the proximity of two otherwise-unrelated components to one another. For example, if the vehicle is raised for any reason, the exhaust can be inspected at the same time as the suspension and steering components.

The first step in this maintenance programme is to prepare yourself before the actual work begins. Read through all the Sections relevant to the work to be carried out, then make a list and gather all the parts and tools required. If a problem is encountered, seek advice from a parts specialist, or a dealer service department.

2 Regular maintenance

If, from the time the vehicle is new, the routine maintenance schedule is followed closely, and frequent checks are made of fluid levels and high-wear items, as suggested throughout this manual, the engine will be kept in relatively good running condition, and the need for additional work will be minimised.

It is possible that there will be times when the engine is running poorly due to the lack of regular maintenance. This is even more likely if a used vehicle, which has not received regular and frequent maintenance checks, is purchased. In such cases, additional work may need to be carried out, outside of the regular maintenance intervals.

If engine wear is suspected, a compression test (refer to Chapter 2A) will provide valuable information regarding the overall performance of the main internal components. Such a test can be used as a basis to decide on the extent of the work to be carried out. If, for example,

a compression test indicates serious internal engine wear, conventional maintenance as described in this Chapter will not greatly improve the performance of the engine, and may prove a waste of time and money, unless extensive overhaul work is carried out first.

The following series of operations are those most often required to improve the performance of a generally poor-running engine:

Primary operations

a) Clean, inspect and test the battery (refer to 'Weekly checks').
b) Check all the engine-related fluids (refer to 'Weekly checks').
c) Check the condition and tension of the auxiliary drivebelts (Section 10).
d) Renew the spark plugs (Section 31).
e) Check the condition of the air filter, and renew if necessary (Section 25).
f) Check the condition of all hoses, and check for fluid leaks (Section 7).

If the above operations do not prove fully effective, carry out the following secondary operations:

Secondary operations

All items listed under Primary operations, plus the following:

a) Check the charging system (refer to Chapter 5A).
b) Check the ignition system (refer to Chapter 5B).
c) Check the fuel system (refer to Chapter 4A).

Every 6000 miles or 6 months

3 Engine oil and filter renewal

Note: To avoid any possibility of scalding, and to protect yourself from possible skin irritants and other harmful contaminants in used engine oils, it is advisable to wear gloves when carrying out this work.

1 Frequent oil and filter changes are the most important preventative maintenance

3.4 Slacken the sump drain plug

procedures which can be undertaken by the DIY owner. As engine oil ages, it becomes diluted and contaminated, which leads to premature engine wear.

2 Before starting this procedure, gather together all the necessary tools and materials. Also make sure that you have plenty of clean rags and newspapers handy, to mop-up any spills. Ideally, the engine oil should be warm, as it will drain more easily, and more built-up sludge will be removed with it.

Caution: Take care not to touch the exhaust or any other hot parts of the engine when working under the vehicle.

3 Firmly apply the handbrake then jack up the front of the vehicle and support it on axle stands (see Jacking and vehicle support). Release the retaining screws and remove the engine undertray.

4 Using a spanner or a suitable socket and bar, slacken the drain plug about half a turn **(see illustration)**. Position the draining container under the drain plug, then remove the plug completely **(see Haynes Hint)**.

5 Allow some time for the oil to drain, noting that it may be necessary to reposition the container as the oil flow slows to a trickle.

6 After all the oil has drained, wipe the drain

plug with a clean rag and discard the sealing washer. Clean the area around the drain plug opening, and refit the plug complete with a new washer and tighten it to the specified torque.

7 Move the container into position under the oil filter on the front side of the cylinder block.

8 Use an oil filter removal tool to slacken the filter initially, then unscrew it by hand the rest

HAYNES HINT

As the drain plug threads release, move it sharply away so the stream of oil issuing from the sump runs into the container, not up your sleeve.

of the way **(see illustration)**. Empty the oil from the old filter into the container.

9 Use a clean rag to remove all oil, dirt and sludge from the filter sealing area on the engine.

10 Apply a light coating of clean engine oil to the sealing ring on the new filter, then screw the filter into position. Screw the filter on until its sealing ring contacts the filter housing then tighten firmly through another half-a-turn by hand only – **do not** use any tools.

11 Remove the old oil and all tools from under the vehicle, refit the engine undertray, then lower the vehicle to the ground.

12 Fill the engine through the filler hole, using the correct grade and type of oil (refer to *Weekly Checks* for details of topping-up). Pour in half the specified quantity of oil first, then wait a few minutes for the oil to drain into the sump. Continue to add oil, a small quantity at a time, until the level is up to the lower mark on the dipstick. Adding approximately a further 1.0 litre will bring the level up to the upper mark on the dipstick **(see illustration)**.

3.8 If necessary, use an oil filter removal tool to slacken the filter

13 Start the engine and run it for a few minutes, while checking for leaks around the oil filter seal and the sump drain plug. Note that there may be a delay of a few seconds before the low oil pressure warning light goes out when the engine is first started, as the oil circulates through the new oil filter and the engine oil galleries before the pressure builds-up.

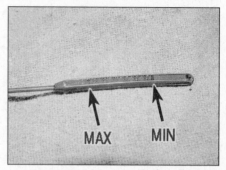

3.12 Oil level dipstick minimum and maximum markings

14 Stop the engine, and wait a few minutes for the oil to settle in the sump once more. With the new oil circulated and the filter now completely full, recheck the level on the dipstick, and add more oil as necessary.

15 Dispose of the used engine oil safely with reference to *General repair procedures*.

Every 12 000 miles or 12 months

4 Body corrosion check

This work should be carried out by a Land Rover dealer in order to validate the vehicle warranty. The work includes a thorough inspection of the vehicle paintwork and underbody for damage and corrosion. **Note:** *This is only applicable to vehicles sold after 24th November 1998.*

5 Power steering fluid level check

1 Park the vehicle on level ground and set the steering wheel straight-ahead. The engine should be turned off.

 HAYNES HINT *For the check to be accurate, the steering must not be turned once the engine has been stopped.*

2 The power steering fluid reservoir is located in the front right-hand corner of the engine compartment. UPPER and LOWER level marks are moulded into the translucent wall of the reservoir. The fluid level should be checked with the engine cold and stopped **(see illustration)**.

3 Check that the fluid is on the upper level mark in the translucent reservoir. Where topping-up is necessary, first wipe clean the area around the filler cap **(see illustration)**.

4 Remove the cap then top-up the fluid level using the specified type of fluid (do not overfill the reservoir). On completion refit the filler cap **(see illustration)**.

6 Manual gearbox oil level check

1 Position the vehicle over an inspection pit, on vehicle ramps, or jack it up, but make sure that it is level (see *Jacking and vehicle support*). Release the retaining screws and remove the engine/transmission undertray. The oil level must be

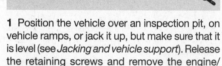

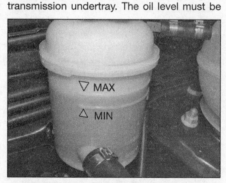

5.2 Power steering fluid reservoir

5.4 Top-up the power steering fluid

checked before the vehicle is driven, or at least 5 minutes after the engine has been switched off. If the oil is checked immediately after driving the vehicle, some of the oil will remain distributed around the gearbox components, resulting in an inaccurate level reading.

2 Remove all traces of dirt from around the filler/level plug located on the left-hand side of the gearbox, where it is situated behind the driveshaft inner joint **(see illustration)**.

5.3 Wipe the reservoir clean

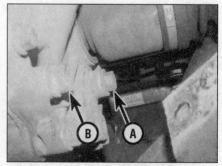

6.2 Gearbox oil filler/level plug (A) and drain plug (B)

6.4 Top-up the gearbox oil level using only the specified type of oil

Unscrew the plug and discard the sealing washer.

3 The oil level should reach the lower edge of the level plug hole. A certain amount of oil will have gathered behind the filler level plug and will trickle out when it is removed; this does not necessarily mean that the level is correct.

4 To ensure that a true level is established, wait until the initial trickle stops then add oil, via the filler/level plug hole, until a new trickle of oil can be seen emerging **(see illustration)**. The level will be correct when the flow ceases. Add only good quality oil of the specified type (see *Lubricants and fluids*).

5 Wipe the filler/level plug with a clean rag fit the new sealing washer. Clean the area around the filler/level plug opening then refit the plug, complete with the washer, tightening it to the specified torque. Refit the engine/transmission undertray, and where necessary, lower the vehicle to the ground.

7 Hose and fluid leak check

1 Visually inspect the engine joint faces, gaskets and seals for any signs of water or oil leaks. Pay particular attention to the areas around the cylinder head cover, cylinder head, oil filter and sump joint faces. Bear in mind that, over a period of time, some very slight seepage from these areas is to be expected – what

A leak in the cooling system will usually show up as white- or antifreeze-coloured deposits on the area adjoining the leak.

you are really looking for is any indication of a serious leak. Should a leak be found, renew the offending gasket or oil seal by referring to the appropriate Chapters in this manual.

2 Also check the security and condition of all the engine-related pipes and hoses, and all braking system pipes and hoses and fuel lines. Ensure that all cable ties or securing clips are in place, and in good condition. Clips which are broken or missing can lead to chafing of the hoses, pipes or wiring, which could cause more serious problems in the future.

3 Carefully check the radiator hoses and heater hoses along their entire length. Renew any hose which is cracked, swollen or deteriorated. Cracks will show up better if the hose is squeezed. Pay close attention to the hose clips that secure the hoses to the cooling system components. Hose clips can pinch and puncture hoses, resulting in cooling system leaks. If the crimped-type hose clips are used, it may be a good idea to update them with standard worm-drive clips.

4 Inspect all the cooling system components (hoses, joint faces, etc) for leaks **(see Haynes Hint)**. Where any problems are found on the system components, renew the component or gasket with reference to Chapter 3.

5 With the vehicle raised, inspect the fuel tank and filler neck for punctures, cracks and other damage. The connection between the filler neck and tank is especially critical. Sometimes a rubber filler neck or connecting hose will leak due to loose retaining clamps or deteriorated rubber.

6 Carefully check all rubber hoses and metal fuel lines leading away from the fuel tank. Check for loose connections, deteriorated hoses, crimped lines, and other damage. Pay particular attention to the vent pipes and hoses, which often loop up around the filler neck and can become blocked or crimped. Follow the lines to the front of the vehicle, carefully inspecting them all the way. Renew damaged sections as necessary. Similarly, whilst the vehicle is raised, take the opportunity to inspect all underbody brake fluid pipes and hoses.

7 From within the engine compartment, check the security of all fuel, vacuum and brake hose attachments and pipe unions, and inspect all hoses for kinks, chafing and deterioration.

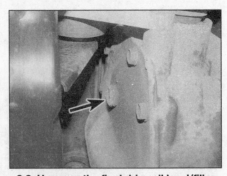

8.2 Unscrew the final drive oil level/filler plug (arrowed)

8 Check the condition of the power steering fluid pipes and hoses.

8 Final drive oil level check

1 Position the vehicle over an inspection pit, on vehicle ramps, or jack it up, but make sure that it is level (see *Jacking and vehicle support*). The oil level must be checked before the vehicle is driven, or at least 5 minutes after the engine has been switched off. If the oil is checked immediately after driving the vehicle, some of the oil will remain distributed around the final drive components, resulting in an inaccurate level reading.

2 Remove all traces of dirt from around the filler/level plug which is located on the rear of the final drive unit **(see illustration)**. Unscrew the plug.

3 The oil level should reach the lower edge of the level plug hole. A certain amount of oil will have gathered behind the filler level plug and will trickle out when it is removed; this does not necessarily mean that the level is correct.

4 To ensure that a true level is established, wait until the initial trickle stops then add oil, via the filler/level plug hole, until a new trickle of oil can be seen emerging. The level will be correct when the flow ceases. Add only good quality oil of the specified type (see *Lubricants and fluids*).

5 Wipe the filler/level plug with a clean rag. Clean the area around the filler/level plug opening then refit the plug, tightening it to the specified torque. Where necessary, lower the vehicle to the ground.

9 Intermediate reduction drive unit oil level check

1 Position the vehicle over an inspection pit, on vehicle ramps, or jack it up, but make sure that it is level (see *Jacking and vehicle support*). Release the retaining screws and remove the engine/transmission undertray. The oil level must be checked before the vehicle is driven, or at least 5 minutes after the engine has been switched off. If the oil is checked immediately after driving the vehicle, some of the oil will remain distributed around the intermediate reduction drive unit components, resulting in an inaccurate level reading.

2 Remove all traces of dirt from around the filler/level plug which is located on the right-hand rear of the unit **(see illustration)**. Unscrew the plug and discard the sealing washer.

3 The oil level should reach the lower edge of the level plug hole. A certain amount of oil will have gathered behind the filler level plug and will trickle out when it is removed; this does not necessarily mean that the level is correct.

4 To ensure that a true level is established, wait until the initial trickle stops then add oil, via the filler/level plug hole, until a new trickle of oil can be seen emerging (see illustration). The level will be correct when the flow ceases. Add only good quality oil of the specified type (see *Lubricants and fluids*).

5 Wipe the filler/level plug with a clean rag fit the new sealing washer. Clean the area around the filler/level plug opening then refit the plug, complete with the washer, tightening it to the specified torque. Refit the engine/transmission undertray, and where necessary, lower the vehicle to the ground.

10 Auxiliary drivebelt(s) check and renewal

Checking

1 Due to their function and material makeup, drivebelts are prone to failure after a long period of time and should therefore be inspected regularly. There are two drivebelts, one for the power steering pump and the other for the alternator and (where fitted) the air conditioning compressor.

2 Turn the steering wheel to the full right-hand lock position. Unscrew the three retaining bolts and remove the splash shield from the wheel arch.

3 With the engine stopped, inspect the full length of the drivebelt(s) for cracks and separation of the belt plies. It will be necessary to turn the engine (using a spanner or socket and bar on the crankshaft pulley bolt) in order to move the belt(s) from the pulleys so that the belt can be inspected thoroughly. Twist the belt(s) between the pulleys so that both sides can be viewed. Also check for fraying, and glazing which gives the belt a shiny appearance. Check the pulleys for nicks, cracks, distortion and corrosion.

4 If a belt shows signs of wear or damage it must be renewed. If the belts are in good condition, check the tension as follows.

5 On models where the alternator belt is manually adjusted (non-air conditioned models and air conditioned models up to 2001 model year), check the tension of the alternator belt at the mid-point between the

9.2 Unscrew the intermediate reduction drive unit oil level/filler plug (arrowed)

crankshaft and alternator pulleys on the upper run of the belt. Apply a force of 10 kg to the belt and check the belt deflection is within the limits given in the Specifications. If adjustment is necessary, adjust the tension as described in the drivebelt renewal procedure.

6 The power steering pump belts, and alternator belts on models with air conditioning from 2001 model year, have automatic tensioning devices. Providing the belts appear to be under tension when examined, no further tension checks are possible.

7 Once the belts have been checked, refit the splash shield, and tighten the retaining screws securely.

Power steering pump drivebelt renewal

8 Turn the steering wheel to the full right-hand lock position. Undo the three retaining screws and remove the splash shield from the wheel arch. If the belt is to be reused, mark the normal direction of rotation of the belt.

9 Using a suitable spanner fitted to the tensioner pulley hexagonal section, lever the tensioner away from the belt until there is sufficient slack to enable the belt to be slipped off from the pulleys. To hold the tensioner in this position, insert a 2 to 3 mm rod into the hole in the centre of the hexagon section into the pulley backplate. Remove the belt from the vehicle (see illustration).

10 Manoeuvre the belt into position, routing it correctly around the pulleys; if the original belt is being fitted use the marks made prior to removal to ensure it is fitted the correct way around.

9.4 Add oil until a trickle of oil emerges

11 Seat the belt on the pulleys. Ensure the belt is centrally located on all pulleys then hold the tensioner pulley in position and pull the rod from the hexagon/backplate. Slowly release the tensioner pulley until the belt is correctly tensioned.

Caution: Do not allow the tensioner to spring back and stress the belt.

12 Refit the splash shield, and tighten the retaining screws securely.

Alternator drivebelt renewal

Models without air conditioning

13 Remove the power steering pump drivebelt as described in this Section.

14 Slacken the alternator upper and lower mounting bolts then release the belt tension using the adjuster bolt on the lower mounting bracket (see illustrations). Slip the drivebelt off from the pulleys and remove it from the engine.

15 Manoeuvre the belt into position, routing it correctly around the pulleys; if the original belt is being fitted use the marks made prior to removal to ensure it is fitted the correct way around. Tension the belt by rotating the adjuster bolt and check the tension as follows.

16 Apply a force of 10 kg to the belt at the mid-point of the upper run of the belt and check the belt deflection is within the limits given in the Specifications. Position the alternator as required by rotating the adjuster bolt then tighten the alternator mounting bolts to the specified torque.

17 Refit the power steering pump belt as

10.9 Using a spanner, push the tensioner away from the belt

10.14a On non-air conditioned models, slacken the alternator upper . . .

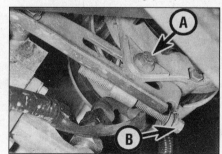

10.14b . . . and lower (A) mounting bolts, then slacken the adjuster bolt (B) to release the belt tension

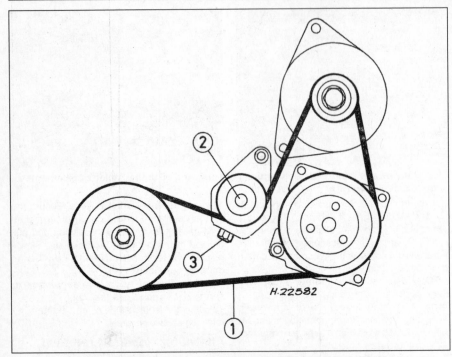

10.30 Lever the tensioner away from the belt, and insert a 2 to 3 mm rod (arrowed) into the hole in the tensioner arm into the pulley backplate

10.21 Alternator drivebelt adjustment – models with air conditioning

1 Drivebelt tension
 checking point

2 Tensioner pulley clamp
 bolt

3 Adjuster bolt

described in this Section, then start the engine and allow it to idle for a few minutes to allow the belts to settle in position.

18 Stop the engine then recheck and, if necessary, adjust the belt tension as described in paragraph 16.

19 Once the belt tension is correctly set, refit the wheel arch splash shield.

Air conditioned models up to 2001

20 Remove the power steering pump drivebelt as described in this Section.

21 Slacken the tensioner pulley retaining nut **(see illustration)**.

22 Release the belt tension by rotating the adjusting bolt anti-clockwise.

23 If the drivebelt is to be re-used, mark the original direction of rotation. Slip the drivebelt from the pulleys and remove it from the engine.

24 Manoeuvre the drivebelt into position,

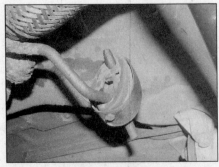

11.3 Check all exhaust mountings are in good condition

routing it correctly around the pulleys; if the original belt is being fitted use the marks made prior to removal to ensure it is fitted the correct way around. Tension the belt by rotating the adjuster bolt and check the tension as follows.

25 Apply a force of 10 kg to the belt at the mid-point of the upper run of the belt, and check the belt deflection is within the limits given in the Specifications. Rotate the adjusting bolt as required, then tighten the tensioner pulley retaining bolt to the specified torque.

26 Refit the power steering pump drivebelt as described in this Section, then start the engine and allow it to idle for a few minutes to allow the belts to settle in position.

27 Stop the engine then recheck and, if necessary, adjust the belt tension as described in paragraph 25.

28 Once the belt tension is correctly set, refit the wheel arch splash shield.

Air conditioned models from 2001

29 Remove the power steering pump drivebelt as described in this Section.

30 Using a suitable spanner fitted to the tensioner pulley hexagonal section, lever the tensioner away from the belt until there is sufficient slack to enable the belt to be slipped off from the pulleys. To hold the tensioner in this position, insert a 2 to 3 mm rod into the hole in the tensioner arm into the pulley backplate. Remove the belt from the vehicle **(see illustration)**.

31 Manoeuvre the belt into position, routing it correctly around the pulleys; if the original

belt is being fitted use the marks made prior to removal to ensure it is fitted the correct way around.

32 Seat the belt on the pulleys. Ensure the belt is centrally located on all pulleys then hold the tensioner pulley in position and pull the rod from the hexagon/backplate. Slowly release the tensioner pulley until the belt is correctly tensioned.

33 Refit the power steering pump drivebelt as described in this Section then start the engine and allow it to idle for a few minutes to allow the belts to settle in position.

34 Stop the engine and refit the wheel arch splash shield.

11 Exhaust system check

1 Park the vehicle on a level surface and switch off the engine. Chock the front wheels and select first gear, then raise the rear of the vehicle and rest it securely on axle stands (see *Jacking and vehicle support*). Release the retaining screws and remove the engine/transmission undertray.

2 With the engine cold (wait at least an hour after switching off the engine), check the complete exhaust system from the engine to the end of the tailpipe.

3 Check the exhaust pipes and connections for evidence of leaks, severe corrosion and damage. Make sure that all brackets and mountings are in good condition, and that all relevant nuts and bolts are tight **(see illustration)**. Leakage at any of the joints or in other parts of the system will usually show up as a black, sooty stain in the vicinity of the leak.

4 Rattles and vibrations can often be traced to the exhaust system. Tap the silencer units with a soft mallet and listen for noises caused by corroded or displaced baffle material. *Caution: Do not strike the catalytic converter, as this may damage the ceramic block inside.*

5 Carefully rock the pipes and silencers

from side to side on their mountings. If the components are able to come into contact with the body or suspension parts, look for broken or worn rubber mountings.

6 Extra clearance can be gained by slackening the clamps between adjacent sections of the exhaust pipe to loosen the joints (where possible – refer to Chapter 4A) and twisting the pipes as necessary to provide the additional clearance. Retighten the clamps on completion.

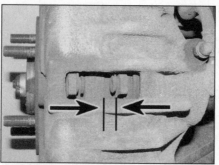

12.2 Measure the thickness of the brake pad lining material

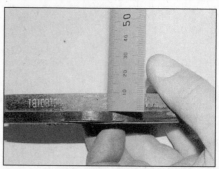

12.4 Check the thickness of the brake pad friction material

12 Brake pad and disc check

1 Firmly apply the handbrake, then jack up the front of the vehicle and support it securely on axle stands (see *Jacking and vehicle support*). Remove the front roadwheels.

2 For a quick check, the pad thickness can be carried out via the inspection hole on the front of the caliper **(see illustration)**. Using a steel rule, measure the thickness of the pad lining material. This must not be less than that indicated in the Specifications.

3 The view through the caliper inspection hole gives a rough indication of the state of the brake pads. For a comprehensive check, the brake pads should be removed and cleaned. The operation of the caliper can then also be checked, and the condition of the brake disc itself can be fully examined on both sides. Chapter 9 contains a detailed description of how the brake disc should be checked for wear and/or damage.

4 If any pad's friction material is worn to the specified thickness or less, *all four pads must be renewed as a set*. Refer to Chapter 9 for details **(see illustration)**.

5 On completion, refit the roadwheels and lower the vehicle to the ground.

13 Brake pipe and hose check

1 Jack up the front and rear of the vehicle and support it on axle stands (see *Jacking and vehicle support*).

2 Check the security and condition of all the braking system pipes and hoses. In particular, check the flexible hoses for signs of cracking by carefully bending them at several points along their lengths. Check the rigid brake lines for corrosion, especially at exposed locations on the underbody.

3 Ensure that all hose and pipe securing clips are in place, and in good condition.

4 Renewal of the brake pipes and hoses is described in Chapter 9.

5 On completion lower the vehicle to the ground.

14 Suspension and steering check

Front suspension and steering

1 Raise the front of the vehicle, and securely support it on axle stands (see *Jacking and vehicle support*).

2 Visually inspect the balljoint dust covers and the steering rack-and-pinion gaiters for splits, chafing or deterioration. Any wear of these components will cause loss of lubricant, together with dirt and water entry, resulting in rapid deterioration of the balljoints or steering gear.

3 On vehicles with power steering, check the fluid hoses for chafing or deterioration, and the pipe and hose unions for fluid leaks. Also check for signs of fluid leakage under pressure from the steering gear rubber gaiters, which would indicate failed fluid seals within the steering gear.

4 Grasp the roadwheel at the 12 o'clock and 6 o'clock positions, and try to rock it **(see illustration)**. Very slight free play may be felt, but if the movement is appreciable, further investigation is necessary to determine the source. Continue rocking the wheel while an assistant depresses the footbrake. If the movement is now eliminated or significantly reduced, it is likely that the hub bearings are at fault. If the free play is still evident with the footbrake depressed, then there is wear in the suspension joints or mountings.

5 Now grasp the wheel at the 9 o'clock and 3 o'clock positions, and try to rock it as before. Any movement felt now may again be caused by wear in the hub bearings or the steering track rod balljoints. If the outer balljoint is worn, the visual movement will be obvious. If the inner joint is suspect, it can be felt by placing a hand over the rack-and-pinion rubber gaiter and gripping the track rod. If the wheel is now rocked, movement will be felt at the inner joint if wear has taken place.

6 Using a large screwdriver or flat bar, check for wear in the suspension mounting bushes by levering between the relevant suspension component and its attachment point. Some movement is to be expected, as the mountings are made of rubber, but excessive wear should be obvious. Also check the condition of any visible rubber bushes, looking for splits, cracks or contamination of the rubber.

7 With the vehicle standing on its wheels, have an assistant turn the steering wheel back-and-forth, about an eighth of a turn each way. There should be very little, if any, lost movement between the steering wheel and roadwheels. If this is not the case, closely observe the joints and mountings previously described. In addition, check the steering column universal joints for wear, and also check the rack-and-pinion steering gear itself.

Rear suspension

8 Chock the front wheels, then jack up the rear of the vehicle and support securely on axle stands (see *Jacking and vehicle support*).

9 Working as described previously for the front suspension, check the rear hub bearings, the suspension bushes and the strut/shock absorber mountings for wear.

Shock absorber

10 Check for any signs of fluid leakage around the front and rear shock absorbers, or from the rubber gaiter around the piston rod. Should any fluid be noticed, the shock absorber is defective internally, and should be renewed. **Note:** *Shock absorbers should always be renewed in pairs on the same axle.*

11 The efficiency of the shock absorber may be checked by bouncing the vehicle at each corner. Generally speaking, the body will

14.4 Grasp the roadwheel at the 12 o'clock and 6 o'clock positions, and try to rock it

15.2 Apply a thin layer of anti-seize compound to the area where the wheel contacts the hub

return to its normal position and stop after being depressed. If it rises and returns on a rebound, the shock absorber is probably suspect. Also examine the shock absorber upper and lower mountings for any signs of wear.

15 Roadwheel anti-seize check

1 In order to prevent the wheel seizing to the hub, Land Rover state that the hub-to-wheel mating surface should be coated with a thin layer of anti-seize compound.
2 With the handbrake fully applied, jack up the front of the vehicle and support on axle stands (see *Jacking and vehicle support*). Remove the front roadwheels. Ensure that the hub/wheel mating surfaces are clean and dry, and apply a thin layer of anti-seize compound **(see illustration)**. Refit the roadwheels to their original positions.
3 Chock the front wheels, jack up the rear of the vehicle and support on axle stands (see *Jacking and vehicle support*). Remove the rear roadwheels. Ensure that the drum/wheel mating surfaces are clean and dry, and apply a thin layer of anti-seize compound. Refit the roadwheels to the **opposite** sides of the rear axle. This is to prevent uneven tyre wear, and subsequent excessive tyre noise. Land Rover state that the wheels must not be swapped diagonally, or the front wheels swapped from side-to-side.

16.1 Inspect the condition of the outer constant velocity (CV) joint rubber gaiters

16 Driveshaft and gaiter check

1 With the vehicle raised and securely supported on stands (see *Jacking and vehicle support*), turn the steering onto full lock then slowly rotate the roadwheel. Inspect the condition of the outer constant velocity (CV) joint rubber gaiters while squeezing the gaiters to open out the folds **(see illustration)**. Check for signs of cracking, splits or deterioration of the rubber which may allow the grease to escape and lead to water and grit entry into the joint. Also check the security and condition of the retaining clips. Repeat these checks on the inner CV joints. If any damage or deterioration is found, the gaiters should be renewed as described in Chapter 8.
2 At the same time check the general condition of the CV joints themselves by first holding the driveshaft and attempting to rotate the wheel. Repeat this check by holding the inner joint and attempting to rotate the driveshaft. Any appreciable movement indicates wear in the joints, wear in the driveshaft splines or loose driveshaft retaining nut.

17 Handbrake check

1 The handbrake should be capable of holding the parked vehicle stationary, even on steep slopes, when applied with moderate force. The mechanism should be firm and positive in feel with no trace of stiffness or sponginess from the cables and should release immediately the handbrake lever is released. If the mechanism is faulty in any of these respects then it must be checked immediately.
2 To check the handbrake setting, first apply the footbrake firmly several times to establish correct shoe-to-drum clearance. Applying normal, moderate pressure, pull the handbrake lever to the fully-applied position whilst counting the number of clicks emitted from the handbrake ratchet mechanism. If adjustment is correct, there should be 4 to 5 clicks before the handbrake is fully applied. If this is not the case, then adjustment is required as described in Chapter 9.

18 Hinge and lock lubrication

1 Work around the vehicle and lubricate the hinges of the bonnet, doors and rear door/tailgate with a light machine oil. Also lubricate the bonnet lock located on the engine compartment front crossmember.
2 Lightly lubricate the bonnet release mechanism and exposed section of the inner cable with a smear of grease.

19 Electrical system check

1 Check the operation of all electrical equipment, ie, lights, direction indicators, horn, wash/wipe system etc. Refer to the appropriate Sections of Chapter 12 for details if any of the circuits are found to be inoperative.
2 Visually check all accessible wiring connectors, harnesses and retaining clips for security, and for signs of chafing or damage. Rectify any faults found.

20 Seat belt and airbag check

1 Check the webbing of each belt for signs of fraying, cuts or other damage, pulling the belt out to its full extent to check its entire length.
2 Check the operation of the belt buckles by pulling the belt hard to ensure that it remains locked in position.
3 Check the inertia reel retractor mechanism by pulling out the belt to the halfway point and jerking hard. The mechanism must lock immediately to prevent any further unreeling but must allow free movement during normal driving.
4 Ensure that all belt mounting bolts are securely tightened. Note that the bolts are shouldered so that the belt anchor points are free to rotate.
5 If there is any sign of damage, or any doubt about a belt's condition, then it must be renewed. If the vehicle has been involved in a collision, then any belt in use at the time must be renewed as a matter of course and all other belts checked carefully.
6 The airbag/SRS warning light on the instrument panel should extinguish 3 seconds after the ignition switch is turned to position II. If this is not the case, have the system checked by a Land Rover dealer. No attempt should be made to carry out repairs to the airbag components.

21 Exhaust emission check

1 The check involves checking the engine management system operation by plugging an electronic tester into the system diagnostic socket to check the electronic control module (ECM) memory for faults (see Chapter 4A).
2 In reality, if the vehicle is running correctly and the engine management warning light in the instrument panel is functioning normally, then this check need not be carried out. On vehicles over 3 years old, the exhaust emissions will be checked every year during the MOT test.

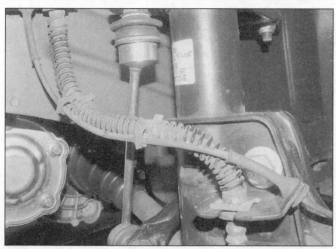

22.2 Check the speed sensors harnesses are correctly routed and secured

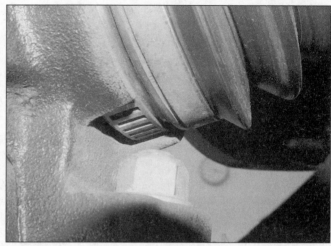

22.3 Check that the reluctor rings are free from debris and damage

22 Roadwheel speed sensors check

1 Raise the vehicle, and securely support it on axle stands (see *Jacking and vehicle support*). Remove the roadwheels.
2 Check the speed sensors harnesses are correctly routed and secured. Check the harnesses for chafing or damage **(see illustration)**.
3 Ensure the sensors are fully inserted in their correct positions, and the reluctor rings are free from debris and damage **(see illustration)**.
4 Refit the roadwheels and lower the vehicle to the ground. Tighten the roadwheel nuts to the specified torque.

23 Pollen filter renewal

1 The pollen filter (if fitted) is located beneath the left-hand side of the facia, in the heater inlet system. To remove the filter on pre-2001 model year vehicles, unscrew the three screws, and pull out the retaining clips **(see illustration)**. On post-2001 model year vehicles, the filter is secured by four screws **(see illustration)**.
2 Pull the filter from the housing **(see illustration)**.
3 Fit the new filter using a reversal of the removal procedure.

24 Road test

Instruments and electrical equipment

1 Check the operation of all instruments and electrical equipment.
2 Make sure that all instruments read correctly, and switch on all electrical equipment in turn, to check that it functions properly.

Steering and suspension

3 Check for any abnormalities in the steering, suspension, handling or road 'feel'.
4 Drive the vehicle, and check that there are no unusual vibrations or noises.
5 Check that the steering feels positive, with no excessive 'sloppiness', or roughness, and check for any suspension noises when cornering and driving over bumps.

Drivetrain

6 Check the performance of the engine, clutch, transmission and driveshafts.
7 Listen for any unusual noises from the engine, clutch and transmission.
8 Make sure that the engine runs smoothly when idling, and that there is no hesitation when accelerating.
9 Check that, where applicable, the clutch action is smooth and progressive, that the drive is taken up smoothly, and that the pedal travel is not excessive. Also listen for any noises when the clutch pedal is depressed.
10 Check that all gears can be engaged smoothly without noise, and that the gear lever action is smooth and not abnormally vague or 'notchy'.
11 Listen for a metallic clicking sound from the front of the vehicle, as the vehicle is driven slowly in a circle with the steering on full-lock. Carry out this check in both directions. If a clicking noise is heard, this indicates wear in a driveshaft joint (see Chapter 8).

Braking system

12 Make sure that the vehicle does not pull to one side when braking, and that the wheels do not lock prematurely when braking hard.
13 Check that there is no vibration through the steering when braking.

23.1a On pre-2001 model year vehicles, unscrew the three screws, and pull out the pollen filter retaining clips

23.1b On post-2001 model year vehicles, the pollen filter is secured by four screws

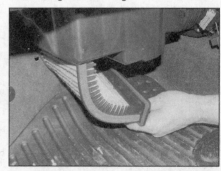

23.2 Pull the pollen filter from the housing

14 Check that the handbrake operates correctly, without excessive movement of the lever, and that it holds the vehicle stationary on a slope.

15 Test the operation of the brake servo unit as follows. Depress the footbrake four or five times to exhaust the vacuum, then start the engine. As the engine starts, there should be a noticeable 'give' in the brake pedal as vacuum builds-up. Allow the engine to run for at least two minutes, and then switch it off. If the brake pedal is now depressed again, it should be possible to detect a hiss from the servo as the pedal is depressed. After about four or five applications, no further hissing should be heard, and the pedal should feel considerably harder.

Every 24 000 miles or 2 years

25 Air filter element renewal

1 The air filter is located in the engine compartment, on the left-hand end of the engine.

2 Release the retaining clips, and lift the air filter cover sufficiently to enable removal of the filter element from its housing **(see illustration)**.

3 Lift out the filter element, noting which way up it is fitted, then wipe out the casing and the cover.

4 Fit the new filter, making sure it is the correct way up, and seat it in the housing **(see illustration)**. Locate the cover on the housing and secure it in position with all the retaining clips.

26 Brake shoe and drum check

Refer to the detailed description given in Chapter 9.

27 Brake caliper and wheel cylinder check

1 Jack up the front and rear of the vehicle and support it on axle stands (see *Jacking and vehicle support*). Remove the front and rear wheels.

2 For a thorough check of the front brake calipers, remove the brake pads as described in Chapter 9. Carefully clean the brake pad locations in the caliper body and mounting bracket taking care not to inhale the brake dust as it may contain asbestos which is a health hazard. Check the caliper for signs of brake fluid leakage. If this is evident at the flexible hose connection, renew the copper washers with reference to Chapter 9. If leakage is evident at the piston, renew the internal sealing ring or renew the caliper complete with reference to Chapter 9.

3 To check the wheel cylinders, remove the drums with reference to Chapter 9, then clean away dust and dirt from the brake shoes and wheel cylinder. Check the wheel cylinders for signs of brake fluid leakage by temporarily lifting the rubber boots **(see illustration)**. If evident, renew the wheel cylinder complete as described in Chapter 9.

28 Handset battery renewal

1 The alarm system handset contains a battery which should last for approximately 3 years. When it requires renewal, the indicator warning lights on the front doors will flash rapidly before the doors are opened and the operating range will reduce considerably.

2 To renew the battery, use a small screwdriver or coin to prise off the handset cover then remove the battery from its clip **(see illustrations)**.

3 Press each button for a minimum of 5 seconds to drain any remaining power from the handset, then fit the new battery (CR2032) taking care not to touch the contact surfaces with the fingers. Make sure the new battery is correctly located with the positive (+) side facing upwards **(see illustration)**.

4 Press on the cover, then unlock the vehicle using the key and operate the lock button on the handset at least four times.

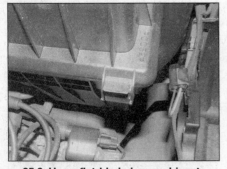

25.2 Use a flat-bladed screwdriver to release the air filter cover retaining clips

25.4 Fit the air cleaner element the right way up

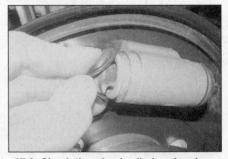

27.3 Check the wheel cylinders for signs of brake fluid leakage by temporarily lifting the rubber boots

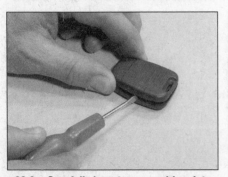

28.2a Carefully insert a screwdriver into the slot . . .

28.2b . . . and prise off the handset cover

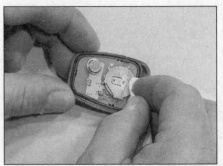

28.3 Ensure the new battery is installed with the positive (+) side facing upwards

29.16 Disconnect the inlet manifold bleed hose from the right-hand rear of the cylinder head – see text

29.17 Unscrew the bleed screw from the heater return hose at the engine compartment bulkhead

Every 36 000 miles or 3 years

29 Coolant/antifreeze renewal

⚠️ **Warning: Wait until the engine is cold before starting this procedure. Do not allow antifreeze to come in contact with your skin, or with the painted surfaces of the vehicle. Rinse off spills immediately with plenty of water. Never leave antifreeze lying around in an open container, or in a puddle in the driveway or on the garage floor. Children and pets are attracted by its sweet smell, but antifreeze can be fatal if ingested.**

Cooling system draining

1 With the engine completely cold, remove the expansion tank filler cap. Turn the cap anti-clockwise, wait until any pressure remaining in the system is released, then unscrew it and lift it off.
2 Jack the front of the vehicle up and support it on axle stands (see *Jacking and vehicle support*). Release the retaining screws and remove the engine undertray. Position a suitable container beneath the left-hand side of the radiator.
3 Position the heater temperature control on its maximum setting.
4 Release the clip and disconnect the bottom hose from the radiator, and allow the coolant to drain into the container.
5 When the flow of coolant stops, refit the bottom hose and refit the clip.
6 If the coolant has been drained for a reason other than renewal, then provided it is clean and less than three years old, it can be re-used, though this is not recommended.

Cooling system flushing

7 If coolant renewal has been neglected, or if the antifreeze mixture has become diluted, then in time, the cooling system may gradually lose efficiency, as the coolant passages become restricted due to rust, scale deposits, and other sediment. The cooling system efficiency can be restored by flushing the system clean.
8 The radiator should be flushed independently of the engine, to avoid unnecessary contamination.

Radiator flushing

9 Disconnect the top and bottom hoses and any other relevant hoses from the radiator, with reference to Chapter 3.
10 Insert a garden hose into the radiator top inlet. Direct a flow of clean water through the radiator, and continue flushing until clean water emerges from the radiator bottom outlet.
11 If after a reasonable period, the water still does not run clear, the radiator can be flushed with a good proprietary cleaning agent. It is important that the manufacturer's instructions are followed carefully. If the contamination is particularly bad, insert the hose in the radiator bottom outlet, and reverse-flush the radiator.

Engine flushing

12 Remove the thermostat as described in Chapter 3 then, if the radiator top hose has been disconnected from the engine, temporarily reconnect the hose.
13 With the top and bottom hoses disconnected from the radiator, insert a garden hose into the radiator top hose. Direct a clean flow of water through the engine, and continue flushing until clean water emerges from the radiator bottom hose.
14 On completion of flushing, refit the thermostat and reconnect the hoses with reference to Chapter 3.

Cooling system filling

15 Before attempting to fill the cooling system, make sure that all hoses and clips are in good condition, and that the clips are tight. Note that an antifreeze mixture must be used all year round, to prevent corrosion of the engine components. Make sure the heater controls are set to maximum heat.
16 Release the retaining clip and disconnect the inlet manifold bleed hose from the right-hand rear of the cylinder head, adjacent to the engine oil dipstick (see illustration). Connect a suitable length of hose to the outlet stub and blow through the tube. This procedure ensures that the bleed valve pin is not stuck in the closed position, which would result in air being trapped in the cylinder head, and engine overheating. Disconnect the tube and refit the original hose and retaining clip.
17 Remove the expansion tank filler cap. Unscrew and remove the bleed screw from the coolant pipe on the left-hand end of the cylinder head, and the bleed screw from the heater return hose at the engine compartment bulkhead (see illustration).
18 Slowly fill the system until bubble-free coolant comes out of the bleed hole in the coolant pipe, then fit and tighten the screw.
19 Continue filling the system until bubble free coolant comes out of the bleed screw in the heater return hose, then fit and tighten the screw.
20 Fill the cooling system until the coolant reaches the MAX mark on the expansion tank, then refit and tighten the filler cap.
21 Refit the undershield beneath the engine compartment, and lower the vehicle to the ground.
22 Start the engine, and allow it to run until it reaches normal operating temperature (until the cooling fan cuts in and out). **Do not** operate the air conditioning at this stage.
23 Stop the engine, and allow it to cool, then recheck the coolant level with reference to *Weekly checks*. Top-up the level if necessary and refit the expansion tank filler cap.

Antifreeze mixture

24 The antifreeze should always be renewed at the specified intervals. This is necessary not only to maintain the antifreeze properties, but also to prevent corrosion which would otherwise occur as the corrosion inhibitors become progressively less effective.

25 Always use an ethylene-glycol based antifreeze which is suitable for use in mixed-metal cooling systems. The quality and quantity of antifreeze, and levels of protection are given in the Specifications.

26 Before adding antifreeze, the cooling system should be completely drained, preferably flushed, and all hoses checked for condition and security.

27 After filling with antifreeze, a label should be attached to the expansion tank, stating the type and concentration of antifreeze used, and the date installed. Any subsequent topping-up should be made with the same type and concentration of antifreeze.

Caution: Do not use engine antifreeze in the windscreen/tailgate washer system, as it will cause damage to the vehicle paintwork. A screenwash additive should be added to the washer system in the quantities stated on the bottle.

30 Brake fluid renewal

⚠️ *Warning: Brake hydraulic fluid can harm your eyes and damage painted surfaces, so use extreme caution when handling and pouring it. Do not use fluid that has been standing open for some time, as it absorbs moisture from the air. Excess moisture can cause a dangerous loss of braking effectiveness.*

1 The procedure is similar to that for the bleeding of the hydraulic system as described in Chapter 9.

2 Working as described in Chapter 9, open the first bleed screw in the sequence, and pump the brake pedal gently until nearly all the old fluid has been emptied from the master cylinder reservoir. Top-up to the MAX level with new fluid, and continue pumping until only the new fluid remains in the reservoir, and new fluid can be seen emerging from the bleed screw. Tighten the screw, and top the reservoir level up to the MAX level line.

> **HAYNES HINT** *Old hydraulic fluid is invariably much darker in colour than the new, making it easy to distinguish the two.*

3 Work through all the remaining bleed screws in the sequence until new fluid can be seen at all of them. Be careful to keep the master cylinder reservoir topped-up to above the MIN level at all times, or air may enter the system and greatly increase the length of the task.

4 When the operation is complete, check that all bleed screws are securely tightened, and that their dust caps are refitted. Wash off all traces of spilt fluid, and recheck the master cylinder reservoir fluid level.

5 Check the operation of the brakes before taking the vehicle on the road.

Every 72 000 miles or 6 years

31 Spark plug renewal and ignition system check

Spark plug renewal

1 The correct functioning of the spark plugs is vital for the correct running and efficiency of the engine. It is essential that the plugs fitted are appropriate for the engine; suitable types are specified at the beginning of this Chapter, or in the vehicle's Owner's Handbook. If the correct type is used and the engine is in good condition, the spark plugs should not need attention between scheduled renewal intervals.

31.2 Undo the retaining screws (arrowed) and remove the spark plug cover from the top of the engine

31.3 Disconnect the HT leads by pulling up the caps – not the leads

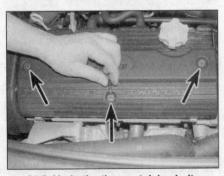

31.5 Undo the three retaining bolts (arrowed) and remove the coil lead cover

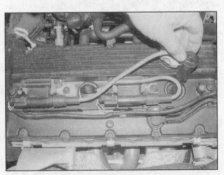

31.6 Disconnect the HT leads by pulling up the caps – not the leads

Spark plug cleaning is rarely necessary, and should not be attempted unless specialised equipment is available, as damage can easily be caused to the firing ends.

Models up to 2001

2 Undo the retaining screws and remove the spark plug cover from the top of the engine **(see illustration)**.

3 If the marks on the original-equipment spark plug (HT) leads cannot be seen, mark the leads to correspond to the cylinder the lead serves. Pull the plug caps from the plugs **(see illustration)**.

Models from 2001

4 Disconnect the battery negative terminal (see Chapter 5A).

5 Undo the three retaining bolts and remove the coil lead cover from the top of the cylinder head **(see illustration)**.

6 Carefully pull the HT leads from the Nos 2 and 4 cylinder spark plugs, and disconnect the wiring plugs form the coil above No 3 cylinder spark plug **(see illustration)**.

7 Unscrew the coil retaining screws (two for each coil), and carefully pull the coils up, disconnecting them from the underlying spark plugs. Disconnect the wiring plug from the coil above No 1 spark plug **(see illustration)**.

All models

8 It is advisable to remove the dirt from the spark plug recesses using a clean brush, vacuum cleaner or compressed air before removing the plugs, to prevent dirt dropping into the cylinders.

9 Unscrew the plugs from the cylinder head using a spark plug spanner, suitable box spanner or a deep socket and extension bar **(see illustration)**. Keep the socket aligned

31.7 Disconnect the wiring plug from the coil above No 1 spark plug after the coil has been removed

31.9 Unscrew the spark plug from the cylinder head

31.14a Measure the spark plug electrode gap using a feeler blade . . .

31.14b . . . or a wire gauge . . .

31.14c . . . and if necessary adjust the gap by bending the outer electrode

with the spark plug – if it is forcibly moved to one side, the ceramic insulator may be broken off. As each plug is removed, examine it as follows.

10 Examination of the spark plugs will give a good indication of the condition of the engine. If the insulator nose of the spark plug is clean and white, with no deposits, this is indicative of a weak mixture or too hot a plug (a hot plug transfers heat away from the electrode slowly, a cold plug transfers heat away quickly).

11 If the tip and insulator nose are covered with hard black-looking deposits, then this is indicative that the mixture is too rich. Should the plug be black and oily, then it is likely that the engine is fairly worn, as well as the mixture being too rich.

12 If the insulator nose is covered with light tan to greyish-brown deposits, then the mixture is correct and it is likely that the engine is in good condition.

13 The spark plug electrode gap is of considerable importance as, if it is too large or too small, the size of the spark and its efficiency will be seriously impaired. The gap should be set to the value given in the Specifications at the beginning of this Chapter.

14 To set the gap, measure it with a feeler blade and then bend open, or closed, the outer plug electrode until the correct gap is achieved. The centre electrode should never be bent, as this may crack the insulator and cause plug failure, if nothing worse. If using feeler blades, the gap is correct when the appropriate-size blade is a firm sliding fit **(see illustrations)**.

15 Special spark plug electrode gap adjusting tools are available from most motor accessory shops, or from some spark plug manufacturers.

16 Before fitting the spark plugs, check that the threaded connector sleeves (where fitted) are tight, and that the plug exterior surfaces and threads are clean **(see Haynes Hint)**.

17 Remove the rubber hose (if used), and tighten the plug to the specified torque using the spark plug socket and a torque wrench. Refit the remaining spark plugs in the same manner.

Models up to 2001

18 Connect the HT leads in their correct order. Refit the spark plug cover to the top of

the engine and securely tighten its retaining screws.

Models from 2001

19 Refit the ignition coils to Nos 1 and 3 spark plugs, insert the coil retaining screws and tighten them to the specified torque.

20 Reconnect the wiring plugs to the coils, and refit the HT lead caps to the spark plugs. The HT lead from the coil over No 1 spark plug connects to No 4 spark plug. Ensure the HT leads are clipped into place securely.

21 Refit the coil lead cover to the top of the engine, and tighten the bolts securely. Reconnect the battery negative lead (see Chapter 5A).

Ignition system check

22 Label the HT leads (if the original marks are not visible) and disconnect them from the spark plugs, as described in the previous sub-section.

23 Check the inside of the end fitting of each lead for signs of corrosion, which will look like a white crusty powder. Remove any such deposits with a stiff brush, or fine grade emery paper. Push the end fitting back onto the spark plug, ensuring that it is a tight fit on the plug. If this is not the case, remove the lead again and use long-nosed pliers to carefully shape the metal connector inside the end fitting, until it fits securely on the end of the spark plug.

24 Using a clean rag sprayed with a little penetrating oil, wipe the entire length of the lead to remove any built-up dirt and grease. Once the lead is clean, check for burns, cracks and other damage.

Caution: Do not bend or kink the lead excessively, or stretch the lead lengthwise, as this may break the conductors inside the lead.

Models up to 2001

25 Disconnect the other end of the lead from the distributor cap. Again, pull only on the end fitting. Check for corrosion and security as described earlier. If an ohmmeter is available, check the resistance of the lead by connecting

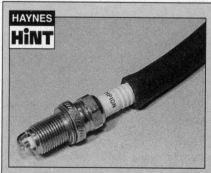

HAYNES HINT

It is very often difficult to insert spark plugs into their holes without cross-threading them. To avoid this possibility, fit a short length of rubber hose over the end of the spark plug. The flexible hose acts as a universal joint to help align the plug with the plug hole. Should the plug begin to cross-thread, the hose will slip on the spark plug, preventing thread damage to the aluminium cylinder head.

the meter between the spark plug end of the lead and the segment inside the distributor cap. Refit the lead securely on completion.

26 Check the remaining leads one at a time, in the same manner.

27 If new HT leads are required, purchase a set for your specific vehicle and engine. Renew the leads one at a time to ensure the firing order is preserved.

28 With reference to Chapter 5B, remove the distributor cap. Wipe it clean, and carefully inspect it inside and out for signs of cracks, black carbon tracks (tracking) and worn, burned or loose contacts.

29 Check that the cap centre carbon brush is in good condition and is free to move against spring pressure, allowing it to make good contact with the top of the rotor arm.

30 Inspect the metal terminals on the inside the cap. Surface corrosion and light deposits can be removed with fine-grade emery paper, but more serious wear will mean the renewal of the distributor cap.

31 Inspect the rotor arm closely. Light deposits can be removed with fine-grade emery paper, but if the contacts are badly pitted, the rotor arm should be renewed. If the rotor arm is to be removed a new retaining screw will be needed; the screw should be renewed whenever it is disturbed.

> **HAYNES HiNT**
> *When fitting a new distributor cap, transfer the HT leads from the old cap to the new one in sequence, one at a time, so that the firing order is preserved.*

32 Timing belt renewal

Refer to the Chapter 2A.

Every 96 000 miles or 8 years

33 Auxiliary drivebelt check and renewal

Refer to Section 10 of this Chapter.

Every 120 000 miles or 10 years

34 Fuel filter renewal

1 Remove the fuel gauge sender unit as described in Chapter 4A.

2 Disconnect the two wiring connectors from the under the top of the pump unit assembly.

3 Release the 3 retaining clips and separate the top of the pump assembly from the base. Take care not to strain the fuel hose, and recover the compression spring from the fuel filter **(see illustrations)**.

4 Carefully release the clips and remove the filter from the base. Discard the O-rings, new ones must be fitted **(see illustration)**.

5 Lubricate the new O-rings with silicone grease, and fit them to the pump base inlet and outlet ports **(see illustration)**.

6 Fit the new filter, ensuring that the sprag clips fully engage.

7 Refit the compression spring into the fuel filter recess, and refit the pump top to the base. Ensure the slots engage correctly with the lugs.

8 Refit the sender unit as described in Chapter 4A.

34.3a Use a small screwdriver to release the retaining clips and separate the pump halves

34.3b Recover the compression spring from the filter

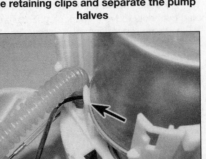

34.4 Release the filter retaining clips (arrowed)

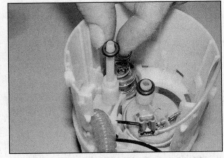

34.5 Lubricate the new O-rings with silicone grease before fitting them

Every 10 years

35 Airbag module renewal

1 The airbag module must be renewed every 10 years on vehicles up to 2001 model year, and every 15 years on subsequent vehicles.

2 Renewal procedures are described in Chapter 12.

36 Seat belt pretensioners renewal

1 The seat belt pretensioners must be renewed every 10 years on vehicles up to 2001 model year, and every 15 years on subsequent vehicles.

2 Renewal procedures are described in Chapter 11.

Chapter 1 Part B:
Routine maintenance and servicing – diesel models

Contents

Degrees of difficulty

Easy, suitable for novice with little experience 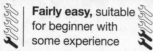	Fairly easy, suitable for beginner with some experience	Fairly difficult, suitable for competent DIY mechanic	Difficult, suitable for experienced DIY mechanic	Very difficult, suitable for expert DIY or professional

Lubricants and fluids................................. Refer to *Weekly checks* on page 0•17

Capacities

Engine oil
Including oil filter*:
L-Series engine............................	4.5 litres
TD4 engine.................................	6.8 litres
Difference between MIN and MAX on dipstick (approximate)........	1.0 litre

* *Capacities shown are for refilling after draining, if the engine is being filled from dry add a further 0.4 litre*

Cooling system
Including reservoir*:
L-Series engine............................	6.5 litres
TD 4 engine.................................	6.6 litres

* *Capacity shown is for refilling after draining, if the cooling system is being filled from dry add a further 0.7 litre*

Automatic transmission
Jatco (TD4 engine)*.........................	4.0 litres

* *Capacity shown is for refilling after draining, if the gearbox is being filled from dry add a further 4.5 litres*

Manual gearbox
PG1 gearbox (L-Series engine)*.............	2.0 litres
Getrag 282 (TD4 engine)...................	1.6 litres

* *Capacity shown is for refilling after draining, if the gearbox is being filled from dry add a further 0.2 litre*

Intermediate reduction drive unit................	1.1 litres
Final drive...................................	0.83 litres
Washer fluid reservoir........................	4.0 litres
Fuel tank...................................	59 litres
Power steering system.......................	0.34 litres

Cooling system
Antifreeze mixture:
50% antifreeze...........................	Protection down to -37°C
55% antifreeze...........................	Protection down to -45°C

Note: *Refer to antifreeze manufacturer for latest recommendations.*

Brakes
Friction material minimum thickness:
Front brake pads.........................	3.0 mm
Rear brake shoes.........................	2.0 mm

Air conditioning compressor drivebelt tension
TD4 engines:
New belt.................................	47 Nm
Used belt................................	38 Nm

Torque wrench settings

	Nm	lbf ft
Air conditioning compressor drivebelt tensioner:		
Clamping bolt............................	24	18
Pivot bolt...............................	24	18
Air filter cover Allen screws...............	8	6
Automatic transmission oil drain plug........	45	33
Automatic transmission oil level/filler plug....	14	10
Engine sump drain plug....................	28	21
Final drive oil plug........................	27	20
Manual gearbox oil filler/level plug..........	35	26
Manual gearbox drain plug.................	35	26
Oil filter housing cap......................	25	18
Oil filter canister (L-Series engine only)......	16	12
Roadwheel nuts...........................	115	85

Maintenance schedule

The maintenance intervals in this manual are provided with the assumption that you, not the dealer, will be carrying out the work. These are the minimum maintenance intervals recommended by us for vehicles driven daily. If you wish to keep your vehicle in peak condition at all times, you may wish to perform some of these procedures more often. We encourage frequent maintenance, because it enhances the efficiency, performance and resale value of your vehicle.

If the vehicle is driven in dusty areas, used to tow a trailer, or driven frequently at slow speeds (idling in traffic) or on short journeys, more frequent maintenance intervals are recommended.

When the vehicle is new, it should be serviced by a dealer service department (or other workshop recognised by the vehicle manufacturer as providing the same standard of service) in order to preserve the warranty. The vehicle manufacturer may reject warranty claims if you are unable to prove that servicing has been carried out as and when specified, using only original equipment parts or parts certified to be of equivalent quality

Every 250 miles or weekly

☐ Refer to *Weekly Checks*

Every 6000 miles or 6 months, whichever comes first

☐ Renew the engine oil and filter (Section 3)

Note: *Land Rover recommend that the engine oil and filter are changed every 12 000 miles or 12 months. However, oil and filter changes are good for the engine and we recommend that the oil and filter are renewed more frequently, especially if the vehicle is used on a lot of short journeys.*

Every 12 000 miles or 12 months, whichever comes first

☐ Check the body and underbody for corrosion protection (Section 4)
☐ Check the power steering fluid level (Section 5)
☐ Check the manual gearbox oil level (Section 6)
☐ Check the automatic transmission oil level (Section 7)
☐ Check all components, pipes and hoses for fluid leaks (Section 8)
☐ Check the final drive oil level (Section 9)
☐ Check the intermediate reduction drive unit oil level (Section 10)
☐ Check the condition and tension of the auxiliary drivebelts (Section 11)
☐ Check the condition of the exhaust system and heat shields (Section 12)
☐ Check the front brake pads and discs for wear (Section 13)
☐ Check the brake pipes and hoses (Section 14)
☐ Check the steering and suspension components for condition and security (Section 15)
☐ Remove the roadwheels, and apply anti-seize compound (Section 16)
☐ Check the condition of the driveshafts and gaiters (Section 17)
☐ Check the operation and adjustment of the handbrake (Section 18)
☐ Lubricate all door locks and hinges, door stops, bonnet lock and release, and tailgate lock and hinges (Section 19)
☐ Check the operation of all electrical systems (Section 20)
☐ Check the seat belts and airbag (Section 21)
☐ Exhaust emission test (Section 22)
☐ Check the roadwheel speed sensor electrical harness – ABS models (Section 23)
☐ Renew the pollen filter (Section 24)
☐ Renew the fuel filter – L-Series engines (Section 25)
☐ Renew the turbocharger boost control solenoid valve vent filter – 2002-on model year only (Section 26)

Every 12 000 miles or 12 months, whichever comes first (continued)

☐ Drain the fuel filter sedimenter – 2003 model year only (Section 27)
☐ Carry out a road test (Section 28)

Every 24 000 miles or 2 years, whichever comes first

☐ Renew the air filter element (Section 29)
☐ Check the rear brake shoes and drums for wear (Section 30)
☐ Check the front brake calipers and rear wheel cylinders (Section 31)
☐ Renew the handset batteries (Section 32)

Every 36 000 miles or 3 years, whichever comes first

☐ Renew the coolant/antifreeze (Section 33)
☐ Renew the brake fluid (Section 34)

Every 48 000 miles or 4 years, whichever comes first

☐ Renew the timing belt and fuel injection pump belt – L-Series engine (Section 35)
☐ Renew auxiliary drivebelt – L-Series engine (Section 11)

Every 60 000 miles or 5 years, whichever comes first

☐ Renew the fuel filter element – TD4 engine (Section 36)
☐ Renew the automatic transmission oil (Section 37)

Every 96 000 miles or 8 years, whichever comes first

☐ Renew the manual gearbox oil – TD4 engine (Section 6)
☐ Renew auxiliary drivebelt – TD4 engine (Section 11)

Every 10 years, regardless of mileage

☐ Renew the airbag module – vehicles up to 2002 model year (Section 38)
☐ Renew the seat belt pretensioners – vehicles up to 2002 model year (Section 39)

Every 15 years, regardless of mileage

☐ Renew the airbag module – 2002 model year-on (Section 38)
☐ Renew the seat belt pretensioners – 2002 model year–on (Section 39)

Underbonnet view of an L-Series engine model

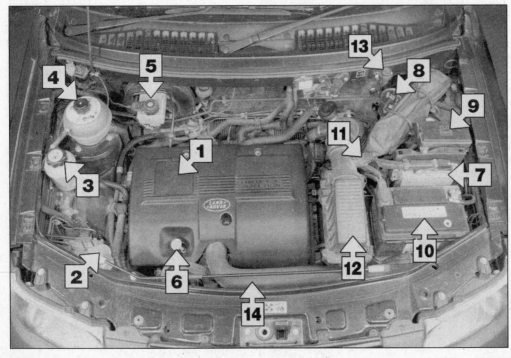

1. Engine oil filler flap
2. Washer fluid reservoir cap
3. Power steering fluid reservoir
4. Cooling system expansion tank
5. Brake fluid reservoir
6. Engine oil level dipstick
7. Engine management ECM
8. Fuel filter
9. Engine compartment fusebox
10. Battery
11. Mass airflow meter
12. Air filter
13. Inertia fuel cut-off switch
14. Intercooler top hose

Underbonnet view of a TD4 engine model

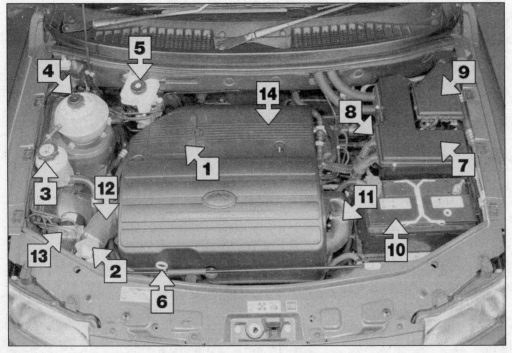

1. Engine oil filler flap
2. Washer fluid reservoir cap
3. Power steering fluid reservoir
4. Cooling system expansion tank
5. Brake fluid reservoir
6. Engine oil level dipstick
7. Engine management ECM
8. Fuel filter
9. Engine compartment fusebox
10. Battery
11. Intercooler-to-manifold hose
12. Air cleaner-to-intercooler hose
13. ABS unit
14. Air cleaner

Front underbody view of an L-Series engine model

1 Front suspension lower arm
2 Front driveshaft
3 Brake caliper
4 Oil filter
5 Lower tie rod
6 Engine sump oil drain plug
7 Auxiliary drivebelt
8 Exhaust pipe flexible joint
9 Radiator bottom hose
10 Intercooler bottom hose
11 Manual transmission
12 Front suspension anti-roll bar
13 Intermediate reduction drive unit
14 Gearchange rod
15 Prop shaft

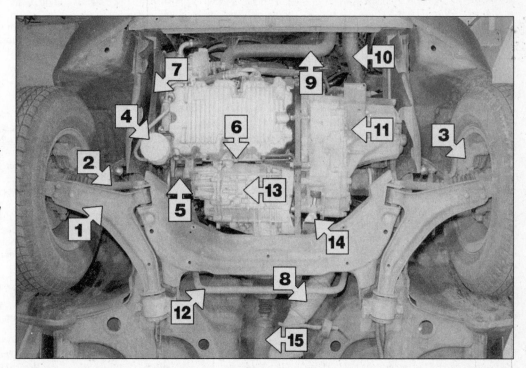

Rear underbody view

1 Fuel tank
2 Handbrake cable
3 Rear silencer box
4 Rear driveshaft
5 Final drive unit
6 Propshaft
7 Fuel filler hose
8 Transverse link
9 Trailing link

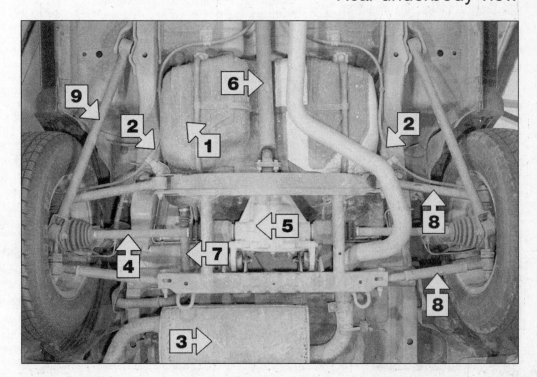

1 General information

This Chapter is designed to help the home mechanic maintain his/her vehicle for safety, economy, long life and peak performance.

The Chapter contains a master maintenance schedule, followed by Sections dealing specifically with each task in the schedule. Visual checks, adjustments, component renewal and other helpful items are included. Refer to the accompanying illustrations of the engine compartment and the underside of the vehicle for the locations of various components.

Servicing your vehicle in accordance with the mileage/time maintenance schedule and the following Sections will provide a planned maintenance programme, which should result in a long and reliable service life. This is a comprehensive plan, so maintaining some items but not others at the specified service intervals will not produce the same results.

As you service your vehicle, you will discover that many of the procedures can – and should – be grouped together, because of the particular procedure being performed, or because of the proximity of two otherwise-unrelated components to one another. For example, if the vehicle is raised for any reason, the exhaust can be inspected at the same time as the suspension and steering components.

The first step in this maintenance programme is to prepare yourself before the actual work begins. Read through all the Sections relevant to the work to be carried out, then make a list and gather all the parts and tools required. If a problem is encountered, seek advice from a parts specialist, or a dealer service department.

2 Regular maintenance

If, from the time the vehicle is new, the routine maintenance schedule is followed closely, and frequent checks are made of fluid levels and high-wear items, as suggested throughout this manual, the engine will be kept in relatively good running condition, and the need for additional work will be minimised.

It is possible that there will be times when the engine is running poorly due to the lack of regular maintenance. This is even more likely if a used vehicle, which has not received regular and frequent maintenance checks, is purchased. In such cases, additional work may need to be carried out, outside of the regular maintenance intervals.

If engine wear is suspected, a compression test (refer to Chapter 2B or 2C) will provide valuable information regarding the overall performance of the main internal components. Such a test can be used as a basis to decide on the extent of the work to be carried out.

If, for example, a compression test indicates serious internal engine wear, conventional maintenance as described in this Chapter will not greatly improve the performance of the engine, and may prove a waste of time and money, unless extensive overhaul work is carried out first.

The following series of operations are those most often required to improve the performance of a generally poor-running engine:

Primary operations

a) Clean, inspect and test the battery (refer to 'Weekly checks').
b) Check all the engine-related fluids (refer to 'Weekly checks').
c) Check the condition and tension of the auxiliary drivebelts (Section 11).
d) Check the condition of the air filter, and renew if necessary (Section 29).
e) Check the condition of all hoses, and check for fluid leaks (Section 8).

If the above operations do not prove fully effective, carry out the following secondary operations:

Secondary operations

All items listed under *Primary operations*, plus the following:

a) Check the charging system (refer to Chapter 5A).
b) Check the preheating system (refer to Chapter 5C).
c) Check the fuel system (refer to Chapter 4B).

Every 6000 miles or 6 months

3 Engine oil and filter renewal

Note: *To avoid any possibility of scalding, and to protect yourself from possible skin irritants and other harmful contaminants in used engine oils, it is advisable to wear gloves when carrying out this work.*

1 Frequent oil and filter changes are the most important preventative maintenance procedures which can be undertaken by the DIY owner. As engine oil ages, it becomes diluted and contaminated, which leads to premature engine wear.

2 Before starting this procedure, gather together all the necessary tools and materials. Also make sure that you have plenty of clean rags and newspapers handy, to mop-up any spills. Ideally, the engine oil should be warm, as it will drain more easily, and more built-up sludge will be removed with it.

Caution: Take care not to touch the exhaust or any other hot parts of the engine when working under the vehicle.

3 Firmly apply the handbrake then jack up the front of the vehicle and support it on axle stands (see *Jacking and vehicle support*). Release the retaining screws and remove the engine undertray.

4 Using a spanner or a suitable socket and bar, slacken the drain plug about half a turn **(see illustrations)**. Position the draining container under the drain plug, then remove the plug completely **(see Haynes Hint)**.

5 Allow some time for the oil to drain, noting that it may be necessary to reposition the container as the oil flow slows to a trickle.

3.4a Engine oil sump plug – L-Series engine

3.4b Engine oil sump plug – TD4 engine

HAYNES HiNT

As the drain plug threads release, move it sharply away so the stream of oil issuing from the sump runs into the container, not up your sleeve.

6 After all the oil has drained, wipe the drain plug with a clean rag and discard the sealing washer. Clean the area around the drain plug opening, and refit the plug complete with a new washer and tighten it to the specified torque.

L-Series engines

7 Move the container into position under the oil filter on the right-hand rear end of the of the cylinder block.
8 Use an oil filter removal tool to slacken the filter initially, then unscrew it by hand the rest of the way **(see illustration)**. Empty the oil from the old filter into the container.
9 Use a clean rag to remove all oil, dirt and sludge from the filter sealing area on the engine.
10 Apply a light coating of clean engine oil to the sealing ring on the new filter, then screw the filter into position. Screw the filter on until its sealing ring contacts the filter housing then tighten firmly through another complete turn by hand. If you are using a filter removal/fitting tool, tighten the filter to 16 Nm (12 lbf ft).

TD4 engines

11 Unscrew the retaining bolts and remove the plastic cover from the top of the engine. Unscrew the oil filter housing cap. Remove the filter element. Examine the 3 seals and renew them if they show any signs of damage or wear **(see illustrations)**.
12 Ensure that the filter cap is clean and dry. Fit the new filter element into the housing **(see illustration)**.
13 Lubricate the new seals (where renewed) with clean engine oil, and fit them to the filter cap. Refit the cap and tighten it to the specified torque.
14 Refit the plastic cover to the top of the engine and tighten the retaining bolts securely.

All models

15 Remove the old oil and all tools from

3.8 If necessary, use a filter removal tool to slacken the oil filter

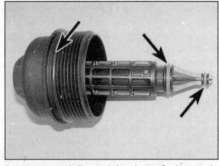
3.11b . . . and discard the three O-ring seals (arrowed) if they are damaged or worn

under the vehicle, refit the engine undertray, then lower the vehicle to the ground.
16 Fill the engine through the filler hole, using the correct grade and type of oil (refer to *Weekly Checks* for details of topping-up). Pour in half the specified quantity of oil first, then wait a few minutes for the oil to drain into the sump. Continue to add oil, a small quantity at a time, until the level is up to the lower mark on the dipstick. Adding approximately a further 1.0 litre will bring the level up to the upper mark on the dipstick.
17 Start the engine and run it for a few minutes, while checking for leaks around the

3.11a Unscrew and remove the oil filter cap . . .

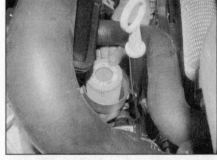
3.12 Fit the new element into the housing

oil filter seal and the sump drain plug. Note that there may be a delay of a few seconds before the low oil pressure warning light goes out when the engine is first started, as the oil circulates through the new oil filter and the engine oil galleries before the pressure builds-up.
18 Stop the engine, and wait a few minutes for the oil to settle in the sump once more. With the new oil circulated and the filter now completely full, recheck the level on the dipstick, and add more oil as necessary.
19 Dispose of the used engine oil safely with reference to *General repair procedures*.

Every 12 000 miles or 12 months

4 Body corrosion check

This work should be carried out by a Land Rover dealer in order to validate the vehicle warranty. The work includes a thorough inspection of the vehicle paintwork and underbody for damage and corrosion. **Note:** *This is only applicable to vehicles sold after 24th November 1998.*

5 Power steering fluid level check

1 Park the vehicle on level ground and set

the steering wheel straight-ahead. The engine should be turned off.

> **HAYNES HiNT** *For the check to be accurate, the steering must not be turned once the engine has been stopped.*

2 The power steering fluid reservoir is located in the front right-hand corner of the engine compartment. UPPER and LOWER level marks are moulded into the translucent wall of the reservoir. The fluid level should be checked with the engine cold and stopped **(see illustration)**.
3 Check that the fluid is on the upper level mark in the translucent reservoir. Where

topping-up is necessary, first wipe clean the area around the filler cap **(see illustration)**.
4 Remove the cap then top-up the fluid level

5.2 Power steering fluid reservoir

5.3 Wipe the reservoir clean

5.4 Top-up the power steering fluid

using the specified type of fluid (do not overfill the reservoir). On completion refit the filler cap **(see illustration)**.

6 Manual gearbox oil level check

Level check

1 Position the vehicle over an inspection pit, on vehicle ramps, or jack it up, but make sure that it is level (see *Jacking and vehicle support*). Release the retaining screws and remove the engine/transmission undertray. The oil level must be checked before the vehicle is driven, or at least 5 minutes after the engine has been switched off. If the oil is checked immediately after driving the vehicle, some of the oil will remain distributed around the gearbox components, resulting in an inaccurate level reading.

2 Remove all traces of dirt from around the filler/level plug which is located on the left-hand side of the gearbox, where it is situated behind the driveshaft inner joint **(see illustrations)**. Unscrew the plug and discard the sealing washer where fitted.

3 The oil level should reach the lower edge of the level plug hole. A certain amount of oil will have gathered behind the filler level plug and will trickle out when it is removed; this does not necessarily mean that the level is correct.

4 To ensure that a true level is established, wait until the initial trickle stops then add oil, via the filler/level plug hole, until a new trickle of oil can be seen emerging **(see illustration)**. The level will be correct when the flow ceases. Add only good quality oil of the specified type (see *Lubricants and fluids*).

5 Wipe the filler/level plug with a clean rag fit the new sealing washer (where fitted). Clean the area around the filler/level plug opening

then refit the plug, complete with the washer, tightening it to the specified torque. Refit the engine/transmission undertray, and where necessary, lower the vehicle to the ground.

Oil renewal

6 Refer to Chapter 7A.

7 Automatic transmission oil level check

1 The oil level must be checked with the fluid at a temperature of 35° to 45°C. To achieve this temperature, take the vehicle for a drive of approximately 5 to 10 miles. If possible, the temperature of the oil should be checked with a thermometer through the oil filler aperture on the top of the transmission.

2 With the transmission oil at the appropriate temperature, position the vehicle over an inspection pit, on vehicle ramps, or jack it up, but make sure that it is level (see *Jacking and vehicle support*). Release the retaining screws and remove the engine/transmission undertray.

3 Start the engine and move the selector lever from P through all the gear positions for 2 to 3 seconds, then return it to the P position.

4 With the engine still running, remove all traces of dirt from around the level plug. Unscrew the plug and allow any excess fluid to drain off **(see illustration)**. Discard the sealing washer, a new one must be fitted.

5 If no fluid spills out, pull out the fluid filler plug from the top of the transmission, and add fluid until it just begins to spill from the level hole.

6 Move the selector lever from P through each gear position and back to P. Allow any excess fluid to spill from the level hole.

7 Wipe the level plug with a clean rag fit the new sealing washer. Clean the area around the level plug opening then refit the plug, complete with the washer, tightening it to the specified torque. Refit the engine/transmission undertray, and where necessary, lower the vehicle to the ground. Refit the filler plug.

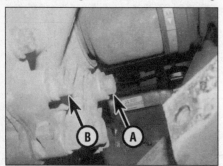

6.2a Transmission oil filler/level plug (A) and drain plug (B) – L-Series engine

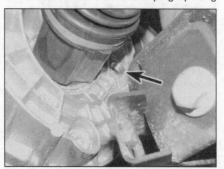

6.2b Transmission oil filler/level plug (arrowed) – TD4 engine

8 Hose and fluid leak check

1 Visually inspect the engine joint faces, gaskets and seals for any signs of water or oil leaks. Pay particular attention to the areas around the cylinder head cover, cylinder head, oil filter and sump joint faces. Bear in mind that, over a period of time, some very slight seepage from these areas is to be expected – what you are really looking for is any indication of a serious leak. Should a leak be found, renew the offending gasket or oil seal by referring to the appropriate Chapters in this manual.

2 Also check the security and condition of all

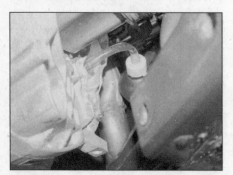

6.4 Top-up the transmission using only the specified oil

7.4 Unscrew the level plug (arrowed) and allow any excess fluid to drain off

A leak in the cooing system will usually show up as white- or antifreeze-coloured deposits on the area adjoining the leak.

the engine-related pipes and hoses, and all braking system pipes and hoses and fuel lines. Ensure that all cable ties or securing clips are in place, and in good condition. Clips which are broken or missing can lead to chafing of the hoses, pipes or wiring, which could cause more serious problems in the future.

3 Carefully check the radiator hoses and heater hoses along their entire length. Renew any hose which is cracked, swollen or deteriorated. Cracks will show up better if the hose is squeezed. Pay close attention to the hose clips that secure the hoses to the cooling system components. Hose clips can pinch and puncture hoses, resulting in cooling system leaks. If the crimped-type hose clips are used, it may be a good idea to update them with standard worm-drive clips.

4 Inspect all the cooling system components (hoses, joint faces, etc) for leaks **(see Haynes Hint)**. Where any problems are found on the system components, renew the component or gasket with reference to Chapter 3.

5 With the vehicle raised, inspect the fuel tank and filler neck for punctures, cracks and other damage. The connection between the filler neck and tank is especially critical. Sometimes a rubber filler neck or connecting hose will leak due to loose retaining clamps or deteriorated rubber.

6 Carefully check all rubber hoses and metal fuel lines leading away from the fuel tank. Check for loose connections, deteriorated hoses, crimped lines, and other damage. Pay particular attention to the vent pipes and hoses, which often loop up around the filler neck and can become blocked or crimped. Follow the lines to the front of the vehicle, carefully inspecting them all the way. Renew damaged sections as necessary. Similarly, whilst the vehicle is raised, take the opportunity to inspect all underbody brake fluid pipes and hoses.

7 From within the engine compartment, check the security of all fuel, vacuum and brake hose attachments and pipe unions, and inspect all hoses for kinks, chafing and deterioration.

8 Check the condition of the power steering fluid pipes and hoses.

9 Final drive oil level check

1 Position the vehicle over an inspection pit, on vehicle ramps, or jack it up, but make sure that it is level (see *Jacking and vehicle support*). The oil level must be checked before the vehicle is driven, or at least 5 minutes after the engine has been switched off. If the oil is checked immediately after driving the vehicle, some of the oil will remain distributed around the final drive components, resulting in an inaccurate level reading.

2 Remove all traces of dirt from around the filler/level plug which is located on the rear of the final drive unit **(see illustration)**. Unscrew the plug.

3 The oil level should reach the lower edge of the level plug hole. A certain amount of oil will have gathered behind the filler level plug and will trickle out when it is removed; this does not necessarily mean that the level is correct.

4 To ensure that a true level is established, wait until the initial trickle stops then add oil, via the filler/level plug hole, until a new trickle of oil can be seen emerging. The level will be correct when the flow ceases. Add only good quality oil of the specified type (see *Lubricants and fluids*).

5 Wipe the filler/level plug with a clean rag. Clean the area around the filler/level plug opening then refit the plug, tightening it to the specified torque. Where necessary, lower the vehicle to the ground.

10 Intermediate reduction drive unit oil level check

1 Position the vehicle over an inspection pit, on vehicle ramps, or jack it up, but make sure that it is level (see *Jacking and vehicle support*). Release the retaining screws and remove the engine/transmission undertray. The oil level must be checked before the vehicle is driven, or at least 5 minutes after the engine has been switched off. If the oil is checked immediately after driving the vehicle, some of the oil will remain distributed around the intermediate

10.2 Intermediate reduction drive unit filler/level plug (arrowed)

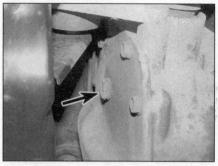

9.2 Final drive oil filler/level plug (arrowed)

reduction drive unit components, resulting in an inaccurate level reading.

2 Remove all traces of dirt from around the filler/level plug which is located on the right-hand rear of the unit **(see illustration)**. Unscrew the plug and discard the sealing washer.

3 The oil level should reach the lower edge of the level plug hole. A certain amount of oil will have gathered behind the filler level plug and will trickle out when it is removed; this does not necessarily mean that the level is correct.

4 To ensure that a true level is established, wait until the initial trickle stops then add oil, via the filler/level plug hole, until a new trickle of oil can be seen emerging **(see illustration)**. The level will be correct when the flow ceases. Add only good quality oil of the specified type (see *Lubricants and fluids*).

5 Wipe the filler/level plug with a clean rag fit the new sealing washer. Clean the area around the filler/level plug opening then refit the plug, complete with the washer, tightening it securely. Refit the engine/transmission undertray and, where necessary, lower the vehicle to the ground.

11 Auxiliary drivebelts check and renewal

Checking

1 Due to their function and material makeup, drivebelts are prone to failure after a long period of time and should therefore be inspected regularly.

10.4 Top-up the IRD unit only with the specified oil

11.9 Rotate the pulley clockwise to relieve the tension on the belt

11.13 Using a suitable spanner, rotate the tensioner anti-clockwise until there is sufficient slack to enable the belt to be slipped off from the pulleys

11.20 Undo the tensioner pivot and clamping bolts

2 Turn the steering wheel to the full right-hand lock position. Unscrew the three retaining bolts and remove the splash shield from the wheel arch.

3 With the engine stopped, inspect the full length of the drivebelt(s) for cracks and separation of the belt plies. It will be necessary to turn the engine (using a spanner or socket and bar on the crankshaft pulley bolt) in order to move the belt(s) from the pulleys so that the belt can be inspected thoroughly. Twist the belt(s) between the pulleys so that both sides can be viewed. Also check for fraying, and glazing which gives the belt a shiny appearance. Check the pulleys for nicks, cracks, distortion and corrosion.

4 If a belt shows signs of wear or damage it must be renewed. If the belts are in good condition, check the tension as follows.

5 The auxiliary drivebelts have an automatic tensioning device. Providing the belts appear to be under tension when examined, no further tension checks are possible. The air conditioning compressor drivebelt is tensioned as described in Paragraph 22.

6 Once the belts have been checked, refit the splash shield, and tighten the retaining screws securely.

Auxiliary drivebelt

7 Undo the retaining bolts and remove the plastic cover from the top of the engine.

8 Firmly apply the handbrake then jack up the front of the vehicle and support it on axle stands (see *Jacking and vehicle support*). Release the retaining screws and remove the engine undertray.

L-Series engine

9 Using a ring spanner on the tensioner pulley bolt, rotate the pulley clockwise, to relieve the tension on the belt **(see illustration)**.

10 With the tension relieved, remove the belt from the pulleys.

11 Fit the new belt around all the pulleys, except the alternator pulley. Hold the tensioner pulley fully clockwise, and fit the belt over the alternator pulley. Release the tensioner.

TD4 engine

12 Turn the steering wheel to the full right-hand lock position. Undo the three retaining screws and remove the splash shield from the wheel arch. If the belt is to be re-used, mark the normal direction of rotation of the belt.

13 Using a suitable spanner fitted to the tensioner pulley bolt, rotate the tensioner anti-clockwise until there is sufficient slack to enable the belt to be slipped off from the pulleys. Remove the belt from the vehicle **(see illustration)**.

14 Manoeuvre the belt into position, routing it correctly around the pulleys as the tensioner is held fully anti-clockwise; if the original belt is being fitted use the marks made prior to removal to ensure it is fitted the correct way around.

15 Seat the belt on the pulleys and slowly release the tensioner pulley until the belt is correctly tensioned.

Caution: Do not allow the tensioner to spring back and stress the belt.

16 Refit the splash shield, and tighten the retaining screws securely.

All models

17 Refit the engine undertray, and lower the vehicle to the ground. Refit the plastic cover to the top of the engine.

Compressor drivebelt

18 Turn the steering wheel to the full right-hand lock position. Undo the three retaining screws and remove the splash shield from the wheel arch. If the belt is to be re-used, mark the normal direction of rotation of the belt.

19 Remove the auxiliary drivebelt as described in Paragraph 13.

20 Undo the tensioner pivot and clamping bolts, and slip the air conditioning compressor drivebelt from the pulleys **(see illustration)**.

21 Manoeuvre the belt into position around the compressor and crankshaft inner pulleys, routing it over the tensioner pulley.

22 Apply the specified torque to the tensioner pivot hexagon, and tighten the tensioner clamping bolt to the specified torque **(see illustration)**. With the tensioner secured, tighten the pivot bolt to the specified torque.

23 Refit and tension the auxiliary drivebelt as described in Paragraphs 14 and 15.

---

12 Exhaust system check

1 Park the vehicle on a level surface and switch off the engine. Chock the front wheels and select first gear, then raise the rear of the vehicle and rest it securely on axle stands (see *Jacking and vehicle support*). Release the retaining screws and remove the engine/transmission undertray.

2 With the engine cold (wait at least an hour after switching off the engine), check the complete exhaust system from the engine to the end of the tailpipe.

3 Check the exhaust pipes and connections for evidence of leaks, severe corrosion and damage. Make sure that all brackets and mountings are in good condition, and that all relevant nuts and bolts are tight **(see illustration)**. Leakage at any of the joints or in other parts of the system will usually show up as a black, sooty stain in the vicinity of the leak.

11.22 Using a torque wrench, apply the specified tension to the belt

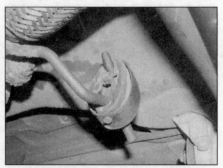

12.3 Check the exhaust system mounting rubbers are in good condition

4 Rattles and vibrations can often be traced to the exhaust system. Tap the silencer units with a soft mallet and listen for noises caused by corroded or displaced baffle material.

Caution: Do not strike the catalytic converter, as this may damage the ceramic block inside.

5 Carefully rock the pipes and silencers from side-to-side on their mountings. If the components are able to come into contact with the body or suspension parts, look for broken or worn rubber mountings.

6 Extra clearance can be gained by slackening the clamps between adjacent sections of the exhaust pipe to loosen the joints (where possible – refer to Chapter 4B) and twisting the pipes as necessary to provide the additional clearance. Retighten the clamps on completion.

13 Brake pad and disc check

1 Firmly apply the handbrake, then jack up the front of the vehicle and support it securely on axle stands (see *Jacking and vehicle support*). Remove the front roadwheels.

2 For a quick check, the pad thickness can be carried out via the inspection hole on the front of the caliper **(see Haynes Hint)**. Using a steel rule, measure the thickness of the pad lining material excluding the backing plate. This must not be less than that indicated in the Specifications.

3 The view through the caliper inspection hole gives a rough indication of the state of the brake pads. For a comprehensive check, the brake pads should be removed and cleaned. The operation of the caliper can then also be checked, and the condition of the brake disc itself can be fully examined on both sides. Chapter 9 contains a detailed description of how the brake disc should be checked for wear and/or damage.

4 If any pad's lining material is worn to the specified thickness or less, *all four pads must be renewed as a set*. Refer to Chapter 9 for details.

5 On completion, refit the roadwheels and lower the vehicle to the ground. Tighten the wheel nuts to the specified torque.

14 Brake pipe and hose check

1 Jack up the front and rear of the vehicle and support it on axle stands (see *Jacking and vehicle support*).

2 Check the security and condition of all the braking system pipes and hoses. In particular, check the flexible hoses for signs of cracking by carefully bending them at several points along their lengths. Check the rigid brake lines

for corrosion, especially at exposed locations on the underbody.

3 Ensure that all hose and pipe securing clips are in place, and in good condition.

4 Renewal of the brake pipes and hoses is described in Chapter 9.

5 On completion lower the vehicle to the ground.

15 Suspension and steering check

Front suspension and steering

1 Raise the front of the vehicle, and securely support it on axle stands (see *Jacking and vehicle support*).

2 Visually inspect the balljoint dust covers and the steering rack-and-pinion gaiters for splits, chafing or deterioration. Any wear of these components will cause loss of lubricant, together with dirt and water entry, resulting in rapid deterioration of the balljoints or steering gear.

3 On vehicles with power steering, check the fluid hoses for chafing or deterioration, and the pipe and hose unions for fluid leaks. Also check for signs of fluid leakage under pressure from the steering gear rubber gaiters, which would indicate failed fluid seals within the steering gear.

4 Grasp the roadwheel at the 12 o'clock and 6 o'clock positions, and try to rock it **(see illustration)**. Very slight free play may be felt, but if the movement is appreciable, further investigation is necessary to determine the source. Continue rocking the wheel while an assistant depresses the footbrake. If the movement is now eliminated or significantly reduced, it is likely that the hub bearings are at fault. If the free play is still evident with the footbrake depressed, then there is wear in the suspension joints or mountings.

5 Now grasp the wheel at the 9 o'clock and 3 o'clock positions, and try to rock it as before. Any movement felt now may again be caused by wear in the hub bearings or the steering track rod balljoints. If the outer balljoint is worn, the visual movement will be obvious. If the inner joint is suspect, it can be felt by placing a hand over the rack-and-pinion rubber gaiter and gripping the track rod. If the wheel is now rocked, movement will be felt at the inner joint if wear has taken place.

6 Using a large screwdriver or flat bar, check for wear in the suspension mounting bushes by levering between the relevant suspension component and its attachment point. Some movement is to be expected, as the mountings are made of rubber, but excessive wear should be obvious. Also check the condition of any visible rubber bushes, looking for splits, cracks or contamination of the rubber.

7 With the vehicle standing on its wheels, have an assistant turn the steering wheel back-and-forth, about an eighth of a turn

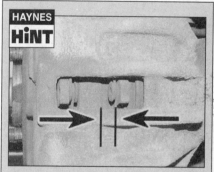

The pad thickness can be carried out via the inspection hole on the front of the caliper.

each way. There should be very little, if any, lost movement between the steering wheel and roadwheels. If this is not the case, closely observe the joints and mountings previously described. In addition, check the steering column universal joints for wear, and also check the rack-and-pinion steering gear itself.

Rear suspension

8 Chock the front wheels, then jack up the rear of the vehicle and support securely on axle stands (see *Jacking and vehicle support*).

9 Working as described previously for the front suspension, check the rear hub bearings, the suspension bushes and the strut/shock absorber mountings for wear.

Shock absorbers

10 Check for any signs of fluid leakage around the front and rear shock absorbers, or from the rubber gaiter around the piston rod. Should any fluid be noticed, the shock absorber is defective internally, and should be renewed. **Note:** *Shock absorbers should always be renewed in pairs on the same axle.*

11 The efficiency of the shock absorber may be checked by bouncing the vehicle at each corner. Generally speaking, the body will return to its normal position and stop after being depressed. If it rises and returns on a rebound, the shock absorber is probably suspect. Also examine the shock absorber upper and lower mountings for any signs of wear.

15.4 Grasp the roadwheel at the 12 o'clock and 6 o'clock positions, and try to rock it

16.2 Apply a thin layer of anti-seize compound to the area where the wheel contacts the hub

16 Roadwheel anti-seize check

1 In order to prevent the wheel seizing to the hub, Land Rover state that the hub-to-wheel mating surface should be coated with a thin layer of anti-seize compound.
2 With the handbrake fully applied, jack up the front of the vehicle and support on axle stands (see *Jacking and vehicle support*). Remove the front roadwheels. Ensure that the hub/wheel mating surfaces are clean and dry, and apply a thin layer of anti-seize compound **(see illustration)**. Refit the roadwheels to their original positions.
3 Chock the front wheels, jack up the rear of the vehicle and support on axle stands (see *Jacking and vehicle support*). Remove the rear roadwheels. Ensure that the drum/wheel mating surfaces are clean and dry, and apply a thin layer of anti-seize compound. Refit the roadwheels to the **opposite** sides of the rear axle. This is to prevent uneven tyre wear, and subsequent excessive tyre noise. Land Rover state that the wheels must not be swapped diagonally, or the front wheels swapped from side-to-side.

17 Driveshaft and gaiter check

1 With the vehicle raised and securely supported on stands (see *Jacking and vehicle*

17.1 Inspect the condition of the outer constant velocity (CV) joint rubber gaiters

support), turn the steering onto full lock then slowly rotate the roadwheel. Inspect the condition of the outer constant velocity (CV) joint rubber gaiters while squeezing the gaiters to open out the folds **(see illustration)**. Check for signs of cracking, splits or deterioration of the rubber which may allow the grease to escape and lead to water and grit entry into the joint. Also check the security and condition of the retaining clips. Repeat these checks on the inner CV joints. If any damage or deterioration is found, the gaiters should be renewed as described in Chapter 8.
2 At the same time check the general condition of the CV joints themselves by first holding the driveshaft and attempting to rotate the wheel. Repeat this check by holding the inner joint and attempting to rotate the driveshaft. Any appreciable movement indicates wear in the joints, wear in the driveshaft splines or loose driveshaft retaining nut.

18 Handbrake check

1 The handbrake should be capable of holding the parked vehicle stationary, even on steep slopes, when applied with moderate force. The mechanism should be firm and positive in feel with no trace of stiffness or sponginess from the cables and should release immediately the handbrake lever is released. If the mechanism is faulty in any of these respects then it must be checked immediately.
2 To check the handbrake setting, first apply the footbrake firmly several times to establish correct shoe-to-drum clearance. Applying normal, moderate pressure, pull the handbrake lever to the fully-applied position whilst counting the number of clicks emitted from the handbrake ratchet mechanism. If adjustment is correct, there should be 4 to 5 clicks before the handbrake is fully applied. If this is not the case, then adjustment is required as described in Chapter 9.

19 Hinge and lock lubrication

1 Work around the vehicle and lubricate the hinges of the bonnet, doors and rear door/tailgate with a light machine oil. Also lubricate the bonnet lock located on the engine compartment front crossmember.
2 Lightly lubricate the bonnet release mechanism and exposed section of the inner cable with a smear of grease.

20 Electrical system check

1 Check the operation of all electrical equipment, ie, lights, direction indicators, horn,

wash/wipe system, etc. Refer to the appropriate Sections of Chapter 12 for details if any of the circuits are found to be inoperative.
2 Visually check all accessible wiring connectors, harnesses and retaining clips for security, and for signs of chafing or damage. Rectify any faults found.

21 Seat belt and airbag check

1 Check the webbing of each belt for signs of fraying, cuts or other damage, pulling the belt out to its full extent to check its entire length.
2 Check the operation of the belt buckles by pulling the belt hard to ensure that it remains locked in position.
3 Check the inertia reel retractor mechanism by pulling out the belt to the halfway point and jerking hard. The mechanism must lock immediately to prevent any further unreeling but must allow free movement during normal driving.
4 Ensure that all belt mounting bolts are securely tightened. Note that the bolts are shouldered so that the belt anchor points are free to rotate.
5 If there is any sign of damage, or any doubt about a belt's condition, then it must be renewed. If the vehicle has been involved in a collision, then any belt in use at the time must be renewed as a matter of course and all other belts checked carefully.
6 The airbag/SRS warning light on the instrument panel should extinguish 3 seconds after the ignition switch is turned to position II. If this is not the case, have the system checked by a Land Rover dealer. No attempt should be made to carry out repairs to the airbag components.

22 Exhaust emission check

1 The check involves checking the engine management system operation by plugging an electronic tester into the system diagnostic socket to check the electronic control module (ECM) memory for faults (see Chapter 4B).
2 In reality, if the vehicle is running correctly and the engine management warning light in the instrument panel is functioning normally, then this check need not be carried out. On vehicles over 3 years old, the exhaust emissions will be checked every year during the MOT test.

23 Roadwheel speed sensors check

1 Raise the vehicle, and securely support it on axle stands (see *Jacking and vehicle support*). Remove the roadwheels.

23.2 Check the speed sensors harnesses are correctly routed and secured

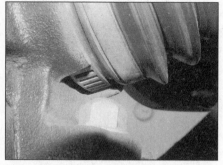

23.3 Check the reluctor rings are free from debris and damage

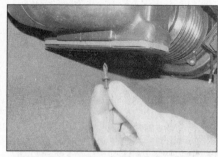

24.1a On pre-2001 model year vehicles, unscrew the three screws, and pull out the pollen filter retaining clips

2 Check the speed sensors harnesses are correctly routed and secured. Check the harnesses for chafing or damage **(see illustration)**.
3 Ensure the sensors are fully inserted in their correct positions, and the reluctor rings are free from debris and damage **(see illustration)**.
4 Refit the roadwheels and lower the vehicle to the ground. Tighten the roadwheel nuts to the specified torque.

24 Pollen filter renewal

1 The pollen filter (if fitted) is located beneath the left-hand side of the facia, in the heater inlet system. To remove the filter on pre-2001 model year vehicles, unscrew the three screws, and pull out the retaining clips **(see illustration)**. On post-2001 model year vehicles, the filter is secured by four screws **(see illustration)**.
2 Pull the filter from the housing **(see illustration)**.
3 Fit the new filter using a reversal of the removal procedure.

24.1b On post-2001 model year vehicles, the pollen filter is secured by four screws

25 Fuel filter renewal (L-Series engine)

1 Undo the retaining straps and remove the vehicle jack from the bracket in the left-hand rear corner of the engine compartment.
2 Place absorbent rag beneath the filter. Release the retaining clips and disconnect the fuel inlet and outlet hoses **(see illustration)**.
3 Remove the filter bracket from the body

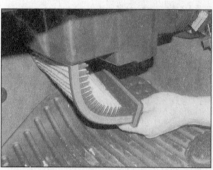

24.2 Pull the pollen filter from the housing

mounting, slacken the filter clamp bolt, and remove the filter from the bracket **(see illustration)**.
4 Fit the new filter to the mounting bracket, and tighten the clamp bolt. Refit the bracket to the body mounting.
5 Reconnect the fuel inlet and outlet hoses, and secure them using the retaining clips.
6 Slacken the bleed screw of the top of the filter, and repeatedly squeeze the hand primer until the fuel coming out of the bleed screw is bubble-free **(see illustration)**. Refit the vehicle jack, and retaining straps.

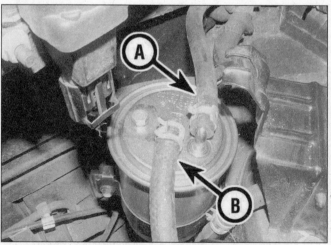

25.2 Fuel filter inlet hose (A) and outlet hose (B) – L-Series engine

25.3 Slacken the filter clamp bolt, and remove the filter from the bracket

26 Turbocharger boost control solenoid valve vent filter renewal

1 The vent filter is located in the right-hand rear corner of the engine compartment, behind the engine. Release the filter hose from the retaining clips, then pull the hoses from the filter **(see illustration)**.
2 Refitting is a reversal of removal, ensuring the hose is securely clipped back into place.

27 Fuel filter sedimenter drainage

1 The fuel filter sedimenter is located just in front of the right-hand rear wheel arch. Position a suitable container under the filter/sedimenter.
2 Slacken the sedimenter drain plug, and allow the fluid to drain until fuel free from water flows **(see illustration)**.
3 Tighten the drain plug.

28 Road test

Instruments and electrical equipment

1 Check the operation of all instruments and electrical equipment.
2 Make sure that all instruments read correctly, and switch on all electrical equipment in turn, to check that it functions properly.

Steering and suspension

3 Check for any abnormalities in the steering, suspension, handling or road 'feel'.
4 Drive the vehicle, and check that there are no unusual vibrations or noises.
5 Check that the steering feels positive, with no excessive 'sloppiness', or roughness, and check for any suspension noises when cornering and driving over bumps.

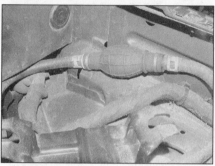

25.6 Repeatedly squeeze the hand primer until the fuel coming out of the bleed screw is bubble-free

Drivetrain

6 Check the performance of the engine, clutch, transmission and driveshafts.
7 Listen for any unusual noises from the engine, clutch and transmission.
8 Make sure that the engine runs smoothly when idling, and that there is no hesitation when accelerating.
9 Check that, where applicable, the clutch action is smooth and progressive, that the drive is taken up smoothly, and that the pedal travel is not excessive. Also listen for any noises when the clutch pedal is depressed.
10 Check that all gears can be engaged smoothly without noise, and that the gear lever action is smooth and not abnormally vague or 'notchy'.
11 Listen for a metallic clicking sound from the front of the vehicle, as the vehicle is driven slowly in a circle with the steering on full-lock. Carry out this check in both directions. If a clicking noise is heard, this indicates wear in a driveshaft joint (see Chapter 8).

Braking system

12 Make sure that the vehicle does not pull to one side when braking, and that the wheels do not lock prematurely when braking hard.
13 Check that there is no vibration through the steering when braking.
14 Check that the handbrake operates correctly, without excessive movement of the

26.1 The turbocharger boost control solenoid valve vent filter is located down the back of the engine (arrowed)

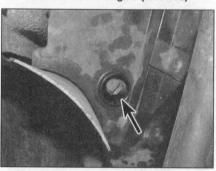

27.2 Slacken the fuel sedimenter drain plug (arrowed – viewed from underneath the vehicle)

lever, and that it holds the vehicle stationary on a slope.
15 Test the operation of the brake servo unit as follows. Depress the footbrake four or five times to exhaust the vacuum, then start the engine. As the engine starts, there should be a noticeable 'give' in the brake pedal as vacuum builds-up. Allow the engine to run for at least two minutes, and then switch it off. If the brake pedal is now depressed again, it should be possible to detect a hiss from the servo as the pedal is depressed. After about four or five applications, no further hissing should be heard, and the pedal should feel considerably harder.

Every 24 000 miles or 2 years

29.2a Release the retaining clips . . .

29.2b . . . and disconnect the mass airflow sensor

29 Air filter element renewal

L-Series engine

1 The air filter is located in the engine compartment, on the left-hand end of the engine.
2 Release the retaining clips, and disconnect the mass airflow sensor from the air filter top cover **(see illustrations)**.
3 Release the retaining clips and remove the air filter top **(see illustration)**.

29.3 Release the retaining clips and remove the air filter top

29.4 Lift out the filter element, noting which way up it is fitted

29.9 Unscrew the five Allen screws (arrowed) and remove the air filter cover

4 Lift out the filter element, noting which up it is fitted, then wipe out the casing and the cover **(see illustration)**.

5 Fit the new filter, making sure it is the correct way up, and seat it in the housing. Locate the cover on the housing and secure it in position with all the retaining clips.

6 Reconnect the mass airflow sensor, and secure the retaining clips.

TD4 engine

7 Slacken the retaining clips, unscrew the mounting bolts and remove the intake air ducting assembly (see Chapter 4B).

8 Remove the engine oil filler cap, and plug the aperture to prevent contamination.

9 Unscrew the five Allen screws and remove the air filter cover and element **(see illustration)**.

10 Clean out the inside of the air filter, and insert the new element **(see illustration)**.

11 Refit the filter cover and tighten the Allen screws to the specified torque.

12 Refit the engine oil filler cap, and the air intake ducting. Tighten the ducting retaining clips.

30 Brake shoe and drum check

Refer to the detailed description given in Chapter 9.

31 Brake caliper and wheel cylinder check

1 Jack up the front and rear of the vehicle and support it on axle stands (see *Jacking and vehicle support*). Remove the front and rear wheels.

2 For a thorough check of the front brake calipers, remove the brake pads as described in Chapter 9. Carefully clean the brake pad locations in the caliper body and mounting bracket taking care not to inhale the brake dust as it may contain asbestos which is a health hazard. Check the caliper for signs of brake fluid leakage. If this is evident at the flexible hose connection, renew the copper

washers with reference to Chapter 9. If leakage is evident at the piston, renew the internal sealing ring or renew the caliper complete, with reference to Chapter 9.

3 To check the wheel cylinders, remove the drums with reference to Chapter 9, then clean away dust and dirt from the brake shoes and wheel cylinder. Check the wheel cylinders for signs of brake fluid leakage by temporarily lifting the rubber boots **(see illustration)**. If evident, renew the wheel cylinder complete as described in Chapter 9.

32 Handset battery renewal

1 The alarm system handset contains a battery which should last for approximately 3 years. When it requires renewal, the indicator warning lights on the front doors will flash rapidly before

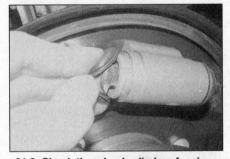

31.3 Check the wheel cylinders for signs of brake fluid leakage by temporarily lifting the rubber boots

29.10 Insert the new air filter element

the doors are opened and the operating range will reduce considerably.

2 To renew the battery, use a small screwdriver or coin to prise off the handset cover then remove the battery from its clip **(see illustrations)**.

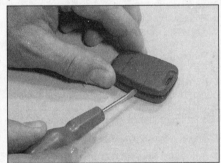

32.2a Carefully insert a screwdriver into the slot . . .

32.2b . . . and prise off the handset cover

32.3 Ensure the new battery is installed with the positive (+) side facing upwards

3 Press each button for a minimum of 5 seconds to drain any remaining power from the handset, then fit the new battery taking care not to touch the contact surfaces with the fingers.

Make sure the new battery is correctly located with the positive (+) side facing upwards **(see illustration)**.
4 Press on the cover, then unlock the vehicle

using the key and operate the lock button on the handset at least four times.

Every 36 000 miles or 3 years

33 Coolant/antifreeze renewal

⚠️ *Warning: Wait until the engine is cold before starting this procedure. Do not allow antifreeze to come in contact with your skin, or with the painted surfaces of the vehicle. Rinse off spills immediately with plenty of water. Never leave antifreeze lying around in an open container, or in a puddle in the driveway or on the garage floor. Children and pets are attracted by its sweet smell, but antifreeze can be fatal if ingested.*

Cooling system draining

1 With the engine completely cold, remove the expansion tank filler cap. Turn the cap anti-clockwise, wait until any pressure remaining in the system is released, then unscrew it and lift it off.
2 Jack the front of the vehicle up and support it on axle stands (see *Jacking and vehicle support*). Release the retaining screws and remove the engine undertray. Position a suitable container beneath the coolant rail.
3 Position the heater temperature control on its maximum setting.
4 Release the clip and disconnect the bottom hose from the coolant rail, and allow the coolant to drain into the container.
5 When the flow of coolant stops, refit the bottom hose and refit the clip.
6 If the coolant has been drained for a reason other than renewal, then provided it is clean and less than three years old, it can be re-used, though this is not recommended.

Cooling system flushing

7 If coolant renewal has been neglected, or if the antifreeze mixture has become diluted, then in time, the cooling system may gradually

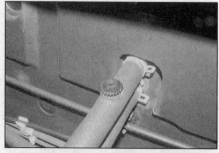

33.16 Unscrew and remove the bleed screw from the heater return hose at the engine compartment bulkhead

lose efficiency, as the coolant passages become restricted due to rust, scale deposits, and other sediment. The cooling system efficiency can be restored by flushing the system clean.
8 The radiator should be flushed independently of the engine, to avoid unnecessary contamination.

Radiator flushing

9 Disconnect the top and bottom hoses and any other relevant hoses from the radiator, with reference to Chapter 3.
10 Insert a garden hose into the radiator top inlet. Direct a flow of clean water through the radiator, and continue flushing until clean water emerges from the radiator bottom outlet.
11 If after a reasonable period, the water still does not run clear, the radiator can be flushed with a good proprietary cleaning agent. It is important that the manufacturer's instructions are followed carefully. If the contamination is particularly bad, insert the hose in the radiator bottom outlet, and reverse-flush the radiator.

Engine flushing

12 Remove the thermostat as described in Chapter 3 then, if the radiator top hose has been disconnected from the engine, temporarily reconnect the hose.
13 With the top and bottom hoses disconnected from the radiator, insert a garden hose into the radiator top hose. Direct a clean flow of water through the engine, and continue flushing until clean water emerges from the radiator bottom hose.
14 On completion of flushing, refit the thermostat and reconnect the hoses with reference to Chapter 3.

Cooling system filling

15 Before attempting to fill the cooling system, make sure that all hoses and clips are in good condition, and that the clips are tight. Note that an antifreeze mixture must be used all year round, to prevent corrosion of the engine components. Make sure the heater controls are set to maximum heat.
16 Remove the expansion tank filler cap. Unscrew and remove the bleed screw from the heater return hose at the engine compartment bulkhead **(see illustration)**.
17 Slowly fill the system until bubble-free coolant comes out of the bleed hole in the coolant pipe, then fit and tighten the screw.
18 Continue filling the system until bubble free coolant comes out of the bleed screw in the heater return hose, then fit and tighten the screw.
19 Fill the cooling system until the coolant

reaches the MAX mark on the expansion tank, then refit and tighten the filler cap.
20 Refit the undershield beneath the engine compartment, and lower the vehicle to the ground.
21 Start the engine, and allow it to run until it reaches normal operating temperature (until the cooling fan cuts in and out). **Do not** operate the air conditioning at this stage.
22 Stop the engine, and allow it to cool, then recheck the coolant level with reference to *Weekly checks*. Top-up the level if necessary and refit the expansion tank filler cap.

Antifreeze mixture

23 The antifreeze should always be renewed at the specified intervals. This is necessary not only to maintain the antifreeze properties, but also to prevent corrosion which would otherwise occur as the corrosion inhibitors become progressively less effective.
24 Always use an ethylene-glycol based antifreeze which is suitable for use in mixed-metal cooling systems. The quality and quantity of antifreeze, and levels of protection are given in the Specifications.
25 Before adding antifreeze, the cooling system should be completely drained, preferably flushed, and all hoses checked for condition and security.
26 After filling with antifreeze, a label should be attached to the expansion tank, stating the type and concentration of antifreeze used, and the date installed. Any subsequent topping-up should be made with the same type and concentration of antifreeze.
Caution: Do not use engine antifreeze in the windscreen/tailgate washer system, as it will cause damage to the vehicle paintwork. A screenwash additive should be added to the washer system in the quantities stated on the bottle.

34 Brake fluid renewal

⚠️ *Warning: Brake hydraulic fluid can harm your eyes and damage painted surfaces, so use extreme caution when handling and pouring it. Do not use fluid that has been standing open for some time, as it absorbs moisture from the air. Excess moisture can cause a dangerous loss of braking effectiveness.*

1 The procedure is similar to that for the bleeding of the hydraulic system as described in Chapter 9.
2 Working as described in Chapter 9, open

the first bleed screw in the sequence, and pump the brake pedal gently until nearly all the old fluid has been emptied from the master cylinder reservoir. Top-up to the MAX level with new fluid, and continue pumping until only the new fluid remains in the reservoir, and new fluid can be seen emerging from the bleed screw. Tighten the screw, and top the reservoir level up to the MAX level line.

HAYNES HINT *Old hydraulic fluid is invariably much darker in colour than the new, making it easy to distinguish the two.*

3 Work through all the remaining bleed screws in the sequence until new fluid can be seen at all of them. Be careful to keep the master cylinder reservoir topped-up to above the MIN level at all times, or air may enter the system and greatly increase the length of the task.
4 When the operation is complete, check that all bleed screws are securely tightened, and that their dust caps are refitted. Wash off all traces of spilt fluid, and recheck the master cylinder reservoir fluid level.
5 Check the operation of the brakes before taking the vehicle on the road.

Every 48 000 miles or 4 years

35 Timing belt and fuel injection pump belt renewal

Refer to Chapter 2B.

Every 60 000 miles or 5 years

36 Fuel filter renewal (TD4 engine)

Up to 2003 model year

1 The fuel filter is located on the left-hand side of the engine compartment bulkhead. Undo the screw securing the filter housing to the bracket, and lift the housing tilting it away from the bracket. Disconnect the wiring multiplug **(see illustration)**.
2 Place absorbent rags under the filter. Note the fitted locations of the fuel hoses, depress the retaining clips, and disconnect the hoses from the filter head **(see illustration)**.
3 Lift the filter and head from the bracket **(see illustration)**.
4 Holding the filter body, unscrew and remove the filter head.
5 Lubricate the sealing ring of the new filter with clean engine oil, and fill the filter with clean diesel. Screw the filter head on to the filter until the seal contacts the head **(see illustration)**. Hand-tighten the filter head a further half a turn (180°).
6 Fit the filter assembly into the housing.

7 Reconnect the fuel hoses and the wiring multiplug, and refit the housing to the bracket. Tighten the retaining screw securely.

2003 model year on

8 Disconnect the battery negative lead as described in Chapter 5A.
9 Jack up the right-hand rear corner of the vehicle (see *Jacking and vehicle support*), and remove the roadwheel.
10 Undo the 2 bolts securing the filter/pump unit to the vehicle body, then prise out the scrivet **(see illustrations)**.

36.1 Undo the screw (arrowed) securing the filter housing to the bracket

36.2 Note the fitted locations of the fuel hoses, depress the retaining clips, and disconnect the hoses from the filter head

36.3 Lift the filter and head from the bracket

36.5 Screw the filter head on to the filter until the seal contacts the head

36.10a Undo the 2 screws (arrowed) ...

36.10b ... and remove the scrivet (arrowed)

36.11 Disconnect the earth lead from the filter (arrowed – shown with the wheel arch liner removed for clarity)

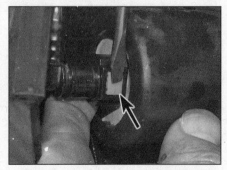

36.12 Depress the release button each side (arrowed) and disconnect the fuel pipes

36.13 Pull back the retaining clip and remove the fuel filter. Note the arrow indicating fuel flow

11 Lower the assembly, then note their fitted positions, and disconnect the earth lead from the filter housing **(see illustration)**.

12 Position a container beneath the assembly to catch any spilled fuel, then press-in the release buttons and disconnect the fuel pipes from the filter **(see illustration)**. Ensure the area around the fuel pipe connections is clean to prevent any ingress of dirt into the system.

13 Pull the retaining clips outwards, and slide the fuel filter from the holder **(see illustration)**.

14 Refitting is a reversal of removal, noting that the OUT marking on the filter must face rearwards. The fuel system is designed to be self-bleeding.

37 Automatic transmission oil renewal

1 Position the vehicle over an inspection pit, on vehicle ramps, or jack it up, but make sure that it is level (see *Jacking and vehicle support*). Release the retaining screws and

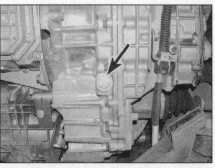

37.2 Unscrew the transmission drain plug (arrowed)

remove the engine/transmission undertray.

2 Position an oil container under the transmission and unscrew the drain plug **(see illustration)**. Discard the sealing washer, a new one must be fitted.

3 When the fluid has finished draining, ensure the drain plug is clean, fit a new sealing washer and refit the drain plug. Tighten it to the specified torque.

37.4 Pull out the filler plug (arrowed) from the top of the transmission

4 Pull out the filler plug from the top of the transmission **(see illustration)**.

5 Pour 3.5 to 4.0 litres of the correct fluid through the filler aperture, and then check the transmission oil level as described in Section 7 of this Chapter.

6 With the oil level correct, refit the engine undertray and lower the vehicle to the ground.

Every 10 years

38 Airbag module renewal

1 The airbag module must be renewed every 10 years on vehicles up to 2002 model year, and every 15 years from 2002-on.

2 Renewal procedures are described in Chapter 12.

39 Seatbelt pretensioners renewal

1 The seat belt pre-tensioners must be renewed every 10 years on vehicles up to 2002 model year, and every 15 years from 2002-on.

2 Renewal procedures are described in Chapter 11.

Chapter 2 Part A:
1.8 litre petrol engine in-car repair procedures

Contents

Degrees of difficulty

Easy, suitable for novice with little experience | **Fairly easy,** suitable for beginner with some experience | **Fairly difficult,** suitable for competent DIY mechanic | **Difficult,** suitable for experienced DIY mechanic | **Very difficult,** suitable for expert DIY or professional

Specifications

General

Engine type. . . . . Four-cylinder in-line, four-stroke, liquid-cooled
Designation . . . . K-Series 1.8 litre
Bore . . . . 80.0 mm
Stroke. . . . . 89.3 mm
Capacity . . . . 1796 cc
Firing order. . . . . 1-3-4-2 (No 1 cylinder at timing belt end)
Direction of crankshaft rotation . . . . Clockwise (seen from right-hand side of vehicle)
Compression ratio 10.5:1
Output:
    Power . . . . 88 kW @ 5500 rpm
    Torque. . . . . 165 Nm @ 2750 rpm
Idle speed. . . . . 775 ± 50 rpm (not adjustable)
Maximum engine speed. . . . . 6750 rpm

Camshaft

Camshaft endfloat:
    Standard. . . . . 0.06 to 0.19 mm
    Service limit . . . . 0.30 mm
Follower outside diameter . . . . 32.959 to 32.975 mm

Lubrication system

System pressure:
    Idle speed. . . . . 1.0 bar minimum
    2500 rpm . . . . 3.75 bar
Pressure relief valve opening pressure. . . . . 4.1 bar
Pressure relief valve spring free length. . . . . 38.9 mm
Low oil pressure warning light comes on. . . . . 0.3 to 0.5 bar
Oil pump clearances:
    Outer rotor-to-body clearance . . . . 0.28 to 0.36 mm
    Inner rotor tip-to-outer rotor clearance . . . . 0.05 to 0.13 mm
    Rotor endfloat. . . . . 0.02 to 0.06 mm

Torque wrench settings

	Nm	lbf ft
Camshaft bearing carrier bolts	10	7
Camshaft cover bolts	8	6
Camshaft oil seal cover plate bolts (2001-on models):		
Exhaust	25	18
Intake	6	4
Camshaft position sensor (2001-on models)	6	4
Camshaft sprocket bolts	65	48
Connecting rod big-end bearing cap bolts*:		
Stage 1	20	15
Stage 2	Angle-tighten a further 45°	
Coolant outlet elbow	9	7
Crankshaft pulley bolt	205	151
Cylinder head bolts*:		
Stage 1	20	15
Stage 2	Angle-tighten a further 180°	
Stage 3	Angle-tighten a further 180°	
Engine/transmission mountings:		
Left-hand mounting-to-body bolts	45	33
Left-hand mounting-to-gearbox bolts	65	48
Left-hand gearbox mounting through-bolt	80	59
Left-hand engine mounting-to-strut bolt	80	59
Lower tie rod-to-bracket bolt	80	59
Lower tie rod-to-subframe bolt	80	59
Lower tie rod bracket to engine sump	80	59
Right-hand mounting-to-body bolts (pre-2001 model year)	45	33
Right-hand mounting/PAS pipe bracket nut (pre-2001 model year)	80	59
Right-hand mounting bracket-to-engine bolts	170	125
Right-hand mounting bracket-to-upper tie bolt	80	59
Right-hand Hydramount to top arm (2001 model year-on)	85	63
Right-hand Hydramount to body (2001 models year-on)	85	63
Tie rod bracket to body	80	59
Upper tie rod-to-engine mounting bolt	80	59
Upper tie rod-to-body bolt	80	59
Flywheel bolts*	80	59
Flywheel cover plate bolts	9	7
Ignition coil bolts (2001 model year-on)	8	6
Ignition coil bracket (pre-2001 model year)	25	18
Intermediate reduction unit support bracket-to-sump bolts	45	33
Main bearing ladder-to-cylinder block bolts*:		
Stage 1	5	4
Stage 2	30	22
Oil pick-up pipe	12	9
Oil pressure switch	17	13
Oil pump retaining bolts	10	7
Oil rail-to-main bearing ladder bolts	9	7
Oil temperature sensor (2001 model year-on)	17	13
Power steering drivebelt automatic tensioner bolts	25	18
Roadwheel nuts	110	81
Spark plugs	27	20
Spark plug cover screws	10	7
Sump bolts:		
Sump to gearbox	45	33
Sump to main bearing ladder:		
M8 x 25	25	18
M8 x 60	30	22
Sump drain plug	25	18
Timing belt cover bolts	10	7
Timing belt tensioner:		
Manual tensioner:		
Backplate bolt	10	7
Pulley Allen bolt	45	33
Automatic tensioner bolt*	22	16

* Do not reuse

1 General information and precautions

How to use this Chapter

This Part of the Chapter describes those repair procedures that can reasonably be carried out on the engine whilst it remains in the vehicle. If the engine has been removed from the vehicle and is being dismantled as described in Part D of this Chapter, any preliminary dismantling procedures can be ignored.

Note that whilst it may be possible physically to overhaul items such as the piston/connecting rod assemblies with the engine in the vehicle, such tasks are not usually carried out as separate operations and usually require the execution of several additional procedures (not to mention the cleaning of components and of oilways). For this reason, all such tasks are classed as major overhaul procedures and are described in Part D of this Chapter.

Engine description

The 1.8 litre engine is from the Rover K-series engine family, and is a four-cylinder, in-line unit, mounted transversely at the front of the vehicle with the clutch and transmission on the left-hand end. The engine is of double overhead camshaft 16-valve design.

The main structure of the engine consists of three major castings – the cylinder head, the cylinder block/crankcase, and the crankshaft main bearing ladder.

The three major castings are made from aluminium alloy, and are clamped together by ten long cylinder head bolts; the bolts also perform the task of crankshaft main bearing bolts as they screw into the main bearing ladder. An oil rail is fitted under the main bearing ladder, and to avoid disturbing the bottom end of the engine when removing the cylinder head bolts, the oil rail is secured independently to the main bearing ladder (by two nuts), and the main bearing ladder is secured to the cylinder block/crankcase (by ten bolts).

The crankshaft runs in five main bearings. Thrustwashers are fitted to the centre main bearing (upper half) to control crankshaft endfloat.

The connecting rods rotate on horizontally-split bearing shells at their big-ends. The pistons are attached to the connecting rods by gudgeon pins which are an interference fit in the connecting rod small-end eyes. The aluminium alloy pistons are fitted with three piston rings, comprising two compression rings and an oil control ring.

The cylinder bores are formed by renewable liners which locate in the cylinder block/crankcase at their top ends. The liners are known as 'damp' liners. To prevent the coolant escaping into the sump the base of each liner is sealed with sealing compound.

The intake and exhaust valves are each closed by coil springs and operate in guides pressed into the cylinder head. The valve seat inserts are pressed into the cylinder head and can be renewed separately if worn.

The camshafts are driven by a toothed timing belt, and operate the valves via followers. Each follower incorporates a hydraulic self-adjusting valve which automatically adjusts the valve clearance. The camshaft rotates in bearings which are line-bored directly into the cylinder head and the (bolted-on) bearing carrier. This means that the bearing carrier and cylinder head are matched, and cannot be renewed independently. The distributor is driven from the left-hand (flywheel end) of the intake camshaft. The coolant pump is driven by the timing belt. The fuel pump is electrically-operated.

Lubrication is by means of an eccentric-rotor type pump driven directly from the right-hand (timing belt end) of the crankshaft. The pump draws oil through a strainer located in the sump. It then forces it through an externally-mounted full-flow cartridge-type oil filter into galleries in the oil rail and the cylinder block/crankcase, from where it is distributed to the crankshaft (main bearings) and camshaft. The big-end bearings are supplied with oil via internal drillings in the crankshaft, while the camshaft bearings and the followers receive a pressurised supply via drillings in the cylinder head. The camshaft lobes and valves are lubricated by oil splash, as are all other engine components.

Operations with engine in vehicle

The following work can be carried out with the engine in the vehicle:

a) Compression pressure – testing.
b) Camshaft cover – removal and refitting.
c) Crankshaft pulley – removal and refitting.
d) Timing belt covers – removal and refitting.
e) Timing belt – removal, refitting and adjustment.
f) Timing belt tensioner and sprockets – removal and refitting.
g) Camshaft oil seals – renewal.
h) Camshafts and followers – removal, inspection and refitting.
i) Cylinder head – removal and refitting.
j) Cylinder head and pistons – decarbonising.
k) Sump – removal and refitting.
l) Oil pump – removal, overhaul and refitting.
m) Crankshaft oil seals – renewal.
n) Engine/transmission mountings – inspection and renewal.
o) Flywheel – removal, inspection and refitting.

Caution: Note that a side-effect of the K-series engine design is that the crankshaft cannot be rotated once the cylinder head bolts have been slackened. During any servicing or overhaul work, the crankshaft must always be rotated to the desired position before the cylinder head bolts are disturbed.

2 Compression test – description and interpretation

Note: *A suitable compression tester will be required for this test.*

1 When engine performance is down, or if misfiring occurs which cannot be attributed to the ignition or fuel systems, a compression test can provide diagnostic clues as to the engine's condition. If the test is performed regularly it can give warning of trouble before any other symptoms become apparent.

2 The engine must be fully warmed-up to normal operating temperature, the battery must be fully-charged and the spark plugs must be removed (see Chapter 1A). The aid of an assistant will be required.

3 Disable the ignition system by disconnecting the two-pin wiring plug that connects the ignition coil to the engine wiring loom (on pre-2001 models), or disconnecting each coil separately (2001-on models – see Chapter 5B).

4 The fuel pump must be disabled by removing fuse No 3 from the engine compartment fusebox on models up to 2001, and by removing the fuel pump relay from the fusebox on models 2001 model year-on.

5 Fit a compression tester to the No 1 cylinder spark plug hole. The type of tester which screws into the plug thread is preferred.

6 Have the assistant hold the throttle wide open and crank the engine on the starter motor. After one or two revolutions, the compression pressure should build-up to a maximum figure and then stabilise. Record the highest reading obtained.

7 Repeat the test on the remaining cylinders, recording the pressure in each.

8 All cylinders should produce very similar pressures; a difference of more than 2 bars between any two cylinders indicates a fault. Note that the compression should build-up quickly in a healthy engine; low compression on the first stroke, followed by gradually-increasing pressure on successive strokes, indicates worn piston rings. A low compression reading on the first stroke, which does not build-up during successive strokes, indicates leaking valves or a blown head gasket (a cracked head could also be the cause). Deposits on the undersides of the valve heads can also cause low compression.

9 Although Land Rover do not specify exact compression pressures, as a guide, any cylinder pressure of below 10 bar can be considered as less than healthy. Refer to a Land Rover dealer or other specialist if in doubt as to whether a particular pressure reading is acceptable.

10 If the pressure in any cylinder is significantly low, carry out the following test to isolate the cause. Introduce a teaspoonful of clean oil into that cylinder through its spark plug hole and repeat the test.

11 If the addition of oil temporarily improves the compression pressure, this indicates that

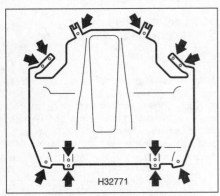

3.5 Undo the screws and remove the engine undertray (arrowed)

bore or piston wear is responsible for the pressure loss. No improvement suggests that leaking or burnt valves, or a blown head gasket, may be to blame.

12 A low reading from two adjacent cylinders is almost certainly due to the head gasket having blown between them and the presence of coolant in the engine oil will confirm this.

13 If one cylinder is about 20 percent lower than the others and the engine has a slightly rough idle, a worn camshaft lobe could be the cause.

14 If the compression reading is unusually high, the combustion chambers are probably coated with carbon deposits. If this is the case, the cylinder head should be removed and decarbonised.

15 On completion of the test, refit the spark plugs (see Chapter 1A), reconnect the ignition coil(s) and refit the No 3 fuse in the engine compartment fusebox.

3 Engine assembly/ valve timing marks – general information and usage

1 The crankshaft pulley, crankshaft and camshaft sprocket(s) all have timing marks which align when the crankshaft is at 90° BTDC. This positions the pistons half-way up the bores, ensuring there is no danger of the

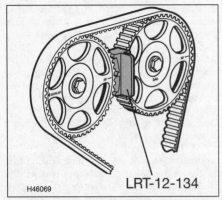

3.9 Use LRT-12-134 to lock the camshafts in position

valves contacting the pistons when refitting the cylinder head/timing belt.

2 Disconnect the battery negative terminal (refer to battery disconnection in Chapter 5A). If necessary, remove all the spark plugs as described in Chapter 1A to enable the engine to be easily turned over.

3 To gain access to the camshaft sprocket timing mark(s), remove the timing belt upper cover as described in Section 6.

4 Firmly apply the handbrake, then jack up the front of the vehicle and support it securely on axle stands (see *Jacking and vehicle support*). Remove the right-hand front roadwheel to improve access to the crankshaft pulley.

5 Undo the screws and remove the engine undertray **(see illustration)**.

6 Remove the three bolts, and withdraw the right-hand splash shield from the inner wheel arch.

7 Using a socket and extension bar on the crankshaft pulley bolt, turn the crankshaft whilst keeping an eye on the camshaft sprockets.

8 Rotate the crankshaft until the EXHAUST mark is at the rear (intake manifold side) of each camshaft sprocket and the IN mark is at the front, and all timing marks are correctly aligned with the mark on the timing belt rear cover (representing the cylinder head upper surface). Once the camshaft sprocket marks are correctly positioned, the notch on the crankshaft pulley rim should align with the mark on the lower timing belt cover **(see illustrations)**.

3.8a Position the sprocket EXHAUST and IN marks correctly, and align the timing marks (A) with the timing mark (B) on the rear cover

4.2 Disconnect the breather hoses from the rear of the camshaft cover

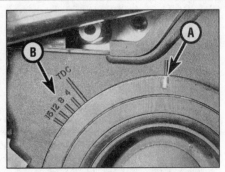

3.8b Align the crankshaft pulley timing notch with the mark (A) on the timing belt lower cover. Ignore the timing marks (B) on the cover (where present)

9 If required, use Land Rover special tool LRT-12-134 to lock the camshaft sprockets in place **(see illustration)**.

10 With the crankshaft pulley and camshaft sprocket timing marks positioned as described, the engine can safely be dismantled.

4 Camshaft cover – removal and refitting

Removal

1 Disconnect the battery negative lead (refer to Chapter 5A).

2 Release the retaining clips and disconnect the breather hoses from the rear of the camshaft cover **(see illustration)**.

3 Undo the retaining screws and remove the spark plug cover from the centre of the camshaft cover.

4 Disconnect the HT leads from the spark plugs then unclip the leads from the cover and position them clear. On 2001-on models, undo the retaining bolts and remove the ignition coils, then disconnect the conventional HT leads form the remaining spark plugs, and remove the camshaft position sensor (Chapter 4A).

5 Working progressively and in the **reverse** of the tightening sequence **(see illustration 4.9)**, slacken and remove the camshaft cover retaining bolts.

6 Carefully remove the cover, complete with the gasket. Check the gasket for signs of damage or deterioration and renew it if damaged. **Note:** *Do not separate the camshaft cover and gasket unless the gasket is to be renewed.*

Refitting

7 If the gasket has been removed from the cover, remove the crankcase ventilation system filters, wash them in solvent then dry them before refitting them to the cover. Ensure the cover is clean and dry then fit the new gasket, making sure its EXHAUST MAN SIDE marking is pointing towards the exhaust manifold.

8 Make sure the mating surfaces are clean

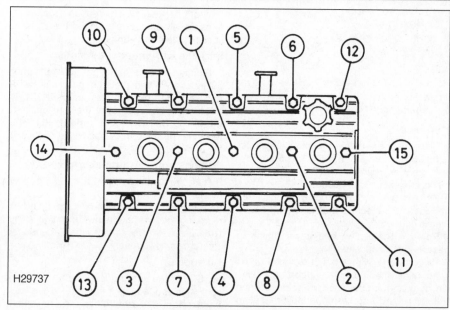

4.9 Camshaft cover bolt tightening sequence

5.8 Ensure the crankshaft pulley notch is correctly engaged with the sprocket lug (arrowed) then refit the retaining bolt and washer

and dry then refit the cover to the cylinder head, ensuring that the gasket remains correctly seated.

9 Refit the cover retaining bolts and tighten them all by hand. Once all bolts are in position, go around in the specified sequence and tighten them to the specified torque setting **(see illustration)**.

10 Reconnect the HT leads securely to the spark plugs. Ensure the leads are clipped correctly into their clips then refit the spark plug cover, tightening its retaining screws securely. On 2001-on models, refit the ignition coils, tighten the bolts to the specified torque, then refit the conventional HT leads to the remaining spark plugs, followed by the camshaft position sensor.

11 The remainder of refitting is a reversal of removal.

<table>
<tr><td>5</td><td>**Crankshaft pulley –**
removal and refitting</td></tr>
</table>

Removal

1 Firmly apply the handbrake then jack up the front of the vehicle and support it securely on axle stands (see *Jacking and vehicle support*). To improve access, remove the right-hand front roadwheel.

2 Undo the screws and remove the engine undertray **(see illustration 3.5)**.

3 Remove the three bolts, and withdraw the right-hand splash shield from the inner wheel arch.

4 If further dismantling is to be carried out, align the engine assembly/valve timing marks as described in Section 3.

5 Remove the auxiliary drivebelt(s) as described in Chapter 1A.

6 Slacken the crankshaft pulley retaining bolt. To prevent crankshaft rotation, have an assistant select top gear and apply the brakes firmly. If the engine is removed from the vehicle it will be necessary to lock the flywheel (see Section 16).

7 Unscrew the pulley bolt and washer, noting which way around the washer is fitted, then remove the pulley from the crankshaft.

Refitting

8 Fit the pulley to the crankshaft, aligning the notch in the pulley with the locating lug on the sprocket, then refit the retaining bolt and washer **(see illustration)**. Make sure that the tapered face of the washer is facing away from the pulley.

9 Lock the crankshaft using the method used on removal, and tighten the pulley retaining bolt to the specified torque setting.

10 Refit and tension the auxiliary drivebelt(s) as described in Chapter 1A.

11 The remainder of refitting is a reversal of removal. Tighten the wheel nuts to the specified torque.

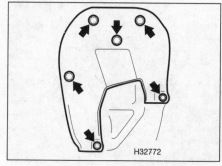

6.1 Unscrew the upper timing cover retaining bolts (arrowed)

<table>
<tr><td>6</td><td>**Timing belt covers –**
removal and refitting</td></tr>
</table>

Upper cover

Removal

1 Slacken the lower bolts securing the upper cover to the engine then unscrew the upper bolts securing it to the rear cover **(see illustration)**.

2 Free the upper cover from the rear cover and remove it from the engine, taking care not to lose the seal which is fitted around the engine mounting bracket. Inspect the seal for signs of damage or deterioration and renew if necessary.

Refitting

3 Refitting is a reversal of removal. Ensure that the rubber seal is positioned correctly and tighten the cover bolts to the specified torque.

Lower cover

Removal

4 Remove the crankshaft pulley as described in Section 5.

5 Remove the upper timing belt cover as described previously in this Section.

6 Unscrew the three bolts and remove the lower cover **(see illustration)**. Check the cover seals for signs of damage or deterioration and renew if necessary.

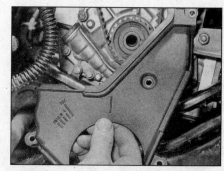

6.6 Remove the timing belt lower cover

6.10 Timing belt rear cover retaining bolts (arrowed)

Refitting

7 Refitting is the reverse of removal ensuring that the seals are correctly fitted. Tighten all bolts to their specified torque settings (where given).

Rear cover

Removal

8 Remove the timing belt as described in Section 7.

9 Remove the camshaft sprockets and the timing belt tensioner as described in Section 8.

10 Undo the retaining bolts securing the cover to the cylinder head/block and remove the cover from the engine **(see illustration)**.

Refitting

11 Refitting is a reversal of removal, refitting the timing belt tensioner, sprockets and belt as described in Sections 7 and 8.

7.5a Remove the two bolts securing the right-hand engine mounting bracket to the engine . . .

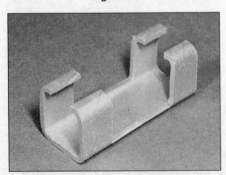

7.6a A sprocket locking tool can be made by cutting a square-section tube as shown . . .

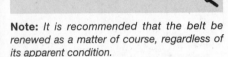

7 Timing belt – removal and refitting

Note: *It is recommended that the belt be renewed as a matter of course, regardless of its apparent condition.*

Removal

1 Disconnect the battery negative lead (refer to battery disconnection in Chapter 5A).

2 Align the engine assembly/valve timing marks as described in Section 3.

3 Remove the crankshaft pulley as described in Section 5, ensuring that all timing marks remain correctly aligned.

4 Remove the timing belt lower cover as described in Section 6.

5 Place a jack, with a block of wood on its head, under the engine to support its weight. Unscrew and remove the two bolts securing the right-hand engine mounting bracket to the engine, and the through-bolt securing the mounting bracket to the upper tie rod. Where applicable, release the power steering cooling pipe from the clip. Undo the retaining nut and remove the right-hand engine mounting bracket **(see illustrations)**.

6 A suitable tool should be used to lock the camshaft sprockets together, so that they cannot move under valve spring pressure when the timing belt is removed. Land Rover technicians use service tool LRT-12-134 which slots in between the sprocket teeth, but an acceptable substitute can be fabricated from

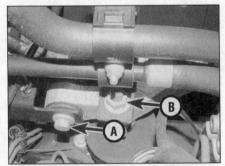

7.5b . . . and undo the upper tie rod through-bolt (A) and the mounting nut (B)

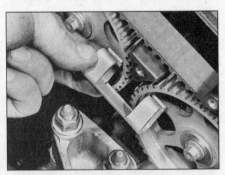

7.6b . . . so that it engages with the sprocket spokes and locks the sprockets together

a length of steel square-section tube cut to fit as closely as possible around the sprocket spokes **(see illustrations)**.

Engines with manual tensioner

7 Slacken both the timing belt tensioner pulley and the backplate bolts through half a turn then push the tensioner pulley fully downwards to remove all the tension from the timing belt **(see illustration)**. Hold the tensioner pulley in this position by tightening the backplate clamp bolt securely.

Engines with automatic tensioner

8 Remove and discard the timing belt tensioner bolt.

9 Disengage the tensioner index spring, whilst removing the tensioner **(see illustration 7.23)**. **Note:** *Land Rover recommend that the tensioner should be renewed every 100 000 miles.*

All engines

10 Slide the timing belt off from its sprockets and remove it from the engine **(see illustration)**. **Do not** rotate the crankshaft or camshafts until the timing belt has been refitted.

11 Due to the low cost of a new belt, it is recommended that the belt be renewed as a matter of course, regardless of its apparent condition. If signs of oil contamination are found, trace the source of the oil leak and rectify it, then wash down the engine timing belt area and all related components to remove all traces of oil.

Refitting

Engines with manual tensioner

12 The tensioner pulley spring and pillar bolt should be used (if a genuine Land Rover belt is being fitted, the spring and a pillar bolt should be supplied as part of a kit). Screw the pillar bolt into the cylinder head between the two camshaft sprockets. Hook the lower end of the new spring onto the tensioner backplate and locate the upper end around the pillar bolt.

13 Thoroughly clean and dry the timing belt sprockets and check that the camshafts and crankshaft are still correctly positioned. The camshaft sprockets timing marks must still be aligned with the cylinder head surface (see Section 3) and the crankshaft sprocket

7.7 Tensioner pulley bolt (A) and backplate (B)

timing dots must be positioned on each side of the raised rib on the oil pump housing **(see illustration)**.

14 Fit the timing belt over the crankshaft and camshaft sprocket(s), ensuring that the belt front run is taut (ie, all slack is on the tensioner side of the belt), then fit the belt over the coolant pump sprocket and tensioner pulley. Do not twist the belt sharply while refitting it. Ensure that the belt teeth are correctly seated centrally in the sprockets, and that the timing marks remain in alignment.

15 Slacken the timing belt tensioner backplate bolt to release the tensioner and apply finger pressure to the backplate to push the pulley against the timing belt. Hold the tensioner in this position and tighten the backplate bolt to the specified torque.

16 Refit the right-hand engine mounting components as described in Section 17. Tighten the bolts/nuts to the specified torque. Remove the jack and block of wood from under the engine.

17 With reference to Section 6, refit the lower timing belt cover ensuring its sealing strips are correctly positioned and tighten the securing bolts to the specified torque.

18 Refit the crankshaft pulley, aligning the notch in the pulley with the locating lug on the sprocket. Refit the retaining bolt and washer, ensuring the tapered face of the washer is facing away from the pulley, but only hand tighten the pulley bolt at this stage. Remove the tool used to lock the camshaft sprockets together, and rotate the crankshaft clockwise two complete revolutions using a spanner or socket on the crankshaft pulley bolt.

19 Check the sprocket timing marks are still correctly aligned. If adjustment is necessary, release the tensioner again then disengage the belt from the sprockets and make any necessary adjustments.

20 When the camshaft and crankshaft timing marks are correctly aligned, slacken the tensioner backplate bolt, and check that tension is being applied to the belt by the tensioner spring. Tighten the tensioner backplate and tensioner pulley bolts to the specified torque.

21 Remove and discard the tensioner spring and pillar bolt.

Engines with automatic tensioner

Note: *Land Rover recommend that the tensioner assembly should be renewed at 100 000 miles.*

22 Thoroughly clean and dry the timing belt sprockets and check that the camshaft(s) and crankshaft are still correctly positioned. The camshaft sprocket timing mark(s) must still be aligned with the cylinder head surface (see Section 3) and the crankshaft sprocket timing dots must be positioned on each side of the raised rib on the oil pump housing **(see illustration 7.13)**.

23 Using a new bolt, refit the tensioner to the engine, ensuring that the index spring is positioned over the pillar bolt, and the tensioner arm is at the 9 o'clock position **(see**

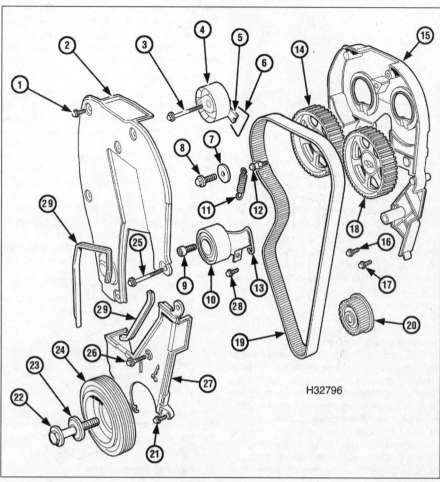

7.10 K-Series timing belt components

1 Screw	11 Spring	20 Crankshaft sprocket
2 Upper timing cover	12 Pillar bolt	21 Screw
3 Tensioner bolt	13 Backplate	22 Pulley bolt
4 Automatic tensioner	14 Inlet camshaft sprocket	23 Washer
5 Pointer	15 Rear timing belt cover	24 Crankshaft pulley
6 Index spring	16 Screw	25 Bolt
7 Washer	17 Screw	26 Screw
8 Bolt	18 Exhaust camshaft	27 Lower timing belt cover
9 Tensioner bolt	sprocket	28 Screw
10 Manual tensioner	19 Timing belt	29 Sealing strips

illustration). Tighten the bolt only to the point where it is just possible to move the tensioner arm.

24 Fit the timing belt over the crankshaft and camshaft sprocket(s), ensuring that the belt front run is taut (ie, all slack is on the tensioner

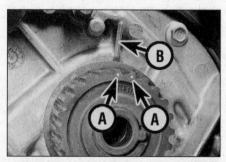

7.13 The timing dots (A) on the crankshaft sprocket must be positioned on each side of the rib (B) on the oil pump housing

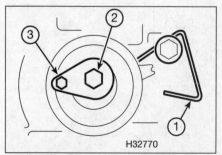

7.23 Hook the index spring (1) over the pillar bolt, position the tensioner arm (3) at 9 o'clock, and tighten the tensioner bolt (2)

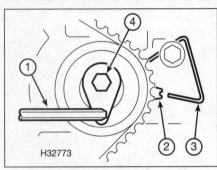

7.25 Using an Allen key (1), rotate the tensioner arm anti-clockwise until the pointer (2) to the right of the tensioner, aligns with the end of the index spring (3). Tighten the tensioner bolt (4) to the specified torque

side of the belt), then fit the belt over the coolant pump sprocket and tensioner pulley. Do not twist the belt sharply while refitting it. Ensure that the belt teeth are correctly seated centrally in the sprockets, and that the timing marks remain in alignment.

25 Using an Allen key, rotate the tensioner arm anti-clockwise until the pointer to the right of the tensioner, aligns with the end of the index spring. Tighten the tensioner bolt to the specified torque **(see illustration)**. **Note:** *Ensure that the pointer only approaches the index spring from above. If the pointer goes past the spring, release the tension completely and repeat the tensioning procedure.*

26 Refit the right-hand engine mounting components as described in Section 17. Tighten the bolts/nuts to the specified torque. Remove the jack and block of wood from under the engine.

27 With reference to Section 6, refit the lower timing belt cover ensuring its sealing strips are correctly positioned and tighten the securing bolts to the specified torque.

28 Refit the crankshaft pulley, aligning the notch in the pulley with the locating lug on the sprocket. Refit the retaining bolt and washer, ensuring the tapered face of the washer is facing away from the pulley, but only hand tighten the pulley bolt at this stage. Remove the tool used to lock the camshaft sprockets together, and rotate the crankshaft clockwise two complete revolutions using a spanner or socket on the crankshaft pulley bolt.

8.3 Using a home-made tool to hold a camshaft sprocket

29 Check the sprocket timing marks are still correctly aligned. If adjustment is necessary, release the tensioner again then disengage the belt from the sprockets and make any necessary adjustments.

All engines

30 Fit the pulley to the crankshaft, aligning the notch in the pulley with the locating lug on the sprocket. Refit the retaining bolt and washer, ensuring the tapered face of the washer is facing away from the pulley, then lock the crankshaft (see Section 5).

31 Tighten the crankshaft pulley retaining bolt to the specified torque, as described in Section 5.

32 Refit the timing belt upper cover, ensuring the seal is correctly positioned, and tighten its retaining bolts to the specified torque.

33 Refit the auxiliary drivebelt(s) as described in Chapter 1A and, where applicable, the undertray/splash shield.

34 Refit the roadwheel, and lower the vehicle to the ground, and tighten the wheel nuts to the specified torque. Reconnect the battery negative lead.

---

8 Timing belt tensioner and sprockets – removal and refitting

Note: *Whenever the tension applied to the timing belt is disturbed, it is recommended that the belt be renewed as a matter of course, regardless of its apparent condition*

Camshaft sprockets

Removal

1 Disconnect the battery negative lead (refer to battery disconnection in Chapter 5A).

2 Remove the timing belt as described in Section 7.

3 Slacken and remove the camshaft sprocket retaining bolt(s), along with the washer(s). To prevent camshaft rotation, Land Rover technicians use the locking tool LRT-12-132 which fits around the sprocket spokes. In the absence of the special tool, a suitable alternative can be fabricated from two lengths of steel strip (one long, the other short) and three nuts and bolts. One nuts and bolt should

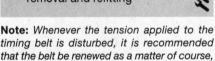

8.8 Engage the exhaust camshaft locating pin with the EX cut-out and the inlet camshaft locating pin in the IN cut-out

form the pivot of the forked tool, with the remaining two nuts and bolts at the tips of the forks to engage with the sprocket spokes **(see illustration)**.

4 Remove the sprockets from the camshafts taking care not to lose the sprocket locating pins. If a pin is a loose fit in the end of the camshaft, remove it and store it with the sprocket for safe-keeping.

5 Check the sprockets for signs of wear or damage and renew if necessary.

Refitting

6 Prior to refitting, check the oil seals for signs of damage or leakage. If necessary, renew as described in Section 9.

7 Ensure the locating pins are in position in the camshaft ends. Note that the pins should be fitted with the split facing inwards.

8 Both intake and exhaust camshaft sprockets are the same but each one is equipped with two locating pin cut-outs. If the sprocket is being fitted to the intake camshaft, engage the locating pin in the IN cut-out, and if the sprocket is being fitted to the exhaust camshaft, engage the locating pin in the EX cut-out **(see illustration)**. Ensure the camshaft locating pin is engaged in the correct sprocket cut-out then refit the washer and retaining bolt.

9 On all engines, retain the sprockets by the method used on removal, and tighten the retaining bolts to the specified torque setting.

10 Ensure the crankshaft pulley mark is still correctly aligned with the mark on the lower cover and the camshaft sprocket marks are correctly aligned with the cylinder head upper surface (see Section 3).

11 Refit the timing belt as described in Section 7.

12 Where applicable, refit the engine undertray and splash shield. Refit the roadwheel, lower the vehicle to the ground, and tighten the wheel nuts to the specified torque. Reconnect the battery negative lead.

Crankshaft sprocket

Removal

13 Remove the timing belt as described in Section 7.

14 Slide the sprocket off from the end of the crankshaft, noting which way around it is fitted.

Refitting

15 Refit the sprocket to the crankshaft, engaging it with the crankshaft flattened section. Check that the sprocket timing marks align – the two dots on the sprocket must be positioned on each side of the raised rib on the oil pump body.

16 Refit the timing belt as described in Section 7.

Tensioner assembly

17 Two types of tensioner are fitted to the 1.8 litre engine. A manual tensioner is secured in place by two bolts, one through the backplate

9.4 Use a socket to tap a camshaft oil seal into position

9.7 Unscrew the ignition coil bracket retaining bolts

9.17 Disconnect the camshaft position sensor wiring plug

and one through the pulley. When the timing belt is renewed, genuine Land Rover belt kits include a spring and pillar bolt. The pillar bolt screws into the cylinder head between the camshaft sprockets, and the spring is fitted between the bolt and the tensioner backplate to set the belt tension. Once the tension has been set and the tensioner secured, the spring and pillar bolt should be removed. The automatic tensioners fitted to some engines are secured by one bolt though the pulley, and incorporate an index spring. This spring provides constant tension to press the pulley against the belt, and a reference point to enable the tensioner to be set initially **(see illustration 7.10)**. Whenever the automatic tensioner mounting bolt is disturbed, it must be renewed.

Removal and refitting

18 As the timing belt must be renewed whenever the tensioner is disturbed, follow the procedure given in Section 7 of this Chapter detailing the timing belt renewal procedure.

9 Camshaft oil seals – renewal

Right-hand seals

1 Remove the camshaft sprocket(s) as described in Section 8.
2 Punch or drill two small holes opposite each other in the oil seal(s). Screw a self-tapping screw into each hole, and pull on the screws with pliers to extract the seal.
3 Clean the seal housing and polish off any burrs or raised edges which may have caused the seal to fail.
4 Lubricate the lips of the new seal (black in colour) with clean engine oil and drive it into position. Use a suitable tubular drift, such as a socket, which bears only on the hard outer edge of the seal **(see illustration)**. Take care not to damage the seal lips during fitting and note that the seal lips should face inwards.
5 Refit the camshaft sprocket(s) as described in Section 8.

Left-hand seal

6 Remove the air cleaner assembly as described in Chapter 4A and proceed as described under the relevant sub-heading.

Exhaust – models up to 2001

7 Release the coolant hose from its clip then unscrew the retaining bolts and remove the ignition coil bracket from the cylinder head **(see illustration)**.
8 Renew the oil seal as described in paragraphs 2 to 4. Note that the oil seals at the flywheel end are red in colour.
9 Ensure the mating surfaces are clean and dry and apply a smear of sealant to the coil bracket. Refit the coil bracket, tightening its retaining bolts to the specified torque.
10 Clip the coolant hose back into position then refit the air cleaner housing (see Chapter 4A).

Exhaust – models 2001-on

11 Slacken and remove the two bolts securing the exhaust camshaft end cover plate to the cylinder head, and remove the plate. Be prepared for oil spillage.
12 Renew the oil seal as described in paragraphs 2 to 4, noting that the oil seal lips must not be oiled. Oil seals at the flywheel end are red in colour.
13 Ensure the mating surfaces are clean and dry and apply a smear of sealant to the cover plate. Refit the plate tightening the retaining bolts to the specified torque.

Intake – models up to 2001

14 Remove the distributor, rotor arm and shield as described in Chapter 5B.
15 Renew the oil seal as described in paragraphs 2 to 4. Oil seals at the flywheel end are red in colour.
16 Refit the distributor components (see Chapter 5B) then refit the air cleaner housing (see Chapter 4A).

Intake – models 2001-on

17 Disconnect the camshaft position sensor wiring plug, and release the connector from the bracket **(see illustration)**.
18 Slacken and remove the two bolts securing the cover plate to the cylinder head, and remove the plate. Be prepared for oil spillage.
19 Renew the oil seal as described in paragraphs 2 to 4, noting that the oil seal lips must not be oiled. Oil seals at the flywheel end are red in colour.
20 Ensure the mating surfaces are clean and

dry, and apply a smear of sealant to the cover plate. Refit the plate, tightening the bolts to the specified torque.

10 Camshafts and followers – removal, inspection and refitting

Note: *Land Rover produce a sealant kit which consists of a plastic scraper, gasket removing compound and the recommended sealant for the camshaft carrier joint. It is recommended that this kit is used during the following procedure. New camshaft oil seals will also be required.*
Note: *Whenever the tension applied to the timing belt is disturbed, it is recommended that the belt be renewed as a matter of course, regardless of its apparent condition*

Removal

1 Remove the camshaft cover as described in Section 4.
2 Remove the air cleaner assembly with reference to Chapter 4A.
3 On models up to 2001, remove the distributor cap, rotor arm and shield, as described in Chapter 5B.
4 On models 2001-on, disconnect the camshaft position sensor wiring plug, and remove the connector from the bracket. Undo the camshaft oil seal cover plates retaining bolts from the left-hand end of the cylinder head, and remove the plates. Be prepared for oil spillage.
5 On all engines, remove the camshaft sprocket(s) as described in Section 8.
6 Unscrew and remove the two bolts securing the rear timing belt cover to the cylinder head.
7 On models up to 2001, release the coolant hose from its clip, then unscrew the retaining bolts and remove the ignition coil mounting bracket from the left hand end of the cylinder head **(see illustration 9.7)**.
8 On all engines, working in the correct sequence, slacken the camshaft bearing carrier retaining bolts evenly progressively, by one turn at a time, to gradually release the pressure of the valve springs **(see illustration)**.
Caution: *If the bearing carrier bolts are carelessly slackened, the carrier might*

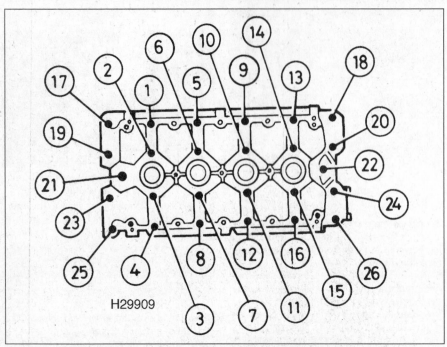

H29909

10.8 Camshaft bearing carrier retaining bolt slackening sequence

break. If the carrier is broken, the complete cylinder head assembly must be renewed; the carrier is matched to the head and is not available separately.

9 Lift the camshaft bearing carrier away from the cylinder, noting the correct fitted positions of the locating dowels. If the dowels are loose,

remove them and store them with the bearing carrier for safe-keeping.

10 Carefully lift the camshaft(s) from the cylinder head. Remove the oil seals and discard them; new ones should be used on refitting. The intake camshaft is easily identified by the distributor rotor arm drive

10.11 Use a sucker or magnet to remove the camshaft followers

10.15 Position the camshaft sprocket locating pins (arrowed) as shown

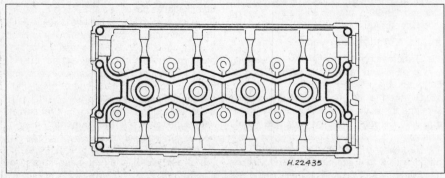

H.22435

10.16 Apply a bead of sealant to the highlighted area of the bearing carrier mating surface

spindle so there is no need to mark the camshafts for identification.

11 If necessary, obtain sixteen small, clean plastic containers, and label them for identification. Alternatively, divide a larger container into compartments. Using a sucker or magnet, withdraw each follower in turn, invert it to prevent oil loss and place it in its respective container, which should then be filled with clean engine oil **(see illustration)**. **Do not** interchange the followers, and do not allow the followers to lose oil, as they will take a long time to refill with oil on restarting the engine, which could result in incorrect valve clearances.

Inspection

12 Examine the camshaft bearing surfaces and cam lobes for signs of wear ridges and scoring. Renew the camshaft if any of these conditions are apparent. Examine the condition of the bearing surfaces both on the camshaft journals and in the cylinder head. If the head bearing surfaces are worn excessively, the cylinder head will need to be renewed.

13 Examine the follower bearing surfaces which contact the camshaft lobes for wear ridges and scoring. Check the followers and their bores in the cylinder head for signs of wear or damage. If a micrometer is available, measure the outside diameter of each follower and compare it to the results given in the Specifications. If the engine's valve clearances have sounded noisy, particularly if the noise persists after initial start-up from cold, then there is reason to suspect a faulty follower. If any follower is thought to be faulty or is visibly worn it should be renewed.

Refitting

14 Liberally oil the camshaft bearings and followers then refit the camshafts to the cylinder head; the intake camshaft is easily identified by the rotor arm drive spindle.

15 Position the camshafts so that the camshaft sprocket locating pins are positioned as shown **(see illustration)**. When viewed from the right-hand end of the engine, the intake camshaft sprocket pin should be in the 4 o'clock position and the exhaust camshaft sprocket pin should be in the 8 o'clock position.

16 Ensure the mating surface of the camshaft bearing carrier and cylinder head are clean and dry. Apply a bead of sealant to the bearing carrier mating surface as shown **(see illustration)**. Spread the sealant to an even film taking care not to allow any sealant to enter the oilway grooves.

17 Ensure that the locating dowels are in position and refit the camshaft bearing carrier to the cylinder head. Ensure the carrier is correctly located then refit the retaining bolts, tightening them all by hand only at this stage.

18 Working in a diagonal sequence, evenly and progressively tighten the retaining bolts to draw the bearing carrier squarely down into contact with the cylinder head. Once the carrier is in contact with the head, go around in the specified sequence and tighten the retaining bolts to the specified torque **(see illustration)**.

Caution: If the bearing carrier bolts are carelessly tightened, the carrier might break. If the carrier is broken then the complete cylinder head assembly must be renewed; the carrier is matched to the head and is not available separately.

19 Fit new camshaft oil seals as described in Section 9.

20 On models up to 2001, ensure the mating surfaces are clean and dry and apply a smear of sealant to the ignition coil mounting bracket. Refit the bracket to the left-hand end of the cylinder head, tightening its retaining bolts to the specified torque.

21 On models 2001-on, ensure the mating surfaces are clean and dry, and apply a smear of sealant to the oil seal cover plates. Refit the plates to the left-hand end of the cylinder head, and tighten the retaining bolts to the specified torque. Refit the camshaft position sensor connector to the bracket, and reconnect the wiring plug.

22 On all engines, insert the two bolts securing the rear timing belt cover to the cylinder head, and tighten the bolts securely.

23 Refit the camshaft sprockets as described in Section 8.

24 Refit the camshaft cover as described in Section 4 then refit the distributor components (where applicable) as described in Chapter 5B.

25 Refit the timing belt as described in Section 7.

---

11 Cylinder head –
removal and refitting

Caution: Before commencing any servicing or overhaul work on the engine, the crankshaft must always be rotated to the desired position before the cylinder head bolts are disturbed. Due to the design of the engine, it will become very difficult, almost impossible, to turn the crankshaft once the cylinder head bolts have been slackened. The manufacturer accordingly states that the crankshaft will be 'tight' and should not be rotated more than absolutely necessary once the head has been removed. If the crankshaft cannot be rotated, then it must be removed for overhaul work to proceed. With this in mind, during any servicing or overhaul work, the crankshaft must always be rotated to the desired position before the bolts are disturbed.

Note: *Whenever the tension applied to the timing belt is disturbed, it is recommended that the belt be renewed as a matter of course, regardless of its apparent condition*

Removal

1 Disconnect the battery negative lead (refer to battery disconnection in Chapter 5A).

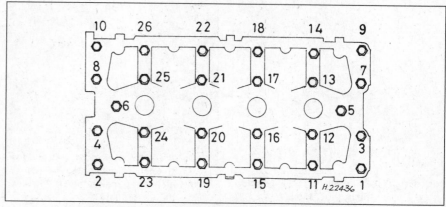

10.18 Camshaft bearing carrier bolt tightening sequence

2 Drain the cooling system, as described in Chapter 1A.

3 Remove the air cleaner housing as described in Chapter 4A.

4 Remove the timing belt rear cover as described in Section 6.

5 Remove the exhaust manifold as described in Chapter 4A. If no work is to be carried out on the cylinder head, the head can be removed complete with the manifold once the exhaust front pipe has been unbolted and the oxygen sensor wiring connector has been disconnected (see Chapter 4A).

6 Remove the intake manifold as described in Chapter 4A. If no work is to be carried out on the cylinder head, the head can be removed complete with the manifold once the following operations have been carried out (see Chapter 4A).

a) *Depressurise the fuel system and disconnect the fuel feed and return hoses from the manifold/fuel rail. Be prepared for fuel spillage.*

b) *Disconnect the various wiring connectors from the manifold components and free all wiring from the manifold.*

c) *Disconnect the various vacuum, breather and (where necessary) coolant hoses from the manifold, noting each one correct fitted location and routing.*

d) *Disconnect the accelerator cable from the throttle housing.*

e) *Unbolt the manifold support bracket (where fitted).*

7 Release the retaining clips and disconnect the coolant hoses from the outlet elbow on the front, left-hand end of the cylinder head. Disconnect the wiring connectors from the coolant temperature sensor(s) which are screwed into the elbow.

Models up to 2001

8 Disconnect the ignition coil HT lead from the centre of the distributor cap and free the lead from its retaining clips. If the cylinder head is to be dismantled, remove the distributor, rotor arm and shield as described in Chapter 5B.

9 Undo the two screws and remove the ignition coil mounting bracket from the left-hand end of the cylinder head **(see illustration 9.7)**.

Disconnect the HT lead and position the coil to one side.

Models 2001-on

10 Disconnect the camshaft position sensor wiring plug from the left-hand end of the cylinder head, and release the connector from the bracket **(see illustration 9.17)**.

All models

11 Remove the camshaft cover as described in Section 4.

12 Working in the **reverse** of the tightening sequence **(see illustration 11.27)**, progressively slacken the cylinder head bolts by a third of a turn at a time until all bolts can be unscrewed by hand. Withdraw the bolts. Land Rover state that new bolts must be fitted.

13 The joint between the cylinder head and gasket and the cylinder block/crankcase must now be broken without disturbing the cylinder liners. Although these liners are better located and sealed than some wet liner engines, there is still a risk of coolant and foreign matter leaking into the sump if the cylinder head is lifted carelessly. If care is not taken and the liners are moved, there is also a possibility of their seals being disturbed, causing leakage after refitting the head.

14 To break the joint, obtain two L-shaped metal bars which fit into the cylinder head bolt holes and gently rock the cylinder head free towards the front of the vehicle **(see illustration)**.

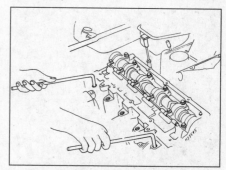

11.14 Use two L-shaped bars to break the cylinder head joint by rocking

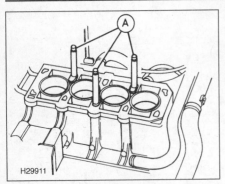

11.16 Cylinder liner clamps (A) in position on the cylinder block

Caution: Do not try to swivel the head on the cylinder block/crankcase as it is located by dowels as well as by the tops of the liners.

15 When the joint is broken, lift the cylinder head away, using assistance if possible as it is a heavy assembly, especially if complete with the manifolds. Remove the gasket and discard it. Support the cylinder head on wooden blocks or stands – do not rest the lower face of the cylinder head on the work surface. Note the fitted positions of the two locating dowels, and remove them for safe-keeping if they are loose. **Note:** *If plastic locating dowels are fitted, discard them. They must be replaced by steel dowels.*

16 Note that further to the warnings given in the note at the beginning of this Section, **do not** attempt to rotate the crankshaft with the cylinder head removed, otherwise the liners may be displaced. Operations that require the rotation of the crankshaft (eg, cleaning the piston crowns) can be carried out after fitting cylinder liner clamps. The manufacturer's liner clamps are secured by the cylinder head bolts as shown **(see illustration).**

 Equivalents can be improvised using large washers and tubular spacers.

17 If the cylinder head is to be dismantled, remove the camshafts, as described in Section 10, then refer to the relevant Sections of Part D of this Chapter.

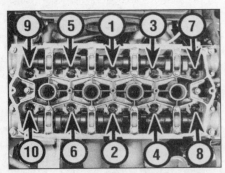

11.27 Cylinder head bolt tightening sequence

11.23 Ensure the locating dowels (arrowed) are in position then fit the new head gasket . . .

Preparation for refitting

18 The mating faces of the cylinder head and cylinder block/crankcase must be perfectly clean before refitting the head. Use a hard plastic or wood scraper to remove all traces of gasket and carbon. Also clean the piston crowns. Take particular care, as the soft aluminium alloy is damaged easily. Also, make sure that the carbon is not allowed to enter the oil and water passages – this is particularly important for the lubrication system, as carbon could block the oil supply to any of the engine components. Using adhesive tape and paper, seal the water, oil and bolt holes in the cylinder block/crankcase. To prevent carbon entering the gap between the pistons and bores, smear a little grease in the gap. After cleaning each piston, use a small brush to remove all traces of grease and carbon from the gap, then wipe away the remainder with a clean cloth. Clean all the pistons in the same way. Take great care not to move the pistons during this procedure.

19 Check the mating surfaces of the cylinder block/crankcase and the cylinder head for nicks, deep scratches and other damage. If slight, they may be removed carefully with a file, but if excessive, machining may be the only alternative to renewal.

20 If warpage of the cylinder head gasket surface is suspected, use a straight-edge to check it for distortion. Refer to Part D of this Chapter if necessary.

21 Discard the cylinder head bolts. New ones must be fitted. **Note:** *In August 2001, Land Rover introduced a new multi-layer head*

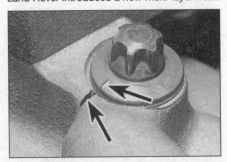

11.28 Make alignment marks between the cylinder head bolt radial marks and the head to check correct bolt tightening

11.24 . . . making sure the TOP mark is upwards and the FRONT arrow points towards the timing belt end

gasket, and a revised thermostat position. It is recommended that all models should have the revised thermostat fitted as described in Chapter 3, as well as the new design of head gasket.

Refitting

22 Remove the cylinder liner clamps (where fitted) and wipe clean the mating surfaces of the cylinder head and cylinder block/crankcase.

23 Ensure the holes in the block are clean, then fit the steel locating dowels into position at each end of the cylinder block surface **(see illustration).** The fitted height of the dowels is between 10 and 11 mm.

24 Position a new gasket on the cylinder block/crankcase surface so that its TOP mark is uppermost and the FRONT arrow points to the timing belt end **(see illustration).**

25 Carefully refit the cylinder head, locating it on the dowels.

26 Lightly oil under the head and on the threads of each new cylinder head bolt, carefully enter them into their holes and screw them in, by hand only, until finger-tight. **Do not** drop the bolts into their holes.

27 Working progressively and in sequence, first tighten all the cylinder head bolts to the Stage 1 torque setting **(see illustration).**

28 Once all bolts have been tightened to the Stage 1 torque, again working in sequence, tighten each bolt through its specified Stage 2 angle, using a socket and extension bar. It is recommended that an angle-measuring gauge is used during this stage of tightening, to ensure accuracy. Prior to tightening, use a felt-tip pen or similar to make alignment marks between the radial mark on each bolt head and the cylinder head **(see illustration).** The second stage torque can then be achieved by tightening each bolt through half-a-turn so that the mark on the bolt head faces away from the corresponding mark on the cylinder head.

29 Finally go around in the specified sequence again and tighten all bolts through the specified Stage 3 angle. Each bolt head radial mark should now be realigned with the corresponding mark on the cylinder head again. If any bolt is overtightened beyond the mark on the cylinder head, slacken the bolt by

a quarter-turn, then retighten until the marks align.

30 Refit the camshaft cover (Section 4).

Models up to 2001

31 Ensure the mating surfaces are clean and dry and apply a smear of sealant to the ignition coil mounting bracket. Refit the bracket to the left-hand end of the cylinder head, tightening its retaining bolts to the specified torque.

32 Reconnect the HT lead to the coil and refit the distributor (see Chapter 5B).

Models 2001-on

33 Refit the camshaft position sensor connector to the bracket on the left-hand intake camshaft oil seal cover plate, and reconnect the wiring plug.

34 Reconnect the coolant hoses to the coolant elbow and secure them in position with the retaining clips. Reconnect the coolant temperature sensor wiring connector(s).

35 Refit the intake manifold (where removed) or reconnect the manifold hoses and wiring as described in Chapter 4A. Ensure all hoses/wiring are correctly routed and securely reconnected then reconnect and adjust the accelerator cable.

36 Refit the exhaust manifold/reconnect the exhaust front pipe (as applicable) as described in Chapter 4A.

37 Refit the timing belt rear cover to the engine, and tighten the bolts to the specified torque.

38 With reference to Section 8, refit the camshaft sprockets.

39 Refit the timing belt with reference to Section 7.

40 Refit the air cleaner housing as described in Chapter 4A.

41 On completion refill the cooling system as described in Chapter 1A.

42 Refit the engine undertray and splash shields as applicable.

43 Reconnect the battery negative lead.

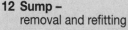

12 Sump –
removal and refitting

Removal

1 Drain the engine oil (with reference to Chapter 1A if necessary), then clean and refit the engine oil drain plug with a new washer, tightening it to the specified torque wrench setting. If the engine is nearing the service interval when the oil and filter are due for renewal, it is recommended that the filter is also removed and a new one fitted. After reassembly, the engine can then be refilled with fresh engine oil.

2 Apply the handbrake, then jack up the front of the vehicle and support it securely on axle stands (see *Jacking and vehicle support*).

3 Remove the exhaust front pipe as described in Chapter 4A.

4 Then lower tie rod is secured by 3 bolts.

12.4 Unscrew the two front bolts and allow the tie rod to swing down

Unscrew and remove the two bolts securing the tie rod at the front, and slacken the bolt at the rear. Allow the tie rod to swing down **(see illustration)**.

5 Unscrew the 9 bolts securing the intermediate reduction drive unit support bracket from between the IRD and the sump.

6 Remove the 2 bolts securing the sump to the gearbox casing.

7 Progressively slacken and remove the bolts securing the sump to the base of the main bearing ladder. Break the sump joint by striking the sump with the palm of the hand, then lower the sump away from the engine. If the sump joint is difficult to break, use a chisel between the cast lug on the sump and the bearing ladder.

8 While the sump is removed, take the opportunity to check the oil pump pick-up/strainer for signs of clogging or splitting. If necessary, unbolt the pick-up/strainer and remove it from the engine along with its sealing ring. The strainer can then be cleaned easily in solvent. Inspect the strainer mesh for signs of clogging or splitting and renew if necessary.

Refitting

9 Clean all traces of sealant from the mating surfaces of the cylinder block/crankcase and sump, then use a clean rag to wipe out the sump and the engine interior.

10 Where necessary, fit a new sealing ring to the oil pump pick-up/strainer groove then carefully refit the pipe, tightening its retaining bolts to the specified torque setting.

11 Apply a bead of suitable sealant (eg, Hylomar 3000) to the sump mating surface.

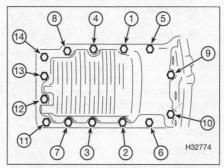

12.14 Sump bolt tightening sequence

12 Offer up the sump to the cylinder block/crankcase then refit the sump-to-main bearing ladder bolts, and tighten the bolts finger-tight only.

13 Insert the sump-to-gearbox bolts (M8 x 40), and tighten the bolts finger tight only at this stage.

14 Working in sequence, tighten the sump-to-main bearing ladder bolts to the specified torque setting **(see illustration)**.

15 Tighten the sump-to-gearbox bolts to the specified torque.

16 Refit the bolts securing the intermediate reduction unit support bracket, and tighten them to the specified torque.

17 Reposition the tie rod at the front of the engine. Refit the tie rod-to-sump bolts, and tighten the bolts to the specified torque. Also tighten the tie rod rear bolt to the specified torque.

18 Refit the exhaust front pipe as described in Chapter 4A.

19 Lower the vehicle to the ground, and refill the engine with oil as described in Chapter 1A.

13 Oil pump –
removal and refitting

Note: *The oil pressure relief valve can be dismantled without removing the oil pump from the vehicle – see Section 14 for details.*

Note: *Whenever the tension applied to the timing belt is disturbed, it is recommended that the belt be renewed as a matter of course, regardless of its apparent condition*

Removal

1 Remove the crankshaft sprocket as described in Section 8.

2 Drain the engine oil, then clean and refit the engine oil drain plug with a new washer, tightening it to the specified torque wrench setting. If the engine is nearing the service interval when the oil and filter are due for renewal, it is recommended that the filter is also removed and a new one fitted. After reassembly, the engine can then be refilled with fresh engine oil (see Chapter 1A).

3 Undo the two bolts and remove the power steering pump drive belt automatic tensioner.

4 Unscrew the two bolts securing the engine wiring harness guide to the oil pump and position the guide clear **(see illustration overleaf)**.

5 Slacken and remove the oil pump retaining bolts, noting the correct fitted location of the shorter bolt.

6 Remove the rear timing belt lower retaining bolt to facilitate removal of the pump.

7 Free the oil pump from the cylinder block then slide it off the end of the crankshaft. Note the correct fitted locations of the pump locating dowels; if the dowels are loose, remove them and store with the pump for safe-keeping. Remove the gasket and discard it.

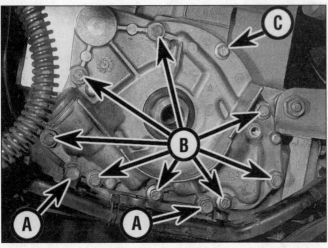

13.4 Oil pump fixings

14.5 The oil pump pressure relief valve can be removed with the engine in the vehicle

A *Engine wiring harness bolts*   C *Oil pump retaining bolt (short)*
B *Oil pump retaining bolts (long)*

Refitting

8 Prior to refitting, carefully lever out the crankshaft oil seal using a flat-bladed screwdriver. Fit the new oil seal, ensuring its sealing lip is facing inwards, and press it squarely into the housing using a tubular drift which bears only on the hard outer edge of the seal. Press the seal into position so that it is flush with the housing and lubricate the oil seal lip with clean engine oil.

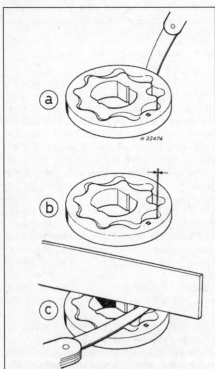

14.7 Oil pump checking

a *Outer rotor-to-pump body clearance*
b *Inner rotor tip-to-outer rotor clearance*
c *Rotor endfloat*

9 Remove all traces of locking compound from the threads of the oil pump bolts and cylinder block and ensure the mating surfaces of the oil pump and cylinder block are clean and dry.
10 Ensure the locating dowels are in position then fit a new gasket to the cylinder block. The gasket must be fitted dry.
11 Carefully manoeuvre the oil pump into position and engage the inner rotor with the crankshaft end. Locate the pump on the dowels, taking great care not to damage the oil seal lip.
12 Apply suitable locking compound to the bolts, fit them, and tighten progressively to the specified torque wrench setting.
13 Refit the rear timing cover retaining bolt, and tighten it to the specified torque.
14 Secure the engine wiring harness guide to the oil pump and securely tighten its retaining bolts.
15 Refit the power steering drivebelt automatic tensioner, and tighten the bolts to the specified torque.
16 Refit the crankshaft sprocket as described in Section 8.
17 On completion, refill the engine with oil as described in Chapter 1A.

> **14 Oil pump –**
> dismantling, inspection
> and reassembly

Note: *If oil pump wear is suspected, check the cost and availability of new parts (only available in the form of a repair kit) against the cost of a new pump. Examine the pump as described in this Section and then decide whether renewal or repair is the best course of action.*

Dismantling

1 Remove the oil pump as described in Section 13.
2 Unscrew the retaining screws and remove

the pump cover plate and sealing ring.
3 Note the identification marks on the outer rotor then remove both the rotors from the body.
4 The oil pressure relief valve can be dismantled, if required, without disturbing the pump. If this is to be done with the pump in position and the engine still installed in the vehicle, it will first be necessary to jack up the front of the vehicle and remove the right-hand roadwheel and wheel arch splash shield to gain access to the valve (see *Jacking and vehicle support*).
5 To dismantle the valve, slacken and remove the threaded plug and washer then recover the valve spring and plunger **(see illustration)**.

Inspection

6 Inspect the rotors for obvious signs of wear or damage and renew if necessary. If the pump body or cover plate is scored or damaged, then the complete oil pump assembly must be renewed.
7 Refit the rotors to the body and, using feeler blades of the appropriate thickness, measure the clearance between the outer rotor and the pump body, then between the inner rotor tip and the outer rotor **(see illustration)**.
8 Using feeler blades and a straight-edge placed across the top of the pump body and the rotors, measure the rotor endfloat.
9 If any measurement is outside the specified limits, the complete pump assembly must be renewed.
10 If the pressure relief valve plunger is scored, or if it does not slide freely in the pump body bore, then it must be renewed, using all the components from the repair kit.
11 Thoroughly clean the threads of the pump cover plate securing screws and renew the cover sealing ring and relief valve washer, if damaged.

Reassembly

12 Lubricate the pump rotors with clean

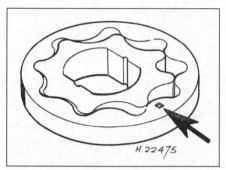

14.12 On reassembly, ensure the identification mark on the outer rotor (arrowed) faces outwards

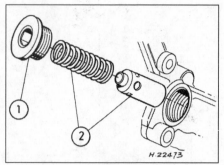

14.15 Oil pump pressure relief valve components

1   Threaded plug and sealing washer
2   Plunger and spring

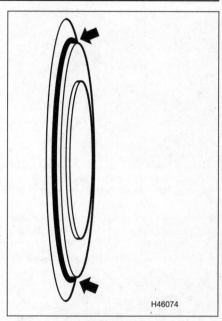

15.9 Apply a 1.5 mm bead of sealant (arrowed) to the oil seal

engine oil and refit them to the pump body, ensuring that the identification mark on the outer rotor faces outwards (ie, towards the pump cover) **(see illustration)**.

13 Fit the sealing ring to the pump body and refit the cover plate. Apply thread-locking compound to the threads of the cover plate screws then refit the screws, tightening them securely.

14 Check that the pump rotates freely, then prime it by injecting oil into its passages and rotating it. If a long time elapses before the pump is refitted to the engine, prime it again before installation.

15 Refit the oil pressure relief valve plunger, ensuring that it is the correct way up, then install the spring **(see illustration)**. Fit the sealing washer to the threaded plug and tighten the plug securely.

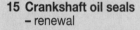

15 Crankshaft oil seals – renewal

Note: *Whenever the tension applied to the timing belt is disturbed, it is recommended that the belt be renewed as a matter of course, regardless of its apparent condition*

Right-hand seal

1 Remove the crankshaft sprocket as described in Section 8,

2 Carefully punch or drill two small holes opposite each other in the oil seal. Screw a self-tapping screw into each and pull on the screws with pliers to extract the seal.
Caution: Great care must be taken to avoid damage to the oil pump.

3 Clean the seal housing and polish off any burrs or raised edges which may have caused the seal to fail in the first place.

4 Lubricate the lips of the new seal with clean engine oil and ease it into position on the end of the shaft. Note that on 2001-on models, the seal must be fitted dry. Press the seal squarely into position until it is flush with the housing. If necessary, a suitable tubular drift, such as a socket, which bears only on the hard outer edge of the seal can be used to tap the seal

into position. Take great care not to damage the seal lips during fitting and ensure that the seal lips face inwards; if a genuine Land Rover seal is being installed, use the seal protector supplied to protect the seal during fitting and remove the protector once the seal is correctly located.

5 Wash off any traces of oil, then refit the crankshaft sprocket as described in Section 8.

Left-hand oil seal

6 Remove the flywheel as described in Section 16.

7 Taking care not to mark either the crankshaft or any part of the cylinder block/crankcase, lever the seal evenly out of its housing, using a large flat-bladed screwdriver or similar tool.

8 Clean the seal housing and polish off any burrs or raised edges which may have caused the original seal to fail.

9 Apply a 1.5 mm wide continuous bead of sealant to the oil seal **(see illustration)**. Once fitted, allow the sealant to cure for at least 30 minutes before rotating the crankshaft or topping-up the engine oil.

10 Ease the sealing lip of the seal over the crankshaft shoulder, by hand only, then press the seal evenly into its housing until its outer flange seats evenly on the housing lip. If necessary, a soft-faced mallet can be used to tap the seal gently into place.

11 Wash off any oil, then refit the flywheel as described in Section 16.

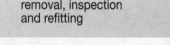

16 Flywheel – removal, inspection and refitting

Note: *New flywheel retaining bolts must be used on refitting.*

Removal

1 Remove the clutch assembly as described in Chapter 6.

2 As a precaution, unbolt the crankshaft position sensor from the cylinder block (see Chapter 4A) to prevent possible damage as the flywheel is removed.

3 Prevent the flywheel from turning by locking the ring gear teeth with a similar arrangement

to that shown in illustration 16.9. Alternatively, bolt a strap between the flywheel and the cylinder block/crankcase. Make alignment marks between the flywheel and crankshaft using paint or a suitable marker pen.

4 Slacken and remove the retaining bolts and remove the flywheel. **Do not** drop it, as it is very heavy. Discard the bolts, they must be renewed whenever they are disturbed.

Inspection

5 If the flywheel clutch mating surface (where applicable) is deeply scored, cracked or otherwise damaged, then the flywheel must be renewed, unless it is possible to have it surface ground. Seek the advice of a Land Rover dealer or engine reconditioning specialist.

6 If the ring gear is badly worn or has missing teeth, then it must be renewed. This job is best left to a Land Rover dealer or engine reconditioning specialist. The temperature to which the new ring gear must be heated for installation (350°C – shown by an even light blue colour) is critical and, if not done accurately, the hardness of the teeth will be destroyed.

Refitting

7 Clean the mating surfaces of the flywheel and crankshaft and remove all traces of locking compound from the crankshaft threaded holes.

8 Fit the flywheel to the crankshaft, engaging it with the crankshaft locating dowel, and fit the new retaining bolts **(see illustration)**.

9 Lock the flywheel using the method employed on dismantling then, working in a diagonal sequence, evenly and progressively tighten the retaining bolts to the specified torque wrench setting **(see illustration)**.

16.8 Position the flywheel over the locating dowel and fit the new retaining bolts

10 Refit the crankshaft position sensor and tighten its retaining bolt to the specified torque (see Chapter 4A).

11 Refit the clutch assembly (see Chapter 6).

17 Engine/transmission mountings – inspection and renewal

Inspection

1 If improved access is required, raise the front of the vehicle and support it securely on axle stands (see *Jacking and vehicle support*). If necessary, undo the retaining screws and fasteners and remove the undertray from beneath the engine/transmission unit.

2 Check the mounting rubber to see if it is cracked, hardened or separated from the metal at any point. Renew the mounting if any such damage or deterioration is evident.

3 Check that all mounting fasteners are securely tightened. Use a torque wrench to check, if possible.

4 Using a large screwdriver or a pry bar, check for wear in the mountings by carefully levering against it to check for free play. Where this is not possible, enlist the aid of an assistant to move the engine/gearbox unit back-and-forth or from side-to-side while you watch the mountings. While some free play is to be expected even from new components, excessive wear should be obvious. If excessive free play is found, check first that the fasteners are correctly secured, then

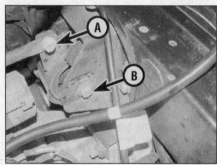

17.10 Disconnect the support bar (A) and the engine mounting through-bolt (B)

16.9 Lock the flywheel as shown, then tighten the retaining bolts to the specified torque

renew any worn components as described below.

Left-hand mounting

5 Firmly apply the handbrake, then jack up the front of the vehicle and support securely on axle stands (see *Jacking and vehicle support*). Undo the screws and remove the engine undertray. Disconnect the battery negative lead with reference to Chapter 5A.

6 Undo the bolts and remove the left-hand front roadwheel.

7 Unscrew the retaining bolts and remove the splash shield from the left-hand wheel arch.

8 Pull back the rubber cover, and disconnect the battery lead from the starter motor (if necessary refer to Chapter 5A).

9 Remove the clip securing the clutch slave cylinder to its mounting bracket (if necessary refer to Chapter 6), and move the slave cylinder to one side. There is no need to disconnect the cylinder fluid pipe.

10 Slacken and remove the bolt securing the support bar to the engine mounting **(see illustration)**.

11 Position a jack under the transmission and take the weight of the unit. Use a piece of wood between the jack head and the transmission casing.

12 Remove the through-bolt securing the engine mounting to the body.

13 Lower the engine/transmission sufficiently to allow access to the mounting retaining bolts. Remove the two mounting bolts and manoeuvre the mounting out of the engine compartment.

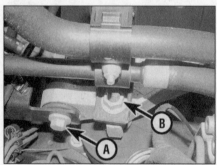

17.25 Disconnect the upper tie rod (A) and the engine mounting bolt (B)

14 Refit the mounting to the transmission and tighten the bolts to the specified torque.

15 Using the jack, raise the engine and align the mounting to allow the mounting-to-body bolt to be inserted. Tighten the bolt to the specified torque.

16 Remove the jack, and refit the bolt securing the support bar to the mounting. Tighten the bolt to the specified torque.

17 Refit the clutch slave cylinder to its bracket, ensuring the push-rod is engaged with the lever, and secure the cylinder in place with its retaining clip (if necessary refer to Chapter 6).

18 Reconnect the battery lead to the starter, tighten the nut securely, and refit the rubber terminal cover.

19 Refit the left-hand wheel arch splash shield, and roadwheel.

20 Fit the engine undertray, and reconnect the battery negative lead.

21 Lower the vehicle to the ground, and tighten the roadwheel nuts to the specified torque.

Right-hand upper mounting

22 Firmly apply the handbrake, then jack up the front of the vehicle and support securely on axle stands (see *Jacking and vehicle support*). Undo the screws and remove the engine undertray.

23 Support the weight of the engine/transmission using a trolley jack with a block of wood placed on its head. Position the jack underneath the engine and raise the engine slightly to remove all load from the mounting. Undo the three bolts, and remove the engine acoustic cover.

24 Where applicable, remove the bolt securing the air conditioning hose clip to the power steering hose support bracket.

25 Remove the power steering hose bracket retaining nut from the engine mounting stud, and position the bracket to one side **(see illustration)**. Note: *On models 2001-on, the power steering hose bracket is not fitted to the engine mounting – simply undo the retaining nut from the engine mounting stud.*

26 Slacken and remove the bolt securing the upper tie rod to the engine mounting bracket.

27 Loosen the bolt securing the upper tie rod to the bracket on the body, then raise it up to clear the engine mounting bracket.

Models up to 2001

28 Using the jack, raise the engine sufficiently for it to clear the engine mounting stud.

29 Unscrew the two bolts and remove the engine mounting.

30 On refitting, position the mounting on the wing valance, and tighten the two retaining bolts to the specified torque.

31 Lower the engine onto the mounting stud.

Models 2001-on

32 Undo the bolts securing the engine mounting top arm to the engine **(see illustration)**.

33 The Hydramount can be unscrewed from

the wing valance, using Land Rover tool LRT-12-169, or using a strap/chain wrench around the circumference of the mounting **(see illustration)**.

34 On refitting, tighten the Hydramount to the specified torque if possible, using the method used for removal.

35 Fit the engine mounting top arm to the engine and mounting stud, and tighten the retaining nuts/bolts to their specified torque settings.

All vehicles

36 Fit the upper tie rod to the mounting bracket, and tighten the both tie rod securing bolts to the specified torque.

37 Remove the jack from under the engine, and refit the power steering hose support bracket to the engine mounting stud. Tighten the retaining nut to the specified torque.

38 Where applicable, fit the air conditioning hose clip to the power steering hose support bracket and tighten the bolt securely. Refit the engine acoustic cover.

39 Refit the engine undertray, and lower the vehicle to the ground.

Lower tie rod

40 Firmly apply the handbrake, then jack up the front of the vehicle and support securely on axle stands (see *Jacking and vehicle support*). Undo the screws and remove the engine undertray.

41 Slacken and remove the tie rod retaining bolts, and manoeuvre the tie rod from the brackets.

42 On refitting, ensure that the large diameter end of the tie rod is at the rear, and position it between the mounting brackets **(see illustration)**.

17.32 Undo the two bolts securing the engine mounting arm to the engine

17.42 The large diameter end of the tie rod is at the rear

43 Fit the tie rod retaining bolts and tighten them to the specified torque.

44 Refit the engine undertray and lower the vehicle to the ground.

Upper tie rod

45 Undo the three bolts and remove the engine acoustic cover.

17.33 If the special tool is not available, use a strap or chain wrench to undo the Hydramount

17.46 Undo the tie rod mounting bolts

46 Slacken and remove the two bolts securing the tie rod to the engine mounting and bracket, and withdraw the tie rod **(see illustration)**.

47 Refit the tie rod and retaining bolts, and tighten them to the specified torque.

48 Refit the engine cover.

Notes

Chapter 2 Part B:
L-Series diesel engine in-car repair procedures

Contents

Degrees of difficulty

Easy, suitable for novice with little experience 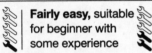	**Fairly easy,** suitable for beginner with some experience 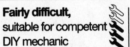	**Fairly difficult,** suitable for competent DIY mechanic	**Difficult,** suitable for experienced DIY mechanic	**Very difficult,** suitable for expert DIY or professional

Specifications

General

Engine type. . . . . Four-cylinder in-line, four-stroke, liquid-cooled, turbocharged and
 intercooled
Designation . . . . L-Series
Emission standard ECD2 (EU2)
Bore . . . . 84.5 mm
Stroke. . . . . 88.9 mm
Capacity . . . . 1994 cc
Firing order. . . . . 1-3-4-2 (No 1 cylinder at timing belt end)
Direction of crankshaft rotation . . . . Clockwise (seen from right-hand side of vehicle)
Maximum power. . . . . 88 kW @ 4200 rpm
Maximum torque . . . . 210 Nm @ 2000 rpm
Compression ratio 19.5:1

Camshaft

Bearing journal running clearance . . . . 0.043 to 0.094 mm
Camshaft endfloat (service limit) . . . . 0.51 mm
Follower outside diameter . . . . 34.959 to 34.975 mm
Timing belt tensioner spring free length. . . . . 65 mm

Lubrication system

Minimum system pressure – at idle . . . . 0.7 bar minimum
Pressure relief valve opening pressure. . . . . 4.5 bar
Pressure relief valve spring free length. . . . . 38.90 mm
Low oil pressure warning light comes on. . . . . 0.2 to 0.6 bar
Oil pump clearances:
 Outer rotor-to-body clearance . . . . 0.05 to 0.10 mm
 Inner rotor tip-to-outer rotor clearance . . . . 0.025 to 0.12 mm
 Rotor endfloat. . . . . 0.03 to 0.08 mm

Torque wrench settings

	Nm	lbf ft
Camshaft bearing carrier bolts	11	8
Camshaft cover bolts	12	9
Camshaft fuel injection pump belt sprocket:		
Sprocket-to-hub bolts	25	18
Hub centre bolt*:		
Stage 1	20	15
Stage 2	Angle-tighten a further 90°	
Camshaft timing belt sprocket bolt*:		
Stage 1	20	15
Stage 2	Angle-tighten a further 90°	
Camshaft timing belt sprocket damper Torx bolts*	10	7
Connecting rod big-end bearing cap bolts*:		
Stage 1	20	15
Stage 2	Angle-tighten a further 85°	
Crankshaft pulley bolt:		
Stage 1	63	46
Stage 2	Angle-tighten a further 90°	
Crankshaft left-hand oil seal housing bolts	10	7
Cylinder head bolts:		
Stage 1	30	22
Stage 2	65	48
Stage 3	Angle-tighten a further 90°	
Stage 4	Angle-tighten a further 90°	
EGR recirculation pipe bolts	10	7
Engine cover screw	4	3
Engine/transmission mountings:		
Left-hand mounting:		
Mounting-to-body bolts	45	33
Mounting bracket through-bolt	80	59
Bracket-to-transmission bolts	65	48
Strut-to-engine mounting bolts	80	59
Right-hand mounting:		
Engine mounting plate-to-engine nuts and bolts:		
Stage 1	30	22
Stage 2	Angle-tighten a further 120°	
Mounting bracket-to-engine bolts	120	89
Mounting bracket to upper tie rod	80	59
Mounting-to-body bolts	45	33
Lower tie rod bolts	80	59
Lower tie rod bracket-to-sump bolts	45	33
Upper tie rod-to-body bolt	80	59
Upper tie rod bracket-to-body bolts	80	59
Upper tie rod to engine mounting bracket	80	59
Strut-to-starter motor bolt	80	59
Flywheel bolts*:		
Stage 1	15	11
Stage 2	Angle-tighten a further 90°	
Fuel injection pump belt cover bolts	8	6
Fuel injection pump belt tensioner bolt	45	33
Main bearing cap bolts	112	83
Main oil gallery plug	12	9
Oil cooler mounting bolts:		
M8 bolts	25	18
M10 bolts	45	33
Oil cooler pipe union nuts	25	18
Oil filter:		
Stage 1	17	13
Stage 2	Angle-tighten a further 180°	
Oil pressure switch	15	11
Oil pump:		
Retaining bolts:		
M6 bolts	10	7
M10 bolt	45	33
Strainer to cylinder block	8	6
Oil pipes to sump	25	18
Pick-up/strainer bolts	8	6
Piston oil jet spray tubes bolts*	12	9

Torque wrench settings (continued)

	Nm	lbf ft
Roadwheel nuts	115	85
Sump bolts	25	18
Sump drain plug	25	18
Sump to gearbox support bracket	25	18
Timing belt cover bolts:		
Rear cover bolts	8	6
All other bolts	5	4
Timing belt idler pulley nut	45	33
Timing belt idler pulley stud	12	9
Timing belt tensioner:		
Pulley bolt*	55	41
Backplate bolt	45	33
Transmission mounting plate	45	33

* Do not re-use

---

1 General information and precautions

How to use this Chapter

This Part of the Chapter describes those repair procedures that can reasonably be carried out on the engine whilst it remains in the vehicle. If the engine has been removed from the vehicle and is being dismantled as described in Part D of this Chapter, any preliminary dismantling procedures can be ignored.

Note that whilst it may be possible physically to overhaul items such as the piston/connecting rod assemblies with the engine in the vehicle, such tasks are not usually carried out as separate operations and usually require the execution of several additional procedures (not to mention the cleaning of components and of oilways). For this reason, all such tasks are classed as major overhaul procedures and are described in Part D of this Chapter.

Engine description

This 2.0 litre diesel engine is from the Rover L-Series engine family, and is a four-cylinder, in-line unit, mounted transversely at the front of the vehicle with the clutch and transmission on the left-hand end.

The cast-iron cylinder block is of the dry-liner type. The crankshaft is supported within the cylinder block on five shell-type main bearings. Thrustwashers are fitted to the centre main bearing to control crankshaft endfloat.

The connecting rods rotate on horizontally-split bearing shells at their big-ends. The pistons are attached to the connecting rods by gudgeon pins which are secured in position with circlips. The aluminium alloy pistons are fitted with three piston rings, comprising two compression rings and an oil control ring.

The inlet and exhaust valves are each closed by coil springs and operate in guides pressed into the cylinder head. The valve seat inserts are pressed into the cylinder head and can be renewed separately if worn.

The camshaft is driven by a toothed timing belt, and operates the valves via followers.

Each follower incorporates a hydraulic self-adjusting valve which automatically adjusts the valve clearance. The camshaft rotates in bearings which are line-bored directly into the cylinder head and the (bolted-on) bearing carrier. This means that the bearing carrier and cylinder head are matched, and cannot be renewed independently.

The fuel injection pump is driven off the left-hand (flywheel) end of the camshaft by a second toothed timing belt and the coolant pump is driven by the auxiliary drivebelt.

Lubrication is by means of an eccentric-rotor type pump driven directly from the right-hand (timing belt end) of the crankshaft. The pump draws oil through a strainer located in the sump, and then forces it through an externally-mounted full-flow cartridge-type oil filter into galleries in the oil rail and the cylinder block/crankcase, from where it is distributed to the crankshaft (main bearings) and camshaft. The big-end bearings are supplied with oil via internal drillings in the crankshaft, while the camshaft bearings and the followers receive a pressurised supply via drillings in the cylinder head. The camshaft lobes and valves are lubricated by oil splash, as are all other engine components. An oil cooler is fitted to keep the oil temperature stable under arduous operating conditions.

Operations with engine in vehicle

The following work can be carried out with the engine in the vehicle:

a) Compression pressure – testing.
b) Camshaft cover – removal and refitting.
c) Crankshaft pulley – removal and refitting.
d) Timing belt covers – removal and refitting.
e) Timing belt – removal and refitting.
f) Fuel injection pump belt – removal and refitting.
g) Timing belt/fuel injection pump belt tensioner and sprockets – removal and refitting.
h) Camshaft oil seals – renewal.
i) Camshafts and followers – removal, inspection and refitting.
j) Cylinder head – removal and refitting.
k) Cylinder head and pistons – decarbonising.

l) Sump – removal and refitting.
m) Oil pump – removal, overhaul and refitting.
n) Oil cooler – removal and refitting.
o) Crankshaft oil seals – renewal.
p) Engine/transmission mountings – inspection and renewal.
q) Flywheel – removal, inspection and refitting.

2 Compression test – description and interpretation

Compression test

Note: *A compression tester specifically designed for diesel engines must be used for this test.*

1 When engine performance is down, or if misfiring occurs which cannot be attributed to the fuel system, a compression test can provide diagnostic clues as to the engine's condition. If the test is performed regularly, it can give warning of trouble before any other symptoms become apparent.

2 A compression tester specifically intended for diesel engines must be used, because of the higher pressures involved. The tester is connected to an adaptor which screws into the glow plug or injector hole. On these models, an adaptor suitable for use in the injector holes will be required, due to there only being glow plugs fitted to Nos 1 to 3 cylinders. It is unlikely to be worthwhile buying such a tester for occasional use, but it may be possible to borrow or hire one – if not, have the test performed by a garage.

3 Unless specific instructions to the contrary are supplied with the tester, observe the following points:

a) The battery must be in a good state of charge, the air filter must be clean, and the engine should be at normal operating temperature.
b) All the injectors should be removed before starting the test (see Chapter 4B).
c) Unscrew the retaining nut and disconnect the wiring connector from the fuel injection pump fuel cut-off solenoid (see

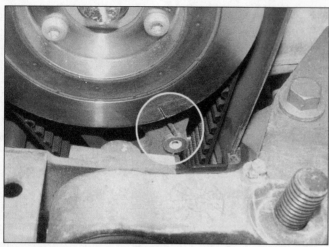

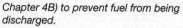

3.6 Rotate the crankshaft until the timing mark on the camshaft sprocket is correctly aligned with the mark on the timing belt rear cover

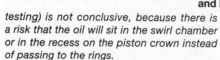

3.8 Lock the crankshaft in position by inserting a 6.75 mm diameter pin through the hole in the rear of the mounting plate, and locating it in the flywheel hole

Chapter 4B) to prevent fuel from being discharged.

4 There is no need to hold the accelerator pedal down during the test, because the diesel engine air inlet is not throttled.

5 Crank the engine on the starter motor; after one or two revolutions, the compression pressure should build-up to a maximum figure, and then stabilise. Record the highest reading obtained.

6 Repeat the test on the remaining cylinders, recording the pressure in each.

7 All cylinders should produce very similar pressures; a difference of more than 2 bars between any two cylinders indicates a fault. Note that the compression should build-up quickly in a healthy engine; low compression on the first stroke, followed by gradually-increasing pressure on successive strokes, indicates worn piston rings. A low compression reading on the first stroke, which does not build-up during successive strokes, indicates leaking valves or a blown head gasket (a cracked head could also be the cause). Deposits on the undersides of the valve heads can also cause low compression. **Note:** *The cause of poor compression is less easy to establish on a diesel engine than on a petrol one. The effect of introducing oil into the cylinders ('wet*

testing) is not conclusive, because there is a risk that the oil will sit in the swirl chamber or in the recess on the piston crown instead of passing to the rings.

8 Although Land Rover do not specify exact compression pressures, as a guide, any cylinder pressure of below 20 bar can be considered as less than healthy. Refer to a Land Rover dealer or other specialist if in doubt as to whether a particular pressure reading is acceptable.

9 On completion of the test, reconnect the injection pump fuel cut-off solenoid wiring connector then refit the injectors as described in Chapter 4B.

Leakdown test

10 A leakdown test measures the rate at which compressed air fed into the cylinder is lost. It is an alternative to a compression test, and in many ways it is better, since the escaping air provides easy identification of where pressure loss is occurring (piston rings, valves or head gasket).

11 The equipment needed for leakdown testing is unlikely to be available to the home mechanic. If poor compression is suspected, have the test performed by a suitably-equipped garage.

3 Engine assembly/ valve timing marks – general information and usage

Note: *A suitable pin will be required to lock the crankshaft in position (see paragraph 8).*

1 The camshaft sprocket has a timing mark which aligns when the crankshaft is at TDC with No 1 and 4 pistons (No 1 piston is at TDC on its compression stroke).

2 Disconnect the battery negative terminal (refer to battery disconnection in Chapter 5A). If necessary, remove all the injectors as described in Chapter 4B to enable the engine to be easily turned over.

3 To gain access to the camshaft sprocket timing mark, remove the timing belt upper cover as described in Section 6.

4 Firmly apply the handbrake, then jack up the front of the vehicle and support it securely on axle stands (see *Jacking and vehicle support*). Remove the right-hand front roadwheel then undo the retaining screws and fasteners and remove the engine/transmission undertray, and the three bolts securing the wheel arch splash shield to gain access to the crankshaft pulley.

5 Using a socket and extension bar on the crankshaft pulley centre bolt, turn the crankshaft whilst keeping an eye on the camshaft sprocket.

6 Rotate the crankshaft until the timing mark on the camshaft sprocket is correctly aligned with the mark on the timing belt rear cover **(see illustration)**.

7 With the camshaft sprocket timing mark positioned as described, the engine can be safely dismantled. If necessary, the crankshaft can be locked in position as follows.

8 To lock the crankshaft in position, a 6.75 mm diameter pin will be required. Land Rover technicians use service tool LRT-12-058, but an acceptable substitute can be a 6.0 or 6.5 mm drill or bolt with tape wrapped around it to bring its diameter up to 6.75 mm. Ensure the camshaft sprocket timing mark is correctly positioned then insert the pin in through the hole in the rear of the transmission mounting plate, situated just below the crankshaft sensor, making sure it is correctly located in the hole in the rear of the flywheel **(see illustration)**.

4 Camshaft cover – removal and refitting

Removal

1 Unscrew the retaining bolts and remove the plastic cover from the top of the engine **(see illustration)**.

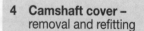

4.1 Unscrew the retaining bolts (arrowed) and remove the engine plastic cover

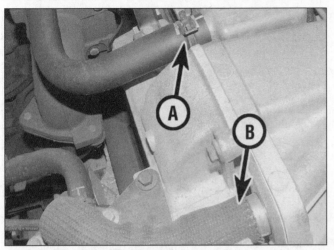

4.3 Disconnect the camshaft cover breather hose (A) and EGR pipe (B)

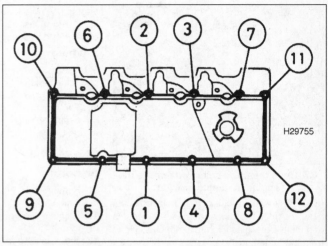

4.10 Camshaft cover bolt tightening sequence

2 Referring to Chapter 4B for further information, carry out the following.
a) *Release the retaining clip and disconnect the hose from the intercooler to the intake pipe above the camshaft cover.*
b) *Undo the bolts securing the intake pipe to the inlet manifold and camshaft cover.*
c) *Undo the bolts securing the EGR pipe to the intake pipe, and remove the intake pipe from the engine.*
3 Release the retaining clip and disconnect the breather hose from the camshaft cover **(see illustration)**.
4 Undo the retaining bolt and free the braking system vacuum hose from the right-hand end of the cover.
5 Remove the oil filler cap and seal from the filler neck.
6 Working in the **reverse** of the tightening sequence **(see illustration 4.10)**, slacken and remove the cover retaining bolts.
7 Remove the cover and discard its gasket.

Refitting

8 Ensure the mating surfaces are clean and dry then fit the new gasket to the cover.
9 Refit the cover to the cylinder head, ensuring that the gasket remains correctly seated.
10 Refit the cover retaining bolts and tighten them all by hand. Once all bolts are in position, go around in sequence and tighten them to the specified torque setting **(see illustration)**.
11 Connect the breather hose to the cover and secure it in position with the retaining clip.
12 Secure the vacuum hose to the right-hand end of the cover, tightening its retaining bolt securely.
13 Refit the seal around the oil filler neck, and fit the oil filler cap.
14 Refit the inlet manifold intake pipe, and the hose from the intercooler to the intake pipe (see Chapter 4B).
15 Reconnect the EGR pipe to the intake pipe.
16 Refit the engine cover.

5 Crankshaft pulley – removal and refitting

Removal

1 Firmly apply the handbrake then jack up the front of the vehicle and support it securely on axle stands (see *Jacking and vehicle support*). Remove the right-hand front roadwheel, undo the three screws and remove the wheel arch splash shield to allow access to the crankshaft pulley.
2 Remove the auxiliary drivebelt as described in Chapter 1B.
3 If further dismantling is to be carried out, align the engine assembly/valve timing marks as described in Section 3.
4 Slacken the crankshaft pulley retaining bolt. To prevent crankshaft rotation, have an assistant select top gear and apply the brakes firmly. If the engine is removed from the vehicle it will be necessary to lock the flywheel (see Section 19).
Caution: Do not be tempted to use the crankshaft locking pin (see Section 3) to prevent rotation as the centre bolt is slackened.
5 Unscrew the retaining bolt and remove the pulley from the crankshaft **(see illustration)**.

Refitting

6 Fit the pulley to the crankshaft and screw in the retaining bolt.
7 Lock the crankshaft by the method used on removal, and tighten the pulley retaining bolt to the specified Stage 1 torque setting then angle-tighten the bolt through the specified Stage 2 angle, using a socket and extension bar. It is recommended that an angle-measuring gauge is used during the final stages of the tightening, to ensure accuracy. If a gauge is not available, use white paint to make alignment marks between the bolt head and pulley prior to tightening; the marks can

then be used to check that the bolt has been rotated through the correct angle.
8 Refit the auxiliary drivebelt as described in Chapter 1B.
9 Refit the wheel arch splash shield, and the roadwheel, then lower the vehicle to the ground and tighten the wheel nuts to the specified torque.

6 Timing belt covers – removal and refitting

Upper cover

Removal

1 Unscrew the retaining bolts and remove the plastic cover from the top of the engine **(see illustration 4.1)**.
2 Firmly apply the handbrake then jack up the front of the vehicle and support it securely on axle stands (see *Jacking and vehicle support*). Undo the retaining screws and remove the engine undertray.
3 Where applicable, remove the bolt securing the air conditioning hose clip to the power steering hose support bracket above the right hand engine mounting.
4 Support the weight of the engine using a

5.5 Unscrew the retaining bolt and remove the pulley from the crankshaft

6.7 Undo the three bolts and remove the engine mounting bracket

trolley jack with a block of wood placed on its head. Position the jack underneath the engine and raise the engine slightly to remove all load from the mounting.

5 Slacken and remove the nut securing the power steering hose support bracket to the engine mounting stud, and remove the bracket.

6 Remove the bolt securing the upper tie rod to the right-hand engine mounting, slacken the bolt at the rear of the tie rod, and pivot the tie rod up and away from the mounting.

7 Remove the three securing bolts, and remove the engine mounting bracket **(see illustration)**.

8 Slacken and remove the four retaining bolts then remove the upper cover from the

engine, complete with its sealing strip **(see illustration)**. Inspect the sealing strip for signs of wear or damage and renew if necessary.

Refitting

9 Ensure the sealing strip is correctly positioned then refit the cover, tightening its bolts to the specified torque.

10 The remainder of refitting is a reversal of removal, tightening all bolts to the specified torque where available.

Lower cover

Removal

11 Remove the crankshaft pulley as described in Section 5.

12 Remove the upper cover as described in paragraph 1.

13 Slacken and remove the six retaining bolts then remove the lower cover from the engine, complete with its sealing strips **(see illustrations)**. Inspect the sealing strips for signs of damage or deterioration and renew if necessary.

Refitting

14 Ensure the sealing strips are correctly positioned then refit the lower cover, tightening its bolts to the specified torque.

15 Refit the upper cover then refit the crankshaft pulley as described in Section 5.

6.8 Unscrew the timing belt upper cover retaining bolts

Rear upper cover

Removal

16 Remove the camshaft sprocket as described in Section 9.

17 Free the wiring harness from the top of the rear cover **(see illustration)**.

18 Slacken and remove the five retaining bolts, complete with their spacers. Remove the rear upper cover from the engine, complete with the rubber sealing strip, noting the rubber grommets which are fitted to the retaining bolt holes **(see illustrations)**. Inspect the sealing strip and grommets for signs of damage or deterioration and renew as necessary.

6.13a Unscrew the retaining bolts . . .

6.13b . . . and remove the timing belt lower cover

6.17 Unclip the harness from the top of the rear cover

6.18a Undo the retaining bolts (arrowed – shown with the engine removed) . . .

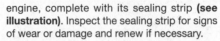

6.18b . . . then remove the rear upper cover from the engine

Refitting

19 Ensure the grommets are correctly fitted to the retaining bolts holes then manoeuvre the rear upper cover into position. Refit the retaining bolts, complete with spacers, and tighten them to the specified torque.
20 Clip the wiring harness back into position.
21 Refit the camshaft sprocket as described in Section 9.

Rear lower cover

Removal

22 Remove the timing belt (see Section 7).
23 Remove the timing belt idler pulley as described in Section 9.
24 Slacken and remove the retaining bolts, complete with their spacers. Remove the rear lower cover from the engine, complete with the rubber sealing strip, noting the rubber grommets which are fitted to the retaining bolt holes **(see illustrations)**. Inspect the sealing strip and grommets for signs of damage or deterioration and renew as necessary.

Refitting

25 Ensure the grommets are correctly fitted to the retaining bolts holes then manoeuvre the cover into position. Refit the retaining bolts, complete with spacers, and tighten them to the specified torque.
26 Refit the idler pulley (Section 9) then refit the timing belt (Section 7).

---

7 Timing belt –
removed and refitting

Note: *A long M6 bolt, nut and washer will be necessary for this procedure (see paragraph 25).*
Note: *Whenever the tension applied to the timing belt is disturbed, it is recommended that the belt be renewed as a matter of course, regardless of its apparent condition*

Removal

1 Disconnect the battery negative lead (refer to battery disconnection in Chapter 5A).
2 Undo the three screws and remove the plastic cover from the top of the engine **(see illustration 4.1)**.
3 Firmly apply the handbrake then jack up the front of the vehicle and support it securely on axle stands (see *Jacking and vehicle support*). Undo the retaining screws and remove the engine undertray, and both front roadwheels.
4 Align the camshaft and crankshaft timing marks as described in Section 3.
5 With reference to Section 5, remove the crankshaft pulley.
6 On models fitted with air conditioning, disconnect the multiplug from the compressor, remove the four securing bolts, and tie the compressor to one side.

 Warning: Do not disconnect the refrigerant pipes from the compressor.

6.24a Slacken and remove the retaining bolts (arrowed) . . .

7 With reference to Chapter 8, remove bolt front driveshafts.
8 Attach a chain or lifting sling/cable to the to the lifting eyes at each end of the cylinder head and, using an engine crossbar or lifting hoist, take the weight of the engine and transmission.
9 Remove the bolts securing the engine lower tie rod to the sump and subframe **(see illustrations)**.
10 With reference to Chapter 4B, remove the air cleaner assembly.
11 Undo the three retaining bolts, and remove the splash shield from the left-hand wheel arch.
12 Pull back the rubber cover, and disconnect the battery lead from the starter motor terminal.
13 Release the clutch slave cylinder retaining clip, and move the cylinder to one side **(see illustration)**.

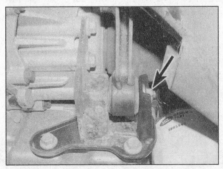

7.9a Unscrew the bolt securing the lower tie rod to the sump (arrowed) . . .

7.13 Prise out the clutch slave cylinder retaining clip

6.24b . . . then remove the timing belt rear lower cover from the engine

14 Remove the bolt securing the support strut to the left-hand engine mounting **(see illustration)**.
15 Slacken and remove the through-bolt securing the left-hand engine mounting to the bracket on the body.
16 Lower the engine/transmission slightly, and remove the two bolts securing the mounting to the transmission. Manoeuvre the mounting from the engine compartment.
17 Undo the bolt and remove the engine mounting strut from the starter motor.
18 Slacken and remove the four securing bolts, and remove the left-hand engine mounting bracket from the body.
19 Carefully push the engine and transmission to the left-hand side of the engine compartment, and if possible use a block of wood to hold it in this position.
20 Undo the six retaining bolts, and remove the timing belt lower cover.

7.9b . . . and the body

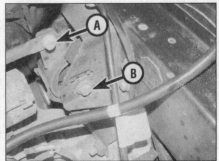

7.14 Remove the support strut bolt (A) and the mounting-to-bracket through-bolt (B)

7.21 Unscrew the three Torx screws securing the damper to the camshaft sprocket

7.22 Undo the retaining nuts and bolts, and remove the cover plate from the right-hand mounting bracket

7.23 Remove the rubber plug to gain access to the rear of the tensioner plunger

21 Slacken and remove the three Torx screws securing the damper to the camshaft sprocket **(see illustration)**.

22 Undo the four nuts and two bolts and remove the right-hand engine mounting plate from the engine **(see illustration)**.

23 Remove the rubber plug from the rear of the timing belt rear lower cover to gain access to the rear of the tensioner spring plunger **(see illustration)**.

24 Slacken the timing belt tensioner pulley Allen bolt.

25 Screw the nut onto the M6 bolt and fit the washer. Screw the bolt into the rear of the tensioner spring plunger then draw the plunger back into the bracket by holding the bolt stationary and rotating the nut **(see illustration)**.

26 Pivot the pulley away from the timing belt and hold it in position by lightly tightening the Allen bolt **(see illustration)**.

27 Slide the timing belt off from its sprockets and remove it from the engine. **Do not** rotate the crankshaft or camshafts until the timing belt has been refitted.

28 Check the timing belt carefully for any signs of uneven wear or oil contamination. If signs of oil contamination are found, trace the source of the oil leak and rectify it, then wash down the engine timing belt area and

all related components to remove all traces of oil.

Refitting

29 Thoroughly clean and dry the timing belt sprockets. Check that the crankshaft is still locked in position and the camshaft sprocket engine assembly mark is still correctly aligned (see Section 3).

30 Fit the timing belt over the crankshaft and camshaft sprockets, ensuring that the belt front run is taut (ie, all slack is on the tensioner side of the belt), then fit the belt over the tensioner pulley. **Do not** twist the belt sharply while refitting it. Ensure that the belt teeth are correctly seated centrally in the sprockets, and that the timing mark remains in alignment.

31 Refit the engine mounting plate to the right-hand side of the engine, and tighten the nuts and bolts to the specified torque.

32 Slacken the timing belt tensioner pulley bolt, then unscrew the M6 bolt from the plunger to tension the belt. Tighten the tensioner pulley Allen bolt securely.

33 Remove the drill bit/bolt inserted through the transmission mounting plate to lock the flywheel.

34 Temporarily refit the crankshaft pulley and retaining bolt and, using a spanner or socket, turn the crankshaft clockwise 2 full revolutions,

until the drill/bolt can be inserted through the hole in the transmission mounting plate and into the flywheel. **Note:** *As the engine/transmission is suspended at this point, the help of an assistant may be required to steady the engine/transmission whilst the crankshaft is turned.*

35 Check the camshaft sprocket timing mark is still correctly aligned, screw the M6 bolt with nut and washer into the tensioner housing and retract the plunger until it is no longer in contact with the pulley backplate. Remove and discard the Allen bolt securing the tensioner pulley. Fit a new Allen bolt to the pulley, but do not tighten it at this stage. It must be possible for the pulley to slide.

36 Carefully release the tensioner spring plunger. Once the plunger is in contact with the pulley backplate, unscrew the M6 bolt from the rear of the plunger and refit the rubber plug to the timing belt cover.

37 Tighten the tensioner pulley Allen bolt to the specified torque, and remove the crankshaft pulley.

38 Clean the camshaft sprocket damper, and refit it to the sprocket, ensuring that the timing groove in the damper is aligned with the groove in the sprocket. Fit new Torx bolts and tighten them to the specified torque.

39 Ensure the sealing strips are correctly

7.25 Screw the M6 bolt (1) into the rear of the tensioner spring plunger and use the nut (2) to draw the plunger back into the mounting bracket

7.26 Pivot the pulley away from the timing belt and hold it in position by lightly tightening the Allen bolt

positioned then refit the timing belt lower cover, tightening its bolts to the specified torque.

40 Centralise the engine/transmission in the engine compartment, and refit the left-hand engine mounting bracket to the body, tightening the bolts to the specified torque.

41 Refit the engine mounting strut to the starter motor, and tighten the bolt to the specified torque.

42 The remainder of refitting is a reversal of removal, noting the following points:
  a) Do not forget to remove the drill/bolt inserted through the transmission mounting plate to lock the flywheel.
  b) Tighten all nuts and bolts to their specified torque setting where available.
  c) Tighten the roadwheel nuts to the specified torque after the vehicle is lowered to the ground

8 Fuel injection pump belt – removal and refitting

Note: Suitable pins will be required to lock the crankshaft (see Section 3) and injection pump sprocket in position (see paragraph 5).

Removal

1 Unscrew the retaining bolts and remove the plastic cover from the top of the engine, taking care not to lose the spacers which are fitted to the cover mounting rubbers **(see illustration 4.1)**.

2 Align the engine assembly/valve timing marks as described in Section 3 and lock the crankshaft in position.

3 Remove the air cleaner housing as described in Chapter 4B.

4 Slacken and remove the retaining bolts, complete with the spacers, and remove the fuel injection pump belt cover and seal from the left-hand end of the engine **(see illustration)**. Inspect the seal and grommets which are fitted to the cover bolt holes; these must be renewed if damaged.

5 To lock the injection pump sprocket in position, a 9.5 mm diameter pin will be required. Land Rover technicians use service tool LRT-12-141, but an acceptable substitute can be a 9.5 mm drill. Insert the pin in through

8.4 Unscrew the retaining bolts, complete with the spacers, and remove the fuel injection pump belt cover and seal

the hole in the sprocket, making sure it is correctly located in the pump mounting plate **(see illustration)**.

6 Loosen the four bolts securing the injection pump belt sprocket to the hub just enough to allow the sprocket to be moved. To prevent camshaft rotation, fit a 3/8 drive ratchet or wrench to the square-section cut-out in the sprocket and hold the sprocket stationary **(see illustrations)**.

7 Slacken the tensioner pulley retaining bolt then slide the injection pump belt off from its sprockets and remove it from the engine **(see illustrations)**. If the belt is to be re-used, use white paint or similar to mark the direction of rotation on the belt.

8 Check the belt carefully for any signs of uneven wear, splitting or oil contamination, and renew it if there is the slightest doubt about its condition. It is recommended that

8.6a Insert a 3/8 drive ratchet or wrench into the square-section hole (arrowed) . . .

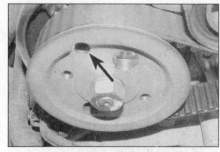

8.5 Insert the 9.5 mm drill bit through the hole in the sprocket (arrowed), making sure it is correctly located in the pump mounting plate

the belt is renewed as a matter of course, regardless of its apparent condition. If signs of oil contamination are found, trace the source of the oil leak and rectify it, then wash down the belt area and all related components to remove all traces of oil. **Note:** Land Rover recommend that a fuel injection pump belt should not be refitted if it has covered more than 24 000 miles.

Refitting

9 Thoroughly clean and dry the sprockets. Check that the crankshaft and injection pump sprockets are still locked in position and the camshaft sprocket engine assembly mark is still correctly aligned (see Section 3).

10 Rotate the camshaft sprocket fully clockwise on its hub then fit the timing belt over the injection pump and tensioner pulley **(see illustration)**. Ensure that the belt lower

8.6b . . . to retain the sprocket then slacken the four bolts securing the sprocket to the hub

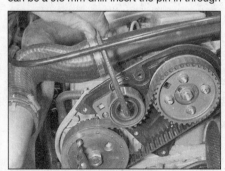

8.7a Slacken the tensioner pulley retaining bolt . . .

8.7b . . . then slip the belt off from the sprockets and remove it from the engine

8.10 Rotate the sprocket fully clockwise on the hub then locate the belt on the sprockets

8.11 Apply the specified torque to the tensioner pulley backplate then securely tighten the pulley retaining bolt

run is taut (ie, all slack is on the tensioner side of the belt), then seat the belt on the camshaft sprocket, rotating the sprocket anti-clockwise on the hub until it engages with the belt teeth. **Do not** twist the belt sharply while refitting it and ensure that the belt teeth are correctly seated centrally in the sprockets. If a used belt is being refitted, ensure that the arrow mark made on removal points in the normal direction of rotation, as before.

11 Using a torque wrench and extension bar fitted to the square-section cut-out in the tensioner backplate, tension the timing belt by applying a torque of 6 Nm (4 lbf ft) to the tensioner. Hold the tensioner in position and securely tighten its retaining bolt **(see illustration)**.

12 Retain the camshaft injection pump belt sprocket (see paragraph 8) and securely tighten the camshaft injection pump belt sprocket bolts.

13 Remove the locking pins from the flywheel and injection pump sprocket then, using a socket on the crankshaft pulley centre bolt, rotate the crankshaft smoothly through two complete turns (720°) in the normal direction of rotation to settle the belt in position.

14 Realign the camshaft sprocket mark then check that the locking tool can be inserted into the rear of the flywheel (see Section 3).

15 Refit the locking pin to the injection pump sprocket then slacken the camshaft injection pump belt sprocket bolts and the tensioner pulley bolt.

16 Refit the torque wrench and extension bar

9.3 Use a home-made tool to retain the camshaft sprocket whilst the retaining bolt is slackened

to the square-section cut-out in the tensioner backplate. Tension the timing belt by applying a torque of 6 Nm (4 lbf ft) to the tensioner then hold the tensioner in position and tighten its retaining bolt to the specified torque.

17 Fit the torque wrench and extension bar to the square-section cut-out on the camshaft sprocket and apply a torque of 25 Nm (18 lbf ft) to the sprocket in an **anti-clockwise** direction. With the correct force applied to the sprocket, tighten the sprocket retaining bolts to the specified torque then remove the torque wrench.

18 Remove the locking pins from the fuel injection pump sprocket and flywheel.

19 Ensure the rubber grommets are correctly fitted to the belt cover holes then locate the seal in the cover groove. Refit the cover then fit the retaining bolts, complete with spacers, and tighten them to the specified torque.

20 The remainder of refitting is a reversal of removal.

9 Timing belt tensioner and sprockets – removal and refitting

Note: *A long M6 bolt, a nut and washer will be required to release the timing belt tensioner spring (see Section 7).*
Note: *Whenever the tension applied to the timing belt is disturbed, it is recommended that the belt be renewed as a matter of course, regardless of its apparent condition*

Camshaft sprocket

Note: *A new sprocket retaining bolt will be required on refitting.*

Removal

1 Align the camshaft and crankshaft timing marks as described in Section 3.

2 Slacken and remove the three Torx bolts securing the damper to the camshaft sprocket. Discard the bolts, new ones must be fitted.

3 Unscrew and remove the camshaft sprocket retaining bolt. To prevent camshaft rotation, Land Rover technicians use the locking tool LRT-12-132 which fits around the sprocket spokes. In the absence of the special tool, a suitable alternative can be fabricated from two

9.15 Slide the sprocket from the crankshaft, noting which way round it is fitted

lengths of steel strip (one long, the other short) and three nuts and bolts. One nut and bolt should form the pivot of the forked tool, with the remaining two nuts and bolts at the tips of the forks to engage with the sprocket spokes **(see illustration)**. Discard the camshaft sprocket bolt, a new one must be fitted.

4 Remove the timing belt as described in Section 7.

5 Slide the camshaft sprocket from the camshaft.

6 Check the sprocket for signs of wear or damage and renew if necessary.

Refitting

7 Prior to refitting check the oil seal for signs of damage or leakage. If necessary, renew as described in Section 11.

8 Ensure the locating pin is in position in the camshaft end. Note that the pin should be fitted with the split facing inwards.

9 Fit the sprocket to the camshaft, aligning the sprocket with the locating pin.

10 Lightly oil the threads of the new sprocket retaining bolt then screw the bolt into position.

11 Prevent camshaft rotation by the method used on removal, and tighten the sprocket retaining bolt to the specified Stage 1 torque setting then angle-tighten the bolt through the specified Stage 2 angle, using a socket and extension bar. It is recommended that an angle-measuring gauge is used during the final stage of the tightening, to ensure accuracy. If a gauge is not available, use white paint to make alignment marks between the bolt head and sprocket prior to tightening; the marks can then be used to check that the bolt has been rotated through the correct angle.

12 Ensure the crankshaft is still locked in position and the camshaft sprocket mark is correctly aligned (see Section 3).

13 Refit timing belt as described in Section 7.

Crankshaft sprocket

Removal

14 Remove the timing belt as described in Section 7.

15 Slide the sprocket off from the end of the crankshaft, noting which way around it is fitted **(see illustration)**.

Refitting

16 Prior to refitting check the oil seal for signs of damage or leakage. If necessary, renew as described in Section 18.

17 Refit the sprocket to the crankshaft, aligning its key with the crankshaft slot.

18 Refit the timing belt as described in Section 7.

Tensioner assembly

Removal

19 Remove the timing belt as described in Section 7.

20 Slacken and remove the Allen screw and bolt securing the tensioner pulley and backplate to the engine **(see illustration)**.

21 With the tensioner removed, carefully release the spring plunger then remove the plunger and spring from the tensioner body **(see illustration)**.

22 Clean the tensioner assembly but **do not** use any strong solvent which may enter the pulley bearing. Check that the pulley rotates freely on the backplate, with no sign of stiffness or free play. Renew the assembly if there is any doubt about its condition or if there are any obvious signs of wear or damage. The same applies to the tensioner spring, which should be checked with great care as its condition is critical for the correct tensioning of the timing belt. The condition of the spring can be judged by measuring its free length; if the spring is less than 65 mm it must be renewed.

Refitting

23 Check that the camshaft timing marks are still correctly aligned and the crankshaft is still locked in position (see Section 3).

24 Lubricate the plunger with a smear of molybdenum disulphide grease then fit the tensioner spring and plunger to the mounting bracket. Use the nut and bolt to draw the plunger fully into the bracket.

25 Fit the tensioner pulley and screw in the backplate and pulley retaining bolts. Tighten the backplate bolt to the specified torque but do not tighten the pulley bolt yet.

26 Refit the timing belt as described in Section 7.

Idler pulley

Removal

27 Remove the timing belt as described in Section 7.

28 Slacken and remove the retaining nut and remove the idler pulley from its mounting stud. If the mounting stud is unscrewed with the pulley, carefully clamp the stud in a vice equipped with soft jaws then remove the retaining nut and separate the pulley and stud.

29 Clean the idler pulley but **do not** use any strong solvent which may enter the pulley bearing. Check that the pulley rotates freely, with no sign of stiffness or free play. Renew the pulley if there is any doubt about its condition or if there are any obvious signs of wear or damage.

Refitting

30 Remove all traces of locking compound from the threads of the retaining nut and mounting stud.

31 Where the mounting stud has been removed, apply locking compound to the stud threads then refit the stud to the engine and tighten it securely.

32 Fit the idler pulley to the mounting stud. Apply locking compound to the threads of the pulley retaining nut then refit the nut and tighten it to the specified torque.

33 Refit the timing belt as described in Section 7.

9.20 Slacken and remove the Allen screw and bolt securing the tensioner pulley and backplate to the engine

10 Fuel injection pump belt tensioner and sprockets – removal and refitting

Camshaft sprocket

Note: *A new sprocket hub retaining bolt will be required on refitting.*

Removal

1 Remove the injection pump belt as described in Section 8.

2 Unscrew the central hub retaining bolt. To prevent camshaft rotation, fit a 3/8 drive ratchet or wrench to the square-section cut-out in the sprocket and hold the sprocket stationary.

3 Unscrew the four retaining bolts and remove the sprocket from the hub **(see illustration)**.

4 Remove the hub from the camshaft, taking care not to lose the locating pin. If a pin is a loose fit in the end of the camshaft, remove it and store it with the hub for safe-keeping.

5 Check the sprocket and hub for signs of wear or damage and renew if necessary.

Refitting

6 Prior to refitting check the oil seal for signs of damage or leakage. If necessary, renew as described in Section 11.

7 Ensure the locating pin is in position in the camshaft end. Note that the pin should be fitted with the split facing inwards.

8 Fit the sprocket hub to the camshaft, aligning its cut-out with the locating pin.

9 Lightly oil the threads of the new retaining bolt then screw the bolt into position.

10.3 Unscrew the four retaining bolts and remove the sprocket from the hub

9.21 Carefully unscrew the bolt and remove the plunger and spring from the tensioner body

10 Refit the sprocket to the hub, tightening its bolts lightly only at this stage.

11 Prevent camshaft rotation by the method used on removal, and tighten the hub retaining bolt to the specified Stage 1 torque setting then angle-tighten the bolt through the specified Stage 2 angle, using a socket and extension bar. It is recommended that an angle-measuring gauge is used during the final stage of the tightening, to ensure accuracy.

> **HAYNES HINT** *If a gauge is not available, use white paint to make alignment marks between the bolt head and hub prior to tightening; the marks can then be used to check that the bolt has been rotated through the correct angle.*

12 Refit the fuel injection pump belt as described in Section 8.

Fuel injection pump sprocket

13 This is described as part of the fuel injection pump removal and refitting procedures. Remove the fuel injection pump belt as described in Section 8 then proceed as described in Chapter 4B, Section 10.

Tensioner pulley

Removal

14 Remove the injection pump belt as described in Section 8.

15 Unscrew the retaining bolt and remove the tensioner assembly from the cylinder head **(see illustration)**.

10.15 Unscrew the retaining bolt and remove the tensioner

10.17 Ensure the tensioner pulley backplate hole is correctly engaged with the pivot pin (arrowed)

16 Clean the tensioner pulley but **do not** use any strong solvent which may enter the pulley bearing. Check that the pulley rotates freely, with no sign of stiffness or free play. Renew the tensioner pulley if there is any doubt about its condition or if there are any obvious signs of wear or damage.

Refitting

17 Refit the tensioner pulley, making sure its backplate is correctly located on the pivot pin, and refit the retaining bolt **(see illustration)**.
18 Refit the fuel injection pump belt as described in Section 8.

11 Camshaft oil seals – renewal

Right-hand seal

Note: *Whenever the tension applied to the timing belt is disturbed, it is recommended that the belt be renewed as a matter of course, regardless of its apparent condition*

1 Remove the camshaft sprocket as described in Section 9.
2 Carefully punch or drill two small holes opposite each other in the oil seal. Screw a self-tapping screw into each hole, and pull on the screws with pliers to extract the seal.
3 Clean the seal housing and polish off any burrs or raised edges which may have caused the seal to fail.
4 Lubricate the lips of the new seal with clean engine oil and drive it fully into position. Use a

11.8a Unscrew the retaining bolts . . .

suitable tubular drift, such as a socket, which bears only on the hard outer edge of the seal. Take care not to damage the seal lips during fitting and note that the seal lips should face inwards.
5 Refit the camshaft sprocket as described in Section 9.

Left-hand seal

6 Remove the fuel injection pump belt as described in Section 8. The belt must be renewed if it has been contaminated with oil.
7 Remove the camshaft sprocket hub and the tensioner pulley as described in Section 10.
8 Slacken and remove the three retaining bolts, noting the correct fitted position of the engine cover bracket, and remove the injection pump belt rear cover from the end of the cylinder head **(see illustrations)**.
9 Renew the oil seal as described in paragraphs 2 to 4.
10 Refit the rear cover to the cylinder head and tighten its retaining bolts to the specified torque, ensuring the engine cover mounting bracket is correctly positioned.
11 Refit the fuel injection pump camshaft sprocket and tensioner as described in Section 10 then refit the belt as described in Section 8.

12 Camshaft and followers – removal, inspection and refitting

Note: *Land Rover produce a sealant kit which consists of a plastic scraper, gasket removing compound and the recommended sealant for the camshaft carrier joint. It is recommended that this kit is used during the following procedure.*
Note: *Whenever the tension applied to the timing belt is disturbed, it is recommended that the belt be renewed as a matter of course, regardless of its apparent condition*

Removal

1 Remove the timing belt rear upper cover as described in Section 6.
2 Remove the fuel injection pump belt camshaft sprocket hub and the tensioner pulley as described in Section 10.
3 Slacken and remove the three retaining

11.8b . . . and remove the injection pump belt rear cover from the cylinder head

bolts, noting the correct fitted position of the engine cover bracket, and remove the injection pump belt rear cover from the end of the cylinder head.
4 Support the weight of the engine using a trolley jack with a block of wood placed on its head and disconnect the lifting chains. Remove the camshaft cover as described in Section 4.
5 Working in the **reverse** of the tightening sequence **(see illustration 12.15)**, slacken the camshaft bearing carrier retaining bolts evenly progressively, by one turn at a time, to gradually release the pressure of the valve springs. Once all bolts are loose, remove them from the cylinder head.
Caution: If the bearing carrier bolts are carelessly slackened, the carrier might break. If the carrier is broken, the complete cylinder head assembly must be renewed; the carrier is matched to the head and is not available separately.
6 Lift the camshaft bearing carrier away from the cylinder, noting the correct fitted positions of the locating dowels. If the dowels are loose, remove them and store them with the bearing carrier for safe-keeping.
7 Carefully lift the camshaft from the cylinder head. Remove the oil seal from each end of the shaft and discard them; new ones should be used on refitting.
8 If necessary, obtain eight small, clean plastic containers, and label them for identification. Alternatively, divide a larger container into compartments. Using a sucker or magnet, withdraw each follower in turn, invert it to prevent oil loss and place it in its respective container, which should then be filled with clean engine oil.
Caution: Do not interchange the followers, and do not allow the followers to lose oil, as they will take a long time to refill with oil on restarting the engine, which could result in incorrect valve clearances.

Inspection

9 Examine the camshaft bearing surfaces and cam lobes for signs of wear ridges and scoring. Renew the camshaft if any of these conditions are apparent. Examine the condition of the bearing surfaces both on the camshaft journals and in the cylinder head. If the head bearing surfaces are worn excessively, the cylinder head will need to be renewed.
10 Examine the follower bearing surfaces which contact the camshaft lobes for wear ridges and scoring. Check the followers and their bores in the cylinder head for signs of wear or damage. If the engine's valve clearances have sounded noisy, particularly if the noise persists after initial start-up from cold, then there is reason to suspect a faulty follower. If any follower is thought to be faulty or is visibly worn it should be renewed.

Refitting

11 Where removed, lubricate the followers with clean engine oil and carefully insert each

one into its original location in the cylinder head **(see illustration)**.

12 Liberally oil the camshaft bearings and followers then refit the camshaft to the cylinder head. Position the shaft so that the timing belt sprocket locating pin is in the 2 o'clock position when viewed from the right-hand end of the engine **(see illustration)**.

13 Ensure the mating surfaces of the camshaft bearing carrier and cylinder head are clean and dry then apply a bead of sealant to the mating surfaces of the bearing carrier **(see illustration)**. Spread the sealant to an even film, taking care not to allow any sealant to enter the oilway grooves.

14 Ensure that the locating dowels are in position and refit the camshaft bearing carrier to the cylinder head. Ensure the carrier is correctly located and screw in the retaining bolts, tightening them all by hand only at this stage.

15 Working in the specified sequence, evenly and progressively tighten the retaining bolts to draw the bearing carrier squarely down into contact with the cylinder head. Once the carrier is in contact with the head, go around in the specified sequence and tighten the retaining bolts to the specified torque **(see illustration)**.

Caution: If the bearing carrier bolts are carelessly tightened, the carrier might break. If the carrier is broken then the complete cylinder head assembly must be renewed; the carrier is matched to the head and is not available separately.

16 Refit the camshaft cover as described in Section 4.

17 Fit a new oil seal to either end of the camshaft as described in Section 11.

18 Refit the timing belt rear cover as described in Section 6 and refit the camshaft sprocket as described in Section 9.

19 Refit the fuel injection pump belt rear cover to the cylinder head and tighten its retaining bolts to the specified torque, ensuring the engine cover mounting bracket is correctly positioned.

20 Refit the fuel injection pump belt camshaft sprocket and tensioner as described in Section 10 then refit the belt as described in Section 8.

12.11 Lubricate the followers with clean engine oil and insert them into their original holes

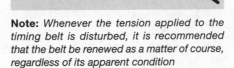

12.13 Apply sealant to the highlighted areas of the cylinder head camshaft bearing carrier

13 Cylinder head – removal and refitting

Note: *Whenever the tension applied to the timing belt is disturbed, it is recommended that the belt be renewed as a matter of course, regardless of its apparent condition*

Removal

1 Disconnect the battery negative lead (refer to battery disconnection in Chapter 5A).

2 Drain the cooling system, as described in Chapter 1B.

3 Align the engine assembly/valve timing marks as described in Section 3 and lock the crankshaft in position.

4 Remove the fuel injection pump belt as described in Section 8.

5 Remove the fuel injection pump belt

12.12 Lay the camshaft in position in the cylinder head, making sure the locating pin (arrowed) is in the 2 o'clock position

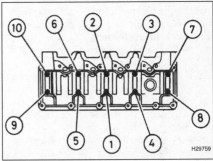

12.15 Camshaft bearing carrier bolt tightening sequence

tensioner, and camshaft sprocket and hub, as described in Section 10. Slacken and remove the three retaining bolts, noting the correct fitted position of the engine cover bracket, and remove the injection pump belt rear cover from the end of the cylinder head.

6 Remove the timing belt upper rear cover as described in Section 6.

7 Remove the camshaft cover as described in Section 4.

8 Support the weight of the engine using a trolley jack with a block of wood placed on its head and disconnect the lifting chains. On models with air conditioning, remove the alternator upper fixing bolt.

9 Disconnect the wiring connector from the coolant temperature sensors which are screwed into the coolant elbow on the front of the cylinder head **(see illustrations)**.

10 Release the retaining clip and disconnect the coolant hose from the cylinder head

13.9a Disconnect the wiring plug from the coolant temperature sensor . . .

13.9b . . . and the temperature gauge sender wiring plug from the cylinder head coolant elbow

13.10 Unscrew the dipstick guide tube retaining bolt

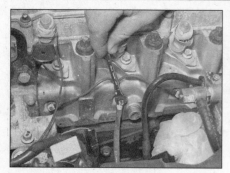

13.12 Unscrew the retaining nut and disconnect the glow plug feed wiring from No 2 glow plug

coolant elbow then slacken and remove the bolt securing the engine oil dipstick tube in position **(see illustration)**.

11 Referring to Chapter 4B, carry out the following operations

a) *Remove the inlet and exhaust manifolds.*

b) *Remove the injector pipes connecting the injection pump to the injectors.*

c) *Disconnect the needle lift sensor wiring connector from No 1 injector.*

d) *If the cylinder head is to be overhauled, remove all the injectors.*

12 Unscrew the retaining nut and disconnect the glow plug feed wiring connector from No 2 glow plug **(see illustration)**. If the cylinder head is to be overhauled, remove the glow plugs as described in Chapter 5C.

13 Slacken the retaining clip securing the braking system servo unit vacuum hose to the pump (which is fitted to the alternator) and position the hose clear of the cylinder head.

14 Make a final check to ensure that all relevant hoses, pipes and wires, etc, have been disconnected.

15 Working in the **reverse** of the tightening sequence **(see illustration 13.36)**, progressively slacken the cylinder head bolts by a third of a turn at a time until all bolts can be unscrewed by hand. Withdraw the bolts, and store them in order, so that they can be refitted in their original locations. The bolts can be stored by pushing them through a clearly-marked cardboard template.

16 Lift the cylinder head from the cylinder block **(see illustration)**. If necessary, tap the

13.16 Remove the cylinder head from the engine

cylinder head gently with a soft-faced mallet to free it from the block, but **do not** lever at the mating faces.

17 When the joint is broken, lift the cylinder head away then remove the gasket. Note the fitted positions of the two locating dowels, and remove them for safe-keeping if they are loose. Keep the gasket for identification purposes (see paragraph 24).

Caution: Do not lay the head on its lower mating surface; support the head on wooden blocks, ensuring each block only contacts the head mating surface not the glow plugs or injector nozzles. The glow plugs and injector nozzles protrude out the bottom of the head and they will be damaged if the head is placed directly onto a bench.

18 If the cylinder head is to be dismantled, remove the camshaft, as described in Section 12, then refer to the relevant Sections of Part D of this Chapter.

Preparation for refitting

19 The mating faces of the cylinder head and block must be perfectly clean before refitting the head. Use a scraper to remove all traces of gasket and carbon, and also clean the tops of the pistons. Take particular care with the aluminium surfaces, as the soft metal is damaged easily. Also, make sure that debris is not allowed to enter the oil and water channels – this is particularly important for the oil circuit, as carbon could block the oil supply to the camshaft or crankshaft bearings. Using adhesive tape and paper, seal the water, oil

and bolt holes in the cylinder block. To prevent carbon entering the gap between the pistons and bores, smear a little grease in the gap. After cleaning the piston, rotate the crankshaft so that the piston moves down the bore, then wipe out the grease and carbon with a cloth rag. Clean the piston crowns in the same way.

20 Check the block and head for nicks, deep scratches and other damage. If slight, they may be removed carefully with a file. More serious damage may be repaired by machining, but this is a specialist job.

21 If warpage of the cylinder head gasket surface is suspected, use a straight-edge to check it for distortion. Refer to Part D of this Chapter if necessary.

22 Ensure that the cylinder head bolt holes in the crankcase are clean and free of oil. Syringe or soak up any oil left in the bolt holes. This is most important in order that the correct bolt tightening torque can be applied and to prevent the possibility of the block being cracked by hydraulic pressure when the bolts are tightened.

23 Check the condition of the cylinder head bolts, particularly their threads. Keeping all bolts in their correct fitted order, wash them and wipe dry. Check each bolt for any sign of visible wear or damage and measure the length of each bolt **(see illustration)**. If any bolt shows signs of wear or damage or is longer than 243.41 mm then all the bolts must be renewed as a complete set. If all bolts are in good condition and are less than 243.41 mm in length, then it is permissible to re-use them. However, as a precaution, we recommend that the bolts are renewed as a complete set, regardless of their apparent condition.

24 On this engine, the cylinder head to piston clearance is controlled by fitting different thickness head gaskets. The gasket thickness can be determined by looking at the tab situated directly in front of No 2 cylinder (the tab is visible once the plastic cover has been removed from the top of the engine) **(see illustration)**.

Holes on gasket tab	Gasket thickness
One hole	1.05 mm
Two holes	1.20 to 1.25 mm
Three holes	1.30 to 1.35 mm

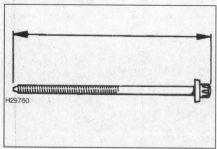

13.23 Measure the length of each cylinder head bolt. If any bolt exceeds the specified limit (see text) all bolts must be renewed as a set

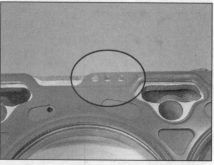

13.24 The cylinder head gasket thickness identification marking can be found at the front of No 2 cylinder

13.26 Measure the protrusion of each piston as described in the text, to calculate the correct thickness of the cylinder head gasket

The correct thickness of gasket required is selected by measuring the piston protrusions as follows.

25 Remove the locking pin from the flywheel and mount a dial test indicator securely on the block so that its pointer can be easily pivoted between the piston crown and block mating surface. Temporarily refit the crankshaft pulley bolt to enable the crankshaft to be easily rotated.

26 Ensure the piston is at exactly TDC then zero the dial test indicator on the gasket surface of the cylinder block. Carefully move the indicator over No 1 piston, taking measurements in line with the gudgeon pin axis, measure the protrusion on both the left-hand and right-hand side of the piston **(see illustration)**. Repeat this procedure on No 4 piston.

27 Rotate the crankshaft half-a-turn to bring Nos 2 and 3 pistons to TDC. Ensure the crankshaft is accurately positioned then measure the protrusions of Nos 2 and 3 pistons, taking two measurements for each piston. Once both pistons have been measured, rotate the crankshaft through half-a-turn to bring Nos 1 and 4 pistons back to TDC and lock the crankshaft in position again.

28 Using the largest protrusion measurement of the four pistons, select the correct thickness of gasket required using the following table.

Largest piston protrusion measurement	Gasket required
0.1 to 0.25 mm	One hole in tab
0.25 to 0.4 mm	Two holes in tab
0.4 to 0.55 mm	Three holes in tab

Refitting

29 Remove the locking pin from the rear of the flywheel and turn the crankshaft slightly **backwards** so that pistons 1 and 4 are positioned approximately 25 mm down their bores. This will ensure the valves do not contact the pistons as the head is refitted. **Note:** *Make a note of the approximate angle through which the crankshaft is rotated; this will be useful when refitting the locking pin prior to fitting the timing belt (see paragraph 48).*

30 Wipe clean the mating faces of the head and block and ensure that the two locating dowels are in position at each end of the cylinder block/crankcase surface **(see illustration)**.

31 Check that the oil restrictor is in position on the front, left-hand end of the cylinder block. Ensure the restrictor is unblocked and does not protrude above the block mating surface.

32 Fit the new cylinder head gasket to the block, making sure it is fitted with the correct way up **(see illustration)**.

33 Prior to refitting the cylinder head, check that the camshaft is still positioned correctly with its timing belt sprocket locating pin in the 2 o'clock position when viewed from the right-hand end of the head **(see illustration 12.12)**.

13.30 Ensure the locating dowels (arrowed) are in position . . .

34 Carefully refit the cylinder head, locating it on the dowels.

35 Keeping all the cylinder head bolts in their correct fitted order, wash them and wipe dry. Lightly oil under the head and on the threads of each bolt, carefully enter it into its original hole and screw it in, by hand only, until finger-tight.

Caution: Do not drop the bolts into their holes.

36 Working progressively and in sequence, first tighten all the cylinder head bolts to the Stage 1 torque setting **(see illustration)**.

37 Once all bolts have been tightened to the Stage 1 torque, go around again in the specified sequence and tighten all bolts to the specified Stage 2 torque setting.

38 Once all bolts have been tightened to the Stage 2 torque, again working in sequence, tighten each bolt through its specified Stage 3 angle, using a socket and extension bar. It is recommended that an angle-measuring gauge is used during this stage of the tightening, to ensure accuracy. Prior to tightening, use a felt-tip pen or similar to make alignment marks between the radial mark on each bolt head and the cylinder head.

39 Finally go around in the specified sequence again and tighten all bolts through the specified Stage 4 angle. Each bolt head radial mark should now be exactly opposite the corresponding mark made on the cylinder head.

40 Refit the glow plugs (where removed) and connect the glow plug wiring to No 2 glow plug (see Chapter 5C).

41 Referring to Chapter 4B, carry out the following:
a) *Refit the injectors (where removed)*
b) *Reconnect the needle lift sensor wiring connector.*
c) *Refit the injector pipes.*
d) *Refit the manifolds.*

42 Reconnect the coolant hose to the cylinder head elbow and secure it in position with the retaining clip. Refit the dipstick tube retaining bolt, tighten it securely, and reconnect the coolant temperature sensor wiring connectors.

43 On models equipped with air conditioning, refit the alternator upper mounting bracket tightening its retaining bolts securely.

13.32 . . . then fit the new gasket, making sure it is the correct way up

44 On all models, refit the camshaft cover as described in Section 4.

45 Attach a chain or lifting sling/cable to the to the lifting eyes at each end of the cylinder head, and using an engine crossbar or lifting hoist, take the weight of the engine and transmission. Remove the jack from under the engine.

46 Reconnect the vacuum hose to the braking system vacuum pump.

47 Refit the timing belt upper cover as described in Section 6 then refit the camshaft sprocket as described in Section 9.

48 Ensure the camshaft sprocket timing mark is correctly aligned with the mark on the cover (see Section 3) then carefully rotate the crankshaft in the normal direction of rotation, to bring Nos 1 and 4 pistons back to TDC. Lock the crankshaft in position by inserting pin into the rear of the flywheel.

Caution: Do not rotate the crankshaft any further than is necessary as there is a risk that the pistons will contact and damage the valves.

49 Refit the timing belt as described in Section 7.

50 Refit the fuel injection pump belt rear cover to the cylinder head and tighten its retaining bolts to the specified torque, ensuring the engine cover mounting bracket is correctly positioned.

51 Refit the fuel injection pump belt camshaft sprocket and tensioner as described in Section 10 then refit the belt as described in Section 8.

52 Reconnect the battery and refill the cooling system as described in Chapter 1B.

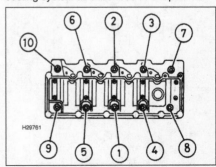

13.36 Cylinder head bolt tightening sequence

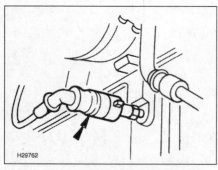

14.6 Disconnect the vacuum pump oil hose union (arrowed) from the sump

14.10 Undo the retaining bolts (arrowed) and remove the oil pump pick-up/strainer

14.12 On refitting, fit a new sealing ring to the oil pump pick-up/strainer groove

14.13 Apply a bead of sealant to the front main bearing cap/cylinder block joints (arrowed) and ensure the cap grooves are filled with sealant

14.14 Apply a bead of sealant to the joint between the crankshaft oil seal housing and the cylinder block (arrowed)

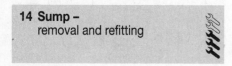

14 Sump –
removal and refitting

Removal

1 Disconnect the battery negative lead (refer to battery disconnection in Chapter 5A).
2 Apply the handbrake, then jack up the front of the vehicle and support it securely on axle stands (see *Jacking and vehicle support*). Remove the retaining screws and fasteners and remove the undertray from beneath the engine and transmission.
3 Drain the engine oil and remove the oil filter as described in Chapter 1B. If the oil filter is

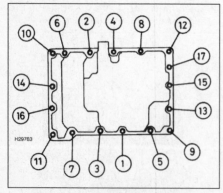

14.16 Sump retaining bolt tightening sequence

damaged on removal (which is likely), then a new filter must be used on refitting and the engine filled with fresh oil. Refit the sump plug with a new sealing washer, and tighten the plug to the specified torque.
4 Slacken and remove the mounting bolts securing the rear engine/transmission steady rod to the bracket and subframe and remove the rod. Unbolt the rod bracket from the sump.
5 Undo the retaining bolts and remove the support bracket securing the rear of the sump to the transmission mounting plate.
6 Wipe clean the area around the vacuum pump hose union on the sump then position a container beneath the union **(see illustration)**. Disconnect the hose from the sump and allow any oil to drain into the container.
7 Unscrew the retaining bolts securing the oil cooler pipes to the sump and bracket. Unscrew the union nut and disconnect the front oil cooler pipe from the pump. Position both pipes clear of the sump and remove the sealing ring which is fitted to the pipe end fitting. Discard the sealing ring; a new one should be used on refitting.
8 Working in the **reverse** of the tightening sequence **(see illustration 14.16)**, progressively slacken and remove the bolts securing the sump to the base of the cylinder block.
9 Break the sump joint by striking the sump with the palm of the hand, then lower the sump away from the engine. Remove the gasket and discard it, a new one should be used on refitting.

10 While the sump is removed, take the opportunity to check the oil pump pick-up/strainer for signs of clogging or splitting. If necessary, unbolt the pick-up/strainer, noting the correct fitted location of the shorter bolt, and remove it from the engine along with its sealing ring **(see illustration)**. The strainer can then be cleaned easily in solvent. Inspect the strainer mesh for signs of clogging or splitting and renew if necessary. If the pick-up/strainer bolts are damaged they must be renewed.

Refitting

11 Clean all traces of gasket from the mating surfaces of the cylinder block/crankcase and sump, then use a clean rag to wipe out the sump and the engine interior.
12 Where necessary, fit a new sealing ring to the oil pump pick-up/strainer groove then carefully refit the pipe **(see illustration)**. Refit the retaining bolts, making sure the shorter bolt is screwed into the main bearing cap, and tighten them to the specified torque setting.
13 Apply a bead of suitable sealant (recommended sealant is available from your Land Rover dealer) to the front main bearing cap joint areas of the cylinder block mating surface and ensure the cap grooves are completely filled with sealant **(see illustration)**.
14 Apply a bead of sealant to the joint between the crankshaft left-hand (flywheel) oil seal housing and cylinder block **(see illustration)**.
15 Fit the gasket to the sump then offer up the sump to the cylinder block/crankcase. Refit the sump retaining bolts, and tighten the bolts finger-tight only.
16 Working in sequence, tighten the sump bolts to the specified torque setting **(see illustration)**. Go around again in the specified sequence and recheck the tightness of each bolt.
17 Fit a new sealing ring to the oil cooler pipe union and reconnect the pipe. Refit the pipe retaining clip bolts, tightening them securely, then tighten the union nut to the specified torque.
18 Securely reconnect the vacuum pipe return hose to the sump.
19 Refit the support bracket connecting the sump to the transmission mounting plate,

tightening its bolts to their specified torque settings.

20 Refit the engine/transmission rear steady rod and tighten its bolts to the specified torque.

21 Fit the oil filter then refit the engine/ transmission undertray. Lower the vehicle to the ground and refill the engine with oil (see Chapter 1B).

15 Oil pump – removal and refitting

Note: *The oil pressure relief valve can be dismantled without removing the oil pump from the vehicle – see Section 16 for details.*
Note: *Whenever the tension applied to the timing belt is disturbed, it is recommended that the belt be renewed as a matter of course, regardless of its apparent condition*

Removal

1 Drain the engine oil and remove the oil filter as described in Chapter 1B. If the oil filter is damaged on removal (which is likely), then a new filter must be used on refitting and the engine filled with fresh oil. Refit the sump plug with a new sealing washer, and tighten the plug to the specified torque.
2 Remove the crankshaft sprocket as described in Section 9.
3 Unbolt the timing belt rear lower cover and remove it from the cylinder block (see Section 6).
4 Wipe clean the area around the oil cooler pipe unions on the front of the oil pump and the turbocharger oil feed pipe union on the rear of the pump. Slacken and remove the pipe retaining clip bolts then unscrew the union nuts and disconnect the pipes from the pump. Remove the sealing rings from the pipe end fittings and discard; new ones must be used on refitting.
5 Working in the **reverse** of the tightening

sequence **(see illustration 15.13)**, progressively slacken and remove the oil pump retaining bolts, noting the correct fitted location of the larger (M10) bolt.
6 Free the oil pump from the cylinder block then slide it off the end of the crankshaft. Note the correct fitted locations of the pump locating dowels; if the dowels are loose, remove them and store with the pump for safe-keeping. Remove the gasket and discard it; if the oil pump bolts are damaged they must also be renewed.
7 Remove the oil pump drive Woodruff key from the crankshaft and store it with the pump for safe-keeping.

Refitting

8 Prior to refitting, carefully lever out the crankshaft oil seal using a flat-bladed screwdriver **(see illustration)**. Fit the new oil seal, ensuring its sealing lip is facing inwards, and press it squarely into the housing using a tubular drift which bears only on the hard outer edge of the seal. Press the seal into position so that it is flush with the housing and lubricate the oil seal lip with clean engine oil.
9 Ensure the mating surfaces of the oil pump and cylinder block are clean and dry.
10 Ensure the locating dowels are in position then fit a new gasket to the cylinder block **(see illustration)**. The gasket must be installed dry.
11 Fit the Woodruff key to the crankshaft slot.
12 Carefully manoeuvre the oil pump into position, aligning the inner rotor slot with the Woodruff key. Locate the pump on the dowels, taking great care not to damage the oil seal lip.
13 Fit the pump retaining bolts, tightening them all by hand, then go around in the specified sequence and tighten them to their specified torque settings **(see illustration)**.
14 Fit new sealing rings to the oil cooler and turbocharger oil pipe end fittings and reconnect the pipes to the pump. Refit the

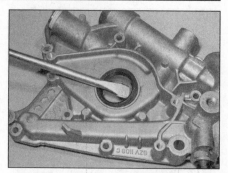

15.8 Prior to refitting the oil pump, renew the crankshaft oil seal

retaining clip bolts, tightening them securely, then tighten the pipe union nuts to the specified torque.
15 Refit the rear lower timing belt cover (see Section 6) then refit the crankshaft sprocket and new timing belt (see Sections 7 and 9).
16 Fit the oil filter then lower the vehicle to the ground and refill the engine with oil as described in Chapter 1B.

16 Oil pump – dismantling, inspection and reassembly

Note: *A new pressure relief valve plug will be required. If oil pump wear is suspected, check the cost and availability of new parts (only the pressure relief valve and thermostatic valve components seem to be available separately) against the cost of a new pump. Examine the pump as described in this Section and then decide whether renewal or repair is the best course of action.*

Dismantling

1 Remove the oil pump as described in Section 15.
2 Make alignment marks between the cover and pump body then unscrew the

15.10 Fit a new gasket over the locating dowels

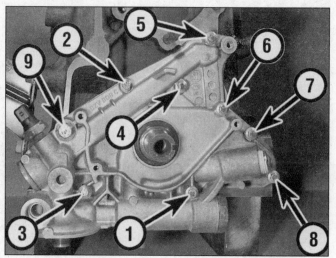

15.13 Oil pump retaining bolt tightening sequence

16.2a Undo the retaining screws . . .

16.2b . . . and remove the cover from the rear of the oil pump housing

16.3 Remove the inner and outer rotors noting which way around they are fitted

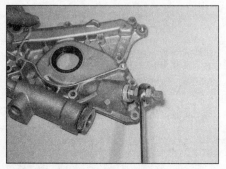

16.5a Unscrew the threaded plug . . .

16.5b . . . and withdraw the oil pressure relief valve spring . . .

16.5c . . . and plunger from the pump body

16.6a Unscrew the oil cooler pipe adaptor . . .

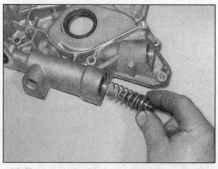

16.6b . . . and withdraw the thermostatic valve and spring from the pump

16.8a Using feeler blades, check the outer rotor-to-body clearance . . .

16.8b . . . and the inner rotor tip-to-outer rotor clearance

retaining screws and remove the cover **(see illustrations)**.

3 Make identification marks on the inner and outer rotors with a suitable marker pen to ensure they are fitted the same way around on reassembly. Remove both the rotors from the body **(see illustration)**.

4 The oil pressure relief valve can be dismantled, if required, without disturbing the pump. If this is to be done with the pump in position and the engine still installed in the vehicle, it will first be necessary to remove the auxiliary drivebelt (see Chapter 1B) and unbolt the drivebelt tensioner.

5 To dismantle the valve, slacken and remove the threaded plug then recover the valve spring and plunger **(see illustrations)**. Discard the threaded plug; a new one should be used on reassembly.

6 To dismantle the thermostatic valve, unscrew the oil cooler pipe adaptor from the front of the pump body then remove the valve and spring, noting each components correct fitted location **(see illustrations)**. Remove the sealing washer from the adaptor and discard it, a new one must be used on refitting.

Inspection

7 Inspect the rotors for obvious signs of wear or damage and renew if necessary. If the pump body or cover plate is scored or damaged, then the complete oil pump assembly must be renewed.

8 Refit the rotors to the body and, using feeler blades of the appropriate thickness, measure the clearance between the outer rotor and the pump body, then between the inner rotor tip and the outer rotor **(see illustrations)**.

9 Using feeler blades and a straight-edge placed across the top of the pump body and the rotors, measure the rotor endfloat **(see illustration)**.

10 If any measurement is outside the specified limits, the complete pump assembly must be renewed.

11 If the pressure relief valve plunger is

16.9 Measure the oil pump rotor endfloat

16.11 If the oil pressure relief valve spring is less than 38.9 mm in length it must be renewed

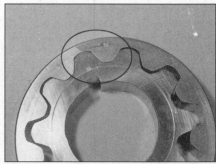

16.14 The oil pump rotors should be fitted with their identification marks facing away from the pump body

scored, or if it does not slide freely in the pump body bore, then it must be renewed. Check the relief valve spring for signs of wear or damage and measure its free length. If the spring shows signs of damage or is less than 38.9 mm in length then it must be renewed **(see illustration)**.

12 Check the thermostatic valve and spring for signs of damage and renew them if there is any doubt about their condition.

Reassembly

13 Remove all traces of sealant and locking compound from the pump and cover mating surfaces and the threads of the body and cover screws. Also clean the adaptor and body threads.

14 Lubricate the pump rotors with clean engine oil and refit them to the pump body, using the marks made on dismantling to ensure they are fitted the correct way around. The rotors should be fitted with their square marks facing away from the pump body **(see illustration)**.

15 Ensure the mating surfaces are clean and dry then apply a bead of sealant (Land Rover recommend the use of Loctite 573), approximately 1.0 mm thick, to the surface of the pump cover. Refit the cover to the pump body, aligning the marks made on dismantling; the cover upper retaining screw hole is marked TOP to avoid the possibility of fitting the cover incorrectly.

16 Ensure the threads of the cover screws are clean and dry and apply a drop of the thread-locking compound to each screw. Refit the screws and tighten them securely.

17 Check that the pump rotates freely, then prime it by injecting oil into its passages and rotating it. If a long time elapses before the pump is refitted to the engine, prime it again before installation.

18 Refit the oil pressure relief valve plunger, ensuring that it is the correct way up, then install the spring. Fit the new threaded plug, tightening it securely.

19 Position the pump so that the thermostatic valve bore is vertical. Lubricate the valve and spring with clean engine oil and fit them to the pump body, making sure the valve is positioned centrally in the pump bore. Fit a new sealing washer to the adaptor then apply

a smear of sealant (Land Rover recommend the use of Loctite 577) to the adaptor threads. Carefully refit the adaptor to the pump body, ensuring that it engages correctly with the valve piston, and tighten it to the specified torque.

17 Oil cooler – removal and refitting

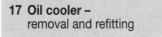

1 The oil cooler is located at the front of the engine cylinder block. At the base of the cooler is located the cooling system thermostat and bottom hose connection from the radiator. The top of the oil cooler has two ports, one to the coolant pump, and the other provides the bypass circuit from the coolant outlet elbow hose. The engine oil temperature is reduced by coolant from the radiator passing through the oil cooler body.

Removal

2 Remove the radiator (see Chapter 3).

3 Wipe clean the area around the oil pipe unions on the base of the oil cooler then undo the retaining bolt and free the pipe retaining clamp from the block **(see illustration)**. Position a container beneath the cooler to catch any spilt oil.

4 Unscrew the union nuts and disconnect both oil pipes from the cooler. Remove the sealing ring from the end of each pipe and discard them, new ones must be used on refitting.

17.3 Undo the retaining bolt and free the pipe retaining clamp

5 Slacken and remove the bolts securing the cooler to the cylinder block.

6 Release the retaining clips then disconnect the coolant hoses and remove the oil cooler from the vehicle.

Refitting

7 Remove all traces of locking compound from the threads of the oil cooler bolts and the cylinder block.

8 Manoeuvre the cooler into position and reconnect the coolant hoses, securing them in position with the retaining clips.

9 Apply a drop of thread locking compound (Land Rover recommend the use of Loctite 242) to the threads of the oil cooler retaining bolts then refit the bolts and tighten them to the specified torque.

10 Fit new sealing rings to the oil pipe end fittings and seat the pipes in the cooler. Refit the pipe retaining clamp, tightening its retaining bolt securely, then tighten the pipe union nuts to the specified torque.

11 Refit the radiator (see Chapter 3).

12 On completion, check the engine oil level as described in *Weekly checks*.

18 Crankshaft oil seals – renewal

Right-hand seal

Note: *Whenever the tension applied to the timing belt is disturbed, it is recommended that the belt be renewed as a matter of course, regardless of its apparent condition*

1 Remove the crankshaft sprocket as described in Section 9.

2 Carefully punch or drill two small holes opposite each other in the oil seal. Screw a self-tapping screw into each and pull on the screws with pliers to extract the seal.

Caution: Great care must be taken to avoid damage to the oil pump.

3 Clean the seal housing and polish off any burrs or raised edges which may have caused the seal to fail in the first place.

4 Lubricate the lips of the new seal with clean engine oil and ease it into position on the end of the shaft. Press the seal squarely

18.10 Carefully ease the crankshaft oil seal into position noting that the protector will be displaced as the housing is fitted

18.11 Refit the housing retaining bolts and tighten them to the specified torque in the sequence shown

into position until it is flush with the housing. If necessary, a suitable tubular drift, such as a socket, which bears only on the hard outer edge of the seal can be used to tap the seal into position. Take great care not to damage the seal lips during fitting and ensure that the seal lips face inwards.

5 Wash off any traces of oil, then refit the crankshaft sprocket as described in Section 9.

Left-hand oil seal

Caution: The new oil seal is supplied complete with housing and is prelubricated with a special coating. The seal must be fitted 'dry' and the seal protector must not be removed until the housing assembly is in position on the engine. Under no circumstances must the oil seal lip be touched, or lubricated with oil or grease, as this will destroy the special coating. If the seal coating is damaged there is a risk of oil leakage once the engine is started.

6 Remove the flywheel as described in Section 19.

7 Remove the sump as described in Section 14.

8 Slacken and remove the retaining bolts and remove the oil seal housing from the end of the crankshaft.

9 Ensure the crankshaft surface and cylinder block mating surface are clean and dry; this is most important to ensure the oil seal coating is not damaged (see Caution at the start of this sub-section).

10 Carefully ease the new seal housing onto the end of the crankshaft, making sure the

sealing lip is not damaged. Slide the housing fully into position, making sure it is correctly located, and carefully remove the oil seal protector **(see illustration)**.

11 Refit the housing retaining bolts and tighten them to the specified torque, working in sequence **(see illustration)**.

12 Refit the sump as described in Section 14.

13 Refit the flywheel as described in Section 19.

19 Flywheel – removal, inspection and refitting

Note: *New flywheel retaining bolts must be used on refitting.*

Removal

1 Remove the clutch assembly as described in Chapter 6.

2 As a precaution, unbolt the crankshaft position sensor from the engine mounting plate (see Chapter 4B) to prevent possible damage as the flywheel is removed.

3 Prevent the flywheel from turning by locking the ring gear teeth with a similar arrangement to that shown **(see illustration)**. Alternatively, bolt a strap between the flywheel and the cylinder block/crankcase.

4 Slacken and remove the retaining bolts and remove the flywheel, noting its locating dowel **(see illustration)**. **Do not** drop it, as it is very heavy. Discard the bolts, they must be renewed whenever they are disturbed.

Inspection

5 If the flywheel clutch mating surface (where applicable) is deeply scored, cracked or otherwise damaged, then the flywheel must be renewed, unless it is possible to have it surface ground. Seek the advice of a Land Rover dealer or engine reconditioning specialist.

6 If the ring gear is badly worn or has missing teeth, then it must be renewed. This job is best left to a Land Rover dealer or engine reconditioning specialist. The temperature to which the new ring gear must be heated for installation (350°C – shown by an even light blue colour) is critical and, if not done accurately, the hardness of the teeth will be destroyed.

Refitting

7 Clean the mating surfaces of the flywheel and crankshaft and remove all traces of locking compound from the crankshaft threaded holes.

8 Fit the flywheel to the crankshaft, engaging it with the crankshaft locating dowel, and fit the new retaining bolts.

9 Lock the flywheel using the method employed on dismantling then, working in a diagonal sequence, tighten all the retaining bolts to the specified Stage 1 torque setting. Go around again in a diagonal sequence and angle-tighten each retaining bolt through the specified Stage 2 angle, using a socket and extension bar. It is recommended that an angle-measuring gauge is used during the final stages of the tightening, to ensure accuracy **(Haynes Hint)**.

> **HAYNES HiNT** *If a gauge is not available, use white paint to make alignment marks between the bolt head and pulley prior to tightening; the marks can then be used to check that the bolt had been rotated through the correct angle.*

10 Refit the crankshaft position sensor and tighten its retaining bolt to the specified torque (see Chapter 4B).

11 Refit the clutch assembly as described in Chapter 6.

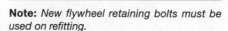

19.3 Lock the flywheel with a tool similar to that shown (arrowed) then slacken the retaining bolts

19.4 Remove the flywheel taking care not to drop it

20 Engine/transmission mountings –
inspection and renewal

Inspection

1 If improved access is required, raise the front of the vehicle and support it securely on axle stands (see *Jacking and vehicle support*). If necessary, undo the retaining screws and fasteners and remove the undertray from beneath the engine/transmission unit.

2 Check the mounting rubber to see if it is cracked, hardened or separated from the metal at any point. Renew the mounting if any such damage or deterioration is evident.

3 Check that all mounting fasteners are securely tightened. Use a torque wrench to check, if possible.

4 Using a large screwdriver or a pry bar, check for wear in the mountings by carefully levering against it to check for free play. Where this is not possible, enlist the aid of an assistant to move the engine/gearbox unit back-and-forth or from side-to-side while you watch the mountings. While some free play is to be expected even from new components, excessive wear should be obvious. If excessive free play is found, check first that the fasteners are correctly secured, then renew any worn components as described below.

Renewal

Left-hand mounting

5 Firmly apply the handbrake, then jack up the front of the vehicle and support securely on axle stands (see *Jacking and vehicle support*). Undo the screws and remove the engine undertray. Disconnect the battery negative lead with reference to Chapter 5A.

6 Undo the bolts and remove the left-hand front roadwheel.

7 Unscrew the retaining bolts and remove the splash shield from the left-hand wheel arch.

8 Pull back the rubber cover, and disconnect the battery lead from the starter motor (if necessary refer to Chapter 5A).

9 Remove the clip securing the clutch slave cylinder to its mounting bracket (if necessary refer to Chapter 6), and move the slave cylinder to one side. There is no need to disconnect the cylinder fluid pipe.

10 Slacken and remove the bolt securing the support bar to the engine mounting **(see illustration)**.

11 Position a jack under the transmission and take the weight of the unit. Use a piece of wood between the jack head and the transmission casing.

12 Remove the bolt securing the engine mounting to the body.

13 Lower the engine/transmission sufficiently to allow access to the mounting retaining bolts. Remove the two mounting bolts and manoeuvre the mounting out of the engine compartment.

14 Refit the mounting to the transmission and tighten the bolts to the specified torque.

15 Using the jack, raise the engine and align the mounting to allow the mounting-to-body bolt to be inserted. Tighten the bolt to the specified torque.

16 Remove the jack, and refit the bolt securing the support bar to the mounting. Tighten the bolt to the specified torque.

17 Refit the clutch slave cylinder to its bracket, ensuring the push-rod is engaged with the lever, and secure the cylinder in place with its retaining clip (if necessary refer to Chapter 6).

18 Reconnect the battery lead to the starter, tighten the nut securely, and refit the rubber terminal cover.

19 Refit the left-hand wheel arch splash shield, and roadwheel.

20 Fit the engine undertray, and reconnect the battery negative lead.

21 Lower the vehicle to the ground, and tighten the roadwheel nuts to the specified torque.

Right-hand upper mounting

22 Firmly apply the handbrake, then jack up the front of the vehicle and support securely on axle stands (see *Jacking and vehicle support*). Undo the screws and remove the engine undertray.

23 Support the weight of the engine/ transmission using a trolley jack with a block of wood placed on its head. Position the jack underneath the engine and raise the engine slightly to remove all load from the mounting. Undo the three bolts and remove the engine acoustic cover.

24 Where applicable, remove the bolt securing the air conditioning hose clip to the power steering hose support bracket.

25 Remove the power steering hose support retaining nut from the engine mounting stud, and position the bracket to one side.

26 Slacken and remove the bolt securing the upper tie rod to the engine mounting bracket.

27 Loosen the bolt securing the upper tie rod to the bracket on the body, then raise it up to clear the engine mounting bracket.

28 Using the jack, raise the engine sufficiently for it to clear the engine mounting stud.

29 Unscrew the two bolts and remove the engine mounting.

30 On refitting, position the mounting on the wing valance, and tighten the two retaining

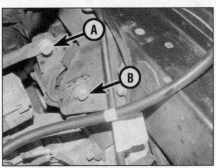

20.10 Remove the support strut bolt (A) and the mounting-to-bracket through-bolt (B)

bolts to the specified torque.

31 Lower the engine onto the mounting stud.

32 Fit the upper tie rod to the mounting bracket, and tighten the tie rod securing bolts to the specified torque.

33 Remove the jack from under the engine, and refit the power steering hose support bracket to the engine mounting stud. Tighten the retaining nut to the specified torque.

34 Where applicable, fit the air conditioning hose clip to the power steering hose support bracket and tighten the bolt securely. Refit the engine acoustic cover.

35 Refit the engine undertray, and lower the vehicle to the ground.

Lower tie rod

36 Firmly apply the handbrake, then jack up the front of the vehicle and support securely on axle stands (see *Jacking and vehicle support*). Undo the screws and remove the engine undertray.

37 Slacken and remove the tie rod retaining bolts, and manoeuvre the tie rod from the brackets.

38 On refitting, ensure that the large diameter end of the tie rod is at the rear, and position it between the mounting brackets.

39 Fit the tie rod retaining bolts and tighten them to the specified torque.

40 Refit the engine undertray and lower the vehicle to the ground.

Upper tie rod

41 Undo the three bolts and remove the engine acoustic cover.

42 Slacken and remove the two bolts securing the tie rod to the engine mounting and bracket, and withdraw the tie rod.

43 On refitting, ensure that the large diameter end of the tie rod is at the rear (mounting bracket) and the small end is connected to the engine mounting.

44 Fit the tie rod retaining bolts and tighten them to the specified torque.

45 Refit the engine cover.

Chapter 2 Part C:
TD4 diesel engine in-car repair procedures

Contents

Degrees of difficulty

Easy, suitable for novice with little experience	Fairly easy, suitable for beginner with some experience	Fairly difficult, suitable for competent DIY mechanic	Difficult, suitable for experienced DIY mechanic	Very difficult, suitable for expert DIY or professional
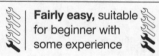				

Specifications

General

Engine type.	Four-cylinder in-line, double overhead camshaft, 16-valve, four-stroke, liquid-cooled
Designation	TD4
Bore	84.0 mm
Stroke.	88.0 mm
Capacity	1951 cc
Firing order.	1-3-4-2 (No 1 cylinder at timing belt end)
Direction of crankshaft rotation	Clockwise (seen from right-hand side of vehicle)
Compression ratio	18.1:1
Output:	
Power	82 kW @ 4000 rpm
Torque.	260 Nm @ 1750 rpm
Idle speed.	780 ± 30 rpm (not adjustable)
Maximum engine speed.	4800 rpm

Camshafts

Camshaft endfloat	0.15 to 0.33 mm

Lubrication system

Minimum system pressure:	
Idle speed (cold)	1.5 bar
3500 rpm (hot)	3.0 to 4.5 bar
Pressure relief valve opening pressure.	4.2 bar
Low oil pressure warning light comes on.	0.2 to 0.5 bar
Oil pump outer rotor-to-body clearance	0.08 to 0.158 mm

Torque wrench settings

	Nm	lbf ft
Acoustic cover-to-engine bolts	8	6
Air conditioning compressor bolts	25	18
Air conditioning compressor mounting bracket	25	18
Auxiliary drivebelt idler pulley Allen bolt*	25	18
Auxiliary drivebelt tensioner pulley arm bolt	10	7
Camshaft bearing cap bolts	10	7
Camshaft cover bolts	10	7
Camshaft position sensor Torx screw	8	6
Camshaft sprocket bolts*:		
Stage 1	20	15
Stage 2	Angle-tighten a further 35°	
Connecting rod big-end bearing cap bolts:		
Stage 1	5	4
Stage 2	25	18
Stage 3	Angle-tighten a further 70°	
Coolant hose connector-to-cylinder head bolts	8	6
Coolant rail:		
Rail-to-cylinder head bolts	20	15
Rail-to-exhaust manifold bolts	20	15
Rail to thermostat housing	10	7
Lower rail-to-sump bolts	10	7
Crankshaft pulley bolt*:		
Stage 1	100	74
Stage 2	Angle-tighten a further 60°	
Stage 3	Angle-tighten a further 60°	
Stage 4	Angle-tighten a further 30°	
Crankshaft left-hand oil seal housing bolts:		
M6	10	7
M8	22	16
Crankshaft position sensor Allen screw	8	6
Cylinder block reinforcing (baffle) plate	22	16
Cylinder head bolts*:		
Stage 1	80	59
Stage 2	Slacken 180°	
Stage 3	50	37
Stage 4	Angle-tighten a further 90°	
Stage 5	Angle-tighten a further 90°	
Stage 6 (41 mm long bolt in position 12 only)	110	81
Cylinder head-to-timing cover Allen screws	15	11
Dipstick tube-to-oil filter housing bolt	10	7
EGR cooler to cylinder head	25	18
Engine/transmission mountings:		
Left-hand mounting:		
Mounting-to-body bolts	45	33
Mounting-to-bracket through-bolt	100	74
Bracket-to-transmission bolts	85	63
Right-hand mounting:		
Mounting bracket-to-engine bracket bolts	100	74
Mounting bracket-to-Hydramount nut	85	63
Lower engine tie rod bolts	100	74
Lower engine tie rod bracket bolts:		
M10	45	33
M12	50	37
Upper engine tie rod mounting bolts	100	74
Flywheel/driveplate bolts*	115	85
Fuel injection pump drive chain lower guide Allen bolt*	24	18
Fuel injection pump sprocket retaining nut	65	48
Fuel pipe union nuts	30	22
Fuel rail Allen bolts	24	18
Main bearing cap bolts*:		
Stage 1	20	15
Stage 2	Angle-tighten a further 70°	
Oil cooler-to-oil filter housing bolts	22	16
Oil feed guide rail bolts	10	7
Oil filter cap	25	18
Oil filter housing bolts	25	18
Oil pressure switch	38	28

Torque wrench settings

	Nm	lbf ft
Oil pump:		
Drive sprocket-to-driveshaft Torx bolt	25	18
Retaining bolts	25	18
Pick-up/strainer bolts	10	7
Piston oil spray jet bolts	10	7
Power steering pump bolts:		
M6	10	7
M8	25	18
Roadwheel nuts	115	85
Sump bolts:		
M6	10	7
M8	28	21
Sump drain plug	28	21
Sump plate bolts	10	7
Timing chain cover bolts	15	11
Timing chain lubrication jet bolt	10	7
Timing chain guide Allen bolt*	20	15
Timing chain guides support pins	20	15
Timing chain tensioner:		
Access plug	30	22
Tensioner bolts	10	7
Turbocharger-to-exhaust manifold bolts	45	33
Turbocharger outlet pipe retaining bolts:		
M6	10	7
M8	25	18
Vacuum pump bolts*	22	16

* Do not re-use

1 General information and precautions

How to use this Chapter

This Part of the Chapter describes those repair procedures that can reasonably be carried out on the engine whilst it remains in the vehicle. If the engine has been removed from the vehicle and is being dismantled as described in Part D of this Chapter, any preliminary dismantling procedures can be ignored.

Note that whilst it may be possible physically to overhaul items such as the piston/connecting rod assemblies with the engine in the vehicle, such tasks are not usually carried out as separate operations and usually require the execution of several additional procedures (not to mention the cleaning of components and of oilways). For this reason, all such tasks are classed as major overhaul procedures and are described in Part D of this Chapter.

Engine description

This 2.0 litre diesel engine is of BMW origin, and is a four-cylinder, double overhead camshaft, 16-valve, in-line unit, mounted transversely at the front of the vehicle with the clutch and transmission on the left-hand end.

The cast-iron cylinder block is of the dry-liner type. The crankshaft is supported within the cylinder block on five shell-type main bearings. Thrustwashers are integral with the No 4 main bearing shells to control crankshaft endfloat.

The cylinder head is of the double overhead camshaft, 16-valve design – two intake and two exhaust valves per cylinder. The valves

are operated by one intake camshaft and one exhaust camshaft, via rocker fingers. One end of each finger acts upon the valve stem, whilst the other end pivots on a support pillar. Valve clearances are maintained automatically by hydraulic compensation elements incorporated within the support pillars. In order to achieve high levels of combustion efficiency, the cylinder head has two intake ports for each cylinder. One port is tangential, whilst the other is helical.

The connecting rods rotate on horizontally-split bearing shells at their big-ends. The pistons are attached to the connecting rods by gudgeon pins which are secured in position with circlips. The aluminium alloy pistons are fitted with three piston rings, comprising two compression rings and an oil control ring.

The intake and exhaust valves are each closed by coil springs and operate in guides pressed into the cylinder head. Valve guides cannot be renewed.

A Simplex chain, driven by the crankshaft, drives the high pressure fuel pump sprocket, which in turn drives the camshafts. The vacuum pump is fitted to the left-hand end of the cylinder head, and is driven by the exhaust camshaft. The coolant pump is driven by the auxiliary drivebelt.

Lubrication is by means of an eccentric-rotor type pump driven by the crankshaft via a Simplex chain. The pump draws oil through a strainer located in the sump, and then forces it through an externally-mounted full-flow paper element type oil filter into galleries in the cylinder block/crankcase, from where it is distributed to the crankshaft (main bearings), timing chain (sprayed by a jet), and camshaft. The big-end bearings are supplied with oil via internal drillings

in the crankshaft, while the camshaft bearings and the followers receive a pressurised supply via drillings in the cylinder head. The camshaft lobes and valves are lubricated by oil splash, as are all other engine components. An oil cooler (integral with the oil filter housing) is fitted to keep the oil temperature stable under arduous operating conditions.

Operations with engine in vehicle

The following work can be carried out with the engine in the vehicle:

a) Compression pressure – testing.
b) Camshaft cover – removal and refitting.
c) Crankshaft pulley – removal and refitting.
d) Camshaft oil seals – renewal.
e) Camshafts and rocker arms – removal, inspection and refitting.
f) Cylinder head – removal and refitting.
g) Cylinder head and pistons – decarbonising.
h) Sump – removal and refitting.
i) Oil pump – removal, overhaul and refitting.
j) Oil filter housing/cooler – removal and refitting.
k) Crankshaft oil seals – renewal.
l) Engine/transmission mountings – inspection and renewal.
m) Flywheel/driveplate – removal, inspection and refitting.

Note: *Although in theory it is possible to remove the timing cover and timing chains with the engine fitted, in practice access is extremely limited, special Land Rover tools are needed, and the cylinder head and sump must be removed. Consequently, it is recommended that the engine is removed prior to timing cover and chains removal.*

3.5 Pull out the blanking plug from the timing pin hole in the engine block

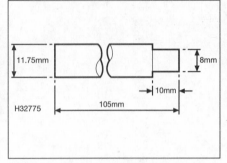

3.7a Crankshaft locking pin dimensions

3.7b Insert the locking pin through the block and into the flywheel indent

2 Compression test – description and interpretation

Compression test

Note: *A compression tester specifically designed for diesel engines must be used for this test.*

1 When engine performance is down, or if misfiring occurs which cannot be attributed to the fuel system, a compression test can provide diagnostic clues as to the engine's condition. If the test is performed regularly, it can give warning of trouble before any other symptoms become apparent.

2 A compression tester specifically intended for diesel engines must be used, because of the higher pressures involved. The tester is connected to an adaptor which screws into the glow plug or injector hole. On these models, an adaptor suitable for use in the injector holes will be required, due to there only being glow plugs fitted to Nos 1 to 3 cylinders. It is unlikely to be worthwhile buying such a tester for occasional use, but it may be possible to borrow or hire one – if not, have the test performed by a garage.

3 Unless specific instructions to the contrary are supplied with the tester, observe the following points:

a) *The battery must be in a good state of charge, the air filter must be clean, and the engine should be at normal operating temperature.*

b) *All the injectors should be removed before starting the test (see Chapter 4B).*

4 There is no need to hold the accelerator pedal down during the test, because the diesel engine air intake is not throttled.

5 Crank the engine on the starter motor; after one or two revolutions, the compression pressure should build-up to a maximum figure, and then stabilise. Record the highest reading obtained.

6 Repeat the test on the remaining cylinders, recording the pressure in each.

7 All cylinders should produce very similar pressures; a difference of more than 2 bars between any two cylinders indicates a fault. Note that the compression should

build-up quickly in a healthy engine; low compression on the first stroke, followed by gradually-increasing pressure on successive strokes, indicates worn piston rings. A low compression reading on the first stroke, which does not build-up during successive strokes, indicates leaking valves or a blown head gasket (a cracked head could also be the cause). Deposits on the undersides of the valve heads can also cause low compression.

Note: *The cause of poor compression is less easy to establish on a diesel engine than on a petrol one. The effect of introducing oil into the cylinders ('wet' testing) is not conclusive, because there is a risk that the oil will sit in the swirl chamber or in the recess on the piston crown instead of passing to the rings.*

8 Although Land Rover do not specify exact compression pressures, as a guide, any cylinder pressure of below 20 bar can be considered as less than healthy. Refer to a Land Rover dealer or other specialist if in doubt as to whether a particular pressure reading is acceptable.

9 On completion of the test, refit the injectors as described in Chapter 4B.

Leakdown test

10 A leakdown test measures the rate at which compressed air fed into the cylinder is lost. It is an alternative to a compression test, and in many ways it is better, since the escaping air provides easy identification of where pressure loss is occurring (piston rings, valves or head gasket).

11 The equipment needed for leakdown testing is unlikely to be available to the home mechanic. If poor compression is suspected, have the test performed by a suitably-equipped garage.

3 Engine assembly/ valve timing settings – general information and usage

Note: *An assistant will be required.*
Note: *Land Rover tool No LRT-12-108 or suitable home-made equivalent will be required to lock the crankshaft in position, and access to Land Rover tool LRT-12-173 or home-made equivalent is required to position the camshafts.*

1 The flywheel is equipped with an indent which aligns with a hole in the engine block when Nos 1 and 4 pistons are at TDC (top dead centre). In this position, if No 1 piston is at TDC on its compression stroke, it must be possible to fit a Land Rover special tool (No LRT-12-173) or home-made equivalent, over the square sections of the intake and exhaust camshafts (with all four No 1 cylinder camshaft lobes pointing upwards).

2 Slacken the right-hand front roadwheel nuts, firmly apply the handbrake then jack up the front of the vehicle and support it securely on axle stands (see *Jacking and vehicle support*). Remove the front right-hand roadwheel.

3 Undo the retaining screws/clips and remove the engine undertray, and right-hand wheel arch splash shield.

4 Remove the camshaft cover and gasket, as described in Section 4.

5 Pull out the blanking plug from the timing pin hole in the engine block **(see illustration)**.

6 Using a socket and extension bar on the crankshaft pulley centre bolt, turn the crankshaft clockwise (viewed from the right-hand end of the engine whilst keeping an eye on the No 1 cylinder camshaft lobes. **Note:** *Do not turn the engine anti-clockwise.*

7 Rotate the crankshaft clockwise until the No 1 cylinder camshaft lobes approach the point where all four lobes are beginning to point up. Have an assistant insert Land Rover tool LRT-12-108 or home-made equivalent into the timing pin hole, and press the pin gently against the flywheel. Continue to slowly turn the crankshaft slowly until the pin is felt to engage in the indent in the flywheel, and the crankshaft locks **(see illustrations)**.

8 With the crankshaft in this position, all four camshaft lobes of No 1 cylinder should be pointing upwards. Fit Land Rover tool No LRT-12-173 over the intake camshaft square section, adjacent to No 1 camshaft bearing cap. If the camshaft is timed correctly, the tool will contact both sides of the camshaft cover gasket face on the cylinder head. If the tool is not available, it is possible to fabricate a home-made equivalent **(see illustrations)**. **Note:** *When fabricating the home-made tool, it is absolutely essential that the dimensions of the illustration are accurately followed where the tool slides over the square section of the camshaft.*

All dimensions in mm

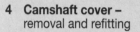

3.8a Camshaft positioning tool dimensions

3.8b If the camshaft is timed correctly, the tool will contact both sides of the camshaft cover gasket face on the cylinder head

9 Remove the tool from the intake camshaft, and position it over the square section of the exhaust camshaft. Again, the tool will contact both sides of the camshaft cover gasket face on the cylinder head if the camshaft is timed correctly.

4 Camshaft cover – removal and refitting

Removal

1 Disconnect the battery negative lead (refer to Chapter 5A).
2 Unscrew the three retaining bolts and remove the plastic cover from the top of the engine (where fitted) **(see illustration)**.
3 With reference to Chapter 4B, remove the fuel injectors.
4 Remove the engine oil filler cap, undo the five Allen screws and remove the air cleaner cover. Lift the air cleaner element from the housing **(see illustration)**.
5 Disconnect the wiring plugs from the camshaft position, and mass airflow/intake air temperature sensors **(see illustrations)**.
6 Using a screwdriver, prise open the two clips securing the turbocharger air duct to the mass airflow sensor, disconnect the duct breather pipe to the air cleaner, and remove the duct.
7 Slacken and remove the bolt securing the breather pipe clip to the mass airflow sensor.
8 Release the wiring harness from the

retaining clip on the camshaft cover.
9 Working in a diagonal pattern, evenly slacken and remove the 14 bolts securing the camshaft cover to the cylinder head.
10 Remove the cover and discard its gasket.

Refitting

11 Ensure the mating surfaces are clean and dry then fit the new gasket to the cover.
12 Refit the engine breather pipe connector to the air cleaner housing.
13 Apply a 2 mm bead of sealant to the cylinder head mating surface **(see illustration)**.
14 Refit the cover to the cylinder head, ensuring that the gasket remains correctly seated.
15 Insert the cover retaining bolts and tighten them all by hand. Once all bolts are in position, go around in a diagonal sequence and evenly tighten them to the specified torque setting.

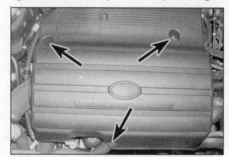

4.2 Unscrew the three retaining bolts (arrowed) and remove the plastic cover from the top of the engine

4.5a Disconnect the wiring plugs from the camshaft position sensor . . .

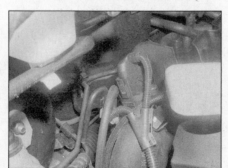

4.5b . . . and the mass airflow sensor

16 The remainder of refitting is a reversal of removal.

5 Crankshaft pulley – removal and refitting

Removal

1 Undo the three retaining bolts, and remove the engine acoustic cover (where fitted).
2 Firmly apply the handbrake then slacken the right-hand front roadwheel nuts. Jack up the front of the vehicle and support it securely on axle stands (see *Jacking and vehicle support*). Unscrew the bolts and remove the right-hand front roadwheel.
3 Remove the auxiliary drivebelt and (where applicable) the air conditioning compressor drivebelt as described in Chapter 1B.

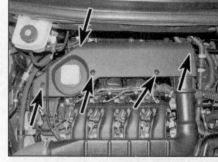

4.4 Undo the five Allen screws and remove the air cleaner cover

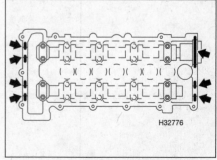

4.13 Apply a 2 mm bead of sealant to the cylinder head mating surface

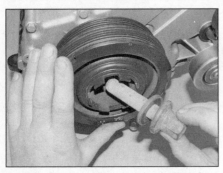

5.6a Unscrew the retaining bolt and washer . . .

5.6b . . . and remove the crankshaft pulley

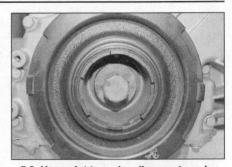

5.8 Use paint to make alignment marks between the bolt head and pulley prior to tightening

4 If further dismantling is to be carried out, align the engine assembly/valve timing settings as described in Section 3.

5 Slacken the crankshaft pulley retaining bolt. To prevent crankshaft rotation (the pulley retaining bolt is extremely tight) remove the starter motor as described in Chapter 5A to expose the flywheel ring gear, and have an assistant insert a wide blade screwdriver between the ring gear teeth and the transmission bellhousing whilst the pulley retaining bolt is slackened. If the engine is removed from the vehicle it will be necessary to lock the flywheel (see Section 13).
Caution: Do not be tempted to use the crankshaft locking pin (see Section 3) to prevent rotation as the centre bolt is slackened.

6 Unscrew the retaining bolt and washer, and remove the pulley from the crankshaft **(see illustrations)**.

Refitting

7 Fit the pulley to the crankshaft and screw in the retaining bolt with the washer fitted.

8 Lock the crankshaft by the method used on removal, and tighten the pulley retaining bolt to the specified Stage 1 torque setting then angle-tighten the bolt through the specified Stages 2, 3 and 4 angles, using a socket and extension bar. It is recommended that an angle-measuring gauge is used during the final stages of the tightening, to ensure accuracy. If a gauge is not available, use paint to make alignment marks between the bolt head and pulley prior to tightening; the marks can then be used to check that the bolt has been rotated through the correct angle **(see illustration)**.

9 Refit the auxiliary drivebelt and (where applicable) air conditioning compressor drivebelt as described in Chapter 1B.

10 Refit the roadwheel then lower the vehicle

to the ground and tighten the wheel nuts to the specified torque.

11 Refit the engine acoustic cover.

6 Camshaft, rocker arms and hydraulic tappets – removal, inspection and refitting

Removal

1 Set the crankshaft and camshafts to TDC on No 1 cylinder as described in Section 3.

2 Remove the auxiliary and air conditioning compressor drivebelts as described in Chapter 1B.

3 With reference to Section 14, remove the right-hand Hydramount (engine mounting).

4 Using a 17 mm Allen key, remove the camshaft timing chain tensioner access plug from the timing chain cover. The plug is located adjacent to the coolant pump pulley.

5 With a spanner on its hexagonal section, rotate the exhaust camshaft slightly clockwise (viewed from the right-hand end of the engine) to fully compress the plunger into the tensioner. Holding the cam in this position, insert LRT-12-172 through the timing cover access hole into the tensioner body to lock the plunger in place. If the tool is not available, a 4 mm drill bit or rod will make a suitable substitute **(see illustrations)**.

6 Undo the two retaining bolts, and remove the oil feed guide rail from between the camshafts **(see illustration)**. Discard the seal.

7 Hold the camshafts with a spanner on their hexagonal sections, and slacken the camshaft sprocket retaining Torx screws.

8 Withdraw the crankshaft locking pin, and rotate the engine 45° backwards (anti-clockwise) using a spanner or socket on the crankshaft pulley. This is to prevent accidental valve-to-piston contact.

9 Completely unscrew the sprocket retaining bolts, and release the sprockets from the camshafts. Discard the bolts, new ones must be fitted.

10 Identify the camshaft bearing caps, to ensure they are refitted to their original positions. The exhaust camshaft is marked A, so mark the exhaust camshaft bearing caps as A1, A2, A3, etc, starting with the cap nearest the timing chain. The intake camshaft

6.5a With a spanner on its hexagonal section, rotate the exhaust camshaft slightly clockwise . . .

6.5b . . . and insert a 4 mm drill bit to lock the tensioner plunger

6.6 Remove the oil feed guide rail from between the camshafts

6.10 Identify the camshaft bearing caps, to ensure they are refitted to their original positions (see text)

6.14 Withdraw each hydraulic tappet in turn, invert it to prevent oil loss

6.17 Lubricate the tappets with clean engine oil and carefully insert each one into its original location

6.18 Refit the rocker arms

is marked E, so repeat the procedure for the intake camshaft starting with E1 adjacent to the timing chain **(see illustration)**.

11 Evenly and progressively, slacken and remove the retaining bolts, and remove the camshaft bearing caps.

12 Remove the camshafts from the cylinder head, disengaging the vacuum pump coupling from the left-hand end of the exhaust camshaft as it is withdrawn.

13 Lift the rocker arms from the cylinder head, and lay them out in order on a clean surface, so that they can be fitted into their original positions – if they are to be re-used.

14 Obtain sixteen small, clean plastic containers, and label them for identification. Alternatively, divide a larger container into compartments. Withdraw each hydraulic tappet in turn, invert it to prevent oil loss and place it in its respective container, which should then be filled with clean engine oil **(see illustration)**.

Caution: Do not interchange the tappets, and do not allow the tappets to lose oil, as they will take a long time to refill with oil on restarting the engine, which could result in incorrect valve clearances. Absolute cleanliness is essential at all times when handling the tappets.

Inspection

15 Examine the camshaft bearing surfaces and cam lobes for signs of wear ridges and scoring. Renew the camshaft if any of these conditions are apparent. Examine the condition of the bearing surfaces both on the camshaft journals and in the cylinder head. If the head bearing surfaces are worn excessively, the cylinder head will need to be renewed.

16 Examine the rocker bearing surfaces which contact the camshaft lobes for wear ridges and scoring. If the engine's valve clearances have sounded noisy, particularly if the noise persists after initial start-up from cold, then there is reason to suspect a faulty tappet. If any tappet is thought to be faulty or is visibly worn it should be renewed.

Refitting

17 Where removed, lubricate the tappets with clean engine oil and carefully insert each one into its original location in the cylinder head **(see illustration)**.

6.19a Position the shafts so that the camshaft lobes for No 1 cylinder are pointing upwards

18 Refit the rocker arms to their original locations, ensuring that they are correctly orientated **(see illustration)**.

19 Ensure that the crankshaft is still at the 45° before TDC position, liberally oil the camshaft bearings and rocker arms then refit the camshafts to the cylinder head. Position the shafts so that the camshaft lobes for No 1 cylinder are pointing upwards. Engage the left-hand end of the exhaust camshaft with the vacuum pump coupling as the camshaft is fitted **(see illustrations)**.

20 Lubricate the camshaft bearing journals with clean engine oil. Refit the camshaft bearing caps to the cylinder head, ensuring that they are fitted to their original positions.

21 Screw in the bearing cap retaining bolts, tightening them all by hand only at this stage.

22 Evenly and progressively tighten the retaining bolts to draw the bearing caps squarely down into contact with the cylinder

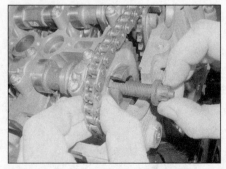

6.23 Fit the new sprocket retaining screws, finger tighten them only

6.19b Engage the left-hand end of the exhaust camshaft with the vacuum pump coupling

head. Once the caps are in contact with the head, tighten the retaining bolts to the specified torque.

Caution: If the bearing caps bolts are carelessly tightened, the caps might break. If the caps are broken then the complete cylinder head assembly must be renewed; the caps are matched to the head and are not available separately.

23 Engage the camshaft sprockets with the timing chain, and position them on the end of the camshafts. Fit the new sprocket retaining screws, finger tighten them only. It must be possible to rotate the sprockets independently of the camshafts **(see illustration)**.

24 Clean the mating surfaces, and fit the oil feed guide rail, with a new seal, to the cylinder head between the camshafts. Tighten the bolts to the specified torque.

25 Whilst holding the exhaust camshaft stationary with a spanner on its hexagonal section, temporarily tighten the exhaust camshaft sprocket retaining screw sufficiently to stop the sprocket rotating independently of the camshaft.

26 With the spanner still on the hexagonal section, rotate the exhaust camshaft clockwise a little, to compress the plunger of the chain tensioner. Remove the tensioner locking pin from the timing cover access plug. Allow the camshaft to return to its previous position, and the tensioner to take up any slack in the chain.

27 Slacken the exhaust camshaft sprocket retaining screw, to allow the sprocket to rotate.

28 Using a spanner or socket on the

6.30 Slide the positioning tool over the square section of the inlet camshaft

crankshaft pulley nut, rotate the crankshaft 45° in the normal direction of rotation (clockwise viewed from the right-hand end of the engine), until the crankshaft locking pin can be inserted through the timing hole in the block and into the locating hole in the flywheel). In this position the crankshaft should be locked at TDC for No 1 cylinder.

29 Refit the timing chain access plug to the chain cover, and tighten it to the specified torque.

30 Slide Land Rover tool No LRT-12-174, or home-made equivalent (see Section 3, paragraph 9), over the square section of the intake camshaft (adjacent to the No 1 bearing cap). Using a spanner on the hexagonal section, rotate the camshaft until both sides of the tool contact the cylinder head-to-camshaft cover mating surface **(see illustration)**. Check that the crankshaft is still locked in the TDC position.

7.3 Disconnect the fuel pressure sensor wiring plug

7.6 Remove the fuel pipe from the fuel pump to the common rail

6.31 Holding the camshaft in this position with the spanner on the hexagonal section, tighten the camshaft sprocket retaining bolt

31 Holding the camshaft in this position with the spanner on the hexagonal section, tighten the camshaft sprocket retaining bolt to the specified Stage 1 torque setting, then tighten it to the Stage 2 angle using an angle-measuring gauge **(see illustration)**.

32 Repeat the procedure detailed in paragraphs 30 and 31 for the exhaust camshaft.

33 Withdraw the crankshaft locking pin, and camshaft aligning tool. Using a spanner on the crankshaft pulley nut, rotate the crankshaft clockwise two complete revolutions, until the locking pin can be inserted again through the timing hole at the front of the block, into the flywheel indent.

34 Following the procedure in paragraphs 30 and 32, check that the camshafts are still aligned correctly. If necessary slacken the camshaft sprocket retaining screws, and repeat the alignment procedure.

7.5 Disconnect the engine coolant temperature sensor wiring plug (arrowed)

7.7 Unscrew the two bolts and remove the common fuel rail (arrowed)

35 With the camshafts and crankshaft ccrrectly aligned, remove the locking pin and alignment tool, and refit the blanking plug to the timing hole in the block.

36 With reference to Section 14, refit the right-hand Hydramount.

37 Refit the camshaft cover as described in Section 4.

38 Refer to Chapter 1B and refit the auxiliary and air conditioning compressor (where applicable) drivebelt.

39 Refit the right-hand wheel arch splash shield and roadwheel, lower the vehicle to the ground, and tighten the roadwheel nuts to the specified torque.

7 Cylinder head –
removal and refitting

Removal

1 Remove the camshafts, rocker arms and tappets as described in Section 6.

2 Drain the cooling system, as described in Chapter 1B.

3 Disconnect the fuel pressure sensor wiring plug, and release the harness grommet from the cylinder head **(see illustration)**.

4 Gently pull the connectors from the glow plugs.

5 Disconnect the engine coolant temperature sensor wiring plug **(see illustration)**.

6 Undo the fuel union nuts and remove the fuel pipe from the fuel pump to the common rail **(see illustration)**. Be prepared for fuel spillage. Plug or cover the rail and pump apertures to prevent contamination.

> **HAYNES HINT** *Cut the fingertips from an old pair of rubber gloves and secure them over the fuel ports with elastic bands.*

7 Unscrew the two bolts and remove the common fuel rail from the cylinder head **(see illustration)**.

8 Slacken and remove the two retaining bolts, and remove the vacuum pump from the left-hand end of the cylinder head. Discard the O-ring seal and bolts, new ones must be fitted.

9 Undo the three retaining bolts, and pull

7.9 Undo the three retaining bolts (arrowed), and pull the coolant hose connector away from the cylinder head

the coolant hose connector away from the cylinder head **(see illustration)**.

10 Release the retaining clip, and disconnect the expansion tank hose from the coolant rail at the right-hand end of the cylinder head **(see illustration)**.

11 Unscrew the bolts securing the coolant rail to the fuel pipe, cylinder head, and exhaust manifold **(see illustrations)**.

12 Release the retaining clips and remove the turbocharger outlet hose.

13 On automatic models, slacken the clamp screw securing the EGR (exhaust gas recirculation) pipe to the cooler, and release the clamp. Remove the three retaining bolts and remove the EGR cooler.

14 Undo the three Allen bolts securing the coolant rail heat shield **(see illustration)**.

15 Slacken and remove the bolt securing the coolant rail to the thermostat housing, and remove the heat shield.

16 Unscrew the three bolts securing the turbocharger to the exhaust manifold, and discard the gasket.

17 Remove the bolts securing the engine lifting eye to the power steering pipe clip and cylinder head.

18 Disengage the camshaft sprockets from the timing chain.

19 Using a Torx key, unscrew and discard the timing chain guide pins. New ones must be fitted **(see illustration)**.

20 Remove the rear chain guide. The front chain guide is easier to remove once the cylinder head has been removed.

21 Unscrew the bolts securing the cylinder head to the timing cover **(see illustration)**.

22 Make a final check to ensure that all relevant hoses, pipes and wires, etc, have been disconnected.

23 Working in the **reverse** of the tightening sequence **(see illustration 7.40)**, progressively slacken the cylinder head bolts by a third of a turn at a time until all bolts can be unscrewed by hand. Withdraw and discard the bolts, new ones must be fitted.

24 Lift the cylinder head from the cylinder block. If necessary, tap the cylinder head gently with a soft-faced mallet to free it from the block, but **do not** lever at the mating faces.

25 When the joint is broken, lift the cylinder

7.10 Disconnect the expansion tank hose from the coolant rail

7.11b . . . and the cylinder head (arrowed) . . .

head away then remove the gasket. Note the fitted positions of the two locating dowels, and remove them for safe-keeping if they are loose. Keep the gasket for identification purposes (see paragraph 31).

Caution: Do not lay the head on its lower mating surface; support the head on wooden blocks, ensuring each block only contacts the head mating surface not the glow plugs. The glow plugs protrude out the bottom of the head and they will be damaged if the head is placed directly onto a bench.

26 If the cylinder head is to be dismantled, refer to the relevant Sections of Part D of this Chapter.

Preparation for refitting

27 The mating faces of the cylinder head and block must be perfectly clean before refitting the head. Use a scraper to remove all traces

7.11a Unscrew the bolt securing the coolant rail to the fuel pipe (arrowed) . . .

7.11c . . . and the exhaust manifold (arrowed)

of gasket and carbon, and also clean the tops of the pistons. Take particular care with the aluminium surfaces, as the soft metal is damaged easily. Also, make sure that debris is not allowed to enter the oil and water channels – this is particularly important for the oil circuit, as carbon could block the oil supply to the camshaft or crankshaft bearings. Using adhesive tape and paper, seal the water, oil and bolt holes in the cylinder block. To prevent carbon entering the gap between the pistons and bores, smear a little grease in the gap. After cleaning the piston, rotate the crankshaft so that the piston moves down the bore, then wipe out the grease and carbon with a cloth rag. Clean the piston crowns in the same way.

28 Check the block and head for nicks, deep scratches and other damage. If slight, they may be removed carefully with a file. More serious damage may be repaired by machining, but this is a specialist job.

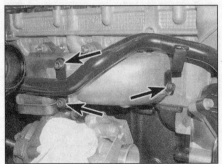

7.14 Undo the three Allen bolts securing the coolant rail heat shield (arrowed)

7.19 Unscrew and discard the timing chain guide pins. New ones must be fitted

7.21 Unscrew the bolts securing the cylinder head to the timing cover (arrowed)

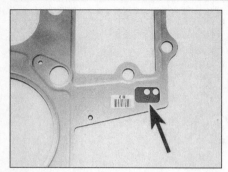

7.31 Gasket identification holes – see text

7.33 Measuring piston protrusion

7.36 Ensure that the locating dowels are in place

29 If warpage of the cylinder head gasket surface is suspected, use a straight-edge to check it for distortion. Refer to Part D of this Chapter if necessary.

30 Ensure that the cylinder head bolt holes in the crankcase are clean and free of oil. Syringe or soak up any oil left in the bolt holes. This is most important in order that the correct bolt tightening torque can be applied and to prevent the possibility of the block being cracked by hydraulic pressure when the bolts are tightened.

31 On this engine, the cylinder head-to-piston clearance is controlled by fitting different thickness head gaskets. The piston protrusion is represented by the number of holes in the gasket next to the timing chain area **(see illustration)**.

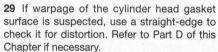

Holes in gasket	Largest piston protrusion
One hole	up to 0.91 mm
Two holes	0.92 to 1.03 mm
Three holes	over 1.03 mm

Select the gasket which has the same thickness/number of holes as the original, unless new piston and connecting rod assemblies have been fitted. In that case, the correct thickness of gasket required is selected by measuring the piston protrusions as follows.

32 Remove the locking pin from the flywheel and mount a dial test indicator securely on the block so that its pointer can be easily pivoted between the piston crown and block mating surface.

33 Ensure the piston is at exactly TDC then zero the dial test indicator on the gasket surface of

the cylinder block. Carefully move the indicator over No 1 piston, taking measurements in line with the gudgeon pin axis, measure the protrusion on both the left-hand and right-hand side of the piston **(see illustration)**. Repeat this procedure on No 4 piston. **Note:** *When turning the crankshaft, ensure that the timing chain does not jam in the timing cover.*

34 Rotate the crankshaft half-a-turn to bring Nos 2 and 3 pistons to TDC. Ensure the crankshaft is accurately positioned then measure the protrusions of Nos 2 and 3 pistons, taking two measurements for each piston. Once both pistons have been measured, rotate the crankshaft through half-a-turn to bring Nos 1 and 4 pistons back to TDC and lock the crankshaft in position again.

35 Use the table in paragraph 31 to select the appropriate gasket.

Refitting

36 Wipe clean the mating faces of the head and block and ensure that the two locating dowels are in position at each end of the cylinder block/crankcase surface **(see illustration)**.

37 Fit the new gasket to the cylinder block, ensuring that it fits correctly over the locating dowels.

38 Carefully refit the cylinder head, locating it on the dowels. Make sure the timing chain can be pulled up through the cylinder head tunnel.

39 Lightly oil under the head and on the threads of each new bolt, carefully enter bolts 1 to 11 into the holes and screw them in, by hand only, until finger-tight. Ensure that the slightly shorter bolt (with the Torx socket head) is fitted

into position 11 **(see illustration)**.

Caution: Do not drop the bolts into their holes.

40 Working progressively and in sequence, first tighten all the cylinder head bolts to the Stage 1 torque setting **(see illustration)**.

41 Slacken all the bolts half a turn (180°), then tighten them in sequence to the Stage 3 setting.

42 Again, in sequence, angle-tighten them 90° (Stage 4), and another 90° (Stage 5), using an angle-measuring gauge **(see illustration)**.

43 Fit and tighten the 41 mm long bolt in the No 12 position to the specified torque **(see illustration 7.40)**.

44 Refit and tighten the five Allen bolts securing the cylinder head to the timing cover to the specified torque. **Note:** *Take great care not to drop the inner screw down the timing chain tunnel **(see illustration 7.21)**.*

45 Ensure that the timing chain guides are in good condition, and refit them into place. Make sure that the front guide is located correctly on its lower support pin. Fit the new upper guide pins and tighten them to the specified torque **(see illustration)**.

46 Clean the camshaft sprockets, and engage them with the timing chain.

47 Refit the lifting eye to the cylinder head and the power steering pipe clip, and tighten the bolts securely.

48 Fit the new gasket, and reconnect the turbocharger to the exhaust manifold. Tighten the bolts to the specified torque.

49 Clean the coolant rail and thermostat housing mating surfaces, fit the heat shield, and with a new seal, fit the coolant rail to the

7.39 Ensure that the slightly shorter bolt (with the Torx socket head) is fitted into position 11

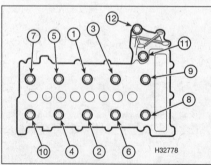

7.40 Cylinder head bolt tightening sequence

7.42 Angle-tightening the cylinder head bolts

thermostat housing. Tighten the bolt to the specified torque **(see illustration)**.
50 Tighten the Allen bolts securing the heat shield securely.
51 On automatic models, align the EGR cooler and coolant rail and tighten the bolts to the specified torque. Refit and tighten the EGR pipe clamp.
52 Refit and tighten the coolant rail to cylinder head and exhaust manifold bolts to the specified torque. Tighten the rail-to-fuel pipe bolt securely.
53 Fit the turbocharger outlet pipe and tighten the retaining clips.
54 Reconnect the expansion tank hose to the coolant rail, and tighten the retaining clip.
55 Clean the coolant hose connector mating surface, with a new seal, fit it to the cylinder head. Tighten the bolts to the specified torque.
56 Ensure that the vacuum pump mating surface is clean, and refit it with a new seal and new bolts. Tighten the bolts to the specified torque.
57 Refit the common fuel rail to the cylinder head and tighten the Allen bolts to the specified torque.
58 Connect the fuel pipe to the pump and fuel rail, and tighten the unions to the specified torque.
59 Reconnect the wiring plugs to the engine coolant temperature sensor, fuel pressure sensor and glow plugs.
60 With reference to Section 6, refit the tappets, rocker arms and camshafts.
61 Refill the cooling system as described in Chapter 1B.

8 Sump –
removal and refitting
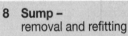

Main sump casting

Removal

1 Disconnect the battery negative lead.
2 Slacken the right-hand front roadwheel nuts, apply the handbrake, then jack up the front of the vehicle and support it securely on axle stands (see *Jacking and vehicle support*). Remove the retaining screws and fasteners and remove the undertray from beneath the engine and transmission. Remove the front

7.45 Make sure that the front guide is located correctly on its lower support pin

right-hand roadwheel and wheel arch splash shield.
3 Drain the engine oil and remove the oil filter as described in Chapter 1B. Refit the sump plug with a new washer and tighten the plug to the specified torque.
4 Slacken and remove the bolt securing the dipstick tube to the oil filter housing, pull the tube out and discard the seal **(see illustration)**.
5 On models with air conditioning, remove the two retaining bolts and remove the compressor drivebelt tensioner.
6 Undo the three bolts securing the coolant rail to the sump and cylinder block **(see illustration)**.
7 On models with air conditioning, undo the retaining bolts, and move the compressor to one side. Do **not** disconnect the refrigerant hoses. Undo the three retaining bolts and remove the compressor mounting bracket.

8.4 Slacken and remove the bolt securing the dipstick tube to the oil filter housing

7.49 With a new seal (arrowed), fit the coolant rail to the thermostat housing

8 Slacken the bolt securing the lower engine tie rod to the subframe, and remove the bolt securing the tie rod to the sump bracket **(see illustration)**.
9 Undo the five bolts securing the tie rod bracket to the sump.
10 Slacken and remove the three bolts securing the transmission casing to the sump.
11 Progressively slacken and remove the 19 bolts securing the sump to the base of the cylinder block **(see illustration)**.
12 Break the sump joint by striking the sump with the palm of the hand, then lower the sump away from the engine. Remove the gasket and discard it, a new one should be used on refitting.
13 While the sump is removed, take the opportunity to check the oil pump pick-up/strainer for signs of clogging or splitting. If necessary, unbolt the pick-up/strainer, and remove it from the engine along with its gasket **(see illustration)**. The strainer can

8.6 Undo the bolts securing the coolant rail to the sump and cylinder block

8.8 Slacken the bolt securing the lower engine tie rod to the subframe, and remove the bolt securing the tie rod to the sump bracket

8.11 Two bolts accessible through the cut-outs in the flywheel

8.13 Unscrew the pick-up/strainer bolts (arrowed)

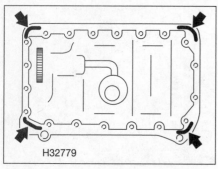

8.16 Apply a bead of suitable sealant to the areas shown

then be cleaned easily in solvent. Inspect the strainer mesh for signs of clogging or splitting and renew if necessary. If the pick-up/strainer bolts are damaged they must be renewed.

Refitting

14 Clean all traces of gasket from the mating surfaces of the cylinder block and sump, then use a clean rag to wipe out the sump and the engine interior.

15 Where necessary, fit a new gasket to the oil pump pick-up/strainer then carefully refit the pipe. Refit the retaining bolts, and tighten them to the specified torque setting.

16 Apply a bead of suitable sealant (recommended sealant is available from your Land Rover dealer) to the cylinder block/crankcase mating surface in the areas shown **(see illustration)**.

17 Fit the gasket to the sump then offer up the sump to the cylinder block/crankcase. Refit the sump retaining bolts, and tighten the bolts finger-tight only.

18 Fit the bolts securing the sump to the gearbox. In order to align the rear sump flange with the gearbox, lightly tighten the bolts, then slacken them. If the sump is being refitted to the engine with the gearbox removed, use a straight-edge to ensure that the sump casting is flush with the end of the engine block **(see illustration)**.

19 Tighten the sump-to-engine block bolts, and then the sump-to-transmission bolts to the specified torque.

20 Position the lower tie rod bracket against the sump, refit the tighten the retaining bolts to the specified torque.

8.18 If the sump is being refitted to the engine with the gearbox removed, use a straight-edge to ensure that the sump casting is flush with the end of the engine block

21 Refit the lower tie rod, and tighten the bolts to the specified torque.

22 On models with air conditioning, refit the compressor mounting bracket, and the compressor, tightening the bolts to the specified torque.

23 Position the lower coolant rail against the sump and tighten the bolts to the specified torque.

24 On models with air conditioning, refit the compressor drivebelt tensioner and drivebelt. Carry out the tensioning procedure described in Chapter 1B.

25 Refit the oil dipstick tube, with a new O-ring, and tighten the bolt to the specified torque.

26 Fit the engine undertray, wheel arch splash shield, and right-hand roadwheel. Lower the vehicle to the ground and tighten the roadwheel nuts to the specified torque.

27 Fit a new oil filter, and fill the engine with the correct quantity of new oil as described in Chapter 1B.

28 Reconnect the battery negative lead.

Lower sump plate

Removal

29 Apply the handbrake, then jack up the front of the vehicle and support it securely on axle stands (see *Jacking and vehicle support*). Remove the retaining screws and fasteners and remove the undertray from beneath the engine and transmission.

30 Drain the engine oil and remove the oil

filter as described in Chapter 1B. Refit the sump plug with a new washer and tighten the plug to the specified torque.

31 Unscrew the sump plate retaining bolts **(see illustration)**.

32 Break the sump plate joint by striking the plate with the palm of the hand, then lower the plate away from the sump. Be prepared for fluid spillage. Remove the gasket and discard it, a new one should be used on refitting.

Refitting

33 Ensure the plate and sump mating surfaces are clean and dry, and fit the new gasket **(see illustration)**.

34 Refit the plate and evenly tighten the bolts to the specified torque.

35 Refit the engine undertray, and lower the vehicle to the ground.

36 Fit a new oil filter, and fill the engine with the correct quantity of new oil, as described in Chapter 1B.

9 Oil pump – removal and refitting

Removal

1 Remove the main sump casting as described in Section 8.

2 Unscrew the three retaining bolts, and remove the oil pump pick-up pipe and strainer **(see illustration 8.13)**. Discard the gasket.

3 Undo the Torx bolt securing the sprocket to the pump driveshaft, and slide the sprocket and chain from the pump.

4 Slacken and remove the four bolts securing the oil pump to the cylinder block **(see illustration)**.

5 Carefully ease the pump down and release it from the locating dowels.

Refitting

6 Ensure the mating surfaces of the oil pump and cylinder block are clean and dry. Make sure the locating dowels are in position.

7 Position the oil pump on the locating dowels. Tighten the bolts to the specified torque.

8 Engage the sprocket with the chain, align the sprocket with the flat machined into the oil

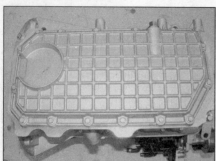

8.31 Unscrew the sump plate retaining bolts

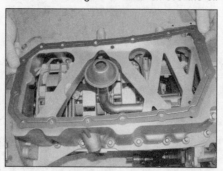

8.33 Fit the new sump plate gasket

9.4 Remove the oil pump from the cylinder block

9.8 Align the flat on the pump shaft with the flat in the sprocket centre

9.9 Refit the pick-up tube with a new gasket

10.2 Undo the bolts and remove the oil pump cover

pump driveshaft, and tighten the Torx bolt to the specified torque setting **(see illustration)**.

9 Using a new gasket, refit the oil pick-up pipe and strainer to the oil pump, and tighten the bolts to the specified torque **(see illustration)**.

10 Refit the sump main casting as described in Section 8.

10 Oil pump – dismantling, inspection and reassembly

Dismantling

1 Remove the oil pump and drive sprocket as described in Section 9.

2 Undo the bolts and remove the pump cover **(see illustration)**.

3 Note the identification marks on the inner and outer rotors to ensure they are

fitted the same way around on reassembly. Remove both the rotors from the body **(see illustration)**.

Inspection

4 Inspect the rotors for obvious signs of wear or damage and renew if necessary. If the pump body or cover plate is scored or damaged, then the complete oil pump assembly must be renewed.

5 Refit the rotors to the body and, using feeler blades of the appropriate thickness, measure the clearance between the outer rotor and the pump body **(see illustration)**.

6 If any measurement is outside the specified limits, the complete pump assembly must be renewed. **Note:** *Although the oil pressure relief valve can be dismantled, at the time of writing, no information was available concerning the fitted depth of the plunger retaining plug. The position of the plug is critical to the performance of the valve. Consequently, consult your Land*

Rover dealer before attempting to dismantle the valve **(see illustrations)**.

Reassembly

7 Remove all traces of locking compound from the threads of the body and cover screws.

8 Lubricate the pump rotors with clean engine oil and refit them to the pump body, using the identification marks to ensure they are fitted the correct way around **(see illustration)**.

9 Refit the cover to the pump body.

10 Ensure the threads of the cover screws are clean and dry and apply a drop of the thread-locking compound to each screw. Refit the screws and tighten them securely.

11 Check that the pump rotates freely, then prime it by injecting oil into its passages and rotating it. If a long time elapses before the pump is refitted to the engine, prime it again before installation.

12 Refit the pump as described in Section 10.

10.3 Note the rotor markings must face out

10.5 Measure the outer rotor-to-body clearance

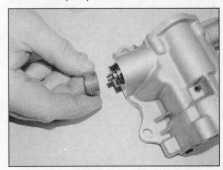

10.6a Unscrew the plunger retaining plug . . .

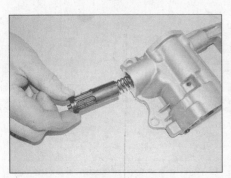

10.6b . . . followed by the plunger

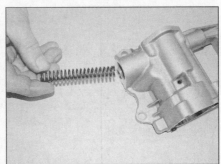

10.6c . . . and spring

10.8 Refit the rotors into the pump body

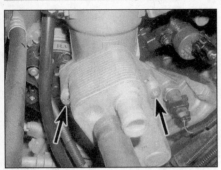

11.5a Undo the three Torx bolts (arrowed – one hidden beneath the oil cooler)

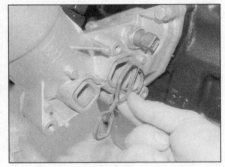

11.5b Renew the oil cooler gasket

4 Lubricate the lips of the new seal with clean engine oil and ease it into position on the end of the shaft. Press the seal squarely into position until it is flush with the housing. If necessary, a suitable tubular drift, such as a socket, which bears only on the hard outer edge of the seal can be used to tap the seal into position. Take great care not to damage the seal lips during fitting and ensure that the seal lips face inwards.

5 Wash off any traces of oil, then refit the crankshaft pulley as described in Section 5.

Left-hand oil seal

6 Remove the flywheel or driveplate as described in Section 13.

7 With reference to Section 8, remove the main sump casting.

8 Undo the retaining bolts and remove the oil seal housing. Using a punch, drive the oil seal from the housing.

9 Clean the seal housing and polish off any burrs or raised edges which may have caused the seal to fail.

10 Press the seal evenly into the housing, until its outer flange is flush with the housing lip **(see illustration)**. If necessary, a soft-faced mallet can be used to tap the seal gently into place.

11 Position a new gasket over the locating dowels **(see illustration)**.

12 Fit the seal protector (supplied with the genuine Land Rover seal) over the end of the crankshaft, and ease the seal and housing over the crankshaft shoulder **(see illustration)**.

13 Refit the oil seal housing bolts, and tighten them to the specified torque.

14 Wash off any oil then refit the flywheel/driveplate as described in Section 13.

11 Oil cooler – removal and refitting

Removal

1 Drain the engine coolant, engine oil, and remove the oil filter as described in Chapter 1B.

2 With reference to Chapter 4B, remove the intake manifold.

3 Remove the starter motor as described in Chapter 5A.

4 Release the clip securing, and disconnect the hose from the oil cooler.

5 Unscrew the three Torx screws and remove the oil cooler from the oil filter housing. Discard the gasket. Be prepared for fluid spillage **(see illustrations)**.

Refitting

6 Ensure the mating surfaces of the oil cooler and oil filter housing are clean and dry and, with a new gasket, fit the cooler to the housing. Tighten the Torx screws to the specified torque.

7 Reconnect the hose to the cooler, and tighten the retaining clip.

8 With reference to Chapter 5A, refit the starter motor.

9 Refit the intake manifold with reference to Chapter 4B.

10 With reference to Chapter 1B, replenish the engine coolant, fit a new oil filter, and fill the engine with the correct quantity of new engine oil.

12 Crankshaft oil seals – renewal

Right-hand seal

1 Remove the crankshaft pulley as described in Section 5.

2 Very carefully punch or drill two small holes opposite each other in the oil seal. Screw a self-tapping screw into each and pull on the screws with pliers to extract the seal **(see illustration)**.

Caution: Great care must be taken to avoid damage to the crankshaft.

3 Clean the seal housing and polish off any burrs or raised edges which may have caused the seal to fail in the first place.

13 Flywheel/driveplate – removal, inspection and refitting

Flywheel

Note: *New flywheel retaining bolts must be used on refitting.*

Removal

1 Remove the clutch assembly as described in Chapter 6.

12.2 Remove the crankshaft oil seal using a self-tapping screw

12.11 Position the new gasket over the locating dowels

12.12 With the seal protector over the end of the crankshaft, ease the oil seal and housing into place

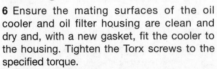

12.10 Press the seal in until it's flush with the housing

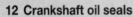

13.2 Lock the flywheel using a similar tool

13.3 Slacken and remove the flywheel bolts, then discard them – new ones must be fitted

13.7 The flywheel will only fit in one position. The one larger flywheel bolt hole, engages with the locating dowel (arrowed)

2 Prevent the flywheel from turning by locking the ring gear teeth with a similar arrangement to that shown **(see illustration)**. Alternatively, bolt a strap between the flywheel and the cylinder block/crankcase.

3 Slacken and remove the retaining bolts and remove the flywheel, noting its locating dowel **(see illustration)**. **Do not** drop it, as it is very heavy. Discard the bolts, they must be renewed whenever they are disturbed.

Inspection

4 If the flywheel-to-clutch mating surface is deeply scored, cracked or otherwise damaged, then the flywheel must be renewed, unless it is possible to have it surface ground. Seek the advice of a Land Rover dealer or engine reconditioning specialist.

5 If the ring gear is badly worn or has missing teeth, then it must be renewed. This job is best left to a Land Rover dealer or engine reconditioning specialist.

Refitting

6 Clean the mating surfaces of the flywheel and crankshaft and remove all traces of locking compound from the crankshaft threaded holes.

7 Fit the flywheel to the crankshaft, engaging it with the crankshaft locating dowel, and fit the new retaining bolts **(see illustration)**. **Note:** *If the new bolts are not supplied precoated with locking compound, apply a few drops prior to fitting the bolts.*

8 Lock the flywheel using the method employed on dismantling then, working in a diagonal sequence, tighten all the retaining bolts to the specified torque setting.

9 Refit the clutch assembly as described in Chapter 6.

Driveplate

Note: *New driveplate retaining bolts must be used on refitting.*

Removal

10 Remove the automatic transmission and torque converter as described in Chapter 7B.

11 Prevent the driveplate from turning by locking the ring gear teeth with a similar arrangement to that shown **(see illustration 13.2)**. Alternatively, bolt a strap between the driveplate and the cylinder block/crankcase.

12 Slacken and remove the retaining bolts and remove the driveplate, noting its locating dowel. Discard the bolts, they must be renewed whenever they are disturbed.

Inspection

13 If the ring gear is badly worn or has missing teeth, then it must be renewed. This job is best left to a Land Rover dealer or engine reconditioning specialist.

Refitting

14 Clean the mating surfaces of the driveplate and crankshaft and remove all traces of locking compound from the crankshaft threaded holes.

15 Fit the driveplate to the crankshaft, engaging it with the crankshaft locating dowel, and fit the new retaining bolts. **Note:** *If the new bolts are not supplied precoated with locking compound, apply a few drops prior to fitting the bolts.*

16 Lock the driveplate using the method employed on dismantling then, working in a diagonal sequence, tighten all the retaining bolts to the specified torque setting.

17 Refit the torque converter and automatic transmission as described in Chapter 7B.

14 Engine/transmission mountings – inspection and renewal

Inspection

1 If improved access is required, firmly apply the handbrake, raise the front of the vehicle and support it securely on axle stands (see *Jacking and vehicle support*). If necessary, undo the retaining screws and fasteners and remove the undertray from beneath the engine/transmission unit.

2 Check the mounting rubber to see if it is cracked, hardened or separated from the metal at any point. Renew the mounting if any such damage or deterioration is evident.

3 Check that all mounting fasteners are securely tightened. Use a torque wrench to check, if possible.

4 Using a large screwdriver or a pry bar, check for wear in the mountings by carefully levering against it to check for free play.

Where this is not possible, enlist the aid of an assistant to move the engine/gearbox unit back-and-forth or from side-to-side while you watch the mountings. While some free play is to be expected even from new components, excessive wear should be obvious. If excessive free play is found, check first that the fasteners are correctly secured, then renew any worn components as described below.

Renewal

Left-hand mounting

5 Firmly apply the handbrake, raise the front of the vehicle and support it securely on axle stands (see *Jacking and vehicle support*). Undo the retaining screws and fasteners and remove the undertray from beneath the engine/transmission unit.

6 With reference to Chapter 4B, remove the air cleaner and intake ducts.

7 Remove the battery carrier, as described in Chapter 5A.

8 Position a jack under the transmission with a block of wood between the jack head and casing, and take the weight if the engine and transmission.

9 Unscrew and remove the through-bolt securing the left-hand mounting to the transmission bracket **(see illustration)**.

10 Using the jack, lower the transmission slightly to gain access to the lower mounting bracket retaining bolts. Undo all four bolts and remove the mounting from the body **(see illustration)**.

14.9 Slacken and remove the left-hand mounting through-bolt

14.10 Remove the left-hand mounting-to-body bolts

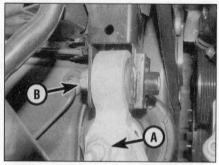

14.18 Undo the engine mounting bracket nut (A) and upper tie rod bolt (B)

14.22 If the Land Rover tool is not available, careful use of a strap/chain wrench can unscrew the Hydramount

11 Upon refitting, position the mounting against the body, and tighten the retaining bolts to the specified torque.

12 Using the jack, raise the engine and transmission to align the mounting with the transmission bracket. Insert the through-bolt and tighten it to the specified torque.

13 Remove the jack from under the vehicle.

14 The remainder of refitting is a reversal of removal.

Right-hand mounting (Hydramount)

15 Raise the front of the vehicle and support it securely on axle stands (see *Jacking and vehicle support*). Undo the retaining screws and fasteners and remove the undertray from beneath the engine/transmission unit.

16 With reference to Chapter 4B, remove the air cleaner and intake ducts.

17 Position a jack under the engine with a block of wood between the jack head and casing, and take the weight if the engine and transmission.

18 Slacken and remove the nut securing the Hydramount to the engine mounting bracket **(see illustration)**.

19 Unscrew the bolt securing the upper tie rod to the engine mounting bracket, and pivot the tie rod to the rear.

20 Unscrew the four retaining bolts and remove the engine mounting bracket from the right-hand end of the engine. Note the locating dowel.

21 Remove the bolt securing the power steering hose clip to the body.

22 The Hydramount can be unscrewed from the wing valance, using Land Rover tool

LRT-12-169, or careful use of a chain/strap wrench around the circumference of the mounting **(see illustration)**.

23 On refitting, tighten the Hydramount to the specified torque if possible, using the method used for removal.

24 Refit the power steering hose clip and tighten the bolt securely.

25 Ensure that the engine and mounting bracket mating faces are clean, and refit the bracket. Tighten the retaining bolts to the specified torque.

26 Lower the engine and transmission, so that the engine mounting bracket fits over the Hydramount stud, and tighten the nut to the specified torque.

27 The remainder of refitting is a reversal of removal.

Upper engine tie rod

28 Undo the retaining bolts and remove the engine acoustic cover.

29 Slacken and remove the retaining bolts and remove the tie rod **(see illustration 14.18)**.

30 To refit, align the tie rod with the brackets, insert the bolts and tighten them to the specified torque.

31 Refit the engine acoustic cover.

Lower engine tie rod

32 Raise the front of the vehicle and support it securely on axle stands (see *Jacking and vehicle support*). Undo the retaining screws and fasteners and remove the undertray from beneath the engine/transmission unit.

33 Undo the two retaining bolts and remove the tie rod.

34 To refit, align the tie rod with the brackets, insert the retaining bolts, and tighten them to the specified torque. Note that the tie rod must be fitted with its 'open' side down **(see illustration)**.

35 Refit the engine undertray, and lower the vehicle to the ground.

15 Crankshaft pilot bearing – inspection, removal and refitting

Inspection

1 The pilot bearing is fitted to the end of the crankshaft, and provides support for the free end of the gearbox input shaft on manual transmission vehicles. It can only be examined once the clutch (Chapter 6) has been removed. Using a finger, rotate the inner race of the bearing and check for any roughness, binding or looseness in the bearing. If any of these conditions are evident, the bearing must be renewed.

Removal

2 Remove the clutch as described in Chapter 6.

3 Using a flat-bladed screwdriver or similar, pack grease through the centre hole of the bearing, until the space between the bearing and the crankshaft, and the centre bearing hole, is completely filled.

4 Select a socket and extension, or rod, which just fits into the centre hole of the bearing. The idea is to tap the tool into the centre hole of the bearing, compress the grease, and force the bearing from the crankshaft. So the tool must be a snug fit in the bearing centre hole, or the grease will escape past it.

5 It may be necessary to repack the bearing with grease several times before the bearing is released **(see illustration)**.

Refitting

6 Using a suitable socket that bears only on the hard outer edge of the bearing, drive the new bearing into the crankshaft until it contacts the shoulder.

7 Refit the clutch as described in Chapter 6.

14.34 The lower tie rod must be fitted with the 'open' side down

15.5 It may be necessary to repack the bearing with grease several times before the bearing is released

Chapter 2 Part D:
Engine removal and overhaul procedures

Contents

Degrees of difficulty

Easy, suitable for novice with little experience	Fairly easy, suitable for beginner with some experience	Fairly difficult, suitable for competent DIY mechanic	Difficult, suitable for experienced DIY mechanic	Very difficult, suitable for expert DIY or professional

Specifications

Petrol engine

Cylinder head

Height	118.95 to 119.05 mm
Reface limit	0.2 mm
Maximum acceptable gasket face distortion	0.05 mm
Valve seat width	1.5 mm

Valves, valve springs and guides

Valve stem diameter:	
Inlet	5.952 to 5.967 mm
Exhaust	5.947 to 5.962 mm
Valve stem installed height:	
New	38.93 to 39.84 mm
Service limit	40.10 mm
Valve guide inside diameter	6.000 to 6.025 mm
Valve stem-to-guide clearance:	
Inlet:	
Standard	0.033 to 0.063 mm
Service limit	0.07 mm
Exhaust:	
Standard	0.038 to 0.078 mm
Service limit	0.11 mm
Valve guide installed height	6.0 mm
Valve spring free length	50.0 mm

Cylinder block/liner

Cylinder liner bore diameter	80.000 to 80.030 mm (nominal)

Petrol engine (continued)

Pistons and rings

Piston diameter	79.975 to 80.005 mm (nominal)
Piston-to-bore clearance	0.010 to 0.040 mm

Piston ring fitted end gaps:

Top compression ring	0.2 to 0.35 mm
Second compression ring	0.28 to 0.48 mm
Oil control ring	0.15 to 0.4 mm

Piston ring-to-groove clearance:

Top compression ring	0.04 to 0.072 mm
Second compression ring	0.03 to 0.062 mm
Oil control ring	0.01 to 0.18 mm

Crankshaft

Main bearing journal diameter	47.979 to 48.000 mm
Big-end (crankpin) journal diameter	47.986 to 48.007 mm
Maximum journal ovality	0.01 mm

Crankshaft endfloat:

Standard	0.1 to 0.25 mm
Service limit	0.34 mm
Thrustwasher thickness	2.61 to 2.65 mm

Torque wrench settings

Refer to Chapter 2A Specifications

L-Series diesel engine

Cylinder head

Maximum acceptable gasket face distortion	0.1 mm

Refacing of the cylinder head is not permitted

Valves, valve springs and guides

Valve stem diameter:

Inlet	6.907 to 6.923 mm
Exhaust	6.897 to 6.913 mm

Valve head recess below cylinder head surface (maximum):

Inlet	1.45 mm
Exhaust	1.35 mm
Valve guide inside diameter	6.95 to 6.963 mm

Valve stem-to-guide clearance:

Inlet	0.056 mm
Exhaust	0.066 mm
Valve guide installed height	61.1 to 61.7 mm
Valve spring free length	37.0 mm

Cylinder block

Cylinder bore diameter	84.442 to 84.46 mm

Pistons and rings

Piston diameter	84.262 mm
Piston-to-bore clearance	0.18 to 0.2 mm

Piston ring fitted end gaps:

Top compression ring	0.25 to 0.27 mm
Second compression ring	0.4 to 0.42 mm
Oil control ring	0.3 to 0.32 mm

Piston ring-to-groove clearance:

Top compression ring	0.115 to 0.135 mm
Second compression ring	0.05 to 0.082 mm
Oil control ring	0.05 to 0.082 mm

Crankshaft

Main bearing journal diameter	60.703 to 60.719 mm
Big-end (crankpin) journal diameter	57.683 to 57.696 mm
Maximum journal ovality	0.01 mm*
Crankshaft endfloat	0.03 to 0.26 mm
Thrustwasher thickness	2.31 to 2.36 mm

* These are suggested figures – no exact figures are quoted by Land Rover. Seek the advice of a Land Rover dealer or engine overhaul specialist before condemning components

Torque wrench settings

Refer to Chapter 2B Specifications

TD4 diesel engine

Cylinder head

Maximum acceptable gasket face distortion . . . . 0.03 mm
Refacing of the cylinder head is not permitted

Valves, valve springs and guides

Valve stem diameter:
  Inlet. . . . . 5.97 ± 0.01 mm
  Exhaust. . . . . 5.97 ± 0.01 mm
Valve head recess below cylinder head surface (maximum):
  Inlet. . . . . 0.73 ± 0.1 mm
  Exhaust. . . . . 0.56 ± 0.1 mm
Valve stem-to-guide clearance. . . . . 0.025 to 0.054 mm
Valve spring free length . . . . 47.5 mm
Valve guides cannot be renewed
Valve seats must not be recut

Cylinder block

Cylinder bore diameter. . . . . 84.000 to 84.268 mm (nominal)
Cylinder block ovality (maximum). . . . . 0.04 mm
Cylinder block taper (maximum). . . . . 0.04 mm

Pistons and rings

Piston diameter (measured 12 mm from base, 90° to gudgeon pin) . . . 83.95 ± 0.009 mm (nominal)
Piston-to-bore clearance . . . . 0.036 to 0.15 mm
Piston ring fitted end gaps:
  Top compression ring. . . . . 0.2 to 0.35 mm
  Second compression ring. . . . . 0.3 to 0.45 mm
  Oil control ring . . . . 0.2 to 0.4 mm
Piston ring-to-groove clearance:
  Top compression ring. . . . . Non specified
  Second compression ring. . . . . 0.05 to 0.09 mm
  Oil control ring . . . . 0.03 to 0.07 mm

Crankshaft

Main bearing journal diameter . . . . 59.977 to 59.469 mm (nominal)
Big-end (crankpin) journal diameter. . . . . 44.975 to 45.009 mm
Maximum journal ovality. . . . . 0.01 mm*
Crankshaft endfloat . . . . 0.08 to 0.163 mm

* These are suggested figures – no exact figures are quoted by Land Rover. Seek the advice of a Land Rover dealer or engine overhaul specialist before condemning components

Torque wrench settings

Refer to Chapter 2C Specifications

1 General information

Included in this Part of Chapter 2 are details of removing the engine/transmission from the vehicle and general overhaul procedures for the cylinder head, cylinder block and all other engine internal components.

The information given ranges from advice concerning preparation for an overhaul and the purchase of parts, to detailed step-by-step procedures covering removal, inspection, renovation and refitting of engine internal components.

After Section 6, all instructions are based on the assumption that the engine has been removed from the vehicle. For information concerning in-vehicle engine repair, as well as the removal and refitting of those external components necessary for full overhaul, refer to the relevant in-vehicle repair procedure section (Chapter 2A to 2C) of this Chapter and to Section 6. Ignore any preliminary dismantling operations described in the relevant in-vehicle repair sections that are no longer relevant once the engine has been removed from the vehicle.

Apart from torque wrench settings, which are given at the beginning of the relevant in-vehicle repair procedure Chapter (2A to 2C), all specifications relating to engine overhaul are at the beginning of this Part of Chapter 2.

2 Engine overhaul – general information

It is not always easy to determine when, or if, an engine should be completely overhauled, as a number of factors must be considered.

High mileage is not necessarily an indication that an overhaul is needed, while low mileage does not preclude the need for an overhaul. Frequency of servicing is probably the most important consideration. An engine which has had regular and frequent oil and filter changes, as well as other required maintenance, should give many thousands of miles of reliable service. Conversely, a neglected engine may require an overhaul very early in its life.

Excessive oil consumption is an indication that piston rings, valve seals and/or valve guides are in need of attention. Make sure that oil leaks are not responsible before deciding that the rings and/or guides are worn. Perform a compression test, as described in the relevant Part of this Chapter, to determine the likely cause of the problem.

Check the oil pressure with a gauge fitted in place of the oil pressure switch, and compare it with that specified. If it is extremely low, the main and big-end bearings, and/or the oil pump, are probably worn out.

Loss of power, rough running, knocking or metallic engine noises, excessive valve gear noise, and high fuel consumption may also point to the need for an overhaul, especially if they are all present at the same time. If a complete service does not remedy the situation, major mechanical work is the only solution.

An engine overhaul involves restoring all internal parts to the specification of a new engine. During an overhaul, the pistons and the piston rings are renewed. New main and big-end bearings are generally fitted; if necessary, the crankshaft may be renewed, to restore the journals. The valves are also serviced as well, since they are usually in less-than-perfect condition at this point. While the engine is being overhauled, other components, such as the starter and alternator, can be overhauled as well. The end result should be an as-new engine that will give many trouble-free miles. **Note:** *Critical cooling system components such as the hoses, thermostat and coolant pump should be renewed when an engine is overhauled. The radiator should be checked carefully, to ensure that it is not clogged or leaking. Also, it is a good idea to renew the oil pump whenever the engine is overhauled.*

Before beginning the engine overhaul, read through the entire procedure, to familiarise yourself with the scope and requirements of the job. Overhauling an engine is not difficult if you carefully follow all of the instructions, have the necessary tools and equipment, and pay close attention to all specifications. It can, however, be time-consuming. Plan on the car being off the road for a minimum of two weeks, especially if parts must be taken to an engineering works for repair or reconditioning. Check on the availability of parts and make sure that any necessary special tools and equipment are obtained in advance. Most work can be done with typical hand tools, although a number of precision measuring tools are required for inspecting parts to determine if they must be renewed. Often the engineering works will handle the inspection of parts and offer advice concerning reconditioning and renewal. **Note:** *Always wait until the engine has been completely dismantled, and until all components (especially the cylinder block and the crankshaft) have been inspected, before deciding what service and repair operations must be performed by an engineering works. The condition of these components will be the major factor to consider when determining whether to overhaul the original engine, or to* buy a reconditioned unit. Do not, therefore, purchase parts or have overhaul work done on other components until they have been thoroughly inspected. As a general rule, time is the primary cost of an overhaul, so it does not pay to fit worn or sub-standard parts.

As a final note, to ensure maximum life and minimum trouble from a reconditioned engine, everything must be assembled with care, in a spotlessly-clean environment.

3 Engine removal – methods and precautions

If you have decided that the engine must be removed for overhaul or major repair work, several preliminary steps should be taken.

Locating a suitable place to work is extremely important. Adequate work space, along with storage space for the vehicle, will be needed. If a workshop or garage is not available, at the very least, a flat, level, clean work surface is required.

Cleaning the engine compartment and engine/transmission before beginning the removal procedure will help keep tools clean and organised.

An engine hoist or A-frame will also be necessary. Make sure the equipment is rated in excess of the combined weight of the engine and transmission. Safety is of primary importance, considering the potential hazards involved in lifting the engine/transmission out of the vehicle.

If this is the first time you have removed an engine, an assistant should ideally be available. Advice and aid from someone more experienced would also be helpful. There are many instances when one person cannot simultaneously perform all of the operations required when lifting the engine out of the vehicle.

Plan the operation ahead of time. Before starting work, arrange for the hire of or obtain all of the tools and equipment you will need. Some of the equipment necessary to perform engine/transmission removal and installation safely and with relative ease (in addition to an engine hoist) is as follows: a heavy duty trolley jack, complete sets of spanners and sockets as described in the rear of this manual, wooden blocks, and plenty of rags and cleaning solvent for mopping-up spilled oil, coolant and fuel. If the hoist must be hired, make sure that you arrange for it in advance, and perform all of the operations possible without it beforehand. This will save you money and time.

Plan for the vehicle to be out of use for quite a while. An engineering works will be required to perform some of the work which the do-it-yourselfer cannot accomplish without special equipment. These places often have a busy schedule, so it would be a good idea to consult them before removing the engine, in order to accurately estimate the amount of time required to rebuild or repair components that may need work.

Always be extremely careful when removing and refitting the engine/transmission. Serious injury can result from careless actions. Plan ahead and take your time, and a job of this nature, although major, can be accomplished successfully.

4 Petrol engine and transmission unit – removal, separation and refitting

Note: *The engine can be removed from the vehicle only as a complete unit with the transmission; the two are then separated for overhaul.*
Note: *It will be necessary to fabricate some engine lifting brackets to attach the hoist to (see paragraph 33).*

Removal

1 Park the vehicle on firm, level ground then open and remove the bonnet as described in Chapter 11. Undo the retaining screws and remove the engine top cover.
2 With reference to Chapters 1A, 7A and 7C, drain the coolant system, engine oil, gearbox and IRD (intermediate reduction unit) oil.
3 Refer to Chapter 8, and remove both driveshafts.
4 Remove the exhaust front pipe (see Chapter 4A).
5 Using a marker pen or similar, mark the relationship of the propeller shaft to the IRD output flange. Unscrew the six nuts and bolts, and move the propeller shaft to one side **(see illustration)**.
6 Push back the gearchange rod roll-pin cover and, using a punch, drive out the roll-pin. Discard the pin, a new one must be fitted **(see illustration)**.
7 Unscrew the retaining bolt and disconnect the gearchange steady rod from the gearbox.
8 Disconnect the earth lead from the left-hand end of the gearbox.
9 Remove the bolt securing the lower tie rod to the engine bracket. Slacken the rear tie rod bolt, and allow it to hang down.
10 With reference to Chapter 5A, remove the battery carrier.

4.5 Mark the relationship of the propeller shaft to the IRD output flange

4.6 Push back the gearchange rod-roll pin cover and, using a punch, drive out the roll pin

4.12 Undo the two screws and release the two positive leads from the fusebox

Models up to 2001

11 Disconnect the engine harness multiplug from the engine compartment fusebox.

12 Open the fusebox, undo the two screws and release the two positive leads from the fusebox **(see illustration)**.

13 Disconnect the engine wiring harness-to-main harness multiplugs, and release the engine harness from the retaining clip **(see illustration)**.

14 Prise out the clutch slave cylinder retaining clip, and move the cylinder to one side. There is no need to disconnect the cylinder supply hose.

Models 2001-on

15 Disconnect the reversing light and 1st gear switch wiring plugs. Release the wiring cables from their retaining clips.

16 Undo the three retaining bolts, and move the clutch slave cylinder and bracket to one side.

17 Refit to Chapter 4A, and remove the engine ECM (electronic control module).

18 An electrical component 'box' is located in the left-hand rear corner of the engine compartment. With reference to the accompanying illustrations, disconnect the engine harness multiplug, air duct and harness rubber sleeve, release the four retaining clips and manoeuvre the component carrier from the box. Undo the nut, release the retainer, and remove the electrical box **(see illustrations)**.

19 Open the fusebox, and unscrew the two bolts securing the battery and starter motor lead to the fusebox. Disconnect the wiring plug from the fusebox **(see illustration)**.

20 Release the clips securing the battery and starter leads to the electrical box mounting bracket.

21 Disconnect the purge control valve wiring plug **(see illustration)**.

All models

22 Squeeze in the two tabs of the retaining clip, and disconnect the fuel feed pipe from the fuel rail.

23 Disconnect the vacuum pipe from the inlet manifold.

24 With reference to Chapter 4A, disconnect the purge valve pipe and accelerator cable from the throttle housing.

4.13 Disconnect the engine harness wiring plugs (1) and release the retaining clip (2)

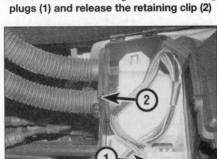

4.18b Engine harness wiring plug (1) and air ducts (2)

Models up to 2001

25 Place a container under the power steering pump, and disconnect the high and low pressure pipes. Be prepared for fluid spillage, and plug the connections to avoid contamination. Undo the high pressure pipe bracket retaining bolt, and position the pipes to one side.

26 Release the retaining clips and disconnect the top hose from the coolant outlet, and the bottom hose from the coolant rail.

27 Disconnect the heater hoses from the coolant outlet elbow and the coolant rail.

28 Release the retaining clips and disconnect the expansion tank hose from the coolant rail, and the expansion tank vent hose from the engine **(see illustration)**.

29 Release the retaining clips, and disconnect the coolant hoses from the IRD unit (see Chapter 3).

4.21 Disconnect the purge control valve wiring plug

4.18a Engine compartment electrical box

4.19 Unscrew the two bolts securing the battery and starter motor lead (A) to the fusebox, and disconnect the wiring plug (B)

Models 2001-on

30 Release the retaining clips and disconnect the following coolant hoses:
   a) *Heater supply and return hoses from the engine bulkhead.*
   b) *Radiator top hose-to-coolant elbow.*
   c) *Expansion tank-to-inlet manifold.*

31 Disconnect the hose from the underside of the expansion tank, and release retaining clip securing the hose to the body.

All models

32 On models with air conditioning, remove the alternator with reference to Chapter 5A, undo the four retaining bolts and move the air conditioning compressor to one side. Do **not** disconnect the refrigerant pipes. **Note:** *On models 2001-on, there is no need to remove the alternator.*

33 Attach suitable engine lifting brackets

4.28 Disconnect the expansion tank vent hose from the engine

4.33 Remove the ignition coil bracket and attach an engine lifting eye

4.35 Slacken and remove the nut securing the power steering hose bracket to the right-hand engine mounting (arrowed)

4.36 Undo the engine mounting bracket bolts

to the cylinder head. The Land Rover lifting brackets (LRT-12-135/1 and LRT-12-135/2) are bolted to the threaded hole on the right-hand end of the rear of the cylinder head and into the inlet camshaft cover plate holes on the left-hand end of the head, once the ignition coil bracket (on models up to 2001) has been removed (see illustration).

34 Attach lifting chains/straps to the lifting brackets and, with an engine crane or hoist, take the weight of the engine and transmission.

Models up to 2001

35 Slacken and remove the nut securing the power steering hose bracket to the right-hand engine mounting (see illustration).

36 Unscrew the two bolts securing the engine mounting bracket to the engine (see illustration).

37 Remove the bolt securing the tie rod to the engine mounting bracket, and withdraw the bracket.

38 Unscrew the left-hand engine mounting through-bolt, and the four bolts securing the mounting to the body.

Models 2001-on

39 Remove the bolts securing the tie rod to the left-hand engine mounting.

40 Slacken and remove the left-hand engine mounting through-bolt, and remove the four

bolts securing the left-hand mounting to the body.

41 Release the power steering reservoir from the mounting bracket, and position to one side.

42 Unscrew the bolt securing the upper tie rod to the engine mounting bracket, slacken the tie rod rear bolt and pivot the tie rod away from the engine (see illustration).

43 Remove the nut and two bolts securing the right-hand engine mounting arm to the engine and Hydramount, and remove the arm.

44 Raise the engine and transmission sufficiently to gain access to the power steering pump. With reference to Chapter 1A, remove the pump drivebelt.

45 Slacken and remove the three power steering pump pulley retaining bolts, then remove the retaining bolts and position the pump to one side.

All models

46 Make a final check that any components which would prevent the removal of the engine/transmission from the vehicle have been removed or disconnected, and with the help of an assistant, manoeuvre the engine and transmission up and out of the engine compartment.

Separation

47 With the engine/transmission assembly

removed, support the assembly on suitable blocks of wood, on a workbench (or failing that, on a clean area of the workshop floor).

48 Disconnect the electrical wiring, undo the retaining bolts and remove the starter motor (see Chapter 5A).

49 Unscrew the retaining bolts, and remove the support bracket between the IRD unit, and the engine.

50 Slacken and remove the four securing bolts, and separate the IRD unit from the gearbox. Discard the IRD unit input shaft O-ring, a new one must be fitted (see illustration).

51 Undo the retaining bolts and remove the flywheel cover plates.

52 Ensure that both engine and transmission are adequately supported, then slacken and remove the remaining bolts securing the transmission housing to the engine. Note the correct fitted positions of each bolt (and the relevant brackets) as they are removed, to use as a reference on refitting.

53 Carefully withdraw the transmission from the engine, ensuring that the weight of the transmission is not allowed to hang on the input shaft while it is engaged with the clutch friction disc.

54 If they are loose, remove the locating dowels from the engine or transmission, and keep them in a safe place.

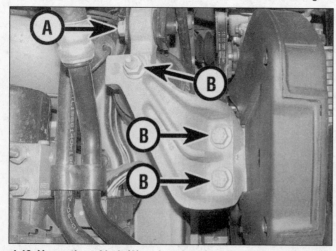

4.42 Upper tie rod bolt (A) and engine mounting arm nut/bolts (B)

4.50 Discard the IRD unit input shaft O-ring, a new one must be fitted

Refitting

55 If the engine and transmission have been separated, perform the operations described below in paragraphs 56 to 62. If not, proceed as described from paragraph 63 onwards.

56 Referring to Chapter 6, apply a smear of molybdenum disulphide grease to the clutch release bearing, fork and guide sleeve contact surfaces and check the operation of the clutch release mechanism. Also apply a smear of grease to the transmission input shaft splines; **do not** apply too much grease otherwise the clutch friction disc may be contaminated.

57 Ensure the locating dowels are correctly positioned then carefully offer the transmission to the engine, until the locating dowels are engaged. Ensure that the weight of the transmission is not allowed to hang on the input shaft as it is engaged with the clutch friction disc.

58 Refit the transmission housing-to-engine bolts, ensuring that all the necessary brackets are correctly positioned, and tighten them to the specified torque setting.

59 Refit the flywheel cover plates.

60 With a new O-ring, refit the IRD unit to the gearbox. Tighten the bolts to the specified torque.

61 Position the support bracket between the IRD unit and the engine, refit the bolts and tighten them to the specified torque.

62 Refit the starter motor and tighten its mounting bolts to the specified torque (see Chapter 5A). Reconnect the starter motor electrical wiring.

63 Reconnect the hoist and lifting tackle to the engine lifting brackets.

64 With the aid of an assistant, carefully lift the assembly into position in the engine compartment, manipulating the hoist and lifting tackle as necessary, taking great care not to trap any components.

65 Refit the left-hand engine/transmission mounting to the body, tighten the bolts to the specified torque.

Models up to 2001

66 Align the engine/transmission with the left-hand mounting bracket and screw in the mounting through-bolt.

67 Refit the right-hand mounting bracket to the engine and mounting, align the upper tie rod with the bracket, and refit the power steering hose support bracket to the engine mounting stud. Tighten all of the engine mounting bolts to the specified torque.

Models 2001-on

68 Align the engine/transmission with the left-hand mounting bracket and tie rod, and screw in the mounting through-bolt and tie rod bolt.

69 Refit the engine mounting top arm, align the upper tie rod, and tighten all engine mounting bolts/nuts to the specified torque.

All models

70 Remove the lifting chains and brackets.

71 On models with air conditioning, refit the compressor to the bracket, refit the alternator

5.4 Separate the links from the anti-roll bar

(models up to 2001 only – see Chapter 5A), and tighten the bolts to the specified torque.

72 The remainder of the refitting procedure is a direct reversal of the removal sequence, noting the following points:

a) *Ensure that all wiring is correctly routed and retained by all the relevant retaining clips and that all connectors are correctly and securely reconnected.*

b) *Ensure that all disturbed hoses are correctly reconnected, and securely retained by their retaining clips.*

c) *Refit the gearchange rod to the shaft using a new roll-pin.*

d) *Renew the transmission differential oil seals (see the relevant part of Chapter 7) before refitting the driveshafts.*

e) *Refill the power steering circuit with the correct quantity and type of fluid, as described in Chapter 1A).*

f) *Refill the transmission and IRD unit with correct quantity and type of oil, as described in the relevant part of Chapter 7. If the oil was not drained, top-up the level as described in Chapter 1A.*

g) *Refit the engine with oil as described in Chapter 1A and also refill the cooling system.*

---

5 Diesel engine and transmission unit – removal, separation and refitting

L-Series engine

Note: *The engine can be removed from the vehicle only as a complete unit with the*

5.13 Disconnect the lower intercooler hose

5.6 Remove the bolt securing the lower tie rod to the engine bracket

transmission. The engine and transmission are lowered out of position, and withdrawn from under the vehicle. Bearing this in mind, ensure that the vehicle is raised sufficiently so that there is enough clearance between the front of the vehicle and the floor to allow the engine/transmission unit to be slid out once it has been lowered out of position.

Removal

1 Park the vehicle on firm, level ground then open and remove the bonnet as described in Chapter 11. Undo the retaining screws and remove the engine top cover.

2 With reference to Chapters 1B, 7A and 7C, drain the coolant system, engine oil, gearbox and IRD (intermediate reduction unit) oil.

3 Refer to Chapter 8, and remove both drive-shafts.

4 Slacken and remove the two nuts, and separate the anti-roll bar links from the bar **(see illustration)**.

5 Using a balljoint breaker, separate the lower arm balljoints from the hub carriers (see Chapter 10).

6 Remove the bolts securing the engine lower tie rod to the bracket on the engine **(see illustration)**.

7 Position a trolley jack under the rear cross-member at the rear of the engine compartment, remove the four bolts securing the lower arm rear mountings to the crossmember and body, and the two bolts securing the crossmember to the body. With the help of an assistant, lower the crossmember and remove it from under the vehicle.

8 Remove the exhaust front pipe (see Chapter 4B).

9 Using a marker pen or similar, mark the relationship of the propeller shaft to the IRD output flange. Unscrew the six nuts and bolts, and move the propeller shaft to one side **(see illustration 4.5)**.

10 Push back the gearchange rod roll-pin cover and, using a punch, drive out the roll-pin. Discard the pin, a new one must be fitted **(see illustration 4.6)**.

11 Unscrew the retaining bolt and disconnect the gearchange steady rod from the gearbox.

12 Disconnect the earth lead from the from left-hand end of the gearbox.

13 Slacken the retaining clip, and disconnect the lower intercooler hose **(see illustration)**.

5.17 Undo the two screws (arrowed) and release the two positive leads from the fusebox

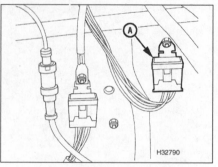

5.19a Disconnect the earth lead multiplug (A) . . .

5.19b . . . and the MAP sensor plug

14 On models with air conditioning, undo the four retaining bolts and move the air conditioning compressor to one side. Do **not** disconnect the refrigerant pipes.

15 With reference to Chapter 5A, remove the battery carrier.

16 Disconnect the engine harness multiplug from the underside of the fusebox.

17 Open the fusebox, undo the two screws and release the two positive leads from the fusebox **(see illustration)**.

18 Disconnect the four engine wiring harness-to-main harness multiplugs, and release the engine harness from the retaining clip **(see illustration 4.13)**.

19 Disconnect the earth lead multiplug from the left-hand side inner wing, and the MAP (manifold absolute pressure sensor) wiring plug **(see illustrations)**.

20 Located in the left-hand side of the engine compartment, disconnect the EGR modulator valve wiring plug **(see illustration)**.

21 Disconnect the EGR valve vacuum pipe.

22 Release the retaining clips and disconnect the following coolant hoses:
a) *Radiator top hose.*
b) *Heater coolant hoses from the engine bulkhead.*
c) *Expansion take outlet hose.*

23 Disconnect the pressure sensing hose from the turbocharger **(see illustration)**.

24 Release the retaining clips and disconnect the fuel supply and return hoses from the fuel pipes **(see illustration)**.

25 Release the retaining clips and disconnect the fuel cooler hoses from the fuel pipe and fuel injection pump. Plug the fuel ports to prevent contamination **(see Haynes Hint)**.

> **HAYNES HINT** *Cut the fingertips from an old pair of rubber gloves and secure them over the fuel ports with elastic bands.*

26 Prise out the clutch slave cylinder retaining clip, and move the cylinder to one side. There is no need to disconnect the cylinder supply hose **(see illustration)**.

27 On models with air conditioning, remove the screw securing the air conditioning pipe clip to the bracket on the right-hand engine mounting.

28 Remove the nut and bolt securing the power steering pipe clamp to the bracket on the right-hand engine mounting.

29 Slacken and disconnect the power steering high-pressure pipe union at the bracket on the right-hand engine mounting. Be prepared for fluid spillage. Discard the union O-ring – a new one must be fitted. Plug the connections to prevent contamination.

30 Remove the bolt securing the upper tie rod to the right-hand engine mounting, slacken the tie rod rear bolt and pivot the tie rod away from the engine **(see illustration)**.

31 Unscrew the nut securing the right-hand engine mounting arm to the mounting.

32 Attach lifting chains/straps to the engine lifting brackets and, with an engine crane or hoist, take the weight of the engine and transmission.

33 Undo the retaining bolts and remove the starter motor-to-left-hand engine mounting support strut.

34 Unscrew the left-hand engine mounting through-bolt, and the four bolts securing the mounting to the body.

35 Make a final check that any components which would prevent the removal of the engine/transmission from the vehicle have been removed or disconnected, and with the help of an assistant, lower the assembly and

5.20 Disconnect the EGR modulator valve wiring plug

5.23 Disconnect the pressure sensing hose from the turbocharger (arrowed)

5.24 Disconnect the fuel supply and return hoses from the fuel pipes

5.26 Prise out the clutch slave cylinder retaining clip

5.30 Remove the bolt securing the upper tie rod to the right-hand engine mounting

manoeuvre the engine and transmission down and out of the engine compartment.

Separation

36 With the engine/transmission assembly removed, support the assembly on suitable blocks of wood, on a workbench (or failing that, on a clean area of the workshop floor).

37 Disconnect the electrical wiring, undo the retaining bolts and remove the starter motor (see Chapter 5A).

38 Unscrew the retaining bolts, and remove the support bracket between the IRD unit and the engine. Undo the bolts and remove the gearbox-to-engine support bracket **(see illustration)**.

39 Slacken and remove the four securing bolts, and separate the IRD unit from the gearbox. Discard the IRD unit input shaft O-ring, a new one must be fitted **(see illustration 4.50)**.

40 Remove the bolt securing the coolant and fuel rails to the gearbox adaptor plate.

41 Ensure that both engine and transmission are adequately supported, then slacken and remove the remaining bolts securing the transmission to the adaptor plate on the engine. Note the correct fitted positions of each bolt (and the relevant brackets) as they are removed, to use as a reference on refitting.

42 Carefully withdraw the transmission from the engine, ensuring that the weight of the transmission is not allowed to hang on the input shaft while it is engaged with the clutch friction disc.

43 If they are loose, remove the locating dowels from the engine or transmission, and keep them in a safe place.

Refitting

44 If the engine and transmission have been separated, perform the operations described below in paragraphs 45 to 50. If not, proceed as described from paragraph 51 onwards.

45 Referring to Chapter 6, apply a smear of molybdenum disulphide grease to the clutch release bearing, fork and guide sleeve contact surfaces and check the operation of the clutch release mechanism. Also apply a smear of grease to the transmission input shaft splines; **do not** apply too much grease otherwise the clutch friction disc may be contaminated.

46 Ensure the locating dowels are correctly positioned then carefully offer the transmission to the engine, until the locating dowels are engaged. Ensure that the weight of the transmission is not allowed to hang on the input shaft as it is engaged with the clutch friction disc.

47 Refit the transmission housing-to-adaptor plate bolts, ensuring that all the necessary brackets are correctly positioned, and tighten them to the specified torque setting.

48 With a new O-ring, refit the IRD unit to the gearbox. Tighten the bolts to the specified torque.

49 Position the support bracket between the IRD unit and the engine, refit the bolts. Refit the gearbox-to-engine support bracket and tighten all of the bolts to the specified torque.

50 Refit the starter motor and tighten its mounting bolts to the specified torque (see

Chapter 5A). Reconnect the starter motor electrical wiring.

51 Reconnect the hoist and lifting tackle to the engine lifting brackets.

52 With the aid of an assistant, carefully lift the assembly into position in the engine compartment, manipulating the hoist and lifting tackle as necessary, taking great care not to trap any components.

53 Refit the left-hand engine/transmission mounting to the body, tighten the bolts to the specified torque.

54 Align the engine/transmission with the left-hand mounting bracket and screw in the mounting through-bolt.

55 Refit the right-hand mounting bracket to the engine and mounting, align the upper tie rod with the bracket, and refit the power steering hose support bracket to the engine mounting stud. Tighten all of the engine mounting bolts to the specified torque.

56 Remove the lifting chains and brackets.

57 The remainder of the refitting procedure is a direct reversal of the removal sequence, noting the following points:

a) *Ensure that all wiring is correctly routed and retained by all the relevant retaining clips and that all connectors are correctly and securely reconnected.*

b) *Ensure that all disturbed hoses are correctly reconnected, and securely retained by their retaining clips.*

c) *Refit the gearchange rod to the shaft using a new roll-pin.*

d) *Renew the transmission differential oil seals (see the relevant part of Chapter 7) before refitting the driveshafts.*

e) *Refill the power steering circuit with the correct quantity and type of fluid, as described in Chapter 1B).*

f) *Refill the transmission and IRD unit with correct quantity and type of oil, as described in the relevant part of Chapter 7. If the oil was not drained, top-up the level as described in Chapter 1B.*

g) *Refill the engine with oil as described in Chapter 1B and also refill the cooling system.*

TD4 engine

Note: *The engine can be removed from the vehicle only as a complete unit with the transmission. The engine and transmission*

5.38 Undo the bolts and remove the gearbox-to-engine support bracket

are lowered out of position, and withdrawn from under the vehicle. Bearing this in mind, ensure that the vehicle is raised so that there is enough clearance between the front of the vehicle and the floor to allow the engine/transmission unit to be slid out once it has been lowered out of position.

Removal

58 Park the vehicle on firm, level ground then open and remove the bonnet as described in Chapter 11. Undo the retaining screws and remove the engine top cover.

59 With reference to Chapters 1B, 7A, 7B and 7C, drain the coolant system, engine oil, transmission and IRD (intermediate reduction unit) oil.

60 Remove the battery carrier as described in Chapter 5A.

61 With reference to Chapter 4B, remove intake ducting assembly and disconnect the engine ECM (electronic control module).

62 Working in the engine compartment electrical box, disconnect the glowplug ECM, and the engine harness multiplug.

63 On automatic transmission models, disconnect the transmission ECM located in the engine compartment electrical box. Release the gearbox harness multiplugs from the retaining clips, and disconnect. Slacken the selector cable-to-selector lever securing bolt on the gearbox, release the cable retaining clip and separate the cable from the gearbox.

64 Remove the four retaining screws, release the clamps and remove the engine wiring harness from the engine compartment electrical box. Lay the harness over the engine **(see illustrations)**.

5.64a Remove the four screws to release the harness clamps . . .

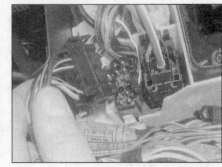

5.64b . . . and then disconnect the wiring plugs

5.65 Pull back the locking collar and separate the clutch slave cylinder pipe connection

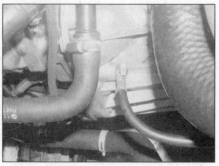

5.66 Disconnect the earth lead from the gearbox

5.69 Undo the retaining clips and disconnect the fuel feed and return hoses

65 On manual transmission models, pull back the locking collar and separate the clutch slave cylinder pipe connection, then disconnect the wiring plug from the 1st gear switch, and the reversing light switch **(see illustration)**.

66 Unscrew the bolt and disconnect the earth lead from the gearbox **(see illustration)**.

67 With reference to Chapter 5A if necessary, disconnect the starter motor solenoid wiring connections.

68 Release the retaining clip and disconnect the intercooler inlet hose.

69 Undo the retaining clips and disconnect the fuel feed and return hoses from the fuel pipes **(see illustration)**. Be prepared for fuel spillage.

70 Release the retaining clips and disconnect the following coolant hoses:

a) *Radiator top hose.*

b) *Heater coolant hoses as shown* **(see illustrations)**.

c) *Expansion tank hose from the coolant rail.*

71 On automatic transmission models, position a suitable container under the transmission fluid cooler hose connections on the radiator, release the retaining clips, and disconnect the hose.

72 Unscrew the bolt securing the power steering pipe clip to the engine lifting eye.

73 Disconnect the hose from the vacuum pump.

74 Note their fitted locations, then disconnect both hoses from the vacuum reservoir, and the EGR solenoid valve **(see illustrations)**.

75 Slacken and remove the bolt securing the lower tie rod to the rear crossmember.

76 Unscrew the two bolts each side securing the anti-roll bar saddle clamps to the crossmember.

77 Slacken the nuts (one each side) securing the mounting bushes to the lower arm **(see illustration)**.

78 Remove the two bolts each side securing the lower arm rear bush housings to the crossmember, and the pivot bolt at the front of each lower arm. Manoeuvre the lower arms from the crossmember.

79 Position a trolley jack under the rear crossmember at the rear of the engine compartment, remove the one bolt each side securing the crossmember to the body **(see illustration)**. With the help of an assistant, lower the crossmember and remove it from under the vehicle.

80 Refer to Chapter 8, and remove both driveshafts.

81 Remove the exhaust front pipe (see Chapter 4B).

82 Using a marker pen or similar, mark the relationship of the propeller shaft to the IRD output flange. Unscrew the six nuts and bolts, and move the propeller shaft to one side **(see illustration 4.5)**.

5.70a Disconnect the heater coolant hoses here . . .

5.70b . . . and here

5.74a Disconnect the hoses from the vacuum reservoir . . .

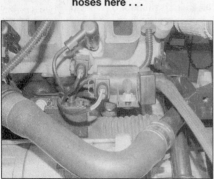

5.74b . . . and the EGR solenoid valve

5.77 Slacken the nuts (one each side) securing the mounting bushes to the lower arm

5.79 Subframe front mounting bolt

83 Carefully prise the gearchange rods from the selector levers – manual transmission only **(see illustration)**.

84 Undo the two bolts securing the gearchange linkage to the engine compartment bulkhead, and tie the linkage to one side – manual transmission only.

85 On models with air conditioning, slacken the compressor drivebelt tensioner pivot and clamp bolts, and remove the drivebelt. Slacken the air conditioning compressor support bracket-to-bolts, but do not remove. Remove the three bolts securing the coolant rail to the sump and cylinder block, then remove the retaining bolts and tie the compressor to one side. Do **not** disconnect the refrigerant pipes.

86 Attach lifting chains/straps to the engine lifting brackets and, with an engine crane or hoist, take the weight of the engine and transmission.

87 Slacken and remove the bolt securing the upper tie rod to the engine mounting. Slacken the tie rod rear bolt, and pivot the tie rod away from the engine.

88 Remove the auxiliary drivebelt, as described in Chapter 1B, unscrew the three retaining screws and remove the power steering pump pulley. Remove the four bolts securing the power steering pump mounting brackets to the engine, and position the pump to one side.

89 Undo the nut and bolts securing the right-hand engine mounting arm to the Hydramount and the engine, and remove the arm.

90 Unclip the fuel cooler hoses from the retaining clips.

91 Unscrew the left-hand engine mounting through-bolt, and the four bolts securing the mounting to the body **(see illustration)**.

92 Make a final check that any components which would prevent the removal of the engine/transmission from the vehicle have been removed or disconnected and, with the help of an assistant, lower the assembly and manoeuvre the engine and transmission down and out of the engine compartment. Ensure that the turbocharger pipe does not foul the gear linkage on the engine compartment bulkhead.

Separation

93 With the engine/transmission assembly removed, support the assembly on suitable blocks of wood, on a workbench (or failing that, on a clean area of the workshop floor).

94 Disconnect the electrical wiring (where necessary), undo the retaining bolts and remove the starter motor (see Chapter 5A).

95 Unscrew the retaining bolts, and remove the support bracket between the IRD unit, and the engine **(see illustration)**.

96 Slacken and remove the four securing bolts, and separate the IRD unit from the transmission **(see illustration)**. Discard the IRD unit input shaft O-ring, a new one must be fitted.

97 Remove the bolt securing the coolant and fuel rails to the gearbox adaptor plate.

5.83 Carefully prise the gearchange rods from the selector levers

98 On automatic transmission models, remove the grommet from the gearbox adaptor plate, to gain access to the torque converter bolts. Mark the relationship of the torque converter to the driveplate, and remove the four bolts, rotating the crankshaft to align the bolts with the aperture as necessary.

99 Ensure that both engine and transmission are adequately supported, then slacken and remove the remaining bolts securing the transmission to the adaptor plate on the engine. Note the correct fitted positions of each bolt (and the relevant brackets) as they are removed, to use as a reference on refitting.

100 Carefully withdraw the transmission from the engine, ensuring that the weight of the transmission is not allowed to hang on the input shaft while it is engaged with the clutch friction disc (manual transmission models), or making sure that the torque converter remains on the transmission input shaft (automatic transmission models).

101 If they are loose, remove the locating dowels from the engine or transmission, and keep them in a safe place.

Refitting

102 If the engine and transmission have been separated, perform the operations described below in paragraphs 103 to 108. If not, proceed as described from paragraph 109 onwards.

103 On manual transmission models, referring to Chapter 6, apply a smear of molybdenum disulphide grease to the clutch release bearing, fork and guide sleeve contact

5.95 Unscrew the retaining bolts, and remove the IRD unit support bracket

5.91 Unscrew the left-hand engine mounting through-bolt

surfaces and check the operation of the clutch release mechanism. Also apply a smear of grease to the transmission input shaft splines; **do not** apply too much grease otherwise the clutch friction disc may be contaminated.

104 Ensure the locating dowels are correctly positioned then carefully offer the transmission to the engine, until the locating dowels are engaged. Ensure that the weight of the transmission is not allowed to hang on the input shaft as it is engaged with the clutch friction disc.

105 Refit the transmission housing-to-adaptor plate bolts, ensuring that all the necessary brackets are correctly positioned, and tighten them to the specified torque setting.

106 On automatic transmission models, align the torque converter with the holes in the driveplate, and tighten the retaining bolts to the specified torque (see Chapter 7B). Rotate the crankshaft as necessary to align the bolts holes with the aperture in the gearbox adaptor plate.

107 With a new O-ring, refit the IRD unit to the gearbox. Tighten the bolts to the specified torque.

108 Position the support bracket between the IRD unit and the engine, refit the bolts and tighten them to the specified torque.

109 Refit the starter motor and tighten its mounting bolts to the specified torque (see Chapter 5A). Reconnect the starter motor electrical wiring.

110 Reconnect the hoist and lifting tackle to the engine lifting brackets.

111 With the aid of an assistant, carefully lift the assembly into position in the engine

5.96 Slacken and remove the IRD unit retaining bolts – two at the top, and two underneath

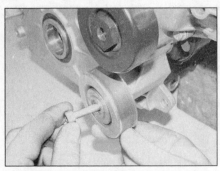

7.5 Undo the Allen bolt, and remove the auxiliary drivebelt idler pulley

7.6a Slacken and remove the retaining nut, and remove the auxiliary drivebelt tensioner arm . . .

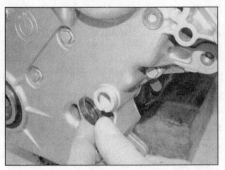

7.6b . . . and discard the seal – a new one must be fitted

compartment, manipulating the hoist and lifting tackle as necessary, taking great care not to trap any components.

112 Refit the left-hand engine/transmission mounting to the body, tighten the bolts to the specified torque.

113 Align the engine/transmission with the left-hand mounting bracket and screw in the mounting through-bolt.

114 Refit the right-hand mounting bracket to the engine and mounting, align the upper tie rod with the bracket, and refit the power steering hose support bracket to the engine mounting stud. Tighten all of the engine mounting bolts to the specified torque.

115 Remove the lifting chains and brackets.

116 The remainder of the refitting procedure is a direct reversal of the removal sequence, noting the following points:

a) Ensure that all wiring is correctly routed and retained by all the relevant retaining clips and that all connectors are correctly and securely reconnected.

b) Ensure that all disturbed hoses are correctly reconnected, and securely retained by their retaining clips.

c) Refit the gearchange rod to the shaft using a new roll-pin.

d) Renew the transmission differential oil seals (see the relevant part of Chapter 7) before refitting the driveshafts.

e) Refill the transmission and IRD unit with correct quantity and type of oil, as described in the relevant part of Chapter 7. If the oil was not drained, top-up the level as described in Chapter 1B.

f) Refill the engine with oil as described in Chapter 1B and also refill the cooling system.

6 Engine overhaul – dismantling sequence

1 It is much easier to dismantle and work on the engine if it is mounted on a portable engine stand. These stands can often be hired from a tool hire shop. Before the engine is mounted on a stand, the flywheel/driveplate should be removed, so that the stand bolts can be tightened into the end of the cylinder block.

2 If a stand is not available, it is possible to

dismantle the engine with it blocked up on a sturdy workbench, or on the floor. Be extra careful not to tip or drop the engine when working without a stand.

3 If you are going to obtain a reconditioned engine, all the external components must be removed first, to be transferred to the new engine (just as they will if you are doing a complete engine overhaul yourself). These components include the following:

a) Inlet and exhaust manifolds (the relevant part of Chapter 4).

b) Alternator/power steering pump/air conditioning compressor bracket(s) (as applicable).

c) Coolant pump (Chapter 3).

d) Fuel system components (the relevant part of Chapter 4).

e) Wiring harness and all electrical switches and sensors.

f) Oil filter (the relevant part of Chapter 1).

g) Flywheel (relevant Part of this Chapter).

h) Transmission mounting plate – L-Series engine.

Note: When removing the external components from the engine, pay close attention to details that may be helpful or important during refitting. Note the fitted position of gaskets, seals, spacers, pins, washers, bolts, and other small items.

4 If you are obtaining a 'short' engine (which consists of the engine cylinder block, crankshaft, pistons and connecting rods all assembled), then the cylinder head, sump, oil pump, and timing belt/chains (as applicable) will have to be removed also.

5 If you are planning a complete overhaul, the engine can be dismantled, and the internal

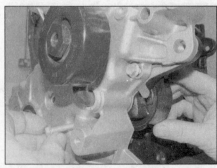

7.8 The removal of the timing cover bolts will release the auxiliary drivebelt tensioner

components removed, in the order given below, referring to the relevant Part of this Chapter unless otherwise stated.

a) Inlet and exhaust manifolds (the relevant part of Chapter 4).

b) Timing belt, sprockets and tensioner.

c) Fuel injection pump belt, sprockets and tensioner – L-Series engine only.

d) Cylinder head.

e) Flywheel.

f) Sump.

g) Oil pump.

h) Timing chains and sprockets – TD4 engine only.

i) Piston/connecting rod assemblies.

j) Crankshaft.

k) Transmission mounting plate – L-Series engine.

6 Before beginning the dismantling and overhaul procedures, make sure that you have all of the correct tools necessary. Refer to the Tools and working facilities Section of this manual for further information.

7 Timing chain cover – removal and refitting (TD4 engine)

Removal

1 Refer to Section 7 of Chapter 2C, and remove the cylinder head.

2 Remove the oil pump as described in Section 9 of Chapter 2C.

3 With reference to Chapter 5A, remove the alternator.

4 Remove the crankshaft pulley as described in Section 5 of Chapter 2C.

5 Undo the Allen bolt, and remove the auxiliary drivebelt idler pulley from the timing cover **(see illustration)**.

6 Slacken and remove the retaining nut, and remove the auxiliary drivebelt tensioner arm from the spring housing. Discard the seal, a new one must be fitted **(see illustrations)**.

7 Undo the two retaining bolts and remove the lower coolant rail support bracket from the timing cover.

8 The timing cover is held by fourteen bolts. Undo the bolts and remove the timing cover. The removal of the bolts will release the auxiliary drivebelt tensioner **(see illustration)**.

9 In order to remove the old gasket and fit the new one, the fuel injection pump drive chain, tensioner and sprocket, and crankshaft sprocket must be removed as described in Section 8 of this Chapter.

10 Undo the retaining bolt and remove the chain lubrication jet **(see illustration)**. Discard the oil seal, a new one must be used.

11 Remove the timing cover gasket.

Refitting

12 Prior to refitting the timing cover, prise out the old crankshaft oil seal, and drive a new one into the cover, using a suitable tubular drift or socket **(see illustrations)**.

13 Ensure that the mating faces of the timing cover and engine block are clean and dry, and fit the new timing cover gasket to the engine block **(see illustration)**.

14 Check to make sure the mating faces are clean, then refit the chain lubrication jet (with the new seal in place), tightening the retaining bolt to the specified torque.

15 Refit the fuel pump drive chain, sprocket, crankshaft sprocket and tensioner as described in Section 8.

16 Fit the camshaft drive chain to the fuel pump sprocket.

17 Position the timing cover in place against the engine block, and temporarily fit the auxiliary drivebelt tensioner pulley arm to align the tensioner.

18 Evenly and progressively tighten the timing cover retaining bolts to the specified torque.

19 Remove the auxiliary drivebelt tensioner

7.10 Undo the retaining bolt and remove the chain lubrication jet

7.12b . . . and drive the seal in until it is flush with the cover

pulley arm, fit the new seal, refit the arm and tighten the retaining nut to the specified torque **(see illustration 7.6b)**.

20 Fit the auxiliary drivebelt idler pulley, and tighten the Allen bolt to the specified torque.

7.12a Use the seal protector supplied with the new seal . . .

7.13 Fit the new timing cover gasket to the engine block

21 Carry out the following operations:
  a) *Refit the alternator (Chapter 5A).*
  b) *Refit the oil pump (Chapter 2C).*
  c) *Refit the crankshaft pulley (Chapter 2C).*
  d) *Refit the cylinder head (Chapter 2C).*
  e) *Refit the air conditioning and auxiliary drivebelts (Chapter 1B).*

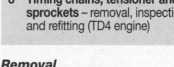

8 Timing chains, tensioner and sprockets – removal, inspection and refitting (TD4 engine)

Removal

Camshaft timing chain

1 Remove the timing chain cover as described in Section 7 of this Chapter.

2 Disengage the timing chain from the fuel pump sprocket.

Timing chains tensioner and guides

3 Remove the timing chain cover as described in Section 7 of this Chapter.

4 Press the lower chain tensioner plunger fully into the tensioner body, and insert Land Rover tool LRT-12-172 into the body to lock the plunger in place. If the tool is not available, a 4 mm drill bit or rod will make a suitable substitute **(see illustration)**.

5 Undo the three bolts and remove the tensioner from the engine block **(see illustration)**.

6 Slide the rear chain guide from the its locating pin. Undo the Allen bolt and remove the front chain guide from its locating pin **(see illustrations)**. Discard the Allen bolt, a new one must be fitted.

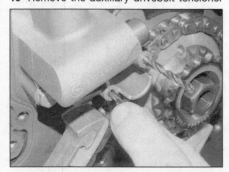

8.4 Push the lower plunger into the tensioner body, and if the Land Rover tool is not available, insert a 4 mm drill bit to lock the plunger in place

8.5 Undo the three bolts (arrowed) and remove the tensioner from the engine block

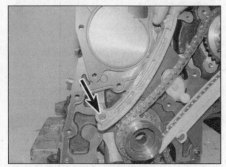

8.6a Slide the rear chain guide from the its locating pin (arrowed)

8.6b Undo the Allen bolt and lift the front chain guide from its locating pin

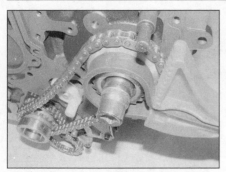

8.10 Use a strap wrench (or similar) to prevent the fuel pump sprocket from rotating

8.11 Using a suitable two- or three-legged puller, remove the fuel injection pump sprocket

8.20 The oil pump chain is fitted to the inside row of teeth on the crankshaft sprocket, and the drive chain is fitted to the inside row of teeth on the fuel injection pump sprocket

Fuel injection pump sprocket, crankshaft sprocket and drive chain

7 Remove the timing chain cover as described in Section 7 of this Chapter.

8 Disengage the camshaft timing chain from the fuel injection pump sprocket.

9 As described in paragraphs 4 to 6 of this Section, remove the chain tensioner and guides.

10 Undo the fuel injection pump central retaining nut. Use a strap wrench (or similar) to prevent the sprocket from rotating **(see illustration)**.

11 Using a suitable two- or three-legged puller, remove the fuel injection pump sprocket from the pump shaft **(see illustration)**.

12 As the fuel pump sprocket is withdrawn, slide the sprocket from the crankshaft. Recover the key from the crankshaft if it is loose. Disengage the sprockets from the chains.

13 Undo the retaining bolt, and remove the chain lubrication jet.

Inspection

14 Examine the teeth on the camshafts, fuel injection pump and crankshaft sprockets for any sign of wear or damage such as chipped or hooked teeth. If there is any sign of wear or damage on either sprocket, *all* sprockets and timing chains should be renewed as a set.

15 Inspect the links of the timing chains for signs of wear or damage on the rollers. The extent of wear can be judged by checking the amount by which the chain can be bent sideways; a new chain will have very little

sideways movement. If there is an excessive amount of side play in either timing chain, it must be renewed.

16 Note that it is a sensible precaution to renew the timing chains, regardless of their apparent condition, if the engine has covered a high mileage, or if it has been noted that the chain(s) have sounded noisy with the engine running. Although not strictly necessary, it is always worth renewing the chains and sprockets as a matched set, since it is false economy to run a new chain on worn sprockets and *vice-versa*. If there is any doubt about the condition of the timing chains and sprockets, seek the advice of a Land Rover dealer service department, who will be able to advise you as to the best course of action, based on their previous knowledge of the engine.

17 Examine the chain guides for signs of wear or damage to their chain contact faces, renewing any which are badly marked.

Refitting

18 Remove the remains of the timing cover gasket from the engine block, and ensure the mating surfaces of the block and timing cover are clean and dry.

19 Position the new timing cover gasket on the engine block, and refit the chain lubrication jet (with a new O-ring seal), tightening its retaining bolt to the specified torque.

20 Engage the crankshaft and fuel injection pump sprockets with the oil pump and fuel injection pump drive chains. The oil pump chain is fitted to the inside row of teeth on

the crankshaft sprocket, and the drive chain is fitted to the inside row of teeth on the fuel injection pump sprocket **(see illustration)**. **Note:** *Due to the common rail design of the fuel injection system, there is no need to 'time' the fuel injection pump to the crankshaft position.*

21 Align the keyway in the crankshaft sprocket with the key in the crankshaft, and slide the sprocket onto the crankshaft. Fit the sprocket to the fuel injection pump at the same time **(see illustration)**.

22 Tighten the fuel injection pump sprocket retaining nut to the specified torque, using a strap wrench (or similar) to prevent the sprocket from rotating **(see illustration)**.

23 Fit the front chain guide to the locating pin, and tighten the new Allen bolt to the specified torque **(see illustration 8.6b)**.

24 Refit the rear chain guide to its locating pin **(see illustration 8.6a)**.

25 Ensure that the tensioner body mating surface and oilways are clean, and fit the tensioner to the engine block, tightening the retaining bolts to the specified torque.

26 Press the lower tensioner plunger into tensioner body, and withdraw the locking tool/rod/drill bit (as applicable).

27 Engage the camshaft drive chain with the fuel injection pump sprocket.

28 Refit the timing chain cover as described in Section 7 of this Chapter.

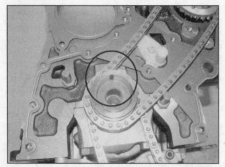

8.21 Align the keyway in the crankshaft sprocket with the key in the crankshaft

8.22 Tighten the fuel injection pump sprocket retaining nut to the specified torque

9 Cylinder head – dismantling

Note: *New and reconditioned cylinder heads are available from the manufacturer, and from engine overhaul specialists. Be aware that some specialist tools are required for the dismantling and inspection procedures, and new components may not be readily available. It may therefore be more practical and economical for the home mechanic to purchase a reconditioned head, rather than dismantle, inspect and recondition the original head.*

1 On petrol engines, referring to Part A of this

9.3a Use a valve spring compressor to compress a valve spring

9.3b Carefully remove the stem oil seal from the valve guide

If the components are to be refitted, place each valve and its associated components in a labelled polythene bag or similar small container, and mark the bag/container with the relevant valve number to ensure that it is refitted in its original location.

Chapter (as applicable), remove the camshafts rockers and tappets, and followers, then remove the cylinder head from the engine. Remove the spark plugs (see Chapter 1A).

2 On diesel engines, remove the glow plugs (Chapter 5C) and injectors (Chapter 4B). Remove the camshaft(s) and followers from the cylinder head then remove the cylinder head from the engine as described in Part B or C of this Chapter.

3 On all engines, using a valve spring compressor, compress each valve spring in turn until the split collets can be removed. Release the compressor, and lift off the spring retainer and spring. Using a pair of pliers, carefully extract the valve stem seal from the valve guide (see illustrations).

4 If, when the valve spring compressor is screwed down, the spring retainer refuses to free and expose the split collets, gently tap the top of the tool, directly over the retainer, with a light hammer. This will free the retainer.

5 Withdraw the valve through the combustion chamber. It is essential that each valve is stored together with its collets, retainer and spring. The valves should also be kept in their correct sequence, unless they are so badly worn that they are to be renewed (see Haynes Hint).

10 Cylinder head and valves – cleaning and inspection

1 Thorough cleaning of the cylinder head and valve components, followed by a detailed

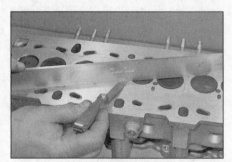

10.6 Use a straight-edge and feeler blade to check the cylinder head surface for distortion

inspection, will enable you to decide how much valve service work must be carried out during the engine overhaul. **Note:** *If the engine has been severely overheated, it is best to assume that the cylinder head is warped – check carefully for signs of this.*

Cleaning

2 Scrape away all traces of old gasket material from the cylinder head.

3 Scrape away the carbon from the combustion chambers and ports, then wash the cylinder head thoroughly with paraffin or a suitable solvent.

4 Scrape off any heavy carbon deposits that may have formed on the valves, then use a power-operated wire brush to remove deposits from the valve heads and stems.

Inspection

Note: *Be sure to perform all the following inspection procedures before concluding that the services of a machine shop or engine overhaul specialist are required. Make a list of all items that require attention.*

Cylinder head

5 Inspect the head very carefully for cracks, evidence of coolant leakage, and other damage. If cracks are found, a new cylinder head should be obtained.

6 Use a straight-edge and feeler blade to check that the cylinder head surface is not

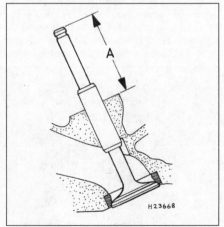

10.8a Valve stem installed height measurement (A) – petrol engine

distorted (see illustration). If it is, it may be possible to resurface it (petrol engine only), provided that the cylinder head is not reduced to less than the minimum specified height.

7 Examine the valve seats in each of the combustion chambers. If they are severely pitted, cracked or burned, then they will need to be renewed or recut by an engine overhaul specialist (petrol and L-Series diesel engines only). If they are only slightly pitted, this can be removed by grinding-in the valve heads and seats with fine valve-grinding compound, as described below.

8 Check valve seat wear by inserting each valve into its relevant guide. On petrol engines, measure the projected height of the valve stem above the cylinder head surface and, on diesel engines, using a straight-edge and feeler blades, measure the valve head recess from the cylinder head mating surface (see illustrations). If any measurement exceeds the specified limit, repeat the check with a new valve. If the measurement still exceeds the specified limit, then the valve seat is excessively worn and must be renewed. The valve seats can only be renewed on petrol and L-Series diesel engines, on TD4 engines the cylinder head must be renewed.

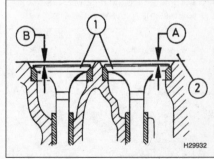

10.8b Valve head recess measurement – diesel engine

1 Valves   A Inlet valve
2 Straight edge   B Exhaust valve

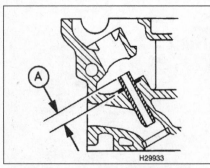

10.10a Valve guide installed height measurement (A) – petrol engine

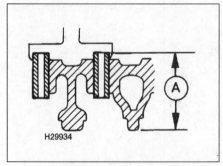

10.10b Valve guide installed height measurement (A) – L-Series diesel engine

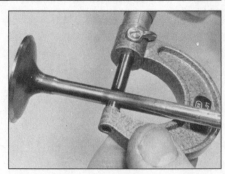

10.13 Use a micrometer to measure the valve stem diameter

9 If the valve guides are worn (indicated by a side-to-side motion of the valve, and accompanied by excessive blue smoke in the exhaust when running) new guides must be fitted. Measure the diameter of the existing valve stems (see below) and the bore of the guides, then calculate the clearance and compare the result with the specified value. If the clearance is not within the specified limits, renew the valves and/or guides as necessary. The valve guides can only be renewed on petrol and L-Series diesel engines, on TD4 engines the cylinder head must be renewed.

10 The renewal of valve guides is best carried out by an engine overhaul specialist. If the work is to be carried out at home, however, on petrol engines, use a stepped, double-diameter drift to drive out the worn guide towards the combustion chamber. Drive the guide into position until it projects the specified amount above the cylinder head surface. On diesel engines, heat the cylinder head up to 120°C, use a stepped double-diameter drift to drive our the worn guide towards the combustion chamber. When fitting the new guide, reheat the cylinder head to 120°C, and position the guide so its upper surface is the specified distance above the cylinder head lower mating surface **(see illustrations)**. On L-Series diesel engines, the valve guides can only be renewed twice. When a guide is renewed the first time, the mark '+' should be stamped next to the guide on the camshaft side of the cylinder head. The second time a guide is renewed, the mark '-' should be stamped in the same area.

HAYNES HiNT *On fitting the new guide, place it first in a deep-freeze for one hour, then drive it into its cylinder head bore from the camshaft side.*

11 If the valve seats are to be recut this must be done only after the guides have been renewed.

Valves

12 Examine the head of each valve for pitting, burning, cracks and general wear, and check the valve stem for scoring and wear ridges. Rotate the valve, and check for any obvious indication that it is bent. Look for pitting and excessive wear on the tip of each valve stem. Renew any valve that shows any such signs of wear or damage.

13 If the valve appears satisfactory at this stage, measure the valve stem diameter at several points using a micrometer **(see illustration)**. Any significant difference in the readings obtained indicates wear of the valve stem. Should any of these conditions be apparent, the valve(s) must be renewed.

14 If the valves are in satisfactory condition, they should be ground (lapped) into their respective seats, to ensure a smooth gas-tight seal. If the seat is only lightly pitted, or if it has been recut, fine grinding compound **only** should be used to produce the required finish. Coarse valve-grinding compound should **not** be used unless a seat is badly burned or deeply pitted; if this is the case, the cylinder head and valves should be inspected by an

expert to decide whether seat recutting, or even the renewal of the valve or seat insert, is required.

15 Valve grinding is carried out as follows. Place the cylinder head upside-down on a bench.

16 Smear a trace of the appropriate grade of valve-grinding compound on the seat face, and press a suction grinding tool onto the valve head. With a semi-rotary action, grind the valve head to its seat, lifting the valve occasionally to redistribute the grinding compound **(see illustration)**. A light spring placed under the valve head will greatly ease this operation.

17 If coarse grinding compound is being used, work only until a dull, matt even surface is produced on both the valve seat and the valve, then wipe off the used compound and repeat the process with fine compound. When a smooth unbroken ring of light grey matt finish is produced on both the valve and seat, the grinding operation is complete. **Do not** grind in the valves any further than absolutely necessary, or the seat will be prematurely sunk into the cylinder head.

18 When all the valves have been ground-in, carefully wash off all traces of grinding compound using paraffin or a suitable solvent before reassembly of the cylinder head.

Valve components

19 Examine the valve springs for signs of damage and discoloration. The condition of each spring can be judged by measuring its free length **(see illustration)**. Stand each spring on a flat surface, and check it for squareness. If any of the springs are less than the specified free length or are damaged or distorted, obtain a complete new set of springs.

11 Cylinder head –
reassembly

1 Lubricate the stems of the valves, and insert them into their original locations **(see illustration)**. If new valves are being fitted, insert them into the locations to which they have been ground.

2 Working on the first valve, fit the seal

10.16 Grinding-in a valve seat

10.19 Measure the valve spring free length

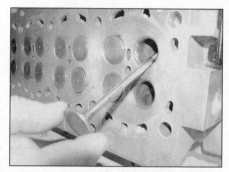

11.1 Insert the valves into their original locations

11.2a Where supplied, fit the seal protector over the valve stem . . .

11.2b . . . then locate the seal over the guide . . .

11.2c . . . and using a socket (or similar) press the seal into place

11.3a Fit the valve spring . . .

11.3b . . . followed by the retainer

protector (where supplied), dip the new valve stem seal in fresh engine oil, then carefully locate it over the valve and onto the guide. Take care not to damage the seal as it is passed over the valve stem. Use a suitable socket or metal tube to press the seal firmly onto the guide **(see illustrations)**.

3 Locate the spring over the seal and fit the spring retainer **(see illustrations)**.

4 Compress the valve spring, and locate the split collets in the recess in the valve stem **(see illustrations and Haynes Hint)**. Release the compressor, then repeat the procedure on the remaining valves.

5 With all the valves installed, using a hammer and interposed block of wood, lightly tap the end of each valve stem to settle the components.

6 On petrol engines, working as described in Part A, refit the cylinder head to the engine and install the followers and camshafts.

7 On diesel engines, working as described in Part B or C, refit the cylinder head to the engine and install the followers, rockers and tappets (TD4 engine only), and camshafts. Refit the injectors and glow plugs as described in Chapters 4B and 5C.

12 Piston/connecting rod assembly – removal

Petrol engine

Note: *Due to the design of the engine, it will become very difficult, almost impossible, to turn the crankshaft once the cylinder head bolts have been slackened. The manufacturer accordingly states that the crankshaft will be 'tight' and should not be rotated more than absolutely necessary once the head has been removed. If the crankshaft cannot be rotated,*

then it must be removed for overhaul work to proceed. With this in mind, during any servicing or overhaul work the crankshaft must always be rotated to the desired position before the bolts are disturbed.

1 Remove the camshafts and followers then remove the sump and oil pump pick-up/strainer as described in Part A of this Chapter.

2 Rotate the crankshaft until Nos 1 and 4 cylinder pistons are at the top of their stroke then remove the cylinder head and clamp the liners securely in position as described in Part A. The crankshaft should not be rotated once the head has been removed **(see illustration)**.

3 Slacken and remove the dipstick tube retaining bolts and remove the tube from the cylinder block/crankcase.

4 Unscrew the two retaining nuts and remove

11.4a Compress the valve spring and retainer . . .

11.4b . . . and locate the collets in position

HAYNES HINT

Use a dab of grease to hold the collets in position on the valve stem whilst the spring compressor is released.

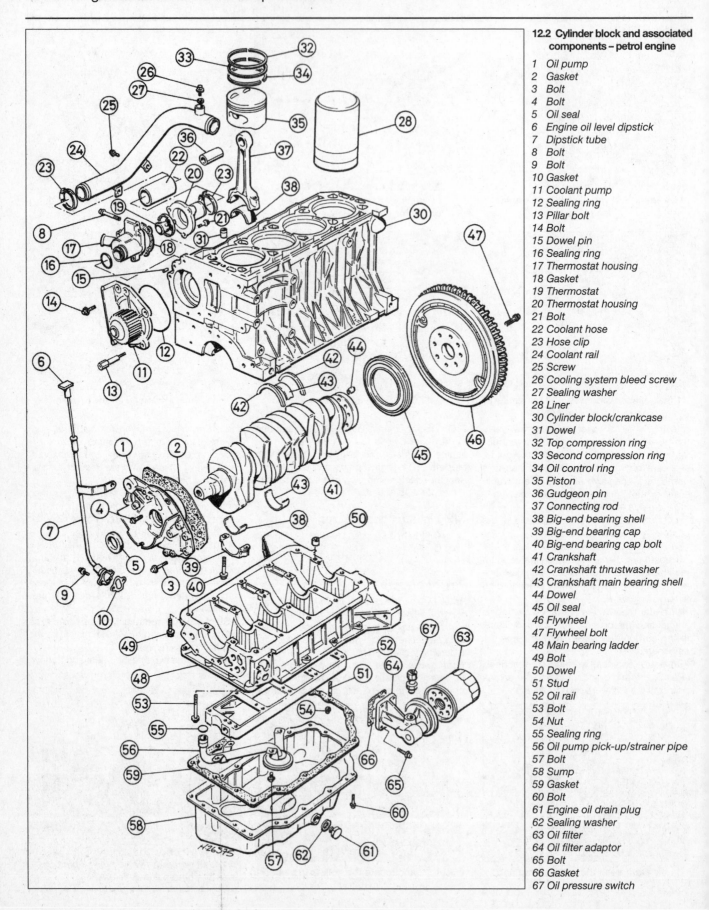

12.2 Cylinder block and associated components – petrol engine

1 Oil pump
2 Gasket
3 Bolt
4 Bolt
5 Oil seal
6 Engine oil level dipstick
7 Dipstick tube
8 Bolt
9 Bolt
10 Gasket
11 Coolant pump
12 Sealing ring
13 Pillar bolt
14 Bolt
15 Dowel pin
16 Sealing ring
17 Thermostat housing
18 Gasket
19 Thermostat
20 Thermostat housing
21 Bolt
22 Coolant hose
23 Hose clip
24 Coolant rail
25 Screw
26 Cooling system bleed screw
27 Sealing washer
28 Liner
30 Cylinder block/crankcase
31 Dowel
32 Top compression ring
33 Second compression ring
34 Oil control ring
35 Piston
36 Gudgeon pin
37 Connecting rod
38 Big-end bearing shell
39 Big-end bearing cap
40 Big-end bearing cap bolt
41 Crankshaft
42 Crankshaft thrustwasher
43 Crankshaft main bearing shell
44 Dowel
45 Oil seal
46 Flywheel
47 Flywheel bolt
48 Main bearing ladder
49 Bolt
50 Dowel
51 Stud
52 Oil rail
53 Bolt
54 Nut
55 Sealing ring
56 Oil pump pick-up/strainer pipe
57 Bolt
58 Sump
59 Gasket
60 Bolt
61 Engine oil drain plug
62 Sealing washer
63 Oil filter
64 Oil filter adaptor
65 Bolt
66 Gasket
67 Oil pressure switch

H26375

12.4 Remove the oil rail from the base of the main bearing ladder

12.5 Mark each connecting rod big-end bearing cap with its respective cylinder number prior to removal

12.12 Make identification markings (arrowed) on each connecting rod and bearing cap prior to removal

the oil rail from the base of the main bearing ladder **(see illustration)**.

5 Using a hammer and centre punch, paint or similar, mark each connecting rod big-end bearing cap with its respective cylinder number on the flat, machined surface provided **(see illustration)**. If the engine has been dismantled before, note carefully any identifying marks made previously. Note that No 1 cylinder is at the timing belt end of the engine.

6 Unscrew and remove the big-end bearing cap bolts and withdraw the cap, complete with bearing shell, from the connecting rod. If only the bearing shells are being attended to, push the connecting rod up and off the crankpin, ensuring that the connecting rod big-ends do not mark the cylinder bore walls, then remove the upper bearing shell. Keep the cap, bolts and (if they are to be refitted) the bearing shells together in their correct sequence.

7 With Nos 2 and 3 cylinder big-ends disconnected, repeat the procedure (exercising great care to prevent damage to any of the components) to remove Nos 1 and 4 cylinder bearing caps.

8 Remove the ridge of carbon from the top of each cylinder bore. Push each piston/connecting rod assembly up and remove it from the top of the bore, and ensure that the connecting rod big-ends do not mark the cylinder bore walls.

9 Note that the number stamped by you on each bearing cap should match the cylinder number stamped on the front of each connecting rod (the letter on the rod is the weight code and the number on the front of bearing cap is the big-end bore size code). If

any connecting rod number does not match its correct cylinder, mark or label it immediately so that each piston/connecting rod assembly can be refitted to its original bore. Fit the bearing cap, shells and bolts to each removed piston/connecting rod assembly, so that they are all kept together as a matched set.

L-Series diesel engine

10 Referring to Part B of this Chapter (as applicable), remove the cylinder head and sump then unbolt the pick-up/strainer from the base of the cylinder block.

11 If there is a pronounced wear ridge at the top of any bore, it may be necessary to remove it with a scraper or ridge reamer, to avoid piston damage during removal. Such a ridge indicates excessive wear of the cylinder bore.

12 Using a hammer and centre-punch, paint or similar, mark each connecting rod and its bearing cap with its respective cylinder number on the flat machined surface provided; make the marks in such a way that there is no possibility in fitting the caps the wrong way around on refitting **(see illustration)**. If the engine has been dismantled before, note carefully any identifying marks made previously. Note that No 1 cylinder is at the timing belt end of the engine.

13 Turn the crankshaft to bring pistons 1 and 4 to BDC (bottom dead centre).

14 Unscrew the nuts/bolts (as applicable) from No 1 piston big-end bearing cap. Take off the cap and recover the bottom half bearing shell. If the bearing shells are to be re-used, tape the cap and the shell together.

Caution: On some engines, the connecting

rod/bearing cap mating surfaces are not machined flat; the big-end bearing caps are 'cracked' (a process known as fracture-split) off from the rod during production and left untouched to ensure the cap and rod mate perfectly. Where this type of connecting rod is fitted, great care must be taken to ensure the mating surfaces of the cap and rod are not marked or damaged in anyway. Any damage to the mating surfaces will adversely affect the strength of the connecting rod and could lead to premature failure.

15 Using a hammer handle, push the piston up through the bore, and remove it from the top of the cylinder block. Recover the bearing shell, and tape it to the connecting rod for safe-keeping.

16 Loosely refit the big-end cap to the connecting rod, and secure with the nuts/bolts – this will help to keep the components in their correct order.

17 Remove No 4 piston assembly in the same way.

18 Turn the crankshaft through 180° to bring pistons 2 and 3 to BDC (bottom dead centre), and remove them in the same way **(see illustrations)**.

TD4 diesel engine

19 Referring to Part C of this Chapter, remove the cylinder head and sump then unbolt the pick-up/strainer and oil pump from the base of the cylinder block.

20 Unscrew the six retaining bolts, and remove the reinforcing plate from the cylinder block **(see illustration)**.

12.18a Slacken and remove the nuts ...

12.18b ... and remove the big-end bearing cap from the connecting rod

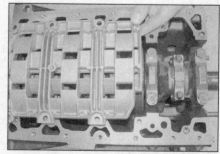

12.20 Unscrew the six retaining bolts, and remove the reinforcing plate from the cylinder block

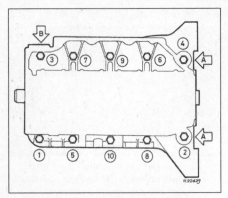

13.4a Main bearing ladder slackening sequence –petrol engine

A Bolts hidden in ladder flanges
B Location of longer bolt

21 If there is a pronounced wear ridge at the top of any bore, it may be necessary to remove it with a scraper or ridge reamer, to avoid piston damage during removal. Such a ridge indicates excessive wear of the cylinder bore.

22 Using a hammer and centre-punch, paint or similar, mark each connecting rod and its bearing cap with its respective cylinder number on the flat machined surface provided; make the marks in such a way that there is no possibility in fitting the caps the wrong way around on refitting. If the engine has been dismantled before, note carefully any identifying marks made previously. Note that No 1 cylinder is at the timing chain end of the engine.

23 Turn the crankshaft to bring pistons 1 and 4 to BDC (bottom dead centre).

24 Unscrew the nuts/bolts (as applicable) from No 1 piston big-end bearing cap. Take off the cap and recover the bottom half bearing shell. If the bearing shells are to be re-used, tape the cap and the shell together. **Note:** *The big-end caps are located on the connecting rods by dowels. Do not tap the caps sideways in an attempt to remove them.*

25 Using a hammer handle, push the piston up through the bore, and remove it from the top of the cylinder block. Recover the bearing shell, and tape it to the connecting rod for safe-keeping.

26 Loosely refit the big-end cap to the

13.6 Remove the crankshaft

13.4b Remove the main bearing ladder from the cylinder block noting the correct fitted locations of the dowels (arrowed)

connecting rod, and secure with the nuts/bolts – this will help to keep the components in their correct order.

27 Remove No 4 piston assembly in the same way.

28 Turn the crankshaft through 180° to bring pistons 2 and 3 to BDC (bottom dead centre), and remove them in the same way.

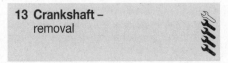

13 Crankshaft – removal

Petrol engine

1 Remove the cylinder head, sump, oil pump and flywheel as described in Part A of this Chapter.

2 Slacken and remove the dipstick tube retaining bolts and remove the tube from the cylinder block/crankcase.

3 Unscrew the two retaining nuts and remove the oil rail from the base of the main bearing ladder.

4 Working in sequence, progressively unscrew the main bearing ladder retaining bolts by a turn at a time, then withdraw the ladder. Note the two locating dowels and the main bearing shells, which should be removed from the ladder and stored in their correct fitted order **(see illustrations)**.

5 Remove the piston and connecting rod assemblies as described in Section 12 **(see illustration)**. If no work is to be done on the pistons and connecting rods, unbolt the caps and push the pistons far enough up the bores

13.13 Remove the main bearing caps noting the locating dowels (one arrowed)

13.5 Remove the No 1 cylinder big-end bearing cap and shell

so that the connecting rods are positioned clear of the crankshaft journals.

6 Check the crankshaft endfloat as described in Section 16, then remove the crankshaft **(see illustration)**.

7 Withdraw the two thrustwashers from the No 3 main bearing upper location. Noting the position of the grooved shells, remove the upper main bearing shells, which must be kept with their correct respective partners from the main bearing ladder so that all shells can be identified and (if necessary) refitted in their original locations.

L-Series diesel engine

8 Referring to Part B of this Chapter, remove the oil pump, flywheel and crankshaft left-hand oil seal housing.

9 Remove the piston and connecting rod assemblies as described in Section 12. If no work is to be done on the pistons and connecting rods, the cylinder head can be left in position then unbolt the caps and push the pistons far enough up the bores so that the connecting rods are positioned clear of the crankshaft journals.

10 Check the crankshaft endfloat as described in Section 16, then proceed as follows.

11 The main bearing caps should be numbered 1 to 5 from the timing belt end of the engine and the arrow on each cap should point towards the timing belt end of the engine. If the bearing caps are not marked, using a hammer and punch or a suitable marker pen, number the caps from 1 to 5 from the timing belt end of the engine and mark each cap to indicate its correct fitted direction to avoid confusion on refitting.
Caution: Do not mark the mating surfaces of number 1 and 5 bearing caps.

12 Working in a diagonal sequence, evenly and progressively slacken the ten main bearing cap retaining bolts by half a turn at a time until all bolts are loose. Remove all bolts, keeping them in the correct fitted order.

13 Carefully remove each cap from the cylinder block, noting the locating dowels, ensuring that the lower main bearing shell remains in position in the cap **(see illustration)**. Note that all lower main bearing shells are plain shells, whereas all upper shells are grooved.

14 Carefully lift out the crankshaft, taking care not to displace the upper main bearing shells.

15 Recover the upper bearing shells from the cylinder block and tape them to their respective caps for safe-keeping. Withdraw the two thrustwasher upper halves from the sides of the centre main bearing.

TD4 diesel engine

16 Referring to Part C of this Chapter, remove the oil pump, flywheel and crankshaft left-hand oil seal housing.

17 Remove the piston and connecting rod assemblies as described in Section 12. If no work is to be done on the pistons and connecting rods, the cylinder head can be left in position then unbolt the caps and push the pistons far enough up the bores so that the connecting rods are positioned clear of the crankshaft journals.

18 Check the crankshaft endfloat as described in Section 16, then proceed as follows.

19 The main bearing caps should be numbered 1 to 5 from the timing chain end of the engine and the arrow on each cap should point towards the timing chain end of the engine. If the bearing caps are not marked, using a hammer and punch or a suitable marker pen, number the caps from 1 to 5 from the timing chain end of the engine and mark each cap to indicate its correct fitted direction to avoid confusion on refitting.

20 Working in a diagonal sequence, evenly and progressively slacken the ten main bearing cap retaining bolts by half a turn at a time until all bolts are loose. Remove all bolts, keeping them in the correct fitted order.

21 Carefully remove each cap from the cylinder block, ensuring that the lower main bearing shell remains in position in the cap **(see illustration)**. Note the No 4 main bearing cap shell incorporates thrustwashers.

22 Carefully lift out the crankshaft, taking care not to displace the upper main bearing shells.

23 Recover the upper bearing shells from the cylinder block and tape them to their respective caps for safe-keeping. Note that the No 4 main bearing upper shell incorporates thrustwashers.

---

14 Cylinder block – cleaning and inspection

Cleaning

1 Remove all external components and electrical switches/sensors from the block. For complete cleaning, the core plugs should ideally be removed. Drill a small hole in the plugs, then insert a self-tapping screw into the hole. Pull out the plugs by pulling on the screw with a pair of grips, or by using a slide hammer.

2 On petrol engines, remove the liners as described in paragraph 13.

3 On diesel engines, undo the retaining bolt(s) and remove each piston oil jet spray tube from inside the cylinder block **(see illustrations)**. Discard the retaining bolts, new ones must be used on refitting.

4 On all engines, scrape all traces of gasket from the cylinder block/crankcase, and from the main bearing ladder/caps (as applicable), taking care not to damage the gasket/sealing surfaces.

5 Remove all oil gallery plugs (where fitted). The plugs are usually very tight – they may have to be drilled out, and the holes re-tapped. Use new plugs when the engine is reassembled.

6 If any of the castings are extremely dirty, all should be steam-cleaned.

7 After the castings are returned, clean all oil holes and oil galleries one more time. Flush all internal passages with warm water until the water runs clear. Dry thoroughly, and apply a light film of oil to all mating surfaces, to prevent rusting. Also oil the cylinder bores. If you have access to compressed air, use it to speed up the drying process, and to blow out all the oil holes and galleries.

⚠️ **Warning: Wear eye protection when using compressed air.**

8 If the castings are not very dirty, you can do an adequate cleaning job with hot (as hot as you can stand), soapy water and a stiff brush. Take plenty of time, and do a thorough job. Regardless of the cleaning method used, be sure to clean all oil holes and galleries very

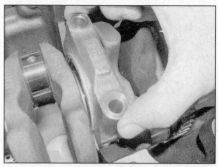

13.21 Carefully remove each cap from the cylinder block

thoroughly, and to dry all components well. Protect the cylinder bores as described above, to prevent rusting.

9 All threaded holes must be clean, to ensure accurate torque readings during reassembly. To clean the threads, run the correct-size tap into each of the holes to remove rust, corrosion, thread sealant or sludge, and to restore damaged threads. If possible, use compressed air to clear the holes of debris produced by this operation. A good alternative is to inject aerosol-applied water-dispersant lubricant into each hole, using the long spout usually supplied.

⚠️ **Warning: Wear eye protection when cleaning out these holes in this way.**

10 Apply suitable sealant to the new oil gallery plugs, and insert them into the holes in the block. Tighten them securely. Similarly, apply a suitable sealant to new core plugs and tap them into place with a close-fitting tube or socket.

11 On diesel engines, apply a drop of thread-locking compound to the threads of the oil jet spray tube new retaining bolts, ensuring that the bolt oil holes are not obstructed. Refit the piston oil jet spray tubes to the cylinder block, then fit the new retaining bolts, tightening them to the specified torque setting **(see illustration)**.

12 If the engine is not going to be reassembled right away, cover it with a large plastic bag to keep it clean; protect all mating surfaces and the cylinder bores as described above, to prevent rusting.

14.3a Unscrew the retaining bolts and remove the piston oil jet spray tubes – L-Series diesel engines . . .

14.3b . . . and TD4 diesel engines

14.11 Apply a drop of thread-locking compound to the threads of the oil jet spray tube new retaining bolts

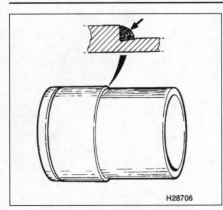

14.20 Apply a continuous bead of sealant (Land Rover part No STC 50552) approximately 2.0 mm thick around the locating shoulder on the liner

Inspection

Note: *On all engines, have the cylinder block inspected by an engine reconditioning specialist. They will be able to determine if the cylinder block is reusable, carry out any machining work, and supply the correct pistons, etc.*

Petrol engine

13 Remove the liner clamps (where used), then use a hard wood drift to tap out each liner from the inside of the cylinder block. When all the liners are released, tip the cylinder block/crankcase on its side and remove each liner from the top of the block. As each liner is removed, stick masking tape on its left-hand (flywheel side) face, and write the cylinder number on the tape. No 1 cylinder is at the timing belt end of the engine.

14 Check each cylinder liner for scuffing and scoring. Check for signs of a wear ridge at the top of the liner, indicating that the bore is excessively worn.

15 If the necessary measuring equipment is available, measure the bore diameter of each cylinder bore. The measurement should be taken 65 mm down from the top of the. Take two measurements, one parallel to the crankshaft axis and the other at right-angles to the crankshaft axis. Compare the results with the figures given in the Specifications.

14.21 Using a hammer and a block of wood, tap each liner lightly but fully onto its locating shoulder

16 If the liner wear exceeds the permitted tolerances at any point, or if the cylinder liner walls are badly scored or scuffed, then renewal of the relevant liner assembly will be necessary. If there is any doubt about the condition of the cylinder bores, seek the advice of a Land Rover dealer or engine reconditioning specialist. If the bores are in reasonably good condition and not worn to the specified limits, then the piston rings should be renewed, but according to Land Rover, the bores should **not** be honed.

17 If renewal is necessary, new liners can be purchased from a Land Rover dealer. New piston/connecting rod assemblies will also be required. Note that the pistons are only supplied as assemblies complete with the connecting rods.

18 To allow for manufacturing tolerances, pistons and liners are separated into two size groups. The size group of each piston is indicated by a letter (A or B) stamped onto its crown, and the size group of each liner is indicated by a paint marking; Red for size group A and Blue for size group B. Ensure that each piston and its respective liner are both of the same size group. It is permissible to have different size group piston and liner assemblies fitted to the same engine, but never fit a piston of one size group to a liner in a different group.

19 Prior to installing the liners, thoroughly clean the liner mating surfaces in the cylinder block, and use fine abrasive paper to polish away any burrs or sharp edges which hinder installation

20 Ensure the liner and block mating surfaces are clean and dry. Apply a continuous bead of sealant (Land Rover part No STC 50552) approximately 2.0 mm thick around the locating shoulder on the liner **(see illustration)**.

21 Carefully insert the liner squarely into the cylinder block and press it fully into position. If the original liners are being refitted, use the marks made on removal to ensure that each is refitted the correct way round, and is inserted into its original bore. Insert each liner into the cylinder block and press it home as far as possible by hand. Using a hammer and a block of wood, tap each liner lightly but fully onto its locating shoulder **(see illustration)**.

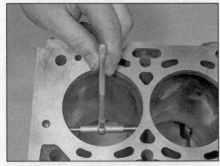

14.26 Use an internal micrometer to measure cylinder bore diameter

Wipe clean, then lightly oil, all exposed liner surfaces, to prevent rusting. If possible, clamp the liners in position.

22 Renew the cylinder head bolts, regardless of their apparent condition.

23 If any of the cylinder head bolt threads in the oil rail are found to be damaged, then the oil rail must be renewed, helicoils (thread inserts) are not an acceptable repair in this instance.

L-Series diesel engine

24 Visually check the castings for cracks and corrosion. Look for stripped threads in the threaded holes. If there has been any history of internal water leakage, it may be worthwhile having an engine overhaul specialist check the cylinder block/crankcase with special equipment. If defects are found, have them repaired if possible, or renew the assembly.

25 Check each cylinder bore for scuffing and scoring. Check for signs of a wear ridge at the top of the cylinder, indicating that the bore is excessively worn.

26 If the necessary measuring equipment is available, measure the bore diameter of each cylinder bore. The measurement should be taken 70 mm down from the top of the bore. Take two measurements, one parallel to the crankshaft axis and the other at right-angles to the crankshaft axis **(see illustration)**. Compare the results with the figures given in the Specifications.

27 At the time of writing, it was not clear whether oversize pistons were available. Consult your Land Rover dealer and/or engine reconditioning specialist for the latest information on piston availability. If oversize pistons are available, then it may be possible to have the cylinder bores rebored and fit the oversize pistons. If oversize pistons are not available, and the bores are worn, renewal of the block seems to be the only option. Seek the advice of a Land Rover dealer or engine reconditioning specialist on the best course of action.

28 If the bores are in reasonably good condition and not worn to the specified limits, then the piston rings should be renewed. If this is the case, the bores should be honed to allow the new rings to bed-in correctly and provide the best possible seal. The conventional type of hone has spring-loaded stones, and is used with a power drill. You will also need some paraffin (or honing oil) and rags. The hone should be moved up-and-down the bore to produce a crosshatch pattern, and plenty of honing oil should be used. Ideally, the crosshatch lines should intersect at approximately a 60° angle. Do not take off more material than is necessary to produce the required finish. If new pistons are being fitted, the piston manufacturers may specify a finish with a different angle, so their instructions should be followed. Do not withdraw the hone from the bore while it is still being turned – stop it first. After honing a bore, wipe out all traces of the honing oil.

If equipment of this type is not available, or if you are not sure whether you are competent to undertake the task yourself, an engine overhaul specialist will carry out the work at moderate cost.

TD4 diesel engine

29 Visually check the castings for cracks and corrosion. Look for stripped threads in the threaded holes. If there has been any history of internal water leakage, it may be worthwhile having an engine overhaul specialist check the cylinder block/crankcase with special equipment. If defects are found, have them repaired if possible, or renew the assembly.

30 Check each cylinder bore for scuffing and scoring. Check for signs of a wear ridge at the top of the cylinder, indicating that the bore is excessively worn.

31 If the necessary measuring equipment is available, measure the bore diameter of each cylinder bore. The measurement should be taken 70 mm down from the top of the bore. Take two measurements, one parallel to the crankshaft axis and the other at right-angles to the crankshaft axis (see illustration 14.26). Compare the results with the figures given in the Specifications.

32 Oversize pistons are available, and it should be possible to have the cylinder block rebored and fit the oversize pistons. Seek the advice of a Land Rover dealer or engine reconditioning specialist on the best course of action.

33 If the bores are in reasonably good condition and not worn to the specified limits, then the piston rings should be renewed. If this is the case, the bores should be honed to allow the new rings to bed-in correctly and provide the best possible seal. The conventional type of hone has spring-loaded stones, and is used with a power drill. You will also need some paraffin (or honing oil) and rags. The hone should be moved up-and-down the bore to produce a crosshatch pattern, and plenty of honing oil should be used. Ideally, the crosshatch lines should intersect at approximately a 60° angle. Do not take off more material than is necessary to produce the required finish. If new pistons are being fitted, the piston manufacturers may specify a finish with a different angle, so their instructions should be followed. Do not withdraw the hone from the bore while it is still being turned – stop it first. After honing a bore, wipe out all traces of the honing oil. If equipment of this type is not available, or if you are not sure whether you are competent to undertake the task yourself, an engine overhaul specialist will carry out the work at moderate cost.

15 Piston/connecting rod assembly – inspection

1 Before the inspection process can begin, the piston/connecting rod assemblies must be cleaned, and the original piston rings removed from the pistons.

2 Carefully expand the old rings over the top of the pistons. The use of two or three old feeler blades will be helpful in preventing the rings dropping into empty grooves (see illustration). Be careful not to scratch the piston with the ends of the ring. The rings are brittle, and will snap if they are spread too far. They're also very sharp – protect your hands and fingers. Note that the third (oil control) ring may consist of a spacer and two side rails, or a one-piece ring. Always remove the rings from the top of the piston. Keep each set of rings with its piston if the old rings are to be re-used.

3 Scrape away all traces of carbon from the top of the piston. A hand-held wire brush (or a piece of fine emery cloth) can be used, once the majority of the deposits have been scraped away. The piston identification markings should now be visible.

4 Remove the carbon from the ring grooves in the piston, using an old ring. Break the ring in half to do this (be careful not to cut your fingers – piston rings are sharp). Be careful to remove only the carbon deposits – do not remove any metal, and do not nick or scratch the sides of the ring grooves.

5 Once the deposits have been removed, clean the piston/connecting rod assembly with paraffin or a suitable solvent, and dry thoroughly. Make sure that the oil return holes in the ring grooves are clear.

6 If the cylinder bores are not damaged or worn excessively (see Section 14), check the piston/connecting rods as follows.

Petrol engine

Note: *Pistons and connecting rods are only supplied as an assembly.*

7 Carefully inspect each piston for cracks around the skirt, around the gudgeon pin holes, and at the piston ring 'lands' (between the ring grooves).

8 Look for scoring and scuffing on the piston skirt, holes in the piston crown, and burned areas at the edge of the crown. If the skirt is scored or scuffed, the engine may have been suffering from overheating, and/or abnormal combustion which caused excessively high operating temperatures. The cooling and lubrication systems should be checked thoroughly. Scorch marks on the sides of the pistons show that blow-by has occurred. A hole in the piston crown, or burned areas at the edge of the piston crown, indicates that abnormal combustion (pre-ignition, knocking, or detonation) has been occurring. If any of the above problems exist, the causes must be investigated and corrected, or the damage will occur again. The causes may include incorrect ignition/injection pump timing (as applicable), or a faulty injector.

9 Corrosion of the piston, in the form of pitting, indicates that coolant has been leaking into the combustion chamber and/or the crankcase. Again, the cause must be

15.2 Use a feeler blade to remove a piston ring

corrected, or the problem may persist in the rebuilt engine.

10 Measure the piston diameter at right angles to the gudgeon pin axis, 8 mm up from the base of the piston skirt, and compare the results with the Specifications at the beginning of this Chapter (see illustration). Note that there are two piston size group to allow for manufacturing tolerances; the size group marking is stamped on the piston crown.

11 To measure the piston-to-bore clearance, measure the bore diameter at right-angles to the crankshaft axis, 20 mm up from the base of the bore (see Section 14). Calculate the clearance by subtracting the piston diameter from the bore measurement. Alternatively, insert each piston into its original bore, then select a feeler blade and slip it into the bore along with the piston. The piston must be aligned exactly in its normal attitude, and the feeler blade must be between the piston and bore, on one of the thrust faces, 20 mm from the bottom of the bore. If the clearance is excessive, a new piston will be required. If the piston binds at the lower end of the bore and is loose towards the top, the bore is tapered. If tight spots are encountered as the piston/feeler blade is rotated in the bore, the bore is out-of-round.

12 Repeat this procedure for the remaining pistons and cylinder bores. Any piston which is worn beyond the specified limits must be renewed.

13 Examine each connecting rod carefully for signs of damage, such as cracks around the big-end and small-end bearings. Check that the rod is not bent or distorted. Damage

15.10 Measure the piston diameter at right angles to the gudgeon pin axis

15.17 Measure the piston diameter in the circular areas left in the graphite coating (arrowed)

is highly unlikely, unless the engine has been seized or badly overheated. Detailed checking of the connecting rod assembly can only be carried out by a Land Rover dealer or engine repair specialist with the necessary equipment.

14 The gudgeon pins are an interference fit in the connecting rod small-end bearings and Land Rover state that the pistons and connecting rods must not be dismantled. Land Rover only supply pistons and connecting rods as an assembly; it is not possible to purchase them separately. Therefore, if either the piston or connecting rod is damaged then both must be renewed as an assembly.

15 Inspect the connecting rod big-end cap bolts closely for signs of wear or damage and check that they screw easily into the connecting rods. Renew any bolt which shows visible signs of damage or does not screw easily into position.

L-Series diesel engine

16 Carry out the checks described in paragraphs 7 to 9.

17 Measure the piston diameter at right angles to the gudgeon pin axis, 44 mm up from the base of the piston skirt, and compare the results with the Specifications at the beginning of this Chapter. **Note:** *The piston diameter should be measured in the exposed circular area left in the graphite coating on the front and rear of the piston* **(see illustration).**

18 To measure the piston-to-bore clearance, measure the bore diameter at right-angles to the crankshaft axis, 70 mm down from the top of the bore (see Section 14). Calculate the

15.21a Remove the piston circlips . . .

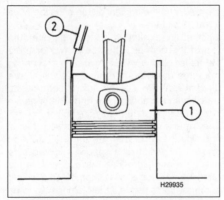

15.18 Position the piston (1) as described in the text then check the piston-to-bore clearance by inserting a feeler blade (2) between the piston and bore

clearance by subtracting the piston diameter from the bore measurement. Alternatively, invert the piston and fit it into its original bore so that the arrow on the piston crown is facing towards the flywheel end of the engine. Position the piston so that the base of its skirt is 25 mm down from the top of the bore then select a feeler blade and slip it into the bore along with the piston. The piston must be aligned exactly in its normal attitude, and the feeler blade must be between the piston and bore, on one of the thrust faces, approximately 70 mm down from the top of the bore **(see illustration).** If the clearance is excessive, a new piston will be required. If the piston binds at the lower end of the bore and is loose towards the top, the bore is tapered. If tight spots are encountered as the piston/feeler blade is rotated in the bore, the bore is out-of-round.

19 Repeat this procedure for the remaining pistons and cylinder bores. Any piston which is worn beyond the specified limits must be renewed.

20 Examine each connecting rod carefully for signs of damage, such as cracks around the big-end and small-end bearings. Check that the rod is not bent or distorted. Damage is highly unlikely, unless the engine has been seized or badly overheated. Detailed checking of the connecting rod assembly can only be carried out by a Land Rover dealer or

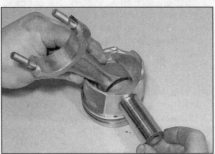

15.21b . . . then press out the gudgeon pin and separate the piston and connecting rod

engine repair specialist with the necessary equipment. The pistons and connecting rods can be separated as follows.

21 Using circlip pliers, remove the circlips from the piston then push out the gudgeon pin **(see illustrations).** Hand pressure should be sufficient to remove the pin. Identify the piston and rod to ensure correct reassembly. Discard the circlips – new ones *must* be used on refitting.

22 Examine the gudgeon pin and connecting rod small-end bearing for signs of wear or damage. Wear will require the renewal of both the pin and connecting rod.

23 The connecting rods themselves should not be in need of renewal, unless seizure or some other major mechanical failure has occurred. Check the alignment of the connecting rods visually, and if the rods are not straight, take them to an engine overhaul specialist for a more detailed check.

24 Examine all components, and obtain any new parts from your Land Rover dealer. If new pistons are purchased, they will be supplied complete with gudgeon pins and circlips. Circlips can also be purchased individually.

25 Assemble the piston and connecting rod so that the arrow on the piston crown is pointing towards from the assembly mark/boss which is cast onto one side of the connecting rod.

26 On all engines, apply a smear of clean engine oil to the gudgeon pin. Slide it into the piston and through the connecting rod small-end. Check that the piston pivots freely on the rod, then secure the gudgeon pin in position with two new circlips, ensuring that each circlip is correctly located in its groove in the piston.

27 Check the condition of the connecting rod big-end bearing cap bolts as described in paragraph 15, renewing them as necessary.

TD4 diesel engine

28 Carry out the checks described in paragraphs 7 to 9.

29 Measure the piston diameter at right angles to the gudgeon pin axis, 12 mm up from the base of the piston skirt, and compare the results with the Specifications at the beginning of this Chapter.

30 To measure the piston-to-bore clearance, measure the bore diameter at 45° to the crankshaft axis, at the top, centre, and bottom of the bore. Remeasure the bore diameter at 90° to the first measurement. Calculate the clearance by subtracting the piston diameter from the bore measurement. If the clearance is excessive, a rebore and new pistons may be required.

31 Repeat this procedure for the remaining pistons and cylinder bores. Any piston which is worn beyond the specified limits must be renewed.

32 Examine each connecting rod carefully for signs of damage, such as cracks around the big-end and small-end bearings. Check that the rod is not bent or distorted. Damage

15.33 Using a small screwdriver, remove the circlips from the piston

15.37a The arrowed on the piston crown (highlighted) must face forward ...

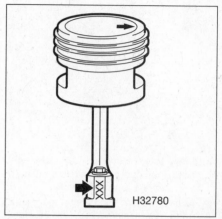

15.37b ... with the grade number on the connecting rod positioned as shown

is highly unlikely, unless the engine has been seized or badly overheated. Detailed checking of the connecting rod assembly can only be carried out by a Land Rover dealer or engine repair specialist with the necessary equipment. The pistons and connecting rods can be separated as follows.

33 Using a small screwdriver, remove the circlips from the piston then push out the gudgeon pin **(see illustration)**. Hand pressure should be sufficient to remove the pin. Identify the piston and rod to ensure correct reassembly. Discard the circlips – new ones *must* be used on refitting.

34 Examine the gudgeon pin and connecting rod small-end bearing for signs of wear or damage. Wear will require the renewal of both the pin and connecting rod.

35 The connecting rods themselves should not be in need of renewal, unless seizure or some other major mechanical failure has occurred. Check the alignment of the connecting rods visually, and if the rods are not straight, take them to an engine overhaul specialist for a more detailed check.

36 Examine all components, and obtain any new parts from your Land Rover dealer. If new pistons are purchased, they will be supplied complete with gudgeon pins and circlips. Circlips can also be purchased individually.

37 Assemble the piston and connecting rod so that if the arrow on the piston crown is pointing forwards, and the grade number cast into the side of the connecting rod is on the right-hand side **(see illustrations)**.

38 Apply a smear of clean engine oil to the gudgeon pin. Slide it into the piston and

through the connecting rod small-end. Check that the piston pivots freely on the rod, then secure the gudgeon pin in position with two new circlips, ensuring that each circlip is correctly located in its groove in the piston.

39 Check the condition of the connecting rod big-end bearing cap bolts as described in paragraph 15, renewing them as necessary.

16 Crankshaft – inspection

Checking crankshaft endfloat

1 If the crankshaft endfloat is to be checked, this must be done when the crankshaft is still installed in the cylinder block, but is free to move (see Section 13). On petrol engines, this means check the endfloat with the connecting rods release from the crankshaft, but the cylinder head still in place and the cylinder head bolts still securing the main bearing ladder.

2 Check the endfloat using a dial gauge in contact with the end of the crankshaft. Push the crankshaft fully one way, and then zero the gauge. Push the crankshaft fully the other way, and check the endfloat **(see illustration)**. The result can be compared with the specified amount, and will give an indication as to whether new thrustwashers are required.

3 If a dial gauge is not available, feeler blades can be used. First push the crankshaft fully towards the flywheel end of the engine, then use feeler blades to measure the gap

between the web of the crankpin and the side of thrustwasher **(see illustration)**. On petrol and L-Series diesel engines the thrustwashers are only fitted to the sides of the upper centre (No 3) main bearing shell, whilst on TD4 diesel engines, they are integral with the No 4 main bearing shells.

Inspection

4 Clean the crankshaft using paraffin or a suitable solvent, and dry it, preferably with compressed air if available. Be sure to clean the oil holes with a pipe cleaner or similar probe, to ensure that they are not obstructed.

⚠️ *Warning: Wear eye protection when using compressed air.*

5 Check the main and big-end bearing journals for uneven wear, scoring, pitting and cracking.

6 Big-end bearing wear is accompanied by distinct metallic knocking when the engine is running (particularly noticeable when the engine is pulling from low speed) and some loss of oil pressure.

7 Main bearing wear is accompanied by severe engine vibration and rumble – getting progressively worse as engine speed increases – and again by loss of oil pressure.

8 Check the bearing journal for roughness by running a finger lightly over the bearing surface. Any roughness (which will be accompanied by obvious bearing wear) indicates that the crankshaft requires regrinding (where possible) or renewal.

9 Check for burrs around the crankshaft oil holes (the holes are usually chamfered, so burrs should not be a problem unless regrinding has been carried out carelessly). Remove any burrs with a fine file or scraper, and thoroughly clean the oil holes as described previously.

10 Using a micrometer, measure the diameter of the main and big-end bearing journals, and compare the results with the Specifications **(see illustration)**. By measuring the diameter at a number of points around each journal's circumference, you will be able to determine whether or not the journal is out-of-round. Take

16.2 Check the endfloat using a dial gauge in contact with the end of the crankshaft

16.3 Using feeler blades to measure the crankshaft endfloat

16.10 Measure the crankshaft main bearing journal diameter

the measurement at each end of the journal, near the webs, to determine if the journal is tapered. Compare the results obtained with those given in the Specifications. If in any doubt have the crankshaft inspected by an engine overhaul specialist. They will be able to determine whether the crankshaft is re-usable, carry out any regrinding as necessary, and supply the correct bearing shells.

11 Check the oil seal contact surfaces at each end of the crankshaft for wear and damage. If the seal has worn a deep groove in the surface of the crankshaft, consult an engine overhaul specialist; repair may be possible, but otherwise a new crankshaft will be required.

12 At the time of writing, it appeared that Land Rover do not produce undersize bearing shells for the petrol or L-Series diesel engines. Therefore, if the crankshaft has worn beyond the specified limits, it will have to be renewed. Undersize bearings are available for the TD4 diesel engine. Consult your Land Rover dealer or engine specialist for further information on parts availability.

13 Carefully inspect the main bearing ladder/cap bolts (as applicable) and renew any bolt which shows signs of damage.

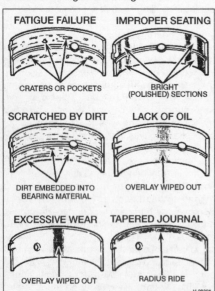

17.2 Typical bearing shell failures

17 Main and big-end bearings – inspection

1 Even though the main and big-end bearings should be renewed during the engine overhaul, the old bearings should be retained for close examination, as they may reveal valuable information about the condition of the engine.

2 Bearing failure can occur due to lack of lubrication, the presence of dirt or other foreign particles, overloading the engine, or corrosion (see illustration). Regardless of the cause of bearing failure, the cause must be corrected (where applicable) before the engine is reassembled, to prevent it from happening again.

3 When examining the bearing shells, remove them from the cylinder block, the main bearing caps, the connecting rods and the connecting rod big-end bearing caps. Lay them out on a clean surface in the same general position as their location in the engine. This will enable you to match any bearing problems with the corresponding crankshaft journal.

4 Dirt and other foreign matter gets into the engine in a variety of ways. It may be left in the engine during assembly, or it may pass through filters or the crankcase ventilation system. It may get into the oil, and from there into the bearings. Metal chips from machining operations and normal engine wear are often present. Abrasives are sometimes left in engine components after reconditioning, especially when parts are not thoroughly cleaned using the proper cleaning methods. Whatever the source, these foreign objects often end up embedded in the soft bearing material, and are easily recognised. Large particles will not embed in the bearing, and will score or gouge the bearing and journal. The best prevention for this cause of bearing failure is to clean all parts thoroughly, and keep everything spotlessly-clean during engine assembly. Frequent and regular engine oil and filter changes are also recommended.

5 Lack of lubrication (or lubrication breakdown) has a number of interrelated causes. Excessive heat (which thins the oil), overloading (which squeezes the oil from the bearing face) and oil leakage (from excessive bearing clearances, worn oil pump or high engine speeds) all contribute to lubrication breakdown. Blocked oil passages, which usually are the result of misaligned oil holes in a bearing shell, will also oil-starve a bearing, and destroy it. When lack of lubrication is the cause of bearing failure, the bearing material is wiped or extruded from the steel backing of the bearing. Temperatures may increase to the point where the steel backing turns blue from overheating.

6 Driving habits can have a definite effect on bearing life. Full-throttle, low-speed operation (labouring the engine) puts very high loads on bearings, tending to squeeze out the oil film. These loads cause the bearings to flex,

which produces fine cracks in the bearing face (fatigue failure). Eventually, the bearing material will loosen in pieces, and tear away from the steel backing.

7 Short-distance driving leads to corrosion of bearings, because insufficient engine heat is produced to drive off the condensed water and corrosive gases. These products collect in the engine oil, forming acid and sludge. As the oil is carried to the engine bearings, the acid attacks and corrodes the bearing material.

8 Incorrect bearing installation during engine assembly will lead to bearing failure as well. Tight-fitting bearings leave insufficient bearing running clearance, and will result in oil starvation. Dirt or foreign particles trapped behind a bearing shell result in high spots on the bearing, which lead to failure.

9 As mentioned at the beginning of this Section, the bearing shells should be renewed as a matter of course during engine overhaul; to do otherwise is false economy.

18 Engine overhaul – reassembly sequence

1 Before reassembly begins, ensure that all new parts have been obtained, and that all necessary tools are available. Read through the entire procedure to familiarise yourself with the work involved, and to ensure that all items necessary for reassembly of the engine are at hand. In addition to all normal tools and materials, thread-locking compound will be needed. A good quality tube of liquid sealant will also be required for the joint faces that are fitted without gaskets.

2 In order to save time and avoid problems, engine reassembly can be carried out in the following order:
a) *Crankshaft.*
b) *Piston/connecting rod assemblies.*
c) *Oil pump.*
d) *Sump.*
e) *Flywheel.*
f) *Cylinder head.*
g) *Timing belt/chain tensioner and sprockets, and belts/chains.*
h) *Inlet and exhaust manifolds (the relevant part of Chapter 4).*
i) *Fuel injection pump sprockets, tensioner and belt – L-Series diesel engine only.*
j) *Engine external components.*

3 At this stage, all engine components should be absolutely clean and dry, with all faults repaired. The components should be laid out (or in individual containers) on a completely clean work surface.

19 Piston rings – refitting

1 Before fitting new piston rings, the ring end gaps must be checked as follows.

19.4 Position the piston ring as described in the text then measure the end gap using feeler blades

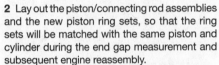

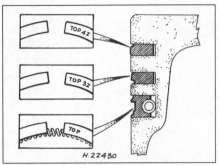

19.9 Piston ring identification – petrol engine

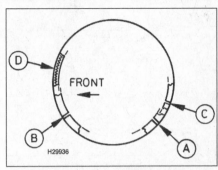

19.10 Piston ring end gap locations – petrol engine

A *Top compression ring*
B *Second compression ring*
C *Oil control ring*
D *Oil control ring expander*

2 Lay out the piston/connecting rod assemblies and the new piston ring sets, so that the ring sets will be matched with the same piston and cylinder during the end gap measurement and subsequent engine reassembly.

3 Insert the top ring into the first cylinder, and push it down the bore using the top of the piston. This will ensure that the ring remains square with the cylinder walls. Push the ring down into the bore until it is positioned 20 mm down from the top edge of the bore on petrol engines, and 30 mm down from the top of the bore on diesel engines. Withdraw the piston.

4 Measure the end gap using feeler blades, and compare the measurements with the figures given in the Specifications **(see illustration)**.

5 If the gap is too small (unlikely if genuine Land Rover parts are used), it must be enlarged, or the ring ends may contact each other during engine operation, causing serious damage. Ideally, new piston rings providing the correct end gap should be fitted. As a last resort, the end gap can be increased by filing the ring ends very carefully with a fine file. Mount the file in a vice with soft jaws, slip the ring over the file with the ends contacting the file face, and slowly move the ring to remove material from the ends. Take care, as piston rings are sharp, and are easily broken.

6 With new piston rings, it is unlikely that the end gap will be too large. If the gaps are too large, check that you have the correct rings for your engine and for the particular cylinder bore size.

7 Repeat the checking procedure for each ring in the first cylinder, and then for the rings in the remaining cylinders. Remember to keep rings, pistons and cylinders matched up.

8 Once the ring end gaps have been checked and if necessary corrected, the rings can be fitted to the pistons as follows, using the same technique as for removal.

Petrol engine

9 Fit the oil control ring expander first (it will be easier if the end gap is correctly positioned at this point), then fit the ring, making sure its identification (eg, TOP) marking is uppermost **(see illustration)**. The second and top rings are different and can be identified by their cross-sections. The second ring is thicker. Fit the

second and top compression rings ensuring that each ring is fitted the correct way up with its identification (TOP) mark uppermost. **Note:** *Always follow any instructions supplied with the new piston ring sets – different manufacturers may specify different procedures. Do not mix up the top and second compression rings.*

10 Check that each ring is free to rotate easily in its groove, then measure the ring-to-groove clearance of each ring, using feeler blades. If the clearance is within the specified range, position the ring end gaps as shown **(see illustration)**.

Diesel engines

11 Fit the oil control ring expander first then carefully fit the ring to the piston, the ring has no identification marking and can be fitted either way up.

12 The second and top rings are different and can be identified by their cross-sections **(see illustrations)**. Fit the second and top compression rings ensuring that each ring is fitted the correct way up with its identification (TOP) mark uppermost. **Note:** *Always follow any instructions supplied with the new piston ring sets – different manufacturers may specify different procedures. Do not mix up the top and second compression rings.*

13 Check that each ring is free to rotate easily in its groove, then measure the ring-to-groove clearance of each ring, using feeler blades. If the clearance is within the specified range, space the ring end gaps at 120° intervals making sure no end gap is in line with the piston thrust (front and rear) faces.

20 Crankshaft – refitting

Note: *It is recommended that new main bearing shells are fitted regardless of the condition of the original ones.*

Petrol engine

1 Clean the backs of the bearing shells and the bearing locations in both the cylinder block/crankcase and the main bearing ladder.

2 Press the bearing shells into their locations, ensuring that the tab on each shell engages in the notch in the cylinder block/crankcase or main bearing ladder location. Take care not to touch any shell bearing surface with your fingers.

3 Press the bearing shells into their locations, ensuring that the tab on each shell engages in the notch in the cylinder block or main bearing cap, noting the following

a) *Make sure that the grooved bearing shells are fitted in the upper (cylinder block) locations of Nos 2, 3 and 4 main bearings.*

b) *If bearing shells of different grades are being fitted to the same bearing, ensure that the thicker shell is fitted in the lower (main bearing ladder) location (see paragraph 1).*

4 Using a little grease, stick the thrustwashers

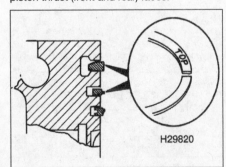

19.12a Piston ring identification – L-Series diesel engine

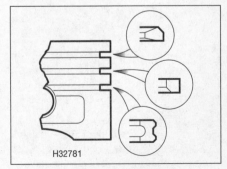

19.12b Piston ring identification – TD4 diesel engine

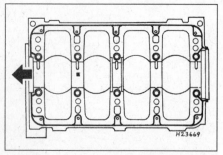

20.7 Apply sealant to the highlighted areas (shown by thick lines) of the cylinder block/ bearing ladder mating surfaces as shown

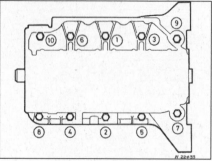

20.10 Crankshaft main bearing ladder bolt tightening sequence

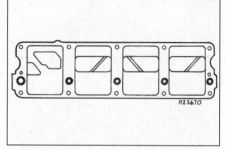

20.11 Apply sealant to the highlighted areas (shown by thick black lines) of the oil rail

to each side of the centre (No 3) main bearing upper location. Ensure that the oilway grooves on each thrustwasher face outwards.

5 Liberally lubricate each bearing shell in the cylinder block/crankcase, then lower the crankshaft into position. Check the crankshaft endfloat as described in Section 16.

6 Refit the piston/connecting rod assemblies to the crankshaft as described in Section 21 and position the crankshaft so the pistons are half-way up the bores.

7 Thoroughly degrease the mating surfaces of the cylinder block and the main bearing ladder. Apply a continuous bead of sealant to the mating surface of the cylinder block/crankcase as shown then spread the sealant to an even film **(see illustration)**. Carefully follow the instructions supplied with the sealant.

8 Ensure the lower bearing shells are correctly fitted to the bearing ladder and lubricate them with clean engine oil.

9 Ensure the locating dowels are in position then refit the main bearing ladder to the cylinder block, taking care to ensure that the shells are not displaced. Once the ladder is correctly located on the dowels, refit the retaining bolts, tightening them all by hand only.

10 Working in the specified sequence, go around and tighten all bolts to the specified Stage 1 torque setting then go around again in the specified sequence and tighten them to the specified Stage 2 torque setting **(see illustration)**. **Note:** *The crankshaft cannot now be rotated until the cylinder head has been refitted.*

11 Thoroughly degrease the mating surfaces of the oil rail and the main bearing ladder. Apply sealant to the oil rail mating surface as shown **(see illustration)**.

12 Refit the oil rail to the main bearing ladder and tighten its retaining nuts to the specified torque.

13 Refit the dipstick tube, using a new gasket, and securely tighten its retaining bolts.

14 Working as described in Part A of this Chapter, carry out the following procedures in order.

 a) *Refit the oil pump, pick-up/strainer and sump.*
 b) *Fit a new left-hand oil seal to the crankshaft and refit the flywheel.*
 c) *Refit the cylinder head and camshaft(s).*
 d) *Refit the timing belt sprockets and belt.*

15 On completion, remove the spark plugs then fit a torque wrench to the crankshaft pulley bolt and rotate the crankshaft in the normal direction of rotation. The crankshaft must rotate smoothly, without any sign of binding, and the amount of force required to rotate the crankshaft should not exceed 31 Nm. If the effort required is greater than this, the engine should be dismantled again to trace and rectify the cause. This value takes into account the increased friction of a new engine and is much higher than the actual pressure required to rotate a run-in engine, so do not make allowances for tight components.

L-Series diesel engine

Selection of bearing shells

16 On these engines all the bearing shells are of the same thickness. Land Rover only produce standard size bearing shells; no undersize shells are available for use with a reground crankshaft. Consult your Land Rover dealer or engine specialist for further information on parts availability.

Refitting

17 Clean the backs of the bearing shells and the bearing locations in both the cylinder block and the main bearing caps.

18 Press the bearing shells into their locations, ensuring that the tab on each shell engages in the notch in the cylinder block or main bearing cap; on shells with no locating tab, ensure the shell is positioned centrally. Fit the grooved bearing shells in the upper (cylinder block) locations and fit the plain shells in the lower (bearing cap) locations **(see illustrations)**. The original bearing shells should never be re-used.

19 Using a little grease, stick the thrustwasher halves to each side of the centre (No 3) main bearing upper location, ensuring that the

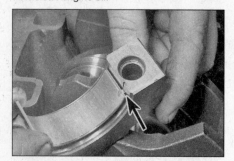

20.18a Fit the plain bearing shells to the bearing caps (locating tab cut-out arrowed) . . .

20.18b . . . and the grooved bearing shells to the cylinder block

20.18c Where the bearing shells have no locating tabs, ensure the shells are positioned centrally in the cap/block

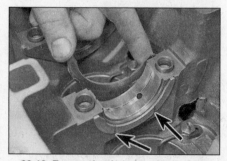

20.19 Ensure the thrustwasher halves are fitted with their oil grooves (arrowed) facing outwards

oilway grooves on each thrustwasher face outwards **(see illustration)**.

20 Lubricate the upper shells with clean engine oil then lower the crankshaft into position **(see illustration)**.

21 Ensure the bearing shells are correctly located in the caps and all locating dowels are in position. Refit the caps to the cylinder block. Ensure the caps are fitted in their correct locations, with number 1 cap at the timing belt end, and are fitted the correct way around so that the arrow on each cap points towards the timing belt end of the engine.

22 Apply a smear of clean engine to oil to the threads and underneath the heads of the main bearing cap bolts **(see illustration)**. Fit the bolts tightening them all by hand.

23 Working in a diagonal sequence from the centre outwards, tighten the main bearing cap bolts evenly and progressively to the specified torque setting.

24 Check that the crankshaft is free to rotate smoothly; if excessive pressure is required to turn the crankshaft, investigate the cause before proceeding further.

25 Check the crankshaft endfloat as described in Section 16.

26 Refit/reconnect the piston connecting rod assemblies to the crankshaft as described in Section 21.

27 Working as described in Part B of this Chapter, carry out the following procedures in order.

a) Refit the oil pump.
b) Oil pump pick-up/strainer and sump.

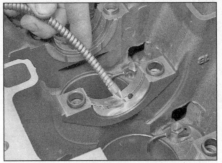

20.20 Lubricate the upper shells with clean engine oil prior to refitting the crankshaft

Ensure the grooves of No 1 main bearing cap are completely filled with sealant, prior to refitting the sump.
c) Fit a new left-hand oil seal to the crankshaft and refit the flywheel.
d) Refit the cylinder head and camshaft.

TD4 diesel engine

28 Clean the backs of the bearing shells and the bearing locations in both the cylinder block and the main bearing caps.

29 Press the bearing shells into their locations, ensuring that the tab on each shell engages in the notch in the cylinder block or main bearing cap; on shells with no locating tab, ensure the shell is positioned centrally. Fit the grooved bearing shells in the upper (cylinder block) locations and fit the plain shells in the lower (bearing cap) locations **(see illustrations)**. Note that the No 4 main

20.22 Lubricate the threads and underside of the heads of the main bearing cap bolts with a smear of oil prior to refitting

bearing shell incorporate the thrustwashers. The original bearing shells should never be re-used.

30 Lubricate the upper shells with clean engine oil then lower the crankshaft into position **(see illustrations)**.

31 Ensure the bearing shells are correctly located in the caps. Refit the caps to the cylinder block. Ensure the caps are fitted in their correct locations, with number 1 cap at the timing chain end, and are fitted the correct way around so that the identification number is on the rear (turbocharger) side of the engine block **(see illustration)**.

32 Apply a smear of clean engine to oil to the threads and underneath the heads of the new main bearing cap bolts. Fit the bolts tightening them all by hand.

33 Working in a diagonal sequence from the centre outwards, tighten the main bearing cap

20.29a Fit the shells with the grooves to the cylinder block . . .

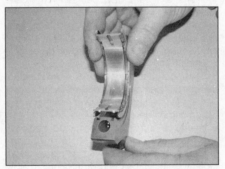

20.29b . . . and the plain shells to the main bearing cap

20.29c No 4 main bearing shell incorporates the thrustwashers

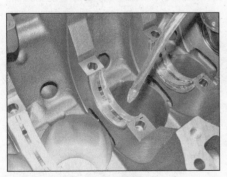

20.30a Lubricate the shells bearings . . .

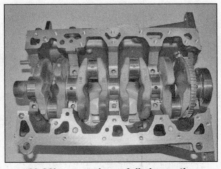

20.30b . . . and carefully lower the crankshaft into place

20.31 Ensure the bearing cap identification number (arrowed) is on the rear (turbocharger) side of the engine block

20.33 Tighten the bolts to the Stage 1 torque . . .

20.34 . . . then to the Stage 2 angle

bolts evenly and progressively to the specified Stage 1 torque setting **(see illustration)**.

34 Using an angle-measuring gauge, tighten the bolts in the same sequence to the Stage 2 angle **(see illustration)**.

35 Check that the crankshaft is free to rotate smoothly; if excessive pressure is required to turn the crankshaft, investigate the cause before proceeding further.

36 Check the crankshaft endfloat as described in Section 16.

37 Refit/reconnect the piston connecting rod assemblies to the crankshaft as described in Section 21.

38 Working as described in Part C of this Chapter, carry out the following procedures in order.

a) *Refit the oil pump and pick-up/strainer.*
b) *Cylinder block reinforcing plate.*
c) *Fit a new left-hand oil seal to the crankshaft and refit the flywheel.*
d) *Refit the cylinder head and camshafts.*
e) *Refit the timing chains, sprockets and tensioner.*

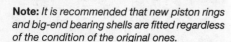

21 Piston/connecting rod assembly – refitting

Note: *It is recommended that new piston rings and big-end bearing shells are fitted regardless of the condition of the original ones.*

Petrol engine

1 Note that the following procedure assumes that the cylinder liners have been refitted

to the cylinder block/crankcase and that the crankshaft and main bearing ladder are in place. It is of course possible to refit the piston/connecting rod assemblies to the cylinder bores, to refit the crankshaft and to reassemble the piston/connecting rods on the crankshaft before refitting the main bearing ladder (see Section 20).

2 Clean the backs of the bearing shells and the bearing recesses in both the connecting rod and the big-end bearing cap. Ensure that all traces of the protective grease are cleaned off using paraffin. Wipe dry the shells and connecting rods with a lint-free cloth.

3 Press the bearing shells into their locations, ensuring that the tab on each shell engages in the notch in the connecting rod or big-end bearing cap and taking care not to touch any shell's bearing surface with your fingers. If bearing shells of differing grades are to be fitted to the same connecting rod, the thicker shell must always be fitted in the lower (bearing cap) location.

4 Lubricate the cylinder bores, the pistons and piston rings, then lay out each piston/connecting rod assembly in its respective position.

5 Starting with assembly No 1, make sure that the piston rings are still correctly spaced (see Section 19) then clamp them in position with a piston ring compressor.

6 Insert the piston/connecting rod assembly into the top of liner No 1, ensuring that the arrow (or FRONT marking) on the piston crown faces the timing belt end of the engine. Note that the stamped marks on the connecting rod and big-end bearing cap should face the

front of the engine **(see illustrations)**. Using a block of wood or hammer handle against the piston crown, tap the assembly into the liner until the piston crown is flush with the top of the liner.

7 Ensure that the bearing shell is still correctly installed. Taking care not to mark the liner bores, liberally lubricate the crankpin and both bearing shells, then pull the piston/connecting rod assembly down the bore and onto the crankpin. Noting that the faces with the stamped marks must match (which means that the bearing shell locating tabs abut each other), refit the big-end bearing cap, tightening the bolts finger-tight at first.

8 Evenly and progressively tighten the big-end bearing cap bolts to the specified Stage 1 torque setting then angle-tighten each bolt through the specified Stage 2 angle. It is recommended that an angle-measuring gauge is used during this stage of the tightening, to ensure accuracy **(see illustration)**.

9 Repeat the procedure for the remaining three piston/connecting rod assemblies, but do not attempt to rotate the crankshaft.

10 Ensure the mating surfaces of the oil rail and the main bearing ladder are clean and dry. Apply sealant to the areas of the oil rail mating surface shown in illustration 20.11.

11 Refit the oil rail to the main bearing ladder and tighten its retaining nuts to the specified torque.

12 Refit the dipstick tube, using a new gasket, and securely tighten its retaining bolts.

13 Working as described in Part A of this Chapter, carry out the following procedures in order.

a) *Refit the oil pump pick-up/strainer and sump.*
b) *Refit the cylinder head and camshaft(s).*
c) *Refit the timing belt sprockets and belt.*

14 On completion, remove the spark plugs then fit a torque wrench to the crankshaft pulley bolt and rotate the crankshaft in the normal direction of rotation. The crankshaft must rotate smoothly, without any sign of binding, and the amount of force required to rotate the crankshaft should not exceed 31 Nm (23 lbf ft). If the effort required is greater than this, the engine should be dismantled again to trace and rectify the cause. This value takes into account the increased friction of a new engine

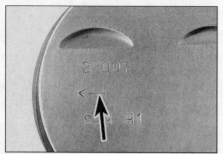

21.6a The arrow (or FRONT marking) (arrowed) on the piston crown must point to the timing belt end of the engine

21.6b Use a piston ring compressor to refit a piston/connecting rod assembly

21.8 Tighten the big-end bearing cap bolts to the specified Stage 1 torque, and then through the specified Stage 2 angle

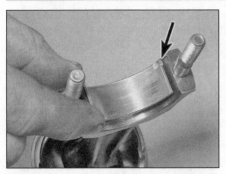

21.17a If the bearing shells are equipped with locating tabs, ensure the tabs are correctly engaged with the cut-outs in the cap/rod (arrowed)

and is much higher than the actual force required to rotate a run-in engine, so do not make allowances for tight components.

L-Series diesel engine

Selection of bearing shells

15 On these engines all the bearing shells are of the same thickness. Land Rover only produce standard size bearing shells; no undersize shells are available for use with a reground crankshaft. Consult your Land Rover dealer or engine specialist for further information on parts availability.

Piston/connecting rods refitting

16 Clean the backs of the bearing shells and the bearing recesses in both the connecting rod and the big-end bearing cap. If new shells are being fitted, ensure that all traces

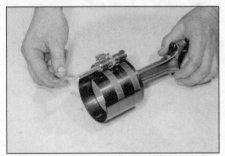

21.19 Ensure the ring gaps are correctly spaced then clamp them in position with the ring compressor

21.21 Insert the piston/connecting rod and tap it gently into position using a hammer handle

21.17b Where the bearing shells have no locating tabs, ensure the shell is positioned centrally in the cap/rod

of the protective grease are cleaned off using paraffin. Wipe dry the shells and connecting rods with a lint-free cloth.

17 Press the bearing shells into their locations, ensuring that the tab on each shell engages in the notch in the connecting rod or big-end bearing cap; on shells with no locating tab, ensure the shell is positioned centrally **(see illustrations)**.

18 Lubricate the bores, the pistons and piston rings then lay out each piston/connecting rod assembly in its respective position **(see illustration)**.

19 Starting with assembly No 1, make sure that the piston rings are still spaced as described in Section 19, then clamp them in position with a piston ring compressor **(see illustration)**.

20 Insert the piston/connecting rod assembly into the top of cylinder No 1, ensuring that the arrow marking on the piston crown is pointing

21.20 The arrow (arrowed) on the piston crown must point towards the timing belt of the engine

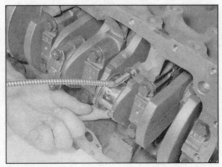

21.22 Lubricate the big-end journal . . .

21.18 Lubricate the piston rings with clean engine oil

towards the timing belt end of the engine **(see illustration)**. The cut-out on the piston skirt should then be aligned with the oil spray jet in the cylinder block.

21 Using a block of wood or hammer handle against the piston crown, tap the assembly into the cylinder until the piston crown is flush with the top of the cylinder **(see illustration)**.

22 Taking care not to mark the cylinder bore, liberally lubricate the crankpin and both bearing shells, then pull the piston/connecting rod assembly down the bore and onto the crankpin **(see illustration)**. Refit the big-end bearing cap using the markings made prior to removal to ensure it is fitted the correct way around; the connecting rod and bearing cap shell locating notches (where fitted) should abut each other.

23 Lubricate the threads of the bolts with clean engine oil then screw them into position in the connecting rod, tightening them both by hand. Evenly and progressively tighten the bolts to the specified Stage 1 torque setting then angle-tighten each bolt through the specified Stage 2 angle. It is recommended that an angle-measuring gauge is used during this stage of the tightening, to ensure accuracy **(see illustration)**.

24 Refit the remaining three piston and connecting rod assemblies in the same way.

25 Rotate the crankshaft, and check that it turns freely, with no signs of binding or tight spots.

26 Refit the oil pump strainer, sump and the cylinder head as described in Part B of this Chapter.

21.23 . . . then refit the bearing cap and tighten the nuts evenly and progressively to the specified torque

21.29a The bearing shell fitted to the connecting rod is of the 'Sputter' type, identified by the letter S or a series of xxx's on the outside of the shell

21.29b Ensure the tab on each shell engages in the notch in the connecting rod and big-end bearing cap

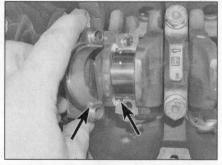

21.34 The connecting rod and bearing cap shell locating notches (arrowed) should abut each other

TD4 diesel engine

Selection of bearing shells

27 Big-end bearings for these engines are available in a range of undersizes to suit reground crankshafts. Details of the exact bearing size options were not available at the time of writing – refer to the your Land Rover dealer or engine reconditioning specialist.

Piston/connecting rods refitting

28 Clean the backs of the bearing shells and the bearing recesses in both the connecting rod and the big-end bearing cap. Ensure that all traces of the protective grease are cleaned off using paraffin. Wipe dry the shells and connecting rods with a lint-free cloth.

29 Press the bearing shells into their locations, ensuring that the tab on each shell engages in the notch in the connecting rod and big-end bearing cap. Note that the bearing shell fitted to the connecting rod is of the 'Sputter' type, identified by the letter S or a series of xxx's on the outside of the shell **(see illustrations)**.

30 Lubricate the bores, the pistons and piston rings then lay out each piston/connecting rod assembly in its respective position.

31 Starting with assembly No 1, make sure that the piston rings are still spaced as described in Section 19, then clamp them in position with a piston ring compressor.

32 Insert the piston/connecting rod assembly into the top of cylinder No 1, ensuring that the arrow marking on the piston crown is pointing towards the timing chain end of the engine **(see illustration 15.37a)**.

33 Using a block of wood or hammer handle against the piston crown, tap the assembly

into the cylinder until the piston crown is flush with the top of the cylinder.

34 Taking care not to mark the cylinder bore, liberally lubricate the crankpin and both bearing shells, then pull the piston/connecting rod assembly down the bore and onto the crankpin. Refit the big-end bearing cap using the markings made prior to removal to ensure it is fitted the correct way around; the connecting rod and bearing cap shell locating notches (where fitted) should abut each other **(see illustration)**.

35 Lubricate the threads of the bolts with clean engine oil then screw them into position in the connecting rod, tightening them both by hand. Evenly and progressively tighten the bolts to the specified Stage 1 torque setting, then the Stage 2 torque setting, followed by angle-tightening each bolt through the specified Stage 3 angle. It is recommended that an angle-measuring gauge is used during this stage of the tightening, to ensure accuracy.

36 Refit the remaining three piston and connecting rod assemblies in the same way.

37 Rotate the crankshaft, and check that it turns freely, with no signs of binding or tight spots.

38 Refit the cylinder block reinforcing plate, oil pump and strainer, sump and the cylinder head as described in Part C of this Chapter.

22 Engine –
initial start-up after overhaul

With the engine refitted in the vehicle,

double-check the engine oil and coolant levels (see *Weekly checks*). Make a final check that everything has been reconnected, and that there are no tools or rags left in the engine compartment.

On petrol engine models, disable the ignition system by disconnect the ignition coil LT wiring connector(s) (see Chapter 5B), then remove the spark plugs. Turn the engine on the starter until the oil pressure warning light goes out then stop and reconnect the wiring connector and refit the spark plugs.

On diesel engine models, switch on the ignition and immediately turn the engine on the starter (without allowing the glow plugs to heat up) until the oil pressure warning light goes out.

On all models, start the engine as normal noting that this may take a little longer than usual, due to the fuel system components having been disturbed.

While the engine is idling, check for fuel, water and oil leaks. Don't be alarmed if there are some odd smells and smoke from parts getting hot and burning off oil deposits.

Assuming all is well, keep the engine idling until hot water is felt circulating through the top hose, then switch off the engine.

Allow the engine to cool then recheck the oil and coolant levels as described in *Weekly checks*, and top-up as necessary.

If new pistons, rings or crankshaft bearings have been fitted, the engine must be treated as new, and run-in for the first 500 miles. *Do not* operate the engine at full-throttle, or allow it to labour at low engine speeds in any gear. It is recommended that the oil and filter be changed at the end of this period.

Chapter 3
Cooling, heating and ventilation systems

Contents

Degrees of difficulty

Easy, suitable for novice with little experience	Fairly easy, suitable for beginner with some experience	Fairly difficult, suitable for competent DIY mechanic	Difficult, suitable for experienced DIY mechanic	Very difficult, suitable for expert DIY or professional

Specifications

System

Type .... Pressurised, pump-assisted with front mounted radiator and ECM-controlled electric cooling fan

Thermostat

Type .... Wax

	Starts to open	**Fully open**
Operating temperatures:		
Petrol engines................................	85°C	100°C
L-Series diesel engines	84°C	96°C
TD4 diesel engines	88 ± 2°C	Not available

Expansion tank

Cap pressure:
  Petrol engines.................................... 1.0 bar
  L-Series diesel engines .... 0.9 to 1.0 bar
  TD4 diesel engines .... 1.43 bar

Cooling fan

	On	**Off**
Petrol engines up to 2001:		
Models without air conditioning............................	102°C	96°C
Models with air conditioning:		
Slow speed..	106°C	100°C
Fast speed	112°C	106°C
Petrol engines 2001-on	Not available	
L-Series diesel engines:		
Models without air conditioning............................	106°C	99°C
Models with air conditioning:		
Slow speed..	106°C	100°C
Fast speed	112°C	106°C
TD4 diesel engines.......................................	Not available	

Air conditioning system

Refrigerant R134a
Refrigerant charge quantity .... 540 ± 25 g
Compressor:
  Pressure (High side) .... 35.3 bar
  Pressure (Low side) .... 1.97 bar
  Lubricating oil...................................... Nippon Denso ND-8
  Lubricating oil quantity............................... 150 ± 20 cc

Torque wrench settings	Nm	lbf ft
Cooling system		
Petrol engines:		
Coolant elbow to cylinder head	9	7
Coolant pump cover	10	7
Coolant pump to cylinder block	10	7
Coolant rail to block	9	7
Cooling fan housing to radiator	6	4
Cooling fan to housing	6	4
Engine coolant temperature sensor	15	11
Thermostat housing cover	9	7
Thermostat housing to block	9	7
L-Series diesel engines:		
Coolant pump	10	7
Cooling fan housing to radiator	6	4
Cooling fan to housing	6	4
Engine coolant temperature sensor	5	4
Outlet elbow to cylinder head	25	18
Radiator to crossmember	9	7
Temperature gauge sender unit	10	7
Thermostat housing to oil cooler	9	7
TD4 diesel engines:		
Coolant hose connector to cylinder head	9	7
Coolant pump to cylinder block	10	7
Coolant rail to exhaust manifold	20	15
Coolant rail-to-cylinder head bolts	20	15
Engine coolant temperature sensor	15	11
Lower coolant rail support bracket bolts	15	11
Thermostat housing to coolant pump	9	7
Upper coolant rail-to-thermostat housing bolts	9	7
Air conditioning system		
Petrol engines:		
Compressor bracket to cylinder block	25	18
Compressor to bracket:		
Up to 2001	45	33
2001-on	25	18
Condenser pipe to compressor	9	7
Condenser to fan housing	9	7
Cooling fan to housing	9	7
Evaporator pipe to compressor	9	7
Receiver/drier to body	9	7
Trinary switch	12	9
L-Series diesel engines:		
Compressor	45	33
Condenser cooling fan	9	7
Condenser pipe union to compressor	25	18
Cooling fan housing to condenser	9	7
Cooling fan to housing	9	7
Pipe to compressor	45	33
Pipe to condenser	5	4
Trinary switch	12	9
TD4 diesel engines:		
Compressor drivebelt tensioner clamp bolt	24	18
Compressor drivebelt tensioner pivot bolt	24	18
Compressor mounting bracket to cylinder block	25	18
Compressor support bracket to sump	10	7
Compressor to mounting bracket	25	18
Condenser bracket to radiator	3	2
Pipe to condenser	5	4
Pressure sensor	10	7

1.1a Cooling system layout – petrol engine

1 Coolant expansion tank
2 Heater matrix
3 Expansion tank-to-coolant rail hose
4 IRD unit cooler
5 Heater inlet hose
6 Bleed screw
7 Heater outlet hose
8 Coolant inlet rail
9 Bleed screw
10 Coolant outlet pipe
11 Radiator bottom hose
12 Air conditioning fan (where fitted)
13 Radiator
14 Engine cooling fan
15 Radiator top hose
16 Thermostat housing
17 Coolant pump
18 Bleed hose
19 Bleed hose

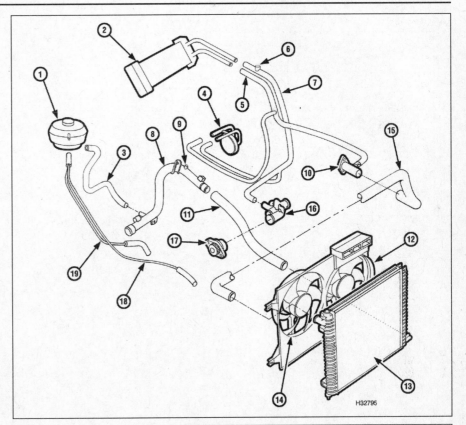

1 General information and precautions

General information

The cooling system is of pressurised type, comprising a front-mounted radiator, an expansion tank mounted in the rear right-hand corner of the engine compartment, electric cooling fan(s) mounted on the rear of the radiator, a thermostat and a centrifugal coolant pump **(see illustrations)**. The cooling fan is controlled by the engine management electronic control module. The thermostat is located in the coolant pump inlet on the rear right-hand side of the cylinder block on petrol engines, in the outlet on the front of the cylinder block, just above the oil cooler on L-Series diesel engines, and on the coolant pump housing on the right-hand end of the engine on the TD4 diesel engines. On petrol engines the coolant pump is located on the right-hand rear end of the cylinder block and is driven by the timing belt. On L-Series diesel engines the coolant pump is located on a bracket attached to the front right-hand end of the cylinder block, and is driven by the power steering pump which is driven from the crankshaft pulley by the auxiliary drivebelt.

1.1b Cooling system layout – L-Series diesel engine

1 Heater matrix
2 Heater inlet hose
3 Heater outlet hose
4 EGR cooler
5 IRD unit cooler
6 Pipe assembly
7 Radiator top hose
8 Cooling fan
9 Radiator
10 Cooling fan
11 Coolant pump
12 Engine inlet hose
13 Radiator bottom hose
14 Outlet elbow
15 Temperature gauge sensor
16 Temperature sensor
17 Oil cooler
18 IRD unit coolant restrictor
19 Bleed hose
20 IRD unit inlet hose
21 Expansion tank hose
22 Expansion tank

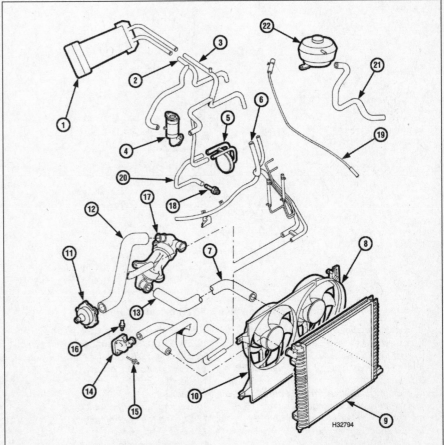

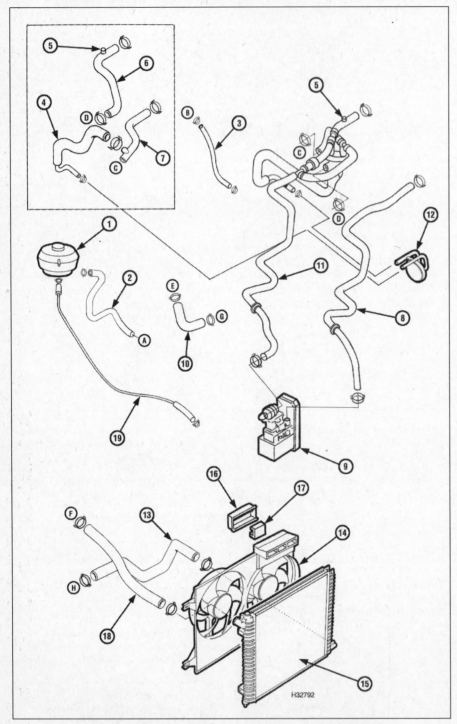

1.1c Cooling system components – TD4 diesel engine (part 1)

1 *Expansion tank*
2 *Expansion tank-to-coolant rail hose*
3 *IRD unit outlet hose*
4 *IRD unit inlet hose (models without FBH)*
5 *Bleed screw*
6 *Heater outlet hose (models without FBH)*
7 *Heater inlet hose (models without FBH)*
8 *Heater inlet hose (models with FBH)*
9 *FBH (fuel burning heater – where fitted)*
10 *Engine outlet-to-coolant rail hose*
11 *Heater outlet hose (models with FBH)*
12 *IRD unit cooler*
13 *Radiator bottom hose*
14 *Cooling fan*
15 *Radiator*
16 *Cooling fan control unit cover*
17 *Cooling fan control unit*
18 *Radiator top hose*
19 *Expansion bleed hose*

On TD4 diesel engines, the coolant pump is located on the right-hand end of the engine, and is driven by the auxiliary drivebelt.

The system functions as follows. With the engine cold, the thermostat is closed and circulation is restricted to the cylinder block, cylinder head and heater matrix; there is no circulation through the radiator. When the coolant reaches a predetermined temperature, the thermostat opens and the coolant is allowed to flow freely through the top hose to the radiator. As the coolant circulates through the radiator, it is cooled by the inrush of air when the vehicle is in forward motion. Airflow is supplemented by the action of the electric cooling fan when necessary. Upon reaching the bottom of the radiator, the coolant is now cooled and the cycle is repeated.

With the engine at normal operating temperature, the coolant expands and some of it is displaced into the expansion tank. This coolant collects in the tank and is returned to the radiator when the system cools.

The operation of the fans is controlled by the engine management electronic control module, which receives engine temperature data from the engine coolant temperature sensor. At a predetermined temperature, the ECM energises the relay which operates the cooling fan.

TD4 models are equipped with a PTC (positive temperature co-efficient) heating element, and an FBH (fuel-burning heater) to shorten the passenger cabin heater warm-up period. The PTC is an electrically-powered element located in the top of the heater box behind the facia, whilst the fuel-burning heater is located behind the front bumper, and burns a small amount of diesel to quickly warm-up the coolant flowing through the heater circuit. A small electrically-powered pump, located behind the right-hand rear wheel arch liner, supplies the diesel to the heater from the fuel tank.

Precautions

Cooling system

Do not attempt to remove the expansion tank filler cap or to disturb any part of the cooling system with the engine hot, as there is a risk of scalding. If the expansion tank filler cap must be removed before the engine and radiator have fully cooled down (even though this is not recommended) the pressure in the cooling system must first be released. Cover the cap with a thick layer of cloth, to avoid scalding, and slowly unscrew the filler cap until a hissing sound can be heard. When the hissing has stopped, showing that the pressure is released, slowly unscrew the filler cap until it can be removed. If more hissing sounds are heard, wait until they have stopped before unscrewing the cap completely. At all times keep well away from the filler opening.

Do not allow antifreeze to come in contact with your skin or painted surfaces of the vehicle. Rinse off spills immediately with plenty of water. Never leave antifreeze lying around; it is fatal if ingested.

1.1d Cooling system components – TD4 diesel engine (part 2)

1 O-ring seal	11 O-ring seal
2 Bolt	12 Coolant pipe
3 Coolant rail	13 Coolant pipe-to-thermostat housing hose
4 Bolt	
5 Bolt	14 Bolt
6 Gasket	15 Coolant pump
7 Coolant outlet elbow	16 Gasket
	17 Gasket
8 Oil cooler-to-coolant rail hose	18 Thermostat housing
9 Torx screw	19 Bolt
10 Oil cooler	

If the engine is hot, the electric cooling fan may start rotating even if the engine is not running, so be careful to keep hands, hair and loose clothing well clear when working in the engine compartment.

Air conditioning system

On models equipped with an air conditioning system, it is necessary to observe special precautions whenever dealing with any part of the system, its associated components and any items which necessitate disconnection of the system. If for any reason the system must be disconnected, entrust this task to your Land Rover dealer or a refrigeration engineer.

Refrigerant must not be allowed to come in contact with a naked flame, otherwise a poisonous gas will be created. **Do not** allow the fluid to come in contact with the skin or eyes.

2 Cooling system hoses – disconnection and renewal

⚠️ **Warning: Never work on the cooling system when it is hot. Release any pressure from the system by loosening the expansion tank cap, having first covered it with a cloth to avoid any possibility of scalding.**

1 If inspection of the cooling system reveals a faulty hose, then it must be renewed as follows.

2 First drain the cooling system (see Chapter 1A or 1B). If the coolant is not due for renewal, it may be re-used if collected in a clean container.

3 To disconnect the hoses, use a screwdriver to slacken the clips then move them along the hose clear of the outlet. Carefully work the hose off its outlets. Note that some hoses are secured using a spring-type clip, where the two ends of the clip must be squeezed together to release, and some hoses are secured using a 'quick-release' system. To release these hoses, prise out the retaining clip a little until it is felt to come to a stop, then pull the hose from the connection **(see illustrations)**.

Caution: Do not attempt to disconnect any part of the system when still hot.

4 Note that the radiator hose outlets are fragile. **Do not** use excessive force when attempting to remove the hoses. If a hose proves stubborn, try to release it by rotating it on its outlets before attempting to work it off.

> **HAYNES HiNT**
> *If all else fails, cut the hose with a sharp knife then slit it so that it can be peeled off in two pieces. While expensive, this is preferable to buying a new radiator.*

5 When refitting a hose, first slide the clips onto the hose then work the hose onto its outlets. If the hose is stiff, use washing-up liquid as a lubricant.

6 Work each hose end fully onto its outlet, check that the hose is settled correctly and is properly routed, then slide each clip along the hose until it is behind the outlet flared end before tightening it securely. Spring type clips

2.3a Hoses may be secured by worm-drive clips . . .

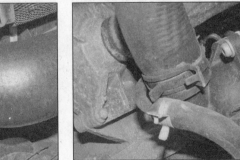

2.3b . . . spring-type clips . . .

2.3c . . . or have quick-release couplings

3.3 Disconnect the expansion tank hose from the outlet stub

3.24a Undo the two bolts securing the condenser to the right-hand side of the radiator ...

must have the ends squeezed together, and the clip positioned over the outlet flared end, then released. Quick-release clips are simply pushed over the outlet until they are heard, or felt, to click into place.

7 Refill the system with coolant (see Chapter 1A or 1B).

8 Check carefully for leaks as soon as possible after disturbing any part of the cooling system.

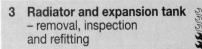

3 Radiator and expansion tank – removal, inspection and refitting

Radiator removal

Petrol engine up to 2001

1 Drain the cooling system (see Chapter 1A).

2 Remove the electric cooling fan assembly as described in Section 6.

3.25 Disconnect the expansion tank hose from the radiator

3.23 Slacken and remove the retaining bolts and remove the intercooler (two arrowed, one hidden)

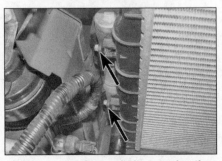

3.24b ... and the two bolts securing the receiver/drier to the left-hand end of the radiator

3 At the top right-hand side of the radiator, loosen the clip and disconnect the expansion tank hose from the outlet stub **(see illustration)**.

4 Loosen the clip and disconnect the top hose from the top right-hand side of the radiator **(see illustration 1.1a)**.

5 Unscrew the retaining pins from the top of the bonnet slam panel **(see illustration 3.27)**.

6 Remove the radiator and recover the lower mounting rubbers.

Petrol engine 2001-on

7 Drain the cooling system (see Chapter 1A).

8 Release the securing clips and disconnect the expansion tank hose and top hose from the radiator.

9 With reference to Chapter 11, remove the front bumper and bumper bar.

10 Remove the electric cooling fan assembly as described in Section 6.

11 On models with air conditioning, unscrew the four retaining bolts and release the

3.27 Unscrew the radiator retaining pins from the bonnet slam panel

condenser from the radiator. Position the condenser to one side – do **not** disconnect the refrigerant pipes.

12 Release the radiator from the lower and upper mountings, and remove it from the vehicle. Recover the rubber mountings. If necessary, the upper mounting brackets can be unscrewed from the radiator.

L-Series diesel engine

13 Drain the cooling system as described in Chapter 1B.

14 Remove the intercooler as described in Chapter 4B.

15 Release the two retaining clips securing the expansion tank hose and the radiator top hose.

16 Unscrew the retaining pins from the top of the radiator slam panel **(see illustration 3.27)**

17 Lift the radiator from the mountings, complete with bottom hose, and remove it from the vehicle. Release the retaining clip and disconnect the bottom hose.

TD4 diesel engine

18 Drain the cooling system as described in Chapter 1B.

19 Undo the three retaining bolts, and remove the engine acoustic cover.

20 Refer to Chapter 11 and remove the front bumper and bumper bar.

21 Release the retaining clips and disconnect the intercooler hoses.

22 Remove the retaining screws and remove the radiator baffles.

23 Slacken and remove the three retaining bolts and remove the intercooler from the radiator **(see illustration)**.

24 Undo the two bolts securing the condenser to the right-hand side of the radiator, and the two bolts securing the receiver/drier to the left-hand end of the radiator **(see illustrations)**. Do **not** disconnect the refrigerant pipes.

25 Release the retaining clips and disconnect the top and bottom hoses, and the expansion tank hose from the radiator **(see illustration)**.

26 Remove the cooling fan assembly as described in Section 6.

27 Unscrew the radiator retaining pins from the bonnet slam panel, and tip the radiator forwards **(see illustration)**.

28 Lift the radiator slightly, and release it from the lower mountings **(see illustration)**.

3.28 Lift the radiator slightly, and release it from the lower mountings

3.39 Undo the expansion tank mounting screw (arrowed)

29 Remove the radiator from the vehicle. On air conditioned models, disengage the radiator from the condenser as the radiator is withdrawn.

Radiator inspection

30 If the radiator was removed because of clogging (causing overheating) then try reverse flushing or, in severe cases, use a radiator cleanser strictly in accordance with the manufacturer's instructions. Refer to Chapter 1A or 1B for further information

31 Use a soft brush and an air line or garden hose to clear the radiator matrix of leaves, insects, etc.

32 Major leaks or extensive damage should be repaired by a specialist, or the radiator should be renewed or exchanged for a reconditioned unit.

33 Examine the mounting rubbers for signs of damage or deterioration and renew if necessary.

Radiator refitting

34 Refitting is a reversal of removal, but tighten all nuts and bolts to the specified torque where given in the Specifications. On completion, refill the cooling system as described in Chapter 1A or 1B.

Expansion tank

Removal

35 With the engine cold, unscrew and remove the filler cap from the expansion tank.

36 Place a suitable container near the expansion tank to collect the drained coolant.

37 Loosen the clip and disconnect the air purge hose from the top of the expansion tank.

38 Release the retaining clip and disconnect the coolant feed hose from the bottom of the tank.

39 Undo the mounting screw and remove the expansion tank **(see illustration)**.

Inspection

40 Empty any remaining coolant from the tank and flush it with fresh water to clean it. If the tank is leaking it must be renewed.

41 The expansion tank cap should be cleaned and checked whenever it is removed. Check that its sealing surfaces and threads are clean and undamaged.

42 The cap's performance can only be checked by using a cap pressure-tester (cooling system tester) with a suitable adaptor. On applying pressure, the cap's pressure relief valve should hold until the specified pressure is reached, at which point the valve should open.

43 If there is any doubt about the cap's performance, then it must be renewed. Ensure that the new one is of the correct type and rating.

Refitting

44 Refitting is a reversal of removal, but tighten the expansion tank mounting securely and top-up the cooling system with reference to *Weekly checks*.

4 Thermostat – removal, testing and refitting

Removal

1 Disconnect the battery negative (earth) lead (see Chapter 5A).
2 Drain the cooling system (see Chapter 1A or 1B).

Petrol models excluding VINs

WA 600000 to YA 699999
YA 500000 to 1A 599999
1A 300000 to 1A 324161
and subsequent models

3 The thermostat is located on the rear right-hand side of the cylinder block, and access to it is best gained from underneath the engine by jacking up the front of the vehicle (see *Jacking and vehicle support*). Undo the retaining screws and remove the engine undertray.
4 Loosen the clip and disconnect the heater hose from the thermostat housing located on the rear of the cylinder block.
5 Unscrew the bolts securing the coolant rail to the cylinder block, then ease the rail from the thermostat housing using a twisting action.
6 Unscrew the bolt securing the thermostat housing to the cylinder block. Ease the thermostat housing from the coolant pump with a twisting action and withdraw.
7 Remove the O-ring seals from the grooves

4.10 The thermostat (arrowed) is located behind the cooling fan on the left-hand side of the engine compartment

in the housing inlet and outlet stubs using a small screwdriver.
8 Unscrew the bolts and separate the cover from the thermostat housing.
9 Remove the thermostat from the housing noting which way round it is fitted, then remove the rubber seal from the periphery of the thermostat.

Petrol models with VINs

WA 600000 to YA 699999
YA 500000 to 1A 599999
1A 300000 to 1A 324161
and subsequent models

10 On the above models, the thermostat position was changed, due to problems with the engines overheating. Instead of being mounted in the cylinder block, the thermostat is now mounted in-line with the radiator hoses at the front left-hand side of the engine compartment **(see illustration)**.
11 To remove the thermostat, release the clips securing the hoses to the thermostat housing, and manoeuvre it from place **(see illustration)**.

L-Series diesel engine

12 The thermostat is located on the front of the cylinder block, bolted to the engine oil cooler. Improved access may be gained from underneath the engine by jacking up the front of the vehicle (see *Jacking and vehicle support*), undoing the retaining screws and removing the engine undertray.
13 Release the retaining clip and disconnect the coolant hose from the thermostat cover **(see illustration)**.

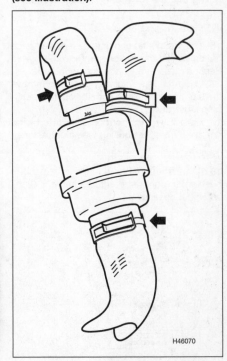

4.11 Release the clips (arrowed) and disconnect the hoses from the thermostat housing

4.13 Release the retaining clip and disconnect the coolant hose from the thermostat cover

4.17 Undo the four retaining bolts (arrowed) and remove the thermostat housing

a) Clean all mating surfaces thoroughly before reassembly.
b) Renew all seals and gaskets, and smear O-rings with a little rubber grease to aid seating **(see illustration)**.
c) Tighten all bolts to their specified torque wrench settings (where given).
d) Ensure the coolant hose clips are positioned so that they do not foul any other component, then tighten them securely.
e) Refill the cooling system (see Chapter 1A or 1B).

4.18a To remove the thermostat, press down, rotate it anti-clockwise ...

4.18b ... and lift it from the housing

5 Coolant pump – removal and refitting

Removal

1 Coolant pump failure is usually indicated by coolant leaking from the gland behind the pump bearing, or by rough and noisy operation, usually accompanied by excessive pump spindle play. If the pump shows any of these symptoms then it must be renewed as follows.
2 Drain the cooling system (see Chapter 1A or 1B).

Petrol engine

3 The coolant pump is located on the right-hand rear end of the cylinder block.
4 Remove the timing belt as described in Chapter 2A.
Caution: Do not rotate the engine with the timing belt removed.
5 Unscrew and remove the single rear bolt securing the coolant pump to the cylinder block flange **(see illustration)**.
6 Note the location of the pillar bolt for the timing cover, then unscrew and remove all the retaining bolts.
7 Withdraw the coolant pump from the cylinder block, then prise out the O-ring seal from the groove in the rear mating face. Discard the seal and obtain a new one. Note the location dowel on the cylinder block.

L-Series diesel engine without air conditioning

8 The coolant pump is located on a bracket

14 Remove the four retaining bolts and remove the thermostat cover. Discard the O-ring, a new one must be fitted.
15 Withdraw the thermostat from the cover, noting that the thermostat spindle locates in the cover recess.

TD4 diesel engine

16 The thermostat can only be renewed once the coolant pump has been removed. Refer to Section 5 and remove the coolant pump.
17 Undo the four retaining bolts and remove the thermostat housing from the coolant pump **(see illustration)**.
18 Note how the thermostat is fitted, and remove it from the housing **(see illustrations)**.

Testing

19 If the thermostat remains in the open position at room temperature, then it is faulty and must be renewed.

20 To test it fully, suspend the (closed) thermostat on a length of string in a container of cold water, with a thermometer beside it **(see illustration)**.
21 Heat the water and check the temperature at which the thermostat begins to open. Compare this value with that specified. Continue to heat the water until the thermostat is fully open. The temperature at which this should happen is usually stamped in the unit's end **(see illustration)**. Allow the thermostat to cool down and check that it closes fully.
22 If the thermostat does not open and close as described, if it sticks in either position, or if it does not open at the specified temperature, then it must be renewed.

Refitting

23 Refitting is a reversal of removal, but note the following additional points:

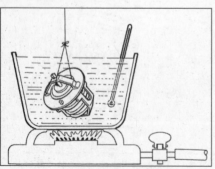

4.20 Testing the thermostat

4.21 The thermostat opening temperature is normally stamped on its end

4.23 Renew the thermostat seal(s)

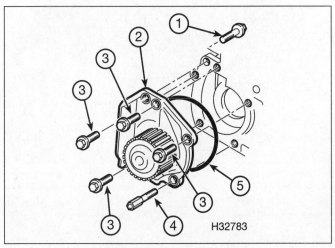

5.5 Coolant pump – petrol models

1 Cylinder block flange
   bolt
2 Coolant pump
3 Coolant pump bolts
4 Pillar bolt
5 O-ring seal

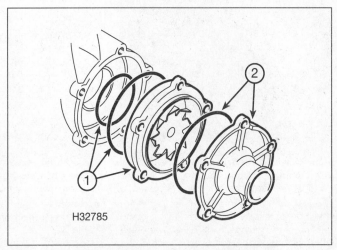

5.10 Coolant pump – L-Series diesel models

1 Coolant pump and O-ring seals
2 Coolant pump cover and O-ring seal

attached to the front right-hand end of the cylinder block, and is driven by the power steering pump which is driven from the crankshaft pulley by the auxiliary drivebelt. The bracket incorporates an internal channel connected to the cylinder block.

9 Release the retaining clip and disconnect the coolant hose from the pump housing.

10 Unscrew the five bolts securing the coolant pump cover, and remove the pump. Discard the O-rings, new ones must be fitted **(see illustration)**.

L-Series diesel engine with air conditioning

11 The coolant pump is located on a bracket attached to the front right-hand end of the cylinder block, and is driven by the power steering pump which is driven from the crankshaft pulley by the auxiliary drivebelt. The bracket incorporates an internal channel connected to the cylinder block.

12 Remove the alternator (see Chapter 5A).

13 Loosen the clips and disconnect the top hose from the radiator, thermostat and engine outlet. Withdraw the hose from the engine compartment.

14 Loosen the clip and disconnect the hose from the coolant pump. Unscrew the five pump cover bolts.

15 Remove the pump cover and prise the O-ring seal from the groove in the water pump flange. Discard the seal and obtain a new one.

16 Remove the coolant pump from the bracket and prise out the O-ring seals. Discard the seals and obtain new ones.

TD4 diesel engine

17 With reference to Chapter 2C, remove the camshaft cover.

18 Slacken the right-hand front roadwheel nuts, firmly apply the handbrake then jack up the front of the vehicle and support it securely on axle stands (see *Jacking and vehicle support*). Remove the front right-hand road wheel.

19 Remove the auxiliary drivebelt (see Chapter 1B).

20 Unscrew the two retaining bolts, and remove the engine lower tie bar.

21 Position a jack under the engine with a block of wood between the jack head and casing, and take the weight if the engine and transmission.

22 Unscrew and remove the two bolts securing the engine upper tie bar.

23 Slacken and remove the four bolts and one nut securing the right-hand engine mounting arm to the engine and the Hydramount. Remove the arm.

24 Working through the right-hand wheel arch aperture, release the retaining clips and disconnect the hose between the thermostat and lower coolant rail **(see illustration)**.

25 Release the clip and disconnect the expansion tank hose from the upper coolant rail.

26 Slacken the retaining clips and disconnect the turbocharger outlet hose.

27 Unscrew the bolts securing the coolant rail to the exhaust manifold, fuel pipe, and cylinder head **(see illustration)**.

28 Undo the three Allen screws securing the coolant rail heat shield adjacent to the thermostat housing **(see illustration)**.

29 Slacken and remove the bolt securing the coolant rail to the thermostat housing (discard the seal – a new one must be fitted), and remove the heat shield **(see illustration)**.

30 Using the jack, adjust the height of the engine for access to the coolant pump bolts. Unscrew the four bolts and remove the coolant pump **(see illustration)**. If this is

5.24 Disconnect the hose between the thermostat and lower coolant rail (arrowed)

5.27 Unscrew the bolts securing the coolant rail to the exhaust manifold

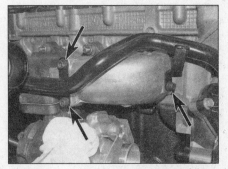

5.28 Undo the three Allen screws securing the coolant rail heat shield (arrowed)

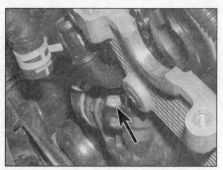

5.29 Remove the bolt securing the coolant rail to the thermostat housing (arrowed)

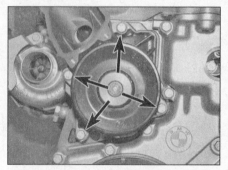

5.30a Unscrew the four bolts (arrowed) and remove the coolant pump

5.30b If necessary, cut the coolant pump section of the timing cover gasket away

the first time the pump has been removed, it will be necessary to cut the coolant pump section of the timing cover gasket away **(see illustration)**. Once removed, discard the gasket.

Refitting

31 Refitting is a reversal of removal, but note the following additional points:
  a) *Clean all mating surfaces thoroughly before reassembly.*
  b) *Renew all seals and gaskets, and smear O-rings with a little rubber grease to aid seating.*
  c) *Tighten all bolts to their specified torque wrench settings (where given).*
  d) *Ensure the coolant hose clips are positioned so that they do not foul any other component, then tighten them securely.*
  e) *Refill the cooling system as described in Chapter 1A or 1B.*

---

6   Electric cooling fan assembly –
testing, removal and refitting

Testing

1 The cooling fan motor is supplied with current via the ignition switch, a fuse and the cooling fan relay. The relay is energised by the engine management ECM (electronic control module).
2 If the fan does not appear to work, first check that the fuse is in good condition and

6.15 Disconnect the wiring plugs from the relay housing

not blown (see Chapter 12). Check all relevant wiring and connectors. Check the relay (see Chapter 12).
3 To check the motor itself, disconnect the wiring loom from the motor, and connect a 12 volt supply directly to it. If the motor does not work then it must be renewed. Further investigation and diagnosis is only possible using dedicated test equipment, which can interrogate the engine management ECM for any stored fault codes. Consult your Land Rover dealer or specialist.

Removal

4 Disconnect the battery negative (earth) lead (see Chapter 5A).

Petrol engine without air conditioning

5 Disconnect the wiring multiplug from the electric cooling fan motor, and release the harness from the retaining clips. On models from 2001-on, disconnect the wiring plugs from the relay housing at the top of the fan assembly.
6 Unscrew and remove the four bolts and the clip securing the fan assembly to the radiator. Remove the fan assembly.
7 To remove the fan motor, unscrew the three fan motor mounting bolts.

Petrol engine with air conditioning up to 2001

8 Remove the air cleaner as described in Chapter 4A.
9 Disconnect the wiring multiplugs from the electric cooling fan motors, and release the wiring harness from the retaining clips.
10 Unscrew and remove the four bolts, and

6.25 Undo the retaining nuts, and move the fuel cooling matrix

the top and bottom clips securing the fan assembly to the radiator. Remove the fan assembly.
11 To remove the fan motors, unscrew the three fan motor mounting bolts.

Petrol engine with air conditioning 2001-on

12 With reference to Chapter 5A, remove the battery tray.
13 Drain the cooling system as described in Chapter 1A.
14 Release the retaining clip and disconnect the radiator top hose.
15 Disconnect the wiring plugs from the fan motors and the relay housing at the top of the fan assembly **(see illustration)**.
16 Undo the four bolts securing the fan assembly to the radiator.
17 Unscrew the two radiator retaining pins from the bonnet slam panel **(see illustration 3.27)**.
18 Manoeuvre the fan assembly from the engine compartment.
19 To remove the fan motors, unscrew the three fan motor mounting bolts.

L-Series diesel engine

20 Undo the retaining screws and remove the engine acoustic cover.
21 Release the retaining clip and disconnect the intercooler top hose.
22 Remove the battery as described in Chapter 5A.
23 Disconnect the air intake elbow from the air cleaner and resonator box pipe.
24 Unscrew the two bolts securing the air cleaner assembly to the battery carrier, and lift the air cleaner from its locating peg and position to one side.
25 Undo the retaining nuts, and move the fuel cooling matrix (fitted to the bonnet slam panel) to one side **(see illustration)**. Do not disconnect the matrix fuel pipes.
26 Disconnect the wiring multiplug from the electric cooling fan motors, and release the wiring harness from the retaining clips.
27 Unscrew and remove the four retaining bolts, the top and bottom clips, and remove the fan assembly **(see illustrations)**.
28 To remove the fan motors, unscrew the three fan motor mounting bolts **(see illustration)**.

TD4 diesel engine up to 2003

29 Undo the three retaining bolts and remove the engine acoustic cover (where fitted).

30 Slacken and remove the mounting nuts, and position the fuel cooler to one side **(see illustration)**. Note: *There is no need to disconnect the fuel pipes from the cooler.*

31 Disconnect the wiring plugs from the fan motors and relay housing, located at the top of the fan assembly. Release the wiring harness from the retaining clips.

32 Unscrew the four securing bolts, and manoeuvre the fan assembly from the engine compartment.

33 To remove the fan motors, unscrew the three fan motor mounting bolts.

TD4 diesel engine from 2003

34 Release the clip and disconnect the radiator bottom hose to drain the coolant system (see Chapter 1B).

35 Slacken and remove the mounting nuts, and position the fuel cooler to one side. **Note:** *There is no need to disconnect the fuel pipes from the cooler.*

36 Release the clips and remove the intercooler inlet hose.

37 Release the clip and disconnect the top hose from the radiator.

38 Disconnect the wiring plugs from the cooling fan control unit.

39 Unscrew the four securing bolts, and manoeuvre the fan assembly from the engine compartment.

40 To remove the fan motors, unscrew the three fan motor mounting bolts.

Refitting

41 Refitting is a reversal of removal, but on completion refill the cooling system as described in Chapter 1A or 1B.

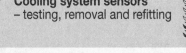

7 Cooling system sensors
– testing, removal and refitting

Temperature sensor testing

1 The engine coolant temperature sensor monitors the temperature of the coolant as it leaves the engine. The sensor is a 'thermistor' with a Negative Temperature Coefficient, ie, the resistance of the sensor decreases as the temperature increases. The signal from the sensor is used by the engine management ECM (electronic control module) to regulate fuel injection quantity and timing, ignition timing, glow plugs, cooling fan operation, and the temperature gauge in the instrument cluster (on L-Series engines, a separate sender unit for the temperature gauge is fitted – see below). Should the sensor fail, the ECM will adopt a predetermined substitute value, and illuminate the MIL (malfunction indicator lamp) on the instrument cluster. No specific test values are available for the sensor. Consequently, testing is limited to

6.27a Unscrew and remove the four fan assembly retaining bolts . . .

6.28 Unscrew the three fan motor mounting bolts

inspecting the wiring and connectors to the sensor. Further investigation can only be carried out by the use of dedicated test equipment. Consult your Land Rover dealer or fuel injection specialist. Testing by any other means could result in ECM damage.

Temperature sensor removal

2 Disconnect the battery negative lead (see Chapter 5A).

Petrol engine

3 The sensor is located in the coolant outlet elbow at the front left-hand end of the cylinder head. Disconnect the wiring plug, and unscrew the sensor from the elbow. Be prepared for coolant spillage **(see illustration)**.

L-Series diesel engine

4 The sensor is located in the coolant outlet elbow at the front right-hand end of the cylinder head. Undo the retaining screws and

7.3 Disconnect the wiring plug, and unscrew the sensor – petrol engine

6.27b . . . and release the retaining clips (upper clip arrowed – lower clip hidden)

6.30 Slacken and remove the fuel cooler mounting nuts

remove the engine acoustic cover.

5 Disconnect the wiring plug, and unscrew the sensor from the outlet. Be prepared for coolant spillage **(see illustration)**.

TD4 diesel engine

6 Drain the cooling system as described in Chapter 1B.

7 With reference to Chapter 4B, remove the intake manifold.

8 Disconnect the wiring plug from the sensor, and using a deep socket, unscrew it from the cylinder head **(see illustration)**. Discard the seal – a new one must be fitted.

Temperature sensor refitting

9 Refitting is a reversal of removal, but apply suitable sealant (Land Rover recommend Loctite 577) to the sensor threads and tighten it to the specified torque. Top-up the cooling system with reference to *Weekly checks*.

7.5 Disconnect the wiring plug, and unscrew the sensor – L-Series diesel engine

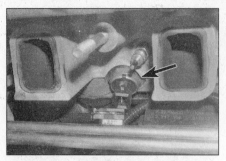

7.8 Disconnect the wiring plug, and unscrew the sensor (arrowed) – TD4 diesel engine

7.11 Disconnect the wiring plug from the temperature gauge sender unit – L-Series diesel engine

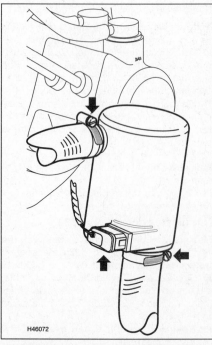

7.16 Disconnect the coolant level sensor wiring plug and hose clips (arrowed)

Temperature gauge sender unit

L-Series diesel engine

10 The sender unit is located on the underside of the coolant elbow at the right-hand side of the engine. On models with air conditioning, it is necessary to remove the alternator as described in Chapter 5A.

11 Disconnect the wiring plug from the sender unit **(see illustration)**.

12 Unscrew the sender from the coolant elbow. Be prepared for coolant spillage, or drain the cooling system as described in Chapter 1B.

13 Ensure that the threads of the sender unit are clean and dry. Apply a smear of sealant to the threads (Land Rover recommend Loctite 577), and screw the gauge in to the elbow, tightening it to the specified torque.

14 The remainder of refitting is a reversal of removal. Replenish the cooling system as described in Chapter 1B.

Coolant level sensor

Petrol engine

Note: *On early models without a coolant level sensor, a retro-fit kit is available from Land Rover dealers.*

15 The sensor is located in the right-hand rear corner of the engine compartment. Clamp the hoses either side of the level sensor housing to prevent coolant loss.

16 Disconnect the unit wiring plug, then release the clips and disconnect the hoses from the sensor housing **(see illustration)**.

17 Refitting is a reversal of removal. Top-up the cooling system as described in Chapter 1A.

---

8 Heating and ventilation system – general information

The heating/ventilation system consists of a blower motor (housed in the heater distribution box in the centre of the facia), face level vents in the centre and at each end of the facia, and air ducts to the front and rear footwells.

The control unit is located in the centre of the facia, and the controls operate flap valves to deflect and mix the air flowing through the various parts of the heating/ventilation system. The flap valves are contained in the air distribution housing, which acts as a central distribution unit, passing air to the various ducts and vents.

Cold air enters the system through the grille at the rear of the engine compartment. If required, the airflow is boosted by the blower fan, and then flows through the various ducts, according to the settings of the controls. Stale air is expelled through ducts at the rear of the vehicle. If warm air is required, the cold air is passed over the heater matrix, which is heated by the engine coolant.

A recirculation switch enables the outside air supply to be closed off, while the air inside the vehicle is recirculated. This can be useful to prevent unpleasant odours entering from outside the vehicle, but should only be used briefly, as the recirculated air inside the vehicle will soon become stale.

---

9 Heating and ventilation system components – removal and refitting

Heater unit

1 Drain the cooling system as described in Chapter 1A or 1B, or alternatively clamp the heater hoses at the bulkhead in the engine compartment using purpose-made hose clamps.

2 With reference to Chapter 11, remove the facia.

3 Undo the two retaining bolts and remove the centre console support bracket **(see illustration)**.

4 Release the clips and disconnect the hoses from the heater matrix tubes on the bulkhead. If the original spring-type clips are fitted, use a pair of grips to release them, as they are very tight **(see illustration)**.

5 Disconnect the wiring plugs from the heater control panel switches, and release the wiring harnesses and relays from the retaining clips on the heater box **(see illustration)**.

9.3 Remove the centre console support bracket

9.4 Release the clips and disconnect the hoses from the heater matrix tubes on the bulkhead

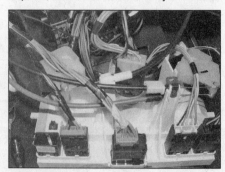

9.5 Disconnect the wiring plugs from the heater control panel switches

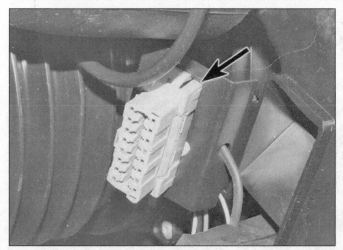

9.6 Depress the retaining clips and release the diagnostic socket from the heater box bracket (arrowed)

9.8 Unscrew the bolt (arrowed) and remove the passenger side outer face level vent/duct. Where fitted, remove the two bolts securing the passenger side airbag mounting bracket (arrowed)

9.10 Remove the left-hand windscreen demister vent ducts

9.11 Remove the air inlet connector hose

9.12a Slacken and remove the two nuts at the top of the heater box

6 Depress the retaining clips and release the diagnostic socket from the heater box bracket **(see illustration)**.

7 On models with air conditioning, disconnect the wiring plug from the evaporator.

8 Undo the bolts and remove the passenger side airbag mounting bracket (where fitted). Unscrew the retaining bolt, and remove the passenger side outer face level vent/duct **(see illustration)**.

9 Unscrew the driver's side outer face level vent/duct retaining bolt to allow the duct to be manoeuvred.

10 Remove the left- and right-hand windscreen demister vent ducts **(see illustration)**.

11 From the passenger side of the heater box, remove the air inlet connector hose **(see illustration)**.

12 Slacken and remove the two nuts at the top of the heater box, and the screw on the lower passenger side of the box, and remove the heater from the vehicle **(see illustration)**. If necessary, the various blend and distribution cables can be disconnected from the heater box. Note the fitted locations of the cables prior to disconnection **(see illustration)**.

13 Refitting is a reverse of the removal procedure, but tighten all nuts and bolts securely and on completion refill the cooling system as described in Chapter 1A or 1B.

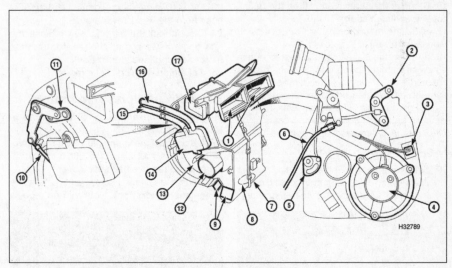

9.12b Heater box details – RHD models (LHD models similar)

1 Centre face level vent outlets
2 Fresh air flap lever
3 Blower motor resistor pack
4 Blower motor
5 Distribution flap lever
6 Distribution control cable
7 Heater box
8 Rear footwells air outlet
9 Front footwells air outlet
10 Control cable – temperature blend flap
11 Temperature blend flap lever
12 Windscreen and side window air outlet
13 Air inlet
14 Heater matrix cover
15 Engine coolant inlet pipe
16 Engine coolant return pipe
17 Outer face level vent outlet

9.16 Remove the screws (arrowed) and lift off the matrix cover

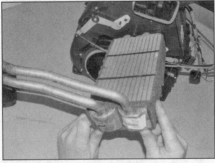

9.17 Slide the matrix from the heater housing

9.20 Slacken and remove the heater blower motor mounting screws

9.24 Release the retaining screws and lift the resistor from the motor housing

9.28 Undo the retaining screw (arrowed), and remove the servo

Heater matrix

14 Remove the heater unit as described previously in this Section.

15 Undo the screw and remove the pipe retaining clamp.

16 Remove the screws and lift off the matrix cover **(see illustration)**.

17 Slide the matrix from the heater housing **(see illustration)**.

18 If the matrix is leaking, it is best to obtain a new or reconditioned unit as home repairs are seldom successful. If it is blocked, it can sometimes be cleared by reverse-flushing using a garden hose. Use a proprietary radiator cleaning product if absolutely necessary.

19 Refitting is a reversal of removal.

Heater blower motor

20 Slacken and remove the mounting screws and pull the blower motor from its housing on the driver's side of the heater box **(see illustration)**.

21 Disconnect the wiring and manoeuvre the motor from under the facia.

22 Refitting is a reversal of removal.

Heater blower motor resistor

23 On LHD models, disconnect the air inlet hose from the heater/evaporator.

24 Disconnect the wiring, then release the retaining screws and lift the resistor from the motor housing **(see illustration)**.

25 Refitting is a reversal of removal.

Air recirculation servo motor

26 Remove the glovebox as described in Chapter 11, Section 27.

27 Disconnect the wiring plug from the servo. Note that on models up to 2001, undo the screws and remove the servo cover.

28 Undo the retaining screw, and remove the servo **(see illustration)**. Note that on models

up to 2001, the servo is retained by three screws, and an operating rod.

29 Refitting is a reversal of removal.

Heater control panel

30 Remove the centre console as described in Chapter 11.

31 Note the position of the outer control cables in their clips as a guide for refitting, then disconnect them.

32 Disconnect the wiring plugs from the rear of the control panel, noting the fitted locations of the plugs **(see illustration 9.5)**.

33 Withdraw the control panel from the facia.

34 Refitting is a reversal of removal, but position the cables to their original settings.

Heater control panel switches

35 To remove the push-button switches, pull the three heater control knobs from the panel.

36 Undo the two screws recessed into the left- and right-hand knob apertures, and remove the trim panel **(see illustrations)**.

37 Pull the relevant switch from its mounting, and disconnect the wiring plug as the switch is withdrawn **(see illustration)**.

38 To remove the blower motor speed control switch, remove the heater control panel as described in this Section.

39 Disconnect the wiring plug from the rear of the switch.

40 Pull the control shaft from the front of the switch.

41 Remove the two retaining screws, and pull the switch from the panel.

42 Refitting is a reversal of removal.

9.36a Undo the two screws recessed into the left- and right-hand knob apertures (arrowed) . . .

9.36b . . . and remove the panel

9.37 Pull the relevant switch from its mounting

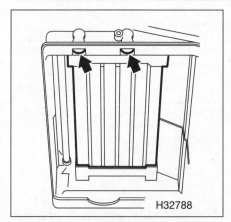

9.50 Disconnect the coolant feed and return hoses from the FBH (arrowed)

9.51 Release the retaining clip and disconnect the fuel feed pipe

9.44 Release the PTC element retaining stud bosses from their locating holes in the heater box (arrowed)

Positive temperature co-efficient (PTC) heater

TD4 diesel engine

43 Remove the heater matrix as described in this earlier in this Section.

44 Release the PTC element retaining stud bosses from their locating holes in the heater box **(see illustration)**.

45 Prise out the PTC element wiring harness grommet from the passenger side of the heater box, and remove the element, guiding the harness through box as the element is withdrawn.

46 Refitting is a reversal of removal.

Fuel-burning heater (FBH)

TD4 diesel engine

47 Disconnect the battery negative lead (see Chapter 5A).

48 Drain the cooling system as described in Chapter 1B.

49 With reference to Chapter 11, remove the front bumper.

50 Release the retaining clips and disconnect the coolant feed and return hoses from the FBH **(see illustration)**. Be prepared for coolant spillage.

51 Position absorbent cloths around the connection, release the retaining clip and disconnect the fuel feed pipe to the FBH **(see**

9.52a Undo the mounting bolts ...

illustration). Be prepared for fuel spillage, and plug the open connections.

52 Undo the two mounting bolts, and remove the FBH. Disconnect the wiring plugs as the unit is withdrawn **(see illustrations)**.

53 Slacken and remove the three retaining bolts and remove the mounting bracket from the FBH.

54 Release the retaining clip and disconnect the air intake hose **(see illustration)**.

55 Undo the two retaining bolts and remove the air intake and exhaust assembly from the FBH. No further dismantling of the unit is recommended. Consult your Land Rover dealer for repair/renewal options.

56 Refitting is a reversal of removal.

Fuel-burning heater (FBH) pump

TD4 diesel engine

57 Disconnect the battery negative lead (see Chapter 5A).

9.52b ... and disconnect the wiring plug

58 With reference to Chapter 11, remove the right-hand rear wheel arch liner.

59 Disconnect the wiring plug from the pump **(see illustration)**.

60 Clean around the fuel pipe connections to prevent dirt ingress, then release the retaining clips and disconnect the fuel pipes from the pump. Note the fitted positions of the pipes prior to disconnection, and be prepared for fuel spillage.

61 Release the pump from the rubber mountings and withdraw from the vehicle.

62 Refitting is a reversal of removal.

Outside temperature sensor

63 Remove the front bumper as described in Chapter 11.

64 Disconnect the wiring plug, remove the sensor from the mounting bracket. Recover the rubber washer and spacer **(see illustration)**.

65 Refitting is a reversal of removal.

9.54 Release the retaining clip and disconnect the air intake hose

9.59 Disconnect the wiring plug from the pump (arrowed)

9.64 Disconnect the sensor wiring plug

10 Air conditioning system
– general information and precautions

General information

1 An air conditioning system is available as an option on all models. The system enables the temperature of incoming air to be lowered, and it also dehumidifies the air, which makes for rapid demisting and increased comfort.

2 The cooling side of the system works in the same way as a domestic refrigerator. Refrigerant gas is drawn into a belt-driven compressor, and passes into a condenser mounted on the front of the radiator, where it loses heat and becomes liquid. The liquid passes through an expansion valve to an evaporator, where it changes from liquid under high pressure to gas under low pressure. This change is accompanied by a drop in temperature, which cools the evaporator. The refrigerant returns to the compressor, and the cycle begins again **(see illustration)**.

3 Air blown through the evaporator passes to the air distribution unit and then into the passenger compartment.

4 The heating side of the system works in the same way as on models without air conditioning.

5 The system is electronically-controlled. Any problems with the system should be referred to a Land Rover dealer or automotive air conditioning specialist **(see Tool tip)**.

Precautions

6 With an air conditioning system, it is necessary to observe special precautions whenever dealing with any part of the system, or its associated components. If for any reason the system must be disconnected, entrust this task to your Land Rover dealer or a refrigeration engineer.

⚠ **Warning: The refrigeration circuit contains a liquid refrigerant which is potentially dangerous, and should only be handled by qualified persons. If it is splashed onto the skin, it can cause frostbite. It is not itself poisonous, but in the presence of a naked flame (including a cigarette), it forms a poisonous gas. Uncontrolled discharging of the refrigerant is dangerous, and potentially damaging to the environment. For all these reasons, it is dangerous to disconnect any part of the system without specialised knowledge and equipment. Note that Land Rover recommend the receiver/drier is renewed every time the air conditioning system is opened.**

7 Do not operate the air conditioning system if it is known to be short of refrigerant, as this may damage the compressor.

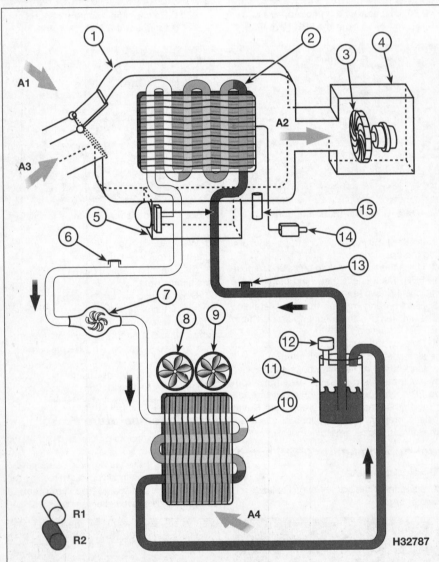

10.2 Air conditioning system

1 Cooling unit	8 Cooling fan	A1 Recirculated air flow
2 Evaporator	9 Condenser fan	A2 Cooled air to the heater
3 Blower	10 Condenser	assembly
4 Heater assembly	11 Receiver/drier	A3 Fresh air flow
5 Thermostatic expansion	12 Trinary pressure switch	A4 Ambient air through the
valve	13 High-pressure servicing	condenser
6 Low pressure servicing	connection	R1 Refrigerant vapour
connection	14 Thermostat	R2 Refrigerant liquid
7 Compressor	15 Water condensate drain	

TOOL TiP

Many car accessory shops sell one-shot air conditioning recharge aerosols. These generally contain refrigerant, compressor oil, leak sealer and system conditioner. Some also have a dye to help pinpoint leaks.

⚠ **Warning: These products must only be used as directed by the manufacturer, and do not remove the need for regular maintenance.**

11.8 Unscrew and remove the compressor mounting bolts

11 Air conditioning system components – removal and refitting

⚠ **Warning: The air conditioning system must be professionally discharged before carrying out any of the following work. Cap or plug the pipe lines as soon as they are disconnected to prevent the entry of moisture. Note also that Land Rover recommend the receiver/drier is renewed every time the system is opened.**

Compressor

1 Have the air conditioning system discharged by a qualified refrigeration engineer.
2 Disconnect the battery negative (earth) lead (see Chapter 5A).
3 Apply the handbrake, then jack up the front of the vehicle and support it on axle stands (see *Jacking and vehicle support*). Undo the retaining screws and remove the engine undertray.
4 Remove the alternator as described in Chapter 5A. On L-Series diesel engines, remove the auxiliary drivebelt, and on TD4 diesel engines, remove the compressor drivebelt (see Chapter 1B).
5 Disconnect the wiring plug from the compressor located in the right-hand corner of the engine compartment.
6 Unscrew the bolt and detach the air conditioning pipe unions from the compressor. Tape over or plug the refrigerant apertures.
7 Remove the seals and discard. New ones must be fitted on refitting.
8 Support the compressor, then unscrew and remove the mounting bolts and lower the unit from under the engine compartment **(see illustration)**.
9 Refitting is a reversal of removal, but renew the receiver/drier and tighten all bolts to the specified torque. Before fitting the new seals, smear a little refrigerant oil on each side. On completion, have the air conditioning system recharged by a refrigeration specialist or suitably-equipped Land Rover dealer.

Condenser

10 Have the air conditioning system discharged by a qualified refrigeration engineer.

11.13 On models 2001 model year-on, undo the four screws (arrowed) and remove the receiver/drier

11 Remove the front bumper and bumper bar as described in Chapter 11.
12 On diesel models, remove the intercooler as described in Chapter 4B.
13 On models 2001 model year-on, undo the four screws and remove the receiver/drier **(see illustration)**.
14 On all models, unscrew the bolts securing the condenser to the radiator, then release the mountings and withdraw the condenser **(see illustration)**.
15 Unscrew the bolts and detach the air conditioning pipes from the condenser. Tape over or plug the refrigerant apertures. Remove the seals and discard. New ones must be fitted on refitting.
16 Refitting is a reversal of removal, tighten all bolts to the specified torque. Before fitting the new seals, smear a little refrigerant oil on them. On completion, have the air conditioning system recharged by a refrigeration specialist or suitably-equipped Land Rover dealer.

Evaporator

17 Have the air conditioning system discharged by a qualified refrigeration engineer.
18 Undo the retaining bolt and disconnect the air conditioning pipes from the thermostatic expansion valve on the engine compartment bulkhead **(see illustration 11.40)**. Discard the O-ring seals, new ones must be fitted.
19 With reference to Chapter 11, remove the facia.
20 Slacken and remove the retaining bolt, and remove the driver's side face level ducting.
21 Pull out the heater control panel, and

11.22a Unscrew the two nuts ...

11.14 Unscrew the bolts securing the condenser to the radiator (arrowed)

disconnect the wiring plugs from the air conditioning switches and the heater harness.
22 Unscrew the two nuts securing the evaporator housing to the body **(see illustrations)**.
23 Disconnect the evaporator air intake and drain hose. Remove the evaporator housing from the vehicle.
24 Remove the retaining screws and lift the top half of the housing away.
25 Lift the evaporator from the housing. If required, unscrew the two Allen screws and remove the thermostatic expansion valve from the evaporator. Discard the O-ring seals, new ones must be used.
26 Refitting is a reversal of removal, but tighten the bolts to the specified torque where given. Before fitting the new seals, smear a little refrigerant oil on each side. On completion, have the air conditioning system recharged by a refrigeration specialist or suitably-equipped Land Rover dealer.

Receiver/drier

Note: *Land Rover recommend that the receiver/drier is renewed every time the air conditioning system is opened.*
27 Have the air conditioning system discharged by a qualified refrigeration engineer.

Models up to 2001

28 Disconnect the air intake elbow from the air cleaner assembly.
29 Release the wiring plug from the trinary switch **(see illustration)**.
30 Unscrew the bolts and detach the air

11.22b ... securing the evaporator housing to the body

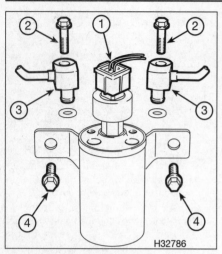

11.29 Receiver/drier components

1 Trinary switch wiring plug
2 Pipe securing bolts
3 Air conditioning pipes
4 Receiver/drier mounting bolts

11.40 Unscrew the bolt securing the air conditioning pipes to the expansion valve

11.44 Disconnect the wiring plug from the refrigerant pressure sensor

conditioning pipe connectors from the receiver/drier. Remove the O-ring seals and discard them; new ones must be fitted on refitting. Tape over or plug the refrigerant apertures.

31 Undo the two bolts and remove the receiver/drier.

Models 2001-on

32 Remove the front bumper and bumper bar as described in Chapter 11.

33 On TD4 models, remove the intercooler as described in Chapter 4B.

34 Undo the four clamping screws and remove the receiver/drier **(see illustration 11.13)**.

All models

35 Refitting is a reversal of removal, but tighten the mounting bolts to the specified

torque where given. Before fitting the new seals, smear a little refrigerant oil on each side. On completion, have the air conditioning system recharged by a refrigeration specialist or suitably-equipped Land Rover dealer.

Trinary pressure switch

Models up to 2001

36 Since the receiver/drier must be renewed whenever the air conditioning system is opened, the removal and refitting procedure for the trinary pressure switch is identical to that given for the receiver/drier. Refer to the previous paragraphs.

Thermostatic expansion valve

Models up to 2001

37 Remove the evaporator as described in this Section.

38 Undo the two Allen screws and remove the valve from the evaporator. Discard the O-ring seals, new ones must be fitted.

Models 2001-on

39 Have the air conditioning system discharged by a qualified refrigeration engineer.

40 Unscrew the bolt securing the air conditioning pipes to the valve on the engine compartment bulkhead **(see illustration)**. Discard the O-ring seals, new ones must be fitted.

All models

41 Refitting is a reversal of removal.

Refrigerant pressure sensor

Models 2001 year-on

42 Have the air conditioning system discharged by a qualified refrigeration engineer.

43 On TD4 models, jack up the front of the vehicle and support it securely on axle stands (see *Jacking and vehicle support*). Undo the retaining screws and remove the engine undertray.

44 Disconnect the wiring plug from the sensor, located on the air conditioning pipe in the left-hand front corner of the engine compartment **(see illustration)**.

45 Unscrew the sensor from the pipe, using another spanner on the pipe union to counter hold the sensor. Discard the O-ring, a new one must be used.

Chapter 4 Part A:
Fuel and exhaust systems – petrol engines

Contents

Degrees of difficulty

Easy, suitable for novice with little experience	**Fairly easy,** suitable for beginner with some experience	**Fairly difficult,** suitable for competent DIY mechanic	**Difficult,** suitable for experienced DIY mechanic	**Very difficult,** suitable for expert DIY or professional

Specifications

System type

Models up to 2001 . . . .   Rover/Motorola multi-point injection Modular Engine Management system MEMS 1.9*

Models 2001-on . . . .   Rover/Motorola multi-point injection Modular Engine Management system MEMS 3*

* See Section 6 for further information

Fuel system data

Fuel pump type . . . .   Electric, immersed in tank
Fuel pump pressure (approximate):
  Regulated . . . .   3.5 ± 0.2 bar
Specified idle speed. . . . .   775 ± 50 rpm not adjustable
Idle mixture CO content . . . .   Regulated by ECM not adjustable

Recommended fuel

Minimum octane rating. . . . .   95 RON unleaded (UK unleaded premium).
Leaded fuel must **not** be used

Torque wrench settings

	Nm	lbf ft
Air cleaner-to-battery bolt	9	7
Alternator mounting bracket	25	18
Alternator mounting bracket stud	25	18
Camshaft sensor bolt (MEMS 3 only)	6	4
Coolant temperature sensor	15	11
Crankshaft position sensor bolt	6	4
Electronic Control Module (ECM) nuts	9	7
Exhaust manifold heat shield:		
Bolts	10	7
Nut	25	18
Exhaust manifold nuts/bolts	45	33
Exhaust system fasteners:		
Front pipe-to-manifold nuts	45	33
Front pipe-to-catalytic converter nuts	60	41
Front pipe mounting nuts	25	18
Intermediate pipe-to-catalytic converter nuts	60	44
Intermediate pipe-to-tailpipe clamp nut	55	40
Fuel breather valve retaining nut	9	7
Fuel filler neck to body	9	7
Fuel pump/sender unit-to-tank locking ring	45	33
Fuel rail bolts	10	7
Fuel tank cradle bolts	45	33
Idle air control valve screws	2	1
Inlet manifold nuts/bolts	17	13
Intake air temperature sensor	7	5
Oxygen sensor	50	37
Rear subframe mounting bolts	190	140
Spark plugs	27	20
Spark plug cover	10	7
Throttle housing retaining bolts	7	5
Throttle position sensor screws*	2	1

* Do not re-use

1.1a Engine management components – MEMS 1.8

1 Air cleaner	5 Intake air temperature sensor	7 Oxygen sensor	9 Fuel injectors
2 Distributor		8 Engine electronic control module (with integral MAP sensor)	10 Idle air control valve
3 Ignition coil	6 Crankshaft position sensor		11 Throttle position sensor
4 Spark plugs			

1 General information and precautions

The fuel system consists of a fuel tank (which is mounted under the rear of the car, with an electric fuel pump immersed in it), a fuel filter and the fuel feed and return lines. The fuel pump supplies fuel to the fuel rail, which acts as a reservoir for the four fuel injectors which inject fuel into the inlet tracts. In addition, there is an Electronic Control Module (ECM) and various sensors, electrical components and related wiring **(see illustrations)**.

Refer to Section 6 for further information on the operation of each fuel injection system, and to Section 16 for information on the exhaust system.

⚠️ *Warning: Many of the procedures in this Chapter require the removal of fuel lines and connections, which may result in some fuel spillage. Before carrying out any operation on the fuel system, refer to the precautions given in 'Safety first!' at the beginning of this manual, and follow them implicitly. Petrol is a highly-dangerous and volatile liquid, and the precautions necessary when handling it cannot be overstressed.*

Note: *Residual pressure will remain in the fuel lines long after the vehicle was last*

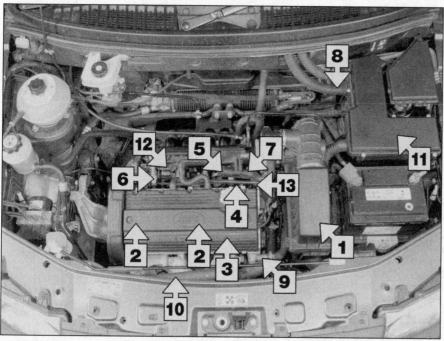

1.1b Engine management components – MEMS 3

1 Air cleaner
2 Ignition coils
3 Camshaft position sensor
4 Intake air temperature sensor
5 Idle air control valve
6 Fuel injectors
7 Throttle position sensor
8 Fuel inertia shut-off valve
9 Coolant temperature sensor
10 Oxygen sensor
11 Engine electronic control module
12 Manifold absolute pressure (MAP) sensor
13 Crankshaft position sensor

used. Before disconnecting any fuel line, first depressurise the fuel system as described in Section 7.

2 Air cleaner assembly and intake ducts – removal and refitting

Removal

1 Remove the battery as described in Chapter 5A.
2 Disconnect the air intake hose from the bottom of the air cleaner **(see illustration)**.
3 Release the retaining clip, and disconnect the hose from the air cleaner to the inlet manifold **(see illustration)**.
4 Slacken and remove the bolts securing the air cleaner housing to the battery tray, and lift the assembly out from the engine compartment **(see illustration)**.

Refitting

5 Refitting is the reverse of removal making sure all the ducts are securely reconnected.

3 Accelerator cable – removal, refitting and adjustment

Removal

1 Unclip the accelerator cable adjustment nut from the mounting bracket then detach the inner cable from the throttle cam **(see illustration)**.
2 Work back along the length of the cable, free it from any retaining clips or ties, noting its correct routing
3 Reaching up behind the facia, squeeze together the nylon clips and unclip the accelerator inner cable from the top of the accelerator pedal **(see illustration)**.
4 Return to the engine compartment then rotate the hard plastic end ferrule of the outer cable anti-clockwise until its lugs align with the slots in the bulkhead hole **(see illustrations)**. Pull the outer cable and grommet from the bulkhead. Remove the cable from the vehicle.
5 Examine the cable for signs of wear or damage and renew if necessary. Check the

2.2 Disconnect the air intake hose from the bottom of the air cleaner

2.3 Release the retaining clip, and disconnect the hose from the air cleaner to the inlet manifold

2.4 Unscrew the bolts securing the air cleaner housing to the battery tray

3.1 Unclip the outer cable from the bracket

3.3 Squeeze together the nylon clips and unclip the accelerator inner cable from the top of the accelerator pedal

3.4a Rotate the hard plastic end ferrule of the outer cable anti-clockwise until . . .

3.4b . . . its lugs align with the slots in the bulkhead hole

3.10 Slide the cable adjustment nut out from the mounting bracket, and rotate the nut to adjust the cable as described in the text

rubber grommet for signs of damage or deterioration and renew it if necessary.

Refitting

6 Feed the cable into position from the engine compartment, and align the lugs of the outer cable ferrule with the slots of the bulkhead hole. Whilst pushing the ferrule squarely into the hole, rotate it 90° clockwise to lock it in place.

7 From inside the vehicle, clip the inner cable into position in the pedal end.

8 From within the engine compartment, ensure the outer cable is correctly seated in the bulkhead, then work along the cable, securing it in position with the retaining clips and ties, and ensuring that the cable is correctly routed.

9 Connect the inner cable to the throttle cam and clip the cable adjusting nut into its mounting bracket and adjust the cable as described below.

Adjustment

10 Slide the cable adjustment nut out from the mounting bracket and position the cable so that the adjustment nut is resting against the upper surface of the bracket **(see illustration)**.

11 Slacken the adjustment nut until the throttle cam is fully against its stop then slowly tighten the nut until the point is found where all freeplay is removed from the cable but the cam is still against its stop.

12 Clip the adjustment nut correctly back into position then have an assistant depress the accelerator pedal. Check that the throttle cam opens fully and returns smoothly to its stop, readjusting the cable if necessary.

4 Accelerator pedal – removal and refitting

Removal

Vehicles up to 2001 model year

1 The accelerator pedal is an integral part of the clutch and brake pedal bracket assembly and is not available separately. Refer to Chapter 6 for removal and refitting details.

Vehicles from 2001 model year

2 Undo the 2 nuts securing the accelerator pedal assembly to the bulkhead, and release the clip securing the accelerator inner cable to the top of the pedal **(see illustration 3.3)**.

3 Disconnect the wiring plug from the pedal switch as the assembly is withdrawn.

Refitting

4 Refitting is a reversal of removal, remembering to tighten the retaining nuts securely.

5 Unleaded petrol – general information and usage

Note: *If travelling abroad, consult one of the motoring organisations (or a similar authority) for advice on the fuel available.*

The fuel recommended by Land Rover is given in the Specifications Section of this Chapter, followed by the equivalent petrol currently on sale in the UK.

All petrol models are designed to run on fuel with a minimum octane rating of 95 (RON) and all models have a catalytic converter, and so must be run on unleaded fuel only. Under no circumstances should leaded, or lead replacement fuel be used, as this may damage the converter.

Super unleaded petrol (98 octane) can also be used in all models if wished, though there is no advantage in doing so.

6 Fuel injection system – general information

The 1.8 litre K-Series petrol engines are equipped with a multi-point Rover/Motorola modular engine management (fuel injection/ignition) system (MEMS). The earlier models (up to 2001 model year) are fitted with MEMS 1.8, and the later models (2001 year-on) are fitted with MEMS 3. The main difference between the two systems is that MEMS 1.8 incorporates a distributor and rotor arm to deliver the HT voltage to the spark plugs, and the injectors are fired semi-sequentially

(injectors 1 and 4, and 2 and 3 are triggered together). Whilst MEMS 3 has fully sequential injection, with spark plugs 1 and 4, and 2 and 3 fired together by two ignition coils mounted directly above Nos 1 and 3 spark plugs (no distributor). MEMS 3 relies on the camshaft position sensor to inform the ECM of the engine firing sequence position. Both systems incorporate a closed-loop catalytic converter and an evaporative emission control system, and complies with the necessary emission control standards. The fuel injection side of the system operates as follows; refer to Chapter 5B for information on the ignition system.

The fuel pump, immersed in the fuel tank, pumps fuel from the fuel tank to the fuel rail, via a filter which is located in the engine compartment. Fuel supply pressure is controlled by the pressure regulator, which is incorporated as part of the pump assembly in the tank. A pressure damper is fitted to the fuel rail, to absorb pressure fluctuations.

The electrical control system consists of the electronic control module (ECM), along with the following sensors.

a) *Throttle position sensor – informs the ECM of the throttle position, and the rate of throttle opening or closing.*

b) *Coolant temperature sensor – informs the ECM of engine temperature.*

c) *Intake air temperature sensor – informs the ECM of the temperature of the air passing through the inlet manifold.*

d) *Oxygen sensor – informs the ECM of the oxygen content of the exhaust gases (explained in greater detail in Part C of this Chapter).*

e) *Crankshaft sensor – informs the ECM of engine speed and crankshaft position.*

f) *Manifold absolute pressure (MAP) sensor (contained within the ECM on MEMS 1.8) – informs the ECM of the engine load by monitoring the pressure in the inlet manifold.*

g) *Camshaft position sensor (MEMS 3 only) – informs the ECM of the camshaft position.*

h) *Idle air control valve*

All the above information is analysed by the ECM and, based on this, the ECM determines the appropriate ignition and fuelling requirements for the engine. The ECM controls the fuel injector by varying its pulse width – the length of time the injector is held open – to provide a richer or weaker mixture, as appropriate. The mixture is constantly varied by the ECM, to provide the best setting for cranking, starting (with either a hot or cold engine), warm-up, idle, cruising, and acceleration.

The ECM also has full control over the engine idle speed. The idle speed is controlled via the idle air control valve; the valve controls the opening of an air passage which bypasses the throttle valve. When the throttle valve is closed, the ECM controls the opening of the valve, which in turn regulates the amount of air entering the manifold, and so controls the idle speed.

The ECM also controls the exhaust and evaporative emission control systems, which are described in detail in Part C of this Chapter.

If there is an abnormality in any of the readings obtained from any sensor, the ECM enters its back-up mode. In this event, the ECM ignores the abnormal sensor signal, and assumes a preprogrammed value which will allow the engine to continue running (albeit at reduced efficiency). If the ECM enters this back-up mode, the warning light on the instrument panel will come on, and the relevant fault code will be stored in the ECM memory.

If the warning light comes on, the vehicle should be taken to a Land Rover dealer at the earliest opportunity. A complete test of the engine management system can then be carried out, using a special electronic diagnostic test unit which is simply plugged into the system's diagnostic connector. The connector is located behind the centre console in the passengers footwell.

7 Fuel injection system – depressurisation

⚠️ **Warning: Refer to the warning note in Section 1 before proceeding. The following procedure will merely relieve the pressure in the fuel system – remember that fuel will still be present in the system components, and take precautions accordingly before disconnecting any of them.**

1 The fuel system referred to in this Section is defined as the tank-mounted fuel pump, the fuel filter, the fuel injector(s) and the pressure regulator, and the metal pipes and flexible hoses of the fuel lines between these components. All these contain fuel which will be under pressure while the engine is running, and/or while the ignition is switched on. The pressure will remain for some time after the ignition has been switched off, and it must be relieved in a controlled fashion when any of these components are disturbed for servicing work.

2 The fuel system is depressurised by disconnecting the fuel rail quick-release coupling.

3 Ensure the ignition is switched off and position wads of rag around the fuel feed pipe connection to the fuel rail to catch the spilled fuel. Squeeze together the two tabs of the quick-release coupling, and slowly release the pipe from the rail **(see illustration)**.

4 Ensure all fuel pressure has been released, then push the feed pipe back into the fuel rail.

8 Fuel pump – removal and refitting

⚠️ **Warning: Refer to the warning note in Section 1 before proceeding.**

Note: *A new fuel pump cover sealing ring will be required on refitting.*

Removal

1 Refer to Chapter 5A and disconnect the battery negative lead, and depressurise the fuel system as described in the previous Section.

2 Open the tailgate, and fold the rear seat forward.

3 Undo the two fasteners, and raise the luggage and passenger compartment carpets for access to the inspection panel.

4 Slacken and remove the six screws, and remove the inspection panel **(see illustration)**.

5 Disconnect the wiring plug from the top of the pump assembly **(see illustration)**.

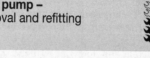

7.3 Squeeze together the two tabs of the quick-release coupling, and slowly release the pipe from the fuel rail

6 Depress the retaining lugs and disconnect the fuel hose **(see illustration)**. Be prepared for fuel spillage.

7 Using Land Rover tool LRT-19-009, unscrew the locking ring from the fuel pump assembly. If the special Land Rover tool is not available, careful use of a large flat-bladed screwdriver and soft hammer will unscrew the locking ring **(see illustration)**.

8 Lift the pump assembly from the tank. Note that the pressure regulator is an integral part of the pump assembly and cannot be renewed separately.

9 To remove the pump filter, remove the fuel gauge sender unit as described in Section 9, then disconnect the remaining two wiring connectors from the underside of the top of the pump assembly **(see illustration)**.

10 Release the three lugs from the slots, and carefully manoeuvre the top of the pump

8.4 Slacken and remove the six screws, and remove the inspection panel

8.5 Disconnect the wiring plug

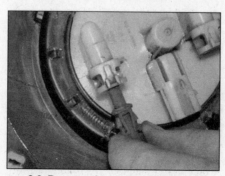

8.6 Depress the retaining lugs and disconnect the fuel hose

8.7 Careful use of a large flat-bladed screwdriver and soft hammer will unscrew the locking ring

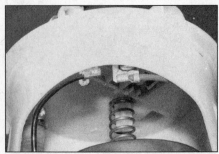

8.9 Disconnect the remaining two wiring connectors from the underside of the top of the pump assembly

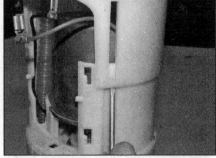

8.10 Release the three lugs from the slots, and separate the two pump halves

8.12 Lubricate the new O-ring seals with silicone grease, and refit them to the ports

assembly away from the base, recovering the compression spring as the top is withdrawn **(see illustration)**.

11 Carefully release the three retaining clips, and release the fuel filter from the connections on the underside. Discard the O-rings, new ones must be fitted.

Refitting

12 If the filter has been removed, lubricate the new O-ring seals with silicone grease, and refit them to the ports **(see illustration)**.
13 Ensure that the earthing spring is correctly located, and refit the filter, making sure that the clips fully engage **See illustration)**.
14 Locate the spring into the top of the filter, and refit the top half of the pump assembly, ensuring that the lugs engage correctly with the slots. Reconnect the two wiring plugs **(see illustration)**.

15 Refit the fuel gauge sender unit, and reconnect the two connectors to the underside of the pump assembly.
16 Clean the tank cover and tank mating surfaces, and fit a new seal to the tank aperture **(see illustration)**. **Note:** *Ensure the seal is fitted with 'This side down' facing downwards.*
17 Manoeuvre the pump assembly into the tank, noting that the locating lug must engage with the notch in the tank **(see illustration)**.
18 Fit the locking ring, and if possible tighten it to the specified torque.
19 Reconnect the fuel hose and wiring plug to the pump assembly.
20 Refit the inspection panel, and tighten the retaining screws securely.
21 Fasten the carpet back into place, and reposition the rear seat.
22 Reconnect the battery negative lead.

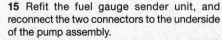 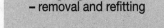

9 Fuel gauge sender unit – removal and refitting

Removal

1 Remove the fuel tank pump assembly as described in the previous Section.
2 Disconnect the two wiring plugs from the underside of the top of the pump assembly **(see illustration)**.
3 Depress the retaining clip and remove the sender from the pump assembly **(see illustration)**.

Refitting

4 Refitting is a reversal of removal.

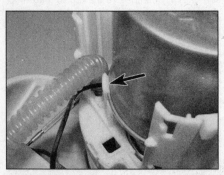

8.13 Refit the filter, making sure that the clips fully engage

8.14 Locate the spring into the top of the filter

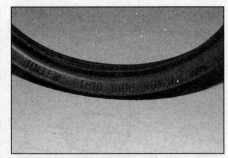

8.16 Ensure the seal is fitted into the tank aperture with 'This side down' facing downwards

8.17 The pump assembly locating lug must engage with the notch in the tank

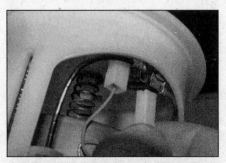

9.2 Disconnect the two wiring plugs from the underside of the top of the pump assembly

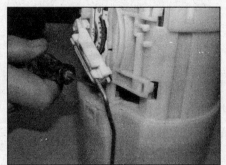

9.3 Release the sender unit retaining clip

10.7 Release the retaining clip and disconnect the two breather hoses from the filler neck

10.8 Remove the tamperproof cover and slacken the retaining clip securing the filler neck to the tank

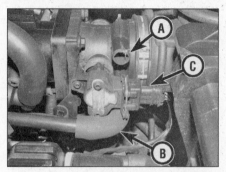

11.3 Disconnect the throttle position sensor wiring plug (C), breather pipe (B), and idle air control valve hose (A)

10 Fuel tank – removal and refitting

> ⚠ **Warning: Refer to the warning note in Section 1 before proceeding.**

 HAYNES HINT *Before removing the fuel tank, all fuel must be drained from the tank. Since a drain plug is not provided, it is therefore preferable to carry out the removal operation when the fuel tank is nearly empty. The remaining fuel can then be syphoned or hand-pumped from the tank.*

Removal

1 Disconnect the battery negative terminal (see Chapter 5A), then depressurise the fuel system as described in Section 7.

2 Remove the fuel pump assembly as described in Section 8. Syphon or hand-pump the fuel from the tank.

3 Chock the front wheels then jack up the rear of the vehicle and support it securely on axle stands (see *Jacking and vehicle support*). Remove the rear roadwheels.

4 With reference to Section 16, remove the exhaust intermediate section.

5 Remove the propshaft with reference to Chapter 8.

6 Undo the screws/clips and remove the right-hand rear wheel arch liner – refer to Chapter 11 if necessary.

7 Release the retaining clips and disconnect the two breather hoses from the filler neck **(see illustration)**.

8 Remove the tamperproof cover, slacken the retaining clip securing the filler neck to the tank **(see illustration)**.

9 Place a trolley jack with an interposed block of wood beneath the rear subframe, then raise the jack until it is supporting the weight of the subframe. Unscrew the four retaining bolts, and lower the subframe. **Note:** *Do not allow the subframe to hang on the rear brake hoses.*

10 Unscrew the four bolts and lower the cradle and fuel tank, disengaging the filler neck tube as the tank is lowered.

11 Separate the tank from the cradle, and recover the heat shields.

12 If the tank is contaminated with sediment or water, swill the tank out with clean fuel. The tank is injection-moulded from a synthetic material – if seriously damaged, it should be renewed. However, in certain cases, it may be possible to have small leaks or minor damage repaired. Seek the advice of a specialist before attempting to repair the fuel tank.

Refitting

13 Refitting is the reverse of the removal procedure, noting the following points:
  a) When lifting the tank back into position, take care to ensure that none of the hoses or the fuel pump wiring become trapped between the tank and vehicle body. Refit the cradle, and tighten the bolts to the specified torque.
  b) Ensure all pipes and hoses are correctly routed and all hoses unions are securely joined.
  c) On completion, refill the tank with a small amount of fuel, and check for signs of leakage prior to taking the vehicle out on the road.

11 Throttle housing – removal and refitting

Removal

1 Disconnect the battery negative lead (see Chapter 5A).

11.7 Unscrew the four throttle body retaining screws (upper screws arrowed)

2 Release the retaining clip and disconnect the air intake hose from the throttle housing.

3 Disconnect the wiring connector from the throttle position sensor **(see illustration)**. Access is much improved by removing the air cleaner assembly as described in Section 2.

4 Release the retaining clip and disconnect the breather hose from the throttle housing.

5 Unclip the accelerator cable adjustment nut from its bracket then detach the inner cable from the throttle cam.

6 Disconnect the idle air control valve hose from the throttle housing.

7 Slacken and remove the four retaining bolts then remove the throttle housing from the manifold. Discard the O-ring seal, a new one must be fitted **(see illustration)**.

Refitting

8 Refitting is the reverse of removal, bearing in mind the following points:
  a) Ensure the sealing ring is in position then refit the throttle housing to the manifold and tighten the retaining bolts to the specified torque.
  b) Ensure all hoses and wiring connectors are correctly and securely reconnected.
  c) Reconnect and adjust the accelerator cable as described in Section 3.

12 Fuel injection system – testing and adjustment

Testing

1 If a fault appears in the fuel injection system, first ensure that all the system wiring connectors are securely connected and free of corrosion. Ensure that the fault is not due to poor maintenance; ie, check that the air cleaner filter element is clean, the spark plugs are in good condition and correctly gapped, the cylinder compression pressures are correct, and that the engine breather hoses are clear and undamaged, referring to Chapters 1A, 2A and 5B for further information (as applicable).

2 If these checks fail to reveal the cause of the problem, the vehicle should be taken to a suitably-equipped Land Rover dealer or

13.4 Release the retaining clip, and disconnect the vacuum pipe from the fuel pressure damper

13.7 Undo the two fuel rail mounting bolts (arrowed)

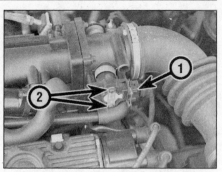

13.15 Disconnect the wiring plug (1), and undo the two Torx screws (2)

specialist for testing. A wiring block connector is incorporated in the engine management circuit, into which a special electronic diagnostic tester can be plugged (see Section 6). The tester will locate the fault quickly and simply, alleviating the need to test all the system components individually, which is a time-consuming operation that carries a risk of damaging the ECM.

Adjustment

3 Experienced home mechanics with a considerable amount of skill and equipment (including a tachometer and an accurately-calibrated exhaust gas analyser) may be able to check the exhaust CO level and the idle speed. However, if these are found to be in need of adjustment, the car will have to be taken to a suitably-equipped Land Rover dealer or specialist who has access to the necessary diagnostic equipment required to test and (where possible) adjust the settings.

13 Fuel injection system components –
removal and refitting

Fuel rail and injectors

Note: *If a faulty injector is suspected, before condemning the injector, it is worth trying the effect of one of the proprietary injector-cleaning treatments.*

⚠ *Warning: Refer to the warning note in Section 1 before proceeding.*

13.21 The intake air temperature sensor is screwed into the left-hand end of the inlet manifold

1 Disconnect the battery negative terminal (see Chapter 5A) then depressurise the fuel system as described in Section 7.
2 On models equipped with MEMS 1.8, refer to Section 2, and remove the air cleaner assembly
3 Disconnect the wiring plug from the IAC (idle air control) valve.
4 Release the retaining clip, and disconnect the vacuum pipe from the fuel pressure damper at the right-hand end of the fuel rail **(see illustration)**.
5 Slide the engine oil dipstick out of the guide tube.
6 On models equipped with MEMS 1.8, release the injector wiring harness wiring plug from its retaining bracket, and disconnect the plug.
7 Undo the two retaining bolts, and release the fuel rail and injectors from the inlet manifold **(see illustration)**.
8 On models equipped with MEMS 3, release and remove the injector spacer, and disconnect the wiring plugs from each injector, and remove the fuel rail with the injectors from the engine.
9 On models equipped with MEMS 1.8, remove the fuel rail, complete with injectors and wiring harness from the engine. Disconnect the wiring plugs from each injector.
10 On all models, remove the lower sealing rings from the injectors and discard them; they must be renewed whenever they are disturbed.
11 Slide off the retaining clips and withdraw the injectors from the fuel rail. Remove the upper sealing ring from the each injector and discard it; all disturbed sealing rings must be renewed.
12 Refitting is a reversal of the removal procedure, noting the following points:
   a) *Renew all disturbed sealing rings and apply a smear of engine oil to them to aid installation.*
   b) *Ease the injector(s) into the fuel rail, ensuring that the sealing ring(s) remain correctly seated. Secure in position with the retaining clips and reconnect the wiring connectors.*
   c) *On refitting the fuel rail, take care not to damage the injectors and ensure that all sealing rings remain in position. Once the fuel rail is correctly seated, tighten its*

retaining bolts to the specified torque.
   d) *On completion start the engine and check for fuel leaks.*

Fuel pressure damper

13 The damper is an integral part of the fuel rail and cannot be renewed separately. If the damper is faulty, renew the fuel rail as described earlier in this Section.

Throttle position sensor

Note: *New retaining screws must be used on refitting.*
14 Disconnect and remove the hose from the IAC (idle air control) valve to the throttle body.
15 Ensure the ignition is switched off then disconnect the wiring connector from the sensor which is fitted to the side of the throttle housing **(see illustration)**.
16 Slacken and remove the two Torx screws securing the sensor to the throttle body. Discard the screws and wave washers – new ones must be fitted **(see illustration 13.15)**. Remove the sensor and specification plate. **Note:** *Do not twist or lever the sensor.*
17 On refitting, carefully align the throttle valve spindle with the sensor slot and seat the sensor on the housing. Gently push the sensor onto the spindle, applying pressure only to the centre portion of the sensor.
18 Rotate the sensor in an anti-clockwise direction to align the fixing holes. Do **not** turn the sensor in a clockwise direction, and ensure that it is not turned beyond its internal stops – the sensor is easily damaged.
19 Fit the retaining plate and new retaining screws and washers, tightening them to the specified torque, and reconnect the wiring connector.
Caution: Do not overtighten the retaining screws as the sensor is easily damaged.
20 Reconnect the wiring connector to the sensor, and refit the IAC hose. Note that after renewing the sensor, the ECM may take a little while to 'relearn' the throttle valve closed position. During this time, the engine may suffer from a raised, or erratic, idle.

Intake air temperature sensor

21 The sensor is screwed into the left-hand end of the inlet manifold, in the side of the No 4 cylinder inlet tract **(see illustration)**.
22 Ensure the ignition is switched off then

disconnect the wiring connector from the sensor.

23 Unscrew the sensor and remove it from the manifold along with its sealing washer (where fitted).

24 On refitting, ensure the manifold and sensor threads are clean and dry. If the sensor was originally fitted with a sealing washer, use a new sealing washer. Where no sealing washer was fitted, clean the threads and apply a smear of sealant to them.

25 Refit the sensor to the manifold, tightening it to the specified torque, and reconnect the wiring connector.

Idle air control valve

26 Ensure the ignition is switched off then disconnect the wiring connector from the valve which is fitted to the top of the inlet manifold (see illustration).

27 On models equipped with MEMS 1.8, undo the two retaining screws then carefully remove the motor from its mounting bracket and lift it away from the engine. Recover the sealing ring and discard it, a new one should be used on refitting.

28 On models equipped with MEMS 3, disconnect the hose from the valve to the throttle body, undo the four Torx screws, and remove the valve. Discard the O-ring seal, a new must be fitted (see illustration).

29 On refitting, ensure the mating surfaces are clean and dry. Fit a new sealing ring then ease the motor into position and tighten its retaining screws to the specified torque. Reconnect the wiring connector, and where applicable, throttle body hose.

Coolant temperature sensor

30 The sensor is screwed into the coolant outlet union on the front, left-hand end of the engine. Refer to Chapter 3 for removal and refitting details.

Manifold absolute pressure (MAP) sensor

31 On models equipped with MEMS 1.8, the sensor is an integral part of the ECM and cannot be renewed separately.

32 On models equipped with MEMS 3, the sensor is located on the right-hand side of the inlet manifold. Slide off the cover, and disconnect the wiring plug from the sensor (see illustration).

33 Unscrew the two Torx screws and remove the sensor.

34 On refitting, ensure the sensor and manifold mating surfaces are clean.

35 Refit the sensor to the manifold, and tighten the Torx screws securely. Reconnect the wiring plug, and fit the plug cover.

Crankshaft position sensor

36 The sensor is fitted into the transmission mounting plate at the rear of the engine. Ensure the ignition is switched off, then disconnect the wiring plug from the sensor (see illustration).

13.26 Idle air control valve wiring plug (1) and upper retaining screw (2)

13.32 Disconnect the wiring plug from the MAP sensor, and undo the two Torx screws

37 Unscrew the retaining bolt and remove the sensor from the engine.

38 Refitting is the reverse of removal, tightening the retaining bolt to the specified torque.

Vehicle speed sensor – non ABS models

39 The sensor is driven by the speedometer drive on the transmission unit. Refer to Chapter 7A, Section 7, for removal and refitting details.

Electronic control module (ECM)

Note: *If a new ECM is to be fitted, it will be necessary to entrust the task to a Land Rover dealer. After fitting, it will be necessary to programme the anti-theft system code into the ECM to enable it function correctly. This can only be done using the special Land Rover equipment which is plugged into the diagnostic connector (see Section 6).*

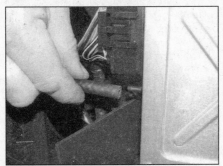

13.41 Disconnect the vacuum hose from the ECM

13.28 On models equipped with MEMS 3, disconnect the hose from the valve to the throttle body, undo the four Torx screws

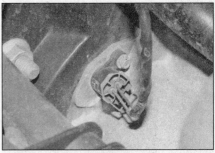

13.36 The crankshaft position sensor is located on the left-hand rear of the engine block

Models equipped with MEMS 1.8

40 The ECM is mounted onto the engine compartment bulkhead. Prior to removal, first disconnect the battery negative terminal (see Chapter 5A).

41 Disconnect the wiring connector and vacuum hose from the ECM (see illustration).

42 Undo the retaining nut, then free the ECM from its lower mounting and remove it from the engine compartment.

43 Refitting is the reverse of removal ensuring the wiring connector and vacuum hose are securely reconnected. Tighten the module nut to the specified torque setting. Note that the ECM lugs must engage with the slots in the bracket (see illustration).

Models equipped with MEMS 3

44 Disconnect the battery negative terminal (see Chapter 5A).

45 Unscrew the five Allen bolts and remove

13.43 The ECM lugs must engage with the slots in the bracket

13.46 Undo the two screws securing the ECM harness clamp

13.48 Depress the two retaining clips (arrowed)

13.53 Unscrew the retaining bolt and remove the camshaft position sensor

13.56a Fuel cut-off inertia switch – MEMS 1.8 . . .

13.56b . . . and MEMS 3

the electrical box cover, located behind the battery.

46 Undo the two screws securing the ECM harness clamp **(see illustration)**.

47 Pull out the locking latches and disconnect the wiring plugs from the ECM.

48 Depress the two retaining clips and remove the ECM **(see illustration)**.

49 Refitting is the reverse of removal, ensuring that the wiring plug locking catches are fully engaged.

Camshaft position sensor

Models equipped with MEMS 3

50 Disconnect the battery negative lead (see Chapter 5A).

51 Slacken and remove the three retaining bolts, and remove the spark plug cover from the engine.

52 Release the sensor harness from the retaining bracket, and disconnect the sensor wiring plug.

53 Unscrew the sensor retaining bolt, and remove the sensor, freeing the harness from

the retaining clips as the sensor is withdrawn **(see illustration)**.

54 On refitting, ensure the sensor and mating face are clean and dry. Refit the sensor, tighten the retaining bolt to the specified torque, and reconnect the wiring connector.

55 Ensure that the harness and connector are refitted to their retaining bracket/clips, and refit the spark plug cover. Tighten the bolts to the specified torque, and reconnect the battery negative lead.

Fuel cut-off inertia switch

56 The fuel cut-off inertia switch is located on the engine compartment bulkhead, in the left-hand corner of the engine compartment. Ensure the ignition is switched off, then disconnect the wiring plug from the switch **(see illustrations)**.

57 Undo the retaining screws and remove the switch.

58 Refitting is the reverse of removal. On completion, reset the switch by depressing the button on the top of the switch.

14 Inlet manifold – removal and refitting

Removal

1 Disconnect the battery negative terminal then depressurise the fuel system as described in Section 7.

2 Drain the cooling system as described in Chapter 1A.

3 Remove the throttle housing as described in Section 11. On models equipped with MEMS 1.8, remove the air cleaner as described in Section 2.

4 Release the retaining clips and disconnect the various vacuum and breather hoses from the manifold. The vacuum servo unit hose is fitted with a quick-release fitting; depress the locking collar with a screwdriver to release the hose.

5 Disconnect the wiring connectors from the idle air control valve and, on models equipped with MEMS 1.8, the intake air temperature sensor.

6 Free the injector wiring harness connector from the left-hand side of the manifold and disconnect the connector.

7 On models equipped with MEMS 3, prise off the MAP sensor connector cover, and disconnect the wiring plug. Undo the screws and remove the spark plug cover from the top of the engine. Disconnect the wiring connectors from the coils. **Note:** *It is only possible to disconnect the No 1 cylinder coil once the coil mounting bolts have been removed.*

8 Slacken the retaining clip and disconnect the coolant hose from the right-hand end of the manifold.

9 Check that all the necessary vacuum/breather hoses have been disconnected then working from the centre outwards, evenly and progressively slacken and remove the manifold retaining bolts and nuts.

10 Remove the manifold from the engine and remove the gasket from the manifold recess.

Refitting

11 Refitting is the reverse of refitting, noting the following:

a) Prior to refitting, check the manifold studs and renew any that are worn or damaged.

b) Ensure the manifold and cylinder mating surfaces are clean and dry and fit the new gasket to the manifold recess. The gasket must be fitted dry. Refit the manifold and tighten the retaining bolts and nuts to the specified torque in sequence **(see illustration)**.

c) Ensure that all relevant hoses are reconnected to their original positions, and are securely held (where necessary) by their retaining clips.

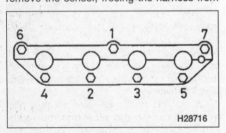

14.11 Inlet manifold nut and bolt tightening sequence

d) Reconnect and adjust the accelerator cable as described in Section 3.

e) On completion refill the cooling system as described in Chapter 1A.

15 Exhaust manifold – removal and refitting

Removal

1 Firmly apply the handbrake then jack up the front of the vehicle and support it securely on axle stands (see *Jacking and vehicle support*). Undo the retaining screws and remove the engine undertray.

Models equipped with MEMS 1.8

2 Remove the air cleaner as described in Section 2.

3 Unscrew the nuts and bolts securing the front exhaust pipe to the IRD (intermediate reduction drive) unit.

4 Remove the two bolts securing the front exhaust pipe to the engine sump.

5 Slacken and remove the four flange nuts and separate the exhaust front pipe from the exhaust manifold. Discard the gasket **(see illustration)**.

6 Release the oxygen sensor harness from the retaining bracket on coolant rail, and disconnect the wiring plug.

7 Undo the retaining nuts securing the manifold to the head. Manoeuvre the manifold out of the engine compartment, complete with the gasket.

Models with MEMS 3

8 On models with air conditioning, remove the compressor drivebelt as described in Chapter 1A. Undo the top alternator mounting bolt and pivot the alternator to the front.

9 On all models, undo the nuts/bolts and remove the exhaust manifold heat shield **(see illustration)**.

10 Undo the two nuts securing the front downpipe to the manifold flange. Disconnect the downpipe, and discard the gasket.

11 Release the oxygen sensor harness from the retaining clip at the left-hand end of the cylinder block, and disconnect the wiring plug.

12 On models with air conditioning, unscrew the alternator mounting bracket bolt, and remove the bracket from the cylinder head. Unscrew the bracket mounting stud.

13 Undo the five retaining nuts, and remove the exhaust manifold from the cylinder head. Discard the gasket.

Refitting

Models with MEMS 1.8

14 Examine all the exhaust manifold studs for signs of damage and corrosion; remove all traces of corrosion, and repair or renew any damaged studs.

15 Ensure that the manifold and cylinder head sealing faces are clean and flat, and fit the new gasket.

15.5 Unscrew the four exhaust flange nuts

16 Refit the manifold then refit the retaining nuts and tighten them to the specified torque.

17 Fit a new gasket and reconnect the front pipe to the manifold. Refit the manifold support bracket (where fitted) then tighten the front pipe retaining nuts to the specified torque. Refit the exhaust front pipe mounting brackets retaining nuts/bolts, and tighten the them to the specified torque.

18 Reconnect the oxygen sensor wiring plug and secure the it to the retaining bracket on the coolant rail.

19 Refit the air cleaner, and engine undertray. Lower the vehicle to the ground.

Models with MEMS 3

20 Ensure the mating faces of the manifold and cylinder head are clean and dry, and fit a new gasket over the studs.

21 Position the exhaust manifold over the studs and tighten the retaining nuts, starting from the centre, evenly and gradually to the specified torque.

22 On models with air conditioning, refit the alternator bracket mounting stud and bracket. Tighten the retaining bolts to the specified torque.

23 Secure the oxygen sensor harness to the retaining clip, and reconnect the wiring plug.

24 Ensure the downpipe and manifold mating surfaces are clean and dry. Using a new gasket, reconnect the downpipe to the manifold, and tighten the nuts to the specified torque.

25 Refit the exhaust manifold heat shield, and tighten the nuts/bolts to the specified torque.

26 On models with air conditioning, refit the

16.6 Front exhaust pipe-to-engine sump bolts

15.9 Undo the nuts/bolts and remove the exhaust manifold heat shield

alternator to the mounting bracket, tightening the retaining bolt to the specified torque, and refit the drivebelt with reference to Chapter 1A. Refit the right-hand wheel arch splash shield.

27 On all models, refit the engine undertray, and lower the vehicle to the ground.

16 Exhaust system – general information, removal and refitting

General information

1 The exhaust system consists of four sections: the front pipe, the catalytic converter, the intermediate pipe with an integral silencer, the tailpipe and main silencer box.

2 The front three exhaust sections are joined by flanged joints, which are secured by nuts, and the system is suspended throughout its entire length by rubber mountings. The rear main silencer box is a sleeve fit over the intermediate pipe.

Removal

3 Each exhaust section can be removed individually, or alternatively, the complete system can be removed as a unit. Even if only one part of the system needs attention, it can sometimes be easier to remove the whole system and separate the sections on the bench.

4 To remove the system or part of the system, first jack up the front or rear of the car and support it securely on axle stands (see *Jacking and vehicle support*). Alternatively, position the car over an inspection pit or on car ramps.

Front pipe – models with MEMS 1.8

5 Slacken and remove the nuts securing the front pipe flange joints to the manifold and catalytic converter.

6 Undo the nuts and bolts securing the front pipe mounting brackets to the engine sump and IRD (intermediate reduction drive) unit **(see illustration)**.

7 Unhook the front pipe from its mounting rubber then free the pipe from its joints and remove it from underneath the vehicle. Recover the gasket from each joint and discard them.

16.8 Prise up the gear lever gaiter and disconnect the wiring connector (arrowed) for the post-catalyst oxygen sensor

Front pipe – models with MEMS 3

8 Working in the passenger cabin, prise up the gear lever gaiter and disconnect the wiring connector for the post-catalyst oxygen sensor **(see illustration)**.

9 Firmly apply the handbrake then jack up the front of the vehicle and support it securely on axle stands (see *Jacking and vehicle support*). Undo the retaining screws and remove the engine undertray.

10 Prise out the harness grommet above the propshaft, and carefully pull the oxygen sensor harness and plug through the aperture.

11 Unscrew the two nuts securing the front pipe to the exhaust manifold. Discard the gasket.

12 Undo the two retaining bolts and separate the front pipe from the intermediate pipe. Discard the gasket.

13 Release the pipe from the rubber mounting, and remove the pipe.

14 If necessary, undo the four retaining nuts and remove the pipe heat shield.

15 If required, use a sleeve socket to remove the oxygen sensor.

Catalytic converter

16 Slacken and remove the nuts securing the catalytic converter to the front pipe and intermediate pipe joints **(see illustration)**.

16.16 Catalytic converter

17 Free the catalytic converter from the flange joints and remove it from underneath the vehicle. Recover the gasket from each joint and discard them.

18 If necessary, undo the retaining bolts and remove the heat shields from the converter.

Intermediate pipe

19 Slacken and remove the nuts securing the intermediate pipe to the catalytic converter and tailpipe joints.

20 Free the intermediate pipe from its mounting rubbers then detach the pipe from the flange joints and remove it from underneath the vehicle. Recover the gasket from each joint and discard them.

21 If necessary, undo the retaining bolts and remove the heat shields from the pipe.

Tailpipe

22 Slacken and remove the clamp nut and bolt securing the tailpipe joint to the intermediate pipe.

23 Free the tailpipe from its mounting rubbers and remove it along with its gasket.

Complete system – models with MEMS 1.8

24 Undo the nuts securing the front pipe flange joint to the manifold. Undo the nuts securing the front pipe to its mounting brackets.

25 Working with the aid of an assistant, free the system from all its mounting rubbers and lower it from under the vehicle. Recover the gasket from the front pipe joint.

Complete system – models with MEMS 3

26 Working in the passenger cabin, prise up the gear lever gaiter and disconnect the wiring connector for the post-catalyst oxygen sensor **(see illustration 16.8)**.

27 Prise out the harness grommet above the propshaft, and carefully pull the oxygen sensor harness and plug through the aperture.

28 Undo the nuts securing the front pipe flange joint to the manifold. Undo the nuts securing the front pipe to its mounting brackets.

29 Working with the aid of an assistant, free the system from all its mounting rubbers and lower it from under the vehicle. Recover the gasket from the front pipe joint.

Heat shield(s)

30 Heat shields are fitted to the catalytic converter and intermediate pipe. Each shield can be removed once its retaining bolts have been undone.

Refitting

31 Each section is refitted by reversing the removal sequence, noting the following points:

a) *Ensure that all traces of corrosion have been removed from the flanges and renew all gaskets.*

b) *Inspect the rubber mountings for signs of damage or deterioration, and renew as necessary.*

c) *If the catalytic converter or intermediate pipe are being renewed, ensure that the heat shields are transferred onto the new components before fitting.*

d) *Prior to tightening the exhaust system fasteners to the specified torque, ensure that all rubber mountings are correctly located, and that there is adequate clearance between the exhaust system and vehicle underbody.*

Chapter 4 Part B:
Fuel and exhaust systems – diesel engines

Contents

Degrees of difficulty

Easy, suitable for novice with little experience		**Fairly easy,** suitable for beginner with some experience		**Fairly difficult,** suitable for competent DIY mechanic		**Difficult,** suitable for experienced DIY mechanic		**Very difficult,** suitable for expert DIY or professional	

Specifications

General

System type:
L-Series .... Direct injection with Bosch Electronic Diesel Control (EDC) system
TD4 .... Direct injection common rail with Bosch high-pressure delivery pump and Electronic Diesel Control with DDE 4.0 ECM

Fuel delivery pump pressure:
L-Series .... Not applicable
TD4 .... 2.5 bar

Fuel injection pump:
L-Series .... Bosch VP37
TD4 .... Bosch Cp1 3 x radial piston pump

Injection pressure:
L-Series .... Not available
TD4 .... 250 to 1350 bar

Turbocharger type:
L-Series .... Garrett GT 1549
TD4 .... Mitsubishi MR1 TD025L3-08T-3.3 or Garrett GT1749

Turbocharger boost pressure:
L-Series .... 1.2 bar (max)
TD4:
  Mitsubishi .... 1.765 ± 0.03 bar (max)
  Garrett. .... Not available

Idle speed*:
L-Series .... 800 ± 50 rpm
TD4 .... 780 ± 30 rpm

Not adjustable – controlled by engine control module (ECM)

Torque wrench settings

	Nm	lbf ft
L-Series engine		
Coolant temperature sensor	5	4
Crankshaft sensor bolt	6	4
Engine electronic control module (ECM) nuts/bolts	9	7
Exhaust gas recirculation (EGR) system:		
EGR modulator to bulkhead	5	4
EGR pipe to plenum chamber	10	7
EGR valve to manifold	25	18
EGR valve to recirculation pipe	25	18
Exhaust manifold to cylinder head:		
Bolts	33	24
Nuts	25	18
Exhaust system fasteners:		
Front pipe-to-manifold nuts	45	33
Front pipe-to-catalytic converter nuts	60	44
Intermediate pipe-to-catalytic converter nuts	60	44
Intermediate pipe-to-tailpipe clamp nut	55	41
Fuel cut-off solenoid	20	15
Fuel hose union bolt	25	18
Fuel injection pump:		
Support bracket bolts	25	18
Sprocket retaining nut	60	44
Vacuum pipe union bolt	10	7
Fuel injector retaining plate bolt	25	18
Fuel tank cradle-to-body bolts	45	33
Injector pipe union nuts	20	15
Inlet manifold fasteners:		
Retaining nuts and bolts	25	18
Intake/turbocharger pipe-to-manifold bolts	9	7
Intake air temperature sensor	12	9
Manifold absolute pressure (MAP) sensor bolt	5	4
Plenum chamber to inlet manifold	9	7
Throttle position sensor lever	10	7
Throttle position sensor to bracket	4	3
Turbocharger fasteners:		
Retaining nuts	25	18
Exhaust flange nuts	25	18
Oil feed hose union bolt	20	15
Oil return hose union bolts	10	7
TD4 engine		
Camshaft position sensor	8	6
Coolant temperature sensor	15	11
Crankshaft position sensor	8	6
EGR cooler to cylinder head	25	18
EGR valve-to-manifold screws	10	7
Electrical box screws	2	1
Engine mounting bracket to engine	100	74
Exhaust front pipe to flange	50	37
Exhaust front pipe to intermediate pipe	60	44
Exhaust intermediate pipe to tailpipe	60	44
Exhaust manifold to cylinder head	25	18
Fuel cooler matrix:		
Matrix to bonnet slam panel	10	7
Mounting brackets to matrix	10	7
Fuel high-pressure sensor	38	28
Fuel injector clamp nuts	10	7
Fuel injector clamp studs	10	7
Fuel injection pump mounting nuts	25	18
Fuel injection pump sprocket retaining nut	65	48
Fuel pipe union nuts	20	15
Fuel pressure regulator Torx screws	9	7
Fuel rail-to-cylinder head bolts	25	18
Fuel rail-to-coolant rail bolts	10	7
Fuel tank cradle-to-body bolts	45	33
Hydramount nut	85	63

Torque wrench settings (continued)

	Nm	lbf ft
TD4 engine (continued)		
Inlet manifold:		
M6	10	7
M7	15	11
Mass airflow/intake air temperature sensor	6	4
Throttle position sensor lever	10	7
Throttle position sensor to bracket	10	7
Timing cover access plug	30	22
Turbocharger boost control solenoid valve bolts	10	7
Turbocharger boost pressure sensor	8	6
Turbocharger oil feed banjo bolts	22	16
Turbocharger oil return flange bolts	8	6
Turbocharger outlet pipe bolts:		
M6	10	7
M8	25	18
Turbocharger-to-exhaust manifold bolts	45	33
Upper tie rod bolts	100	74

1 General information and precautions

General information

The operation of the fuel injection system is described in more detail in Section 5.

L-Series engine

Fuel is supplied from a tank under the rear of the vehicle, and then passes through a filter to the fuel injection pump, which delivers the fuel to the injectors. The injection pump is controlled by an engine control module (ECM) on the basis of information provided by various sensors. Excess fuel is returned to the tank via a fuel cooler matrix located at the rear of the bonnet slam panel.

The inducted air passes through an air cleaner, which incorporates a paper filter element to filter out potentially-harmful particles (serious internal engine damage can be caused if foreign particles enter through the air intake system).

The engine control module (ECM) controls both the fuel injection pump and the preheating system, integrating the two into a complete engine management system. Refer to Chapter 5C for details of the preheating side of the system.

The exhaust system incorporates a turbocharger and a catalytic converter. Further details of the emission control systems can be found in Chapter 4C.

The EDC (electronic diesel control) system fitted, incorporates a 'drive by wire' system, where the traditional accelerator cable is replaced by an accelerator pedal position sensor. The position and rate-of-change of the accelerator pedal is reported by the position sensor to the ECM, which then adjusts the fuel injection pump to deliver the required amount of fuel, and optimum combustion efficiency **(see illustration)**.

TD4 engines

Fuel is drawn from a tank under the rear of the vehicle by a tank-immersed electric pump, then by an electrically powered lift pump (on vehicles up to 2003 model year), or by a pump/filter assembly mounted under the right-hand rear wheel arch (on vehicles from 2003 model year), and then forced through a filter to the injection pump. The chain driven injection pump supplies very high pressure fuel to the common fuel rail, which is connected to each individual injector. The injectors are operated by solenoids controlled by the ECM, based on information supplied by various sensors. If the fuel temperature is

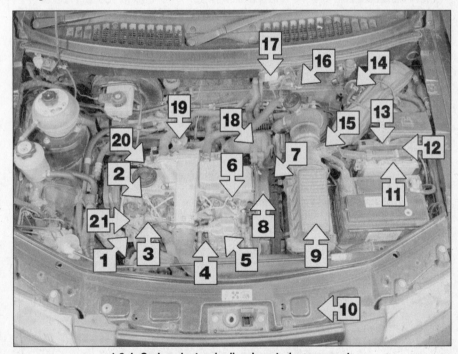

1.6 L-Series electronic diesel control components

1 Coolant temperature gauge sender	8 Crankshaft position sensor	16 EGR modulator valve
2 Needle lift sensor	9 Air cleaner	17 Manifold absolute pressure sensor (MAP)
3 Glow plugs	10 Intercooler	18 Turbocharger
4 Fuel shut-off solenoid	11 Engine control module	19 EGR valve
5 Fuel injection pump	12 Glow plug relay	20 Intake air temperature sensor
6 Injectors	13 Fuel injection pump relay	21 Engine coolant temperature sensor
7 Vehicle speed sensor	14 Fuel filter	
	15 Mass airflow sensor	

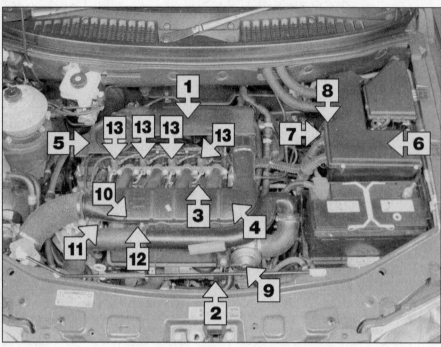

1.9 TD4 electronic diesel control components

1 Air cleaner	5 Mass airflow/intake air
2 Crankshaft position	temperature sensor
sensor	6 Engine electronic control
3 Coolant temperature	module
sensor	7 Fuel low-pressure
4 Fuel high-pressure	sensor
sensor	8 Fuel lift pump

9 EGR control valve	
10 Turbocharger boost	
pressure sensor	
11 High pressure fuel	
pump	
12 Fuel pressure regulator	
13 Fuel injectors	

sufficient, the returning fuel, passes through a fuel cooling radiator mounted at the front of the engine compartment, and then returns to the fuel tank. The engine ECM also controls the preheating side of the system – refer to Chapter 5C for more details.

The EDC (electronic diesel control) system fitted, incorporates a 'drive by wire' system, where the traditional accelerator cable is replaced by an accelerator pedal position sensor. The position and rate-of-change of the accelerator pedal is reported by the position sensor to the ECM, which then adjusts the fuel injectors to deliver the required amount of fuel, and optimum combustion efficiency

The exhaust system incorporates a turbocharger, and an EGR. Further detail of the emission control systems can be found in Chapter 4C (see illustration).

Precautions

• When working on diesel fuel system components, scrupulous cleanliness must be observed, and care must be taken not to introduce any foreign matter into fuel lines or components.
• After carrying out any work involving disconnection of fuel lines, it is advisable to check the connections for leaks; pressurise the system by cranking the engine several times.

• Electronic control units are very sensitive components, and certain precautions must be taken to avoid damage to these units as follows.
• When carrying out welding operations on the vehicle using electric welding equipment, the battery and alternator should be disconnected.
• Although the underbonnet-mounted modules will tolerate normal underbonnet conditions, they can be adversely affected by excess heat or moisture. If using welding equipment or pressure-washing equipment in the vicinity of an electronic module, take care not to direct heat, or jets of water or steam, at the module. If this cannot be avoided, remove the module from the vehicle, and protect its wiring plug with a plastic bag.
• Before disconnecting any wiring, or removing components, always ensure that the ignition is switched off.
• Do not attempt to improvise ECM fault diagnosis procedures using a test lamp or multimeter, as irreparable damage could be caused to the module.
• After working on fuel injection/engine management system components, ensure that all wiring is correctly reconnected before reconnecting the battery or switching on the ignition.

2 Air cleaner assembly – removal and refitting

Removal

L-Series

1 Remove the battery as described in Chapter 5A.
2 Pull out the air intake hose from the base of the air cleaner.
3 Release the two retaining clips, and disconnect the air cleaner-to-turbo hose, complete with mass airflow sensor, from the air cleaner (see illustration).
4 Slacken and remove the two bolts securing the air cleaner assembly to the battery tray (see illustration).
5 The various intake duct(s) can be removed once the engine cover has been unbolted and removed.

TD4

6 The air cleaner housing is integral with the camshaft cover, and cannot be removed separately.

Refitting

7 Refitting is a reversal of removal. **Do not** forget to fit the sealing ring to the airflow meter and make sure the meter and intake duct are clipped securely into position.

2.3 Release the two retaining clips, and disconnect the air cleaner-to-turbo hose

2.4 Remove the two bolts securing the air cleaner assembly to the battery tray

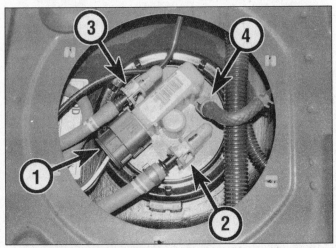

3.4 Fuel gauge sender unit (1) fuel return (2) fuel feed (3) and fuel feed (4) to the fuel burning heater (TD4 only)

3.9a Disconnect the two breather hoses from the filler neck

3 Fuel tank – removal and refitting

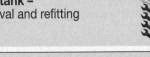

HAYNES HINT

Before removing the fuel tank, all fuel must be drained from the tank. Since a drain plug is not provided, it is therefore preferable to carry out the removal operation when the fuel tank is nearly empty. The remaining fuel can then be syphoned or hand-pumped from the tank.

Removal

1 Disconnect the battery negative terminal (see Chapter 5A).
2 Fold the rear seat forward, and release the front right-hand corner of the luggage compartment carpet.
3 Undo the six retaining screws, and remove the fuel gauge cover.
4 Disconnect the fuel gauge sender unit wiring plug, and, noting their fitted locations, depress the quick-release connections locking collars and disconnect the fuel feed and return pipes **(see illustration)**. Where fitted, disconnect the small diameter hose which supplies fuel to the fuel burning heater.

5 Chock the front wheels then jack up the rear of the vehicle and support it securely on axle stands (see *Jacking and vehicle support*). Remove the rear roadwheels.
6 With reference to Section 20, remove the exhaust intermediate section.
7 Remove the propshaft with reference to Chapter 8.
8 Undo the screws/clips and remove the right-hand rear wheel arch liner – refer to Chapter 11 if necessary.
9 Release the retaining clip and disconnect the two breather hoses from the filler neck **(see illustration)**. Release the hoses from the retaining clips in the wheel arch **(see illustration)**.
10 Remove the tamperproof cover, slacken the retaining clip securing the filler neck to the tank **(see illustration)**.
11 Undo the filler neck bracket retaining bolt, and disconnect the filler neck from the fuel filler hose **(see illustration)**.
12 Place a trolley jack with an interposed block of wood beneath the rear subframe, then raise the jack until it is supporting the weight of the subframe. Unscrew the four retaining bolts, and lower the subframe. **Note:** *Do not allow the subframe to hang on the rear brake hoses.*
13 Unscrew the four bolts and lower the cradle and fuel tank, pulling the breather hoses through the body aperture as the tank is lowered **(see illustrations)**.

3.9b Release the breather hoses from the retaining clip

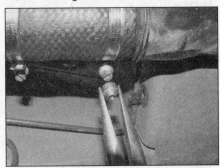

3.10 Hose clip cover

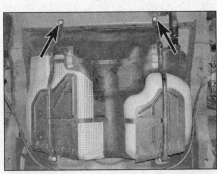

3.11 Undo the filler neck bracket retaining bolt

3.13a Undo the tank cradle retaining bolts (arrowed)

3.13b Pull the breather hoses through the body aperture as the tank is lowered

4.1 Unscrew the nut securing the pedal position sensor lever to the accelerator pedal

4.2 Prise off the retaining clip, and slide the pedal pivot to one side

4.4 Undo the bolts (arrowed), and disconnect the sensor wiring plug

14 Separate the tank from the cradle, and recover the heat shields.

15 If the tank is contaminated with sediment or water, swill the tank out with clean fuel. The tank is injection-moulded from a synthetic material – if seriously damaged, it should be renewed. However, in certain cases, it may be possible to have small leaks or minor damage repaired. Seek the advice of a specialist before attempting to repair the fuel tank.

Refitting

16 Refitting is the reverse of the removal procedure, noting the following points:
  a) When lifting the tank back into position, take care to ensure that none of the hoses or the fuel gauge sender unit wiring become trapped between the tank and vehicle body.
  b) Remember to feed the breather hoses through the body aperture as the tank is refitted.
  c) Refit the cradle, and tighten the bolts to the specified torque.
  d) Ensure all pipes and hoses are correctly routed and all hoses unions are securely joined.
  e) On completion, refill the tank with a small amount of fuel, and check for signs of leakage prior to taking the vehicle out on the road.

4 Accelerator pedal – removal and refitting

Removal

Vehicles up to 2003 model year

1 Working underneath the driver's side facia, unscrew the nut securing the pedal position sensor lever to the accelerator pedal (see illustration).
2 Prise off the retaining clip, and slide the pedal pivot to one side. Disconnect the return spring, and remove the pedal (see illustration).
3 The accelerator pedal mounting bracket is part of the clutch and brake pedal mounting bracket. In order to remove the bracket, refer to Chapter 6.

Vehicles from 2003 model year

4 Undo the 3 bolts securing the pedal and sensor assembly to the bulkhead bracket (see illustration). Disconnect the wiring plug as the pedal/sensor assembly is withdrawn. The pedal is available only as a complete assembly with the sensor – no further dismantling is recommended.

Refitting

5 Reconnect the return spring and position the pedal in the mounting bracket.
6 Slide the pivot into place, and secure it with a new retaining clip.
7 With the throttle pedal in the closed position, refit the sensor lever and tighten the nut to the specified torque.

5 Fuel injection system – general information

L-Series engines

The system is under the overall control of the Electronic Diesel Control (EDC) system, which also controls the preheating system (see Chapter 5C).

Fuel is supplied from the rear-mounted fuel tank, via a fuel filter, to the fuel injection pump. The fuel injection pump supplies the exact amount of fuel required by the engine, according to the prevailing engine operating conditions.

The engine is fitted with various sensors, which monitor the engine operating conditions, and transmit data to the engine control module (ECM). The control module processes the data from the various sensors, and determines the optimum amount of fuel required, and the injection timing for the prevailing running conditions. Additionally, the control module activates the fuel injection pump stop solenoid, the preheating system, and the exhaust gas recirculation (EGR) system (see Chapter 4C).

The system uses the following sensors.
  a) Crankshaft sensor – informs the ECM of the crankshaft speed and position.
  b) Coolant temperature sensor – informs the ECM of engine temperature.
  c) Fuel temperature sensor – informs the

ECM of fuel temperature (in the injection pump).
  d) Airflow meter – informs the ECM of the mass of air entering the intake tract.
  e) Fuel injector needle lift sensor – informs the ECM of the start of the injection sequence.
  f) Vehicle speed sensor – informs the ECM of the vehicle speed (non-ABS models only).
  g) Fuel quantity servo position sensor – informs the ECM of the quantity of fuel supplied to the injectors by the fuel injection pump.
  h) Throttle position sensor – informs the ECM of throttle position, and the rate of throttle opening/closing.
  i) Manifold absolute pressure (MAP) sensor – informs the ECM of the pressure of air entering the intake tract (used in conjunction with the intake air temperature sensor to calculate the volume of oxygen in the air entering the engine).
  j) Intake air temperature sensor – informs the ECM of the temperature of air entering the engine.
  k) Stop-light switch – informs the ECM when the brakes are being applied.

TD4 engines

The system is under the overall control of the Electronic Diesel Control (EDC) system, which also controls the preheating system (see Chapter 5C).

Fuel is supplied from the rear-mounted fuel tank, via an electrically powered lift pump, and fuel filter, to the fuel injection pump. The fuel injection pump supplies fuel under high pressure to the common fuel rail. The fuel rail provides a reservoir of fuel under pressure ready for the injectors to deliver direct to the combustion chamber. The individual fuel injectors incorporate solenoids which, when operated, allow the high pressure fuel to be injected. The solenoids are controlled by the ECM. The fuel injection pump purely provides high pressure fuel. The timing and duration of the injection is controlled by the ECM, based on the information received from the various sensors. In order to increase combustion efficiency and reduce combustion noise (diesel 'knock'), a small amount of fuel is injected before the main injection takes place – this is known as Pre- or Pilot-injection.

Additionally, the control module activates the preheating system, and the exhaust gas recirculation (EGR) system (see Chapter 4C). The system uses the following sensors.

a) *Crankshaft sensor – informs the ECM of the crankshaft speed and position.*

b) *Coolant temperature sensor – informs the ECM of engine temperature.*

c) *Mass airflow/intake temperature sensor – informs the ECM of the mass and temperature of air entering the intake tract.*

d) *Wheel speed sensor – informs the ECM of the vehicle speed.*

e) *Throttle position sensor – informs the ECM of throttle position, and the rate of throttle opening/closing.*

f) *Fuel high-pressure sensor – informs the ECM of the pressure of the fuel in the common rail.*

g) *Fuel low pressure sensor – informs the ECM of the pressure of the fuel in the filter.*

h) *Fuel pressure regulator – controls the pressure produced by the high pressure fuel pump.*

i) *Camshaft position sensor – informs the ECM of the camshaft position so that the engine firing sequence can be established.*

j) *Stop-light switch – informs the ECM when the brakes are being applied*

k) *Turbocharger boost pressure sensor – informs the ECM of the boost pressure generated by the turbocharger.*

All models

On all models, a 'drive-by-wire' throttle control system is used. The accelerator pedal is not physically connected to the fuel injection pump, but instead is connected by a cable to a throttle position sensor, mounted in the engine compartment, which provides the engine control module (ECM) with a signal relating to accelerator pedal movement.

The signals from the various sensors are processed by the ECM, and the optimum fuel quantity and injection timing settings are selected for the prevailing engine operating conditions.

A catalytic converter and an exhaust gas recirculation (EGR) system is fitted, to reduce harmful exhaust gas emissions. Details of this and other emissions control system equipment are given in Chapter 4C.

If there is an abnormality in any of the readings obtained from any sensor, the ECM enters its back-up mode. In this event, the ECM ignores the abnormal sensor signal, and assumes a preprogrammed value which will allow the engine to continue running (albeit at reduced efficiency). If the ECM enters this back-up mode, the warning light on the instrument panel will come on, and the relevant fault code will be stored in the ECM memory.

If the warning light comes on, the vehicle should be taken to a Land Rover dealer

6.2a Slacken the bleed screw on top of the fuel filter . . .

6.2b . . . and squeeze the priming pump

or specialist at the earliest opportunity. A complete test of the Electronic Diesel Control (EDC) system can then be carried out, using a special electronic test unit which is simply plugged into the system's diagnostic connector. The connector is located behind the driver's side of the facia; to gain access to the connector unclip the storage pocket and reach in through the facia aperture.

6 Fuel system – priming and bleeding

1 On L-Series engines, after any operation which requires the disconnection of any fuel hose, it is necessary to prime and bleed the fuel system; the priming pump is located in the left-hand rear corner of the engine compartment, where it is fitted to the fuel filter intake pipe. On models fitted with the TD4 engine, the system is self-priming.

2 Position wads of absorbent rag around the fuel filter then slacken the bleed screw which is fitted to the top of the fuel filter **(see illustrations)**. Gently squeeze and release the pump until fuel which is free of air bubbles is flowing out of the filter. Once all traces of air have been removed, squeeze and hold the pump then securely tighten the bleed screw before releasing the pump. Remove the rag from around the filter and mop-up any spilt fuel.

3 Turn on the ignition switch and gently squeeze and release the pump until resistance is felt. Once the lines are full of fuel (indicated

7.2 Undo the six screws, and remove the fuel gauge sender cover

by the resistance felt when the pump is squeezed), stop pumping and turn off the ignition.

4 On all models, depress the accelerator pedal to the floor then start the engine as normal (this may take longer than usual, especially if the fuel system has been allowed to run dry – operate the starter in ten second bursts with 5 seconds rest in between each operation). Run the engine at a fast idle speed for a minute or so to purge any remaining trapped air from the fuel lines. After this time the engine should idle smoothly at a constant speed.

5 If the engine idles roughly, then there is still some air trapped in the fuel system. Increase the engine speed again for another minute or so then recheck the idle speed. Repeat this procedure as necessary until the engine is idling smoothly.

7 Fuel gauge sender unit – removal and refitting

Removal

1 Fold the rear seat forward, and release the luggage compartment carpet.

2 Undo the six screws, and remove the fuel gauge sender cover **(see illustration)**.

3 Disconnect the wiring connector from the sender unit.

4 Note their fitted locations, then depress the retaining clips and disconnect the fuel feed and return pipes. On TD4 models, the small diameter hose feeds the fuel burning heater **(see illustration 3.4)**.

5 Unscrew the locking ring and remove it from the tank. In the absence of the special Land Rover ring spanner (tool number LRT 19-009), a pair of slip-jointed pliers can be used to slacken the ring or the ring may be tapped around using a large flat-bladed screwdriver against one of the ring tabs.

6 Carefully lift the sender unit out from the fuel tank, taking care not to damage the sender unit float. Recover the sealing ring and discard it; a new one must be used on refitting.

7 Disconnect the two spade terminals in the upper section of the assembly, and using a flat-bladed screwdriver, release the retaining

7.7 Release the retaining clip, and remove the sender unit

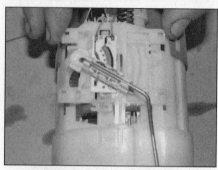

7.8 Position the sender unit in the location slots, and engage the retaining clip

7.10 Fit the new sealing ring to the tank

7.11 Ensure the sender unit tag is correctly engaged with the tank cut-out

clip, and remove the sender unit **(see illustration)**.

Refitting

8 Position the sender unit in the location slots, and engage the retaining clip **(see illustration)**.

9 Reconnect the electrical terminals to the upper section of the assembly.

10 Ensure the tank and sender unit faces are clean and dry then fit the new sealing ring to the tank **(see illustration)**.

11 Carefully ease the sender unit into position, taking care not to bend the float arm, and seat it in the tank. Ensure the sender unit tag is correctly engaged with the tank cut-out then secure it in position with the locking ring **(see illustration)**.

12 Reconnect the fuel burning heater, fuel feed, and return pipes.

13 Reconnect the wiring connector to the sender unit.

14 Refit the fuel gauge sender unit cover, and tighten the six retaining screws.

15 Fit the luggage compartment carpet, and reposition the rear seat.

---

8 Fuel pump unit – removal and refitting

Tank mounted pump unit

Note: *Only diesel vehicles fitted with the TD4 engine up to 2003 model year have a fuel tank mounted pump.*

Removal

1 Remove the fuel gauge sender unit as described in the previous Section.

2 Using a small screwdriver, carefully prise apart the retaining clips, and slide off the lower section of the pump assembly **(see illustrations)**.

3 Again using a small screwdriver, very carefully release the clip securing the filter to the base of the pump. Clean the filter in fresh fuel **(see illustration)**. Further dismantling of the pump unit is not recommended, as the pump is only available as a complete unit.

Refitting

4 Refitting is a reversal of removal, noting that the lower section of the pump assembly will only fit in one position.

Wheel arch mounted pump unit

Note: *Only diesel vehicles fitted with the TD4 engine from 2003 model year have a wheel arch mounted pump.*

Removal

5 Disconnect the battery negative lead as described in Chapter 5A.

6 Slacken the right-hand rear wheel nuts, then jack up the right-hand rear of the vehicle (see *Jacking and vehicle* support). Remove the road wheel.

7 Undo the 2 bolts securing the pump/filter assembly to the vehicle body **(see illustration)**.

8 Prise out the scrivet **(see illustration)**.

9 Lower the pump/filter assembly and disconnect the wiring plugs, including the earth lead **(see illustration)**.

10 Place a container beneath the assembly to catch any spilled fuel, then release the clips and disconnect the pipes from the fuel sedimenter and fuel filter **(see illustration)**.

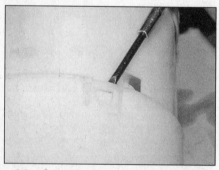

8.2a Carefully prise apart the retaining clips . . .

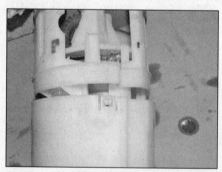

8.2b . . . and slide off the lower section of the pump assembly

8.3 Release the clip securing the filter to the base of the pump

8.7 Undo the 2 bolts securing the pump/filter cover (arrowed) . . .

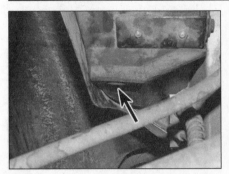

8.8 . . . and remove the scrivet (arrowed)

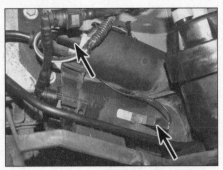

8.9 Disconnect the wiring plug and the earth lead (arrowed)

8.10 Disconnect the fuel pipes from the filter and sedimenter (arrowed)

The connection on the filter is released by depressing the button each side, and the connection on the sedimenter is released by lifting the light-coloured collar.

11 Remove the assembly from under the vehicle, then release the clips and disconnect the pipes from the pump. Pull the clip away and slide the pump from the housing **(see illustrations)**.

Refitting

12 Ensure the pipe fittings are clean, then reconnect the pipes to the pump, filter and sedimenter.

13 The remainder of refitting is a reversal of removal, ensuring the earth lead is refitted, and the retaining bolts are tightened securely.

9 Fuel injection system – testing and adjustment

Testing

1 If a fault appears in the fuel injection system, first ensure that all the system wiring connectors are securely connected and free from corrosion. Ensure that the fault is not due to poor maintenance; ie, check that the air cleaner filter element is clean, that the cylinder compression pressures are correct (see Chapter 2B or 2C), and that the engine breather hoses are clear and undamaged (see Chapter 4C).

2 If the engine will not start, check the condition of the glow plugs (see Chapter 5C).

3 If these checks fail to reveal the cause of the problem, the vehicle should be taken to a Land Rover dealer or specialist for testing using special electronic equipment which is plugged into the diagnostic connector (see Section 5). The tester should locate the fault quickly and simply, avoiding the need to test all the system components individually, which is time-consuming, and also carries a risk of damaging the ECM.

Adjustment

4 The engine idle speed, maximum speed and fuel injection pump timing are all controlled by the ECM. Whilst in theory it is possible to check the settings, if they are found to be in

8.11a Lower the pump/filter assembly . . .

need of adjustment, the vehicle will have to be taken to a suitably-equipped Land Rover dealer or specialist. They will have access to the necessary diagnostic equipment required to test and (where possible) adjust the settings.

10 Fuel injection pump – removal and refitting

Caution: Be careful not to allow dirt into the injection pump or injector pipes during this procedure.

L-Series engines

Note: *Renew all sealing washers disturbed on removal. A new inlet manifold intake pipe gasket will also be required.*

Removal

1 Disconnect the battery negative lead (see Chapter 5A).

2 Unscrew the retaining bolts and remove the plastic cover from the top of the engine, taking care not to lose the spacers which are fitted to the cover mounting rubbers.

3 Drain the cooling system as described in Chapter 1B.

4 Release the retaining clip and disconnect the intercooler duct from the inlet manifold intake pipe.

5 Undo the two bolts securing the EGR pipe to the inlet manifold intake pipe **(see illustration)**.

6 Unscrew the bolts securing the intake pipe to the inlet manifold, and the bolt securing the

8.11b . . . disconnect the pipes from the pump, release the clip (arrowed) and slide the pump from the housing

intake pipe support bracket. Remove the pipe and discard the gasket, a new one must be fitted.

7 Remove the fuel injection pump timing belt as described in Chapter 2B.

8 To improve access to the pump, release the retaining clips and remove the radiator top hose.

9 Working at the front of the fuel injection pump, slacken the pump shaft clamp bolt and remove the spacer plate from the bolt **(see illustration)**. With the spacer plate removed, tighten the bolt to 31 Nm (23 lbf ft). Take care not to lose the spacer plate.

Caution: Do not exceed the specified torque when tightening the pump shaft clamp bolt, as this could damage the pump shaft. If the pump shaft is damaged, the injection pump will have to be renewed.

10 Ensure that the locking pin is correctly fitted to the fuel injection pump sprocket,

10.5 Undo the bolts securing the EGR pipe to the inlet manifold intake pipe

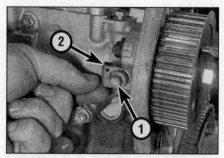

10.9 Slacken the injection pump shaft clamp bolt (1) and slide out the spacer plate (2)

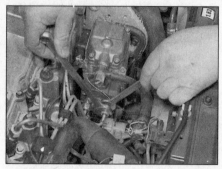

10.19a Slacken the injector pipe union nuts . . .

10.19b . . . and remove the pipes from the engine

then slacken and remove the sprocket retaining nut and washer. If the Land Rover locking pin (LRT 12-141) is not available, a 9.5 mm diameter rod or drill bit will suffice.

11 Remove the locking pin from the sprocket and remove the sprocket from the injection pump shaft. The sprocket is a tight fit on the shaft and a puller will be needed to remove it. In the absence of the special Land Rover puller (tool number LRT 12-066), the sprocket can be removed using a two M8 bolts and a length of bar with two holes drilled in it. Fit the bar and screw the bolts into the sprocket, tightening them evenly and progressively until the sprocket is freed from the pump shaft.

Caution: The pump shaft clamp screw must not be slackened until after the sprocket has been refitted and its retaining nut tightened to the specified torque. Failure to heed this warning will lead to the injection pump timing setting being

lost. If the injection pump timing is lost, the vehicle will have to be taken to a Land Rover dealer or specialist to have the pump timing reset.

12 Unscrew the retaining nut and disconnect the glow plug feed wiring from the No 2 cylinder glow plug.

13 Release the fuel injection pump wiring connector(s) from the pump mounting bracket and separate the two halves of each connector. Detach the engine wiring harness from the pump.

14 Place a wad of absorbent cloth around the injection pump to catch any spilt fuel.

15 Slacken and remove the union bolt securing the fuel feed pipe union to the pump. Recover and discard the sealing washers. Plug or cover the open ends of the pipe and the pump to prevent dirt entry.

16 Unscrew the cap nut and disconnect the fuel return pipe/hose union from the injection

pump. Recover and discard the sealing washers. Release the retaining clip and disconnect the fuel return hose from the union then position the union clear of the pump. Plug or cover the open ends of the pump and the hose to prevent dirt entry.

17 Remove the injector pipe clamps.

18 Place a wad of absorbent cloth around the fuel feed pipe unions on Nos 1 and 2 cylinder fuel injectors, then working on each of the two injectors in turn, slacken the union nut (counterhold the union on the injector using a second spanner), and disconnect the fuel pipe from the injector. Plug or cover the open ends of the pipes and fuel injectors to prevent dirt entry.

19 Repeat the procedure to disconnect Nos 1 and 2 cylinder fuel injector pipes from the pump, then remove the pipe assembly **(see illustrations)**.

20 Repeat the procedure given in paragraphs 18 and 19 and remove Nos 3 and 4 cylinder fuel injector pipes.

21 Remove the bolt securing the oil dipstick guide tube to the engine.

22 Unscrew the four bolts securing the injection pump support bracket to the engine. Slacken and remove the two nuts and bolts securing the bracket to the pump and remove the bracket **(see illustrations)**.

23 Slacken and remove the three nuts securing the pump to the engine/transmission mounting plate, then lift the pump away from the engine **(see illustrations)**.

Refitting

24 Thoroughly clean the mating faces of the injection pump and the engine/transmission mounting plate.

25 Manoeuvre the injection pump into position then refit the pump retaining nuts.

26 Refit the support bracket to the pump and refit its retaining nuts and bolts, tighten them all by hand only. Tighten the bolts securing the bracket to the pump to the specified torque first, then tighten the bolts securing the bracket to the cylinder block to the specified torque.

27 Ensure the unions are clean and dry then refit Nos 3 and 4 injector pipes, tightening their union nuts to the specified torque. Refit the Nos 1 and 2 pipes, tightening their union nuts to the specified torque then refit the clamp to the pipes.

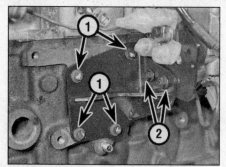

10.22a Slacken and remove the bolts (1) and the nuts and bolts (2) . . .

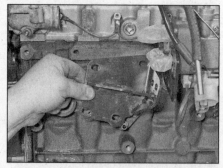

10.22b . . . then remove the pump support bracket from the engine

10.23a Unscrew the pump mounting nuts (arrowed) . . .

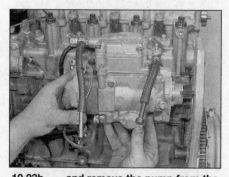

10.23b . . . and remove the pump from the engine

10.46 Unscrew the large access plug in the timing chain cover

10.48a Screw the tool into the timing chain cover . . .

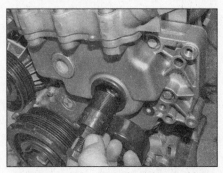

10.48b . . . then screw the other tool into the fuel pump drive sprocket

28 Reconnect all the fuel/vacuum pipes to the injection pump. Position a new sealing washer on each side of all hose unions and tighten the union bolts/cap nut (as applicable) to the specified torque. Reconnect the leak-off pipe to the injector.

29 Fit and tighten the oil dipstick guide tube bolt.

30 Reconnect the injection pump wiring connector(s) and clip the connector onto the bracket. Also clip the engine wiring harness into position on the bracket.

31 Reconnect the glow plug feed wiring to No 2 cylinder glow plug, and securely tighten the retaining nut.

32 Ensure the pump shaft and sprocket are clean and dry then fit the sprocket, washer and retaining nut to the pump. Insert the locking pin then tighten the sprocket retaining nut to the specified torque.

33 Slacken the pump shaft clamp bolt, then refit the spacer plate under the bolt head, and tighten the clamp bolt to 10 Nm (7 lbf ft).

34 Refit the fuel injection pump timing belt as described in Chapter 2B.

35 Reconnect the hose to the coolant pump and refit the radiator top hose, ensure the retaining clips are securely refitted.

36 Refit the intake pipe to the manifold, using a new gasket, and reconnect the EGR pipe. Tighten all the intake pipe bolts to the specified torque setting.

37 Refill the cooling system as described in Chapter 1B.

38 Refit the cover to the engine, ensuring the spacers are correctly fitted to the mounting rubbers, and securely tighten its retaining bolts.

39 Reconnect the battery negative lead then prime the fuel system (see Section 6).

TD4 engines

Removal

40 Disconnect the battery negative lead (see Chapter 5A).

41 Unscrew the retaining bolts and remove the plastic cover from the top of the engine, taking care not to lose the spacers which are fitted to the cover mounting rubbers.

42 Refer to Section 19, and remove the inlet manifold.

43 With reference to Chapter 5A, remove the starter motor.

44 Undo the bolts securing the upper tie rod to the right-hand engine mounting bracket. Undo the retaining screws and remove the engine undertray (see Chapter 11). Position a jack underneath the engine, with a block of wood on the jack head, and take the weight of the engine. Unscrew the four bolts and one nut securing the right-hand engine mounting bracket to the engine and Hydramount (see Chapter 2C).

45 With reference to Chapter 1B, remove the auxiliary drive belt.

46 Using a 17 mm Allen key, unscrew the large access plug in the timing chain cover **(see illustration)**. Discard the seal, a new one must be fitted.

47 Slacken and remove the fuel pump sprocket nut.

48 Screw Land Rover tool No LRT 12-178/1 into the timing chain cover, then screw Land Rover tool No LRT 12-178 into the fuel pump

drive sprocket. Carefully tighten the centre bolt of the tool, and free the sprocket from the pump shaft **(see illustrations)**. If the special Land Rover tools are not available, the only other alternative is to remove the timing chains and pull the sprocket from the shaft as described in Chapter 2D – this necessitates the removal of the engine and transmission. Although in theory it would be possible to free the sprocket from the shaft using a drift or similar, the position of the sprocket, and therefore the tension of the timing chains, would be lost.

49 Disconnect wiring plug from the fuel pump.

50 Unscrew and remove the bolt securing the fuel pipe bracket to the oil filter housing **(see illustration)**.

51 Remove the bolt securing the fuel pipe to the coolant rail.

52 Place a wad of absorbent cloth under the fuel pump, then release the retaining clips and disconnect the fuel hoses from the pump **(see illustration)**.

53 Undo the two union nuts, and remove the high-pressure fuel pipe from the pump to the common fuel rail **(see illustration)**.

54 Disconnect the wiring plugs from Nos 1 and 2 glow plugs.

55 Undo the three mounting nuts and remove the fuel pump **(see illustration)**. Discard the gasket, a new one must be fitted.

Refitting

56 Ensure that the mating surfaces of the pump and engine are clean and dry, and fit the new pump gasket.

10.50 Remove the bolt (arrowed) securing the fuel pipe bracket to the oil filter housing

10.52 Release the retaining clips and disconnect the fuel hoses (arrowed)

10.53 Remove the high-pressure fuel pipe from the pump to the common fuel rail

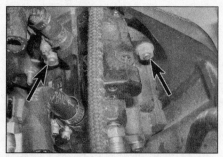

10.55 Undo the three mounting nuts (two arrowed, lower one hidden) and remove the fuel pump

57 Position the fuel pump, and tighten the mounting nuts to the specified torque.
58 Refit the glow plug wiring connectors.
59 Ensure that the high-pressure fuel pipe unions are clean, and refit the pipe. Tighten the unions to the specified torque.
60 Reconnect the fuel hoses to the pump, and secure them in place with the retaining clips.
61 Refit the bolts securing the fuel pipes to oil filter housing and coolant rail.
62 Reconnect the wiring plug to the fuel pump.
63 If the Land Rover special tools were used to release the fuel pump drive sprocket, and hold the sprocket in position, unscrew the tools, fit and tighten the sprocket retaining nut to the specified torque. If the tools were not available, refit the timing chains, sprockets and covers, as described in Chapter 2D.
64 Ensure that the timing cover access plug is clean, and tighten it to the specified torque.

11.6 Unscrew the union bolt and detach the return hose union from the injector

11.8a ... then remove the injector (No 1 shown) from the cylinder head ...

11.5 Retain the injector and unscrew the injector pipe union nut

65 With reference to Chapter 1B, refit the auxiliary drivebelt.
66 Refit the right-hand engine mounting bracket to the Hydramount and the engine. Fit the nut/bolts and tighten them to the specified torque. Refit the upper tie rod to the engine mounting bracket and tighten the bolt to the specified torque. Remove the jack from under the engine. Refit the engine undertray.
67 With reference to Chapter 5A, refit the starter motor.
68 Refer to Section 19, and refit the inlet manifold.
69 Refit the engine acoustic cover, and reconnect the battery negative lead.
70 Depress the accelerator pedal to the floor then start the engine as normal (this may take longer than usual – operate the starter in ten second bursts with 5 seconds rest in between each operation). Run the engine at a fast idle speed for a minute or so to purge any

11.7 Undo the retaining bolt and slide out the injector retaining plate ...

11.8b ... complete with its sealing washer

remaining trapped air from the fuel lines. After this time the engine should idle smoothly at a constant speed.

11 Fuel injectors – removal and refitting

Caution: Be careful not to allow dirt into the injection pump or injector pipes during this procedure.

L-Series engines

Removal

Note: *Renew all sealing washers disturbed on removal.*

1 Disconnect the battery negative lead (see Chapter 5A).
2 Unscrew the retaining bolts and remove the plastic cover from the top of the engine, taking care not to lose the spacers which are fitted to the cover mounting rubbers.
3 Referring to Section 18, disconnect the intercooler duct from the intake pipe then unbolt the pipe and remove it from the inlet manifold. Discard the gasket, a new one should be used on refitting. **Note:** *If Nos 2 and 3 injectors are not to be disturbed then the intake pipe can be left in position.*
4 Wipe clean the area around each injector then remove the injector pipe clamp which is situated at the rear of the injection pump. Each injector can then be removed as follows.
5 Position a wad of absorbent cloth around the fuel feed pipe union on the injector, then slowly unscrew the union nut, and disconnect the pipe from the injector (counterhold the union on the injector using a second spanner) **(see illustration)**. Slacken the union on the rear of the injection pump then pivot the pipe away from the injector. Plug or cover the open ends of the injector and pipe to prevent dirt entry.
6 Slacken and remove the union bolt securing the return hose union to the injector **(see illustration)**. Recover the sealing washer fitted to each side of the union and discard them; new ones must be used on refitting.
7 Slacken and remove the retaining bolt and slide the retaining plate out from the injector **(see illustration)**.
8 Withdraw the injector from the cylinder head along with its sealing washer; discard the washer, a new one must be used on refitting **(see illustrations)**. Note that if No 1 cylinder injector is being removed, it will be necessary to disconnect the needle lift sensor wiring connector (the sensor is an integral part of the injector).

Refitting

9 Thoroughly clean the injector, and the injector seat in the cylinder head.
10 Fit a new sealing washer to the injector making sure the domed surface of the washer is facing the top of the injector.
11 Fit the retaining plate to the injector and

11.20 Release the clips and slacken the pipe unions

11.23 Disconnect the wiring plugs from the injectors

11.24 Push in the closed end of the clips, and remove the fuel return hoses

carefully refit the injector to the cylinder head, aligning the retaining plate bolt hole with the threaded hole in the cylinder head. Ensure the injector is correctly seated then refit the retaining bolt and tighten to the specified torque.

12 Position a new sealing washer on each side of the return hose union then refit the union bolt, tightening it to the specified torque.

13 If No 1 cylinder injector has been removed, ensure the needle lift sensor wiring is correctly routed then securely reconnect the connector.

14 Reconnect the injector pipe to the injector and pump, tightening its union nuts to the specified torque. Ensure all pipe union nuts are correctly tightened then refit the clamp to the injection pump end of the pipes.

15 On models with an intercooler, referring to Section 18, refit the intake pipe (where removed) to the manifold and securely reconnect the intercooler duct.

16 Refit the cover to the engine, ensuring the spacers are correctly fitted to the mounting rubbers, and securely tighten its retaining bolts.

17 Reconnect the battery negative lead then prime the fuel system (see Section 6).

TD4 engines

Removal

18 Disconnect the battery negative lead, as described in Chapter 5A.

19 Remove the inlet manifold as described in Section 19.

20 Release the clips from the injector pipe(s),

slacken the pipe unions (where possible, counterhold the union on the common fuel rail and the injector), and remove the relevant injector pipe **(see illustration)**.

21 Free the injector fuel return hose from the clip on the camshaft cover.

22 In order to remove No 1 injector (nearest the timing chain), undo the five screws and remove the air cleaner cover.

23 Disconnect the wiring plugs from the injectors, and if removing injector Nos 2, 3 or 4, undo the retaining bracket screws and move the wiring harness to one side **(see illustration)**.

24 Push in the closed end of the clips, and remove the fuel return hoses from the injectors **(see illustration)**. Discard the return hose seals, new ones must be fitted.

25 Unscrew the two nuts securing each injector clamp, and using a Torx socket, unscrew the injector clamp studs until the injectors and clamps can be removed **(see illustrations)**. Discard the sealing washers – new ones must be fitted.

Refitting

26 Ensure that the injectors and seats in cylinder head are clean and dry.

27 Refit the clamp studs, tightening them to the specified torque.

28 Fit new sealing washers to the injectors, and refit them with the clamps **(see illustration)**. Tighten the clamp nuts to the specified torque.

29 With new seals fitted, squeeze together the closed ends of the clips and refit the fuel return hoses to the injectors.

30 If injector Nos 2, 3 or 4 were removed, reposition the wiring harness, and secure the harness brackets in place with the screws.

31 If No 1 injector was removed, refit the air cleaner cover, and tighten the retaining screws securely.

32 Secure the fuel return hose to the camshaft cover using the retaining clip.

33 Reconnect the wiring plugs to the injectors.

34 Refit the injection pipe(s, and tighten the unions to the specified torque. Refit the pipe retaining clips.

35 With reference to Section 19, refit the inlet manifold.

36 Reconnect the battery negative lead, as described in Chapter 5A.

12 Electronic Diesel Control (EDC) system components – removal and refitting

Crankshaft sensor

1 On L-Series engines the sensor is located at the rear of the engine, where it is mounted onto the engine/transmission mounting plate at the rear of the flywheel. To gain access to the sensor, refer to Section 19, and remove the inlet and exhaust manifolds. On TD4 engines, the sensor is mounted on the front face of the engine block. To gain access, remove the starter motor as described in Chapter 5A.

2 Ensure the ignition is switched off, then disconnect the wiring connector from the sensor.

11.25a Unscrew the injector clamp studs . . .

11.25b . . . until the injectors and clamps can be removed

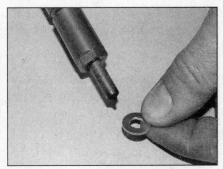

11.28 Fit new sealing washers to the injectors

12.3a Crankshaft position sensor – L-Series engines

12.3b Crankshaft position sensor – TD4 engines

12.5 Disconnect the wiring plug from the airflow meter

3 Slacken and remove the retaining bolt and carefully remove the sensor from the engine **(see illustrations)**.
4 Refitting is the reverse of removal, tightening the retaining bolt to the specified torque.

Airflow meter

L-Series engines

5 Ensure the ignition is switched off then release the retaining clip and disconnect the wiring connector from the airflow meter **(see illustration)**.
6 Slacken the retaining clip and detach the intake duct from the airflow meter.
7 Release the retaining clips then remove the airflow meter from the air cleaner housing, along with its sealing ring.
8 Refitting is the reverse of removal, using a new sealing ring. Make sure the meter is clipped securely in position and the intake duct is securely retained by its clip.

Fuel injector needle lift sensor

L-Series engines

9 The fuel injector needle lift sensor is an integral part of No 1 cylinder fuel injector and cannot be renewed separately. Refer to Section 11 for injector removal and refitting details.

Coolant temperature sensor

10 The sensor is screwed into the coolant outlet union on the front, right-hand end of the cylinder head (L-Series engines), or directly into the cylinder head (TD4 engines). Refer to Chapter 3 for removal and refitting details.

Note that on L-Series engines, the temperature gauge sender unit is also fitted to the coolant elbow.

Fuel temperature sensor

L-Series engines

11 The sensor is an integral part of the fuel injection pump, and cannot be renewed separately (see Section 10).

Vehicle speed sensor

Non-ABS models

12 The sensor is driven by the speedometer drive on the transmission unit. Refer to Chapter 7, Section 7, for removal and refitting details.

Fuel quantity servo position sensor

L-Series engines

13 The sensor is integral with the fuel injection pump, and cannot be renewed separately (see Section 10).

Throttle pedal position sensor

14 The sensor is secured to the accelerator pedal bracket. Disconnect the battery negative lead, as described in Chapter 5A.
15 On LHD models, it is necessary to remove the facia as described in Chapter 11.
16 Working underneath the driver's side facia, undo the throttle pedal/sensor assembly mounting nuts, release the throttle sensor wiring plug from its bracket, then disconnect the wiring plug as the assembly is withdrawn.
17 On vehicles up to 2003 model year,

unscrew the nut securing the lever to the sensor **(see illustration)**. On vehicles from 2003 model year, the sensor and pedal is a complete assembly and must not be dismantled.
18 Unscrew the retaining bolts/nuts then remove the sensor (up to 2003 model year vehicles only).
19 Refitting is the reverse of removal. **Note:** *If the pedal operation is unsatisfactory after fitting a new sensor, have the sensor operation confirmed by means of dedicated test equipment – consult your Land Rover dealer or specialist.*

Manifold absolute pressure (MAP) sensor

L-Series engines

20 The sensor is mounted onto the engine compartment bulkhead, where it is located left of centre adjacent to the EGR modulator valve **(see illustration)**.
21 Ensure the ignition is switched off then disconnect the wiring connector and vacuum hose from the sensor.
22 Slacken and remove the retaining bolt and remove the MAP sensor from the vehicle.
23 Refitting is the reverse of removal, tightening the sensor retaining bolt to the specified torque.

Intake air temperature sensor

L-Series engines

24 Unscrew the retaining bolts and remove the plastic cover from the top of the engine, taking care not to lose the spacers which are fitted to the cover mounting rubbers.
25 Ensure the ignition is switched off then disconnect the wiring connector from the intake air temperature sensor which is screwed into the right-hand end of the inlet manifold **(see illustration)**.
26 Unscrew the sensor and remove it from the manifold.
27 On refitting, remove all traces of sealant from the sensor and manifold threads and apply a smear of fresh sealant (Land Rover recommend the use of Loctite 577) to the sensor threads. Refit the sensor, tightening it to the specified torque, and reconnect the wiring connector. Refit the cover to the engine.

12.17 Unscrew the nut securing the lever to the sensor

12.20 Manifold absolute pressure (MAP) sensor

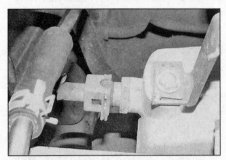

12.25 The intake air temperature sensor is screwed into the right-hand end of the inlet manifold

12.32 Free the vacuum hose and wiring harness from the turbocharger duct

12.33 Release the two retaining clips and disconnect the turbocharger duct from the sensor

Mass airflow/ intake air temperature sensor

TD4 engines

28 Unscrew the retaining bolts and remove the plastic cover from the top of the engine, taking care not to lose the spacers which are fitted to the cover mounting rubbers.

29 Slacken the retaining clips and release the intake ducting assembly. Unscrew the two retaining screws and remove the assembly from the camshaft cover.

30 Remove the engine oil filler cap, unscrew the five Allen screws and remove the air cleaner cover. Refit the oil filler cap.

31 Disconnect the wiring plug from the sensor.

32 Free the vacuum hose and wiring harness from the turbocharger duct (see illustration).

33 Release the two retaining clips and disconnect the turbocharger duct from the sensor (see illustration). Recover the duct seal and engine breather tube connector.

34 Unscrew the breather pipe retaining bracket bolt and move the pipe to one side.

35 Slacken and remove the two Torx screws, and withdraw the sensor (see illustration).

36 Refitting is a reversal of removal.

Stop-light switch

37 The engine control module receives a signal from the stop-light switch which indicates when the brakes are being applied. Stop-light switch removal and refitting details can be found in Chapter 9.

Fuel cut-off solenoid

L-Series engines

Caution: Be careful not to allow dirt into the injection pump during this procedure.

38 The fuel cut-off solenoid is fitted to the top of the fuel injection pump.

39 Unscrew the retaining bolts and remove the plastic cover from the top of the engine, taking care not to lose the spacers which are fitted to the cover mounting rubbers. Slacken the retaining clip and disconnect the intercooler duct from the manifold to improve access to the pump.

40 Ensure the ignition is switched off then unscrew the retaining nut and disconnect the wire from the solenoid terminal (see illustration).

41 Wipe clean the area around the solenoid and position a wad of absorbent cloth around the pump to absorb escaping fuel.

42 Slacken and remove the solenoid from the injection pump and recover the solenoid plunger and spring, noting each components correct fitted location. Remove the sealing ring and discard it; a new one must be used on refitting.

43 Refitting is the reverse of removal using a new sealing ring. Ensure the plunger and spring are fitted the correct way around and tighten the solenoid to the specified torque.

Electronic control module (ECM)

Note: If a new ECM is to be fitted, it will be necessary to entrust the task to a Land Rover dealer or specialist. After fitting, it will be necessary to programme the anti-theft system code into the ECM to enable it function correctly. This can only be done using

12.35 Slacken and remove the two Torx screws (arrowed), and withdraw the sensor

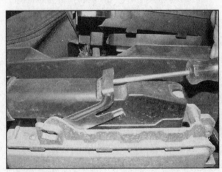

12.45a Release the locking clamp . . .

the special Land Rover equipment which is plugged into the diagnostic connector (see Section 5).

L-Series engines

44 The electronic control module (ECM) is mounted on the left-hand side of the engine compartment, behind the battery. With reference to Chapter 5A, remove the battery.

45 Using a flat-bladed screwdriver, release the locking clamp and disconnect the wiring plug from the ECM (see illustrations).

46 Undo the two bolts and move the engine compartment fusebox to one side.

47 Slacken and remove the four retaining nuts/bolts and withdraw the ECM from its mounting bracket (see illustration)

48 Refitting is the reverse of removal ensuring the wiring connector is securely reconnected. Tighten the ECM retaining nuts/bolts to the specified torque setting.

12.40 Unscrew the retaining nut and disconnect the wire from the fuel cut-off solenoid terminal

12.45b . . . and disconnect the wiring plug from the ECM

12.47 Undo the four nuts/bolts securing the ECM (arrowed)

12.50 Unscrew the five Allen screws and remove the electrical box cover

12.51a Disconnect the five wiring plugs from the ECM

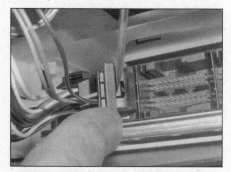

12.51b Depress the lug and pivot the locking lever over

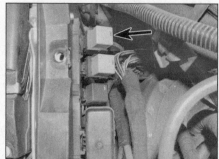

12.54 Main relay – L-Series engine

12.58 Fuel pump relay – TD4 engine up to 2003 model year

TD4 engines

49 Disconnect the battery negative lead (see Chapter 5A).

50 Unscrew the five Allen screws and remove the electrical box cover, located on the left-hand side of the engine compartment, behind the battery **(see illustration)**.

51 Note their fitted locations, and disconnect the five wiring plugs from the ECM. Some of the plugs are locked in place. To release these plugs, depress the lug and pivot the locking lever over **(see illustrations)**.

52 Release the two retaining clips and remove the ECM.

53 Refitting is the reverse of removal.

Relays

L-Series engines

54 On these models, the main (fuel injection pump) relay and the glow plug relay are

12.59 Fuel pump relay (arrowed) – TD4 engine from 2003 model year

mounted adjacent to the main engine compartment fusebox, located in the left-hand side corner; the glow plug relay is the one nearest the wing and the main relay is situated next to the glow plug relay **(see illustration)**.

55 In order to improve access, unscrew the two screws and position the fusebox to one side.

56 Release the relay from the mounting bracket, and disconnect the two wiring plugs.

57 Refitting is a reversal of removal.

TD4 engines

58 On vehicles up to 2003 model year, the fuel pump relay is located in the fusebox in the driver's side glovebox. Open the glovebox, and unclip the fusebox cover. Carefully pull the relay from the holder. The fuel pump relay is lower of the two on the far right-hand side of the fusebox **(see illustration)**.

59 On vehicles from 2003 model year, the relay is located in the engine compartment

12.62 Fuel temperature switch – TD4 engine

fusebox. Open the fusebox and pull the relay from the holder **(see illustration)**.

60 Refitting is a reversal of removal.

Fuel temperature switch

TD4 engines

61 Fitted to the fuel return circuit, this purely mechanical switch diverts hot fuel through the fuel cooler matrix, prior to it being returned to the plastic tank. The switch is located in the left-hand front area of the engine compartment. On vehicles from 2003 model year, slacken the clips and disconnect the intake ducting from the EGR valve.

62 Note their fitted locations, and disconnect the fuel hoses from the switch. Some of the connections are of the 'quick-release' type. On these, squeeze the two plastic lugs together and pull the connection apart **(see illustration)**.

63 Refitting is a reversal of removal.

Inertia fuel cut-off switch

TD4 engines

64 The inertia fuel cut-off switch is designed to cut-off the fuel supply from the tank should the vehicle be involved in an accident. The switch is located on the engine compartment bulkhead, adjacent to the brake fluid reservoir.

65 Ensure that the ignition is switched off, and disconnect the wiring plug from the switch.

66 Unscrew the securing bolt and remove the switch from the bulkhead **(see illustration)**. If required the switch can be separated from

12.66 Inertia fuel cut-off switch – TD4 engine

12.71 The turbo boost pressure sensor is mounted on the right-hand end of the inlet manifold – TD4 engine

12.80 Turbo boost pressure control solenoid valve – TD4 engine

the mounting bracket by unscrewing the two nuts.

67 Refitting is a reversal of removal. **Note:** *If the fuel cut-off switch has been activated by an accident or similar, reset the switch by pressing the top down.*

Turbocharger boost pressure sensor

Note: *On L-Series engines the turbo boost pressure is 'sensed' by the wastegate actuator. The mechanism contains no serviceable parts.*

TD4 engines

68 Undo the retaining bolts and remove the plastic cover from the top of the engine. Ensure that the ignition is switched off.
69 Release the two retaining clips and remove the intercooler outlet hose.
70 Release the wiring harness and the fuel return hose from the retaining clips on the inlet manifold, adjacent to the right-hand engine mounting bracket.
71 Disconnect the wiring plug, undo the retaining bolt, and remove the sensor **(see illustration)**.
72 Ensure that the mating surfaces of the sensor and manifold are clean and dry. With a new seal, refit the sensor to the manifold, and tighten the securing bolt to the specified torque.
73 The remainder of refitting is a reversal of removal.

Turbocharger boost pressure control solenoid valve

TD4 engines

74 Unscrew the retaining bolts and remove the plastic cover from the top of the engine, taking care not to lose the spacers which are fitted to the cover mounting rubbers.
75 Slacken the retaining clips and release the intake ducting assembly. Unscrew the two retaining screws and remove the assembly from the camshaft cover.
76 Remove the engine oil filler cap, unscrew the five Allen screws and remove the air cleaner cover. Refit the oil filler cap.
77 Free the vacuum hose and wiring harness from the turbocharger duct.
78 Release the two retaining clips, and disconnect the turbocharger duct from the mass air flow/intake air temperature sensor.

Recover the duct seal and breather pipe connector.
79 Chock the rear wheels then jack up the front of the vehicle and support it securely on axle stands (see *Jacking and vehicle support*). Undo the screws and remove the engine undertray.
80 Ensure that the ignition is switched off, and disconnect the wiring plug from the solenoid valve **(see illustration)**.
81 Note their fitted locations, and disconnect the vacuum hoses from the solenoid valve.
82 Unscrew the two retaining nuts and remove the solenoid from the mounting bracket.
83 Refitting is a reversal of removal.

Fuel high-pressure sensor

TD4 engines

84 Unscrew the retaining bolts and remove the plastic cover from the top of the engine, taking care not to lose the spacers which are fitted to the cover mounting rubbers.
85 Slacken the retaining clips and release the intake ducting assembly. Unscrew the two retaining screws and remove the assembly from the camshaft cover.
86 The fuel high-pressure sensor is located in the left-hand end of the common fuel rail. Ensure that the ignition is switched off, and disconnect the wiring plug from the sensor **(see illustration)**.
87 Using a suitable deep socket, unscrew the sensor, and discard the seal. A new one must be fitted. Plug the port of the common rail to prevent contamination.

12.86 The fuel high-pressure sensor is located in the left-hand end of the common fuel rail – TD4 engine

88 Ensure that the mating surfaces of the sensor and common rail are clean and dry, and refit the sensor with a new seal, tightening the sensor to the specified torque.
89 The remainder of refitting is a reversal of removal.

Fuel low-pressure sensor

TD4 engines

90 Up to 2003 model year, the low pressure sensor is integral with the fuel filter head, and cannot be renewed separately. If faulty the complete filter should be renewed. On vehicles from 2003 model year, the sensor is located on the left-hand side of the engine compartment, adjacent to the steering track rod. Disconnect the sensor wiring plug, then undo the retaining bolt, release the clips and disconnect the hoses from the sensor **(see illustration)**. Be prepared for fuel spillage.

Fuel pressure regulator

TD4 engines

91 With reference to Section 19, remove the inlet manifold.
92 Disconnect the wiring plug from the regulator, located in the left-hand end of the fuel pump **(see illustration)**.
93 Undo the two Torx screws and remove the regulator. Discard the two seals, new ones must be fitted.
94 Ensure the pump and regulator mating faces are clean, and with new seals fitted, refit the regulator. Tighten the Torx screws to the specified torque.

12.90 The fuel low-pressure sensor is located on the adjacent to the left-hand steering track rod

12.92 The fuel pressure regulator is located in the end of the fuel pump (arrowed)

95 Refit the manifold as described in Section 19.

Camshaft position sensor

TD4 engines

96 Undo the three retaining bolts and remove the plastic cover from the top of the engine.

97 Ensure that the ignition is switched off, and disconnect the wiring plug from the sensor, located on the right-hand side of the camshaft cover (see illustration).

98 Undo the Torx screw and remove the sensor. Discard the seal, a new one must be fitted.

99 To refit the sensor, ensure the mating face of the camshaft cover and sensor are clean, and fit the new seal.

100 Fit the sensor into the cover, and tighten the Torx screw to the specified torque.

13.3a The fuel cooler matrix is secured by two nuts on the left-hand side . . .

14.2 Undo the screw securing the pump housing to the mounting bracket

12.97 Undo the Torx screw and remove the camshaft position sensor. The O-ring seal must be renewed

13 Fuel cooler matrix – removal and refitting

Removal

1 Unscrew the retaining bolts and remove the plastic cover (where fitted) from the top of the engine, taking care not to lose the spacers which are fitted to the cover mounting rubbers.

2 The fuel cooler matrix is located at the front of the engine compartment, under the bonnet slam panel. Ensure the area around the cooler fuel connections is clean, and free from debris. Place a suitable container under the fuel connections. Release the two retaining clips and, noting their fitted locations, disconnect the fuel hoses from the

13.3b . . . and two nuts on the right-hand side

14.4 Squeeze together the plastic lugs, and disconnect the quick-release fuel connections

matrix . Plug the fuel ports of the matrix to prevent contamination.

3 Unscrew the retaining nuts and remove the matrix (see illustrations). If required the mounting brackets and rubbers can be removed from the matrix by undoing the 2 bolts.

Refitting

4 If removed, refit the mounting brackets and rubbers to the matrix. Tighten the bolts to the specified torque.

5 Refit the matrix to the slam panel, and tighten the nuts to the specified torque.

6 Ensure that the fuel hose and connections are clean, and reconnect the hoses to the matrix. Secure the hoses with the retaining clips.

7 Refit the engine plastic cover (where fitted).

14 Fuel lift pump – removal and refitting

Removal

Models up to 2003 model year

1 Disconnect the battery negative lead, as described in Chapter 5A.

2 Undo the screw securing the pump housing to the mounting bracket (see illustration).

3 Lift and tilt the pump housing away from the bracket, and disconnect the wiring plug.

4 By squeezing together the plastic lugs, disconnect the quick-release fuel connections to the pump and fuel filter (see illustration). Be prepared for fuel spillage.

5 Lift the pump up and out of the housing (see illustration).

6 If required, the fuel hose can be removed from the pump by releasing the retaining clips.

Models from 2003 model year

7 The wheel arch mounted pump removal and refitting procedure is described in Section 8.

Refitting

8 Refitting is a reversal of removal, ensuring that the hose connections are clean prior to reconnection. The fuel system should self-prime.

14.5 Lift the pump up and out of the housing

15 Turbocharger –
description and precautions

Description

A turbocharger is fitted to all diesel engines. It increases engine efficiency by raising the pressure in the inlet manifold above atmospheric pressure. Instead of the air simply being sucked into the cylinders, it is forced in. Additional fuel is supplied by the injection pump in proportion to the increased air intake.

Energy for the operation of the turbocharger comes from the exhaust gas. The gas flows through a specially-shaped housing (the turbine housing) and, in so doing, spins the turbine wheel. The turbine wheel is attached to a shaft, at the end of which is another vaned wheel known as the compressor wheel. The compressor wheel spins in its own housing and compresses the inducted air on the way to the inlet manifold.

The compressed air passes through an intercooler. This is an air-to-air heat exchanger, mounted with the radiator at the front of the vehicle. The purpose of the intercooler is to remove from the inducted air some of the heat gained in being compressed. Because cooler air is denser, removal of this heat further increases engine efficiency.

On L-Series engines, boost pressure (the pressure in the inlet manifold) is limited by a wastegate, which diverts the exhaust gas away from the turbine wheel in response to a pressure-sensitive actuator.

On TD4 engines the turbocharger has nine adjustable guide vanes controlling the flow of exhaust gas into the turbine. The vanes are swivelled by the boost pressure control solenoid valve, controlled by the engine management ECM (see Section 12). At lower engine speeds, the vanes close together, giving a smaller exhaust gas entry port, and therefore higher gas speed, which increases boost pressure at low engine speed. At high engine speed, the vanes are turned to give a larger exhaust gas entry port, and therefore lower gas speed, effectively maintaining a reasonably constant boost pressure over the engine rev range. This is known as a Variable Nozzle Turbocharger (VNT).

The turbo shaft is pressure-lubricated by an oil feed pipe from the main oil gallery. The shaft 'floats' on a cushion of oil. A drain pipe returns the oil to the sump.

Precautions

• The turbocharger operates at extremely high speeds and temperatures. Certain precautions must be observed to avoid premature failure of the turbo or injury to the operator.
• **Do not** operate the turbo with any parts exposed. Foreign objects falling onto the rotating vanes could cause excessive damage and (if ejected) personal injury.

• **Do not** race the engine immediately after start-up, especially if it is cold. Give the oil a few seconds to circulate.
• **Always** allow the engine to return to idle speed before switching it off – do not blip the throttle and switch off, as this will leave the turbo spinning without lubrication.
• Allow the engine to idle for several minutes before switching off after a high-speed run.
• Observe the recommended intervals for oil and filter changing, and use a reputable oil of the specified quality (see *Lubricants and fluids*). Neglect of oil changing, or use of inferior oil, can cause carbon formation on the turbo shaft and subsequent failure.

16 Turbocharger –
removal and refitting

L-Series engines

Note: *A new oil return pipe union gasket, and exhaust front pipe gasket will be required on refitting, as will new oil feed pipe union sealing washers.*

Removal

1 Remove the exhaust manifold as described in Section 19.
2 Unscrew the three retaining nuts, and separate the turbocharger from the exhaust manifold **(see illustration)**.
3 If necessary, unscrew the four retaining nuts and remove the outlet elbow from the turbocharger.

Refitting

4 Remove all traces of dirt from the manifold and turbocharger mating surfaces.
5 Fit the exhaust flange (where removed), using a new gasket, and tighten its retaining nuts to the specified torque.
6 Fit a new gasket to the turbocharger flange then refit it to the exhaust manifold. Refit the retaining nuts and tighten them evenly and progressively to the specified torque.
7 Refit the exhaust manifold, as described in Section 19.
8 Check and, if necessary, top-up the oil level as described in *Weekly checks*.
9 Before refitting the engine cover, disconnect the wiring from the injection pump fuel cut-off solenoid (see Section 12) then turn the engine over on the starter until the oil pressure warning light goes out; this will allow oil to be circulated around the turbocharger bearings before the engine is started. Reconnect the solenoid then refit the engine cover and start the engine as normal.

TD4 engines

Removal

10 Disconnect the battery negative lead, as described in Chapter 5A.
11 Unscrew the retaining bolts and remove the plastic cover from the top of the engine (where fitted), taking care not to lose the

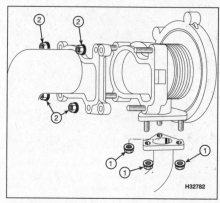

16.2 Turbocharger-to-exhaust manifold nuts (1) and outlet nuts (2)

spacers which are fitted to the cover mounting rubbers.
12 Slacken the retaining clips and release the intake ducting assembly. Unscrew the two retaining screws and remove the assembly from the camshaft cover.
13 Remove the engine oil filler cap, unscrew the five Allen screws and remove the air cleaner cover. Remove the air filter element, and refit the oil filler cap.
14 With reference to Chapter 7C, remove the intermediate reduction drive unit.
15 Free the vacuum hose and wiring harness from the turbocharger duct.
16 Release the two retaining clips, and disconnect the turbocharger duct from the mass air flow/intake air temperature sensor. Recover the duct seal and breather pipe connector.
17 Slacken the two retaining clips and remove the turbocharger outlet hose **(see illustration)**.
18 Disconnect the wiring plug and the vacuum hose from the turbocharger boost control solenoid valve. Note their fitted locations.
19 Undo the two retaining bolts, and remove the turbocharger boost control solenoid valve, complete with its bracket.
20 Unscrew the two bolts securing the turbocharger outlet pipe to the coolant rail. Slacken, but do not remove, the remaining turbocharger-to-coolant rail retaining bolt.
21 Prise out the three rubber access plugs from the base of the air cleaner housing.

16.17 Slacken the two retaining clips and remove the turbocharger outlet hose

16.22 Press down the rearmost holes in the heat shield access plate, and slide the plate to the rear

22 Working in the base of the air cleaner housing, press down the rear most holes in the heat shield access plate, and slide the plate to the rear to expose the turbocharger-to-manifold bolts **(see illustration)**.

23 Unscrew and remove the turbocharger oil feed banjo bolt from the cylinder block. Discard the sealing washers, new ones must be fitted. Plug the hose and block openings to prevent contamination.

24 Slacken the two retaining clips and disconnect the turbocharger oil return hose from the cylinder block. Undo the two bolts and remove the return hose bracket from the cylinder block **(see illustration)**.

25 Unscrew the three bolts through the base of the air cleaner housing, and remove the turbocharger. Discard the gasket, a new one must be fitted.

26 If required, note the fitted positions of the turbocharger oil feed and return pipes,

undo the bolts and remove them. Discard the sealing washers/gaskets, new ones must be fitted.

Refitting

27 Refitting is a reversal of removal, noting the following points:

a) *Ensure all mating surfaces are clean and dry.*
b) *Renew all O-rings, seals and gasket.*
c) *Tighten all fasteners to the specified torque, where available.*
d) *Prior to starting the engine, remove the fuel pump relay as described in Section 12, and operate the starter until the oil pressure warning light extinguishes. Replace the relay, start the engine and check for leaks.*

17 Turbocharger – examination and overhaul

1 With the turbocharger removed, inspect the housing for cracks or other visible damage.

2 Spin the turbine or the compressor wheel to verify that the shaft is intact and to feel for excessive shake or roughness. Some play is normal since in use the shaft is 'floating' on a film of oil. Check that the wheel vanes are undamaged.

3 The wastegate and actuator are integral with the turbocharger, and cannot be checked or renewed separately. Consult a Land Rover dealer or other specialist if it is thought that the wastegate may be faulty.

4 If the exhaust or induction passages are oil-

16.24 Slacken the two retaining clips and disconnect the turbocharger oil return hose from the cylinder block

contaminated, the turbo shaft oil seals have probably failed. (On the induction side, this will also have contaminated the intercooler, where applicable, which if necessary should be flushed with a suitable solvent.)

5 No DIY repair of the turbo is possible. A new unit may be available on an exchange basis.

18 Intercooler – removal and refitting

Removal

L-Series engines

1 Remove the front grille as described in Chapter 11.

2 With reference to Chapter 3, remove the cooling fan assembly.

3 Slacken the retaining clip and disconnect the lower hose from the intercooler **(see illustration)**.

4 Unscrew the two intercooler retaining bolts. One down through the bonnet slam panel, and one on the right-hand side of the intercooler top hose connection **(see illustration)**.

5 Lift the intercooler, and remove it from the engine compartment.

TD4 engines

6 With reference to Chapter 11, remove the front bumper.

7 Working in the engine compartment, slacken the retaining clips, and disconnect the intercooler intake and outlet hoses.

8 Undo the retaining bolts and remove both

18.3 Disconnect the lower hose from the intercooler

18.4 Remove the intercooler bolt through the slam panel

18.8 Remove both plastic radiator baffles from the front panel

18.10a The intercooler is secured by two bolts (arrowed) on the right-hand side . . .

18.10b . . . and one on the left-hand side (arrowed)

plastic radiator baffles from the front panel (see illustration).

9 On models with air conditioning, unscrew the two bolts securing the condenser to the left-hand side of the radiator, and lower it a little to gain access to the intercooler bolt. Do **not** disconnect the air conditioning pipes.

10 Unscrew the three retaining bolts, and remove the intercooler from the radiator (see illustrations).

Refitting

11 Refitting is the reverse of removal.

19 Manifolds –
removal and refitting

L-Series engines

Note: *Although the inlet and exhaust manifolds are separate, they are retained by the same nuts and bolts and share the same gasket. Therefore, in order to renew the gasket both manifolds must be removed at the same time.*

Note: *Renew all gaskets disturbed on removal. New turbocharger oil feed pipe union sealing washers will also be required.*

Removal

1 Remove the battery as described in Chapter 5A.

2 Pull out the air intake hose from the base of the air cleaner.

3 Release the two retaining clips, and disconnect the air cleaner-to-turbo hose, complete with mass airflow sensor, from the air cleaner.

4 Slacken and remove the two bolts securing the air cleaner assembly to the battery tray.

5 With reference to Section 20, remove the front exhaust pipe.

6 Slacken the retaining clip, and disconnect the breather hose from the camshaft cover.

7 Disconnect the mass airflow sensor wiring plug, slacken the retaining clip, and remove the intake hose from the turbocharger.

8 Release the retaining clip, and disconnect the boost pressure sensing pipe from the turbocharger (see illustration).

9 Unscrew the banjo bolt, and disconnect the oil turbocharger oil feed pipe (see illustration). Recover the two sealing washers, and plug the oil ports to prevent contamination.

10 Slacken the retaining clip and disconnect the turbocharger air outlet hose.

11 Disconnect the wiring plug from the intake air temperature sensor, located at the right-hand end of the inlet manifold.

12 Disconnect the EGR valve vacuum pipe, undo the four bolts and remove the EGR valve-to-inlet manifold intake pipe.

13 Slacken and remove the two bolts securing the inlet manifold intake pipe to the inlet manifold.

14 Working underneath the unit, unscrew the two retaining bolts, and disconnect the oil return pipe from the turbocharger.

19.8 Disconnect the boost pressure sensing pipe from the turbocharger (arrowed)

15 Remove the two bolts securing the exhaust manifold to the engine lifting bracket.

16 Slacken and remove the six bolts and six nuts securing the inlet and exhaust manifolds to the cylinder head, and remove the manifolds complete with the turbocharger.

17 Remove the exhaust manifold and turbocharger assembly from the cylinder head then lift off the inlet manifold. Remove the gasket from the manifold studs and discard it.

Refitting

18 Examine all the manifold studs for signs of damage and corrosion; remove all traces of corrosion, and repair or renew any damaged studs.

19 Ensure that the manifolds and cylinder head sealing faces are clean and flat, and fit the new gasket.

20 Refit the inlet manifold followed by the exhaust manifold and after applying a few drops of thread-locking compound, refit the retaining nuts and bolts. Tighten all nuts and bolts by hand only then evenly and progressively tighten them to the specified torque setting.

21 The remainder of refitting is a reversal of removal, noting the following points:

a) *Tighten all fasteners to their specified torque, where available.*

b) *Check and, if necessary, top-up the oil level as described in 'Weekly checks'.*

c) *Before refitting the engine cover, disconnect the wiring from the injection pump fuel cut-off solenoid (see Section 12) then turn the engine over on the starter*

19.23 Undo the 3 screws (arrowed) and remove the injector cover

19.9 Unscrew the banjo bolt, and disconnect the oil turbocharger oil feed pipe

until the oil pressure warning light goes out; this will allow oil to be circulated around the turbocharger bearings before the engine is started. Reconnect the solenoid then refit the engine cover and start the engine as normal.

TD4 engines

Inlet manifold removal

22 Disconnect the battery negative lead, with reference to Chapter 5A.

23 Unscrew the retaining bolts and remove the plastic cover from the top of the engine (where fitted), taking care not to lose the spacers which are fitted to the cover mounting rubbers. On 2003-on model year vehicles, undo the 3 screws and remove the cover from the injectors (see illustration).

24 Slacken the retaining clips and release the intake ducting assembly. Unscrew the two retaining screws and remove the assembly from the camshaft cover.

25 Disconnect the EGR valve vacuum hose.

26 Completely unscrew the retaining clip, and disconnect the EGR pipe from the EGR valve (see illustration).

27 Release the wiring harness and fuel return hose from the retaining clips on the inlet manifold.

28 Disconnect the wiring plug from the turbocharger boost pressure sensor.

29 Release the fuel pressure sensor harness grommet from the inlet manifold (see illustration).

30 Undo the nine bolts and four nuts, and remove the inlet manifold.

19.26 Completely unscrew the EGR pipe retaining clip

19.29 Release the wiring harness grommet from the inlet manifold

19.31 Position new seals on the inlet manifold

19.37 Disconnect the expansion tank hose from the coolant rail

19.40 Undo the bolt securing the coolant rail to the exhaust manifold

19.42 Unscrew the three Allen screws securing the heat shield to the coolant rail

19.45 Undo the three bolts securing the turbocharger to the exhaust manifold (arrowed)

Inlet manifold refitting

31 Ensure the manifold and cylinder head mating surfaces are clean and dry, and position new seals on the inlet manifold **(see illustration)**.

32 Refit the manifold to the cylinder head, and evenly tighten the bolts and nuts to the specified torque.

33 The remainder of refitting is a reversal of removal.

Exhaust manifold removal

34 Disconnect the battery negative lead, as described in Chapter 5A.

35 Drain the cooling system as described in Chapter 1B.

36 With reference to Chapter 2C, remove the camshaft cover.

37 Slacken the retaining clip, and disconnect the expansion tank hose from the coolant rail **(see illustration)**.

38 On manual transmission models, remove the bolt securing the fuel pipe to the coolant rail.

39 On models with automatic transmission, Remove the bolts securing the fuel pipe and turbocharger outlet pipe to the support bracket. Slacken the EGR pipe-to-cooler clamp screw, and unscrew the three bolts securing the cooler to the cylinder head and lifting bracket.

40 Unscrew the bolts securing the coolant rail to the cylinder head, and the exhaust manifold **(see illustration)**.

41 Release the retaining clips and remove the turbocharger outlet hose.

42 Unscrew the three Allen screws securing

the heat shield to the coolant rail **(see illustration)**.

43 Slacken and remove the retaining bolt and release the coolant rail from the thermostat housing. Discard the seal, and new one must be fitted. Now it is possible to remove the heat shield.

44 On manual transmission models, slacken the bolt securing the EGR pipe to the cylinder head, and remove the two bolts securing the pipe to the exhaust manifold.

45 Undo the three bolts securing the turbocharger to the exhaust manifold **(see illustration)**.

46 Unscrew the eight nuts, and remove the exhaust manifold.

Exhaust manifold refitting

47 Examine all the manifold studs for signs of damage and corrosion; remove all traces of corrosion, and repair or renew any damaged studs.

48 Ensure the mating surfaces of the exhaust manifold and cylinder head are clean and dry. Position new gaskets, and refit the exhaust manifold to the cylinder head. Tighten the nuts to the specified torque.

49 The remainder of refitting is a reversal of removal, noting the following points:

 a) Tighten all fasteners to their specified torque, where available.

 b) Check and, if necessary, top-up the oil level as described in 'Weekly checks'.

 c) Before restarting the engine, remove the fuel pump relay (see Section 12) then turn the engine over on the starter until the oil pressure warning light goes out; this

will allow oil to be circulated around the turbocharger bearings before the engine is started. Refit the relay and start the engine as normal.

20 Exhaust system – general information and component renewal

General information

1 The exhaust system consists of four sections: the front pipe, the catalytic converter, the intermediate pipe, the tailpipe and main silencer box.

2 The tailpipe is a sleeve fit over the end of the intermediate pipe, whilst all other exhaust sections are joined by flanged joints, which are secured by nuts, and the system is suspended throughout its entire length by rubber mountings.

Removal

3 Each exhaust section can be removed individually, or alternatively the complete system can be removed as a unit. Even if only one part of the system needs attention, it can sometimes be easier to remove the whole system and separate the sections on the bench.

4 To remove the system or part of the system, first jack up the front or rear of the vehicle and support it securely on axle stands (see *Jacking and vehicle support*). Alternatively, position the vehicle over an inspection pit or on vehicle ramps.

Front pipe

5 Remove the retaining screws and remove the engine undertray.

6 Slacken and remove the nuts securing the front pipe flange joints to the turbocharger flange and catalytic converter.

7 Unhook the front pipe from its mounting rubber then free the pipe from its joints and remove it from underneath the vehicle. Recover the gasket from each joint and discard them.

Catalytic converter

8 Slacken and remove the nuts securing the catalytic converter to the front pipe and intermediate pipe joints.

9 Free the catalytic converter from the flange joints and remove it from underneath the vehicle. Recover the gasket from each joint and discard them.

Intermediate pipe

10 Slacken and remove the nuts securing the intermediate pipe to the catalytic converter.

11 Slacken the clamp bolt and separate the tail pipe from the intermediate pipe.

12 Free the intermediate pipe from its mounting rubbers then detach the pipe from the flange joints and remove it from underneath the vehicle. Recover the gasket from each joint and discard them.

Tailpipe

13 Slacken clamp bolt securing the tailpipe joint to the intermediate pipe. Separate the tailpipe from the intermediate pipe.

14 Free the tailpipe from its mounting rubbers and remove it along with its gasket.

Complete system

15 Slacken and remove the retaining screws, and remove the engine undertray.

16 Undo the nuts securing the front pipe flange joint to the turbocharger flange.

17 Working with the aid of an assistant, free the system from all its mounting rubbers and lower it from under the vehicle. Recover the gasket from the front pipe joint.

Heat shields

18 Heat shield(s) are fitted to the underside of the vehicle body. Each shield can be removed once its retaining bolts have been undone.

Refitting

19 Each section is refitted by reversing the removal sequence, noting the following points:

  a) *Ensure that all traces of corrosion have been removed from the flanges and renew all gaskets.*

  b) *Inspect the rubber mountings for signs of damage or deterioration, and renew as necessary.*

  c) *Prior to tightening the exhaust system fasteners to the specified torque, ensure that all rubber mountings are correctly located, and that there is adequate clearance between the exhaust system and vehicle underbody.*

Chapter 4 Part C:
Emission control systems

Contents

Degrees of difficulty

| Easy, suitable for novice with little experience | Fairly easy, suitable for beginner with some experience | Fairly difficult, suitable for competent DIY mechanic | Difficult, suitable for experienced DIY mechanic | Very difficult, suitable for expert DIY or professional 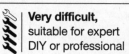 |

Specifications

Torque wrench settings

	Nm	lbf ft
Depression limiter valve and filter assembly Allen screws	8	6
Exhaust gas recirculation (EGR) cooler-to-cylinder head	25	18
Exhaust gas recirculation (EGR) valve/pipe bolts:		
M6 bolts	10	7
M8 bolts	25	18
Oxygen sensor	55	41

1 General information

All petrol engine models use unleaded petrol and also have various other features built into the fuel system to help minimise harmful emissions. All models are equipped with a crankcase emission control system, a catalytic converter and an evaporative emission control system to keep fuel vapour/ exhaust gas emissions down to a minimum.

All diesel engine models are also designed to meet strict emission requirements. All models are fitted with a crankcase emission control system, a catalytic converter and an exhaust gas recirculation (EGR) system to keep exhaust emissions down to a minimum.

The emission control systems function as follows.

Petrol models

Crankcase emission control

To reduce the emission of unburned hydrocarbons from the crankcase into the atmosphere, the engine is sealed and the blow-by gases and oil vapour are drawn from inside the crankcase, through a wire mesh oil separator, into the intake tract to be burned by the engine during normal combustion.

Under conditions of high manifold depression (idling, deceleration) the gases will be sucked positively out of the crankcase through a small diameter pipe and into the intake tract 'downstream' of the throttle valve. A larger diameter pipe, 'upstream' of the throttle valve, allows fresh air to be drawn back into the crankcase, and mix with the crankcase gases. Under conditions of low manifold depression (acceleration, full-throttle running) the gases are forced out of the crankcase by the (relatively) higher crankcase pressure; and drawn through both pipes upstream and downstream of the throttle valve.

Exhaust emission control

To minimise the amount of pollutants which escape into the atmosphere, all models are fitted with a catalytic converter in the exhaust system. The system is of the closed-loop type, in which an oxygen sensor(s) in the exhaust system supplies a voltage signal to the engine management system ECM, enabling the ECM to adjust the mixture to provide the best possible conditions for the converter to operate. Models with MEMS 1.8 engine management systems have one oxygen sensor fitted to the exhaust manifold, whilst models equipped with the MEMS 3 engine management system are fitted with two oxygen sensors; one fitted to the exhaust manifold (pre-catalyst sensor), and one 'downstream' of the catalytic converter (post-catalyst sensor). The oxygen sensor(s) has a built-in heating element which is controlled by the ECM; the heating element is used to warm the sensor when the engine is cold to bring it quickly to an efficient operating temperature.

The oxygen sensor's tip is sensitive to oxygen and sends the ECM a varying voltage depending on the amount of oxygen in the exhaust gases; the leaner the air/fuel mixture, the higher the oxygen content, and the lower the voltage from the sensor(s). If the intake air/ fuel mixture is too rich, the exhaust gases are low in oxygen so the sensor sends a higher-voltage signal. Peak conversion efficiency of all major pollutants occurs if the intake air/fuel mixture is maintained at the chemically-correct ratio for the complete combustion of petrol of 14.7 parts (by weight) of air to 1 part of fuel (the 'stoichiometric' ratio). The sensor output voltage alters in a large step at this point, the ECM using the signal change as a reference point and correcting the intake air/fuel mixture accordingly by altering the fuel injector pulse width.

2.4 Disconnect the canister hose from the throttle body (arrowed)

2.7 Disconnect the wiring connector from the top of the canister

2.10 The canister is located under the vehicle, just ahead of the right-hand side rear roadwheel

Evaporative emission control

To minimise the escape into the atmosphere of unburned hydrocarbons, an evaporative emissions control system is also fitted to all models. The fuel tank filler cap is sealed and a charcoal canister is mounted in the engine compartment. The canister collects the petrol vapours generated in the tank when the vehicle is parked and stores them until they can be cleared from the canister (under the control of the engine management system ECM) via the purge valve into the intake tract to be burned by the engine during normal combustion.

To ensure that the engine runs correctly when it is cold and/or idling, and to protect the catalytic converter from the effects of an over-rich mixture, the purge control valve is not opened by the ECM until the engine has warmed-up, and the engine is under load; the valve solenoid is then modulated on and off to allow the stored vapour to pass into the intake tract.

Diesel models

Crankcase emission control

To reduce the emission of unburned hydrocarbons from the crankcase into the atmosphere, the engine is sealed and the blow-by gases and oil vapour are drawn from inside the crankcase, through a wire mesh oil separator, into the intake tract to be burned by the engine during normal combustion. Crankcase gases are drawn via a depression limiting valve. The valve closes progressively as the engine speed increases, so limiting the maximum depression in the crankcase.

2.11 Squeeze together the union lugs and disconnect the tank, air and purge pipes

Exhaust emission control

To minimise the level of exhaust pollutants released into the atmosphere, a catalytic converter is fitted in the exhaust system of some models.

The catalytic converter consists of a canister containing a fine mesh impregnated with a catalyst material, over which the hot exhaust gases pass. The catalyst speeds up the oxidation of harmful carbon monoxide, unburned hydrocarbons and soot, effectively reducing the quantity of harmful products released into the atmosphere via the exhaust gases.

Exhaust gas recirculation system

This system is designed to recirculate small quantities of exhaust gas into the intake tract, and therefore into the combustion process. This process reduces the level of unburnt hydrocarbons present in the exhaust gas before it reaches the catalytic converter. The system is controlled by the engine management system ECM, using the information from its various sensors, via the EGR valve which is fitted to the metal pipe connecting the inlet and exhaust manifolds. The exhaust gasss are cooled prior to entering the inlet manifold by passing through a cooler mounted on the side of the EGR valve. Engine coolant circulates through the cooler. The EGR valve is vacuum operated and is switched on and off by an electrical solenoid valve.

2 Petrol engine emission control systems – testing and component renewal

Crankcase emission control

1 The components of this system require no attention other than to check that the hose(s) are clear and undamaged at regular intervals.

Evaporative emission control

Testing

2 If the system is thought to be faulty, disconnect the hoses from the charcoal canister and purge control valve and check that they are clear by blowing through them. Full testing of the system can only be carried out

using specialist electronic equipment which is connected to the engine management system diagnostic wiring connector (see Chapter 4A). If the purge control valve or charcoal canister are thought to be faulty, they must be renewed.

Charcoal canister renewal

Models with MEMS 1.8

3 The charcoal canister is located on the left-hand side of the engine compartment.
4 Trace the outlet hose back from the canister to the throttle body. Release the retaining clip and disconnect the hose from the throttle body **(see illustration)**.
5 Trace the intake hose back from the canister then release the retaining clip and disconnect it from the fuel vapour pipe.
6 Release the breather hose from its retaining clips so that it is free to be removed with the canister.
7 Disconnect the wiring connector from the canister purge valve **(see illustration)**.
8 Unclip the canister mounting bracket from the body and remove the assembly from the engine compartment. If necessary, slacken the clamp bolt and separate the canister and bracket.
9 Refitting is a reverse of the removal procedure ensuring the hoses are correctly and securely reconnected.

Models with MEMS 3

10 The canister is located under the vehicle, just ahead of the right-hand side rear roadwheel **(see illustration)**. Working underneath the vehicle, unscrew the retaining nut (at the front of the canister) and remove the canister from the bracket.
11 Note the fitted locations of the pipes. Squeeze together the union lugs and disconnect the tank, air and purge pipes from the canister **(see illustration)**.
12 Refitting is a reverse of the removal procedure, ensuring the hoses are correctly and securely reconnected.

Purge valve renewal

Models with MEMS 1.8

13 The purge valve is mounted onto the top of the charcoal canister, which is located on the left-hand side of the engine compartment.

14 To renew the valve, ensure the ignition is switched off then disconnect the wiring connector from the valve.

15 Release the retaining clip and disconnect the hose from the valve.

16 Release the retaining clips and remove the purge valve from the top of the canister. Recover the sealing ring from the valve union and discard it; a new one must be used on refitting.

17 Refitting is the reverse of removal, using a new sealing ring. Ensure the valve and the hose are securely held by the retaining clips.

Models with MEMS 3

18 The valve is located on the left-hand side inner wing in the engine compartment, below the electrical box (see illustration).

19 Ensure the ignition is switched off, and disconnect the wiring plug from the valve.

20 Disconnect the quick release connector from the valve, and release the hose.

21 Release the clip and slide the valve from the bracket.

22 Refitting is a reversal of removal. Ensure the valve and hose are securely held by the retaining clips.

2-way valve renewal

23 The 2-way valve is mounted onto the top of the fuel tank. To gain access, remove the fuel tank as described in Chapter 4A.

24 Release the retaining clips then disconnect the hoses from the valve, noting each hose's correct fitted position.

25 Unscrew the retaining nut and remove the valve from the tank.

26 Refitting is the reverse of removal ensuring the hoses are correctly and securely reconnected.

Exhaust emission control

Testing

27 The performance of the catalytic converter can be checked only by measuring the exhaust gases using a good-quality, carefully-calibrated exhaust gas analyser.

28 If the CO level at the tailpipe is too high, the vehicle should be taken to a Land Rover dealer or specialist so that the complete fuel injection and ignition systems, including the oxygen sensor, can be thoroughly checked using the special diagnostic equipment. Once these have been checked and are known to be free from faults, the fault must be in the catalytic converter, which must be renewed.

Catalytic converter renewal

29 Refer to Chapter 4A.

Oxygen sensor(s) renewal

Note: *The oxygen sensor is delicate and will not work if it is dropped or knocked, if its power supply is disrupted, or if any cleaning materials are used on it.*

Exhaust manifold sensor

30 Ensure the ignition is switched off then trace the wiring back from the oxygen sensor.

2.18 The purge valve is located on the left-hand side inner wing in the engine compartment

Free the connector from its retaining clip and disconnect the two halves of the connector.

31 Unscrew the sensor and remove it from the manifold. Note that the use of a special deep, split socket is recommended (see illustration). Recover the sensor sealing washer and discard it; a new one must be used on refitting.

32 Refitting is a reverse of the removal procedure, using a new sealing washer. Tighten the sensor to the specified torque and ensure that the wiring is correctly routed and in no danger of contacting either the exhaust manifold or the engine.

Post-catalyst sensor (MEMS 3)

33 Ensure the ignition is switched off, then working in the passenger compartment, release the clips and free the gear lever gaiter from the centre console.

34 At the rear of the gaiter aperture, disconnect the oxygen sensor wiring plug (see illustration 16.8 in Chapter 4A).

35 Working underneath the vehicle, prise out the grommet and withdraw the oxygen sensor harness through the hole.

36 Unscrew the sensor from the rear of the catalytic converter. Note that the use of a special deep, split socket is recommended.

37 Refitting is a reverse of the removal procedure, using a new sealing washer. Tighten the sensor to the specified torque, and ensure the wiring is correctly routed and in no danger of contacting the exhaust system.

<table>
<tr><td>3</td><td>Diesel engine emission control systems – testing and component renewal</td><td></td></tr>
</table>

Crankcase emission control

Testing

1 The components of this system require no attention other than to check that the hose(s) are clear and undamaged at regular intervals. If the system is thought to be faulty, renew the crankcase pressure limiting valve as follows.

Pressure limiting valve renewal

L-Series engine

2 Slacken the retaining clip and disconnect

2.31 Unscrew the sensor and remove it from the manifold

the breather hose then ease the valve out from the intake duct and remove it from the engine compartment.

3 Refitting is the reverse of removal ensuring that the valve is positioned the correct way around with the outlet marked F fitted to the intake duct.

TD4 engine

4 With reference to Chapter 4B, remove the air cleaner cover.

5 Disconnect the injector wiring plugs, unscrew the three retaining screws, and move the injector harness to one side.

6 Unscrew the four Allen screws, and remove the depression limiting valve complete with filter (see illustration).

7 Ensure the mating surfaces are clean and dry, refit the valve housing. Tighten the Allen screws to the specified torque.

8 The remainder of refitting is a reversal of removal.

Exhaust emission control

Testing

9 The performance of the catalytic converter can be checked only by measuring the exhaust gases using a good-quality, carefully-calibrated exhaust gas analyser.

10 Before assuming that the catalytic converter is faulty, it is worth checking whether the problem is not due to a faulty injector(s). Refer to your Land Rover dealer for further information.

3.6 Remove the depression limiting valve complete with filter

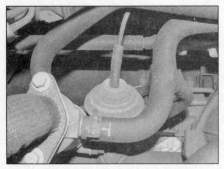

3.14 Disconnect the vacuum hose from the EGR valve – L-Series engine

3.19 Disconnect the vacuum hose from the EGR valve – TD4 engine

3.20 Completely slacken the clamp screw and disconnect the EGR pipe from the valve

Catalytic converter renewal

11 Refer to Chapter 4B for removal and refitting details.

Exhaust gas recirculation (EGR)

Testing

12 Comprehensive testing of the system can only be carried out using specialist electronic equipment which is connected to the injection system diagnostic wiring connector (see Chapter 4B). If the EGR valve or solenoid valve are thought to be faulty, they must be renewed as follows.

EGR valve renewal

L-Series engine

13 Unscrew the retaining bolts and remove the plastic cover from the top of the engine unit, taking care not to lose the spacers from the engine cover mounting rubbers. The EGR valve is fitted to the metal pipe linking the inlet and exhaust manifolds.

14 Disconnect the vacuum hose from the EGR valve **(see illustration)**.

15 Slacken and remove the Allen screws securing the valve to the manifold and connecting pipe and remove it from the engine. Recover the gaskets and discard them; new ones must be used on refitting. If necessary, the connecting pipe can then be unbolted and removed from the other manifold.

16 Refitting is the reverse of the removal, using new gaskets and tightening the valve retaining bolts to the specified torque.

TD4 engine

17 Unscrew the retaining screws, and remove the plastic cover from the top of the engine (where fitted).

18 Slacken the retaining clips and disconnect the air intake ducting assembly. Unclip the injector wiring harness, unscrew the two retaining bolts, and remove the ducting assembly.

19 Disconnect the vacuum hose from the EGR valve **(see illustration)**.

20 Completely slacken the clamp screw and disconnect the EGR pipe from the valve **(see illustration)**.

21 Unscrew the four retaining bolts, and remove the EGR valve.

22 Refitting is a reversal of removal, using a new seal and tightening the valve retaining bolts to the specified torque.

EGR solenoid valve renewal

L-Series engine

23 The EGR solenoid valve is located on the left-hand side of the engine compartment bulkhead.

24 Disconnect the wiring connector and vacuum hoses from the valve then undo the retaining screws and remove the valve from its mounting **(see illustration)**. Note the fitted locations of the vacuum pipes.

25 Refitting is the reverse of removal.

TD4 engine

26 With reference to Chapter 4B, remove the inlet manifold.

27 Disconnect the wiring plug from the solenoid **(see illustration)**.

28 Unscrew the two bolts securing the solenoid bracket to the cylinder block. Note their fitted locations then disconnect the vacuum hoses. If necessary, the solenoid can be separated from the mounting bracket by unscrewing the two retaining nuts.

29 Refitting is a reversal of removal.

EGR cooler renewal

30 With reference to Chapter 2C, remove the camshaft cover.

31 Completely slacken and remove the clamps securing the EGR pipes to the cooler.

32 Remove the bolt securing the fuel rails to the support bracket.

33 Undo the bolt securing the turbo outlet pipe to the support bracket at the front left-hand side of the engine.

34 Apply the handbrake, then jack up the front of the vehicle and support it securely on axle stands (see *Jacking and vehicle support*). Remove the retaining screws and fasteners and remove the undercover from beneath the engine and transmission.

35 Working underneath the vehicle, remove the bolt securing the turbo outlet pipe to the upper coolant rail.

36 Remove the two bolts securing the turbo outlet pipe support bracket to the left-hand end of the cylinder head.

37 Release the retaining clip and disconnect the hose from the vacuum pump.

38 Undo the three bolts securing the EGR cooler to the left-hand end of the cylinder head.

39 Be prepared for coolant spillage, and disconnect the coolant hoses from the cooler.

40 Refitting is a reversal of removal. Top-up the coolant level as described in Chapter 1B.

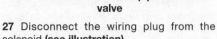

4 Catalytic converter –
general information
and precautions

1 The catalytic converter is a reliable and simple device which needs no maintenance in itself, but there are some facts of which an owner should be aware if the converter is to function properly for its full service life.

3.24 EGR solenoid valve – L-Series engine

3.27 EGR solenoid valve – TD4 engine

Petrol engine

a) DO NOT use leaded petrol or LRP in a vehicle equipped with a catalytic converter – the lead will coat the precious metals, reducing their converting efficiency and will eventually destroy the converter.

b) Always keep the ignition and fuel systems well-maintained in accordance with the manufacturer's schedule.

c) If the engine develops a misfire, do not drive the vehicle at all (or at least as little as possible) until the fault is cured.

d) DO NOT push- or tow-start the vehicle – this will soak the catalytic converter in unburned fuel, causing it to overheat when the engine does start.

e) DO NOT switch off the ignition at high engine speeds.

f) DO NOT use fuel or engine oil additives – these may contain substances harmful to the catalytic converter.

g) DO NOT continue to use the vehicle if the engine burns oil to the extent of leaving a visible trail of blue smoke.

h) Remember that the catalytic converter operates at very high temperatures. DO NOT, therefore, park the vehicle in dry undergrowth, over long grass or piles of dead leaves after a long run.

i) Remember that the catalytic converter is FRAGILE – do not strike it with tools during servicing work.

j) In some cases a sulphurous smell (like that of rotten eggs) may be noticed from the exhaust. This is common to many catalytic converter-equipped vehicles and once the vehicle has covered a few thousand miles the problem should disappear. Sometimes the smell is a result of the fuel used.

k) The catalytic converter, used on a well-maintained and well-driven vehicle, should last for between 50 000 and 100 000 miles – if the converter is no longer effective it must be renewed.

Diesel engine

2 Refer to the information given in parts f, g, h and i of the petrol engine information given above.

Chapter 5 Part A:
Starting and charging systems

Contents

Degrees of difficulty

Easy, suitable for novice with little experience

Fairly easy, suitable for beginner with some experience

Fairly difficult, suitable for competent DIY mechanic

Difficult, suitable for experienced DIY mechanic

Very difficult, suitable for expert DIY or professional

Specifications

System type.................................... 12 volt, negative earth

Battery
Charge condition:
Poor.................................... 12.5 volts
Normal.................................... 12.6 volts
Good.................................... 12.7 volts

Torque wrench settings	Nm	lbf ft
Alternator fixings:		
Petrol engine:		
Mounting bolts	45	33
Upper mounting bracket nut/bolt (non-air conditioned models)	10	7
Upper mounting bracket nut/bolt (air conditioned models)	45	33
L-Series diesel engine:		
Lower mounting bolt	45	33
Upper mounting bolt	25	18
TD4 diesel engine:		
M8	25	18
M10	45	33
Alternator drivebelt tensioner bolt	25	18
Oil pressure switch:		
Petrol engine	15	11
L-Series diesel engine	15	11
TD4 diesel engine	38	28
Oil temperature sensor	12	9
Starter motor bolts:		
Petrol engine	80	59
L-Series diesel engine	85	63
TD4 diesel engine	45	33

1 General information and precautions

General information

The engine electrical system consists mainly of the charging and starting systems. Because of their engine-related functions, these components are covered separately from the body electrical devices such as the lights, instruments, etc (which are covered in Chapter 12). On petrol engine models refer to Part B for information on the ignition system, and on diesel models refer to Part C for information on the preheating system.

The electrical system is of the 12 volt negative earth type.

The battery is of the low maintenance or 'maintenance-free' (sealed for life) type and is charged by the alternator, which is belt-driven from the crankshaft pulley.

The starter motor is of the pre-engaged type incorporating an integral solenoid. On starting, the solenoid moves the drive pinion into engagement with the flywheel ring gear before the starter motor is energised. Once the engine has started, a one-way clutch prevents the motor armature being driven by the engine until the pinion disengages from the flywheel.

Precautions

Further details of the various systems are given in the relevant Sections of this Chapter. While some repair procedures are given, the usual course of action is to renew the component concerned. The owner whose interest extends beyond mere component renewal should obtain a copy of the *Automotive Electrical & Electronic Systems Manual*, available from the publishers of this manual.

It is necessary to take extra care when working on the electrical system to avoid damage to semi-conductor devices (diodes and transistors), and to avoid the risk of personal injury. In addition to the precautions given in *Safety first!* at the beginning of this manual, observe the following when working on the system:

• *Always remove rings, watches, etc before working on the electrical system.* Even with the battery disconnected, capacitive discharge could occur if a component's live terminal is earthed through a metal object. This could cause a shock or nasty burn.

• *Do not reverse the battery connections.* Components such as the alternator, electronic control units, or any other components having semi-conductor circuitry could be irreparably damaged.

• If the engine is being started using jump leads and a slave battery, connect the batteries *positive-to-positive* and *negative-to-negative* (see *Jump starting*). This also applies when connecting a battery charger.

• Never disconnect the battery terminals,

the alternator, any electrical wiring or any test instruments when the engine is running.

• Do not allow the engine to turn the alternator when the alternator is not connected.

• Never 'test' for alternator output by 'flashing' the output lead to earth.

• Never use an ohmmeter of the type incorporating a hand-cranked generator for circuit or continuity testing.

• Always ensure that the battery negative lead is disconnected when working on the electrical system.

• Before using electric-arc welding equipment on the vehicle, disconnect the battery, alternator and components such as the fuel injection/ignition electronic control unit to protect them from the risk of damage.

• The radio/cassette unit fitted as standard equipment by Land Rover is equipped with a built-in security code to deter thieves. If the power source to the unit is cut, the anti-theft system will activate. Even if the power source is immediately reconnected, the radio/cassette unit will not function until the correct security code has been entered. Therefore, if you do not know the correct security code for the radio/cassette unit do not disconnect the battery negative terminal of the battery or remove the radio/cassette unit from the vehicle.

2 Electrical fault finding – general information

Refer to Chapter 12.

3 Battery – testing and charging

Testing

Standard and low maintenance battery

1 If the vehicle covers a small annual mileage, it is worthwhile checking the specific gravity of the electrolyte every three months to determine the state of charge of the battery. Use a hydrometer to make the check and compare the results with the following table. Note that the specific gravity readings assume an electrolyte temperature of 15°C; for every 10°C below 15°C subtract 0.007. For every 10°C above 15°C add 0.007.

	Ambient temperature above 25°C	below 25°C
Fully-charged	1.210 to 1.230	1.270 to 1.290
70% charged	1.170 to 1.190	1.230 to 1.250
discharged	1.050 to 1.070	1.110 to 1.130

2 If the battery condition is suspect, first check the specific gravity of electrolyte in each cell. A variation of 0.040 or more between any cells indicates loss of electrolyte or deterioration of the internal plates.

3 If the specific gravity variation is 0.040 or more, the battery should be renewed. If the

cell variation is satisfactory but the battery is discharged, it should be charged as described later in this Section.

Maintenance-free battery

4 In cases where a 'sealed for life' maintenance-free battery is fitted, topping-up and testing of the electrolyte in each cell is not possible. The condition of the battery can therefore only be tested using a battery condition indicator or a voltmeter.

5 Models may be fitted with a 'Delco' type maintenance-free battery, with a built-in charge condition indicator. The indicator is located in the top of the battery casing, and indicates the condition of the battery from its colour. If the indicator shows green, then the battery is in a good state of charge. If the indicator turns darker, eventually to black, then the battery requires charging, as described later in this Section. If the indicator shows clear/yellow, then the electrolyte level in the battery is too low to allow further use, and the battery should be renewed. **Do not** attempt to charge, load or jump start a battery when the indicator shows clear/yellow.

All batteries

6 If testing the battery using a voltmeter, connect the voltmeter across the battery and compare the result with those given in the Specifications under 'charge condition'. The test is only accurate if the battery has not been subjected to any kind of charge for the previous six hours. If this is not the case, switch on the headlights for 30 seconds, then wait four to five minutes before testing the battery after switching off the headlights. All other electrical circuits must be switched off, so check that the doors and tailgate are fully shut when making the test.

7 If the voltage reading is less than 12.2 volts, then the battery is discharged, whilst a reading of 12.2 to 12.4 volts indicates a partially discharged condition.

8 If the battery is to be charged, remove it from the vehicle (Section 4) and charge it as described later in this Section.

Charging

Note: *The following is intended as a guide only. Always refer to the manufacturer's recommendations (often printed on a label attached to the battery) before charging a battery.*

Standard and low maintenance battery

9 Charge the battery at a rate of 3.5 to 4 amps and continue to charge the battery at this rate until no further rise in specific gravity is noted over a four hour period.

10 Alternatively, a trickle charger charging at the rate of 1.5 amps can safely be used overnight.

11 Specially rapid 'boost' charges which are claimed to restore the power of the battery in 1 to 2 hours are not recommended, as they can cause serious damage to the battery plates through overheating.

4.2 Slacken the clamp nut and disconnect the clamp from the battery negative (earth) terminal

4.3 Disconnect the positive terminal

4.4 Unscrew the bolt and remove the battery retaining clamp

12 While charging the battery, note that the temperature of the electrolyte should never exceed 37.8°C.

Maintenance-free battery

13 This battery type takes considerably longer to fully recharge than the standard type, the time taken being dependent on the extent of discharge, but it can take anything up to three days.

14 A constant voltage type charger is required, to be set, when connected, to 13.9 to 14.9 volts with a charger current below 25 amps. Using this method, the battery should be usable within three hours, giving a voltage reading of 12.5 volts, but this is for a partially discharged battery and, as mentioned, full charging can take considerably longer.

15 If the battery is to be charged from a fully discharged state (condition reading less than 12.2 volts), have it recharged by your Land Rover dealer or local automotive electrician, as the charge rate is higher and constant supervision during charging is necessary.

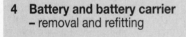

4 Battery and battery carrier – removal and refitting

Note: *If a Land Rover radio/cassette unit is fitted, refer to Section 1 of this Chapter.*

Battery

Removal

1 The battery is located on the left-hand side of the engine compartment.

4.6a Unscrew the fusebox retaining bolts (arrowed)

2 Slacken the clamp nut and disconnect the clamp from the battery negative (earth) terminal **(see illustration)**.

3 Lift the insulation cover and disconnect the positive terminal lead in the same way **(see illustration)**.

4 Unscrew the bolt and remove the battery retaining clamp then lift the battery out of the engine compartment **(see illustration)**.

Refitting

5 Refitting is a reversal of removal, but smear petroleum jelly on the terminals after reconnecting the leads, and always reconnect the positive lead first, and the negative lead last. **Note:** *Upon reconnection of the battery, the tailgate glass mechanism may need to be recalibrated. If the battery was disconnected (or discharged) with the alarm armed, reconnect the battery and disarm the alarm. The tailgate glass will now lower fully (this will happen automatically if the alarm was not armed). Fully raise the tailgate glass to recalibrate the mechanism. If the glass is not fully raised, an error 'beep' will sound. If the alarm handset fails to lock, or unlock the door locks, it may be that the handset requires resynchronisation by operating the button at least five times in quick succession, in close proximity to the vehicle.*

Battery carrier removal

Vehicles up to 2001

6 To remove the battery tray, remove the two mounting bolts, and move the engine compartment fusebox to one side. Slide the electrical components up from the brackets

4.6b Slide the various electrical components from the battery tray brackets

on the rear of the carrier under the fusebox **(see illustrations)**

7 Release the wiring harness from the retaining clip.

8 With the battery removed, slacken and remove the two bolts securing the battery carrier to the air cleaner housing. Release the retaining clip, and disconnect the air cleaner outlet and inlet hoses. Remove the air cleaner from the engine compartment.

9 Unscrew the retaining nut, and move the engine ECM to one side. There is no need to disconnect the ECM.

10 Slacken and remove the four retaining bolts, and remove the battery carrier.

Vehicles 2001-on

11 With the battery removed, release the wiring harness from the retaining clip on the battery carrier. On models equipped with cruise control, disconnect the wiring plug and vacuum hose from the vacuum pump.

12 Slacken and remove the four retaining bolts, and remove the battery tray **(see illustration)**.

Battery carrier refitting

13 Refitting is a reversal of removal.

5 Charging system – testing

Note: *Refer to the warnings given in 'Safety first!' and in Section 1 of this Chapter before starting work.*

1 If the ignition warning light fails to illuminate

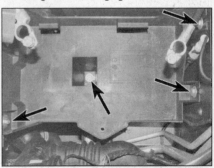

4.12 Battery tray retaining bolts (arrowed) – vehicles from 2001

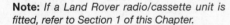

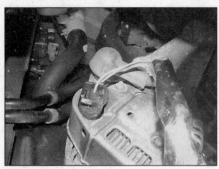

7.3 Peel back the rubber cover, unscrew the terminal nut and pull out the wiring plug

7.8 Alternator upper mounting bolt

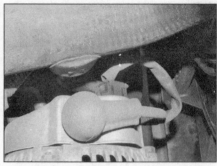

7.11 Prise up the rubber cover, undo the terminal nut and disconnect the wiring plug

when the ignition is switched on, first check the alternator wiring connections for security. If satisfactory, check that the warning light bulb has not blown, and that the bulbholder is secure in its location in the instrument panel. If the light still fails to illuminate, check the continuity of the warning light feed wire from the alternator to the bulbholder. If all is satisfactory, the alternator is at fault and should be renewed or taken to an auto-electrician for testing and repair.

2 If the ignition warning light illuminates when the engine is running, stop the engine and check that the drivebelt is correctly tensioned (see Chapter 1A or 1B) and that the alternator connections are secure. If all is so far satisfactory, have the alternator checked by an auto-electrician for testing and repair.

3 If the alternator output is suspect even though the warning light functions correctly, the regulated voltage may be checked as follows.

4 Connect a voltmeter across the battery terminals and start the engine.

5 Increase the engine speed until the voltmeter reading remains steady; the reading should be approximately 12 to 13 volts, and no more than 14 volts.

6 Switch on as many electrical accessories (eg, the headlights, heated rear window and heater blower) as possible, and check that the alternator maintains the regulated voltage at around 13 to 14 volts.

7 If the regulated voltage is not as stated, the fault may be due to worn brushes, weak brush springs, a faulty voltage regulator, a

7.12 Release the retaining clip and disconnect the vacuum pipe

faulty diode, a severed phase winding or worn or damaged slip-rings. The alternator should be renewed or taken to an auto-electrician for testing and repair.

6 Alternator drivebelt – removal, refitting and tensioning

Refer to the procedure given for the auxiliary drivebelt(s) in Chapter 1A or 1B.

7 Alternator – removal and refitting

Removal

1 Firmly apply the handbrake then jack up the front of the vehicle and support it securely on axle stands (see *Jacking and vehicle support*). Undo the retaining bolts/clips and remove the undercover from beneath the engine/transmission unit. Disconnect the battery negative lead and proceed as described under the relevant sub-heading.

Petrol engine without air conditioning

2 Release the auxiliary drivebelt as described in Chapter 1A and disengage it from the alternator pulley.

3 Remove the rubber covers (where fitted) from the alternator terminals, then unscrew the retaining nut and disconnect the wiring plug from the rear of the alternator **(see illustration)**. Where fitted, unscrew the bolts and remove the exhaust manifold heat shield.

4 Unscrew the nuts and remove the alternator upper and lower mounting bolts.

Petrol engine with air conditioning

5 Release the auxiliary drivebelt as described in Chapter 1A and disengage it from the alternator pulley.

6 With reference to Chapter 3, remove the electric cooling fan assembly.

7 Remove the rubber covers (where fitted) from the alternator terminals, then unscrew the retaining nut and disconnect the wiring plug from the rear of the alternator.

8 Slacken and remove the alternator upper and lower mounting nuts and bolts, and free the alternator from its mountings **(see illustration)**.

L-Series diesel engine

9 Undo the retaining screws and remove the cover from the top of the engine, noting the spacers which are fitted to the cover mounting rubbers.

10 Release the auxiliary drivebelt as described in Chapter 1B and disengage it from the alternator pulley.

11 Peel back the rubber cover from the alternator terminal, then unscrew the retaining nut and disconnect the wiring. Also disconnect the wiring connector from the rear of the alternator **(see illustration)**.

12 Release the retaining clip and disconnect the vacuum pipe from the vacuum pump which is fitted to the front of the alternator **(see illustration)**. On models with air conditioning, unscrew the bolt securing the brake servo pipe to the camshaft cover.

13 Wipe clean the area around the vacuum pump oil feed and return pipes unions on the cylinder block. Position a container beneath the unions then unscrew the feed pipe union nut and disconnect the return pipe union and allow any oil to drain into the container.

14 Slacken and remove the mounting bolts and free the alternator from its mountings.

15 Unscrew the oil feed pipe union nut from the vacuum pump then remove the alternator assembly from the vehicle.

16 If necessary, referring to Chapter 9, remove the vacuum pump from the alternator.

TD4 diesel engine without air conditioning

17 Working underneath the vehicle, slacken and remove the three bolts securing the coolant rail to the sump/engine block.

18 Disconnect the alternator wiring plug, and undo the nut securing the battery cable to the alternator **(see illustration)**.

19 Unscrew the three retaining bolts and remove the alternator.

TD4 diesel engine with air conditioning

20 With reference to Chapter 1B, remove the compressor drivebelt.

7.18 Alternator connections – TD4 diesel models

7.24 Undo the compressor bracket bolts

7.26 Lower the alternator from the mountings

21 Unscrew the three bolts securing the coolant rail to the sump/engine block.
22 Slacken the bolt securing the compressor bracket to the sump, but do not remove it.
23 Unscrew the three bolts securing the compressor to the bracket, and position the compressor to one side. Do **not** disconnect the refrigerant pipes.
24 Remove the retaining bolts and remove the compressor bracket from the cylinder block **(see illustration)**.
25 Disconnect the alternator wiring plug, and undo the nut securing the battery cable to the alternator **(see illustration 7.18)**.
26 Unscrew the three retaining bolts and remove the alternator **(see illustration)**.

Refitting

27 Refitting is the reverse of removal tightening all mounting bolts to their specified torque settings (where given). Ensure the drivebelt is correctly refitted and tensioned as described in Chapter 1A or 1B (as applicable). Top-up the cooling system as described in *Weekly Checks*. **Note:** *On TD4 diesel models, fit the top retaining bolt to the alternator prior to installation, as once fitted it is impossible to insert the bolt due to access limitations.*

8 Alternator – testing and overhaul

If the alternator is thought to be suspect, it should be removed from the vehicle and taken to an auto-electrician for testing. Most auto-electricians will be able to supply and fit brushes at a reasonable cost. However, check on the cost of repairs before proceeding as it may prove more economical to obtain a new or exchange alternator.

9 Starting system – testing

Note: *Refer to the precautions given in 'Safety first!' and in Section 1 of this Chapter before starting work.*
1 If the starter motor fails to operate when the ignition key is turned to the appropriate position, the following possible causes may be to blame:
a) *The battery is faulty.*
b) *The electrical connections between the switch, solenoid, battery and starter motor are somewhere failing to pass the necessary current from the battery through the starter to earth.*
c) *The solenoid is faulty.*
d) *The starter motor is mechanically or electrically defective.*
2 To check the battery, switch on the headlights. If they dim after a few seconds, this indicates that the battery is discharged – recharge (see Section 3) or renew the battery. If the headlights glow brightly, operate the ignition switch and observe the lights. If they dim, then this indicates that current is reaching the starter motor, therefore the fault must lie in the starter motor. If the lights continue to glow brightly (and no clicking sound can be heard from the starter motor solenoid), this indicates that there is a fault in the circuit or solenoid – see following paragraphs. If the starter motor turns slowly when operated, but the battery is in good condition, then this indicates that either the starter motor is faulty, or there is considerable resistance somewhere in the circuit.
3 If a fault in the circuit is suspected, disconnect the battery leads (including the earth connection to the body), the starter/solenoid wiring and the engine/transmission earth strap. Thoroughly clean the connections, and reconnect the leads and wiring, then use a voltmeter or test lamp to check that full battery

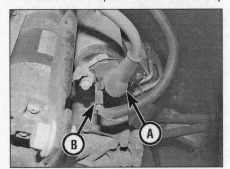

10.3 Starter motor main supply connection (A) and solenoid terminal (B)

voltage is available at the battery positive lead connection to the solenoid, and that the earth is sound. Smear petroleum jelly around the battery terminals to prevent corrosion – corroded connections are amongst the most frequent causes of electrical system faults.
4 If the battery and all connections are in good condition, check the circuit by disconnecting the wire from the solenoid blade terminal. Connect a voltmeter or test lamp between the wire end and a good earth (such as the battery negative terminal), and check that the wire is live when the ignition switch is turned to the 'start' position. If it is, then the circuit is sound – if not the circuit wiring can be checked as described in Chapter 12.
5 The solenoid contacts can be checked by connecting a voltmeter or test lamp between the battery positive feed connection on the starter side of the solenoid, and earth. When the ignition switch is turned to the 'start' position, there should be a reading or lighted bulb, as applicable. If there is no reading or lighted bulb, the solenoid is faulty and should be renewed.
6 If the circuit and solenoid are proved sound, the fault must lie in the starter motor. In this event, it may be possible to have the starter motor overhauled by a specialist, but check on the cost of spares before proceeding, as it may prove more economical to obtain a new or exchange motor.

10 Starter motor – removal and refitting

Removal

1 Disconnect the battery negative lead, firmly apply the handbrake then jack up the front of the vehicle and support it on axle stands (see *Jacking and vehicle support*).

Petrol engine

2 Remove the air cleaner housing assembly as described in Chapter 4A.
3 Remove the rubber cover then unscrew the retaining nut and disconnect the main supply lead from the solenoid. Disconnect the wiring connector from the solenoid terminal **(see illustration)**.

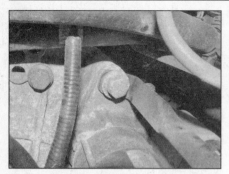

10.4 Undo the bolts and remove the support bracket

10.11a Unscrew the nut (arrowed) and disconnect the two cables . . .

10.11b . . . then disconnect the wiring plug

4 Slacken and remove the retaining nuts and bolts and remove the support bracket from the rear of the starter motor and the transmission mounting bracket **(see illustration)**.

5 Slacken and remove the starter motor lower mounting bolt, noting the correct fitted location of any earth leads, then manoeuvre the starter motor out of position and remove it from the vehicle.

L-Series diesel engine

6 Remove the air cleaner housing assembly as described in Chapter 4B.

7 Remove the rubber cover then unscrew the retaining nut and disconnect the main supply lead from the solenoid. Disconnect the wiring connector from the solenoid terminal.

8 Remove the starter motor mounting bolts then manoeuvre the motor out of position and remove it from the vehicle.

TD4 diesel engine

9 On models with automatic transmission, remove the battery and carrier as described in Section 4.

10 Unscrew the retaining bolts, and remove the plastic cover from the top of the engine (where fitted).

11 Remove the rubber cover, unscrew the nut and disconnect the two cables from the starter motor solenoid. Disconnect the single wiring plug from the solenoid **(see illustrations)**.

12 Slacken and remove the mounting bolts, and remove the starter motor.

Refitting

13 Refitting is a reversal of removal tightening

the mounting bolts to the specified torque. Ensure all wiring is correctly routed and its retaining nuts are securely tightened.

11 Starter motor – testing and overhaul

If the starter motor is thought to be suspect, it should be removed from the vehicle and taken to an auto-electrician for testing. Most auto-electricians will be able to supply and fit brushes at a reasonable cost. However, check on the cost of repairs before proceeding as it may prove more economical to obtain a new or exchange motor.

12 Ignition switch – removal and refitting

The ignition switch is integral with the steering column lock and can be removed as described in Chapter 10.

13 Oil pressure warning light switch – removal and refitting

Removal

Petrol and L-Series diesel engines

1 On petrol engines, the switch is screwed into the oil filter housing which is mounted

onto the front of the cylinder block, and on L-Series diesel engines the switch is screwed into the rear of the oil pump housing which is mounted onto the right-hand end of the cylinder block **(see illustrations)**.

2 To improve access to the switch, firmly apply the handbrake then jack up the front of the vehicle and support it on axle stands (see *Jacking and vehicle support*).

3 Turn the steering wheel to the right-hand full lock, unscrew the retaining bolts and remove the right-hand splash shield.

4 Disconnect the wiring connector then unscrew the switch and remove it from the engine. Be prepared for oil spillage, and if the switch is to be left removed from the engine for any length of time, plug the switch aperture.

TD4 diesel engines

5 Remove the starter motor as described in Section 10 of this Chapter.

6 Disconnect the wiring plug from the switch **(see illustration)**.

7 Unscrew the switch and discard the sealing washer, a new one must be fitted.

Refitting

8 Ensure the switch threads are clean and dry. Apply a smear of sealant to the switch threads then refit the switch to the housing and tighten it to the specified torque. Where applicable, renew the sealing washer.

9 Reconnect the wiring connector.

10 The remainder of refitting is a reversal of removal. Lower the vehicle to the ground then check and, if necessary, top-up the engine oil as described in *Weekly checks*.

13.1a Oil pressure switch – petrol models

13.1b Oil pressure switch – L-Series diesel models

13.6 Oil pressure switch – TD4 diesel models

14 Oil temperature sensor
– removal and refitting

Note: *The oil temperature sensor is only fitted to post-2001 model year vehicles fitted with the petrol engine.*

Removal

1 The sensor is screwed into the oil filter housing which is mounted onto the front of the cylinder block **(see illustration)**.

2 To improve access to the switch, firmly apply the handbrake then jack up the front of the vehicle and support it on axle stands (see *Jacking and vehicle support*).

3 Turn the steering wheel to the right-hand full lock, unscrew the retaining bolts and remove the right-hand splash shield.

4 Disconnect the wiring connector then unscrew the sensor and remove it form the engine. Be prepared for oil spillage, and if the sensor is to be left removed from the engine for any length of time, plug the aperture.

Refitting

5 Ensure the sensor threads are clean and dry. Apply a smear of sealant to the threads then refit the sensor to the housing and tighten it to the specified torque. Where applicable, renew the sealing washer.

6 Reconnect the wiring connector.

7 The remainder of refitting is a reversal of removal. Lower the vehicle to the ground then

**14.1 Oil temperature sensor –
2001-on petrol models only**

check and, if necessary, top-up the engine oil as described in *Weekly checks*.

Chapter 5 Part B:
Ignition system – petrol engine models

Contents

Degrees of difficulty

Easy, suitable for novice with little experience	Fairly easy, suitable for beginner with some experience	Fairly difficult, suitable for competent DIY mechanic	Difficult, suitable for experienced DIY mechanic	Very difficult, suitable for expert DIY or professional

Specifications

System type
Models up to 2001 . . . . Rover/Motorola Modular Engine Management System 1.8 (MEMS 1.8)
– see Chapter 4A for further information

Models 2001-on . . . . Rover/Motorola Modular Engine Management System 3 (MEMS 3)
– see Chapter 4A for further information

Firing order. . . . . 1-3-4-2 (No 1 cylinder at timing belt end)

Ignition coil
Type:
    MEMS 1.8. . . . . Denso Dry – single output
    MEMS 3 . . . . NEC 100730 – twin output
Primary resistance:
    MEMS 1.8. . . . . 0.71 to 0.81 ohm
    MEMS 3 . . . . 0.7 ohm
Secondary resistance:
    MEMS 1.8. . . . . Not specified
    MEMS 3 . . . . 10 ohm

Ignition timing
The ignition timing is constantly altered by the ECM and cannot be checked without specialist equipment

Torque wrench settings

	Nm	lbf ft
Ignition coil retaining bolts:		
MEMS 1.8:		
Ignition coil to bracket	9	7
Coil bracket to cylinder head	25	18
MEMS 3	8	6
Rotor arm screw (MEMS 1.8)*	8	6

* Do not re-use

3.2 Disconnect the wiring connector and HT lead from the coil

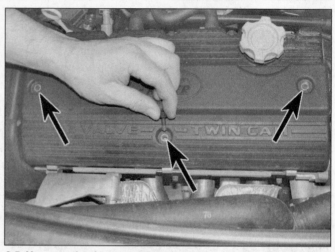

3.5 Unscrew the three retaining screws (arrowed) and remove the coil lead cover

1 Ignition system – general information

The ignition system is integrated with the fuel injection system to form a combined engine management system under the control of one ECM (See Chapter 4A for further information).

Two different systems are fitted to the range. Models up to 2001 are equipped with the MEMS 1.8 engine management system, whereas models 2001-on are fitted with the MEMS 3 system.

On MEMS 1.8 equipped models, the ignition side of the system incorporates an ignition coil and a distributor, which is driven off the end of the inlet camshaft. The ECM uses its inputs from the various sensors to calculate the required ignition advance setting and coil charging time. This causes a high voltage to be induced in the coil secondary (HT) windings which then travels down the HT lead to the distributor and onto the relevant spark plug.

The MEMS 3 system does not use a distributor. Instead, two dual-output coils are fitted to the camshaft cover. One above No 1 spark plug, and the other above No 3 spark plug. Whilst one output from each coil goes directly to the spark plug below it, the other output is sent via an HT lead to another spark plug. The coil over No 1 spark plug connects to No 4 spark plug, and the coil above No 3 spark plug connects to No 2 spark plug. Each coil fires both spark plugs simultaneously. The engine management ECM uses inputs from the various sensors to calculate the required ignition advance setting.

The easiest method of differentiating between the systems, is to check for a distributor on the left-hand end of the camshaft cover.

⚠ **Warning: Voltages produced by an electronic ignition system are considerably higher than those produced by conventional ignition systems. Extreme care must be taken when working on the system with the ignition switched on. Persons with surgically-implanted cardiac pacemaker devices should keep well clear of the ignition circuits, components and test equipment.**

2 Ignition system – testing

1 If a fault appears in the engine management (fuel injection/ignition) system first ensure that the fault is not due to a poor electrical connection or poor maintenance; ie, check that the air cleaner filter element is clean, the spark plugs are in good condition and correctly gapped, that the engine breather hoses are clear and undamaged, referring to Chapter 1A for further information. Also check that the accelerator cable is correctly adjusted as described in Chapter 4A. If the engine is running very roughly, check the compression pressures as described in Chapter 2A.

2 If these checks fail to reveal the cause of the problem the vehicle should be taken to a suitably-equipped Land Rover dealer or specialist for testing. A wiring block connector is incorporated in the engine management

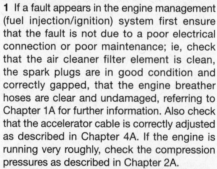

3.6 Disconnect the HT leads by pulling up the cap – not the leads

circuit into which a special electronic diagnostic tester can be plugged. The connector is located behind the centre console in the passenger side footwell. The tester will locate the fault quickly and simply alleviating the need to test all the system components individually, which is a time-consuming operation that carries a high risk of damaging the ECM.

3 The only ignition system checks which can be carried out by the home mechanic are those described in Chapter 1A, relating to the spark plugs, HT leads and (where fitted) distributor cap and rotor arm. If necessary, the system wiring and wiring connectors can be checked as described in Chapter 12 ensuring that the ECM wiring connector(s) have first been disconnected.

3 Ignition HT coil(s) – removal and refitting

Removal

MEMS 1.8

1 Disconnect the battery negative terminal (see Chapter 5A). The ignition coil is mounted left-hand end of the camshaft cover.

2 Disconnect the wiring connector and HT lead from the coil **(see illustration)**.

3 Slacken and remove the retaining bolts and remove the coil from the mounting bracket.

MEMS 3

4 Disconnect the battery negative terminal (see Chapter 5A). The coils are mounted under a cover at the top of the engine.

5 Unscrew the three retaining screws and remove the coil lead cover **(see illustration)**.

6 Disconnect the two HT leads from the two spark plugs, and release them from the retaining clips **(see illustration)**.

7 Undo the retaining bolts and release each coil from the spark plug underneath it **(see illustration)**. Disconnect the wiring plugs from the coils as they are removed.

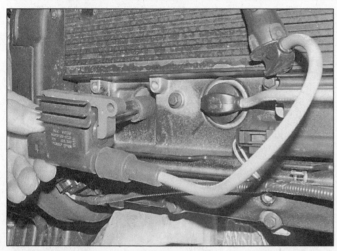

3.7 Undo the retaining bolts and release the coils from the spark plugs

4.2 Unscrew the distributor cap retaining screws

Refitting

8 Refitting is the reverse of removal, tightening the coil retaining bolts to the specified torque. Ensure the HT lead(s) and wiring connectors are correctly and securely reconnected. Note that on the MEMS 3 system, the HT lead from the coil above No 1 spark plug connects to No 4 spark plug.

4 Distributor – removal and refitting

Note: *A new rotor arm retaining screw will be needed on refitting.*

Removal

1 Ensure the ignition is switched off. To improve access, refer to Chapter 4A and remove the air cleaner assembly.
2 Slacken the distributor cap retaining screws then release the cap from the cylinder head and position it clear of the rotor arm **(see illustration)**. If renewing the distributor cap or HT leads, transfer the HT leads one at a time to prevent losing the firing order.
3 Slacken the retaining screw then remove the rotor arm from the end of the camshaft. Slide the oil splash shield off from the camshaft, noting which way around it is fitted.
4 Examine all components for signs of wear or damage and renew as necessary.

Refitting

5 Refitting is the reverse of removal, using a new rotor arm retaining screw and tightening it to the specified torque.

5 Ignition timing – checking and adjustment

The timing is constantly being monitored and adjusted by the engine management ECM. The only way in which the ignition timing can be checked and (where possible) adjusted is by using special electronic test equipment, connected to the engine management system diagnostic connector (refer to Chapter 4A for further information). Refer to your Land Rover dealer or specialist for further information.

Chapter 5 Part C:
Preheating system – diesel engine models

Contents

Degrees of difficulty

Easy, suitable for novice with little experience		Fairly easy, suitable for beginner with some experience		Fairly difficult, suitable for competent DIY mechanic		Difficult, suitable for experienced DIY mechanic		Very difficult, suitable for expert DIY or professional	

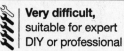

Specifications

Torque wrench settings	Nm	lbf ft
Coolant outlet elbow bolts.	25	18
Glow plugs.	20	15
Inlet manifold intake pipe bolts	9	7

1 General information

To assist cold starting, diesel engine models are fitted with a preheating system, which comprises a relay, and four glow plugs. The system is controlled by the Electronic Diesel Control (EDC) system.

The glow plugs are miniature electric heating elements, encapsulated in a metal case with a probe at one end, and an electrical connection at the other. The combustion chambers have a glow plug threaded into it. When the glow plug is energised, it heats up rapidly causing the temperature of the air charge drawn into each of the combustion chambers to rise. Each glow plug probe is positioned directly in line with the incoming spray of fuel from the injector. Hence the fuel passing over the glow plug probe is also heated, allowing its optimum combustion temperature to be achieved more readily.

The duration of the preheating period is governed by the Electronic Diesel Control (EDC) system control module (ECM), using information provided by the coolant temperature sensor (see Chapter 4B). The ECM alters the preheating time (the length for which the glow plugs are supplied with current) to suit the prevailing conditions.

A warning light informs the driver that preheating is taking place. The lamp extinguishes when sufficient preheating has taken place to allow the engine to be started, but power will still be supplied to the glow plugs for a further period until the engine is started. If no attempt is made to start the engine, the power supply to the glow plugs is switched off to prevent battery drain and glow plug burn-out.

3.6 Undo the dipstick guide tube mounting bolt (arrowed)

3.11a Unscrew the retaining nut and disconnect the wiring connector . . .

3.11b . . . then unscrew the glow plug from the cylinder head

2 Preheating system – testing

1 Full testing of the system can only be carried out using specialist diagnostic equipment which is connected to the engine management system diagnostic wiring connector (see Chapter 4B). If the preheating system is thought to be faulty, some preliminary checks of the glow plug operation may be made as described in the following paragraphs.

2 Connect a voltmeter or 12 volt test lamp between the glow plug supply cable, and a good earth point on the engine. *Caution: Make sure that the live connection is kept well clear of the engine and bodywork.*

3 Have an assistant activate the preheating system by turning the ignition key to the second position, and check that battery voltage is applied to the glow plug electrical connection. **Note:** *The supply voltage will be less than battery voltage initially, but will rise and settle as the glow plug heats up. It will then drop to zero when the preheating period ends and the safety cut-out operates.*

4 If no supply voltage can be detected at the glow plug, then the glow plug relay or the supply cable may be faulty.

5 To locate a faulty glow plug, first operate the preheating system to allow the glow plugs to reach working temperature, then disconnect the battery negative cable and position it away from the battery terminal.

6 Refer to Section 3, and remove the supply

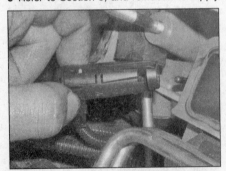

3.13 Squeeze the end of the connector and pull it from the glow plug

cable from No 2 glow plug terminal. Measure the electrical resistance between the glow plug terminal and the engine earth. A reading of anything more than a few ohms indicates that the glow plug is defective.

7 As a final check, remove the glow plugs and inspect them visually, as described in Section 3.

8 If no problems are found, take the vehicle to a Land Rover dealer for testing using the appropriate diagnostic equipment.

3 Glow plugs – removal, inspection and refitting

Removal – L-Series engine

1 Disconnect the battery negative lead (see Chapter 5A).

2 Unscrew the retaining bolts and remove the plastic cover from the top of the engine, taking care not to lose the spacers which are fitted to the cover mounting rubbers.

No 1 cylinder glow plug

3 Drain the cooling system as described in Chapter 1B, and remove the fuel injection pump as described in Chapter 4B.

4 On models with air conditioning, remove the alternator, as described in Part A of this Chapter.

5 Disconnect the wiring connectors from the coolant temperature sensor and sender which are screwed into the coolant outlet elbow on the front, right-hand of the cylinder head.

6 Unscrew the retaining bolts securing

3.14 Unscrew and remove the glow plug

the dipstick tube to the coolant outlet **(see illustration)**.

7 Slacken the retaining clip and disconnect the coolant hose then unscrew the retaining bolts and remove the coolant outlet from the front of the cylinder head. Discard the outlet seal, a new one should be used on refitting.

8 Unscrew the terminal nut securing the feed wiring to the glow plugs, then disconnect the wiring, and move it to one side.

9 Unscrew the glow plug and remove it from the cylinder head.

Nos 2, 3 and 4 cylinder glow plugs

10 To improve access on models with an intercooler, slacken the retaining clip and disconnect the intercooler duct from the inlet manifold intake pipe. Slacken and remove the two bolts securing the exhaust gas recirculation (EGR) pipe to the rear of the intake pipe then unscrew the bolts securing the pipe to the manifold. Undo the bolt securing the pipe to the cylinder head cover then remove the pipe from the engine, along with its gasket. Recover and discard the gasket.

11 Remove the glow plug(s) as described in paragraphs 8 and 9 **(see illustrations)**.

Removal – TD4 engine

12 With reference to Chapter 4B, remove the inlet manifold.

13 Squeeze together the lugs at the end of the connectors and pull them from the glow plugs **(see illustration)**.

14 Using a deep socket, unscrew and remove the glow plugs **(see illustration)**.

Inspection

15 Inspect the glow plugs for signs of damage. Burnt or eroded glow plug tips can be caused by a bad injector spray pattern. Have the injectors checked if this sort of damage is found.

16 If the glow plugs are in good condition, check them electrically, as described in Section 2.

17 The glow plugs can be energised by applying 12 volts to them to verify that they heat up evenly and in the required time. Observe the following precautions:

a) *Support the glow plug by clamping it carefully in a vice or self-locking pliers. Remember it will be red hot.*

4.4 Glow plug relay (arrowed)

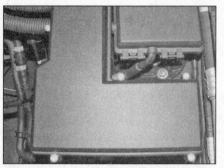

4.6 Undo the five screws and remove the lid of the electrical box

4.7a Disconnect the glow plug ECM – up to 2003

b) Make sure that the power supply or test lead incorporates a fuse or overload trip to protect against damage from a short-circuit.

c) After testing, allow the glow plug to cool for several minutes before attempting to handle it.

18 A glow plug in good condition will start to glow red at the tip after drawing current for 5 seconds or so. Any plug which takes much longer to start glowing, or which starts glowing in the middle instead of at the tip, is probably defective.

Refitting – L-Series engine

No 1 cylinder glow plug

19 Thoroughly clean the glow plugs, and the glow plug seating areas in the cylinder head.

20 Apply a smear of anti-seize compound to the glow plug threads, then refit the glow plug and tighten it to the specified torque.

21 Reconnect the wiring to the glow plug and securely tighten the terminal nut.

22 Ensure the coolant outlet and cylinder head surfaces are clean and dry. Fit a new gasket to the cylinder head then refit the outlet, tightening its retaining bolts to the specified torque.

23 Reconnect the coolant hose, tightening its retaining clip securely, then refit the dipstick tube bolts, tightening them securely.

24 Reconnect the coolant temperature sensor/sender wiring connectors.

25 On models with air conditioning refit the alternator as described in Part A.

26 Refit the fuel injection pump as described in Chapter 4B.

27 Refill the cooling system as described in Chapter 1B then refit the cover to the engine.

Nos 2, 3 and 4 cylinder glow plugs

28 Refit the glow plug(s) as described in

4.7b Press-in the clip (arrowed) and slide the glow plug relay assembly upwards (from 2003) . . .

paragraphs 19 to 21, ensuring that the main feed wire is connected to No 2 glow plug.

29 Where necessary, fit a new gasket to the inlet manifold then refit the intake pipe. Tighten all the bolts to the specified torque and securely reconnect the intercooler duct.

Refitting – TD4 engine

30 Thoroughly clean the glow plugs, and the glow plug seating areas in the cylinder head.

31 Apply a smear of anti-seize compound to the glow plug threads, then refit the glow plug and tighten it to the specified torque.

32 Reconnect the wiring to the glow plug. The connectors are a push-fit.

33 Refit the inlet manifold as described in Chapter 4B.

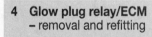

4 Glow plug relay/ECM – removal and refitting

Removal

L-Series engine

1 The relay is located under the engine

4.7c . . . then pull the relay from the holder

compartment fusebox, behind the engine management ECM, on the left-hand side of the engine compartment.

2 Disconnect the battery negative terminal as described in Chapter 5A.

3 Unscrew the two retaining bolts, and position the engine compartment fusebox to one side.

4 Release the relay holder from the battery carrier, and pull from the relay out of the wiring connector **(see illustration)**.

TD4 engine

5 The glow plug ECM/relay unit is located in the left-hand corner of the engine compartment. Disconnect the battery negative terminal as described in Chapter 5A.

6 Slacken the five retaining screws and remove the lid from the electrical box **(see illustration)**.

7 Disconnect the wiring plug from the ECM/relay unit **(see illustrations)**.

8 Where fitted, unscrew the retaining nut and disconnect the lead to the ECM. Remove the ECM from the box.

Refitting

9 Refitting is a reversal of removal.

Chapter 6
Clutch

Contents

Degrees of difficulty

Easy, suitable for novice with little experience	**Fairly easy,** suitable for beginner with some experience	**Fairly difficult,** suitable for competent DIY mechanic	**Difficult,** suitable for experienced DIY mechanic	**Very difficult,** suitable for expert DIY or professional

Specifications

Type . . . . Single dry plate with diaphragm spring, hydraulically-operated

Friction disc
Diameter. . . . . 228 mm
Friction material-to-rivet head depth:
    New (approximate) . . . . 1.2 mm
    Service limit . . . . 0.2 mm
Friction disc thickness:
    New . . . . 7.4 to 6.9 mm
    Service limit . . . . 5.6 mm

Pressure plate
Maximum diaphragm spring finger height difference. . . . . 1.0 mm
Maximum warpage or machined surface. . . . . 0.18 mm

Torque wrench settings

	Nm	lbf ft
Pressure plate retaining bolts.	25	18
Release fork-to-shaft bolt.	29	21
Slave cylinder mounting bracket-to-gearbox bolts	25	18

1 General information

The clutch consists of a friction disc, a pressure plate assembly, a release bearing and the release mechanism; all of these components are contained in the large cast-aluminium alloy bellhousing, sandwiched between the engine and the transmission. The clutch release mechanism is hydraulically-operated.

The friction disc is fitted between the engine flywheel and the clutch pressure plate, and is allowed to slide on the transmission input shaft splines.

The pressure plate assembly is bolted to the engine flywheel. When the engine is running, drive is transmitted from the crankshaft, via the flywheel, to the friction disc (these components being clamped securely together by the pressure plate assembly) and from the friction disc to the transmission input shaft.

To interrupt the drive, the spring pressure must be relaxed. Depressing the pedal pushes on the master cylinder pushrod. On petrol and L-Series diesel engines, this hydraulically forces the slave cylinder piston which is connected to the end of the clutch release fork lever. The release fork acts on its pivot and presses the release bearing against the pressure plate spring fingers. On TD4 diesel engines, the hydraulic pressure causes

the centrally-mounted slave cylinder/release bearing to act against the pressure plate fingers. This causes the springs to deform and releases the clamping force on the pressure plate. The hydraulic clutch is self-adjusting and requires no manual adjustment.

On models fitted with petrol and L-Series diesel engines, the master cylinder, slave cylinder and connecting pipe work is one assembly and can only be renewed in its entirety. The new assembly is prefilled with hydraulic fluid, and is described by Land Rover as 'sealed for life'.

On models fitted with the TD4 diesel engine, the slave cylinder, master cylinder and connecting pipe work are available as separate units.

2.2 Prise the pushrod from the pivot

3.2 Clutch master cylinder

3.8 Prise apart the two halves of the clutch pipe connection

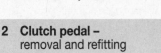

2 Clutch pedal –
removed and refitting

Removal

1 With reference to Chapter 11, remove the facia.
2 Unclip the clutch master cylinder pushrod from the pedal **(see illustration)**.
3 Slacken and remove the nuts and bolt securing the pedal assembly to the bulkhead then manoeuvre the assembly out from underneath the facia. Do not attempt to dismantle the pedal assembly, if it is worn or damaged the complete assembly must be renewed; no individual components are available.

Refitting

4 Manoeuvre the pedal assembly into position, ensuring it is correctly engaged with the pushrod clevis. Refit the bracket mounting nuts and bolt and tighten them securely.
5 Press the master cylinder pushrod back onto the clutch pedal.
6 Check the operation of the clutch pedal then refit the facia.

3 Clutch master cylinder
– removal and refitting

Petrol and L-Series diesel engines

Note: *As the master cylinder, slave cylinder and connecting pipe are one assembly, it is necessary to renew the slave cylinder and pipe along with the master cylinder.*

Removal

1 Reach up underneath the driver's side facia, and unclip the master cylinder pushrod from the clutch pedal.
2 Working in the engine compartment, rotate the master cylinder clockwise, and release it from the bulkhead **(see illustration)**.
3 Do not attempt to dismantle the master cylinder, as no parts are available. If the cylinder was removed for renewal, it is now

necessary to remove the slave cylinder and connecting pipe, as described in Section 4.

Refitting

4 With the slave cylinder renewed, position the cylinder reservoir 45° from the vertical position then seat the cylinder firmly in the bulkhead and secure it in position by rotating it 45° anti-clockwise. Ensure the connecting pipe is secured by its retaining clips.
5 Clip the master cylinder pushrod to the clutch pedal.
6 Check the operation of the clutch pedal (the clutch hydraulic system is sealed and does not need bleeding).

TD4 diesel engine

Removal

7 With reference to Chapter 4B, remove the air cleaner element
8 Use Land Rover tool No LRT-37-051 to release and disconnect the hydraulic pipe connection to the master cylinder. If the Land Rover tool is not available, use a pair of thin-nosed pliers **(see illustration)**.
9 Note the routing of the pipe, and release it from the inner wing and engine compartment bulkhead retaining clips.
10 Reach under the driver's side facia, prise the master cylinder pushrod from the clutch pedal.
11 Working in the engine compartment, rotate the master cylinder clockwise, and manoeuvre it from the bulkhead.

Refitting

12 Fit the master cylinder into position, rotate

4.2 Remove the C-clip and release the slave cylinder

it 45° anti-clockwise to secure it. Reach under the driver's side of the facia and clip the master cylinder pushrod to the clutch pedal.
13 Ensure that the end of the hydraulic pipe and master cylinder are clean, and reconnect the pipe by pushing it into the master cylinder connection.
14 Secure the hydraulic pipe into the retaining clips.
15 Refit the air cleaner element as described in Chapter 4B.
16 Check the operation of the pedal, and if necessary bleed the system as described in Section 5.

4 Clutch slave cylinder
– removal and refitting

Petrol and L-Series diesel engines

Removal

1 With reference to Chapter 4A or 4B, remove the air cleaner assembly.
2 Remove the C-clip and release the slave cylinder from the support bracket **(see illustration)**. Do **not** attempt to dismantle the slave cylinder/pipe assembly; if it is faulty the complete assembly must be renewed, no individual components are available.

Refitting

3 Manoeuvre the cylinder into position and locate it in the mounting bracket. Ensure the pushrod is correctly engaged with the release lever then secure the slave cylinder in position with the C-clip.
4 Ensure the slave cylinder pipe is correctly routed and retained by all the necessary clips.
5 Check the operation of the clutch pedal (the clutch hydraulic system is sealed and does not need bleeding) then refit the air cleaner housing (see Chapter 4).

TD4 diesel engine

Removal

6 With reference to Chapter 7A, remove the gearbox.
7 Carefully prise out the grommet sealing the slave cylinder pipes into the gearbox housing.

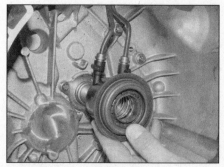

4.8 Pull the release bearing from the guide tube

4.10 Fit the slave cylinder to the guide tube and press it into place

5.3 Check that the slave cylinder bleed screw is closed (arrowed)

8 Pull the release bearing from the guide tube, and manoeuvre the bearing and pipes from the gearbox housing **(see illustration)**.

9 Check that the release bearing contact surface rotates smoothly and easily, with no sign of noise or roughness. Also check that the surface itself is smooth and unworn, with no signs of cracks, pitting or scoring. If there is any doubt about its condition, the bearing must be renewed along with the slave cylinder.

Refitting

10 Manoeuvre the slave cylinder pipes through the gearbox casing hole, as the slave cylinder and release bearing are positioned over the guide tube **(see illustration)**. Fit the slave cylinder to the guide tube by pressing it into place.

11 Refit the sealing grommet to the gearbox casing and slave cylinder pipes.

12 Refit the gearbox as described in Chapter 7A.

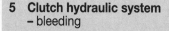

5 Clutch hydraulic system – bleeding

Petrol and L-Series diesel engines

The clutch hydraulic system is a sealed system and never requires topping-up or bleeding. If a problem develops then either the master cylinder or slave cylinder is faulty and renewal is the only option.

TD4 diesel engine

 Warning: Hydraulic fluid is poisonous; thoroughly wash off spills from the bare skin without delay. Seek immediate medical advice if any fluid is swallowed or gets into the eyes. Certain types of fluid are inflammable and may ignite when brought into contact with hot components. Hydraulic fluid is also an effective paint stripper. If spillage occurs onto painted bodywork or fittings, it should be washed off immediately, using copious quantities of cold water. It is also hygroscopic (ie, it can absorb moisture from the air) which then renders it useless. Old fluid may have suffered contamination, and should never by re-used.

1 If any part of the hydraulic system is dismantled, or if air has accidentally entered the system, the system will need to be bled. The presence of air is characterised by the pedal having a spongy feel and it results in difficulty in changing gear.

2 During the bleeding procedure, add only clean, unused hydraulic fluid of the recommended type; never re-use fluid that has already been bled from the system. Ensure that sufficient fluid is available before starting work.

3 Check that the slave cylinder bleed screw is closed. Remove the dust cap, and clean any dirt from around the bleed screw **(see illustration)**.

4 It is recommended that pressure-bleeding equipment is used to bleed the system. Pressure-bleeding kits are usually operated by the reservoir of pressurised air contained in the spare tyre. However, note that it will probably be necessary to reduce the pressure to a lower level than normal; refer to the instructions supplied with the kit.

5 By connecting a pressurised, fluid-filled container to the brake fluid reservoir, bleeding can be carried out simply by opening the bleed screw on the slave cylinder bleed pipe, and allowing the fluid to flow out until no more air bubbles can be seen in the expelled fluid.

6 This method has the advantage that the large reservoir of fluid provides an additional safeguard against air being drawn into the system during bleeding.

7 Collect a clean glass jar, a suitable length of plastic or rubber tubing which is a tight fit over the bleed screw, and a ring spanner to fit the screw.

8 Fit the spanner and tube to the slave cylinder bleed screw, place the other end of the tube in the jar, and pour in sufficient fluid to cover the end of the tube.

9 Connect the pressure-bleeding equipment to the brake fluid reservoir in accordance with the manufacturers instructions.

10 Slacken the bleed screw using the spanner, and allow fluid to drain into the jar until no more air bubbles emerge.

11 When bleeding is complete, tighten the bleed screw, and disconnect the hose and pressure bleeding equipment.

12 Wash off any spilt fluid, check once more

that the bleed screw is tightened securely, and refit the dust cap.

13 Check the hydraulic fluid level in the reservoir, and top-up if necessary (see *Weekly checks*).

14 Discard any hydraulic fluid that has been bled from the system; it will not be fit for re-use.

15 Check the feel of the clutch pedal. If it feels at all spongy, air must still be present in the system, and further bleeding is required. Failure to bleed satisfactorily after a procedure may be due to worn master or slave cylinder seals.

6 Clutch assembly – removal, inspection and refitting

 Warning: Dust created by clutch wear and deposited on the clutch components may contain asbestos, which is a health hazard. DO NOT blow it out with compressed air, or inhale any of it. DO NOT use petrol or petroleum-based solvents to clean off the dust. Brake system cleaner or methylated spirit should be used to flush the dust into a suitable receptacle. After the clutch components are wiped clean with rags, dispose of the contaminated rags and cleaner in a sealed, marked container.

Note: *Although some friction materials may no longer contain asbestos, it is safest to assume that they do, and to take precautions accordingly.*

Removal

1 Unless the complete engine/transmission unit is to be removed from the car and separated for major overhaul (see the relevant Part of Chapter 2), the clutch can be reached by removing the gearbox and intermediate reduction drive unit as described in Chapters 7A and 7C.

2 Before disturbing the clutch, use chalk or a marker pen to mark the relationship of the pressure plate assembly to the flywheel.

3 Working in a diagonal sequence, slacken the pressure plate bolts by half a turn at a time, until spring pressure is released and the bolts can be unscrewed by hand **(see illustration)**.

4 Prise the pressure plate assembly off its

6.3 Working in a diagonal sequence, slacken the pressure plate bolts by half a turn at a time

6.4 Remove the clutch pressure plate and friction disc from the flywheel

6.7 Use a vernier to measure the friction disc rivet head depth below the friction material

locating dowels, and collect the friction disc, noting which way round the friction disc is fitted **(see illustration)**.

Inspection

Note: *Due to the amount of work necessary to remove and refit clutch components, it is usually considered good practice to renew the clutch friction disc, pressure plate assembly and release bearing as a matched set, even if only one of these is actually worn enough to require renewal. It is also worth considering the renewal of the clutch components on a preventative basis if the engine and/or transmission have been removed for some other reason.*

5 Remove the clutch assembly.

6 When cleaning clutch components, read first the warning at the beginning of this Section; remove dust using a clean, dry cloth, and working in a well-ventilated atmosphere.

7 Check the friction disc facings for signs of wear, damage or oil contamination. If the friction material is cracked, burnt, scored or damaged, or if it is contaminated with oil or grease (shown by shiny black patches), the friction disc must be renewed. Measure the friction disc thickness and check the depth of the rivets below the friction material surface **(see illustration)**. If the friction disc thickness or the depth of any rivet is equal to, or less than, the service limit given

in the Specifications, then the friction disc must be renewed.

8 If the friction material is still serviceable, check that the centre boss splines are unworn, that the torsion springs are in good condition and securely fastened, and that all the rivets are tight. If any wear or damage is found, the friction disc must be renewed.

9 If the friction material is fouled with oil, this must be due to an oil leak from the crankshaft left-hand oil seal, from the sump-to-cylinder block joint, or from the transmission input shaft. Renew the seal or repair the joint, as appropriate, as described in the relevant Part of Chapter 2 or 7, before installing the new friction disc.

10 Check the pressure plate assembly for obvious signs of wear or damage; shake it to check for loose rivets or worn or damaged fulcrum rings, and check that the drive straps securing the pressure plate to the cover do not show signs (such as a deep yellow or blue discoloration) of overheating. Check the diaphragm spring fingers for signs of wear or damage and check that the height of each finger above the pressure plate machined face. If the finger height exceeds the specified service limit or the diaphragm spring is worn or damaged, or if its pressure is in any way suspect, the pressure plate assembly should be renewed.

11 Examine the machined bearing surfaces of the pressure plate and of the flywheel; they should be clean, completely flat, and free from scratches or scoring. If either is discoloured from excessive heat, or shows signs of cracks, it should be renewed – although minor damage of this nature can sometimes be polished away using emery paper. Using a straight-edge and feeler blades check the pressure plate surface for warpage at several points around its diameter, if the warpage exceeds the specified limit the plate must be renewed.

12 Check that the release bearing contact surface rotates smoothly and easily, with no sign of noise or roughness. Also check that the surface itself is smooth and unworn, with no signs of cracks, pitting or scoring. If there is any doubt about its condition, the bearing must be renewed.

Refitting

13 On reassembly, ensure that the friction surfaces of the flywheel and pressure plate are completely clean, smooth, and free from oil or grease. Use solvent to remove any protective grease from new components.

14 Fit the friction disc so that its spring hub assembly faces away from the flywheel; there may also be a marking showing which way round the plate is to be refitted. On genuine

6.14a The friction disc should be fitted with the GETRIEBESEITE (gearbox side) marking facing away from the flywheel . . .

6.14b . . . or SCHWUNGRADSEITE (flywheel side) towards the flywheel

Land Rover clutches the friction disc should be fitted with the GETRIEBESEITE (GEARBOX SIDE) marking facing away from the flywheel, or SCHWUNGRADSEITE (FLYWHEEL SIDE) towards the flywheel **(see illustrations)**.

15 Refit the pressure plate assembly, aligning the marks made on dismantling (if the original pressure plate is re-used), and locating the pressure plate on its locating dowels. Fit the pressure plate bolts, but tighten them only finger-tight, so that the friction disc can still be moved.

16 The friction disc must now be centralised, so that when the transmission is refitted, its input shaft will pass through the splines at the centre of the friction disc.

17 Centralisation can be achieved by passing a screwdriver or other long bar through the friction disc and into the hole in the crankshaft; the friction disc can then be moved around until it is centred on the crankshaft hole. Alternatively, a clutch-aligning tool can be used to eliminate the guesswork; these can be obtained from most accessory shops **(see illustration)**.

 TOOL TiP *A home-made aligning tool can be fabricated from a length of metal rod or wooden dowel which fits closely inside the crankshaft hole, and has insulating tape wrap around it to match the diameter of the friction disc splined hole.*

18 When the friction disc is centralised, tighten the pressure plate bolts evenly and in a diagonal sequence to the specified torque setting **(see illustration)**. Ensure the pressure plate is drawn squarely onto the flywheel, to prevent the pressure plate being distorted.

19 Refit the transmission as described in the relevant Part of Chapter 7.

6.17 A typical clutch aligning tool

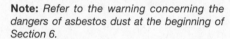

7 Clutch release mechanism – removal, inspection and refitting

Note: *Refer to the warning concerning the dangers of asbestos dust at the beginning of Section 6.*

Removal

1 Unless the complete engine/transmission unit is to be removed from the car and separated for major overhaul (see Chapter 2), the clutch release mechanism can be reached by removing the transmission only, as described in Chapter 7A.

Petrol and L-Series diesel engines

2 Slide the release bearing off from the transmission shaft guide sleeve and disengage it from the release fork **(see illustration)**.

3 Slacken and remove the retaining bolt and washer securing the release fork to the lever shaft **(see illustration)**.

4 Slide the lever and shaft out through the casing and the release fork. Note which way around the release fork is fitted. If dislodged, recover the shaft oil seal.

6.18 Ensure the friction disc is centralised then progressively tighten the pressure plate bolts to the specified torque

TD4 diesel engines

5 On these models, the release bearing is integral with the clutch slave cylinder, and can only be renewed as a complete unit. Refer to Section 4.

Inspection

6 Check the release mechanism, renewing any component which is worn or damaged. Carefully check all bearing surfaces and points of contact.

7 When checking the release bearing itself, note that it is often considered worthwhile to renew it as a matter of course. Check that the contact surface rotates smoothly and easily, with no sign of noise or roughness, and that the surface itself is smooth and unworn, with no signs of cracks, pitting or scoring. If there is any doubt about its condition, the bearing must be renewed.

8 Check if the seal in the outer lever shaft hole in the casing is split, worn or perished. If it shows any sign of deterioration, prise it from the casing, noting which way around it fits, and renew it. Use a suitable tubular drift, such as a socket, which bears only on the hard outer edge of the seal, and tap the seal into place with a few light hammer blows.

7.2 Slide the release bearing off from the transmission shaft guide sleeve

7.3 Remove the retaining bolt and washer securing the release fork to the lever shaft

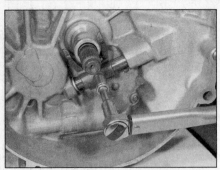

7.11 Refit the retaining bolt and washer, and tighten it to the specified torque

Refitting

Petrol and L-Series diesel engines

9 Ensure all components are clean and dry then apply molybdenum disulphide grease (Land Rover recommend the use of Molykote BR2 plus, G-n plus or G-Rapid plus) to the contact areas of the release fork and release bearing.

10 Manoeuvre the fork into position. Slide the lever shaft down and through the release fork and engage it in the locating hole in the casing.

11 Align the fork with the shaft hole then refit the retaining bolt and washer, tighten it to the specified torque **(see illustration)**.

12 Slide the release bearing onto the transmission shaft guide sleeve and engage it with the release fork.

13 Check the operation of the release mechanism then refit the transmission as described in Chapter 7A.

TD4 diesel engine

14 Refer to Section 4.

Chapter 7 Part A:
Manual transmission

Contents

Degrees of difficulty

Easy, suitable for novice with little experience 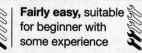	**Fairly easy,** suitable for beginner with some experience 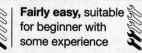	**Fairly difficult,** suitable for competent DIY mechanic 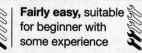	**Difficult,** suitable for experienced DIY mechanic 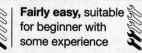	**Very difficult,** suitable for expert DIY or professional

Specifications

General

Type:

Petrol and L-Series diesel engines . . . . PG1, five forward speeds and reverse.
Synchromesh on all forward speeds

TD4 diesel engine . . . . Getrag 282, five forward speeds and reverse.
Synchromesh on all speeds

Ratios:	**PG1**	**Getrag 282**
First	3.250 : 1	3.577 : 1
Second	1.894 : 1	1.887 : 1
Third	1.222 : 1	1.192 : 1
Fourth	0.848 : 1	0.848 : 1
Fifth	0.649 : 1	0.686 : 1
Reverse	3.000 : 1	3.308 : 1

Lubrication

Recommended oil . . . . See *Lubricants and fluids*
Capacity:
  PG1:
    From dry . . . . 2.2 litres
    Drain and refill . . . . 2.0 litres
  Getrag 282:
    From dry . . . . 1.67 litres
    Drain and refill . . . . 1.6 litres

Torque wrench settings

	Nm	lbf ft
PG1		
Drain plug	35	26
Filler/level plug	45	33
First gear switch	25	18
Flywheel top cover nut/bolt (petrol engine)	9	7
Gearbox mountings:		
Mounting-to-gearbox bolts	65	48
Mounting-to-body bracket bolts	83	61
Gearbox mounting bracket bolts	45	33
Gearbox-to-adapter plate/engine bolts	80	59
Gearbox-to-sump bolts	45	33
Gearchange mechanism-to-body bolt	22	16
Gearchange mechanism-to-gearbox nut/bolt	22	16
Gearchange steady rod-to-gearbox bolt	25	18
Intermediate reduction drive unit-to-gearbox bolts	80	59
Reversing light switch	25	18
Speedometer drive pinion retaining plate bolt	5	4
Support bracket-to-gearbox bolt	80	59
Support bracket-to-sump bolt	45	33
Getrag 282		
Drain plug	35	26
Filler/level plug	35	26
First gear switch	25	18
Gearbox mounting bracket bolts	85	63
Gearbox-to-engine bolts	85	63
Gearchange cover Torx bolts*	25	18
Left-hand mounting bracket through-bolt	100	74
Left-hand mounting bracket-to-gearbox bolts	100	74
Release bearing sleeve bolts	12	9
Reversing light switch	25	18

* Do not re-use

1 General information

The manual gearbox is contained in a cast-aluminium alloy casing bolted to the engine's left-hand end. In contrast to traditional FWD gearboxes, the casing does not include a differential to distribute drive to the front wheels. Instead drive is transmitted, via a splined hub in the gearbox final drive gear carrier, to the input shaft of the IRD (Intermediate Reduction Drive) unit. The IRD unit contains a differential to drive the front wheels, and an output shaft to transmit power to the rear wheels – see Chapter 7C for further details of the IRD unit.

Drive is transmitted from the crankshaft via the clutch to the input shaft, which has a splined extension to accept the clutch friction disc, and rotates in sealed ball-bearings. From the input shaft, drive is transmitted to the output shaft, which rotates in a roller bearing at its right-hand end, and a sealed ball-bearing at its left-hand end. From the output shaft, the drive is transmitted to the final drive gear, and to the IRD unit input shaft.

The input and output shafts are arranged side-by-side, parallel to the crankshaft and driveshafts, so that their gear pinion teeth are in constant mesh. In the neutral position, the output shaft gear pinions rotate freely, so that drive cannot be transmitted to the final drive gear.

Gear selection is via a floor-mounted lever and selector rod mechanism. The selector rod causes the appropriate selector fork to move its respective synchro-sleeve along the shaft, to lock the gear pinion to the synchro-hub. Since the synchro-hubs are splined to the output shaft, this locks the pinion to the shaft, so that drive can be transmitted. To ensure that gearchanging can be made quickly and quietly, a synchromesh system is fitted to all forward gears (and reverse gear on the Getrag 282), consisting of baulk rings and spring-loaded fingers, as well as the gear pinions and synchro-hubs. The synchromesh cones are formed on the mating faces of the baulk rings and gear pinions.

2 Gearbox oil – draining and refilling

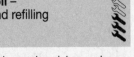

1 This operation is much quicker and more efficient if the vehicle is first taken on a journey of sufficient length to warm the engine/gearbox up to normal operating temperature.
2 Park the vehicle on level ground, switch off the ignition and apply the handbrake firmly. For improved access, jack up the front of the vehicle and support it securely on axle stands (see *Jacking and vehicle support*). Note that the vehicle must be lowered to the ground and level, to ensure accuracy when refilling and checking the oil level. Undo the retaining screws and fasteners then remove the engine/

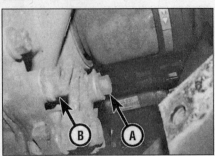

2.3a Gearbox level plug (A) and drain plug (B) – petrol and L-Series diesel engines ...

2.3b ... and level plug (arrowed) on the TD4 diesel engine

gearbox undertray from the vehicle to gain access to the filler/level and drain plugs.

3 Remove all traces of dirt from around the filler/level plug which is located on the left-hand side of the gearbox behind the left-hand driveshaft inner joint **(see illustrations)**. Unscrew the plug and recover the sealing washer (where fitted).

4 Position a suitable container under the drain plug which is also situated on the left-hand side of the gearbox housing, but underneath the driveshaft inner joint.

5 Unscrew the drain plug and allow the oil to drain completely into the container **(see illustration)**. If the oil is hot, take precautions against scalding. Clean both the filler/level and the drain plugs, being especially careful to wipe any metallic particles off the magnetic inserts. Discard the original sealing washers (where fitted); they should be renewed whenever they are disturbed.

6 When the oil has finished draining, clean the drain plug threads and those of the gearbox casing, fit a new sealing washer (where applicable) and refit the drain plug, tightening it to the specified torque. It the vehicle was raised for the draining operation, now lower it to the ground.

7 Refilling the gearbox is an extremely awkward operation **(see illustration)**. Above all, allow plenty of time for the oil level to settle properly before checking it. Note that the vehicle must be parked on flat level ground when checking the oil level.

8 Refill the gearbox with the exact amount of the specified type of oil (see *Lubricants and fluids*) then check the oil level as described in the relevant Part of Chapter 1. When the level is correct, refit the filler/level plug with a new sealing washer (where applicable) and tighten it to the specified torque. Refit the undertray.

HAYNES HINT *If the correct amount was poured into the gearbox and a large amount flows out on checking the level, refit the filler/level plug and take the vehicle on a short journey so that the new oil is distributed fully around the gearbox components, then check the level again on your return.*

2.5 Unscrew the drain plug and allow the oil to drain

3 Gearchange linkage – removal and refitting

1 Park the vehicle on level ground, switch off the ignition, and apply the handbrake firmly. Jack up the front of the vehicle and support it securely on axle stands (see *Jacking and vehicle support*), release the retaining screws and remove the engine/transmission undertray. Proceed as described under the relevant sub-heading.

PG1 gearbox

Removal

2 Although not strictly necessary, access to the gearchange linkage is greatly improved if the exhaust front pipe is first removed (see Chapter 4A or 4B).

3 Working at the gearbox end of the selector shaft, remove the roll-pin retaining clip from the selector rod. Tap the roll-pin out of position and disconnect the selector rod from the gearbox **(see illustrations)**.

4 Slacken and remove the nut and pivot bolt securing the selector rod to the base of the gearchange lever and remove the rod from the vehicle.

5 Working inside the vehicle, remove the centre console as described in Chapter 11. Unscrew the gear knob. Release the gearchange lever rubber gaiter from the housing and slide it off the top of the lever.

6 Disconnect the wiring plug from the hill descent switch on the gearchange lever.

2.7 Refilling the gearbox is an extremely awkward operation

7 From underneath the vehicle, slacken and remove the bolts and retaining plate securing the steady rod rear mounting to the body. Remove the mounting rubber from the steady rod, taking care not to lose its spacers.

8 Remove the bolt securing the gearchange steady rod to the IRD unit adapter plate and recover the washers and mounting rubber. Manoeuvre the steady rod and gearchange lever assembly out from underneath the vehicle.

9 Thoroughly clean all components and check them for wear or damage, renewing all worn or faulty items.

Refitting

10 Refitting is the reverse of the removal procedure, applying a smear of the specified grease to all linkage pivot points (see *Lubricants and fluids*). Ensure all nuts and bolts are securely tightened. **Note:** *Do not overtighten the gear knob. The profile of the trigger must remain flush with the hill descent switch* **(see illustration)**.

Getrag 282 gearbox

Removal

11 Using a suitable flat-bladed screwdriver, carefully lever the link rod balljoints off the gearbox levers. Make a note of each link rods correct fitted location and which way around they are fitted then detach them from the bellcrank assembly and remove them from the vehicle **(see illustration)**.

12 Prise the selector rod from its balljoints on the gearchange lever and bellcrank assembly and manoeuvre it out from underneath the vehicle.

3.3a Remove the roll-pin retaining clip from the selector rod . . .

3.3b . . . and tap the roll-pin out of position

3.10 Do not overtighten the gear knob. The profile of the trigger must remain flush with the hill descent switch

3.11 Carefully lever the link rod balljoints off the gearbox levers

4.4 Prise the oil seal out of the gearbox using a large flat-bladed screwdriver

4.5 Ensure the seal is correctly positioned, with its sealing lip facing inwards

13 Thoroughly clean all components and check them for wear or damage, renewing all worn or faulty items.

Refitting

14 Refitting is the reverse of the removal procedure, applying a smear of the specified grease to all linkage pivot points and balljoints (see *Lubricants and fluids*). Ensure all nuts and bolts are securely tightened and that all gearchange linkage balljoints are pressed firmly together. **Note:** *Do not overtighten the gear knob. The profile of the trigger must remain flush with the hill descent switch.*

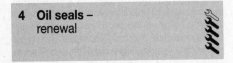

4 Oil seals –
renewal

Left-hand driveshaft oil seal

Note: *Renewal of the right-hand oil seal is detailed in Chapter 7C.*

1 Chock the rear wheels, apply the handbrake, then jack up the front of the vehicle and support it on axle stands (see *Jacking and vehicle support*). Remove the left-hand front roadwheel.
2 Drain the gearbox oil as described in Section 2 or be prepared for some fluid loss as the driveshaft is removed.
3 Working as described in Chapter 8, remove the left-hand driveshaft.
4 Carefully prise the oil seal out of the

gearbox using a large flat-bladed screwdriver **(see illustration)**.
5 Remove all traces of dirt from the area around the oil seal aperture. Ensure the seal is correctly positioned, with its sealing lip facing inwards, and drive it squarely into position, using a suitable tubular drift (such as a socket) which bears only on the hard outer edge of the seal **(see illustration)**.
6 Ensure the seal is correctly located in the gearbox housing then refit the driveshaft as described in Chapter 8.
7 Refill/top-up the gearbox with the specified type of oil (see *Lubricants and fluids*) and check the oil level as described in the relevant Part of Chapter 1.

Input shaft oil seal

PG1 gearbox

8 To renew the input shaft oil seal, the gearbox must be dismantled. This task should therefore be entrusted to a Land Rover dealer or gearbox specialist.

Getrag 282 gearbox

9 Remove the gearbox unit from the vehicle and slide off the clutch release bearing/slave cylinder (see Chapter 6).
10 Undo the three bolts securing the clutch release bearing guide sleeve in position and slide the guide off the input shaft **(see illustration)**. Discard the O-ring seal **(see illustration)**. **Note:** *The bearing guide sleeve contains an oil seal. However, this seal is only supplied complete with the guide sleeve.*
11 Ensure that the release bearing sleeve and mating face are clean.

12 Using a new O-ring, refit the bearing sleeve to the gearbox casing. Apply locking compound to the threads and tighten the retaining bolts to the specified torque.
13 Refit the release bearing/slave cylinder as described in Chapter 6.

Gearchange selector shaft oil seal

PG1 gearbox

14 Chock the rear wheels, apply the handbrake, then jack up the front of the vehicle and support it on axle stands (see *Jacking and vehicle support*). Release the retaining screws and remove the engine/transmission undertray.
15 Remove the bolt securing the gearchange steady rod to the IRD support bracket. Release the rod and recover the two washers.
16 Move the selector shaft roll-pin clip to one side, and using a punch, drive out the roll-pin.
17 Detach the selector lever from the gearbox shaft, and remove the gaiter **(see illustration)**.
18 Carefully lever the seal out of position, taking great care not to damage the shaft or casing **(see illustration)**. Be prepared for fluid spillage.
19 Before fitting a new seal, check the selector shaft's seal rubbing surface for signs of burrs, scratches or damage which may have caused the seal to fail in the first place. It may be possible to polish away minor faults of this sort using fine abrasive paper, however, more serious defects will require the renewal of the shaft.

4.10a Undo the three bolts securing the clutch release bearing guide sleeve in position and slide the guide off the input shaft . . .

4.10b . . . then remove the O-ring seal

4.17 Slide off the rubber gaiter

4.18 Prise out the selector shaft oil seal

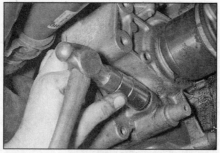

4.20 Tap the new oil seal into position using a socket which bears on the outer edge of the seal

4.30 Using a pin punch, drive out the roll-pin securing the gearchange selector quadrants to the selector shaft

20 Press the seal squarely into position, ensuring its sealing lip is facing inwards, using a socket which bears only on the hard outer edge of the seal **(see illustration)**.
21 Refit the gaiter to the selector shaft, ensuring that the gaiter lip is located over the lip on the oil seal.
22 Refit the selector shaft to the gearbox shaft and secure it in position with the new roll-pin. Reposition the clip over the roll-pin.
23 Position the washers and refit the gearchange steady rod to the IRD unit support bracket.
24 Refit the engine/transmission undertray, and lower the vehicle to the ground. Check and if necessary, top-up the gearbox oil as described in the relevant Part of Chapter 1.

Gettrag 282 gearbox

25 Chock the rear wheels, apply the handbrake, then jack up the front of the vehicle and support it on axle stands (see *Jacking and vehicle support*). Release the retaining screws and remove the engine/transmission undertray.
26 With reference to Chapter 5A, remove the battery and battery carrier.
27 Position a jack under the gearbox, with a block of wood on the jack head. Take the weight of the transmission.
28 Slacken and remove the left-hand gearbox mounting through-bolt, and the four bolts securing the mounting bracket to the gearbox casing. Lower the jack and remove the mounting bracket.
29 Using a large flat-bladed screwdriver, carefully prise the gearchange rods' sockets from the selector quadrants' balljoints **(see illustration 3.11)**.
30 Using a pin punch, drive out the roll-pin securing the gearchange selector quadrants to the selector shaft **(see illustration)**. Slide the quadrant from the shaft.
31 Unscrew the five Torx bolts and remove the gearchange cover **(see illustration)**.
32 At the time of writing, the oil seal was only available complete with the gearchange cover. Consequently, if the seal is leaking, a new cover will be required.
33 Ensure the mating faces of the gearchange cover and gearbox are clean and dry.
34 Lubricate the gearchange cover bearing with clean gearbox oil, and apply a 1 mm

bead of silicone sealant to the gearchange cover **(see illustration)**.
35 Refit the cover to the gearbox, and tighten the new Torx bolts to the specified torque.
36 Position the quadrant on the selector shaft, and drive in a new roll-pin. Check the operation of the selector mechanism.
37 Press the gearchange rods sockets onto the selector quadrants balljoints using a large pair of pliers.
38 Refit the left-hand gearbox mounting bracket to the gearbox casing, and adjust the height of the assembly using the jack, until the mounting through-bolt can be inserted. Tighten the mounting bracket bolts and through-bolt to the specified torque. Remove the jack from under the vehicle.
39 With reference to Chapter 5A, refit the battery carrier and battery.
40 Refit the engine/transmission undertray, and lower the vehicle to the ground.

5 Reversing light switch – testing, removal and refitting

Testing

1 The reversing light circuit is controlled by a plunger-type switch that is screwed into the gearbox casing, on the Getrag 282 gearbox the switch is screwed into the top of the casing and on PG1 gearboxes it is screwed into the bottom of the casing. If a fault develops in the circuit, first ensure that the circuit fuse has not blown (see Chapter 12).

4.31 Unscrew the five Torx screws and remove the gearchange cover

2 To test the switch, disconnect the wiring connector. Use a multimeter (set to the resistance function) or a battery-and-bulb test circuit to check that there is continuity between the switch terminals only when reverse gear is selected. If this is not the case, and there are no obvious breaks or other damage to the wires, the switch is faulty and must be renewed.

Removal

Note: *A new sealing washer will be required on refitting.*

PG1 gearbox

3 Chock the rear wheels, apply the handbrake, then jack up the front of the vehicle and support it on axle stands (see *Jacking and vehicle support*). Release the retaining screws and remove the engine/transmission undertray.
4 Trace the wiring back from the switch, freeing it from any retaining clips, and disconnect the wiring connector.
5 Be prepared for oil loss when the switch is removed and have ready a suitable plug to plug the gearbox aperture whilst the switch is removed. Unscrew the switch and remove it from bottom of the gearbox casing along with its sealing washer **(see illustration)**.

Getrag 282 gearbox

6 Firmly apply the handbrake then jack up the front of the vehicle and support it on axle stands (see *Jacking and vehicle support*). Remove the retaining screws and fasteners and remove the undertray to gain access to the switch.

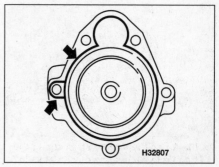

4.34 apply a 1 mm bead of silicone sealant to the gearchange cover

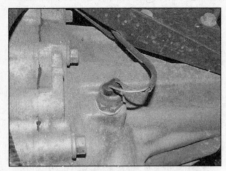

5.5 Unscrew the switch and remove it from bottom of the gearbox casing

7 Disconnect the wiring connector from the switch **(see illustration)**.

8 Wipe clean the area around the switch then unscrew it and remove it from the gearbox unit.

Refitting

PG1 gearbox

9 Fit a new sealing washer to the switch, then screw it back into position in the bottom of the gearbox housing and tighten it to the specified torque.

10 Work back along the switch wiring, securing it in position with all the relevant clips and ties, and reconnect the wiring connector.

11 Refit the engine/transmission undertray, and lower the vehicle to the ground. Check the gearbox oil level as described in the relevant Part of Chapter 1, and top-up if necessary.

Getrag 282

12 Screw the switch into the gearbox casing, and tighten it to the specified torque.

13 Reconnect the wiring connector, and test the operation of the switch.

14 Refit the undertray then lower the vehicle to the ground.

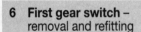

6 First gear switch –
removed and refitting

Removal

PG1 gearbox

1 Chock the rear wheels, apply the handbrake, then jack up the front of the vehicle and

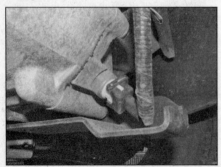

6.2 1st gear switch – PG1 gearbox

5.7 Reversing light switch – TD4 engine

support it on axle stands (see *Jacking and vehicle support*). Release the retaining screws and remove the engine/transmission undertray.

2 Unscrew the retaining nuts and remove the cover from the 1st gear switch **(see illustration)**.

3 Disconnect the wiring plug, and unscrew the switch from the casing. Be prepared for fluid spillage.

Getrag 282 gearbox

4 Chock the rear wheels, apply the handbrake, then jack up the front of the vehicle and support it on axle stands (see *Jacking and vehicle support*). Release the retaining screws and remove the engine/transmission undertray.

5 Disconnect the wiring plug, and unscrew the switch from the casing **(see illustration)**. Be prepared for fluid spillage.

Refitting

PG1 gearbox

6 Ensure that the mating faces of the switch and casing are clean and dry. Fit the switch and switch and tighten it to the specified torque. Reconnect the wiring plug.

7 Refit the cover over the switch, and tighten the retaining nuts to the specified torque. Tighten the nuts securely.

8 Refit the engine/transmission undertray, and lower the vehicle to the ground. Check and top-up the gearbox oil level, as described in the relevant Part of Chapter 1.

Getrag 282 gearbox

9 Ensure that the mating faces of the switch and casing are clean and dry. Fit the switch

6.5 1st gear switch – Getrag 282 gearbox

and switch and tighten it to the specified torque. Reconnect the wiring plug.

10 Refit the engine/transmission undertray, and lower the vehicle to the ground. Check and top-up the gearbox oil level, as described in Chapter 1B.

7 Speedometer drive –
removal and refitting

Removal

1 All models are fitted with an electrically-operated speedometer which is operated by either the vehicle speed sensor (non-ABS models) or ABS control unit/wheel speed sensors (ABS models). The vehicle speed sensor is mounted on the top of the speedometer drive. As all later models were equipped with ABS, the speedometer drive is only fitted to pre-June 2000 PG1 gearboxes. The speedometer drive is situated on the top of the gearbox housing, next to the inner end of the right-hand driveshaft. Access to the drive is poor from above; to gain access from below, firmly apply the handbrake then jack up the front of the vehicle and support it on axle stands (see *Jacking and vehicle support*). Release the retaining screws and remove the engine/transmission undertray.

2 Disconnect the wiring connector from the vehicle speed sensor then unscrew the sensor and remove it from the top of the speedometer drive.

3 Slacken and remove the retaining bolt and withdraw the speedometer drive assembly from the gearbox housing, along with its sealing ring.

Refitting

4 Fit a new sealing ring to the speedometer housing and lubricate it with a smear of oil to ease installation.

5 Ease the speedometer drive into position in the gearbox, ensuring that the drive and driven pinions are correctly engaged, and securely tighten the retaining bolt.

6 Fit the speed sensor to the top of the drive, ensuring its drive pin is correctly engaged with the pinion, and securely tighten its retaining nut.

7 Reconnect the wiring connector to the speed sensor.

8 Refit the engine/transmission undertray, then lower the vehicle to the ground.

8 Gearbox –
removal and refitting

Removal

Petrol engine

1 Chock the rear wheels, then firmly apply the handbrake. Jack up the front of the vehicle, and securely support it on axle stands (see

8.7a On early models, the exhaust pipe is secured to the sump by two bolts

8.7b The exhaust pipe is secured to the exhaust manifold by two nuts on later models

8.9 Separate the hub carrier from the base of the suspension strut

Jacking and vehicle support). Remove both front roadwheels then undo the retaining screws and fasteners and remove the undertray from beneath the engine/gearbox unit.

2 Drain the gearbox oil as described in Section 2 then refit the drain plug, and tighten it to the specified torque setting.

3 With reference to Chapter 7C, drain the IRD (Intermediate Reduction Drive) unit oil, then refit the drain plug and tighten it to the specified torque.

4 Working as described in Chapter 8, remove the left-hand driveshaft.

5 Undo the three retaining screws, and remove the splash shield from the left-hand front wheel arch.

6 Slacken and remove the three nuts securing the exhaust front pipe to the catalytic converter, and the two nuts securing the pipe support bracket to the IRD unit.

7 Unscrew the two bolts securing the front exhaust pipe to the engine sump, and the flange nuts securing the pipe to the exhaust manifold **(see illustrations)**. Remove the pipe and discard the gaskets.

8 Release the retaining clip and remove the front right-hand flexible brake hose from the bracket. Do not disconnect the hose.

9 Undo the two retaining nuts and bolts, and separate the right-hand hub carrier from the base of the suspension strut **(see illustration)**.

10 With reference to Chapter 5A, remove the battery, battery carrier and starter motor.

11 Disconnect the first gear switch wiring plug, and the reversing light switch connections. Refer to Sections 5 and 6 if necessary.

12 Unscrew the three retaining bolts, and position the clutch slave cylinder bracket and earth lead to one side **(see illustration)**.

Caution: Whilst the cylinder is removed from the gearbox, do not depress the clutch pedal.

13 On non-ABS models, disconnect the wiring plug from the vehicle speed sensor located at the top-rear of the gearbox. Refer to Section 7 if necessary.

14 Slacken and remove the three retaining bolts, and remove the lower tie rod bracket from the engine sump **(see illustration)**.

8.12 Unscrew the three retaining bolts, and position the clutch slave cylinder bracket to one side

15 Unscrew the nine retaining bolts and remove the IRD support bracket. On 2001-on models, unscrew the bolt securing the gearchange steady rod to the IRD unit.

16 The IRD unit is secured to the gearbox by four bolts. Slacken and remove the bolts, and carefully separate the IRD unit from the gearbox. With a block of wood, support the IRD unit on the subframe.

17 Slide the gearchange selector rod roll-pin retaining clip to one side and, using a punch, drive the roll-pin out. Disconnect the rod from the gearbox shaft.

18 Unscrew the three bolts securing the IRD adaptor plate to the gearbox **(see illustration)**.

19 Undo the nut/bolts and remove the front flywheel cover plate. Where fitted remove the lower flywheel cover plate.

20 Unscrew the top gearbox-to-engine bolt, attach a suitable lifting eye, and screw the bolt back in. Attach a lifting hoist or engine crane to the eye.

21 Slacken and remove the left-hand gearbox mounting though bolt. Lower the engine/gearbox approximately 50 mm.

22 Undo the two retaining bolts and remove the left-hand mounting bracket from the gearbox.

23 Position a jack underneath the engine with a block of wood on the jack head. Take the weight of the engine.

24 Slacken and remove the remaining bolts securing the gearbox housing to the engine. Note the correct fitted positions of each bolt, and the necessary brackets, as they are removed, to use as a reference on refitting.

8.14 Undo the three retaining bolts, and remove the lower tie rod bracket from the engine sump

Make a final check that all components have been disconnected, and are positioned clear of the gearbox so that they will not hinder the removal procedure.

25 With the bolts removed, and the help of an assistant, carefully separate the gearbox from the engine, and disengage the gearbox from the clutch and IRD unit shaft. Once the gearbox is free, lower the unit to the floor and manoeuvre it out from under the vehicle. Remove the locating dowels from the gearbox or engine if they are loose, and keep them in a safe place. Discard the IRD unit input shaft O-ring, a new one must be fitted.

L-Series diesel engine

26 Chock the rear wheels, then firmly apply the handbrake. Jack up the front of the

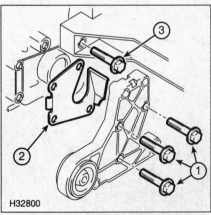

8.18 IRD adaptor plate bolts (1), flywheel cover plate (2) and 'dowel' bolt (3)

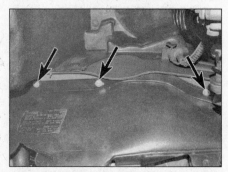

8.31 Undo the retaining screws (arrowed) and remove the left- and right-hand wheel arch splash shields

vehicle, and securely support it on axle stands (see *Jacking and vehicle support*). Remove both front roadwheels then undo the retaining screws and fasteners and remove the undertray from beneath the engine/gearbox unit.

27 Drain the gearbox oil as described in Section 2 then refit the drain plug, and tighten it to the specified torque setting.

28 With reference to Chapter 7C, drain the IRD (Intermediate Reduction Drive) unit oil, then refit the drain plug and tighten it to the specified torque.

29 Remove the battery, battery carrier and starter motor as described in Chapter 5A.

30 Slacken and remove the three flange nuts securing the front exhaust pipe to the catalytic converter, and the three flange nuts securing the pipe to the exhaust manifold. Release the pipe from the rubber mounting, and undo the two bolts securing the pipe to the support bracket on the gearbox. Remove the exhaust pipe and discard the gaskets.

31 Unscrew the retaining screws and remove the left- and right-hand wheel arch splash shields **(see illustration)**.

32 With reference to Chapter 8, remove both front driveshafts.

33 On non-ABS models, disconnect the wiring plug from the vehicle speed sensor. Refer to Section 7.

34 Disconnect the wiring plug from the first gear switch, and the wiring connectors for the reverse light switch. Refer to Sections 5 and 6 if necessary.

35 Release the retaining clip and remove

8.37a Undo the retaining bolt (arrowed) and remove the engine lower tie rod from the sump . . .

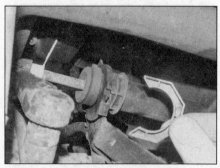

8.35 Release the retaining clip and remove the clutch slave cylinder from the bracket

the clutch slave cylinder from the bracket. Position the cylinder to one side. There is no need to disconnect the hydraulic pipe **(see illustration)**.

36 Unscrew the three retaining bolts and remove the clutch slave cylinder bracket from the gearbox. Release the first gear switch wiring loom from the retaining clip.

37 Undo the retaining bolts, and remove the engine lower tie rod from the sump and subframe **(see illustrations)**.

38 Slacken and remove the bolts securing the tie rod bracket to the sump and IRD unit, and remove the bracket.

39 Unscrew the six retaining bolts, and remove the support bracket from the cylinder block and IRD unit.

40 Undo the two bolts securing the IRD unit support bracket to the sump.

41 The IRD unit is secured to the gearbox by four bolts. Slacken and remove the bolts, and carefully separate the IRD unit from the gearbox. With a block of wood, support IRD unit on the subframe.

42 Unscrew the bolt securing the gearchange steady rod to the IRD adaptor plate.

43 Slide the gearchange selector rod roll-pin retaining clip to one side, and using a punch, drive the roll-pin out. Disconnect the rod from the gearbox shaft.

44 Slacken and remove the three retaining bolts and remove the IRD unit adaptor plate.

45 Unscrew the top gearbox-to-engine bolt, attach a suitable lifting eye, and screw the bolt back in. Attach a lifting hoist or engine crane to the eye.

8.37b . . . and subframe

46 Slacken and remove the left-hand gearbox mounting though bolt. Lower the engine/gearbox approximately 50 mm.

47 Remove the bolt securing the coolant rail and fuel pipes to the adaptor plate.

48 Undo the two retaining bolts and remove the left-hand mounting bracket from the gearbox.

49 Position a jack underneath the engine with a block of wood on the jack head. Take the weight of the engine.

50 Slacken and remove the remaining bolts securing the gearbox housing to the engine. Note the correct fitted positions of each bolt, and the necessary brackets, as they are removed, to use as a reference on refitting. Make a final check that all components have been disconnected, and are positioned clear of the gearbox so that they will not hinder the removal procedure.

51 With the bolts removed, and the help of an assistant, carefully separate the gearbox from the engine, and disengage the gearbox from the clutch and IRD unit shaft. Once the gearbox is free, lower the unit to the floor and manoeuvre it out from under the vehicle. Remove the locating dowels from the gearbox or engine if they are loose, and keep them in a safe place. Discard the IRD unit input shaft O-ring, a new one must be fitted.

TD4 diesel engine

52 Chock the rear wheels, then firmly apply the handbrake. Jack up the front of the vehicle, and securely support it on axle stands (see *Jacking and vehicle support*). Remove both front roadwheels then undo the retaining screws and fasteners and remove the undertray from beneath the engine/gearbox unit.

53 Drain the gearbox oil as described in Section 2 then refit the drain plug, and tighten it to the specified torque setting.

54 With reference to Chapter 7C, drain the IRD (Intermediate Reduction Drive) unit oil, then refit the drain plug and tighten it to the specified torque.

55 Remove the battery, battery carrier and starter motor as described in Chapter 5A.

56 Release the retaining clips and disconnect the air intake ducting assembly. Unscrew the retaining screws and remove the assembly from the engine.

57 Refer to Chapter 7C, and remove the IRD unit.

58 Working as described in Chapter 8, remove the left-hand driveshaft.

59 Using a flat-bladed screwdriver, carefully prise apart the gearchange selector rods balljoints **(see illustration 3.11)**.

60 Trace the wiring back from the reversing light switch, and pull apart the connectors.

61 Disconnect the first gear switch wiring plug. Refer to Section 6 if necessary.

62 Use Land Rover tool No LRT-37-051 to release and disconnect the hydraulic pipe connection to the master cylinder above the gearbox. If the Land Rover tool is not available, use a pair of thin-nosed pliers.

63 Slacken and remove the bolt and disconnect the earth lead from the gearbox.

64 Attach a lifting hoist or engine crane to the lifting eye on the top of the gearbox casing **(see illustration)**.

65 Slacken and remove the left-hand gearbox mounting though-bolt. Where fitted, undo the bolt and remove the weight attached to the top of the gearbox **(see illustration)**. Lower the engine/gearbox approximately 50 mm.

66 Undo the four retaining bolts and remove the left-hand mounting bracket from the gearbox **(see illustration)**.

67 Using a pin punch, drive out the roll-pin and remove the quadrant **(see illustration 4.30)**.

68 Unscrew the retaining bolt from the flywheel cover plate at the rear of the gearbox **(see illustration)**.

69 Position a jack underneath the engine with a block of wood on the jack head. Take the weight of the engine.

70 Slacken and remove the remaining bolts securing the gearbox housing to the engine. Note the correct fitted positions of each bolt, and the necessary brackets, as they are removed, to use as a reference on refitting. Make a final check that all components have been disconnected, and are positioned clear of the gearbox so that they will not hinder the removal procedure.

71 With the bolts removed, and the help of an assistant, carefully separate the gearbox from the engine. Once the gearbox is free, lower the unit to the floor and manoeuvre it out from under the vehicle. Remove the locating dowels from the gearbox or engine if they are loose, and keep them in a safe place.

Refitting

72 The gearbox is refitted by a reversal of the removal procedure, bearing in mind the following points:

a) *Apply a smear of molybdenum disulphide grease (Land Rover recommend the use of Molykote BR2 plus, G-n plus or G-Rapid plus) to the clutch release bearing, fork and guide sleeve contact surfaces and check the operation of the clutch release mechanism (see Chapter 6). Also apply a smear of grease to the gearbox input shaft splines; do not apply too much grease otherwise the clutch friction disc may be contaminated.*

b) *Ensure the locating dowels are correctly positioned prior to installation.*

c) *Tighten all nuts and bolts to the specified torque (where given).*

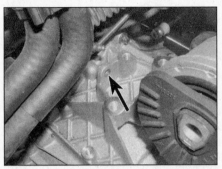

8.64 Attach a lifting hoist or engine crane to the lifting eye on the top of the gearbox casing (arrowed)

8.66 Undo the four retaining bolts and remove the left-hand mounting bracket from the gearbox

d) *Renew the driveshaft oil seals (see Section 4) then refit the driveshafts as described in Chapter 8, renewing the inner joint circlips prior to refitting.*

e) *Renew all roll-pins.*

f) *On completion, refill the gearbox with the specified type and quantity of lubricant (see 'Lubricants and fluids') then check the oil level as described in the relevant Part of Chapter 1.*

9 Gearbox overhaul – general information

Overhauling a manual gearbox unit is a difficult and involved job for the DIY home mechanic. In addition to dismantling and reassembling many small parts, clearances must be precisely measured and, if necessary, changed by selecting shims and spacers. Internal gearbox components are also often difficult to obtain, and in many instances, extremely expensive. Because of this, if the gearbox develops a fault or becomes noisy,

8.65 Where fitted, remove the weight attached to the top of the gearbox

8.68 Unscrew the retaining bolt (arrowed) from the flywheel cover plate at the rear of the gearbox

the best course of action is to have the unit overhauled by a specialist repairer, or to obtain an exchange reconditioned unit.

Nevertheless, it is not impossible for the more experienced mechanic to overhaul the gearbox, provided the special tools are available, and the job is done in a deliberate step-by-step manner, so that nothing is overlooked.

The tools necessary for an overhaul include internal and external circlip pliers, bearing pullers, a slide hammer, a set of pin punches, a dial test indicator, and possibly a hydraulic press. In addition, a large, sturdy workbench and a vice will be required.

During dismantling of the gearbox, make careful notes of how each component is fitted, to make reassembly easier and more accurate.

Before dismantling the gearbox, it will help if you have some idea what area is malfunctioning. Certain problems can be closely related to specific areas in the gearbox, which can make component examination and renewal easier. Refer to the *Fault finding* Section of this manual for more information.

Chapter 7 Part B:
Automatic transmission

Contents

Degrees of difficulty

Easy, suitable for novice with little experience	**Fairly easy,** suitable for beginner with some experience	**Fairly difficult,** suitable for competent DIY mechanic	**Difficult,** suitable for experienced DIY mechanic	**Very difficult,** suitable for expert DIY or professional

Specifications

General

Type	Jatco, five forward speeds and reverse.

Torque wrench settings	Nm	lbf ft
Inhibitor switch bolts	3	2
Oil drain plug	45	33
Oil filler/level plug	14	10
Selector housing nuts	10	7
Selector lever-to-transmission selector shaft nut	25	18
Sump securing bolts	8	6
Torque converter access plate bolts	9	7
Torque converter-to-driveplate bolts	45	33
Transmission housing-to-engine bolts	85	63
Transmission housing-to-sump bolts	85	63
Transmission mounting bracket bolts	85	63
Transmission mounting through bolt	100	74

1 General information

A 5-speed fully-automatic transmission is available as an option on models equipped with the TD4 duesel engine. The transmission consists of a torque converter, an epicyclic geartrain, and hydraulically-operated clutches and brakes.

The torque converter provides a fluid coupling between the engine and transmission, acts as an automatic 'clutch', and also provides a degree of torque multiplication when accelerating.

Three modes of operation are available: Normal, Sport or Steptronic. In Normal mode, the traditional lever positions of P, R, N, D are available, with the addition of 4 which excludes 5th gear, 2 which permits only 1st and 2nd gears, and 1 to hold the transmission in 1st gear. In Sport/Manual mode, the software programme shifts the transmission up and down at higher engine speeds for better acceleration and response. In this position, the lever can be used to select the forwards speeds in Steptronic mode, where pulling the lever back causes the transmission to shift down, and pushing the lever forwards causes the transmission to shift up. The software retains ultimate control over the shift points, preventing up or downshifts which

could result in damaging engine speeds. The Steptronic mode is not available when HDC (Hill Descent Control) function is active. Sophisticated adaptive software programming of the transmission control unit enables it to recognise driving situations such as towing, downhill overrun, steep mountain roads, etc, and select the optimum shift strategies for each.

Due to the complexity of the automatic transmission, any repair or overhaul work must be entrusted to a Land Rover dealer, or a suitably-qualified transmission specialist, with the necessary specialist equipment and knowledge for fault diagnosis and repair. Refer to the *Fault finding* Section at the end of this manual for further information.

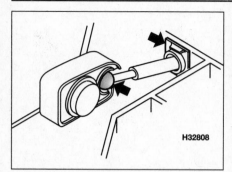

2.3 Slide the selector inner cable end (arrowed) from the selector lever, and remove the clip (arrowed) securing the outer cable to the selector housing

3.5a Slacken the selector inner cable clamp nut (arrowed) at the transmission end of the cable ...

3.5b ... and remove the outer cable-to-transmission bracket retaining clip (arrowed)

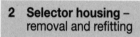

2 Selector housing –
removal and refitting

Removal

1 Park the vehicle on level ground, switch off the ignition, and apply the handbrake firmly. Jack up the front of the vehicle and support it securely on axle stands (see *Jacking and vehicle support*), release the retaining screws and remove the engine/transmission undertray.
2 Working as described in Chapter 11, remove the front section of the centre console.
3 Slide the selector inner cable end from the selector lever **(see illustration)**.
4 Remove the clip securing the outer cable to the selector housing.
5 Where fitted, release the mirror ECM retaining screw and place to one side.
6 At the rear of the housing, disconnect the wiring plug from the shift interlock solenoid.
7 Where fitted, remove the bolt and disconnect the cable from the key interlock mechanism.
8 Working underneath the vehicle, unscrew the six retaining screws and remove the selector housing.

Refitting

9 Refitting is a reversal of removal.

3 Selector cable –
removal, refitting and adjustment

Removal and refitting

1 Working as described in Chapter 11, remove the front section of the centre console.
2 Slide the barrelled end of the inner selector cable from the selector lever, pull out the retaining clip and release the outer cable from the selector housing **(see illustration 2.3)**.
3 Park the vehicle on level ground, switch off the ignition, and apply the handbrake firmly. Jack up the front of the vehicle and support it securely on axle stands (see *Jacking and*

vehicle support), release the retaining screws and remove the engine/transmission undertray.
4 Release the selector cable from the retaining clips on the vehicle body.
5 Slacken the selector inner cable clamp nut at the transmission end of the cable, and remove the outer cable-to-transmission bracket retaining clip **(see illustrations)**. Remove the cable.
6 Refitting is a reversal of removal. However, before refitting the engine/transmission undertray, carry out the cable adjustment procedure.

Adjustment

7 Park the vehicle on level ground, switch off the ignition, and apply the handbrake firmly. Jack up the front of the vehicle and support it securely on axle stands (see *Jacking and vehicle support*), release the retaining screws and remove the engine/transmission undertray.
8 Slacken the selector inner cable clamp nut at the transmission end of the cable **(see illustration 3.5a)**.
9 Move the selector lever in the passenger compartment into position P.
10 Move the selector lever on the transmission fully clockwise to engage P position.
11 At the transmission end, gently pull the inner cable to eliminate any slack, and then tighten the inner cable clamp nut securely.
12 Check that all selector lever operation is correct, and that the engine can only be started in positions P and N.
13 Refit the engine/transmission undertray, and lower the vehicle to the ground.

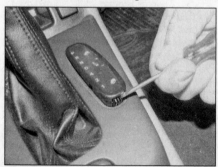

4.1 Carefully prise the indicator from the selector lever trim panel

4 Selector indicator –
removal and refitting

Removal

1 Carefully prise the indicator from the selector lever trim panel **(see illustration)**.
2 Disconnect the indicator wiring plug.

Refitting

3 Reconnect the wiring plug to the underside of the indicator.
4 Refit the indicator to the selector lever trim panel.

5 Inhibitor switch –
description, removal, refitting and adjustment

Description

1 The starter inhibitor switch is screwed into the top of transmission casing. The function of the switch ensures that the engine can only be started with the selector lever in either the N or the P positions, therefore preventing the engine from being started with the transmission in gear. If at any time it is noted that the engine can be started with the selector lever in any position other than N or P, then it is likely that the inhibitor function of the switch is faulty, or the selector cable adjustment is incorrect (see Section 3).

4.2 Disconnect the indicator wiring plug

Removal

2 Park the vehicle on level ground, switch off the ignition, and apply the handbrake firmly. Jack up the front of the vehicle and support it securely on axle stands (see *Jacking and vehicle support*), release the retaining screws and remove the engine/transmission undertray.

3 Move the selector lever to position N.

4 Release the inhibitor switch wiring plug from the retaining clip on the transmission fluid pan, and disconnect it **(see illustration)**.

5 Unscrew the two retaining bolts and remove the switch from the transmission casing.

Refitting

6 Commence refitting by cleaning the switch, and the switch mating face in the transmission casing.

7 Align the internal lugs with the mark on the inhibitor switch.

8 Align the two lugs of the switch with the machined grooves in the selector lever shaft, and fit the switch. Do not tighten the switch bolts at this stage.

9 Reconnect the switch wiring plug, and refit the connector to the retaining clip.

10 Carry out the adjustment procedure.

Adjustment

11 Ensure the selector lever is in position N.

12 Slacken the inhibitor switch screws.

13 Fit Land Rover special tool No LRT-44-018 over the selector lever shaft, and rotate the switch so that the tool alignment pin can be inserted through the tool lever, and into the inhibitor switch. If the Land Rover tool is not available, a suitable home-made equivalent can be fabricated **(see illustrations)**.

14 Tighten the inhibitor switch bolts to the specified torque, and remove the alignment tool.

15 Check the inhibitor switch operation by attempting to start the engine with the selector lever in positions other than P or N.

---

6 Automatic transmission – removal and refitting

Note: *Although the following procedure is not difficult, the transmission assembly is heavy, and awkward to handle. Read through the entire procedure before proceeding, to familiarise yourself with the steps. The help of an assistant will prove invaluable during this operation. A suitable engine lifting crane and tackle will be required.*

Removal

1 Disconnect the battery negative terminal (see Chapter 5A).

2 Slacken the retaining clips, unscrew the retaining bolts and remove the air intake ducting assembly.

3 Jack up the vehicle, and support securely on axle stands placed under the axle tubes

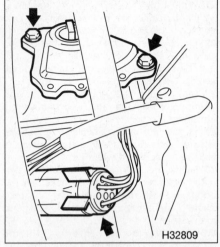

5.4 Disconnect the inhibitor switch wiring plug (arrowed) from the retaining clip, and undo the two switch retaining bolts (arrowed)

(see *Jacking and vehicle support*). Remove bolt front roadwheels. Note that the vehicle must be raised sufficiently to give enough clearance for the transmission assembly to be removed from under the vehicle. Release the retaining screws and remove the engine/transmission undertray.

4 Remove the fluid cooler as described in Section 8.

5 With reference to Chapter 5A, remove the starter motor.

6 Working as described in Chapter 7C, remove the IRD unit.

5.13a Land Rover inhibitor switch aligning tools

7 Remove the left-hand front driveshaft as described in Chapter 8.

8 Slacken the selector inner cable clamp bolt at the transmission end. Release the retaining clip and remove the outer cable from the transmission.

9 Working at the rear of the cylinder block, unscrew the nut securing the cover plate to the rear of the transmission/cylinder block. Prise out the grommet in the cover plate to gain access to the torque converter bolts **(see illustration)**.

10 Mark the relationship of the driveplate to the torque converter to aid refitment. Rotate the crankshaft using a spanner or socket on the crankshaft pulley, to access and unscrew the four torque converter bolts one at a time.

11 Unscrew the retaining bolt and disconnect the earth lead from the transmission.

12 Slacken the retaining clip and disconnect the turbocharger outlet pipe.

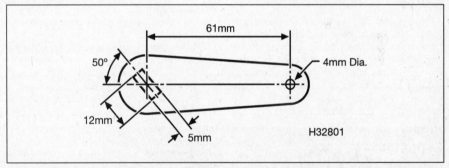

5.13b If the Land Rover tool is not available, it may be possible to fabricate an equivalent using the dimensions shown

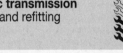

5.13c Aligning tool and pin fitted

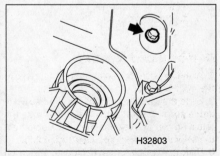

6.9 Prise out the grommet in the cover plate to gain access to the torque converter bolts

13 Working underneath the vehicle, release the transmission wiring plugs from the retaining clips, and disconnect them.

14 Position a jack under the engine with a block of wood on the jack head. Take the weight of the engine.

15 Unscrew the left-hand transmission mounting through-bolt and, using the jack, lower the transmission sufficiently to unscrew the four bolts securing the mounting bracket to the transmission.

16 Attach lifting eyes and a chain/sling to the transmission. Using a crane or hoist, take the weight of the transmission.

17 Slacken and remove the remaining bolts securing the transmission housing to the engine. Note the correct fitted positions of each bolt, and the necessary brackets, as they are removed, to use as a reference on refitting. Make a final check that all components have been disconnected, and are positioned clear of the transmission so that they will not hinder the removal procedure.

18 With the bolts removed, and the help of an assistant, carefully separate the transmission from the engine. Ensure that the torque converter remains on the transmission input shaft. Once the transmission is free, lower the unit to the floor and manoeuvre it out from under the vehicle. Remove the locating dowels from the transmission or engine if they are loose, and keep them in a safe place. Fit a suitable strip of metal across the bellhousing, to retain the torque converter. **Do not** allow the torque converter to fall out of the transmission.

Refitting

19 If required, the torque converter oil seal can be renewed as described in Section 9.

20 Ensure that the mating surfaces of the engine and transmission are clean and dry. Check that the engine end plate is correctly located on its dowels. Make sure that the torque converter is correctly fitted to transmission input shaft (see Section 9).

21 With lifting eyes and chains/slings attached, raise the transmission up into position in the engine compartment.

22 Engage the transmission with the locating dowels on the end of the cylinder block. Fit the transmission-to-engine retaining bolts, and tighten them to the specified torque.

23 Make sure the engine/transmission is supported by the jack, and remove the transmission lifting eyes and chains/slings.

24 Fit the left-hand transmission mounting bracket to the transmission, and tighten the bolts to the specified torque.

25 Using the jack, align the transmission mounting bracket with the bracket on the body, and refit the mounting through-bolt. Tighten the through-bolt to the specified torque.

26 Align the torque converter with the driveplate, and tighten the securing bolts to the specified torque. Refit the grommet to cover plate. If the original torque converter and driveplate components are being refitted, ensure that the marks made on the torque converter and the driveplate before removal are aligned

27 The remainder of the refitting procedure is a reversal of removal, bearing in mind the following points:
  a) Ensure that all wiring is routed correctly, and that all plugs are reconnected to their correct locations.
  b) Refit the IRD unit as described in Chapter 7C.
  c) Refit the exhaust front section with reference to Chapter 4B.
  d) Refit the driveshafts as described in Chapter 8.
  e) Refit the starter motor as described in Chapter 5A.
  f) Adjust the selector cable as described in Section 3.
  g) Where applicable, on completion, refill the transmission and IRD unit with fluid and oil of the correct type, as described in Chapter 1B.

7 Automatic transmission overhaul – general information

In the event of a fault occurring on the transmission, it is first necessary to determine whether it is of an electrical, mechanical or hydraulic nature, and to achieve this special test equipment is required. It is therefore essential to have the work carried out by a Land Rover dealer, or a suitably-equipped specialist if a transmission fault is suspected.

Do not remove the transmission from the vehicle for possible repair before professional fault diagnosis has been carried out, since most tests require the transmission to be in the vehicle.

8 Fluid cooler – removal and refitting

Removal

1 Jack up the vehicle, and support securely on axle stands placed under the axle tubes (see *Jacking and vehicle support*). Release the retaining screws and remove the engine/ transmission undertray. The fluid cooler is located at the front of the transmission.

2 Release the retaining clips, and disconnect the coolant hoses from the fluid cooler. Be prepared for coolant spillage.

3 Slacken the unions and disconnect the fluid hoses from the cooler. Discard the O-rings, new ones must be refitted **(see illustration)**.

4 Unscrew the three retaining bolts, and remove the cooler **(see illustration)**.

Refitting

5 Position the cooler and tighten the mounting bolts securely.

6 Using new O-rings, reconnect the fluid hoses to the cooler.

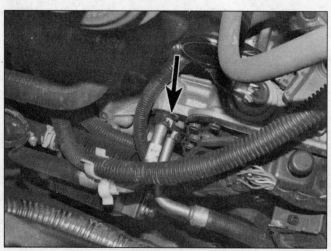

8.3 Slacken the unions (arrowed) and disconnect the fluid hoses from the cooler

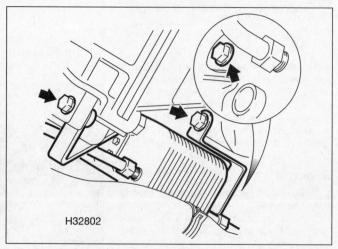

H32802

8.4 Unscrew the three retaining bolts (arrowed), and remove the cooler

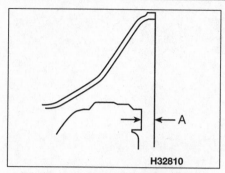

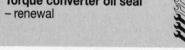

9.5 When the torque converter is fully located in the oil pump drive, the distance (A) should be 27 mm

10.3 Release the two retainers, and withdraw the electronic control module (ECM) from the box

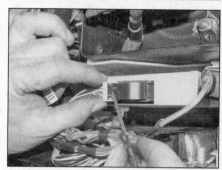

10.4 Prise back the locking lever, and disconnect the ECM wiring plug

7 Reconnect the coolant hoses, and tighten the retaining clips.

8 Refit the engine/transmission undertray, and lower the vehicle to the ground.

9 Check and top-up the cooling system as described in *Weekly checks*, and the transmission fluid as described in Chapter 1B.

---

9 Torque converter oil seal – renewal

1 Remove the transmission as described in Section 6, and slide the torque converter from the transmission input shaft.

2 Discard the O-ring seal from the input shaft and, using a flat-bladed screwdriver, prise the oil seal from the input shaft housing. Note the fitted depth of the seal.

3 Ensure that the oil seal recess in the transmission, and the torque converter

spigot are clean and dry. Lubricate the new oil seal with clean transmission fluid, and fit it to the transmission. Use a tubular drift that bears only on the hard outer edge of the seal. Fit the seal squarely into the housing, with the inner lip facing the transmission.

4 Fit a new O-ring to the transmission input shaft.

5 Position the torque converter over the input shaft, and check that it is fully located **(see illustration)**.

---

10 Electronic control module – removal and refitting

Removal

1 With reference to Chapter 5A, disconnect the battery negative terminal.

2 Undo the five retaining screws and remove the electrical box cover from the left-hand corner of the engine compartment.

3 Release the two retainers, and withdraw the electronic control module (ECM) from the box **(see illustration)**.

4 Disconnect the wiring plug from the ECM **(see illustration)**.

Refitting

5 Reconnect the wiring plug, and insert the ECM into the electrical box. Ensure the ECM is secured by the retainers.

6 Refit the electrical box cover, and tighten the screws securely. Reconnect the battery negative terminal.

Chapter 7 Part C:
Intermediate Reduction Drive unit

Contents

Degrees of difficulty

Easy, suitable for novice with little experience	Fairly easy, suitable for beginner with some experience	Fairly difficult, suitable for competent DIY mechanic	Difficult, suitable for experienced DIY mechanic	Very difficult, suitable for expert DIY or professional

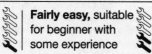

Specifications

Lubrication

Recommended oil	See *Lubricants and fluids*
Capacity	1.1 litres

Torque wrench settings

	Nm	lbf ft
Drain plug	35	26
Filler/level plug	35	26
IRD unit support bracket to sump (petrol engine)	45	33
IRD unit support bracket-to-cylinder block bolt	45	33
IRD unit support bracket-to-lower engine tie rod bolts		
(TD4 diesel engine)	100	74
IRD unit-to-transmission bolts	80	59
Lower tie rod bracket to sump (L-Series diesel engine)	90	66
Main case end cover bolts	30	22
Pinion housing nuts	25	18
Pinion nut	150	111
Prop shaft-to-IRD flange bolts	40	30
Support bracket to IRD unit	50	37

1 General information

The Intermediate Reduction Drive (IRD) unit is attached to the transmission and distributes drive to the front and rear wheels. Drive is taken from the transmission, through the IRD unit primary shaft, via a layshaft and hypoid gear set, to the rear drive pinion, where the rear propshaft connects. The primary shaft also drives the front wheels via a differential assembly within the IRD unit, to control the proportion of drive delivered to each front wheel. In order to prevent the IRD unit lubricating oil from overheating, an oil cooler is connected to the vehicles cooling system **(see illustration)**.

2 Intermediate Reduction Drive unit oil – draining and refilling

1 This operation is much quicker and more efficient if the vehicle is first taken on a journey of sufficient length to warm the engine/transmission up to normal operating temperature.

2 Jack up the front of the vehicle and support it securely on axle stands (see *Jacking and vehicle support*). Note that the vehicle must be lowered to the ground and level, to ensure accuracy when refilling and checking the oil level. Undo the retaining screws and fasteners then remove the engine/transmission undertray from the vehicle to gain access to the filler/level and drain plugs.

3 Remove all traces of dirt from around the filler/level plug which is located on the right-hand rear side of the IRD unit. Unscrew the plug and recover the sealing washer **(see illustration)**.

4 Position a suitable container under the drain plug.

5 Unscrew the drain plug and allow the oil to drain completely into the container **(see illustration)**. If the oil is hot, take precautions against scalding. Clean both the filler/level and the drain plugs, being especially careful to wipe any metallic particles off the magnetic inserts. Discard the original sealing washers;

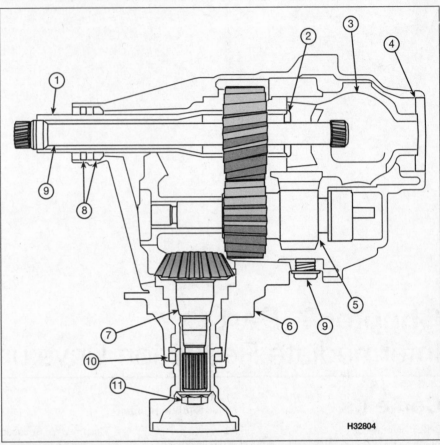

1.1 Intermediate Reduction Drive unit

1 Primary shaft	5 Layshaft	9 Intermediate shaft
2 Oil seal	6 Pinion housing	10 Oil seal
3 Differential unit	7 Rear output pinion	11 Pinion nut
4 Oil seal for RH driveshaft	8 Oil seals	

they should be renewed whenever they are disturbed.

6 When the oil has finished draining, clean the drain plug threads and those of the IRD unit casing, fit a new sealing washer and refit the drain plug, tightening it to the specified torque. Lower the vehicle to the ground.

7 Refilling the IRD is an awkward operation. Above all, allow plenty of time for the oil level to settle properly before checking it. Note that the vehicle must be parked on flat level ground when checking the oil level.

8 Refill the transmission with the exact amount of the specified type of oil (see *Lubricants and fluids*) then check the oil level as described in the relevant Part of Chapter 1. When the level is correct, refit the filler/level plug with a new sealing washer and tighten it to the specified torque. Refit the undertray.

> **HAYNES HiNT**
>
> *If the correct amount was poured into the transmission and a large amount flows out on checking the level, refit the filler/level plug and take the vehicle on a short journey so that the new oil is distributed fully around the drive unit components, then check the level again on your return.*

3 Oil seals – renewal

1 The IRD unit is fitted with two external oil seals to prevent oil escaping from the transmission and the IRD unit, and three

2.3 The filler/level plug which is located on the right-hand rear side of the IRD unit (arrowed)

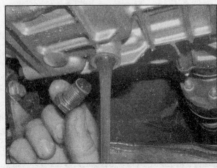

2.5 Unscrew the drain plug and allow the oil to drain

3.3 Carefully prise the oil seal out of the transmission

3.5 Position the seal in the recess with the sealing lip facing towards the IRD unit

3.10 Unscrew the retaining bolts, and remove the IRD unit main case end cover

internal seals prevent transmission oil from contaminating the IRD unit oil. **Note:** *At the time of writing, the only internal seal available was the rear pinion housing-to-IRD unit housing O-ring. If It is suspected that any of the other internal seals are leaking, consult your local Land Rover dealer.*

Right-hand driveshaft oil seal

Note: *Renewal of the left-hand side driveshaft oil seal is detailed in Chapter 7A.*

2 Remove the right-hand drive shaft as described in Chapter 8.

3 Carefully prise the oil seal out of the transmission using a large flat-bladed screwdriver **(see illustration).**

4 On refitting, ensure that the oil seal recess of the casing is clean and dry, lubricate the new oil seal with clean IRD unit oil.

5 Position the seal in the recess with the sealing lip facing towards the IRD unit **(see illustration).** Using a tubular drift that bears only on the hard outer edge of the seal, drive the seal squarely and evenly into the casing recess, until it is fully seated.

6 Refit the driveshaft as described in Chapter 8.

7 With the vehicle parked on level ground, check and top up the IRD unit oil as described in the relevant Part of Chapter 1.

Primary shaft oil seals

Note: *The following procedure description is given on the assumption that new seals are available – see the note in Paragraph 1.*

8 The primary shaft oil seals prevent transmission oil from contaminating the IRD unit oil, and *vice-versa*. One seal is located at each end of the shaft, to seal between the primary shaft and intermediate shaft, and two seals are fitted between the primary shaft and the unit casing **(see illustration 1.1).** The left-hand shaft-to-casing seal prevents transmission oil from leaking into the IRD unit, and the right-hand shaft-to-casing seal prevents IRD unit oil leaking into the transmission. Located between these two seals is a drain hole in the casing. If either seal should fail, escaping oil will leak from the drain hole, indicating the necessity for seal renewal.

9 With reference to Section 5, remove the IRD unit from the vehicle.

10 Unscrew the retaining bolts, and remove the IRD unit main case end cover **(see illustration).**

11 Working through the casing end cover aperture, remove the differential, complete with intermediate shaft, from the casing.

12 Carefully pull the primary shaft assembly through the casing end cover.

13 Note the fitted positions of the oil seals located in each end of the primary shaft and, using a flat-bladed screwdriver, carefully prise the oil seals from the shaft.

14 Carefully prise the two oil seals from the main casing. Note their fitted locations.

15 On refitting, ensure that the seal areas of the primary shaft are clean and dry. Fit the new seals to each end of the primary shaft, using a suitable tubular drift (such as a socket). Ensure that the oil seal lips face outwards.

16 Refit the primary shaft into the IRD unit casing. Ensure that the helical gear on the primary shaft engages properly with the layshaft.

17 Wrap a layer of insulating tape around the end of the intermediate shaft to prevent the shaft splines damaging the oil seals lips. Carefully insert the intermediate shaft into the primary shaft.

18 With all traces of old sealant removed from the casing and end cover, apply a thin bead of silicone sealant to the end cover.

19 Refit the end cover, and tighten the retaining bolts to the specified torque.

20 Land Rover specify the use of special tool No LRT-41-015 to install the two casing-to-primary shaft seals. The tool is fitted with a flange at one end to control the fitted depth of

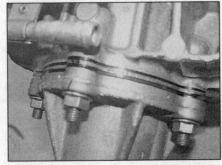

4.4 Unscrew the five nuts/bolts securing the rear pinion housing to the main casing

the outer seal. The inner seal is driven into the casing until it contacts the casing shoulder, whilst the outer seal must be fitted to a depth of 8.5 mm (from the outer edge of the seal to the casing edge). If the tool is not available, use a suitable-sized tubular drift which bears only on the hard outer edge of the seals, or take the IRD unit to a Land Rover dealer or specialist, and have them install the seals. Ensure the seals are fitted squarely, with the main sealing lips facing away from each other.

21 Refit the IRD unit, as described in Section 5.

Pinion oil seal

22 Although the pinion housing removal is straightforward (see Section 4), renewal of the oil seal necessitates resetting the pinion bearing preload. Consequently, renewal of the oil seal is best entrusted to a Land Rover dealer or specialist.

---

4 Pinion housing O-ring – renewal

1 Chock the rear wheels, apply the handbrake, then jack up the front of the vehicle and support it on axle stands (see *Jacking and vehicle support*). Release the retaining screws, and remove the engine/transmission undertray.

2 Drain the IRD unit oil as described in Section 2 or be prepared for some fluid loss as the housing is removed.

3 Disconnect the front flange of the propshaft from the IRD unit, as described in Chapter 8. Tie the shaft to one side.

Caution: *Do not allow the tripod joint on the front of the propshaft to fully extend or be dropped, as this could damage the joint.*

4 Mark the relationship of the pinion housing to the IRD unit using a maker pen, and unscrew the five nuts/bolts securing the rear pinion housing to the main casing. Note that on petrol models the upper three nuts/bolts also secure the mass damper. Carefully remove the pinion housing from the rear of the IRD unit. If the housing is reluctant to separate from the main casing, a gentle tap with a soft-faced hammer should be sufficient **(see illustration).**

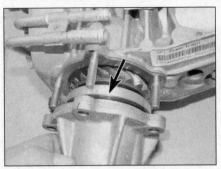

4.6 Pinion housing O-ring (arrowed)

5.7 Mark the relationship between the front propshaft flange and the pinion flange

5.9 Disconnect the coolant hoses from the IRD unit

5 Discard the O-ring, and recover the spacer from the pinion housing.

6 With the main casing, pinion housing and spacer mating faces clean and dry, refit the spacer to the housing, and lubricate the new O-ring with IRD unit oil, prior to installing it into the locating groove in the housing **(see illustration)**.

7 Refit the pinion housing to the rear of the IRD unit casing and evenly and gradually tighten the retaining bolts/nuts to the specified torque. On petrol models, do not omit the mass damper, fitted to the upper three housing retaining bolts/nuts.

8 With reference to Chapter 8, refit the propshaft.

9 Lower the vehicle to the ground, and check/top-up the IRD unit oil level as described in the relevant Part of Chapter 1.

10 Refit the engine/transmission undertray.

5 Intermediate Reduction Drive unit – removal and refitting

Removal

1 Chock the rear wheels, then firmly apply the handbrake. Jack up the front of the vehicle, and securely support it on axle stands (see *Jacking and vehicle support*). Remove both front roadwheels then undo the retaining screws and fasteners and remove the undertray from beneath the engine/transmission unit.

2 Drain the transmission as described in the relevant Part of Chapter 7 then refit the drain and filler/level plugs, and tighten them to their specified torque settings.

3 On 2001-on model year vehicles, remove the front subframe as described in Chapter 10.

4 With reference to Section 2, drain the IRD unit oil.

5 As described in Chapter 8, remove the right-hand front driveshaft.

6 On all models except those fitted with the L-Series diesel engine, remove the exhaust front downpipe as described in the relevant Part of Chapter 4.

7 To aid refitting, mark the relationship between the front propshaft flange, and the pinion flange at the rear of the IRD unit **(see illustration)**.

8 Undo the bolts/nuts and separate the propshaft from the pinion flange.
Caution: Do not allow the tripod joint on the front of the propshaft to fully extend or be dropped, as this could damage the joint.

9 Release the retaining clips, and disconnect the coolant hoses from the IRD unit **(see illustration)**. Note that the heat shield is fitted to the rearmost pipe.

10 Disconnect the breather hose from the top of the IRD unit **(see illustration)**.

11 Slacken and remove the bolts securing the lower tie rod to the subframe and engine bracket. Unscrew the nuts/bolts and remove the tie rod bracket from the engine/IRD unit.

12 Unscrew the retaining bolts and remove the IRD unit support bracket **(see illustration)**. On L-Series diesel engines, Undo the two bolts and remove the stiffener bracket between the engine block and transmission adaptor plate **(see illustration)**. On petrol models, unscrew the three rear pinion housing upper bolts/nuts, and remove the mass damper.

13 Slacken and remove the four bolts securing the IRD unit to the transmission.

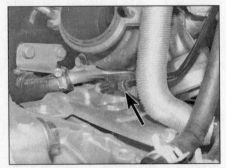

5.10 Disconnect the breather hose (arrowed) from the top of the IRD unit

5.12a Remove the IRD unit support bracket

5.12b Remove the stiffener bracket between the engine block and transmission adaptor plate (L-Series diesel engine)

5.13a IRD unit lower bolts (arrowed) . . .

5.13b . . . and upper bolts

5.14 Lubricate the new O-ring with clean oil and fit it to the IRD unit

With assistance, separate the IRD unit from the transmission and manoeuvre the unit from the vehicle. Discard the IRD unit O-ring, a new one must be fitted **(see illustrations)**.

Refitting

14 Ensure the mating faces of the IRD unit and transmission are clean and dry. Lubricate the new O-ring with clean oil, and fit it to the IRD unit **(see illustration)**.

15 Refit the IRD unit to the transmission. Fit the retaining bolts, but only finger tighten the bolts at this stage. Position a jack to support the IRD unit.

16 Position the various IRD unit support bracket(s), and tie rod brackets. Finger tighten the bolts at this stage. On L-Series diesel engines, do not omit the stiffener bracket between the engine block and the transmission adaptor plate.

17 Now tighten the IRD unit-to-transmission bolts evenly to the specified torque setting, then tighten the various support and tie rod brackets bolts/nuts (stiffener bracket bolts on L-Series engines) to the specified torque.

18 Refit the lower tie rod to the engine bracket and subframe, tightening the retaining bolts to the specified torque. Note that on TD4 models, the tie rod must be fitted with the mark TOP uppermost **(see illustration)**.

19 The remainder of refitting is a reversal of removal, bearing in mind the following points:
a) *Tighten all fasteners to the correct torque setting where specified.*
b) *When the vehicle is lowered to the ground, top-up the transmission and IRD unit as described in the relevant Part of Chapter 1, and the cooling system as described in 'Weekly Checks'.*

5.18 The tie rod must be fitted with the mark TOP uppermost

6 Intermediate Reduction Drive unit overhaul – general information

At the time of writing, only new or exchange IRD units are available. Consequently, although the unit can be dismantled with common hand tools, no overhaul parts are available.

If a fault develops, consult a Land Rover dealer or specialist on the best course of action.

Chapter 8
Driveshafts, propeller shafts & final drive

Contents

Degrees of difficulty

Easy, suitable for novice with little experience	Fairly easy, suitable for beginner with some experience	Fairly difficult, suitable for competent DIY mechanic	Difficult, suitable for experienced DIY mechanic	Very difficult, suitable for expert DIY or professional

Specifications

General

Driveshaft type	Solid shaft, with constant velocity (CV) joints. Tripod inner joints, ball-and-cage outer joints. Early front shafts have dynamic dampers
Propeller shaft type	Front and rear tubular sections, with centre viscous coupling unit (VCU). Front tripod-type CV joint, three universal joints with renewable sealed needle-roller bearings
Final drive type	Hypoid gears, drive pinion centre-line below centre of ring gear. Aluminium alloy housing

Final drive pinion preload	1.7 to 2.8 Nm (1.3 to 2.1 lbf ft)

Torque wrench settings

	Nm	lbf ft
Driveshaft nut (renew)	400	295
Engine/transmission undertray bolts	45	33
Final drive mounting-to-subframe bolt	120	89
Final drive oil plug	27	20
Final drive pinion nut (renew):		
Initial tightening	190	140
Maximum tightening	373	275
Final drive rear cover bolts	25	18
Final drive-to-mounting bolts	65	48
Front propeller shaft to IRD flange	40	30
Front suspension strut to wheel hub	205	151
Propeller shafts to viscous coupling	65	48
Rear propeller shaft to rear axle flange	65	48
Roadwheel nuts	115	85
Trailing link to wheel hub	120	89
Transverse links to subframe	120	89
Viscous coupling support bearing bolts	28	21

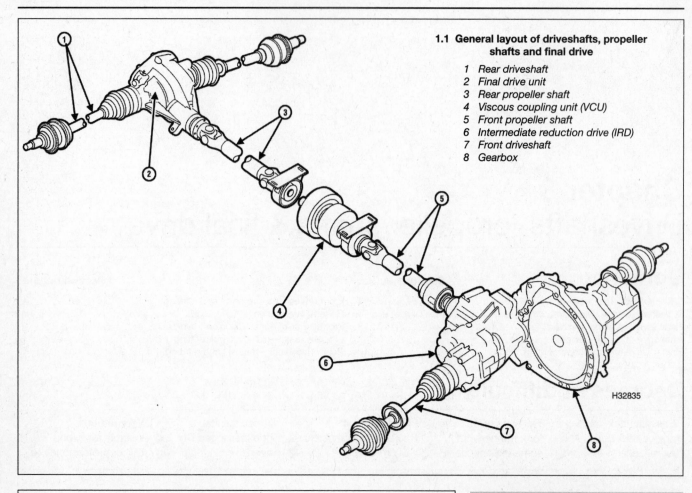

1.1 General layout of driveshafts, propeller shafts and final drive

1 Rear driveshaft
2 Final drive unit
3 Rear propeller shaft
4 Viscous coupling unit (VCU)
5 Front propeller shaft
6 Intermediate reduction drive (IRD)
7 Front driveshaft
8 Gearbox

H32835

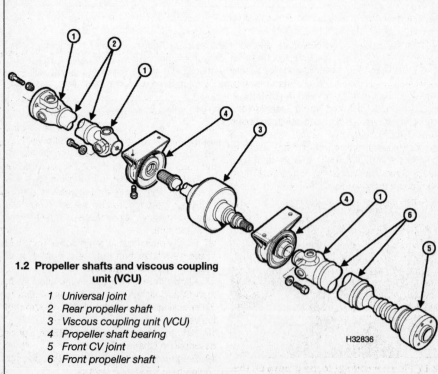

1.2 Propeller shafts and viscous coupling unit (VCU)

1 Universal joint
2 Rear propeller shaft
3 Viscous coupling unit (VCU)
4 Propeller shaft bearing
5 Front CV joint
6 Front propeller shaft

H32836

1   General information

The drive is transmitted from the intermediate reduction drive (IRD) unit (front differential or transfer box) to the front wheels, via conventional unequal-length driveshafts. The driveshafts have a constant velocity (CV) joint at each end, splined into the wheel hubs and IRD; the inner joints are tripod type, and the outer joints are ball-and-cage type **(see illustration)**.

From the IRD unit, drive is taken to the rear wheels via a two-section tubular propeller ('prop') shaft, with a centre viscous coupling unit (VCU). The VCU has a sealed-for-life support bearing pressed onto its input and output shafts – these bearings also serve to support the prop shafts **(see illustration)**. Although the Freelander is essentially a permanent four-wheel-drive vehicle, when used on-road, it is effectively front-wheel-drive only, thanks to the viscous coupling, which only transmits power to the rear wheels when the front wheels lose traction, and the speed of the front prop shaft exceeds that of the rear shaft.

The prop shafts have flexible couplings at each end, to cater for the varying angles

2.3 Undo the three bolts (arrowed) and remove the wheel arch splash shield

2.4 Using a hammer and suitable chisel, release the staking (arrowed) from the driveshaft nut

2.7 Remove the two bolts securing the suspension strut to the wheel hub

between the axle and IRD unit, caused by suspension movement. The front prop shaft has a flexible CV-type coupling at the front, with a conventional universal joint (UJ) at the rear. The rear shaft has UJs front and rear – all universal joints have renewable sealed needle-roller bearings.

The final drive (or rear differential) distributes drive from the rear prop shaft to the rear wheels, via two driveshafts. The shafts are similar to those used at the front, having a CV joint at either end, and are splined into the final drive and wheel hubs. The final drive housing is of alloy, and is mounted to the rear subframe by three rubber bushes. The three final drive oil seals (prop shaft seal and two driveshaft seals) are specially designed to prevent ingress of dirt and water, and are referred to as 'labyrinth' type seals; the seals also have a pressed-on steel shield, or 'flinger'. A breather is located in the top of the housing. Apart from maintaining the final drive oil level, as described in the relevant part of Chapter 1, no oil changes are necessary.

2 Front driveshafts – removal and refitting

Removal

1 Loosen the wheel nuts, then jack up the relevant front wheel and support on axle stands (see *Jacking and vehicle support*). Remove the front wheel.
2 Remove the engine/transmission undertray and its frame, as follows. Remove the two screws securing the panel to the front bumper, then on early models, pull the lower edge of the bumper down for access to the two front frame bolts. Now remove a total of eight bolts around the frame – the two at the rear are smaller than the rest, so note their locations.
3 Remove the wheel arch splash shield, which is secured by three bolts **(see illustration)**.
4 Using a hammer and suitable chisel, release the staking from the driveshaft nut **(see illustration)**.

 Warning: Before attempting to loosen the driveshaft nut, which is done up extremely tight, make

sure the front of the vehicle is securely supported. Do not use poor-quality, badly-fitting tools for this task, due to the risk of personal injury.
5 While an assistant presses the brake pedal firmly, loosen and remove the driveshaft nut. Discard the nut once removed – owing to the extremely high tightening torque, it is **not** recommended that the nut is re-used.
6 With reference to Chapter 9, remove the ABS wheel sensor and brake caliper. Tie the caliper up to prevent straining the brake hose.
7 Remove the two bolts securing the suspension strut to the wheel hub, noting which way round they are fitted **(see illustration)**.
8 Release the hub from the base of the strut, then pivot the hub to withdraw the end of the driveshaft from it. Do not let the right-hand driveshaft hang down at too steep an angle from the transmission, as this could cause damage to the inner joint.
9 The inner end of the driveshaft must now be released from the IRD unit. Be prepared for oil spillage as the shaft is released, by placing a container under the inner end of the shaft.
10 The shafts are secured in place with a circlip. Land Rover recommend prising between the driveshaft and the IRD unit, but care must be taken not to damage the driveshaft oil seal as this is done – the dealers use a special collar tool (which resembles a narrow exhaust clamp) around the shaft, to provide a levering surface (LRT-54-026) **(see illustration)**. If an assistant is available, have them pull **gently** outwards on the shaft as it is

2.14 Fit a new circlip to the groove on the driveshaft

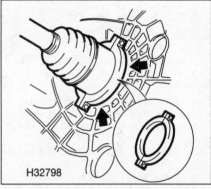

2.10 Land Rover special tool used to provide a levering point for removing the front driveshafts

prised out – pulling too hard on the shaft may well damage the CV joints.
11 When the driveshaft is free, remove the circlip from its groove, and discard it – a new one should be obtained for refitting.

Refitting

12 Inspect the driveshaft oil seal for signs of damage, and renew it if necessary, as described in the relevant part of Chapter 7.
13 Wipe clean the ends of the driveshaft, and the oil seal and hub, then lubricate the oil seal running surfaces with fresh gear oil/fluid.
14 Fit a new circlip to the groove on the driveshaft splined inner end **(see illustration)**.
15 Taking care not to damage the oil seal as the shaft is offered in, fit the driveshaft inner end into the IRD unit until the circlip is felt to engage. Pull gently on the shaft to ensure that the circlip is correctly seated. **Note:** *The longer of the two driveshafts is fitted to the left-hand side.*
16 Fit the driveshaft into the wheel hub, and fit the new driveshaft nut, hand-tight only at this stage **(see illustration)**.
17 Align the hub into the suspension strut, then fit and tighten the strut-to-hub bolts to the specified torque (bolt heads to the front of the vehicle).
18 Refit the brake caliper and ABS sensor as described in Chapter 9.
19 Refit the driveshaft splash shield, and the engine/transmission undertray.
20 Referring to the Warning earlier in this

Section, tighten the new driveshaft nut to the specified torque. If a torque wrench capable of reading to such a high torque is not available, do the nut up as tight as possible, stake it, and drive slowly to the nearest garage to have the nut correctly torqued – this is a vital safety item, and tightening by guesswork is not advisable.

21 Stake the driveshaft nut's collar into the groove in the end of the shaft **(see illustration)**.

22 Refit the wheel, then lower the vehicle to the ground and tighten the wheel nuts to the specified torque.

23 Check and if necessary top-up the IRD unit oil level, as described in the relevant part of Chapter 1.

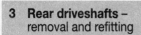

3   Rear driveshafts – removal and refitting

Removal

1 Loosen the wheel nuts, then jack up the relevant rear wheel and support on axle stands (see *Jacking and vehicle support*). Remove the rear wheel.

2 Using a hammer and suitable chisel, release the staking from the driveshaft nut.

> ⚠ **Warning: Before attempting to loosen the driveshaft nut, which is done up extremely tight, make sure the rear of the vehicle is securely supported. Do not use poor-quality, badly-fitting tools for this task, due to the risk of personal injury.**

3.4 Unbolt the trailing link arm from the base of the hub

3.5b . . . and adjustable (rear) transverse link arms from the rear subframe

2.16 Fit the driveshaft into the wheel hub

3 While an assistant presses the brake pedal firmly, loosen and remove the driveshaft nut. Discard the nut once removed – owing to the extremely high tightening torque, it is **not** recommended that the nut is re-used.

4 The rear hub must now be freed of all linkages to it, so that it can be pulled outwards to allow the driveshaft to be removed. First, unbolt the trailing link arm from the base of the hub **(see illustration)**.

5 Unbolt the fixed (front) and adjustable (rear) transverse link arms from the rear subframe – these links need only be detached at the inner ends **(see illustrations)**.

6 Unbolt the handbrake cable securing clip from the rear subframe.

7 Have an assistant pull outwards on the hub to release the splined outer end of the driveshaft from the hub. Do not let the driveshaft hang down at too steep an angle from the final drive, as this could cause damage to the inner joint.

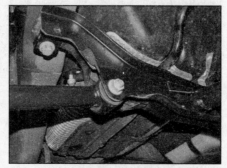

3.5a Unbolt the fixed (front) . . .

3.9 Land Rover forked tool used for prising the rear driveshafts out of the final drive

2.21 Stake the driveshaft nut's collar into the groove in the end of the shaft

8 The inner end of the driveshaft must now be released from the final drive. Be prepared for oil spillage as the shaft is released, by placing a container under the inner end of the shaft.

9 The shafts are secured in place with a circlip. Land Rover recommend prising between the driveshaft and the final drive, but care must be taken not to damage the driveshaft oil seal 'flinger' as this is done – the dealers use a special forked tool as a levering device (LRT-51-014) **(see illustration)**. Have an assistant pull **gently** outwards on the shaft as it is prised out – pulling too hard on the shaft may damage the CV joints.

10 When the driveshaft is free, remove the circlip from its groove, and discard it – a new one should be obtained for refitting.

Refitting

11 Inspect the driveshaft oil seal for signs of damage, and renew it if necessary, as described in Section 9.

12 Wipe clean the ends of the driveshaft, and the oil seal and hub, then lubricate the oil seal running surfaces with fresh gear oil.

13 Fit a new circlip to the groove on the driveshaft splined inner end **(see illustration)**.

14 Taking care not to damage the oil seal as the shaft is offered in, fit the driveshaft inner end into the final drive until the circlip is felt to engage. Pull gently on the shaft to ensure that the circlip is correctly seated.

15 With an assistant again pulling the rear hub outwards, fit the driveshaft into the wheel hub, and fit the new driveshaft nut, hand-tight only at this stage.

16 Fit the nuts and bolts securing the two

3.13 Fit a new circlip to the groove on the driveshaft splined inner end

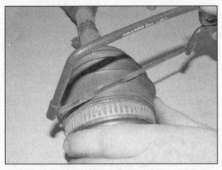

4.3 If necessary, the clips can be cut from the gaiter

4.5a Drive the CV joint off the shaft using a drift in the inner part of the joint

4.5b Check the circlip for damage and, if necessary, fit a new one

transverse links, and the trailing link, to the rear subframe and wheel hub respectively. These fasteners should only be tightened once the weight of the vehicle is again resting on its wheels. Therefore, tighten these hand-tight for now, and delay torquing them to the specified figure until later.

17 Referring to the Warning earlier in this Section, tighten the new driveshaft nut to the specified torque. If a torque wrench capable of reading to such a high torque is not available, do the nut up as tight as possible, stake it, and drive slowly to the nearest garage to have the nut correctly torqued – this is a vital safety item, and tightening by guesswork is not advisable.

18 Stake the driveshaft nut's collar into the groove in the end of the shaft (see illustration 2.21).

19 Refit the wheel, then lower the vehicle to the ground and tighten the wheel nuts to the specified torque.

20 Tighten the two transverse link bolts, and the trailing link bolt, to the specified torques.

21 Check and if necessary top-up the final drive oil level, as described in the relevant part of Chapter 1.

4 Driveshaft gaiters – renewal

1 Remove the driveshaft as described in Section 2 or 3, as applicable.

Outer joints

2 Mount the driveshaft in a vice.

3 Release the gaiter securing clips, and discard them. If necessary, the clips can be cut from the gaiter, but great care must be taken to ensure that the ABS reluctor ring is not damaged (see illustration).

4 Slide the old gaiter back up the shaft to expose the CV joint itself.

5 The CV joint is held onto the shaft by means of a circlip. Taking care not to damage the CV joint, use a suitable drift to tap the joint off the shaft (see illustration). Check the circlip for damage and, if necessary, fit a new one (see illustration).

6 Remove the gaiter from the shaft, and discard it.

7 Clean up the driveshaft before fitting the new gaiter. If the gaiter has been split for some time, there is a danger that the CV joint will have suffered from dust and dirt entry, causing wear in the joint. Simply packing it with grease and fitting a new gaiter will only delay the need for a new joint. If wished, there's nothing to lose by washing the joint clean in a suitable solvent, but let it dry completely before packing it liberally with fresh grease.

8 Fit the new gaiter onto the shaft, taking care not to damage it over the circlip.

9 Slide the outer joint into place, using a small screwdriver to press the circlip down into its groove as the joint passes over it (see illustration). Once the joint is in position, pull on the joint to make sure the circlip has engaged.

10 Pack the joint with the grease which should have been supplied with the new gaiter, and place any excess inside the gaiter itself (see illustration).

11 Fit the gaiter onto the joint, and secure it with the two clips usually supplied. A special pair of crimping pliers will be needed for the metal-type clips (see illustration).

12 Refit the driveshaft as described in Section 2 or 3, as applicable.

Inner joints

13 Remove the outer joint and gaiter as described previously in this Section.

14 Release the gaiter securing clips, then slide the gaiter off the outer end of the shaft.

15 Clean up the driveshaft before fitting the new gaiter.

16 Fit the new gaiter onto the shaft, taking care not to damage it over the circlip (see illustration).

17 Pack the inner joint with the grease which should have been supplied with the new gaiter, and place any excess inside the gaiter itself (see illustration 4.10).

4.9 Tap the outer joint into place

4.10 Place any excess grease inside the gaiter itself

4.11 A special pair of crimping pliers will be needed for the metal-type clips

4.16 Fit the new gaiter onto the shaft

4.18 Secure the inner gaiter with the clips supplied

18 Fit the gaiter onto the joint, and secure it with the two clips again usually supplied (see illustration). A special pair of crimping pliers will be needed for the metal-type clips.
19 Refit the outer joint as described previously in this Section.
20 Refit the driveshaft as described in Section 2 or 3, as applicable.

5 Driveshaft overhaul –
general

1 To check the front driveshafts, listen for a metallic clicking from the front as the vehicle is driven slowly in a circle with the steering on full-lock. Repeat the check on full-left and full-right lock. This noise may also be apparent when pulling away from a standstill with lock applied. If a clicking noise is heard, this indicates wear in the outer constant velocity joints.

6.2 Make alignment marks on the prop shaft flanges at the IRD and the final drive

6.5 Unscrew the four nuts and Torx bolts securing the rear prop shaft

2 If vibration, consistent with roadspeed, is felt through the vehicle when accelerating, there is a possibility of wear in the inner constant velocity joints.
3 The outer constant velocity joints can be removed as described in Section 4. If wear is apparent, the joints should be renewed.

6 Propeller shaft –
removal and refitting

⚠️ **Warning: Note the following points before working on the prop shafts:**
• **Always remove the prop shafts and viscous coupling (VCU) as an assembly – dismantling on the vehicle may cause damage to the individual components.**
• **Never unbolt the VCU support bearings from the underbody without first detaching the prop shafts at the IRD and final drive – the weight of the centre section will pull the front CV joint apart, causing irreparable damage.**
• **Do not allow the front CV joint to bend at too acute an angle, or the internal roller bearings will break up and cause the joint to fail.**

Removal

1 Jack up the front and rear of the vehicle, and support securely on axle stands, as described in *Jacking and vehicle support*.
2 If the original propeller shaft is to be refitted, make alignment marks on the prop shaft

6.3 Remove the six nuts, Torx bolts, and curved washers securing the front CV joint

6.6 The four bolts securing the VCU support bearings

flanges at the IRD and the final drive (see illustration).
3 Remove the six nuts, Torx bolts, and curved washers securing the front CV joint to the IRD flange (see illustration).
4 Separate the CV joint from the IRD flange by pulling on the main CV joint casing. If necessary, a method similar to that used for prising out the front driveshafts from the IRD can be employed here – see Section 2. When the joint is free, support the front of the prop shaft to prevent the damage described in the Warning at the start of this Section.
5 Unscrew the four nuts and Torx bolts securing the rear prop shaft to the final drive flange. Support the rear of the prop shaft when the flange has been separated (see illustration).
6 Support the weight of the viscous coupling to avoid the damage mentioned in the Warning at the start of this Section. Make alignment marks between the VCU support bearing mountings and the vehicle body, then loosen and remove the four bolts securing the VCU support bearings (see illustration). With the aid of at least one assistant, lower the complete prop shaft assembly to the ground, keeping it as level as reasonably possible.

Refitting

7 Before fitting, clean the prop shaft flanges, and the corresponding mating faces on the IRD and final drive – take care, however, that the alignment marks made prior to removal are not destroyed by this process.
8 With assistance, raise the complete prop shaft assembly into position under the vehicle.
9 Align the viscous coupling support bearings with their alignment marks previously made, and fit the bolts hand-tight at this stage, so that the bearings can still move.
10 Offer the rear prop shaft up to the final drive flange, check that the previously-made marks align, then fit and tighten the four nuts and bolts to the specified torque.
11 Similarly, offer up the front CV joint so that the flange marks align, then fit the CV joint and tighten the six IRD flange nuts and bolts (complete with the curved washers) to the specified torque.
12 The VCU support bearings must be aligned so that they are at exactly 90° to the centre-line of the VCU, and are therefore

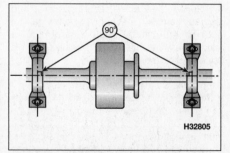

6.12 The VCU support bearings must be aligned so that they are at exactly 90° to the centre-line of the VCU

7.9 Slacken the bolt and slide out the U-shaped washer

7.10 Use a tapered rod to separate the prop shaft from the VCU

7.12 Discard the seal fitted between the joint body and the 'can'

running as freely as possible. When the alignment is satisfactory, tighten first the rear, then the front support bolts to the specified torque **(see illustration)**.

13 On completion, lower the vehicle to the ground. Check the oil level in the IRD unit and final drive, as described in the relevant part of Chapter 1.

7 Propeller shaft – 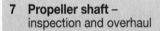 inspection and overhaul

Inspection

1 Wear in the universal joint needle roller bearings is characterised by vibration in the transmission, 'clonks' on taking up the drive, and in extreme cases, unpleasant metallic noises as the bearings break up (lack of lubrication).

2 To test the universal joints for wear with the propeller shaft in place, apply the handbrake, and chock the wheels.

3 Working under the vehicle, apply leverage between the yokes using a large screwdriver or a flat metal bar. Wear is indicated by movement between the shaft yoke and the coupling flange yoke. Check all the universal joints in this way.

4 To check the front CV joint, try to push the shafts from side-to-side, and look for any excessive movement between the sleeve and the shaft. A further check can be made by gripping the shaft and sleeve, and turning them in opposing directions, again looking for excessive movement. As a rough guide, if *any*

movement can be seen, the splines are worn, and the shaft assembly should be renewed.

5 If a universal joint is worn, a new joint must be obtained and fitted as described later in this Section.

6 If the CV joint splines are excessively worn, the complete shaft assembly must be renewed. Check with a Land Rover dealer on the availability of spare parts, before proceeding further.

7 To work on any part of the prop shaft assembly, the whole assembly **must** be removed first, as described in Section 6.

Overhaul

Dismantling prop shafts

8 The front or rear prop shafts can be detached from the viscous coupling as follows.

9 Knock back the locktab on the bolt securing the prop shaft to the viscous coupling, then loosen the bolt and slide out the U-shaped washer **(see illustration)**.

10 To separate the prop shaft splines, Land Rover dealers have a special wedge tool (LRT-51-017) which is inserted between the head of the bolt just loosened and the yoke of the universal joint **(see illustration)**. However, in the absence of the special tool, any tapered rod can be used. The bolt can be screwed in or out to ideally position the wedge/rod, and the wedge/rod is then driven in squarely to separate the components. Finally, the bolt and its tab washer can be removed – fit a new tab washer if it was damaged during removal.

11 Refitting the prop shafts is a reversal of dismantling. Clean the splines before

assembly, and use the bolt to draw the components together initially, before finally tightening to the specified torque and securing with the tab washer.

Dismantling front CV joint

12 Mount the CV joint in a vice, and carefully release the gaiter's metal 'can' at the front of the gaiter. Separate the joint body from the gaiter, and discard the seal fitted between it and the 'can' **(see illustration)**.

13 With the prop shaft held securely in a vice, clean off the grease to expose the tripod inner joint and circlip.

14 Using circlip pliers, remove the inner joint circlip, then slide the inner joint off the splines **(see illustrations)**.

15 Remove the clip securing the rear end of the gaiter, and remove the gaiter from the prop shaft.

16 Fit the new clip and gaiter to the shaft, but do not secure the rear of the gaiter at this stage.

17 Fit the inner joint to the shaft, and secure with the circlip.

18 Liberally lubricate the inner joint and gaiter with the grease normally supplied with a new gaiter.

19 Fit the new seal to the groove in the joint body, securing it in place with a smear of grease, and ensuring that the six bolt holes are aligned **(see illustration)**.

20 Fit the joint body to the prop shaft, and align the gaiter 'can' holes with those in the joint body. Temporarily fit and tighten the six nuts and Torx bolts to draw the 'can' onto the joint body.

7.14a Using circlip pliers, remove the inner joint circlip . . .

7.14b . . . then slide the inner joint off the splines

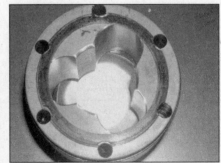

7.19 Fit the new seal to the groove in the joint body

7.21 Crimp the gaiter 'can' at three equally-spaced points to secure it to the joint body

21 Crimp the gaiter 'can' at three equally-spaced points to secure it to the joint body, and secure the rear of the gaiter with the clip. Remove the six nuts and bolts prior to refitting the prop shaft **(see illustration)**.

Dismantling universal joints

22 Before removing the universal joints, mark the position of the joint spider pin relative to the journal yoke ears on the prop shaft joint, to ensure correct assembly without introducing imbalance problems. If no such marks are visible, scribe your own.

23 Clean away all traces of dirt and grease from the circlips located on the ends of the joint spiders. Using a suitable pair of circlip pliers, remove the four joint circlips **(see illustration)**. If a circlip proves difficult to remove, as a last resort, place a drift on the bearing cup, in the centre of the circlip, and tap the top of the bearing cup to ease the

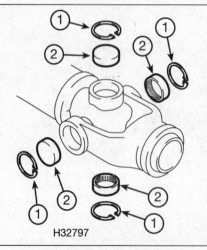

H32797

7.23 Universal joint exploded view, showing circlips (1) and bearing cups (2)

pressure on the circlip. Remove the circlips.

24 Support the end of the shaft in a vice, with the yoke in a vertical plane. Using a hammer and a suitable drift (a socket of appropriate size, for example), tap the uppermost bearing cup until the bottom bearing cup protrudes from the yoke **(see illustration)**.

25 Remove the shaft from the vice, then securely grip the protruding bearing cup in the vice jaws. Turn the shaft from side-to-side, at the same time lifting the shaft until the bearing cup comes free. Note how each component is fitted, as it is removed.

26 Refit the shaft to the vice, with the exposed spider uppermost. Tap the spider with the

7.24 Tap the uppermost bearing cup until the bottom bearing cup protrudes from the yoke

hammer and drift until the lower bearing cup protrudes, then remove the cup as described previously **(see illustration)**.

27 The coupling flange and the spider can now be removed from the shaft, and the remaining two bearing cups can be removed as described previously.

28 Clean all components thoroughly, and assess the wear of each.

29 Remove the bearing cups from the new spider. Check that all the needle rollers are present, and correctly positioned in the bearing cups.

30 Ensure that the bearing cups are one-third full of fresh grease.

31 Fit the new spider, complete with seals, into the coupling flange yoke.

32 Partially insert one of the bearing cups into the yoke, and enter the spider trunnion into the bearing cup, taking care not to dislodge the needle rollers **(see illustration)**.

33 Similarly, insert a bearing cup into the opposite yoke.

34 Using the vice, carefully press both bearing cups into place, ensuring that the spider trunnions do not dislodge any of the needle rollers.

35 Using a suitable tube or socket of a slightly smaller diameter than the bearing cups, press each cup into its respective yoke, until the top of the cup just reaches the lower land of the circlip groove. **Do not** press the cups below this point, as damage may be caused to the cups and seals **(see illustrations)**.

36 Fit the new circlips to retain the bearing cups.

37 Engage the spider with the yokes on the relevant propeller shaft section, then partially fit both bearing cups to the yokes, taking care not to dislodge any of the needle rollers.

38 Press the bearing cups into position, and fit the new circlips, as described in paragraphs 34 to 36.

Dismantling viscous coupling

39 The viscous coupling can be separated from both prop shafts as described earlier in this Section. Further work, including removal of the support bearings, will require the use of a press, and is a job for a Land Rover dealer or specialist, as the viscous coupling can be damaged if care is not taken.

7.26 Tap the lower bearing cap free

7.32 Partially insert one of the bearing cups into the yoke, and enter the spider trunnion into the bearing cup

7.35a Press each cup into its respective yoke . . .

7.35b . . . until the top of the cup just reaches the lower land of the circlip groove

8 Final drive – removal and refitting

Removal

1 Remove both rear driveshafts as described in Section 3.

2 Using the information in Section 6, separate the rear prop shaft from the final drive flange. Make sure that, once separated, the prop shaft is either supported or tied up – do not let it hang down unsupported.

3 Anticipate oil spillage as the final drive is removed – put down plenty of rags or newspaper if necessary.

4 Support the weight of the final drive on a large trolley jack, supplemented by a pair of axle stands. This is a heavy assembly, and it must be adequately supported while the mountings are removed.

5 Land Rover dealers use a special centralising jig to align the final drive with the prop shaft when it is refitted. If this jig is not available, it is advisable to make as many alignment markings as possible on the front and rear mountings, to give some chance of retaining the correct alignment after refitting.

6 Remove the two bolts securing the final drive to the front mounting, noting which way round they are fitted **(see illustration)**.

7 Depress the red locking collar, and remove the breather pipe from the top of the casing.

8 Check once more that the final drive is supported, then remove the two bolts from each of the two rear mountings **(see illustration)**.

9 With the aid of an assistant, tip the final drive through 90° (rear down), and remove it from the rear subframe.

10 If required, any of the final drive mountings can now be unbolted from the subframe, for renewal. Tighten the mounting-to-subframe bolt to the specified torque on completion. Note that at the time of writing, the final drive mounting bushes were only available complete with the mountings.

Refitting

11 Refitting is a reversal of removal, noting the following points:

  a) *Align the marks made prior to dismantling, if the centralising jig is not available.*

8.6 Remove the two bolts securing the final drive to the front mounting

  b) *Tighten the front mounting bolts before the rear mounting bolts, all to the specified torque.*
  c) *Refit the rear prop shaft using the information in Section 6.*
  d) *Refit the driveshafts as described in Section 3.*
  e) *On completion, check and top-up the final drive oil level, as described in the relevant part of Chapter 1.*

9 Final drive oil seals – renewal

Prop shaft pinion oil seal

1 Renewal of the oil seal necessitates resetting the pinion bearing preload. Consequently, renewal of the oil seal is best entrusted to a Land Rover dealer or specialist.

Driveshaft seals

2 Remove the relevant driveshaft as described in Section 3.

3 Using a flat-bladed screwdriver, carefully extract the old oil seal, noting its fitted depth and ensuring that the oil seal recess is not damaged in the process **(see illustration 3.3 in Chapter 7C)**.

4 Clean the oil seal recess. If the seal recess shows any sign of scoring or rough edges, clean it up now, or the new seal will also be damaged.

5 Lightly lubricate the new oil seal with gear oil, then press it into place using a suitable drift which bears on the seal edges. Press the seal in to the same depth noted on the old seal.

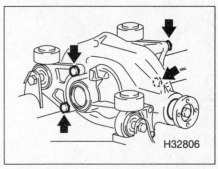

8.8 Final drive rear mounting bolts (arrowed)

6 Refit the driveshaft as described in Section 3.

10 Final drive overhaul – general information

Overhauling a final drive unit is a difficult and involved job for the DIY home mechanic. In addition to dismantling and reassembling many small parts, clearances must be precisely measured and, if necessary, changed by selecting shims and spacers. Components are also often difficult to obtain and in many instances, extremely expensive. Because of this, if the final drive develops a fault or becomes noisy, the best course of action is to have the unit overhauled by a specialist repairer, or to obtain an exchange reconditioned unit.

Nevertheless, it is not impossible for the more experienced mechanic to overhaul the final drive, if the special tools are available and the job is done in a deliberate step-by-step manner so that nothing is overlooked.

The tools necessary for an overhaul include internal and external circlip pliers, bearing pullers, a slide hammer, a set of pin punches, a dial test indicator, and possibly a hydraulic press. In addition, a large, sturdy workbench and a vice will be required.

During dismantling, make careful notes of how each component is fitted, to make reassembly easier and more accurate.

Before dismantling, it will help if you have some idea what area is malfunctioning. Refer to *Fault finding* at the end of this manual for more information.

Chapter 9
Braking system

Contents

Degrees of difficulty

Easy, suitable for novice with little experience	**Fairly easy,** suitable for beginner with some experience	**Fairly difficult,** suitable for competent DIY mechanic	**Difficult,** suitable for experienced DIY mechanic	**Very difficult,** suitable for expert DIY or professional

Specifications

General

System type . . . .   Diagonal-split, dual-circuit, servo-assisted. Optional 4-channel Anti-Lock Braking System (ABS), Hill Descent Control (HDC), traction control and Electronic Brake force Distribution (EBD)

Handbrake . . . .   Mechanically-operated, via twin cables to rear brakes

Front brakes

Type . . . .   Solid or ventilated disc, with single-piston caliper
Disc diameter . . . .   262 mm
Disc thickness:
    Solid . . . .   14.0 mm
    Ventilated . . . .   20.8 to 21.0 mm
    Service limit:
        Solid . . . .   11.0 mm
        Ventilated . . . .   18.0 mm
Maximum disc run-out . . . .   0.040 mm
Brake pad friction material minimum thickness . . . .   3.0 mm

Rear brakes

Type . . . .   Drums, with leading/trailing shoes
Drum internal diameter. . . . .   254 mm
Drum wear limit . . . .   255.49 mm
Drum ovality limit . . . .   0.012 mm
Brake shoe friction material minimum thickness . . . .   2.0 mm

Master cylinder bore diameter. . . . .   23.8 mm

Torque wrench settings

	Nm	lbf ft
ABS modulator mounting nuts	14	10
Brake pipe unions	17	13
Brake servo mounting nuts	22	16
Caliper bleed screw	10	7
Caliper brake hose banjo bolt	27	20
Caliper guide pin bolts	27	20
Caliper mounting bracket bolts:		
Models with solid discs	83	61
Models with ventilated discs	100	74
Handbrake cable mounting brackets	22	16
Handbrake lever bolts	22	16
Master cylinder-to-servo nuts	25	18
Rear brake backplate bolts	45	33
Rear wheel cylinder bleed screw	7	5
Rear wheel cylinder bolts	8	6
Roadwheel nuts	115	85
Vacuum pump bolts:		
L-Series engine	8	6
TD4 engine (renew)	22	16

1 General information

The braking system is of the servo-assisted, dual-circuit hydraulic type, operating from a tandem master cylinder; in the event of hydraulic failure in one circuit, braking force will still be available at least two wheels. All non-ABS models are fitted with pressure-conscious reducing valves (PCRVs) in the brake pipes feeding the rear wheels – the purpose of the valves is to limit the hydraulic pressure supplied to the rear brakes, to prevent the rear wheels from locking-up under heavy braking. Models with ABS up to 2001 model year also have these valves, but after 2001 model year, they were discontinued, and the pressure-reducing function is contained within the ABS modulator itself.

On diesel models, since there is insufficient vacuum in the inlet manifold to operate the braking system servo unit, a vacuum pump is fitted to the engine, to provide the required vacuum.

All models have front disc and rear drum brakes. An Anti-lock Braking System (ABS) was fitted to higher-specification models (and to all from 2001 model year onwards), and offered as an option on all other models (refer to Section 19 for further information on ABS operation). Models with ABS are also equipped with various other traction-related systems, which rely on the ABS wheel sensors to operate – these being the Hill Descent Control (HDC), traction control (anti-wheelspin), and Electronic Brake force Distribution (EBD). From 2001 model year onwards, the speedometer receives its speed signal from the ABS ECU – the signal is derived from the average of the four readings from the wheel sensors.

On all models, the handbrake is cable-operated, to the rear drums, unlike some other Land Rover models, which have a parking brake which acts on the transmission.

When servicing any part of the system, work carefully and methodically; also observe scrupulous cleanliness when overhauling any part of the hydraulic system. Always renew components (in axle sets, where applicable) if in doubt about their condition, and use only genuine Land Rover parts, or at least those of known good quality. Note the warnings given in *Safety first!* and at relevant points in this Chapter concerning the dangers of asbestos dust and hydraulic fluid.

2 Hydraulic system – bleeding

⚠️ **Warning: Hydraulic fluid is poisonous; wash off immediately and thoroughly in the case of skin contact, and seek immediate medical advice if any fluid is swallowed or gets into the eyes. Certain types of hydraulic fluid are inflammable, and may ignite when allowed into contact with hot components. When servicing any hydraulic system, it is safest to assume that the fluid IS inflammable, and to take precautions against the risk of fire as though it is petrol that is being handled. Finally, it is hygroscopic (it absorbs moisture from the air) – old fluid may be contaminated and unfit for further use. When topping-up or renewing the fluid, always use the recommended type, and ensure that it comes from a freshly-opened sealed container. Brake fluid is an effective paint stripper, and will attack plastics; if any is spilt, it should be washed off immediately using copious quantities of fresh water.**

General

1 The correct operation of any hydraulic system is only possible after removing all air from the components and circuit; this is achieved by bleeding the system.

2 During the bleeding procedure, add only clean, unused hydraulic fluid of the recommended type; never re-use fluid that has already been bled from the system. Ensure that sufficient fluid is available before starting work.

3 If there is any possibility of incorrect fluid being already in the system, the brake components and circuit must be flushed completely with uncontaminated, correct fluid, and new seals should be fitted to the various components.

4 If hydraulic fluid has been lost from the system (or air has entered) because of a leak, ensure that the fault is cured before proceeding further.

5 Park the vehicle on level ground, switch off the engine and select first or reverse gear, then chock the wheels and release the handbrake. On models with ABS, to be absolutely safe, ensure that the ignition is switched off (take out the key) – this will prevent the ABS pump from operating.

6 Check that all pipes and hoses are secure, unions tight and bleed screws closed. Clean any dirt from around the bleed screws.

7 Unscrew the master cylinder reservoir cap, and top the master cylinder reservoir up to the MAX level line; refit the cap loosely. Remember to maintain the fluid level at least above the MIN level line throughout the procedure, or there is a risk of further air entering the system.

8 There is a number of one-man, do-it-yourself brake bleeding kits currently available from motor accessory shops. It is recommended that one of these kits is used whenever possible, as they greatly simplify the bleeding operation, and also reduce the risk of expelled air and fluid being drawn back into the system. If such a kit is not available, use the basic (two-man) method which is described in detail below.

9 If a kit is to be used, prepare the vehicle as described previously, and follow the kit manufacturer's instructions as the procedure may vary slightly according to the type being

used; generally, they are as outlined below in the relevant sub-section.

10 Whichever method is used, the same sequence must be followed (paragraphs 11 and 12) to ensure the removal of all air from the system.

Bleeding sequence

11 If the system has been only partially disconnected, and suitable precautions were taken to minimise fluid loss, it should be necessary only to bleed that part of the system (ie, the primary or secondary circuit).

12 If the complete system is to be bled, then it should be done working in the following sequence (specified by Land Rover, which goes against the norm of bleeding from rear to front):

   a) Left-hand front brake.
   b) Right-hand front brake.
   c) Left-hand rear brake.
   d) Right-hand rear brake.

Bleeding

Basic (two-man) method

13 Collect a clean glass jar, a suitable length of plastic or rubber tubing which is a tight fit over the bleed screw, and a ring spanner to fit the screw. The help of an assistant will also be required.

14 Remove the dust cap from the bleed screw on the left-hand front brake – if the front wheels are turned onto full-lock, it should not be necessary to remove the wheel for access. Fit the spanner and tube to the screw, place the other end of the tube in the jar, and pour in sufficient fluid to cover the end of the tube (see illustration).

15 Ensure that the master cylinder reservoir fluid level is maintained at least above the MIN level line throughout the procedure.

16 Have the assistant fully depress the brake pedal several times to build-up pressure, then maintain it on the final stroke.

17 While pedal pressure is maintained, unscrew the bleed screw (approximately one turn) and allow the compressed fluid and air to flow into the jar. The assistant should maintain pedal pressure, following it down to the floor if necessary, and should not release it until instructed to do so. When the flow stops, tighten the bleed screw again, release the pedal slowly and recheck the reservoir fluid level.

18 Repeat the steps given in paragraphs 16 and 17 until the fluid emerging from the bleed screw is free from air bubbles. If the master cylinder has been drained and refilled, and air is being bled from the first screw in the sequence, allow approximately five seconds between cycles for the master cylinder passages to refill.

19 When no more air bubbles appear, tighten the bleed screw securely, remove the tube and spanner, and refit the dust cap. Do not overtighten the bleed screw.

20 Repeat the procedure on the remaining brakes, in the sequence given – it will be

necessary to crawl under the rear of the vehicle for access to the rear brake bleed screws if the vehicle isn't raised.

Using a one-way valve kit

21 As their name implies, these kits consist of a length of tubing with a one-way valve fitted, to prevent expelled air and fluid being drawn back into the system; some kits include a translucent container, which can be positioned so that the air bubbles can be more easily seen flowing from the end of the tube.

22 The kit is connected to the bleed screw, which is then opened. The user returns to the driver's seat and depresses the brake pedal with a smooth, steady stroke and slowly releases it; this is repeated until the expelled fluid is clear of air bubbles.

23 Note that these kits simplify work so much that it is easy to forget the master cylinder reservoir fluid level; ensure that this is maintained at least above the MIN level line at all times.

Using a pressure-bleeding kit

24 These kits are usually operated by the reservoir of pressurised air contained in the spare tyre, although note that it will probably be necessary to reduce the tyre pressure to a lower level than normal; refer to the instructions supplied with the kit.

25 By connecting a pressurised, fluid-filled container to the master cylinder reservoir, bleeding can be carried out simply by opening each screw in turn (in the specified sequence) and allowing the fluid to flow out until no more air bubbles can be seen in the expelled fluid.

26 This method has the advantage that the large reservoir of fluid provides an additional safeguard against air being drawn into the system during bleeding.

27 Pressure-bleeding is particularly effective when bleeding 'difficult' systems, or when bleeding the complete system at the time of routine fluid renewal.

All methods

28 When bleeding is complete and firm pedal feel is restored, wash off any spilt fluid, tighten the bleed screws securely and refit their dust caps.

29 Check the hydraulic fluid level, and top-up if necessary (see Weekly checks).

30 Discard any hydraulic fluid that has been

2.14 Remove the dust cap from the bleed screw

bled from the system; it will not be fit for re-use.

31 Check the feel of the brake pedal. If it feels at all spongy, air must still be present in the system, and further bleeding is required. Failure to bleed satisfactorily after a reasonable repetition of the bleeding procedure may be due to worn master cylinder seals.

3 Hydraulic pipes and hoses – renewal

Note: Before starting work, refer to the warning at the beginning of Section 2 concerning the dangers of hydraulic fluid.

1 If any pipe or hose is to be renewed, minimise fluid loss as follows. Remove the master cylinder reservoir cap, then tighten it down onto a piece of polythene to obtain an airtight seal. Alternatively, flexible hoses can be sealed, if required, using a proprietary brake hose clamp, while metal brake pipe unions can be plugged (if care is taken not to allow dirt into the system) or capped immediately they are disconnected (see illustration). Place a wad of rag under any union that is to be disconnected, to catch any spilt fluid.

2 If a flexible hose is to be disconnected, unscrew the brake pipe union nut before removing the spring clip which secures the hose to its mounting bracket (where fitted).

3 To unscrew the union nuts, it is preferable to obtain a brake pipe spanner of the correct size; these are available from most large motor accessory shops (see illustration). Failing

3.1 Flexible hoses can be sealed using a proprietary brake hose clamp

3.3 To unscrew the union nuts, use a brake pipe spanner of the correct size

4.2a Unscrew and remove the lower caliper guide pin bolt . . .

4.2b . . . pivot the caliper upwards from the disc

4.3 Remove the brake pads from the caliper mounting bracket

this, a close-fitting open-ended spanner will be required, though if the nuts are tight or corroded, their flats may be rounded-off if the spanner slips. In such a case, a self-locking wrench is often the only way to unscrew a stubborn union, but it follows that the pipe and the damaged nuts must be renewed on reassembly. Always clean a union and surrounding area before disconnecting it.

 HAYNES HiNT *If disconnecting a component with more than one union, make a careful note of the connections before disturbing any of them.*

4 If a brake pipe is to be renewed, it can be obtained, cut to length and with the union nuts and end flares in place, from Land Rover dealers. All that is then necessary is to bend it to shape, following the line of the original, before fitting it to the vehicle. Alternatively, most motor accessory shops can make up brake pipes from kits, but this requires very careful measurement of the original to ensure that the new one is of the correct length. The safest answer is usually to take the original to the shop as a pattern.

5 On refitting, do not overtighten the union nuts. It is not necessary to exercise brute force to obtain a sound joint.

6 Ensure that the pipes and hoses are correctly routed with no kinks, and that they are secured in the clips or brackets provided. After fitting, remove the polythene from the reservoir, and bleed the hydraulic system as

described in Section 2. Wash off any spilt fluid, and check carefully for fluid leaks.

4 Front brake pads – renewal

 Warning: Renew BOTH sets of front brake pads at the same time – NEVER renew the pads on only one wheel, as uneven braking may result. Note that the dust created by wear of the pads may contain asbestos, which is a health hazard. Never blow it out with compressed air, and don't inhale any of it. An approved filtering mask should be worn when working on the brakes. DO NOT use petroleum-based solvents to clean brake parts – use brake cleaner or methylated spirit only.

1 Apply the handbrake, then loosen the front roadwheel nuts. Jack up the front of the vehicle and support it on axle stands. Remove both front roadwheels.

2 Unscrew and remove the lower caliper guide pin bolt. Pivot the caliper upwards from the disc to gain access to the brake pads, and tie it to the suspension strut using a piece of wire **(see illustrations)**.

3 Remove the brake pads from the caliper mounting bracket, noting the correct position of the pad retainer springs **(see illustration)**.

4 Measure the thickness of friction material remaining on each brake pad. If either pad is worn at any point to the specified minimum thickness or less, all four front pads must be

renewed **(see illustration)**. The pads should also be renewed if any are fouled with oil or grease, as there is no satisfactory way of degreasing friction material once contaminated. If any of the brake pads are worn unevenly or fouled with oil or grease, trace and rectify the cause before reassembly. New brake pad kits are available from Land Rover dealers, and include new pad retainer springs.

5 If the brake pads are still serviceable, carefully clean them using a clean, fine wire brush or similar, paying particular attention to the sides and back of the metal backing. Carefully clean the pad retainer springs and the pad locations in the caliper body and mounting bracket.

6 Scrape any rust from the periphery of the brake disc.

7 If new brake pads are to be fitted, the caliper piston must be pushed back into the cylinder to make room for them. Either use a piston retraction tool, a G-clamp or use suitable pieces of wood as levers. Clamp off the flexible brake hose leading to the caliper then connect a brake bleeding kit to the caliper bleed nipple. Open the bleed nipple as the piston is retracted; the surplus brake fluid will then be collected in the bleed kit vessel **(see illustration)**.

8 Check that the caliper guide pins are free to slide easily in the caliper bracket, and that the rubber guide pin gaiters are undamaged. Inspect the dust seal around the piston for damage and the piston for evidence of fluid leaks, corrosion or damage. Renew as necessary.

Refitting

9 Commence refitting by fitting the pad retainer springs to the caliper mounting bracket.

10 Apply a thin smear of high-temperature copper brake grease or anti-seize compound to the sides and back of each pad's metal backing, and to the pad contact surfaces on the caliper body and mounting bracket.

11 Install the brake pads in the caliper mounting bracket, ensuring that the friction material is against the disc. The pads are not identical – look carefully; the pad with the horizontally chamfered top corner of the friction material is the outboard pad **(see illustrations)**.

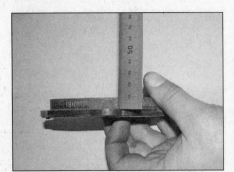

4.4 Measure the thickness of friction material remaining on each brake pad

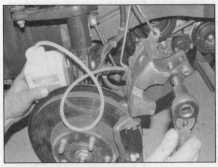

4.7 Open the bleed nipple as the piston is retracted

4.11a Install the brake pads in the caliper mounting bracket, ensuring that the friction material is against the disc

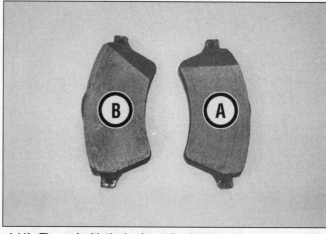

4.11b The pad with the horizontally chamfered top corner of the friction material (A) is the outboard pad, and the pad with the sloping chamfer (B) is the inboard pad

12 Pivot the caliper body down over the brake pads, then refit the bottom guide pin bolt and tighten it to the specified torque wrench setting.

13 Check that the caliper body slides smoothly in the mounting bracket, then depress the brake pedal repeatedly until the pads are pressed into firm contact with the brake disc and normal pedal pressure is restored.

14 Repeat the above procedure on the remaining front brake caliper.

15 Refit the roadwheels, then lower the vehicle to the ground and tighten the roadwheel nuts to the specified torque setting.

16 On completion, check and if necessary top-up the hydraulic fluid level as described in *Weekly checks*.

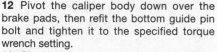

5 Rear brake shoes – renewal

Warning: Brake shoes must be renewed on both rear wheels at the same time – never renew the shoes on only one wheel, as uneven braking may result. Also, the dust created by wear of the shoes may contain asbestos, which is a health hazard. Never blow it out with compressed air, and do not inhale any of it. DO NOT use petrol or petroleum-based solvents to clean brake parts; use brake cleaner or methylated spirit only.

Removal and inspection

1 Remove the brake drum as described in Section 7.

2 Remove all traces of brake dust from the brake drum, backplate and shoes, but take care not to inhale the dust.

3 Measure the thickness of friction material remaining on each brake shoe at several points. If either shoe is worn at any point to the specified minimum thickness or less, **all four** shoes must be renewed as a set

(see illustration). Also, the shoes should be renewed if any are fouled with oil or grease, as there is no satisfactory way of degreasing friction material once contaminated.

4 If any of the brake shoes are worn unevenly or fouled with oil or grease, trace and rectify the cause before reassembly. If the shoes are to be renewed, proceed as described below. If all is well, refit the drum as described in Section 7.

> **HAYNES HINT**
> *When working on rear drums, only ever dismantle one side at a time, as this will give you a pattern to work to, for spring locations, etc, on the opposite side of the vehicle.*

5 To remove the brake shoes, first remove the shoe retainer springs and pins, using a screwdriver to press in each retainer clip until it can be slid from under the retaining pin head and released **(see illustration)**.

Vehicles up to 2001 model year

6 Ease the shoes out one at a time from the lower pivot point to release the tension of the return spring, then disconnect the lower return spring from both shoes. Ease the upper end

5.3 Measure the thickness of friction material remaining on each brake shoe at several points

of both shoes out from their wheel cylinder locations, taking care not to damage the wheel cylinder seals. The brake shoe and adjuster strut assembly can now be manoeuvred out of position and away from the backplate **(see illustration overleaf)**.

7 Unhook the handbrake cable from the bracket on the trailing shoe.

8 Do not depress the brake pedal until the brakes are reassembled. Wrap a strong elastic band around the wheel cylinder pistons to retain them.

9 With the brake shoe assembly on the bench, make a note of the fitted positions of the adjuster strut and springs to use as a guide on reassembly **(see illustration)**. Carefully ease the adjuster strut from its slot in the trailing shoe and remove the short spring which secures the two components together. Detach the upper return spring and separate the shoes and strut.

10 Examine the adjuster strut assembly for signs of wear or damage, paying particular attention to the adjuster quadrant and knurled wheel. If damaged, the strut assembly must be renewed. Renew all the brake shoe return springs if necessary.

Vehicles from 2001 model year

11 Using a pair of thin-nosed pliers, release

5.5 Use a screwdriver to press in each retainer clip until it can be slid from under the retaining pin head and released

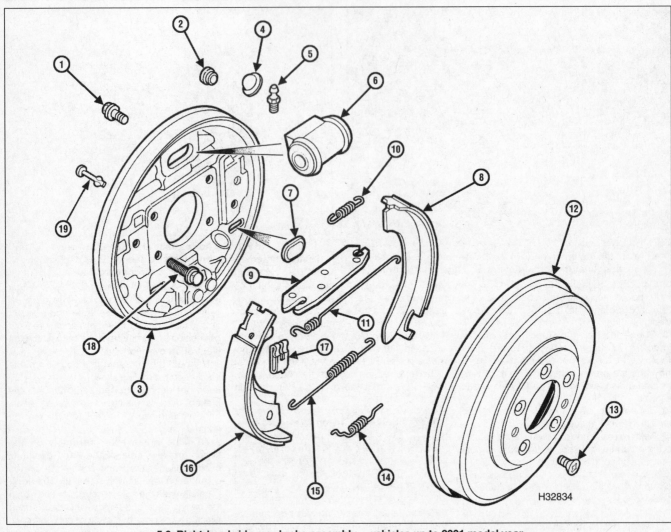

5.6 Right-hand side rear brake assembly – vehicles up to 2001 model year

1 Wheel cylinder bolt	6 Wheel cylinder	11 Upper shoe return	15 Lower shoe return spring
2 Blanking plug	7 Blanking plug	spring	16 Trailing brake shoe
3 Backplate	8 Leading brake shoe	12 Brake drum	17 Shoe retainer clip
4 Dust cap	9 Adjuster strut	13 Drum retaining screw	18 Backplate fixing bolt
5 Bleed nipple	10 Adjuster spring	14 Spring	19 Shoe retaining pin

the handbrake inner cable from the lever **(see illustration)**.

12 Ease one shoe out at a time from the lower pivot point, then manoeuvre the brake shoe assembly around the wheel cylinder and hub flange and remove from the vehicle. Ensure that the ends of the brake shoes do not damage the wheel cylinder rubber dust covers.

13 Do not depress the brake pedal until the brakes are reassembled. Wrap a strong elastic band around the wheel cylinder pistons to retain them **(see illustration)**.

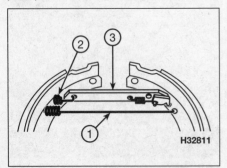

5.9 Upper return spring (1), adjuster strut spring (2) and adjuster strut (3)

5.11 Using a pair of thin-nosed pliers, release the handbrake inner cable

5.13 Wrap a strong elastic band around the wheel cylinder

5.14a Upper spring assembly . . .

5.14b . . . lower spring assembly . . .

5.14c . . . rear spring assembly . . .

5.14d . . . and front spring assembly

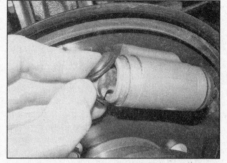

5.15 Peel back the rubber protective caps and check the wheel cylinder for fluid leaks

5.22 Fit the upper return spring and adjuster strut

14 With the brake shoe assembly on the bench, note the fitted position of the various springs and remove them. Remove the adjuster and expander strut **(see illustrations)**.

All models

15 Peel back the rubber protective caps and check the wheel cylinder for fluid leaks or other damage – a certain amount of dampness is normal **(see illustration)**. Check that both cylinder pistons are free to move easily.

Refitting

16 Prior to fitting, clean the backplate and apply a little high-temperature copper grease to all the shoe contact surfaces on the backplate, adjuster and wheel cylinder pistons. Do not allow the grease to foul the friction material.

Vehicles up to 2001 model year

17 Ensure the handbrake stop lever on the trailing shoe is correctly engaged with the lever, and is pressed tight against the brake shoe.

18 Fully extend the adjuster strut quadrant and fit the leading brake shoe into the adjuster strut slot, ensuring that the strut spring and knurled wheel are situated on the underside of the strut assembly. Using a screwdriver, move the quadrant away from the knurled wheel and set it in the minimum adjustment position.

19 Fit the upper return spring to its respective location on the leading shoe. Fit the trailing shoe to the upper return spring and carefully ease the shoe into position in the adjuster strut slot. Once in position, fit the small spring

which secures the trailing shoe to the strut assembly **(see illustration 5.9)**.

20 Remove the elastic band fitted to the wheel cylinder, and manoeuvre the shoe and strut assembly into position on the backplate. Locate the upper end of both shoes with the wheel cylinder pistons and fit the handbrake cable to the trailing shoe clip. Fit the lower return spring to both shoes and ease the shoes into position on the lower pivot point.

21 Tap the shoes to centralise them with the backplate, then refit the shoe retainer pins and springs and secure them in position with the retainer clips. Check that the adjuster quadrant is still in the minimum adjuster position and, if necessary, reset it by levering the leading shoe away from the wheel cylinder then moving the adjustment cam back. Once the adjuster strut is correctly set, ease the leading shoe back into position and check that the shoes are still central.

5.23 Position the brake shoes either side of the wheel cylinder

Vehicles from 2001 model year

22 Fit the upper return spring and adjuster strut **(see illustration)**. Ensure the adjuster wheel is set in the minimum position (fully compressed).

23 Remove the elastic bands, and position the brake shoes either side of the wheel cylinder, and ensure that the ends of the shoes align with the cylinder pistons **(see illustration)**.

24 Refit the lower return spring and handbrake strut **(see illustration)**.

25 Carefully refit the adjuster wheel ratchet mechanism and spring **(see illustration)**, and the expander strut spring **(see illustration 5.14d)**.

26 Using a pair of thin-nosed pliers, reconnect the handbrake inner cable to the brake shoe lever.

27 Insert the retaining pins through the corresponding holes in the shoes, and secure them in place with the clips **(see illustration)**.

5.24 Refit the lower return spring and handbrake strut

5.25 Carefully refit the adjuster wheel ratchet mechanism and spring

All models

28 Refit the brake drum (Section 7) and repeat the above operations on the remaining rear brake assembly.

29 On completion, apply the footbrake repeatedly to set the shoe-to-drum clearance, until normal brake pedal operation returns.

30 Check handbrake operation and, if necessary, adjust as described in the relevant part of Chapter 1.

31 Refit the roadwheels then lower the vehicle to the ground and tighten the roadwheel nuts to the specified torque.

32 On completion, check and if necessary top-up the hydraulic fluid level as described in *Weekly checks*.

---

6 Front brake disc – inspection, removal and refitting

Note: *Before starting work, refer to the warning at the beginning of Section 4.*

Inspection

Note: *If either disc requires renewal, BOTH should be renewed at the same time, to ensure even and consistent braking.*

1 Firmly apply the handbrake, then loosen the front roadwheel nuts. Jack up the front of the vehicle and support it on axle stands. Remove the appropriate front roadwheel.

2 Slowly rotate the brake disc, so that the full area of both sides can be checked; remove the brake pads if better access is required to the inner surface. Light scoring is normal in

6.3 The disc's thickness must be measured using a micrometer

5.27 Note the position of the shoe retaining pin clips

the area swept by the brake pads, but if heavy scoring is found, the disc must be renewed.

3 It is normal to find a lip of rust and brake dust around the disc's perimeter; this can be scraped off if required. If, however, a lip has formed due to excessive wear of the brake pad swept area, then the disc's thickness must be measured using a micrometer **(see illustration)**. Take measurements at several places around the disc, at the inside and outside of the pad swept area. If there's any doubt as to the condition of the discs, renew them both – discs are often less expensive than you might think, and it's never worth taking any risks where brakes are concerned.

4 If the disc is thought to be warped, it can be checked for run-out as follows (note that the run-out specs at the start of this Chapter assume that the roadwheel is fitted while checking). Either use a dial gauge mounted on any convenient fixed point, while the disc is slowly rotated, or use feeler blades to measure (at several points all around the disc) the clearance between the disc and a fixed point such as the brake caliper **(see illustration)**. If the measurements obtained are at the specified maximum or beyond, the disc is excessively warped and must be renewed; however, it is worth checking first that the wheel bearing is in good condition (Chapter 10).

5 Check the disc for cracks, especially around the wheel studs, and any other wear or damage.

Removal

6 Remove the caliper as described in Section 8.

6.4 Use a dial gauge to check the brake disc run-out

---

7 Using chalk or paint, make alignment marks between the disc and hub.

8 Slacken and remove the two bolts securing the brake disc to the hub assembly, and separate the two components. If the screws are tight, or more likely rusted-in, make sure first that a close-fitting screwdriver is used, to avoid damaging the screw head (an impact driver may ultimately be needed). If the discs are to be re-used, clean off any penetrating oil used to free the screws before refitting them **(see illustration)**.

Refitting

9 Refitting is the reverse of the removal procedure, noting the following points:

a) Ensure that the mating surfaces of the disc and hub are clean and flat.

b) If a new disc has been fitted, use a suitable solvent to wipe any preservative coating from the disc before refitting the caliper.

c) Fit the disc to the hub, aligning (if applicable) the marks made prior to removal.

d) Fit the disc retaining bolts and tighten them securely – remember, these only locate the disc in place – the disc is clamped in position by the roadwheel studs and nuts.

e) Refit the brake caliper as described in Section 8.

f) Refit the roadwheel, lower the vehicle to the ground, and tighten the roadwheel nuts to the specified torque. On completion, repeatedly depress the brake pedal, until normal (non-assisted) pedal pressure returns.

---

7 Rear brake drum – inspection, removal and refitting

> ⚠ **Warning: The rear brake drums must be renewed as an axle set at the same time, otherwise uneven braking may result.**

Removal

1 Chock the front wheels, then jack up the rear of the vehicle and support on axle stands (see *Jacking and vehicle support*). Remove the appropriate rear wheel.

6.8 Slacken and remove the two bolts securing the brake disc to the hub assembly (arrowed)

7.3 Unscrew the drum retaining screws (arrowed)

2 Use chalk or paint to mark the relationship of the drum to the hub.

3 With the handbrake firmly applied to prevent drum rotation, unscrew the drum retaining screws. Fully release the handbrake cable, then withdraw the drum **(see illustration)**.

4 If the drum will not pull away, first check that the handbrake is fully released. If the drum will still not come away, remove the grommet from the rear of the backplate and, using a small screwdriver (or two), release the shoe adjuster ratchet and turn the adjuster to increase the shoe-to-drum clearance **(see illustration)**.

Inspection

5 Remove all traces of brake dust from the drum, but avoid inhaling the dust as it is a health hazard.

6 Clean the outside of the drum and check it for obvious signs of wear or damage, such as cracks around the wheel stud holes. Renew the drum if necessary.

7 Examine the inside of the drum. Light scoring of the friction surface is normal, but if heavy scoring is found, the drum must be renewed. It is usual to find a rusty lip on the drum's inboard edge, and this can be scraped away to leave a smooth surface – this also makes refitting (and any subsequent removal) much easier.

8 If the drum is thought to be excessively worn or oval, its internal diameter must be measured at several points by using an internal micrometer. Take measurements in pairs, the second at right angles to the first, and compare the two to check for signs of ovality. Provided that it does not enlarge the drum to beyond the specified maximum diameter, it may be possible to have the drum refinished by skimming or grinding but if this is not possible, the drums on both sides must be renewed.

Refitting

9 Refitting is the reverse of the removal procedure, noting the following:

a) *If fitting a new brake drum, use a suitable solvent to remove any preservative coating that may have been applied to its interior.*

b) *Remove all traces of dirt, brake dust and corrosion from the mating surfaces of the drum and the hub flange.*

c) *Align (if applicable) the marks made on removal.*

d) *If the drum is difficult to refit (when the brake shoes haven't been removed), check that the leading shoe hasn't been pulled out of its location in the wheel cylinder during drum removal.*

e) *Tighten the drum retaining screws securely. Refit the wheels, then lower the vehicle to the ground and tighten the roadwheel nuts to the specified torque.*

8 Brake caliper –
removal, overhaul and refitting

Note: *Before starting work, refer to the warning at the beginning of Section 2 concerning the dangers of hydraulic fluid, and to the warning at the beginning of Section 4.*

Removal

1 Apply the handbrake, then jack up the front of the vehicle and support it on axle stands (see *Jacking and vehicle support*). Remove the appropriate front roadwheel.

As part of another procedure

2 If the caliper is being removed for reasons other than to overhaul it, there are two options – either remove the guide pin bolts and take the caliper off its mounting bracket, or unbolt the mounting bracket itself.

3 If just the caliper is removed, the brake pads can be left in the mounting bracket – otherwise, remove them as described in Section 4. Either way avoids disconnecting the fluid hose from the caliper, which saves bleeding the brakes on completion, but the caliper must be hung up under the wheel arch so that the hose is not strained. If necessary, remove the clips securing the brake hose, to increase the range of movement available (the clips must be refitted on completion).

Removal for overhaul

4 If the caliper is to be overhauled, do not unbolt it until the fluid hose has been disconnected. Minimise brake fluid loss either by removing the master cylinder reservoir cap and then tightening it down onto a piece of polythene to obtain an airtight seal (taking care

8.6 Carefully lift the caliper assembly off the brake pads

7.4 Remove the grommet from the rear of the backplate to allow access to the adjuster wheel

not to damage the sender unit), or by using a brake hose clamp to clamp the flexible hose.

5 Clean the area around the union, then unscrew the brake hose union bolt and disconnect the hose from the caliper. Plug or tape over the end of the hose and the aperture in the caliper, to prevent dirt entering the hydraulic system. Discard the union sealing washers, as they must be renewed.

6 Unscrew the two caliper guide pin bolts, then carefully lift the caliper assembly off the brake pads **(see illustration)**. Note that the brake pads need not be disturbed, and can be left in position in the caliper mounting bracket.

Overhaul

7 With the caliper on the bench, wipe away all traces of dust and dirt.

> ⚠️ **Warning: Avoid inhaling the dust, as it is a health hazard.**

8 Withdraw the piston from the caliper body, and remove the dust seal. The piston can be withdrawn by hand or, if necessary, pushed out by applying compressed air to the union bolt hole. Only low pressure should be required such as is generated by a foot pump **(see illustration overleaf)**.

9 Using a small screwdriver, extract the piston seal, taking care not to damage the caliper bore.

10 Withdraw the guide pins from the caliper mounting bracket, and remove the guide pin gaiters.

11 Thoroughly clean all components, using only methylated spirit or clean hydraulic fluid as a cleaning medium. Never use mineral-based solvents such as petrol or paraffin, which will attack the hydraulic system's rubber components. Dry the components using compressed air or a clean, lint-free cloth. Use compressed air to blow clear the fluid passages.

12 Check all components and renew any that are worn or damaged. Check particularly the cylinder bore and piston; if these are scratched, worn or corroded in any way, renew the complete body assembly. Similarly, check the condition of the guide pins and their bores in the mounting bracket. Both guide pins should be undamaged and a reasonably

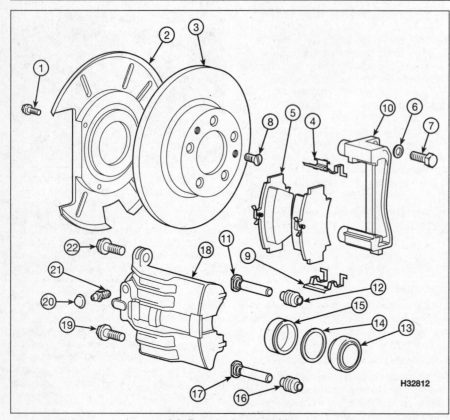

8.8 Front brake assembly

1 Backplate bolt
2 Backplate
3 Brake disc
4 Retaining spring
5 Brake pads
6 Washer
7 Bolt
8 Disc retaining screw
9 Retaining spring
10 Caliper bracket
11 Caliper guide pin
12 Dust cover
13 Piston dust cover
14 Piston seal
15 Piston
16 Dust cover
17 Caliper guide pin
18 Caliper
19 Guide pin bolt
20 Dust cap
21 Bleed screw
22 Guide pin bolt

H32812

tight sliding fit in the mounting bracket bores. If there is any doubt about the condition of any component, renew it.

13 If the assembly is fit for further use, obtain the appropriate repair kit. Components are available from Land Rover dealers.

14 Renew the rubber seals, dust covers and caps, and the copper sealing washers.

15 On reassembly, ensure that all components are absolutely clean and dry.

16 Dip the piston and new seal in clean hydraulic fluid. Smear clean fluid on the cylinder bore surface.

17 Fit the new seal using only the fingers to manipulate it into the cylinder bore groove. Fit the new dust seal to the piston and refit it to the cylinder bore using a twisting motion, ensuring that the piston enters squarely into the bore. Press the piston fully into the bore, then secure the dust seal to the caliper body.

18 Apply the grease supplied in the repair kit (do not use any other type of grease) to the guide pins, and fit the new gaiters. Fit the guide pins to the caliper mounting bracket, ensuring that the gaiters are correctly located

in the grooves on both the guide pin and mounting bracket.

Refitting

Overhauled caliper

19 Carefully slide the caliper into position over the brake pads. Refit the caliper guide pin bolts and tighten them to the specified torque setting.

20 Position a new copper sealing washer on each side of the hose union and refit the brake hose union bolt. Ensure that the brake hose union is correctly positioned between the lugs on the caliper, then tighten the union bolt to the specified torque setting.

21 Remove the brake hose clamp, where fitted, and bleed the hydraulic system (see Section 2). Providing the precautions described were taken to minimise brake fluid loss, it should only be necessary to bleed the relevant front brake. On completion, refit the roadwheel then lower the vehicle to the ground and tighten the roadwheel nuts to the specified torque.

Removed caliper

22 Where removed, refit the caliper mounting bracket, and tighten the bolts to the specified torque **(see illustration)**.

23 Again where removed, refit the brake pads as described in Section 4.

24 Carefully slide the caliper into position over the brake pads. Refit the caliper guide pin bolts and tighten them to the specified torque setting.

25 Check that the brake hose is secured in position by all of its clips.

26 Refit the roadwheel, then lower the vehicle to the ground and tighten the roadwheel nuts to the specified torque.

---

9 Master cylinder – removal, overhaul and refitting

Note: *Before starting work, refer to the warning at the beginning of Section 2 concerning the dangers of hydraulic fluid.*

Removal

1 Remove the master cylinder reservoir cap, and syphon the hydraulic fluid from the reservoir. **Note:** *Do not syphon the fluid by mouth, as it is poisonous; use a syringe or an old poultry baster.*

2 On petrol-engine models, unscrew the servo vacuum hose from the inlet manifold, then trace the hose back to the master cylinder, and unclip it from the reservoir.

3 Wipe clean the area around the brake pipe unions on the side of the master cylinder, and place absorbent rags beneath the pipe unions to catch any surplus fluid. Make a note of the correct fitted positions of the unions, then unscrew the union nuts and carefully withdraw the pipes **(see illustration)**. Wash off any spilt fluid immediately with cold water.

8.22 Refit the caliper mounting bracket, and tighten the bolts to the specified torque

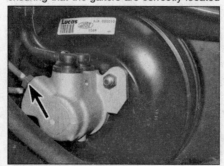

9.3 Unscrew the union nuts and carefully withdraw the pipes

HAYNES HiNT *Plug or tape over the pipe ends and master cylinder orifices to minimise the loss of brake fluid, and to prevent the entry of dirt into the system.*

4 Remove the nut and two bolts securing the master cylinder reservoir **(see illustration)**.

5 Slacken and remove the two nuts and washers securing the master cylinder to the vacuum servo unit. Withdraw the master cylinder assembly from the engine compartment. Recover the O-ring from the rear of the master cylinder.

Overhaul

6 At the time of writing, master cylinder overhaul was not possible, since spares were not available. If the cylinder is thought to be faulty, it must be renewed.

7 The only parts available individually are the fluid reservoir and its mounting seals.

Refitting

8 Inspect the master cylinder O-ring for signs of damage or deterioration and, if necessary, renew it.

9 Remove all traces of dirt from the master cylinder and servo unit mating surfaces, then fit the master cylinder, ensuring that the servo unit pushrod enters the master cylinder bore centrally. Refit the master cylinder washers and mounting nuts, and tighten them to the specified torque.

10 Wipe clean the brake pipe unions, then refit them to the master cylinder ports and tighten them to the specified torque setting.

11 Refill the master cylinder reservoir with new fluid.

12 Slowly depress the brake pedal to the floor, and then slowly release it – repeat this five times. Wait for 10 seconds, then repeat this process. As this is done, air bubbles will rise into the reservoir, effectively bleeding the master cylinder.

13 Repeat the operations described in paragraph 10 until resistance is felt at the brake pedal, then bleed the complete hydraulic system as described in Section 2.

10 Rear wheel cylinder –
removal, overhaul and refitting

Removal

1 Remove the brake shoes as described in Section 5.

2 Minimise fluid loss by removing the master cylinder reservoir cap and then tightening it down onto a piece of polythene to obtain an airtight seal (taking care not to damage the sender unit), or by using a brake hose clamp to clamp the flexible hose.

3 Wipe away all traces of dirt around the brake pipe union at the rear of the wheel cylinder, and unscrew the union nut. Carefully

9.4 Remove the nut and two bolts securing the master cylinder reservoir

ease the pipe out of the wheel cylinder and plug or tape over its end to prevent dirt entry **(see illustration)**.

4 Unscrew the two wheel cylinder retaining bolts from the rear of the backplate and remove the cylinder.

Overhaul

5 Remove the wheel cylinder from the vehicle and clean it thoroughly **(see illustration)**.

6 Mount the wheel cylinder in a soft-jawed vice, and remove the rubber protective caps. Extract the piston assemblies.

7 Thoroughly clean all components using only methylated spirit or clean hydraulic fluid as a cleaning medium.

Caution: Never use mineral-based solvents such as petrol or paraffin, which will attack the hydraulic system's rubber components. Dry the components immediately using compressed air or a clean, lint-free cloth.

8 Check all components and renew any that are worn or damaged. Check particularly the cylinder bore and pistons. The complete assembly must be renewed if these are scratched, worn or corroded. If there is any doubt about the condition of the assembly or of any of its components, renew it. Remove the bleed screw and check that the fluid entry port and bleed screw passages are clear.

9 If the assembly is fit for further use, obtain a repair kit (if available). Renew the rubber protective caps, dust caps and seals removed on dismantling; these should never be re-used. Renew also any other items included in the repair kit.

10 On reassembly, dip the pistons and the

10.3 Wipe away all traces of dirt around the brake pipe union at the rear of the wheel cylinder, and unscrew the union nut

new seals in clean hydraulic fluid. Smear clean fluid on the cylinder bore surface.

11 Fit the new seals to their pistons using only the fingers to manipulate them into the grooves. Ensure that all components are refitted in the correct order and the right way round.

12 Insert the pistons into the bore using a twisting motion to avoid trapping the seal lips. Apply a smear of rubber lubricant to each piston before fitting the new rubber protective caps.

Refitting

13 Clean the cylinder's location in the brake backplate, removing all dirt and corrosion.

14 Place the cylinder in position on the backplate, fit the wheel cylinder retaining bolts and tighten them to the specified torque.

15 Tighten the brake pipe union nut to the specified torque. Remove the clamp from the brake hose if fitted.

16 Refit the brake shoes as described in Section 5.

17 Bleed the hydraulic braking system (see Section 2). If precautions were taken to minimise fluid loss, it should only be necessary to bleed the relevant rear brake. On completion, check that both footbrake and handbrake function correctly before taking the vehicle on the road.

11 Brake pedal –
removal and refitting

Refer to the clutch pedal removal details given in Chapter 6.

12 Vacuum servo unit –
testing, removal and refitting

Testing

1 To test the operation of the servo unit, with the engine switched off, depress the footbrake several times to exhaust the vacuum. Keeping the pedal depressed, start the engine. As the engine starts, there should be a noticeable 'give' in the brake pedal as the vacuum builds-

10.5 Remove the wheel cylinder from the vehicle and clean it thoroughly

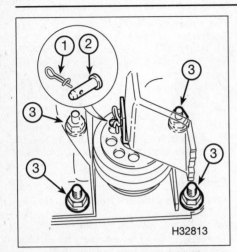

12.9 Brake servo removal details

1 Spring clip
2 Clevis pin
3 Servo mounting
   nuts

up. Allow the engine to run for at least two minutes, then switch it off. If the brake pedal is now depressed it should feel normal, but further applications should result in the pedal feeling firmer, with the pedal stroke decreasing with each application.

2 If the servo does not operate as described, first test the servo unit check valve as described in Section 13. On diesel models, any problems with servo operation could also be due to a fault with the vacuum pump – see Section 18.

3 If the servo unit still fails to operate satisfactorily, the fault lies within the unit itself. Repairs to the unit are not possible, and if faulty, the servo unit must be renewed.

Removal

4 On models with the TD4 diesel engine, remove the air cleaner cover, as described in Chapter 1B.

5 Remove the master cylinder as described in Section 9.

6 Prise out the vacuum hose from the rubber grommet on the front of the servo, then remove and discard the grommet – a new one should be fitted on reassembly.

7 Release the brake pipes from their clips on the bulkhead, as necessary for access.

8 From inside the vehicle, release the

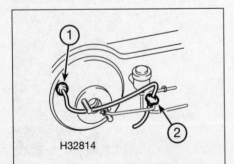

13.2 Servo pipe grommet (1) and check valve (2)

fasteners and release the driver's side lower facia panel.

9 Slide out the spring clip, and withdraw the clevis pin securing the pedal to the servo unit pushrod **(see illustration)**.

10 Undo the four retaining nuts securing the servo unit.

11 Return to the engine compartment, and lift the servo unit out of position. Recover the spacer which is fitted between the servo unit and bulkhead.

Refitting

12 Apply a smear of grease to the pushrod fork, then refit the spacer to the rear of the servo unit, and manoeuvre the assembly into position.

13 From inside the vehicle, ensure that the servo unit pushrod is correctly engaged with the brake pedal. Refit the mounting nuts, and tighten them to the specified torque setting.

14 Refit the servo unit pushrod-to-brake pedal clevis pin, and secure it in position with the spring clip.

15 Return to the engine compartment, and reconnect the vacuum hose to the servo unit.

16 Refit the master cylinder as described in Section 9.

17 On models with the TD4 diesel engine, refit the air cleaner cover, as described in Chapter 1B.

18 On completion, re-test the servo operation, as described at the start of this Section.

13 Vacuum servo unit check valve – removal, testing and refitting

Removal

1 Unscrew the vacuum hose from the inlet manifold (petrol models) or release the clip and pull it from the connection on the vacuum pump (diesel models).

2 Trace the hose back to the brake servo itself. On petrol models, unclip the hose from the brake fluid reservoir. Carefully prise the end fitting out of its rubber grommet on the brake servo, and remove the hose complete **(see illustration)**.

Testing

3 The valve may be tested by blowing through the hose in both directions, air should flow through the valve in one direction only – when blown through from the servo unit end of the valve. If this is not the case, renew the hose – the valve does not appear to be available separately.

4 Examine the servo's rubber sealing grommet for signs of damage or deterioration – a new one should be fitted as a matter of course.

Refitting

5 Fit the new sealing grommet into position in the servo unit.

6 Carefully ease the hose into position, taking great care not to displace or damage

the grommet. On petrol models, clip the hose back onto the brake fluid reservoir.

7 Reconnect the other end of the hose to the inlet manifold or vacuum pump, as applicable.

8 On completion, start the engine, and check the connections for signs of air leaks. Retest the servo operation as described in Section 12.

14 Handbrake – check and adjustment

1 Handbrake adjustment is normally only necessary at the first major service, according to Land Rover. After that, it is only necessary to adjust the handbrake after renewing or dismantling the rear brake shoes, or renewing the drum.

2 Depress the brake pedal firmly at least 30 times to set the self-adjusting rear brake shoe mechanism. The brake pedal must be released fully each time, to ensure a correct setting.

3 Apply the handbrake fully, counting the number of clicks from the ratchet. The handbrake should be fully applied after a minimum of four, and a maximum of seven, clicks, using normal effort. If adjustment is required, proceed as follows.

4 On pre-2001 model year vehicles, remove the rear section of the centre console, as described in Chapter 11.

5 On 2001 model year vehicles onwards, unclip the ashtray from the rear console, then disconnect the power socket wiring plug and remove the ashtray completely, to gain access to the handbrake adjusting nut.

6 Apply the handbrake lever and check that the equaliser and cables move freely and smoothly **(see illustration)**, then set the lever on the first notch of the ratchet mechanism.

7 Chock the front wheels, then jack up the rear of the vehicle and support on axle stands (see Jacking and vehicle support).

8 With the lever on its first notch, turn the handbrake lever adjusting nut clockwise until the rear wheels are just dragging slightly **(see illustration)**.

9 Fully release the handbrake lever, and check that the wheels rotate freely.

10 Now confirm the adjustment by applying the handbrake lever one notch at a time until

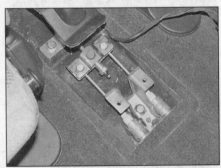

14.6 View of the handbrake cables and equaliser – centre console removed

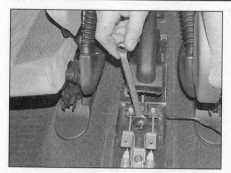

14.8 Adjusting the handbrake

both rear wheels are locked. The rear wheels must be locked with the lever applied between four and five notches.

11 Lower the vehicle to the ground, and recheck the adjustment.

15 Handbrake cables –
removal and refitting

Removal

1 The handbrake cable consists of two sections (right- and left-hand), which are linked to the lever assembly by an equaliser plate. Each section can be removed individually.

2 Chock the front wheels, then jack up the rear of the vehicle and support on axle stands (see *Jacking and vehicle support*). Remove both rear wheels.

3 On models without electric rear windows, remove the rear section of the centre console, as described in Chapter 11.

4 On models with electric rear windows, unclip the ashtray from the rear console, then disconnect the power socket wiring plug and remove the ashtray completely, to gain access to the handbrake adjusting nut.

5 Unscrew and remove the handbrake cable adjusting nut from the rear of the lever **(see illustration 14.8)**.

6 Undo the two bolts securing the outer cable retaining plate to the floorpan **(see illustration)**. Remove the retaining plate then detach the equaliser plate from the adjusting rod.

7 Detach the relevant inner cable from the equaliser plate.

8 Working under the vehicle, remove the two bolts securing the handbrake cable clips to the underside; also release the cable from the push-in clip between the bolted-on clips **(see illustration)**.

9 Prise the cable grommet from the floorpan, and withdraw the front section of cable through it, under the vehicle.

10 Remove the rear brake shoes as described in Section 5.

11 The cable is secured to the brake backplate by an expanding fastener which is pushed through from the inboard side of the backplate. Use pliers to compress this

fastener, while pulling on the cable from the inboard side of the backplate. Remove the cable from the vehicle **(see illustration)**.

Refitting

12 Refitting is a reversal of the removal procedure noting the following:
- a) *Lubricate all exposed linkages and cable pivots with a good-quality multi-purpose grease.*
- b) *Ensure the cable outer grommet is correctly located in the floorpan and that all retaining bolts are tightened to the specified torque.*
- c) *Refit the rear brake shoes as described in Section 5.*
- d) *Adjust the handbrake cable as described in Section 14.*

16 Handbrake lever –
removal and refitting

Removal

1 Remove the rear section of the centre console as described in Chapter 11.

2 Disconnect the wiring connector from the handbrake warning light switch. Note that the switch is clipped around the lever's front mounting bolt.

3 Slacken and remove the cable adjusting nut at the equaliser quadrant behind the handbrake lever **(see illustration 14.8)**.

15.6 Undo the two bolts securing the outer cable retaining plate to the floorpan (arrowed)

15.11 Compress the fastener while pulling on the cable from the inboard side of the backplate

4 Undo the two mounting bolts, then free the adjusting rod from the equaliser, and lift the lever assembly out of the vehicle. Recover the spring from the adjusting rod **(see illustration)**.

Refitting

5 Refit the handbrake lever assembly, making sure the spring is refitted to the adjusting rod, and that the rod is fed through the equaliser correctly.

6 Refit the handbrake lever mounting bolts, and tighten them to the specified torque.

7 Refit the cable adjustment nut, and tighten it to take up the slack.

8 Reconnect the wiring connector to the handbrake warning light switch.

9 Adjust the handbrake cable as described in Section 14, then refit the centre console as described in Chapter 11.

17 Braking system switches
– removal and refitting

Stop-light switch

1 The stop-light switch is located on the pedal bracket behind the facia. To remove the switch, first disconnect the battery negative lead.

2 Disconnect the wiring connector plugs from the stop-light switch. On models with cruise control, the stop-light switch is the

15.8 Working under the car, remove the bolt securing the handbrake cable clip to the underside

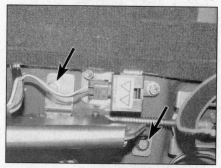

16.4 Undo the two handbrake lever mounting bolts (arrowed)

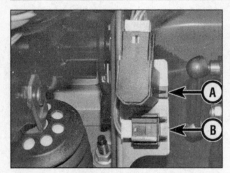

17.2 Stop-light switch (A) and brake pedal position switch (B)

17.3 Twist the switch body clockwise slightly to disengage its bayonet fitting

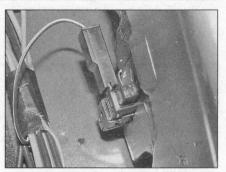

17.11 Disconnect the wiring connector from the handbrake warning light switch

upper-mounted of the two switches **(see illustration)**.

3 Twist the switch body clockwise slightly, to disengage its bayonet fitting, and remove it from the pedal bracket **(see illustration)**.

4 Refitting is a reversal of removal, but adjust the switch as follows. With the switch refitted in the pedal bracket, depress and hold the brake pedal, then pull out the switch plunger to its full extent. Release the pedal, and the switch plunger will automatically be set to the correct position. Test the operation of the switch on completion.

Brake pedal position switch

5 The brake pedal position switch is fitted to models with cruise control, and is located on the pedal bracket behind the facia **(see illustration 17.2)**.

6 To remove the switch, first disconnect the battery negative lead.

7 Disconnect the wiring connector plug from the position switch. Carefully prise the switch body from the pedal bracket, and remove it.

8 Refitting is a reversal of removal, but adjust the switch as follows. With the switch refitted, hold the brake pedal depressed, and push the switch plunger fully into the pedal bracket. Release the pedal slowly to set the switch position.

9 Refit the brake light switch as described previously in this Section.

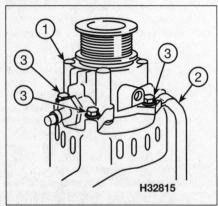

18.3 Vacuum pump details – L-Series diesel engine

1 Vacuum pump
2 Oil return hose
3 Mounting bolts (three of four shown)

Handbrake warning light switch

10 Remove the rear section of the centre console as described in Chapter 11.

11 Disconnect the wiring connector from the handbrake warning light switch **(see illustration)**.

12 The switch is clipped around the handbrake lever's front mounting bolt – either remove the bolt, or twist the switch to work it off.

13 Refitting is a reversal of removal. If the handbrake lever mounting bolt was removed, tighten it to the specified torque. Test the operation of the switch on completion.

---

18 Vacuum pump (diesel models) – removal and refitting

L-Series engine

Removal

1 The brake vacuum pump is located on the rear of the alternator. First remove the alternator as described in Chapter 5A.

2 With the alternator on the bench, release the clip and disconnect the oil return hose from the vacuum pump. If the pump is likely to be refitted at a later date, plug or cap off the oil and vacuum connections, to prevent dirt entry.

3 Unscrew the four mounting bolts, and withdraw the vacuum pump from the alternator **(see illustration)**.

18.11 Release the retaining clip and disconnect the vacuum hose from the pump

Refitting

4 Wipe clean the mating faces of the alternator and vacuum pump.

5 Locate the pump on the alternator, then insert the mounting bolts and tighten to the specified torque.

6 Fit the oil return hose pipe and secure with the clip.

7 Refit the alternator with reference to Chapter 5A. Test the operation of the servo as described in Section 12.

TD4 engine (manual gearbox)

Removal

8 The vacuum pump is driven from the end of the exhaust camshaft, and is mounted on the left-hand side of the engine. Disconnect the battery negative terminal, and move the lead away from the terminal.

9 Refer to Chapter 1B and remove the air cleaner cover.

10 Release the retaining clips as necessary, and move the injector wiring harness clear of the vacuum pump.

11 Release the retaining clip and disconnect the vacuum hose from the pump **(see illustration)**.

12 Unscrew the two mounting bolts, then remove and discard them – new bolts should be obtained for refitting.

13 Withdraw the pump from the engine, noting how its drivegear engages with the end of the camshaft. Recover the O-ring seal, and discard it – a new one should be used when refitting **(see illustration)**.

18.13 Recover the O-ring seal and discard it – a new one should be used when refitting

Refitting

14 Clean the mating faces of the vacuum pump and engine, then fit a new O-ring to the vacuum pump.

15 Offer the pump into position, rotating the drivegear as necessary to align with the end of the camshaft **(see illustration)**.

16 Insert the two new mounting bolts, and tighten them to the specified torque.

17 Reconnect the vacuum hose to the pump, securing with the clip.

18 Refit the air cleaner element as described in Chapter 1B, then reconnect the battery. Test the operation of the servo as described in Section 12.

TD4 engine (automatic transmission)

Removal

19 The vacuum pump is driven from the end of the exhaust camshaft, and is mounted on the left-hand side of the engine. Disconnect the battery negative terminal, and move the lead away from the terminal.

20 Remove the camshaft cover as described in Chapter 2C.

21 Using the information in Chapter 4C, remove the EGR cooler. The cooler pipes need not be disconnected, just unbolt the cooler and move it to one side for access to the vacuum pump.

22 Unscrew the two pump mounting bolts, then remove and discard them – new bolts should be obtained for refitting.

23 Withdraw the pump from the engine, noting how its drivegear engages with the end of the camshaft. Recover the O-ring seal, and discard it – a new one should be used when refitting **(see illustration 18.13)**.

Refitting

24 Clean the mating faces of the vacuum pump and engine, then fit a new O-ring to the vacuum pump.

25 Offer the pump into position, rotating the drivegear as necessary to align with the end of the camshaft **(see illustration 18.15)**.

26 Insert the two new mounting bolts, and tighten them to the specified torque.

27 Refit the EGR cooler as described in Chapter 4C, and the camshaft cover as described in Chapter 2C. Reconnect the battery on completion. Test the operation of the servo as described in Section 12.

19 Anti-lock braking system (ABS) – general information

ABS was fitted as standard to most models, and was available as an option on lesser models in the range. It was a popular option to take up, since the ABS is used to provide other valuable features, such as traction control and the Freelander's unique selling point, its Hill Descent Control, or HDC. The system is a full-time four-channel type,

18.15 Note how the vacuum pump drive engages with the camshaft

offering individual speed control at each of the four wheels. In addition to the components of the non-ABS system, models with ABS have an ABS modulator (which contains the hydraulic solenoid valves and accumulators, and the electrically-driven return pump), four roadwheel sensors and an ABS electronic control unit (ECU).

The purpose of the system is to detect and counter any unacceptable acceleration or deceleration in any of the four wheels, relative to the vehicle speed, and to the wheel speeds of any of the other three wheels. In braking mode, the system will prevent wheel(s) locking-up, while in traction control mode, the system prevents wheelspin. Control of either situation is achieved by automatic release of the brake on the relevant wheel, followed by reapplication of the brake, or *vice-versa*.

Control of each wheel's speed is achieved through the modulator's solenoid valves, which switch the supply of brake fluid to each wheel's brake on and off. The modulator is controlled by the ABS ECU, which itself receives signals from the four wheel sensors (one fitted on each hub), which monitor the speed of rotation of each wheel. By comparing these speed signals from the four wheels, the ECU can determine the speed at which the vehicle is travelling. It can then use this speed to determine when a wheel is accelerating or decelerating at an abnormal rate compared to the speed of the vehicle, and therefore predicts when a wheel is about to spin or lock.

The operation of the ABS is entirely dependent on electrical signals. To prevent the system responding to any inaccurate signals, a built-in safety circuit monitors all signals received by the ECU. The first time the vehicle exceeds 5 mph after the ignition has been switched on, the ECU tests the readings from each wheel sensor, and the operation of the modulator solenoid valves. If a fault is present, some or all of the ABS functions will be disabled, and the warning light on the instrument panel is illuminated to inform the driver of an ABS fault.

If a fault does develop in the ABS, normal braking will still be available, but the vehicle must be taken to a Land Rover dealer or competent specialist as soon as possible for fault diagnosis and repair.

Anti-lock braking

During normal operation, the solenoid valves in the modulator are closed, and the governor valves are in the at-rest position. The system then functions in the same way as a non-ABS braking system does.

If the ECU senses that a wheel is about to lock, the ABS operates the relevant solenoid valve in the modulator assembly, which then isolates the brake caliper on the wheel which is about to lock from the master cylinder, effectively sealing-in the hydraulic pressure.

If the speed of rotation of the wheel continues to decrease at an abnormal rate, the electrically-driven return pump operates, and pumps the hydraulic fluid back into the master cylinder, releasing pressure on the brake caliper so that the brake is released. Once the speed of rotation of the wheel returns to an acceptable rate, the pump stops and the solenoid valve opens, allowing the hydraulic master cylinder pressure to return to the caliper, which then reapplies the brake. This cycle can be carried out at many times a second.

The action of the solenoid valves and return pump creates pulses in the hydraulic circuit. When the ABS is functioning, these pulses can be felt through the brake pedal.

ABS will not necessarily reduce braking distances under all conditions – the primary aim of the system is to help the driver retain steering control in emergency braking situations.

Electronic Brake Force Distribution

When the ABS is in operation, the brakes are operated in axle pairs, and the braking force is distributed between the front and rear axles as necessary, to maintain the stability of the vehicle. Distribution of the braking effort is dependent on direction of travel and the amount of braking effort being applied.

Electronic Traction Control

In addition to detecting when a wheel is locking under braking, the system also detects a wheel that is spinning under acceleration. When this condition is detected, the brake on that wheel is momentarily applied to reduce, or eliminate the wheelspin. When the rotational speed of the spinning wheel is detected to be equal to the other wheels, the brake is released. The ETC system is automatically enabled at speeds up to 31 mph, provided the brakes are off. If the brakes are pressed while the ETC is active, the system will revert to ABS mode.

Hill Descent Control

The Hill Descent Control is a very specialised system, intended for use when descending slippery slopes off-road. Normal practice here is to select first or reverse gear, and to allow the vehicle to descend the slope using only engine braking – touching the brake pedal would result in locked wheels and no steering

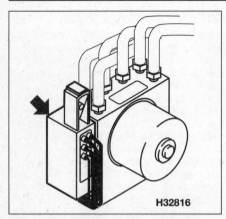

20.9 Slide up the catch and disconnect the multiplug from the modulator

control. The HDC uses intermittent application of the brakes to limit descent speeds further, while retaining steering control. When HDC is selected (using the gear lever switch), the descent speed can be controlled by the throttle alone – if the throttle is not pressed, the HDC will select its minimum target speed, which is just a few mph. If a fault occurs with

the HDC, or the clutch pedal is pressed, or the brakes overheat through prolonged use, the system will 'fade out' gradually, indicated by the HDC warning light flashing.

The system only operates in 1st or reverse gear. Manual gearbox models have a special 1st gear sensor fitted to the gearbox casing, while on automatic models selector position 1 is sensed by the transmission ECU – reverse gear is sensed on all models through the reversing light switch.

20 Anti lock braking system (ABS) components – removal and refitting

Modulator assembly

Note: *Before starting work, refer to the warning at the beginning of Section 2 concerning the dangers of hydraulic fluid.*

Removal – up to 2001 model year

1 Disconnect the battery negative terminal.
2 Remove the right-hand headlight unit as described in Chapter 12.

HAYNES HINT *Place a piece of polythene over the master cylinder filler neck, and securely refit the cap. This will minimise brake fluid loss during subsequent operations. As a precaution, place absorbent rags beneath the modulator brake pipe unions.*

3 Disconnect the three wiring connectors from the ABS modulator assembly.
4 Wipe clean the area around the modulator brake pipe unions, then make a note of how the pipes are arranged, to use as a reference on refitting. Unscrew the union nuts, and carefully withdraw the pipes – there are eight in all to disconnect. Plug or tape over the pipe ends and modulator orifices, to minimise the loss of brake fluid and to prevent the entry of dirt into the system. Wash off any spilt fluid immediately with cold water.
5 Working under the right-hand front wheel arch (jack up and remove the front wheel to improve access), trace the brake hose up from the caliper, and disconnect the brake pipe union where it joins the hose.
6 Slacken and remove the three mounting nuts, and release the modulator assembly from its mounting bracket. If a new modulator is being fitted, unscrew the modulator rubber mounting bushes, and remove them for transfer to the new modulator. **Note:** *Do not attempt to dismantle the modulator block hydraulic assembly; overhaul of the unit is not possible.*

Removal – 2001 model year onwards

7 On TD4 models, remove the engine acoustic cover as described in Chapter 2C. Release and remove the air intake duct, then loosen two clips and remove the intercooler outlet hose (see Chapter 4B).
8 Remove the two bolts securing the power steering fluid cooler pipes, then release the power steering fluid reservoir from its mounting bracket and move it to one side – try to keep it as upright as possible, to avoid fluid spillage.
9 The modulator is mounted in the right-hand front corner of the engine compartment. Release the catch by sliding it upwards, and disconnect the main multiplug from the modulator **(see illustration)**.

HAYNES HINT *Place a piece of polythene over the master cylinder filler neck, and securely refit the cap. This will minimise brake fluid loss during subsequent operations. As a precaution, place absorbent rags beneath the modulator brake pipe unions.*

10 Wipe clean the area around the modulator brake pipe unions, then make a note of how the pipes are arranged, to use as a reference on refitting. Unscrew the union nuts, and carefully withdraw the pipes – there are six

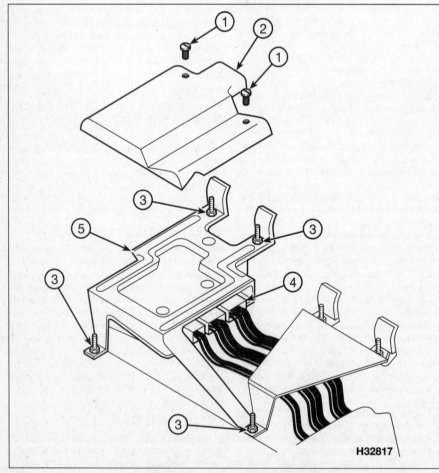

20.14 ABS ECU – vehicles up to 2001 model year

1 Torx screws	*3 Nuts*	*5 Support bracket*
2 ECU cover	*4 Wiring plugs*	

20.23 ABS sensor harness

20.24a Prise out the sensor . . .

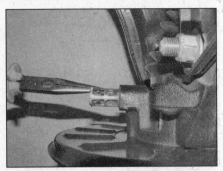

20.24b . . . and recover the bush

to disconnect. Plug or tape over the pipe ends and modulator orifices, to minimise the loss of brake fluid and to prevent the entry of dirt into the system. Wash off any spilt fluid immediately with cold water.

11 Slacken and remove the three mounting bolts, and release the modulator assembly from its mounting bracket. **Note:** *Do not attempt to dismantle the modulator block hydraulic assembly; overhaul of the unit is not possible.*

Refitting

12 Refitting is the reverse of the removal procedure, noting the following points:

a) *Examine the rubber mounting bushes for signs of wear or damage, and renew if necessary.*

b) *Refit the brake pipes to their respective unions, and tighten the union nuts to the specified torque.*

c) *Ensure that the wiring is correctly routed, and that the connectors are firmly pressed into position.*

d) *On completion, prior to refitting the battery, bleed the complete braking system as described in Section 2.*

e) *If a new modulator has been fitted, Land Rover state that the system must be tested using their Testbook diagnostic equipment, to ensure that the system is functioning correctly.*

Electronic control unit (ECU)

Removal

13 On vehicles up to 2001 model year, the ABS electronic control unit (ECU) is mounted on a bracket below the right-hand front seat, under a protective cover. Prior to removing the ECU, disconnect the battery negative terminal. On vehicles from 2001 model year, the ECU is integral with the modulator – check with your Land Rover dealer or specialist for parts availability.

14 Slide the right-hand front seat fully rearwards for access to the ECU. Remove the two Torx screws securing the ECU cover, and remove the cover **(see illustration opposite).**

15 Unscrew and remove the two nuts at the front of the ECU bracket, then slide the seat fully forwards and remove the remaining two nuts at the rear of the bracket.

16 Disconnect the three ECU wiring plugs,

and remove the ECU and its bracket from under the seat.

17 The ECU is secured to the bracket by three Torx screws.

Refitting

18 Refitting is a reversal of removal. If a new ECU has been fitted, Land Rover state that the system must be tested using their Testbook diagnostic equipment, to ensure that the system is functioning correctly.

Front wheel sensor

Note: *A new sensor mounting bush and seal will be required on refitting.*

Removal

19 The front wheel sensors are mounted on the front of the hubs. Prior to removal, disconnect the battery negative terminal. If working on the left-hand sensor, the battery and battery tray must be removed – see Chapter 5A.

20 Firmly apply the handbrake, then loosen the relevant front roadwheel nuts. Jack up the front of the vehicle and support on axle stands. Remove the appropriate front roadwheel.

21 Remove the front wheel arch liner, which is held to the wing by five screws at the rear edge, and a total of eight 'scrivets' inside.

22 Under the bonnet, trace the wheel sensor wiring back to its wiring connector on the inner wing, and release it from its retaining clip. Disconnect the connector, then release the wiring grommet from the inner wing and feed the wiring through into the wheel arch.

23 Under the wheel arch, the sensor wiring is held by two grommets (one on the wing, one on the strut), and by two clips to the brake hose **(see illustration).**

24 The sensor itself is a push-fit into the hub (this is why it's essential to buy a new mounting bush when removing the sensor). Prise out the sensor, and recover the bush **(see illustrations).**

Refitting

25 Refitting is a reversal of removal, noting the following points:

a) *Clean the sensor and hub mating surfaces thoroughly.*

b) *Always fit a new mounting bush into the hub.*

c) *Apply a little grease to the sensor, and ensure that it's fully seated in the*

mounting bush. In this position, the sensor will be touching the sensor ring. The sensor will then be pushed back by the ring, to set the correct air gap the first time the vehicle is driven.

d) *Ensure that the sensor wiring is securely clipped in place, routed as before, and that the inner wing grommet is correctly located.*

e) *If a new sensor has been fitted, Land Rover state that the system must be tested using their Testbook diagnostic equipment, to ensure that the system is functioning correctly.*

Rear wheel sensor

Note: *A new sensor mounting bush and seal will be required on refitting.*

Removal

26 The rear wheel sensors are mounted onto the rear of the hub assemblies, inboard of the rear brake backplates. Prior to removal, disconnect the battery negative terminal.

27 Chock the front wheels and loosen the relevant rear wheel nuts, then jack up the rear of the vehicle and support it on axle stands. Take off the rear wheel.

28 Trace the wiring back from the sensor to its wiring connector. Free the connector from its retaining clip, disconnect it from the main wiring loom, then work back along the sensor wiring and free it from any relevant retaining clips. The wiring has three grommets along its length, pushed into mounting points on the brake hose end fitting and suspension strut – there's a further clip securing the wiring to the brake hose **(see illustration).**

20.28 Release the ABS sensor harness grommets

20.29 Recover the ABS sensor bush

20.31 The wheel speed sensor toothed rings are an integral part of the constant velocity (CV) joints, and cannot be renewed separately

29 Where applicable, remove the sensor securing bolt. The sensor itself is a push-fit into the hub (this is why it's essential to buy a new mounting bush when removing the sensor). Prise out the sensor, and recover the bush **(see illustration)**.

Refitting

30 Refitting is a reversal of removal, noting the following points:

  a) *Clean the sensor and hub mating surfaces thoroughly.*

  b) *Always fit a new mounting bush into the hub.*

  c) *Apply a little grease to the sensor, and ensure that it's fully seated in the mounting bush. In this position, the sensor will be touching the sensor ring. The sensor will then be pushed back by the ring, to set the correct air gap the first time the vehicle is driven.*

  d) *Refit and tighten the sensor securing bolt, where applicable.*

  e) *Ensure that the sensor wiring is securely clipped in place.*

  f) *If a new sensor has been fitted, Land Rover state that the system must be tested using their Testbook diagnostic equipment, to ensure that the system is functioning correctly.*

Wheel sensor toothed rings

31 The toothed rings are an integral part of the constant velocity (CV) joints, and cannot be renewed separately. If renewal is necessary, the complete constant velocity joint must be renewed as described in Chapter 8 **(see illustration)**.

Relays

32 Only two relays are associated with the ABS – the modulator return pump relay, and the brake light relay. See Chapter 12.

Hill Descent Control switch

Manual gearbox models

33 Unscrew and remove the gear lever knob, then carefully unclip the top of the gear lever gaiter from its locating groove, and slide it down for access to the switch.

34 Disconnect the switch multi-plug, then remove the mounting bolt which secures the switch assembly to the gear lever, and lift it off the gear lever **(see illustrations)**.

35 If required, the microswitch at the base of the assembly can be unclipped – make sure, however, that a new part is available separately before dismantling.

36 Refitting is a reversal of removal. It is important that the gear lever knob is not overtightened – the profile of the trigger should remain flush with the HDC switch, to ensure that the trigger is not overloaded unnecessarily.

Automatic transmission models

37 Remove the front section of the centre console, as described in Chapter 11.

38 The HDC switch is pressed out from inside to remove it. Prising it out is not recommended, as it carries a high risk of damage to the switch.

39 Refitting is a reversal of the removal procedure.

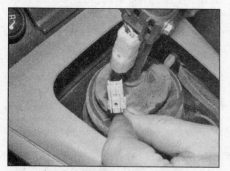

20.34a Disconnect the switch multi-plug . . .

20.34b . . . then remove the mounting bolt which secures the switch assembly . . .

20.34c . . . and lift it off the gear lever

Chapter 10
Suspension and steering

Contents

Degrees of difficulty

Easy, suitable for novice with little experience	Fairly easy, suitable for beginner with some experience	Fairly difficult, suitable for competent DIY mechanic	Difficult, suitable for experienced DIY mechanic	Very difficult, suitable for expert DIY or professional

Specifications

Front suspension

Type . . . . Independent MacPherson strut, coil springs, lower suspension arms
mounted to front subframe, anti-roll bar
Spring free length . . . . 359 to 375 mm, depending on model

Rear suspension

Type . . . . Independent MacPherson strut, coil springs, trapezoidal suspension
links mounted to rear subframe
Spring free length . . . . 350 mm

Steering

Type . . . . Rack-and-pinion, power-assisted

Front wheel alignment and steering angles

Note: *All measurements should be taken with the vehicle unladen*

Camber angle (negative)...	-0° 15' ± 0° 45' (-0.25° ± 0.75°)
5 1/2 J x 15 wheel	1.710 mm ± 5.11 mm
6 J x 16 wheel...	1.811 mm ± 5.323 mm
Castor angle..	3° 25' ± 1° (3.42° ± 1.0°)
5 1/2 J x 15 wheel	21.322 mm ± 6.71 mm
6 J x 16 wheel...	24.872 mm ± 7.11 mm
Kingpin inclination	12° 18' (12.3°)
5 1/2 J x 15 wheel	83.05 mm
6 J x 16 wheel...	88.61 mm
Front wheel alignment – total toe-out	-0°14' ± 0°14'
5 1/2 J x 15 wheel	-0.57 mm to -4.13 mm
6 J x 16 wheel...	-0.61 mm to -4.46 mm
17 inch wheel	-0.65 mm to -4.73 mm

Rear wheel alignment

Note: *All measurements should be taken with the vehicle unladen*

Camber angle (negative)...	-0° 30' ± 0° 45' (-0.5° ± 0.75°)
5 1/2 J x 15 wheel	3.314 mm ± 1.710 mm
6 J x 16 wheel...	3.551 mm ± 1.811 mm
Thrust angle	0° 0' ± 0° 6' (0° ± 0.10°)
5 1/2 J x 15 wheel	0 mm ± 0.601 mm
6 J x 16 wheel...	0 mm ± 0.611 mm
Rear wheel alignment – total toe-in	0° 20' ± to 0° 15'
5 1/2 J x 15 wheel	0.57 mm to 4.13 mm
6 J x 16 wheel...	0.61 mm to 4.46 mm
17 inch wheel	0.65 mm to 4.73 mm

Roadwheels

Type	Pressed-steel or aluminium alloy, 5 1/2 J x 15 or 6 J x 16 (depending on model)

Tyres

Size...	195/80 R 15 or 215/65 R 16 (depending on model)
Pressures	See end of *Weekly checks*

Torque wrench settings

	Nm	lbf ft
Front suspension		
Anti-roll bar clamp bolts...	23	17
Anti-roll bar drop link balljoint nuts*..............................	45	33
Driveshaft nut*...	400	295
Engine lower tie-bar bolts	100	74
Front subframe-to-body front bolts*.................................	190	140
Lower arm front pivot bolt**.......................................	190	140
Lower arm rear bush housing bolts to body**........................	105	77
Lower arm-to-rear bush housing nut**...............................	140	103
Lower balljoint nut*...	65	48
Roadwheel nuts	115	85
Strut inner locknut*...	57	42
Strut-to-body upper mounting nuts..................................	45	33
Strut-to-hub nuts/bolts..	205	151
Rear suspension		
Adjustable link locknuts	90	66
Brake backplate-to-hub bolts	45	33
Brake pipe unions	14	10
Driveshaft nut*...	400	295
Final drive mounting-to-subframe bolt...............................	120	89
Final drive-to-mounting bolts.......................................	65	48
Rear propeller shaft to rear axle flange	65	48
Rear subframe-to-body bolts..	190	140
Roadwheel nuts	115	85
Strut inner locknut*...	57	42
Strut-to-body upper mounting nuts..................................	45	33
Strut-to-hub nuts/bolts**..	205	151
Trailing link to wheel hub*...	120	89
Transverse links to wheel hub/subframe**:		
Stage 1..	35	26
Stage 2..	Angle-tighten a further 360°	

Torque wrench settings (continued)

	Nm	lbf ft
Steering		
Fluid outlet hose high-pressure unions	25	18
PAS pump mounting bolts:		
M6 bolts	10	7
M8 bolts	25	18
PAS pump mounting-to-block bolts.	45	33
PAS pump pulley bolts.	10	7
Roadwheel nuts	115	85
Steering column bracket side support bolt	10	7
Steering column height adjuster clamp bolt	12	9
Steering column-to-facia support Nyloc nuts*	14	10
Steering column-to-steering rack pinion pinch-bolt**	32	24
Steering rack feed pipe union nuts:		
Small (6 mm).	18	13
Large (10 mm).	24	18
Steering rack mounting bolts*	45	33
Steering wheel nut*	45	33
Track rod adjuster sleeve locknuts.	90	66
Track rod end balljoint nut*	55	41
Track rod end balljoint pinch-bolt.	28	21
Track rod-to-rack bolts*	100	74

* Use new nut/bolt
** Tighten when vehicle is resting on its wheels

1 General information

Unlike previous Land Rovers, the Freelander has fully-independent front and rear suspension, by conventional coil springs and MacPherson struts, bolted to the wheel hubs. Subframes are fitted front and rear, to provide mounting points for the suspension components.

At the front, the hubs are attached to pressed-steel lower arms, which pivot on bushes mounted to the subframe; the bushes are designed to deform progressively under load, to reduce any unwanted suspension 'steering' effects. An anti-roll bar is fitted, attached directly to the front subframe, with the bar ends attached to the struts by balljointed drop links.

At the rear, the hubs are connected to the subframe and underbody via three link arms – two transverse, one trailing – known as 'trapezoidal' links. The rear of the two transverse links has a threaded section at each end, to provide adjustment of the rear wheel toe setting. The non-adjustable front link is slightly shorter than the adjustable link, and features a specially-designed softer inboard bush, which promotes rear wheel toe-in under hard cornering, to improve handling response. The trailing link further controls rear suspension movement, and provides another fixed attachment point from the hub to the underside of the vehicle.

The steering system comprises an impact-absorbing telescopic steering column, power-assisted steering rack and engine-

driven fluid pump, with a fluid reservoir, fluid cooler, and connecting pipes and hoses. The adjustable steering column has upper mountings which are designed to detach or deform in the event of a collision, allowing the column to collapse and reduce the risk of injuring the driver. The upper section of the column is splined to accept the steering wheel; the intermediate shaft is joined to the lower shaft by a universal joint, and a further universal joint at the base of the column joins to the splined adaptor which attaches the column to the rack pinion.

The steering rack, which is mounted on the engine compartment bulkhead, is unusual in having both track rods mounted centrally on the rack – the long track rods and optimised steering geometry reduce the incidence of 'bump steer', which is especially useful off-road.

Power-assisted steering is standard on all models. The hydraulic steering system is powered by a vane-type pump, which is belt-driven off the crankshaft pulley; a self-adjusting tensioner maintains the correct belt tension. Rotary movement of the steering wheel is transferred via the steering column to the valve unit mounted on the steering rack; depending on direction of rotation, fluid pressure is applied to one side of the valve or the other, to boost the turning force applied to the pinion, which in turn moves the rack left or right.

Note: *Many of the suspension and steering components are secured in position with self-locking 'Nyloc' nuts, recognisable by having a plastic thread insert (often coloured blue). Whenever a self-locking nut is disturbed, it must be discarded and a new nut fitted.*

2 Front suspension strut –
removal, overhaul and refitting

Removal

1 Remove the front brake caliper (and, where applicable, the ABS wheel sensor) on the side concerned, as described in Chapter 9.
2 Loosen fully, but do not remove, the nut which secures the steering track rod to the arm at the top of the strut body. Using a balljoint splitter, separate the tapered joint from the arm, then unscrew the nut completely.
3 Remove the top nut from the anti-roll bar drop link, using a spanner or an Allen key to stop the link rotating. Separate the link from the strut, and move it to one side **(see illustration)**.
4 Loosen and remove the two nuts and bolts securing the lower end of the strut to the hub

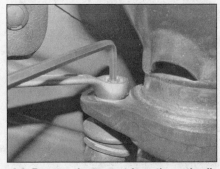

2.3 Remove the top nut from the anti-roll bar drop link, using an Allen key to stop the link rotating

2.4 Undo the two nuts and bolts securing the lower end of the strut to the hub

2.7 Loosen the suspension strut upper mounting nuts

2.8 Fit the spring compressors to the coils of the spring

(note which way round the bolts are fitted – bolt head to the front of the vehicle), and separate the strut at the base **(see illustration)**.

5 If the left-hand strut is being removed, proceed as follows:

a) *If not already done, disconnect the battery negative lead, and place the lead away from the battery terminal.*

b) *Open the engine compartment fusebox, and remove the bolt(s) securing the positive and negative (where fitted) leads from the fusebox.*

c) *Remove the three nuts securing the fusebox, and move the fusebox to one side, for access to the strut upper mounting nuts.*

6 If the right-hand strut is being removed, remove the coolant expansion tank mounting bolt, and move the tank to one side.

7 Loosen the strut upper mounting nuts then, with one hand supporting the strut from below,

remove the nuts and lower the strut out from under the wheel arch **(see illustration)**.

Overhaul

⚠️ *Warning: Before attempting to dismantle the suspension strut, a suitable tool to hold the coil spring in compression must be obtained. Adjustable coil spring compressors are readily available, and are recommended for this operation. Any attempt to dismantle the strut without such a tool is likely to result in damage or personal injury.*

8 Fit the spring compressors to the coils of the spring **(see illustration)**. Tighten the compressors evenly until the load is taken off the spring seats.

9 Before removing the strut inner locknut, note the alignment of the top mounting plate, spring end and dust boot.

10 Hold the strut piston with an Allen key, then use a spanner to loosen the strut locknut. Remove the nut, and discard it – a new nut must be used for reassembly **(see illustration)**.

11 Take off the rebound washer and the upper mounting plate, followed by the upper spring seat and gaiter **(see illustrations)**.

12 Taking care not to disturb the spring clamps, lift off the spring.

13 Remove the washer, bump stop, and bump stop lower seat **(see illustrations)**.

14 With the strut assembly now completely dismantled, examine all the components for wear, damage or deformation. Renew any of the components as necessary.

15 Check the rubber components for deterioration. Examine the shock absorber for damage and signs of fluid leakage, and check the piston rod for pitting along its entire length. While holding it in an upright position,

2.10 Remove the nut, and discard it – a new nut must be used for reassembly

2.11a Take off the rebound washer and the upper mounting plate . . .

2.11b . . . followed by the upper spring seat . . .

2.11c . . . and gaiter

2.13a Remove the washer . . .

2.13b . . . bump stop . . .

test the operation of the shock absorber by moving the rod through a full stroke, and then through short strokes of 50 to 100 mm. In both cases, the resistance felt should be smooth and continuous. If the resistance is jerky, or uneven, or if there is any visible sign of wear or damage to the shock absorber, renewal is necessary.

16 If any doubt exists about the condition of the coil spring, gradually release the spring compressor, and check the spring for distortion and signs of cracking. Check the spring free length against the specified figures. Renew the spring if it is damaged or distorted, or if there is any doubt as to its condition. Note that springs should only be renewed with those that have the same colour-coding – mixing them up will result in a difference in ride heights; springs, like shock absorbers, should be renewed in axle pairs.

17 Inspect all other components for signs of damage or deterioration, and renew any that are suspect. The bump stops, for instance, are likely to be in less-than-perfect condition after a high mileage, or prolonged off-road use.

18 If a new shock absorber is being fitted, hold it vertically and pump the piston a few times to prime it.

19 Reassembly is a reversal of dismantling, noting the following points:

a) Compress the spring before fitting it.

b) Use a new strut locknut, and using a torque wrench and adaptor, tighten it to the specified torque while holding the strut piston against rotation with an Allen key.

c) Ensure the arrow on the top face of the upper mounting plate, points to the outside of the vehicle, in line with the hub mounting brackets at the lower end of the strut **(see illustration)**.

Refitting

21 Refitting is a reversal of the removal procedure, noting the following points:

a) Use a new anti-roll bar link rod nut and track rod balljoint nut.

b) Tighten all fixings to the specified torque.

c) Refit the ABS wheel sensor and brake caliper as described in Chapter 9.

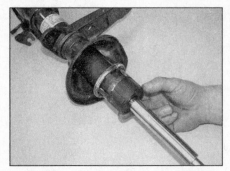
2.13c . . . and bump stop lower seat

3 Front suspension lower arm – removal, overhaul and refitting

Note: *If the arm is being removed to renew either bush, this can be achieved without removing the arm completely. If care is taken, the lower arm mountings can be unbolted from the raised vehicle, and either bush can then be worked on in situ. However, if the Land Rover puller tool mentioned below (or an equivalent) for pressing out/in the bushes is not available, it would be better to work on the arm once it has been removed completely.*

Removal

1 Loosen the wheel nuts, apply the handbrake, then jack up the relevant front wheel and support on axle stands (see *Jacking and vehicle support*). Remove the front wheel.

2 Remove the engine/transmission undertray, as follows. Remove the two screws securing the panel to the front bumper then, on early models, pull the lower edge of the bumper down for access to the two front frame bolts. Now remove a total of eight bolts around the frame – the two at the rear are smaller than the rest, so note their locations.

3 Using a hammer and suitable chisel, release the staking from the driveshaft nut.

⚠ **Warning: Before attempting to loosen the driveshaft nut, which is done up extremely tight, make sure the front of the vehicle is securely supported. Do not use poor-quality, badly-fitting tools for this task, due to the risk of personal injury.**

2.19 Ensure the arrow on the top face of the upper mounting plate (arrowed), points to the outside of the vehicle, in line with the hub mounting brackets (arrowed) at the lower end of the strut

4 While an assistant presses the brake pedal firmly, loosen and remove the driveshaft nut. Discard the nut once removed – owing to the extremely high tightening torque, it is **not** recommended that the nut is re-used.

5 Remove the front brake caliper (and, where applicable, the ABS wheel sensor) on the side concerned, as described in Chapter 9.

6 Loosen and remove the two nuts and bolts securing the lower end of the strut to the hub (note which way round the bolts are fitted – bolts heads to the front of the vehicle) **(see illustration)**.

7 Tilt the hub outwards to separate it from the strut, and also from the driveshaft's splined end fitting. Make sure that the driveshaft is supported once it has been released from the hub – do not let it hang down unsupported, or the CV joints could be damaged.

8 Loosen fully, but do not remove, the nut which secures the lower balljoint to the hub. Using a balljoint splitter, separate the tapered joint from the hub, then unscrew the nut completely. Remove the hub from the vehicle **(see illustration)**.

9 Remove the two bolts securing the lower arm rear housing, then remove the lower arm front pivot bolt, and remove the lower arm from under the vehicle **(see illustrations)**. Note that the rear bush housing is located over a dowel on the vehicle's underbody.

10 If required, the nut securing the rear bush housing to the arm can now be undone, and the bush housing removed. Note the OUT

3.6 Undo the two nuts and bolts securing the lower end of the strut to the hub

3.8 Loosen fully, but do not remove, the nut which secures the lower balljoint to the hub

3.9a Remove the two bolts securing the lower arm rear housing . . .

3.9b . . . then remove the lower arm front pivot bolt

3.10 Note the OUT marking (arrowed) on the outboard side of the large snubber washer

3.12 To extract the bush make up your own puller using a bolt, with several large washers and large sockets

marking on the outboard side of the large snubber washer fitted to the bush housing **(see illustration)**.

Overhaul

11 Overhaul is limited to renewing the bush at either end of the arm – if the arm has suffered damage (from, for example, careless jacking-up or off-road abuse), the arm is best renewed complete. It is advisable to consider renewing both arms in an axle set, rather than just one.

12 Land Rover dealers have a special puller tool and adaptors for extracting the front bushes from the lower arms (LRT-60-008). In the absence of this tool, mount the arm in a vice, and drive the bushes out using a suitable drift (such as a large socket); alternatively, make up your own puller, using a bolt, with several large washers and large sockets **(see illustration)**. If the DIY approach fails, entrust bush renewal to a Land Rover dealer. The rear bush is supplied as an assembly, complete with the aluminium bush housing.

Refitting

13 Refitting is a reversal of the removal procedure, noting the following points:

a) Locate the rear bush housing correctly on its dowel on the underbody.

b) Do not fully tighten the lower arm mounting/pivot bolts until the vehicle is resting on its wheels.

c) Use a new lower balljoint nut and driveshaft nut.

d) Refit the ABS wheel sensor and brake caliper as described in Chapter 9.

e) Tighten all fixings to the specified torque.

4 Front wheel bearing
– renewal

1 Loosen the wheel nuts, apply the handbrake, then jack up the relevant front wheel and support on axle stands (see *Jacking and vehicle support*). Remove the front wheel.

2 Remove the engine/transmission undertray as follows. Remove the two screws securing the panel to the front bumper then, on early models, pull the lower edge of the bumper down for access to the two front frame bolts. Now remove a total of eight bolts around the frame – the two at the rear are smaller than the rest, so note their locations.

3 Remove the driveshaft splash shield, which is secured by three bolts **(see illustration)**.

4 Using a hammer and suitable chisel, release the staking from the driveshaft nut.

⚠ *Warning: Before attempting to loosen the driveshaft nut, which is done up extremely tight, make sure the front of the vehicle is securely supported. Do not use poor-quality, badly-fitting tools for this task, due to the risk of personal injury.*

5 While an assistant presses the brake pedal firmly, loosen and remove the driveshaft nut. Discard the nut once removed – owing to the extremely high tightening torque, it is **not** recommended that the nut is re-used.

6 With reference to Chapter 9, remove the brake disc and ABS wheel sensor.

7 Remove the two bolts securing the suspension strut to the wheel hub, noting which way round they are fitted.

8 Release the hub from the base of the strut, then pivot the hub to withdraw the end of the driveshaft from it. Do not let the right-hand driveshaft hang down at too steep an angle from the gearbox/transmission, as this could cause damage to the inner joint.

9 Loosen fully, but do not remove, the nut which secures the lower balljoint to the hub. Using a balljoint splitter, separate the tapered joint from the hub, then unscrew the nut completely **(see illustration 3.8)**. Remove the hub from the vehicle.

10 Remove the three bolts securing the brake disc splash shield – the shield cannot be removed completely until the hub's drive flange (with five studs on it) has been removed.

11 Mount the hub securely in a vice, and using a suitable drift (such as a large socket) drive out the hub flange from the inboard side **(see illustration)**. Remove the brake disc splash shield.

12 Remove the bearing sealing plate from the drive flange, then mount the drive flange in a vice.

13 With careful use of a chisel, progressively tap off the bearing race **(see illustration)**. If a bearing puller is available, this is preferable, to avoid risking any damage to the drive flange surfaces.

14 Remove the bearing retaining circlip from the outboard side of the hub **(see illustration)**.

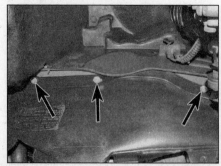

4.3 Remove the driveshaft splash shield, which is secured by three bolts (arrowed)

4.11 Use a suitable drift to drive out the hub flange

4.13 With careful use of a chisel, progressively tap off the bearing race

15 Mount the hub in a vice, and drive out the bearing from the inboard side, using a suitable drift.

16 Clean up the hub and drive flange, removing all old grease, and any metal debris from removing the old bearing.

17 Support the inboard side of the hub below the bearing location, and progressively press in the new bearing using a suitable socket or tube which bears only on the bearing outer race. Make sure that the bearing is kept square in the hub until it is fully seated **(see illustration)**.

18 Secure the bearing using a new circlip (usually supplied with the new bearing), then refit the brake disc shield and secure with the three bolts **(see illustration)**.

19 Again supporting the inboard side of the hub below the bearing location, align the drive flange squarely into the hub, and tap it fully into position **(see illustration)**.

20 Refitting the hub is a reversal of removal, noting the following points:

a) *Tighten all fasteners to the specified torque.*
b) *Use a new lower balljoint nut.*
c) *Refit the brake disc and ABS wheel sensor as described in Chapter 9.*
d) *Use a new driveshaft nut, and tighten it to the specified torque, taking the same precautions tightening it as when it was loosened previously.*

5 Front anti-roll bar bushes – renewal

1 Loosen the wheel nuts, apply the handbrake, then jack up the front of the vehicle and support it securely on axle stands (see *Jacking and vehicle support*).

2 Remove the engine/transmission undertray as follows. Remove the two screws securing the panel to the front bumper then, on early models, pull the lower edge of the bumper down for access to the two front frame bolts. Now remove a total of eight bolts around the frame – the two at the rear are smaller than the rest, so note their locations.

3 Loosen and remove the two bolts per clamp, and remove the clamp plates from the top of the subframe **(see illustrations)**.

4.14 Remove the bearing retaining circlip from the outboard side of the hub

4.18 Refit the brake disc shield and secure with the three bolts

4 The rubber bushes are of split design, so they can be twisted around and removed with the bar *in situ* **(see illustration)**. Once the old bushes are removed, clean up their locations on the bar, and also clean the inner surfaces of the clamp plates.

HAYNES HINT *When fitting the new bushes, it is helpful to coat them in soapy water (such as washing-up liquid) prior to fitting. This will make it much easier to slip them into place, and to twist them round into position on the bar.*

5 Locate the new bushes in place, then refit the clamp plates and tighten the bolts to the specified torque.

6 Refit the engine/transmission undertray and the front wheels, then lower the vehicle to the ground.

4.17 Press the new bearing into the hub

4.19 Align the drive flange squarely into the hub, and tap it fully into position

6 Front anti-roll bar drop links – removal and refitting

Removal

1 Loosen the wheel nuts, apply the handbrake, then jack up the front of the vehicle and support it securely on axle stands (see *Jacking and vehicle support*). Remove the front wheels.

2 Unscrew the nut securing the lower end of each drop link to the anti-roll bar. It may be necessary to use a second spanner on the inboard side of the roll bar, to prevent the drop link balljoint shank from turning as the nut is unscrewed **(see illustration)**.

3 Now unscrew the nut at the top end of each link. This time, the shank can be prevented

5.3a Loosen and remove the two bolts per clamp . . .

5.3b . . . and remove the clamp plates from the top of the subframe

5.4 The rubber bushes are of split design, so they can be twisted around and removed with the bar *in situ*

6.2 It may be necessary to use a second spanner on the inboard side of the roll bar, to prevent the drop link balljoint shank from turning as the nut is unscrewed

from turning using an Allen key in the end of the shank **(see illustration 2.3)**. Remove the drop link from the vehicle – the nuts should be discarded, and new ones obtained for refitting.

Refitting

4 If a new link is not being fitted, clean up the balljoint tapers and their mating faces in their fitted locations on the strut and anti-roll bar. Do not apply any lubricant to the tapers, or tightening the new balljoint nuts will be made more difficult.
5 Offer the links into position, making sure they are the right way up. Using a new nut at each end, and holding the balljoint shanks against rotation as necessary, tighten the upper and lower balljoint nuts to the specified torque.
6 Refit the front wheels, then lower the vehicle to the ground and tighten the wheel nuts to the specified torque.

7 Front anti-roll bar – removal and refitting

Removal

1 Loosen the wheel nuts, apply the handbrake, then jack up the front of the vehicle and support it securely on axle stands (see *Jacking and vehicle support*). Note that the front subframe has to be lowered to remove

8.5 Loosen the nut securing each lower arm to the rear bush housing

7.5 Remove the bolt securing the front end of the engine lower tie-bar to the sump (arrowed)

the anti-roll bar, so do not support the vehicle there. Remove the front wheels.
2 Remove the engine/transmission undertray as follows. Remove the two screws securing the panel to the front bumper then, on early models, pull the lower edge of the bumper down for access to the two front frame bolts. Now remove a total of eight bolts around the frame – the two at the rear are smaller than the rest, so note their locations.
3 Unscrew the nut securing the lower end of each drop link to the anti-roll bar. It may be necessary to use a second spanner on the inboard side of the roll bar, to prevent the drop link balljoint shank from turning as the nut is unscrewed **(see illustration 6.2)**.
4 Unscrew and remove the four bolts securing the anti-roll bar clamps to the subframe **(see illustration 5.3a**. If required, new bushes can be fitted as described in Section 5.
5 Remove the bolt securing the front end of the engine lower tie-bar to the sump **(see illustration)**.
6 Before proceeding further, securely support the weight of the front subframe. It may also be useful to have an assistant on hand, to help with lowering the subframe and removing the roll bar.
7 Remove the total of four bolts securing the lower arm rear housings **(see illustration 3.9a)**, then remove the two large bolts securing the front subframe to the underside of the vehicle. Carefully lower the subframe until the anti-roll bar is released, and remove the roll bar from under the vehicle.

8.8 Remove the two large bolts each side securing the front subframe to the underside of the car

Refitting

8 Refitting is a reversal of removal, noting the following points:
  a) *New subframe-to-body bolts should be used, and new drop link balljoint nuts.*
  b) *Tighten all fasteners to the specified torque.*
  c) *If a new roll bar has been fitted, it is advisable to fit new bushes also, as described in Section 6.*

8 Front subframe – removal and refitting

Removal

1 Loosen the wheel nuts, apply the handbrake, then jack up the front of the vehicle and support it securely on axle stands (see *Jacking and vehicle support*). Do not support under the front subframe, for obvious reasons. Remove the front wheels.
2 Remove the engine/transmission undertray as follows. Remove the two screws securing the panel to the front bumper then, on early models, pull the lower edge of the bumper down for access to the two front frame bolts. Now remove a total of eight bolts around the frame – the two at the rear are smaller than the rest, so note their locations.
3 Remove the bolt securing the front end of the engine lower tie-bar to the sump **(see illustration 7.5)**.
4 Unscrew and remove the four bolts securing the anti-roll bar clamps to the subframe. Tie the roll bar up to the underside of the vehicle.
5 Loosen the nut securing each lower arm to the rear bush housing, then remove the two rear housing bolts each side **(see illustration)**. Note that the rear bush housings are located over a dowel on the vehicle's underbody.
6 Remove the lower arm pivot bolt each side, and release the lower arms from the subframe.
7 Before proceeding further, securely support the weight of the front subframe. It may also be useful to have an assistant on hand, to help with lowering the subframe.
8 Remove the two large bolts securing the front subframe to the underside of the vehicle. Carefully lower the subframe, and remove it from under the vehicle **(see illustration)**.

Refitting

9 With the help of an assistant, offer up the subframe, and secure it using two new subframe-to-body bolts. Do not fully tighten the bolts at this stage.
10 Refit the lower arms to the subframe, starting with the front pivot bolts. Do not fully tighten the bolts yet.
11 Fit the lower arm rear bush housings, aligning the dowels. Tighten the two bush housing bolts each side to the specified torque.
12 Tighten the front subframe-to-body bolts to the specified torque.

9.3 Remove the clip which secures the brake hose to the strut bracket

9.5 Undo the two nuts and bolts securing the lower end of the strut to the hub

9.6 On 5-door models, unscrew the rear seat belt lower Torx bolt

13 Relocate the anti-roll bar into position, then fit the clamp plates and tighten the bolts to the specified torque.

14 Refit the bolt securing the engine lower tie-bar to the subframe, and tighten it to the specified torque.

15 Refit the wheels, and lower the vehicle to the ground. Tighten the wheel nuts to the specified torque.

16 With the weight of the vehicle on its wheels, tighten the lower arm pivot bolts, and the lower arm rear bush nuts, to the specified torques.

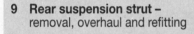

9 Rear suspension strut – removal, overhaul and refitting

Removal

1 Loosen the relevant rear wheel nuts, then chock the front wheels and jack up the rear of the vehicle and support on axle stands (see *Jacking and vehicle support*). Remove the relevant rear wheel.

2 Clamp the rear brake flexible hose to reduce fluid spillage (if wished, unclip the brake hose to make it easier to work on). Place some absorbent cloth under the hose-to-pipe union, and disconnect the union.

3 If not already done, remove the clip which secures the brake hose to the strut bracket. Release the brake hose and the ABS wiring from their various locations on and around the strut **(see illustration)**.

4 Remove the ABS wheel sensor from its location on the rear hub. Depending on model, the sensor may have a retaining bolt fitted; otherwise, the sensor just prises out.

5 Loosen and remove the two nuts and bolts securing the lower end of the strut to the hub (note which way round the bolts are fitted – bolt heads to the front of the vehicle), and separate the strut at the base **(see illustration)**.

6 Inside the vehicle, fold the rear seat forwards. On 5-door models, unscrew the rear seat belt lower Torx bolt **(see illustration)**.

7 Prise out the luggage compartment light, then disconnect the two connectors from it, and remove it from the luggage area side trim panel.

8 Remove the screws securing the carpet

retainer at the rear edge of the luggage area, and release the retainer and carpet as necessary so that the side trim panel will be free to be removed.

9 Turn the four turn-buckle fasteners securing the side trim panel to release them **(see illustration)**.

10 The side trim panel is clipped in place by five clips, mainly along the front and top edges. Carefully prise along the edges of the trim panel to release the clips, and remove it from the vehicle for access to the strut upper mounting nuts.

11 Loosen the strut upper mounting nuts then, with one hand supporting the strut from below, remove the nuts and lower the strut out from under the wheel arch **(see illustration)**.

Overhaul

⚠️ *Warning: Before attempting to dismantle the suspension strut, a suitable tool to hold the coil spring in compression must be obtained. Adjustable coil spring compressors are readily available, and are recommended for this operation. Any attempt to dismantle the strut without such a tool is likely to result in damage or personal injury.*

12 Fit the spring compressors to catch at least four coils of the spring. Tighten the compressors evenly until the load is taken off the spring seats **(see illustration 2.8)**.

13 Before removing the strut inner locknut, note the alignment of the top mounting plate, spring end and dust boot.

14 Hold the strut piston with an Allen key, then use a spanner to loosen the strut locknut.

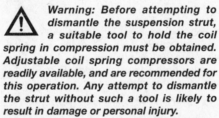

9.9 Turn the four turn-buckle fasteners securing the side trim panel to release them

Remove the nut, and discard it – a new nut must be used for reassembly.

15 Take off the rebound washer and the upper mounting plate, followed by the spacer, the upper spring seat and gaiter **(see illustrations 2.11a to 2.11c)**.

16 Taking care not to disturb the spring clamps, lift off the spring.

17 Remove the bump stop, dust boot and bump stop lower seat **(see illustration 2.13a to 2.13c)**.

18 With the strut assembly now completely dismantled, examine all the components for wear, damage or deformation. Renew any of the components as necessary.

19 With the shock absorber assembly now dismantled, examine all the components for wear and damage. Check the rubber components for deterioration. Examine the shock absorber for damage and signs of fluid leakage, and check the piston rod for pitting along its entire length. While holding it in an upright position, test the operation of the shock absorber by moving the rod through a full stroke, and then through short strokes of 50 to 100 mm. In both cases, the resistance felt should be smooth and continuous. If the resistance is jerky, or uneven, or if there is any visible sign of wear or damage to the shock absorber, renewal is necessary.

20 If any doubt exists about the condition of the coil spring, gradually release the spring compressor, and check the spring for distortion and signs of cracking. Check the spring free length against the specified figure. Renew the spring if it is damaged or distorted, or if there is any doubt as to its condition.

9.11 Loosen the strut upper mounting nuts

10.2 Remove the nut and bolt securing the outboard end of the link to the hub

10.3 Remove the nut and bolt from the inboard end of the link

10.5 Remove the nut, bolt and washers securing the adjustable link to the hub

10.6 Disconnect the inner end of the adjustable link from the subframe

10.8 Remove the nut and bolt securing the outboard end of the link to the hub

10.9 Remove the nut and bolt from the bracket at the inboard end of the link

Note that springs should only be renewed with those that have the same colour-coding – mixing them up will result in a difference in ride heights; springs, like shock absorbers, should be renewed in axle pairs.

21 Inspect all other components for signs of damage or deterioration, and renew any that are suspect. The bump stops, for instance, are likely to be in less-than-perfect condition after a high mileage, or prolonged off-road use.

22 If a new shock absorber is being fitted, hold it vertically and pump the piston a few times to prime it.

23 Reassembly is a reversal of dismantling, noting the following points:
a) Compress the spring before fitting it.
b) Use a new strut locknut, and using a torque wrench with an adaptor, tighten it to the specified torque while holding the strut piston against rotation with an Allen key.
c) Check the alignment of the top mounting plate, spring end and dust boot, as noted before dismantling **(see illustration 2.19)**.

Refitting

24 Refitting is a reversal of the removal procedure, noting the following points:
a) The two strut-to-hub bolts are inserted from the front.
b) Tighten all fixings to the specified torque.
c) Refit the ABS wheel sensor as described in Chapter 9. Make sure that the sensor wiring and the brake hose are clipped back into place correctly on the strut.
d) On completion, top-up the brake fluid level and bleed the brakes as described in Chapter 9.

10 Rear suspension links
– removal and refitting

1 Loosen the relevant rear wheel nuts, chock the front wheels, then jack up the rear of the vehicle and support it on axle stands (see *Jacking and vehicle support*). Remove the relevant rear roadwheel.

Fixed transverse link (front)

2 Remove the nut and bolt securing the outboard end of the link to the hub, noting which way round the bolt is fitted **(see illustration)**.

3 Similarly, remove the nut and bolt from the inboard end of the link, and remove the link from the vehicle **(see illustration)**.

4 Refitting is a reversal of removal, noting the following points:
a) Check the condition of the bushes at either end of the link before fitting, and renew if necessary as described in Section 11.
b) Fit the nuts/bolts hand-tight initially, and only tighten to the specified torque once the wheels have been refitted and the vehicle has been lowered.

Adjustable transverse link (rear)

5 Remove the nut, bolt and washers securing the adjustable link to the hub – note which way round the bolt is fitted, and the arrangement of the washers, for use when refitting **(see illustration)**.

6 Disconnect the inner end of the adjustable

link from the subframe, again noting how the bolt is fitted **(see illustration)**.

7 Refitting is a reversal of removal, noting the following points:
a) Check the condition of the bushes at either end of the link before fitting, and renew if necessary as described in Section 11.
b) At the outboard (hub) end of the link, make sure the washers are correctly refitted at each end of the bolt.
c) Fit the nuts/bolts hand-tight initially, and only tighten to the specified torque once the wheels have been refitted and the vehicle has been lowered.
d) Particularly if a new link has been fitted, have the rear wheel alignment checked as soon as possible.

Trailing link

8 Remove the nut and bolt securing the outboard end of the link to the hub, noting which way round the bolt is fitted **(see illustration)**.

9 Similarly, remove the nut and bolt from the bracket at the inboard end of the link, and remove the link from the vehicle **(see illustration)**.

10 Refitting is a reversal of removal, noting the following points:
a) Check the condition of the bushes at either end of the link before fitting, and renew if necessary as described in Section 11.
b) Fit the nuts/bolts hand-tight initially, and only tighten to the specified torque once the wheels have been refitted and the vehicle has been lowered.

11 Rear suspension link bushes
– renewal

1 In all cases, renewal of the trailing arm bushes is essentially the same procedure. It's not essential to remove any link completely, if a bush at one end only is to be renewed, but removing the link in question (as described in Section 10) will make work easier, as the link can then be mounted in a vice.
2 Land Rover dealers have several special tools used to press out the old bushes, and to fit new ones, but these amount to simple arrangements of washers/spacers and a draw-bolt, which could easily be fabricated at home. Otherwise, the bushes can be pressed out using sockets or tubes of suitable diameter **(see illustration)**. If the DIY approach fails, entrust bush renewal to a Land Rover dealer or specialist.
3 When renewing bushes, note that the alignment of the bush in its location is often important – the bushes are designed to flex in particular directions, so if they are incorrectly fitted, this could lead to peculiar handling. Mark the old bush relative to its location in the arm before removing it, and check that the new one is fitted the same way round.

> **HAYNES HiNT**
> *When fitting the new bushes, it is helpful to coat them in soapy water (such as washing-up liquid) prior to fitting. This will make it much easier to slip them into position.*

12 Rear wheel bearing – renewal

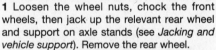

1 Loosen the wheel nuts, chock the front wheels, then jack up the relevant rear wheel and support on axle stands (see *Jacking and vehicle support*). Remove the rear wheel.
2 Using a hammer and suitable chisel, release the staking from the driveshaft nut.

> ⚠ *Warning: Before attempting to loosen the driveshaft nut, which is done up extremely tight, make sure the rear of the vehicle is securely supported. Do not use poor-quality, badly-fitting tools for this task, due to the risk of personal injury.*

3 While an assistant presses the brake pedal firmly, loosen and remove the driveshaft nut. Discard the nut once removed – owing to the extremely high tightening torque, it is **not** recommended that the nut is re-used.
4 Remove the brake shoes as described in Chapter 9.
5 Using a pair of thin-nosed pliers, compress and release the handbrake cable retaining clip from the brake backplate, and withdraw the cable.

6 Clamp the rear brake flexible hose to reduce fluid spillage (if wished, unclip the brake hose to make it easier to work on). Place some absorbent cloth under the wheel cylinder pipe union, and disconnect the union.
7 If not already done, remove the clip which secures the brake hose to the strut bracket. Release the brake hose and the ABS wiring from their various locations on and around the strut.
8 Remove the ABS wheel sensor from its location on the rear hub. Depending on model, the sensor may have a retaining bolt fitted; otherwise, the sensor just prises out.
9 Loosen and remove the two nuts and bolts securing the lower end of the strut to the hub (note which way round the bolts are fitted), and separate the strut at the base **(see illustration 9.5)**.
10 Referring to Section 10 if necessary, disconnect all the link arms from the hub – the links do not have to be removed completely, but note the arrangement of the various nuts, bolts and washers used.
11 Slide the hub off the driveshaft splines, and mount it in a vice.
12 With the hub securely in a vice, use a suitable drift (such as a large socket) to drive out the hub flange from the inboard side **(see illustration 4.11)**.
13 Remove the bearing sealing plate from the drive flange, then mount the drive flange in a vice.
14 With careful use of a chisel, progressively tap off the bearing race **(see illustration 4.13)**. If a bearing puller is available, this is preferable, to avoid risking any damage to the drive flange surfaces.
15 Mount the hub in the vice, and remove the four bolts securing the brake backplate to the hub. Take off the backplate.
16 Remove the bearing retaining circlip from the outboard side of the hub, then drive out the bearing from the inboard side, using a suitable drift **(see illustration)**.
17 Clean up the hub and drive flange, removing all old grease, and any metal debris from removing the old bearing.
18 Support the inboard side of the hub below the bearing location, and progressively press in the new bearing using a suitable socket or tube which bears only on the bearing outer race. Make sure that the bearing is kept square in the hub until it is fully seated.
19 Secure the bearing using a circlip, then refit the brake backplate and secure with the four bolts, tightened to the specified torque.
22 Again supporting the inboard side of the hub below the bearing location, align the drive flange squarely into the hub, and tap it fully into position **(see illustration 4.19)**.
23 Refitting the hub is a reversal of removal, noting the following points:
a) *Tighten all fasteners to the specified torque, with the exception of the link arm nuts/bolts, which should be initially tightened by hand only (see Section 10).*

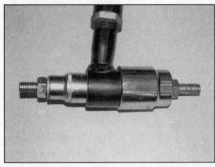

11.2 The bushes can be pressed out using sockets or tubes of suitable diameter

b) *Refit the brake shoes and ABS wheel sensor as described in Chapter 9.*
c) *Use a new driveshaft nut, and tighten it to the specified torque, taking the same precautions tightening it as when it was loosened previously.*
d) *On completion, refit the wheel and lower the vehicle to the ground. Tighten the wheel nuts to the specified torque, then tighten the link arm nuts/bolts to the specified torques.*
e) *Top-up the brake fluid level, then bleed the brakes as described in Chapter 9.*

13 Rear subframe – removal and refitting

Removal

1 Remove both rear driveshafts as described in Chapter 8.
2 Again using the information in Chapter 8, disconnect the rear propeller shaft from the final drive flange, and tie it to one side.
3 With reference to the relevant Part of Chapter 4, remove the exhaust intermediate and tailpipe/silencer.
4 Support the weight of the subframe on a jack (or preferably, a pair of jacks). The help of an assistant will also prove useful in lowering the subframe.
5 Remove the bolt securing each of the handbrake cables to the subframe, and move the cables clear of the working area **(see illustration)**.

12.16 Remove the bearing retaining circlip from the outboard side of the hub

13.5 Remove the bolt securing each of the handbrake cables to the subframe

6 Ensuring that the subframe is adequately supported, remove the four bolts securing the subframe to the body.

7 With the help of an assistant, lower the subframe and remove from under the vehicle. Note as the subframe is removed that it is located on dowels – note their locations to aid refitting **(see illustration)**.

8 If the final drive is to be removed from the subframe, note the comments in Chapter 8 regarding the importance of aligning the final drive and propshaft – make alignment markings between the final drive and subframe if they are to be reassembled later, or transfer the marks made to any new components.

Refitting

9 Refitting is a reversal of removal, noting the following points:

 a) Locate the subframe on its locating dowels when offering it into position.

14.3 Disconnect the wiring plug from the rotary contact unit

14.5 Make an alignment mark between the wheel boss and the top of the column, to ensure the wheel goes back on straight

13.7 The rear subframe locates on dowels (arrowed)

 b) Land Rover do not actually state that new subframe-to-body bolts must be used, but they are done up to an extremely high torque, and it would seem sensible to fit new ones. New ones should certainly be fitted if there is any doubt about the old ones' condition.

 c) Tighten all fasteners to the specified torque.

 d) Reconnect the rear prop shaft, and refit the driveshafts, as described in Chapter 8.

 e) Refit the exhaust intermediate and tail-pipe/silencer as described in Chapter 4.

14 Steering wheel – removal and refitting

Removal

1 Release the steering lock by inserting the ignition key.

14.4 Undo the steering wheel retaining nut

15.2 The upper shroud is clipped to the lower shroud (steering wheel removed for clarity)

2 Remove the airbag unit as described in Chapter 12, then return the steering wheel to the straight-ahead position.

3 Disconnect the wiring plug from the rotary contact unit **(see illustration)**.

4 Hold the steering wheel to prevent it turning (don't rely on the steering lock for this, as it may not be strong enough, and damage could result), and undo the steering wheel retaining nut **(see illustration)**.

5 Make an alignment mark between the wheel boss and the top of the column, to ensure the wheel goes back on straight. Pull the steering wheel from the splined end of the steering column. This should not require great effort, but if it sticks, put the wheel nut back on by a few threads (to prevent it flying off), and tap the wheel off from behind the boss **(see illustration)**.

6 The steering wheel nut is a self-locking type, and should not be re-used. Its importance to vehicle safety should be obvious.

> **HAYNES HINT** *Whilst the steering wheel is removed, wrap adhesive tape around the airbag contact unit. This will prevent unnecessary rotation of the contact unit, and will ensure that it remains correctly positioned until the steering wheel is refitted.*

Refitting

7 Remove the tape from the contact unit, then feed the airbag unit wiring up through the wheel.

8 Locate the steering wheel on the column splines, aligning the marks made on removal.

9 Fit a new retaining nut, and tighten it to the specified torque setting, holding the wheel against rotation as before.

10 Reconnect the contact unit, feed the airbag wiring back into the steering wheel, then refit the airbag unit as described in Chapter 12.

15 Ignition switch/ steering column lock – removal and refitting

Removal

1 Disconnect the battery negative lead, and remove the ignition key.

2 Remove the steering column upper and lower shrouds. The upper shroud is clipped to the lower shroud, and there are two clips either side – take care when releasing them to avoid damage **(see illustration)**. Lift out the upper shroud.

3 The lower shroud is secured by two screws from below – remove the screws, then lower the steering column tilt lever **(see illustration)**.

4 Remove the cover from the ignition switch, taking care not to damage the reader coil fitted round the switch **(see illustration)**.

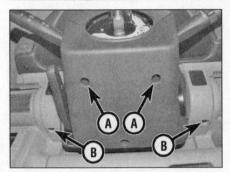

15.3 Lower steering column shroud screws (A) and lower trim panel screws (B)

15.4 Remove the cover from the ignition switch

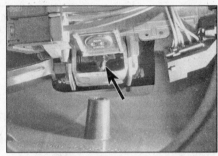

15.5 Carefully pull the lower shroud down, releasing it from the clip (arrowed) on the ignition switch

5 Carefully pull the lower shroud down, releasing it from the clip on the ignition switch, and remove it **(see illustration)**.

6 Disconnect the multiplugs from the ignition switch, and from the switch reader coil (for the passive immobiliser) **(see illustration)**.

7 Unclip the reader coil from the ignition switch, and remove it.

8 Remove the ignition switch unit by taking out its two retaining screws **(see illustration)**.

9 Move the column rubber cover to one side, to gain access to the switch clamp bolts mounted in from above the column.

10 Mark both bolts with a centre-punch (they are of shear-head type, so cannot be unscrewed), and drill them out.

11 Take off the ignition switch upper clamp, and remove the switch body.

12 On automatic models, unscrew the large union nut and detach the ignition switch interlock cable from the switch assembly.

Refitting

13 Refitting is a reversal of removal, noting the following points:
a) New shear-head bolts will obviously be needed. Before tightening them fully, refit the switch hand-tight (including refitting the interlock cable, on automatic models), and test the operation of the steering lock (and automatic gearbox interlock). When everything is working correctly, remove the ignition key and tighten the shear-head bolts until their heads snap off.
b) On completion, reconnect the battery and confirm correct switch operation.

16 Ignition switch interlock cable (automatic models) – removal, refitting and adjustment

Removal

1 Remove the front section of the centre console, as described in Chapter 11.

2 Loosen the cable clamp bolt in front of the selector lever, and disconnect the cable end from the interlock mechanism.

3 Remove the steering column upper and lower shrouds. The upper shroud is clipped to the lower shroud, and there are two clips

15.6 Disconnect the multi-plugs (arrowed) from the ignition switch, and from the switch reader coil

either side – take care when releasing them to avoid damage. Lift out the upper shroud.

4 The lower shroud is secured by two screws from below **(see illustration 15.3)** – remove the screws, then lower the steering column tilt lever.

5 Remove the cover from the ignition switch, taking care not to damage the reader coil fitted round the switch.

6 Carefully pull the lower shroud down, releasing it from the clip on the ignition switch, and remove it.

7 Remove the bolt securing the steering column height adjuster lever – this bolt has a **left-hand** thread (ie, it unscrews **clockwise**). Take off the height adjuster lever.

8 Remove the nut from the height adjuster clamp bolt, and take out the bolt and its plastic collar.

9 Loosen the large union nut, and disconnect the cable end fitting from the steering column lock **(see illustration)**.

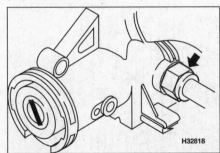

16.9 Loosen the large union nut (arrowed), and disconnect the cable end fitting from the steering column lock

15.8 Remove the ignition switch unit by taking out its two retaining screws

10 Noting how the cable is routed, release it from the two retaining clips, and feed the cable out from under the heater and steering column bracket.

Refitting

11 Refitting is a reversal of removal, noting the following points:
a) The steering column height adjuster lever should be refitted in the 'up' position.
b) Before refitting the centre console as described in Chapter 11, check the operation of the interlock mechanism, and adjust the cable if necessary, as described below.

Adjustment

12 With the selector lever in P, and the ignition key removed from the switch, the selector lever should be locked in position. If the ignition key is now inserted and turned to position II, with the brake pedal pressed, the selector lever can be moved out of P. Once the lever is out of P, it should not be possible to remove the ignition key. If any of these conditions are not met, the interlock cable requires adjustment, as described below.

13 Select P and remove the ignition key.

14 If not already done, remove the front section of the centre console, as described in Chapter 11.

15 Loosen the cable clamp bolt in front of the selector lever, and try to pull the cable away from the interlock mechanism until spring pressure is felt. The correct adjustment is when all freeplay is removed from the cable, without compressing the spring.

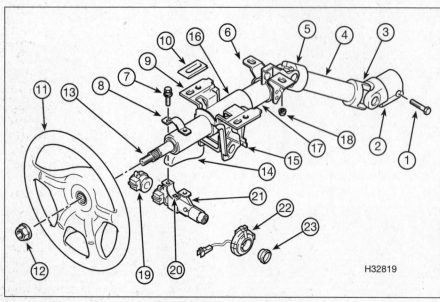

17.9 At the very base of the column, unscrew and remove the pinch-bolt (arrowed) which secures the column to the rack pinion

17.1 Steering column exploded view

1 Clamp bolt	9 Upper mounting bracket	17 Lower column tube
2 Adaptor	10 U-clip	18 Mounting nut (x4)
3 Lower universal joint	11 Steering wheel	19 Ignition switch
4 Intermediate shaft	12 Steering wheel nut	20 Lock bolt
5 Upper universal joint	13 Upper column	21 Steering column lock
6 Lower mounting bracket	14 Column adjuster lever	22 Ignition key
7 Shear-head bolt	15 Upper mounting/column adjuster assembly	23 Passive reader coil (immobiliser)
8 Clamp plate	16 Upper column tube	24 Light ring, ignition switch

16 Adjust the cable as necessary, then tighten the cable clamp bolt.

17 Recheck the interlock operation, and when satisfactory, refit the centre console as described in Chapter 11.

17 Steering column – removal and refitting

Removal

1 Remove the steering wheel as described in Section 14. This is not absolutely essential, but it makes working on and around the column much easier (see illustration).

2 Remove the steering column multi-function switches as described in Chapter 12.

3 Disconnect the multiplugs from the ignition switch and reader coil (for passive immobiliser).

4 Remove the two screws securing the steering column lower trim panel, and remove the panel (see illustration 15.3).

5 Open the driver's glovebox lid, and remove the fusebox cover.

6 Taking care not to damage any wiring, cut the cable-ties securing the wiring harness at the left-hand side of the column.

7 Release the harness clips at the right-hand side of the column, and manoeuvre the harness away from the column.

8 On automatic models, remove the interlock cable at the ignition switch end, using the information in Section 16. When the cable has been removed, refit the height adjuster clamp

bolt and spacer, and secure loosely with the nut.

9 At the very base of the column, unscrew and remove the pinch-bolt which secures the column to the rack pinion (see illustration).

10 Remove the bolt which secures the steering column to the fusebox support bracket (see illustration).

11 Remove the two nuts and two bolts which secure the steering column to the facia support rail (see illustrations).

12 Lift the column to release it from the rack pinion, and manoeuvre it out of the vehicle. Collect the rubber mounting fitted to the column pivot bracket.

13 With the column removed, take out the remains of the harness cable-ties – if the column is to be refitted, fit new cable-ties now. If required, the ignition switch and steering column lock can be removed, using the information in Section 15.

Refitting

14 Refitting is a reversal of removal, noting the following points:
a) When the column is first offered in, only tighten the mounting nuts and bolts hand-tight until the column has been engaged correctly with the rack pinion, and the pinch-bolt tightened to the specified torque.
b) On automatic models, reconnect the interlock cable to the ignition switch using the information in Section 16.
c) Use new steering column upper mounting nuts.

17.10 Remove the bolt which secures the steering column to the fusebox support bracket

17.11a Remove the two nuts and two bolts . . .

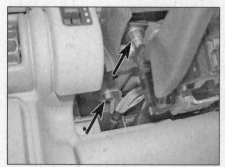

17.11b . . . which secure the steering column to the facia support rail

18.7 At the left-hand end of the steering rack, remove the two bolts and washers from the steering rack clamp plate

18.8 At the right-hand end of the rack, remove the two bolts which secure the rack mounting flange to the bulkhead

18.11 Disconnect the pipe unions from the rack

d) *Tighten all fasteners to the specified torque.*

e) *On completion, check the operation of the steering column lock, indicator self-cancelling (and interlock cable) before taking the vehicle out on the road.*

18 Steering rack – removal and refitting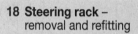

Removal

1 Loosen the wheel nuts, apply the handbrake, then jack up the front of the vehicle and support it on axle stands (see *Jacking and vehicle support*). Remove the front wheels.

2 Loosen fully, but do not remove, the nut which secures each steering track rod to the arm at the top of the strut body. Using a balljoint splitter, separate the tapered joint from the arm, then unscrew the nut completely – if necessary, refer to Section 23.

3 Inside the vehicle, unscrew and remove the pinch-bolt at the base of the steering column, which secures the column to the rack pinion **(see illustration 17.9)**.

4 On TD4 manual models, working under the vehicle, disconnect the gearchange rods from the gear linkage, using the information in Chapter 7A. Remove the two bolts securing the gear linkage to the bulkhead, and tie the linkage to one side.

5 Also on TD4 manual models, working in the right-hand front wheel arch, remove the bolt securing the IRD unit coolant hose. Trace the coolant hose up from the IRD unit to the wheel arch, and remove the wheel arch liner if necessary.

6 On TD4 automatic models, remove the bolt which secures the IRD unit coolant hose to the steering rack.

7 At the left-hand end of the steering rack, remove the two bolts and washers from the steering rack clamp plate **(see illustration)**. Remove the plate from the rack, and take off the rack rubber mount.

8 At the right-hand end of the rack, remove the two bolts which secure the rack mounting flange to the bulkhead **(see illustration)**. Note the large washer fitted to the lower bolt.

9 The rack should now be free from the bulkhead, though the fluid pipes will still be connected. Release the rack from the connection to the steering column, and pull it and the column rubber gaiter through the bulkhead.

10 Remove the bolt which secures the fluid pipe bracket to the rack. Position a container below the rack fluid pipe unions, in anticipation of some fluid spillage.

11 Wrap some absorbent cloth around the pipe unions, then disconnect them from the rack. Remove and discard the union O-rings – new ones should be obtained for refitting **(see illustration)**. If possible, plug or tape over the opened connections, to reduce further fluid loss, and prevent the entry of dirt into the system.

12 Trace the fluid pipes along to their clamp. Remove the bolt securing the pipes to the clamp, and loosen the clamp bolt.

13 With the help of an assistant, manoeuvre the rack out from the passenger side.

Refitting

14 Refitting is a reversal of removal, noting the following points:

a) *Before reconnecting the fluid pipe unions, make sure they are clean, and use new O-rings. Tighten the unions by hand only until the rack is fully located in position, and the bulkhead mounting bolts have been tightened to the specified torque.*

b) *Likewise, engage the rack pinion with the steering column at an early stage, but do not tighten the pinch-bolt more than hand-tight until the rack has been located on its bulkhead mountings.*

c) *Use new rack mounting bolts and track rod balljoint nuts.*

d) *Tighten all fasteners and unions to the specified torque.*

e) *On TD4 manual models, reconnect the gearchange linkage with reference to Chapter 7A.*

f) *On completion, top-up and bleed the power steering system as described in Section 22. Have the front wheel alignment checked and if necessary adjusted as soon as possible.*

19 Steering rack gaiter – renewal

1 Remove the rack as described in Section 18.

2 Remove the two Torx bolts which secure the track rods to the rack, then remove the support plate, track rods and spacers, noting their order of fitting and orientation for reassembly **(see illustration overleaf)**. New Torx bolts will be needed for reassembly, but keep hold of the old ones for the moment.

3 Remove the clips from the rack fluid feed pipes.

4 Loosen the four pipe unions, and remove both the fluid feed pipes from the rack. Be aware of the need to keep dirt out of the fluid pipes and connections while working on the rack – cap them or tape over them if necessary.

5 Remove the clamp bolt from the fluid pipe support bracket, and remove the bracket.

6 Remove the two gaiter securing clips and the gaiter sealing ring, and slide the gaiter off the rack.

7 Remove the gaiter sealing band from the rack, then take off the slider and clip assembly from the front of the rack **(see illustration 19.2)**.

8 Clean any old grease from the slider and clip, then apply fresh grease (which should be supplied with a new gaiter) to the slider, clip, and to the exposed rack shaft.

9 Fit the gaiter sealing band and slide on the new gaiter, together with its sealing ring.

10 Align the new gaiter with the rack slider, and when it is correctly located, loosely fit the old track rod bolts to hold the gaiter in position. Do not fit the new bolts yet – they are coated with locking compound, and should only be fitted when they are about to be tightened.

11 Fit and secure the gaiter securing clips, making sure that the gaiter is not twisted.

12 Fit the fluid pipe support bracket, and secure with its bolt.

13 Check that the fluid feed pipe unions are clean, then reconnect the unions, tightening them to the specified torques according to size. Refit the pipe clips.

14 Remove the old track rod bolts used to locate the gaiter. Fit the spacers, track rods

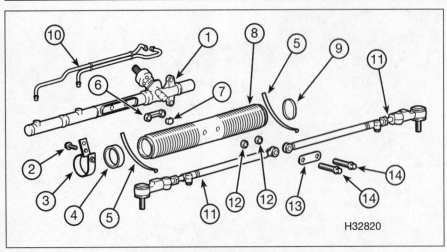

19.2 Steering rack gaiter renewal details

1 Steering rack (LHD shown)	5 Gaiter securing clip (cable-tie)	10 Fluid pipes
2 Clamp bolt	6 Slider	11 Track rods
3 Fluid pipe support bracket	7 Clip	12 Spacers
4 Gaiter sealing ring	8 Rack gaiter	13 Support plate
	9 Gaiter sealing band	14 Torx bolts

and the support plate to the rack using the new bolts, ensuring that all components are refitted as noted during removal.

15 Hold the track rods parallel to the rack, and tighten the Torx bolts to the specified torque **(see illustration)**.

16 Refit the rack as described in Section 18.

20 Power steering pump
– removal and refitting

Petrol engine

1 Apply the handbrake, then jack up the front

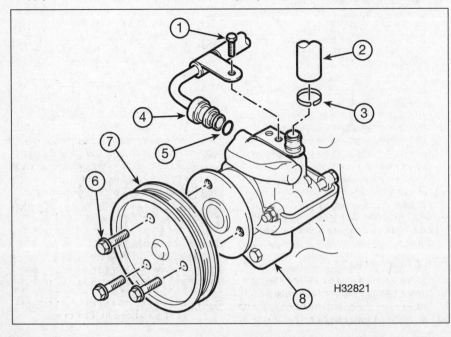

of the vehicle and support it on axle stands (see *Jacking and vehicle support*).

2 Loosen the power steering pump pulley bolts – if this is done before removing the drivebelt, the pulley will not be able to turn, making the bolts easier to loosen. Note the FRONT mark on the face of the pulley.

3 Referring to Chapter 1A, remove the power steering pump drivebelt.

4 Position a container under the fluid inlet hose connection on the pump – be prepared for the contents of the fluid reservoir to drain into it **(see illustration)**.

5 Using pliers, release the spring clip securing the fluid inlet hose, and disconnect it from the pump. Clean the connection on the pump,

19.15 Tighten the Torx bolts to the specified torque

then plug it or tape over it to prevent dirt getting in.

6 Remove the bolt securing the fluid outlet pipe clamp to the pump bracket.

7 Move the fluid container under the fluid outlet union. Loosen the union, disconnect the outlet pipe, and recover the O-ring. Clean the connection on the pump, then plug it or tape over it to prevent dirt getting in.

8 Remove the three pump pulley bolts, and remove the pulley.

9 Loosen and remove the two through-bolts and nuts, and the single bolt securing the pump to its mounting bracket, and remove the pump from the engine bay **(see illustration)**.

10 Refitting is a reversal of removal, noting the following points:

a) Tighten all fasteners and unions to the specified torque.

b) When refitting the pump pulley, fit the bolts by hand only, and tighten when the drivebelt has been refitted. Make sure the FRONT mark on the pulley faces outwards.

c) Clean around the pump fluid outlet union, use a new O-ring, and tighten the union to the specified torque.

d) Refit the drivebelt as described in Chapter 1A.

e) On completion, fill the fluid reservoir and bleed the system as described in Section 22.

L-Series diesel engine

11 Apply the handbrake, then jack up the front of the vehicle and support it on axle stands (see *Jacking and vehicle support*).

12 Remove the engine/transmission undertray, which is secured by two screws and a total of ten bolts – the frame bolts are of

20.4 Petrol engine power steering pump pulley and connections

1 Fluid outlet pipe clamp bolt
2 Fluid inlet hose
3 Spring clip
4 Fluid outlet pipe union
5 O-ring
6 Pulley bolts
7 Pulley
8 Power steering pump

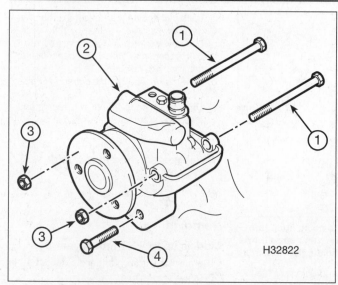

20.9 Petrol engine power steering pump mountings

1 Through-bolts   3 Nuts
2 Power steering pump   4 Bolt

20.24 L-Series diesel engine power steering pump details

1 Support bracket upper bolts (short)
2 Support bracket lower bolts (long)
3 Support bracket
4 Pump high-pressure union
5 O-ring
6 Fluid feed hose
7 Power steering pump

a different size to the panel bolts, so note their locations.

13 Remove the engine acoustic cover, as described in Chapter 2B.

14 Using a jack with a large flat piece of wood placed on the jack head, support the weight of the engine under the sump.

Models without air conditioning

15 Remove the three bolts securing the engine right-hand mounting to the engine, then lower the engine on the jack until the pump is accessible from below. Remove the right-hand front wheel and wheel arch liner to improve access.

Models with air conditioning

16 Unbolt and unclip the power steering hose from the support bracket attached to the engine right-hand mounting – the bracket is held by a nut on one of the engine mounting studs.

17 Remove the bolt securing the engine upper tie-bar to the engine right-hand mounting.

18 Loosen the bolt which secures the engine tie-bar to the body bracket, and raise the tie-bar to clear the engine mounting.

19 Remove the three engine right-hand mounting bolts, and lift off the mounting bracket. Raise the engine sufficiently to give access to the power steering pump.

All models

20 Loosen the three pump pulley Torx bolts, then remove the auxiliary drivebelt as described in Chapter 1B.

21 Remove the pulley bolts, and take off the pulley.

22 Position a container under the pump's high-pressure union. Loosen the union

(using two spanners, to prevent damage to the pump), disconnect the outlet pipe, and recover the O-ring. Clean the connection on the pump, then plug it or tape over it to prevent dirt getting in.

23 Move the fluid container under the fluid feed hose connection at the base of the fluid reservoir. Using pliers, release the spring clip and disconnect the hose from the reservoir – be prepared for the contents of the reservoir to be lost.

24 Remove the five bolts (three short, at the top, and two long, at the base) which secure the support bracket to the power steering pump and coolant pump **(see illustration)**. Take off the bracket, then remove the pump from the engine.

25 Refitting is a reversal of removal, noting the following points:

a) *Tighten all fasteners and unions to the specified torque. Refer to Chapter 2B for the engine mounting tightening torques.*

b) *When refitting the pump pulley, fit the bolts by hand only, and tighten when the drivebelt has been refitted.*

c) *Clean around the pump fluid outlet union, use a new O-ring, and tighten the union to the specified torque.*

d) *Refit the drivebelt as described in Chapter 1B.*

e) *On completion, fill the fluid reservoir and bleed the system as described in Section 22.*

TD4 diesel engine

26 Remove the 'Hydramount' engine right-hand mounting as described in Chapter 2C.

27 Loosen the three power steering pump pulley bolts, then remove the auxiliary

drivebelt as described in Chapter 1B. Take off the pulley, noting which way round it fits.

28 Using a suitable hoist or engine crane, raise the engine for access to the power steering pump.

29 Before proceeding, cover the alternator to prevent it getting covered in power steering fluid as the pump is removed.

30 Position a suitable container below the fluid feed hose connection to the pump, from the fluid reservoir. Be prepared for the contents of the fluid reservoir to be lost.

31 Using pliers, release the spring clip securing the fluid feed hose to the pump, then disconnect the hose and allow the fluid to drain **(see illustration)**.

32 Clean the pump around the fluid high-pressure hose connection. Loosen and remove the banjo bolt, then disconnect the hose and recover the sealing washers (new washers must be used when refitting). Clean the connection on the pump, then plug it or tape over it to prevent dirt getting in **(see illustration)**.

20.31 Release the spring clip securing the fluid feed hose to the pump

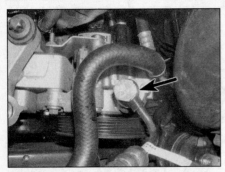

20.32 Remove the banjo bolt (arrowed), disconnect the hose and recover the sealing washers

33 Remove the pump mounting bolts, and remove the pump together with its mounting bracket. If a new pump is being fitted, the mounting bracket can be transferred to the new pump after removing the five Torx bolts **(see illustration)**.

34 Refitting is a reversal of removal, noting the following points:

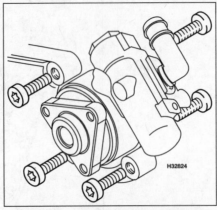

20.33 If a new pump is being fitted, the mounting bracket can be transferred to the new pump after removing the five Torx bolts

a) *Tighten all fasteners and unions to the specified torque. Refer to Chapter 2C for the engine mounting tightening torques.*

b) *When refitting the pump pulley, fit the*

bolts by hand only, and tighten when the drivebelt has been refitted.

c) *Use new washers on the high-pressure connection, and tighten the banjo bolt to the specified torque.*

d) *Refit the drivebelt as described in Chapter 1B.*

e) *On completion, fill the fluid reservoir and bleed the system as described in Section 22.*

21 Power steering fluid cooler – removal and refitting

Removal

Models up to 2001 model year

1 Remove the front bumper as described in Chapter 11.

2 Position a suitable container below the fluid cooler connections on the steering rack.

3 Remove the bolt securing the power steering fluid pipe bracket to the steering rack **(see illustration)**.

4 Loosen the union nut on the high-pressure fluid supply pipe, disconnect the pipe, and recover the O-ring (a new O-ring should be obtained for reassembly).

5 Using pliers, release the spring clip on the fluid return hose connection, and disconnect it.

6 Similarly, disconnect the fluid return hose from the base of the fluid reservoir – anticipate the loss of the entire reservoir contents into the container.

7 Remove the nut and bolt securing the power steering pipes to the bracket attached to the engine right-hand mounting.

8 Also remove the power steering pipe bracket on the right-hand inner wing, recovering the rubber mounting piece clipped around the pipes.

9 Two brackets of the same type, with a rubber mounting piece, are used to mount the fluid cooler pipes to the front crossmember – remove the two bolts from each bracket, then carefully withdraw the fluid cooler from under the vehicle.

Models from 2001 model year

10 On TD4 engine models, to gain access to the fluid cooler lower mounting bracket, carry out the following:

a) *Remove the engine acoustic cover.*

b) *Remove the air intake duct and intercooler outlet hose.*

c) *Remove the engine oil dipstick.*

11 Remove the bolt securing the fluid cooler pipe lower mounting bracket, at the base of the right-hand inner wing. Trace the pipes around the engine, noting how they are routed, then remove the bolt securing one of the pipes to the right-hand suspension strut turret **(see illustration)**.

12 Position a suitable container below the fluid reservoir – anticipate losing the reservoir contents when the hose is removed.

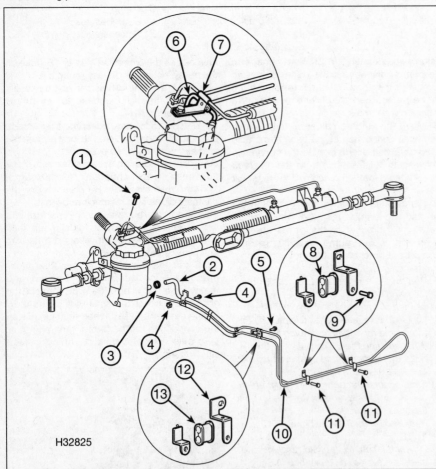

21.3 Power steering cooler components – up to 2001 model year

1 *Pipe bracket-to-rack bolt*	5 *Fluid pipe-to-front panel bracket bolt*	9 *Bolt*
2 *Fluid hose from reservoir*		10 *Cooler*
3 *Hose clip*	6 *Fluid return pipe union*	11 *Bolts*
4 *Fluid pipe-to-engine mounting bracket nut/bolt*	7 *Return pipe clip*	12 *Bracket*
	8 *Rubber sleeve*	13 *Rubber sleeve*

13 Using pliers, release the spring clip securing the fluid feed hose, disconnect the hose and allow the fluid to drain.

14 Reposition the container under the fluid hose quick-release connection just below the strut top mounting on the inner wing.

15 Release the connection by depressing the locking tab, and separate the hose sections.

16 Unclip and lift out the power steering fluid reservoir, feeding out the hoses as necessary.

17 Taking care not to damage the pipes, withdraw the fluid cooler from the engine bay.

Refitting

18 Refitting is a reversal of removal. Ensure that all pipework is routed correctly, with no kinks which might restrict fluid flow, and with no risk of pipework coming into contact with hot or moving components. On completion, refill the fluid reservoir, and bleed the system as described in Section 22.

22 Power steering system – bleeding

1 With the engine stopped, top-up the fluid reservoir up to the maximum mark with the specified type of fluid.

2 Have an assistant start the engine, while you keep watch on the fluid level. If the system has been drained during servicing work, be prepared to add more fluid as soon as the engine starts – the fluid level is likely to drop quickly.

3 Once the fluid level has stabilised, turn the engine off.

4 Check that the power steering fluid level is still up to the maximum mark, topping-up if necessary.

5 Start the engine and allow it idle for about 10 seconds, without turning the steering. Stop the engine, then check and top-up the fluid level if necessary.

6 Restart the engine, and turn the steering onto full left-hand lock, holding it there for a few seconds, and then onto full right-hand lock; check all steering hose/pipe unions for signs of leakage. **Note:** *Do not hold the steering at full lock for more than 10 seconds at a time, otherwise the hydraulic system may be damaged.*

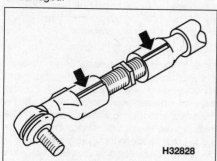

23.2 The slots (arrowed) in the track rod balljoint and the track rod should be aligned

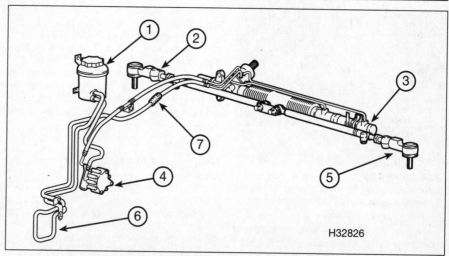

21.11 Power steering cooler components – from 2001 model year

1 Reservoir	4 Pump	6 Cooler
2 Right-hand track rod	5 Left-hand track rod	7 Quick-release connection
3 Steering rack		

7 Stop the engine, and top-up the fluid level if necessary.

8 Start the engine once more, and this time run it for about 2 minutes, turning the steering fully to the right and left.

9 Once all air is removed from the system, stop the engine, and check the fluid level as described in Chapter 1A or 1B. Take the vehicle for a journey of a few miles, then recheck the fluid level with the system fully up to operating temperature – repeat the bleeding process completely if there is any suggestion that air is still present.

23 Track rod end balljoint – removal and refitting

Removal

1 Loosen the wheel nuts, apply the handbrake, then jack up the relevant front wheel and support on axle stands (see *Jacking and vehicle support*). Remove the front wheel.

2 There are slots in the track rod balljoint and the track rod itself, which should be aligned, and can be used as a guide for refitting (this applies to old and new components) **(see illustration)**. If the slots cannot be seen, clean both components thoroughly. If necessary, use a straight-edge and a scriber, or similar, to mark its relationship to the track rod.

3 Slacken and remove the balljoint pinch-bolt, which secures the balljoint to the threaded adjuster sleeve (this is the outer pinch-bolt – leave the inner pinch-bolt alone) **(see illustration)**.

4 Loosen fully, but do not remove, the nut which secures each steering track rod to the steering arm at the top of the strut body. Using a balljoint splitter, separate the tapered joint from the arm, then unscrew the nut completely **(see illustration)**.

5 Counting the **exact** number of turns necessary to do so, unscrew the balljoint from the threaded adjuster sleeve.

6 Carefully clean the balljoint/strut tapers and the track rod threads. Renew the balljoint

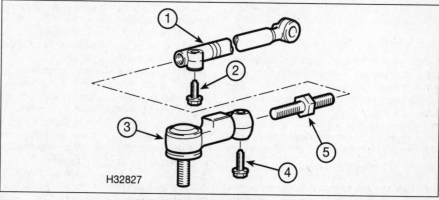

23.3 Track rod end balljoint details

1 Track rod	3 Track rod end balljoint	5 Threaded adjuster sleeve
2 Track rod pinch-bolt	4 Balljoint pinch-bolt	

23.4 Loosen fully, but do not remove, the nut which secures each steering track rod to the steering arm at the top of the strut body

if its movement is sloppy or too stiff, if it is excessively worn, or if it is damaged in any way; carefully check the stud taper and threads. If the balljoint gaiter is damaged, the complete balljoint assembly must be renewed; it is not possible to obtain the gaiter separately.

Refitting

7 Screw the balljoint onto the threads by the number of turns noted on removal – this should line up the slots or alignment marks that were made on removal.
8 Fit the pinch-bolt, but leave it hand-tight at this stage.
9 Fit the balljoint into the steering arm on the strut, then fit a new nut and tighten it to the specified torque.
10 If the tracking is not going to be adjusted immediately the vehicle is lowered, tighten the pinch-bolt to the specified torque now.
11 Refit the wheel, then lower the vehicle to the ground and tighten the wheel nuts to the specified torque.
12 On completion, have the tracking (front wheel alignment) checked as soon as possible. A good indication of the need for this will be whether the steering wheel is centralised, but even this isn't foolproof.

24 Track rods – removal and refitting

Removal

1 Loosen the wheel nuts, apply the handbrake, then jack up the front of the vehicle and support it on axle stands (see *Jacking and vehicle support*). Remove the front wheels.
2 On TD4 engine models, it will be necessary to remove the steering rack completely in order to proceed – refer to Section 18.
3 Remove the track rod end balljoints, as described in Section 23.
4 Remove the two Torx bolts which secure the track rods to the rack, then remove the support plate, track rods and spacers, noting their order of fitting and orientation for reassembly. New Torx bolts will be needed for reassembly. If the rack has been removed for this work, consider

fitting a new rack gaiter at the same time, as a precaution – see Section 19.
5 If necessary, the threaded adjuster section for setting the tracking can be unscrewed from each track rod, after removing the second pinch-bolt. The adjuster threaded section has a **left-hand** thread (ie, unscrews **clockwise**). To preserve the setting for refitting, note the number of turns required to remove the threaded section.

Refitting

6 Refitting is a reversal of removal, noting the following points:
a) Use new Torx bolts, and a new track rod balljoint nut.
b) Make sure that the track rod support plate and spacers are correctly refitted.
c) Hold the track rods parallel to the rack when tightening the track rod bolts.
d) Tighten all fasteners to the specified torque.
e) On completion, have the front wheel alignment checked at the earliest opportunity.

25 Wheel alignment and steering angles – general information

1 Accurate wheel alignment is essential for precise steering and handling, and for even tyre wear. Before carrying out any checking or adjusting operations, make sure that the tyres are correctly inflated, that all steering and suspension joints and linkages are in sound condition, and that the wheels are not buckled or distorted, particularly around the rims. It will also be necessary to have the vehicle positioned on flat, level ground, with enough space to push the vehicle backwards and forwards through about half its length.
2 Front wheel alignment consists of four factors:
Camber is the angle at which the road-wheels are set from the vertical, when viewed from the front or rear of the vehicle. 'Positive' camber is the angle (in degrees) that the wheels are tilted outwards at the top from the vertical.
Castor is the angle between the steering axis and a vertical line when viewed from each side of the vehicle. 'Positive' castor is indicated when the steering axis is inclined towards the rear of the vehicle at its upper end.
Steering axis or kingpin inclination is the angle, when viewed from the front or rear of the vehicle, between the vertical and an imaginary line drawn between the upper and lower front suspension strut mountings.
Toe setting is the amount by which the distance between the front inside edges of the roadwheels differs from that between the rear inside edges, when measured at hub height. If the distance between the front edges is less than at the rear, the wheels are said to 'toe-in'. If it is greater than at the rear, the wheels are said to 'toe-out'.
3 On the Freelander, the rear wheel toe

setting is also adjustable. Land Rover also quote specifications for the rear wheel camber angle, and the 'thrust angle' (about which no further details were forthcoming).
4 Camber, castor, steering axis inclination and 'thrust angle' are set during manufacture, and are not adjustable. Unless the vehicle has suffered accident damage, or there is gross wear in the suspension mountings or joints, it can be assumed that these settings are correct. If for any reason it is believed that they are not correct, the task of checking them should be left to a Land Rover dealer, who will have the necessary special equipment needed to measure the small angles involved.
5 It is, however, within the scope of the home mechanic to check and adjust the front and rear wheel toe setting. To do this, a tracking gauge must first be obtained. Two types of gauge are available, and can be obtained from motor accessory shops. The first type measures the distance between the front and rear inside edges of the roadwheels, as previously described, with the vehicle stationary. The second type, known as a 'scuff plate', measures the actual position of the contact surface of the tyre, in relation to the road surface, with the vehicle in motion. This is achieved by pushing or driving the front tyre over a plate, which then moves slightly according to the scuff of the tyre, and shows this movement on a scale. Both types have their advantages and disadvantages, but either can give satisfactory results if used correctly and carefully.
6 Many tyre specialists will also check toe settings free, or for a nominal charge.
7 Make sure that the steering is in the straight-ahead position when making measurements, and the vehicle is at normal kerb weight (ie, no-one inside, and no significant load or luggage carried).

Front wheel toe adjustment

8 If adjustment is necessary, apply the handbrake, then jack up the front of the vehicle and support it securely on axle stands. Slacken the track rod adjuster sleeve pinch-bolts, then rotate the adjuster threaded section using the nut provided to alter the length of the track rod (as necessary); shortening the track rod will reduce toe-in/increase toe-out.
9 When the setting is correct, tighten both the pinch-bolts to the specified torque setting.
10 Recheck the toe setting and, if necessary, repeat the adjustment procedure.

Rear wheel toe adjustment

11 If adjustment is necessary, chock the front wheels, then jack up the rear of the vehicle and support it securely on axle stands. Slacken the track rod adjuster sleeve locknuts, then rotate the adjuster sleeve to alter the length of the track rod (as necessary); shortening the track rod will reduce toe-in/increase toe-out.
12 When the setting is correct, hold the sleeve and tighten both the locknuts to the specified torque setting.
13 Recheck the toe setting and, if necessary, repeat the adjustment procedure.

Chapter 11
Bodywork and fittings

Contents

Degrees of difficulty

Easy, suitable for novice with little experience	Fairly easy, suitable for beginner with some experience	Fairly difficult, suitable for competent DIY mechanic	Difficult, suitable for experienced DIY mechanic	Very difficult, suitable for expert DIY or professional

Specifications

Torque wrench settings	Nm	lbf ft
Bonnet hinge bolts	9	7
Door hinge bolts	30	22
Driver's airbag module screws	9	7
Front seat bolts	45	33
Passenger's airbag module screws	9	7
Rear seat bolts	25	18
Roof rack side rail bolts	22	16
Seat belt buckle bolts	32	24
Seat belt mountings:		
Front:		
Slider bar and lower mounting bolts	40	30
Upper mounting	31	23
Rear:		
Lower mounting bolt:		
3-door	50	37
5-door	40	30
Upper mounting bolt	32	24
Seat belt pretensioner to seat	32	24
Seat belt reel bolt:		
Front, and rear centre	31	23
Rear side	50	37
Seat mounting bolts:		
Front seat	45	33
Rear seat	25	18
Soft back (roof) support bracket bolts	25	18
Spare wheel mounting bracket:		
Bolts	13	10
Nuts	25	18
Spare wheel-to-bracket nuts	45	33
Underbelly panel to body:		
Bolts	45	33
Rear screws	8	6

1 General information

Unlike previous Land Rovers, the Freelander does not have a separate 'ladder-frame' chassis and body, but instead has a car-like 'unitary' bodyshell, made of pressed-steel sections. The Freelander is available in three- and five-door versions, with the three-door model featuring a fold-down softback roof (with optional hardback section). Most components are welded together, but some use is made of structural adhesives; the front wings are bolted on.

Extensive use is made of plastic materials, mainly for the interior but also for exterior components. The front wings are made of a polymer-composite material, designed to be flexible enough to shrug off minor bumps, while the front and rear bumpers are injection-moulded from a synthetic material, which is very strong and yet light. Plastic components such as wheel arch liners are fitted to the underside of the vehicle, to improve the body's resistance to corrosion.

2 Maintenance – bodywork and underframe

The general condition of a vehicle's bodywork is the one thing that significantly affects its value. Maintenance is easy, but needs to be regular. Neglect, particularly after minor damage, can lead quickly to further deterioration and costly repair bills. It is important also to keep watch on those parts of the vehicle not immediately visible, for instance the underside, inside all the wheel arches, and the lower part of the engine compartment.

The basic maintenance routine for the bodywork is washing – preferably with a lot of water, from a hose. This will remove all the loose solids which may have stuck to the vehicle. It is important to flush these off in such a way as to prevent grit from scratching the finish. The wheel arches and underframe need washing in the same way, to remove any accumulated mud, which will retain moisture and tend to encourage rust. Paradoxically enough, the best time to clean the underframe and wheel arches is in wet weather, when the mud is thoroughly wet and soft. In very wet weather, the underframe is usually cleaned of large accumulations automatically, and this is a good time for inspection.

Periodically, except on vehicles with a wax-based underbody protective coating, it is a good idea to have the whole of the underframe of the vehicle steam-cleaned, engine compartment included, so that a thorough inspection can be carried out to see what minor repairs and renovations are necessary. Steam-cleaning is available at many garages, and is necessary for the removal of the accumulation of oily grime, which sometimes is allowed to become thick in certain areas. If steam-cleaning facilities are not available, there are some excellent grease solvents available which can be brush-applied; the dirt can then be simply hosed off. Note that these methods should not be used on vehicles with wax-based underbody protective coating, or the coating will be removed. Such vehicles should be inspected annually, preferably just prior to Winter, when the underbody should be washed down, and any damage to the wax coating repaired. Ideally, a completely fresh coat should be applied. It would also be worth considering the use of such wax-based protection for injection into door panels, sills, box sections, etc, as an additional safeguard against rust damage, where such protection is not provided by the vehicle manufacturer.

After washing paintwork, wipe off with a chamois leather to give an unspotted clear finish. A coat of clear protective wax polish will give added protection against chemical pollutants in the air. If the paintwork sheen has dulled or oxidised, use a cleaner/polisher combination to restore the brilliance of the shine. This requires a little effort, but such dulling is usually caused because regular washing has been neglected. Care needs to be taken with metallic paintwork, as special non-abrasive cleaner/polisher is required to avoid damage to the finish. Always check that the door and ventilator opening drain holes and pipes are completely clear, so that water can be drained out. Windscreens and windows can be kept clear of the smeary film which often appears, by the use of proprietary glass cleaner. Never use any form of wax or other body polish on glass.

3 Maintenance – upholstery and carpets

Mats and carpets should be brushed or vacuum-cleaned regularly, to keep them free of grit. If they are badly stained, remove them from the vehicle for scrubbing or sponging, and make quite sure they are dry before refitting. Seats and interior trim panels can be kept clean by wiping with a damp cloth. If they do become stained (which can be more apparent on light-coloured upholstery), use a little liquid detergent and a soft nail brush to scour the grime out of the grain of the material. Do not forget to keep the headlining clean in the same way as the upholstery. When using liquid cleaners inside the vehicle, do not over-wet the surfaces being cleaned. Excessive damp could get into the seams and padded interior, causing stains, offensive odours or even rot.

 HAYNES HiNT *If the inside of the vehicle gets wet accidentally, it is worthwhile taking some trouble to dry it out properly, particularly where carpets are involved. Do not leave oil or electric heaters inside the vehicle for this purpose.*

4 Minor body damage – repair

Minor scratches

If the scratch is very superficial, and does not penetrate to the metal of the bodywork, repair is very simple. Lightly rub the area of the scratch with a paintwork renovator, or a very fine cutting paste, to remove loose paint from the scratch and to clear the surrounding bodywork of wax polish. Rinse the area with clean water.

In the case of metallic paint, the most commonly-found 'scratches' are not in the paint, but in the lacquer top coat, and appear white. If care is taken , these can sometimes be rendered less obvious by very careful use of paintwork renovator (which would otherwise not be used on metallic paintwork); otherwise, repair of these scratches can be achieved by applying lacquer with a fine brush.

Apply touch-up paint to the scratch using a thin paintbrush; continue to apply thin layers of paint until the surface of the paint in the scratch is level with the surrounding paintwork. Allow the new paint at least two weeks to harden, then blend it into the surrounding paintwork by rubbing the paintwork in the scratch area with a paintwork renovator or a very fine cutting paste. Finally, apply wax polish.

Where the scratch has penetrated right through to the metal of the bodywork, causing the metal to rust, a different repair technique is required. Remove any loose rust from the bottom of the scratch with a penknife, then apply rust-inhibiting paint, to prevent the formation of rust in the future. Using a rubber or nylon applicator fill the scratch with bodystopper paste. If required, this paste can be mixed with cellulose thinners, to provide a very thin paste which is ideal for filling narrow scratches. Before the stopper-paste in the scratch hardens, wrap a piece of smooth cotton rag around the top of a finger. Dip the finger in cellulose thinners, and then quickly sweep it across the surface of the stopper-paste in the scratch; this will ensure that the surface of the stopper-paste is slightly hollowed. The scratch can now be painted over as described earlier in this Section.

Dents

When deep denting of the vehicle's bodywork has taken place, the first task is to pull the dent out, until the affected bodywork almost attains its original shape. There is little point in trying to restore the original shape completely, as the metal in the damaged area will have stretched on impact, and cannot be reshaped fully to its original contour. It is better to bring the level of the dent up to a point which is about 3 mm below the level of the surrounding bodywork. In cases where the dent is very shallow anyway, it is not worth trying to pull it out at all. If the underside of the dent is accessible, it can be hammered out gently from behind, using a mallet with a wooden or plastic head. Whilst doing this, hold a suitable block of wood firmly against the outside of the panel to absorb the impact from the hammer blows and thus prevent a large area of the bodywork from being 'belled-out'.

Should the dent be in a section of the bodywork which has a double skin or some other factor making it inaccessible from behind, a different technique is called for. Drill several small holes through the metal inside the area – particularly in the deeper section. Then screw long self-tapping screws into the holes just sufficiently for them to gain a good purchase in the metal. Now the dent can be pulled out by pulling on the protruding heads of the screws with a pair of pliers.

The next stage of the repair is the removal of the paint from the damaged area, and from an inch or so of the surrounding 'sound' bodywork. This is accomplished most easily by using a wire brush or abrasive pad on a power drill, although it can be done just as effectively by hand using sheets of abrasive paper. To complete the preparation for filling, score the surface of the bare metal with a screwdriver or the tang of a file, or alternatively, drill small holes in the affected area. This will provide a really good 'key' for the filler paste.

To complete the repair, see the Section on filling and re-spraying.

Rust holes or gashes

Remove all paint from the affected area, and from an inch or so of the surrounding 'sound' bodywork, using an abrasive pad or a wire brush on a power drill. If these are not available, a few sheets of abrasive paper will do the job just as effectively. With the paint removed, you will be able to gauge the severity of the corrosion, and therefore decide whether to renew the whole panel (if this is possible) or to repair the affected area. New body panels are not as expensive as most people think, and it is often quicker and more satisfactory to fit a new panel than to attempt to repair large areas of corrosion.

Remove all fittings from the affected area, except those which will act as a guide to the original shape of the damaged bodywork. Then, using tin snips or a hacksaw blade, remove all loose metal and any other metal badly affected by corrosion. Hammer the edges of the hole inwards in order to create a slight depression for the filler paste.

Wire-brush the affected area to remove the powdery rust from the surface of the remaining metal. Paint the affected area with rust-inhibiting paint; if the back of the rusted area is accessible treat this also.

Before filling can take place, it will be necessary to block the hole in some way. This can be achieved by the use of aluminium or plastic mesh, or aluminium tape.

Aluminium or plastic mesh or glass fibre matting is probably the best material to use for a large hole. Cut a piece to the approximate size and shape of the hole to be filled, then position it in the hole so that its edges are below the level of the surrounding bodywork. It can be retained in position by several blobs of filler paste around its periphery.

Aluminium tape should be used for small or very narrow holes. Pull a piece off the roll and trim it to the approximate size and shape required, then pull off the backing paper (if used) and stick the tape over the hole; it can be overlapped if the thickness of one piece is insufficient. Burnish down the edges of the tape with the handle of a screwdriver or similar, to ensure that the tape is securely attached to the metal underneath.

Before using this Section, see the Sections on dent, deep scratch, rust holes and gash repairs.

Many types of bodyfiller are available, but generally speaking those proprietary kits which contain a tin of filler paste and a tube of resin hardener are best for this type of repair; some can be used directly from the tube. A wide, flexible plastic or nylon applicator will be found invaluable for imparting a smooth and well contoured finish to the surface of the filler.

Mix up a little filler on a clean piece of card or board – measure the hardener carefully (follow the maker's instructions on the pack) otherwise the filler will set too rapidly or too slowly. Using the applicator, apply the filler paste to the prepared area; draw the applicator across the surface of the filler to achieve the correct contour and to level the filler surface. As soon as a contour that approximates to the correct one is achieved, stop working the paste – if you carry on too long the paste will become sticky and begin to 'pick up' on the applicator. Continue to add thin layers of filler paste at twenty-minute intervals until the level of the filler is just proud of the surrounding bodywork.

Once the filler has hardened, excess can be removed using a metal plane or file. From then on, progressively finer grades of abrasive paper should be used, starting with a 40-grade production paper and finishing with a 400-grade wet-and-dry paper. Always wrap the abrasive paper around a flat rubber, cork, or wooden block – otherwise the surface of the filler will not be completely flat. During the smoothing of the filler surface the wet-and-dry paper should be periodically rinsed in water. This will ensure that a very smooth finish is imparted to the filler at the final stage.

At this stage the 'dent' should be surrounded by a ring of bare metal, which in turn should be encircled by the finely 'feathered' edge of the good paintwork. Rinse the repair area with clean water, until all of the dust produced by the rubbing-down operation has gone.

Spray the whole repair area with a light coat of primer – this will show up any imperfections in the surface of the filler. Repair these imperfections with fresh filler paste or bodystopper, and once more smooth the surface with abrasive paper. If bodystopper is used, it can be mixed with cellulose thinners to form a really thin paste which is ideal for filling small holes. Repeat this spray and repair procedure until you are satisfied that the surface of the filler, and the feathered edge of the paintwork are perfect. Clean the repair area with clean water and allow to dry fully.

The repair area is now ready for final spraying. Paint spraying must be carried out in a warm, dry, windless and dust free atmosphere. This condition can be created artificially if you have access to a large indoor working area, but if you are forced to work in the open, you will have to pick your day very carefully. If you are working indoors, dousing the floor in the work area with water will help to settle the dust which would otherwise be in the atmosphere. If the repair area is confined to one body panel, mask off the surrounding panels; this will help to minimise the effects of a slight mis-match in paint colours. Bodywork fittings (e.g. chrome strips, door handles etc) will also need to be masked off. Use genuine masking tape and several thicknesses of newspaper for the masking operations.

Before commencing to spray, agitate the aerosol can thoroughly, then spray a test area (an old tin, or similar) until the technique is mastered. Cover the repair area with a thick coat of primer; the thickness should be built up using several thin layers of paint rather than one thick one. Using 400 grade wet-and-dry paper, rub down the surface of the primer until it is really smooth. While doing this, the work area should be thoroughly doused with water, and the wet-and-dry paper periodically rinsed in water. Allow to dry before spraying on more paint.

Spray on the top coat, again building up the thickness by using several thin layers of paint. Start spraying at the top of the repair area and then, with a side-to-side motion, work downwards until the whole repair area and about 50 mm of the surrounding original paintwork is covered. Remove all masking material 10 to 15 minutes after spraying on the final coat of paint.

Allow the new paint at least two weeks to harden, then, using a paintwork renovator or a very fine cutting paste, blend the edges of the paint into the existing paintwork. Finally, apply wax polish.

Plastic components

With the use of more and more plastic body components by the vehicle manufacturers (e.g. bumpers, spoilers, and in some cases major body panels), rectification of more serious damage to such items has become a matter of either entrusting repair work to a specialist in this field, or renewing complete components. Repair of such damage by the DIY owner is not really feasible owing to the cost of the equipment and materials required for effecting such repairs. The basic technique involves making a groove along the line of the

6.3a Remove the four screws (arrowed) along the top edge of the grille . . .

6.3b . . . then release the two catches at the base of the grille

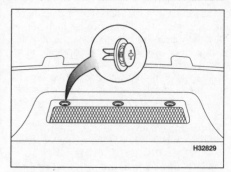

6.4 Remove the three 'scrivets' (arrowed) in the central recess below the number plate

crack in the plastic using a rotary burr in a power drill. The damaged part is then welded back together by using a hot-air gun to heat up and fuse a plastic filler rod into the groove. Any excess plastic is then removed and the area rubbed down to a smooth finish. It is important that a filler rod of the correct plastic is used, as body components can be made of a variety of different types (e.g. polycarbonate, ABS, polypropylene).

Damage of a less serious nature (abrasions, minor cracks etc) can be repaired by the DIY owner using a two-part epoxy filler repair material. Once mixed in equal proportions, this is used in similar fashion to the bodywork filler used on metal panels. The filler is usually cured in twenty to thirty minutes, ready for sanding and painting.

If the owner is renewing a complete component himself, or if he has repaired it with epoxy filler, he will be left with the problem of finding a suitable paint for finishing which is compatible with the type of plastic used. At one time the use of a universal paint was not possible owing to the complex range of plastics encountered in body component applications. Standard paints, generally speaking, will not bond to plastic or rubber satisfactorily. However, it is now possible to obtain a plastic body parts finishing kit which consists of a pre-primer treatment, a primer and coloured top coat. Full instructions are normally supplied with a kit, but basically the method of use is to first apply the pre-primer to the component concerned and allow it to dry for up to 30 minutes. Then the primer is

applied and left to dry for about an hour before finally applying the special coloured top coat. The result is a correctly-coloured component where the paint will flex with the plastic or rubber, a property that standard paint does not normally possess.

5 Major body damage – repair

Where serious damage has occurred, or large areas need renewal due to neglect, it means that complete new panels will need welding in, and this is best left to professionals. If the damage is due to impact, it will also be necessary to check completely the alignment of the bodyshell, and this can only be carried out accurately by a Land Rover dealer using special jigs. If the body is left misaligned, it is primarily dangerous, as the vehicle will not handle properly. Secondly, uneven stresses will be imposed on the steering, suspension and possibly transmission, causing abnormal wear, or complete failure, particularly to such items as the tyres.

6 Front bumper – removal and refitting

Removal

1 Open the bonnet. It is useful to have an assistant on hand for bumper removal, and

almost essential when refitting it.
2 To avoid the risk of damaging the number plate when the bumper is lowered, unscrew and remove it now if preferred.

Up to 2001 model year

3 Remove the radiator grille panel as follows (on models after this date, the grille is part of the front bumper moulding). Remove the four screws along the top edge of the grille, then release the two catches at the base of the grille, and remove it from the front of the vehicle (see illustrations).
4 Working from below, remove the three 'scrivets' in the central recess below the number plate. Remove the three screws, and prise out the plastic plugs (see illustration).
5 Remove the two upper screws in the centre which secure the top of the bumper to the front crosspanel, and the two lower centre screws which secure the bumper to the underbelly panel brackets (see illustration).
6 Remove the front wheel arch liners, which are held to the wings by five screws at the rear edge, and to the bumpers by a total of eight 'scrivets' inside. Prise out the centre of the 'scrivets' and then pull the outer section away.
7 With the wheel arch liners removed, loosen and remove the two bolts securing the bumper ends to the front wings.
8 With the help of an assistant if possible, pull out the bumper ends from the inner wings, and withdraw the bumper from the front of the vehicle, and lower it to the ground. If required, undo the eight bolts and remove the bumper bar. Disconnect the ambient temperature sensor (where fitted) from the bumper as it is withdrawn.

2001 model year onwards

9 Working from below, remove the three 'scrivets' in the central recess below the number plate. Remove the three screws, and prise out the plastic plugs (see illustration).
10 Remove the four upper screws in the centre which secure the top of the bumper to the front crosspanel (see illustration), and the two lower centre screws which secure the bumper to the underbelly panel brackets.
11 Remove the front wheel arch liners, which are held to the wings by five screws at the rear edge, and to the bumpers by a total of eight

6.5 Undo the two lower centre screws which secure the bumper to the underbelly panel brackets (arrowed)

6.9 Remove the three 'scrivets' in the central recess below the number plate (arrowed)

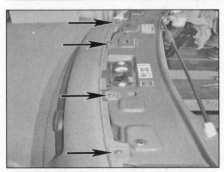

6.10 Unscrew the four upper screws in the centre which secure the top of the bumper to the front crosspanel

'scrivets' inside. Prise out the centre of the 'scrivets' and then pull the outer section away.

12 With the wheel arch liners removed, loosen and remove the two bolts securing the bumper ends to the front wings **(see illustration)**.

13 With the help of an assistant if possible, pull out the bumper ends from the inner wings, and withdraw the bumper from the front of the vehicle, and lower it to the ground. If required, undo the eight bolts and remove the bumper bar **(see illustration)**. Disconnect the ambient temperature sensor (where fitted) from the bumper as it is withdrawn.

Refitting

14 Refitting is a reversal of removal. Have an assistant ready to help with offering the bumper into position, and tighten all fixings securely.

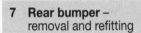

7 Rear bumper –
removal and refitting

Removal

1 Remove both rear mudflaps, which are secured by three screws each side. Also remove the mudflap mounting brackets either side **(see illustration)**.

2 Remove both bumper-mounted rear light clusters, as described in Chapter 12.

3 Remove the rear wheel arch extension mouldings on both sides, as follows:

a) On 3-door models, unscrew and remove the six 'scrivets' from inside the wheel

6.12 Undo the two bolts (one each side) securing the bumper ends to the front wings

arch then, taking care not to damage the paintwork, carefully prise off the extension moulding, which is clipped onto a total of eight studs on the outside.

b) On 5-door models, the procedure is similar to that for 3-door models, but there are only two 'scrivets' and two studs **(see illustration)**.

4 Remove five 'scrivets' from the top centre section of the bumper **(see illustration)**.

5 Work around the edges of the bumper, and remove a total of ten screws (five each side – two at the front upper corner, two from below, and one below the light cluster location).

6 Working through the bumper light apertures, undo the two nuts each side securing the bumper bar to the vehicle **(see illustration)**. With the help of an assistant if possible, withdraw the bumper from the rear of the vehicle, and lower it to the ground.

7.1 Remove both rear mudflaps

6.13 Undo the eight bolts (four each side) and remove the bumper bar

7 If required, the bumper cover can be separated from the bumper bar by unscrewing the two Torx bolts and nuts on the underside of the cover, and the 'scrivet' on the inside face **(see illustration)**.

Refitting

8 Refitting is a reversal of removal. Have an assistant ready to help with offering the bumper into position, and tighten all fixings securely.

8 Bonnet –
removal, refitting and adjustment

Removal

1 Open the bonnet, and have an assistant support it. Using a pencil or felt tip pen, mark

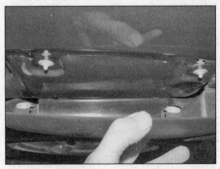

7.3 Carefully prise off the wheel arch extension moulding

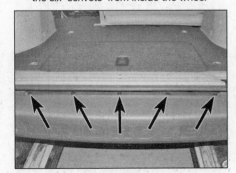

7.4 Remove five 'scrivets' (arrowed) from the top centre section of the bumper

7.6 Working through the bumper light apertures, undo the two nuts each side securing the bumper bar to the vehicle

7.7 Don't overlook the 'scrivet' on the inside face of the rear bumper

8.3 Undo the bonnet retaining bolts

the outline position of each bonnet hinge relative to the bonnet, to use as a guide on refitting.
2 Disconnect the washer tube from the elbow joint on the base of the driver's side washer jet.
3 Undo the bonnet retaining bolts and, with the help of an assistant, carefully lift the bonnet clear **(see illustration)**.

Refitting and adjustment

4 With the aid of an assistant, offer up the bonnet, and loosely fit the retaining bolts. Align the hinges with the marks made on removal, then tighten the retaining bolts securely.
5 Close the bonnet, and check for alignment with the adjacent panels. If necessary, slacken the bonnet bolts and realign the bonnet to suit, or screw the rubber buffers at the front corners in or out. Once the bonnet is correctly aligned, securely tighten the bolts. Check that the bonnet fastens and releases in a satisfactory manner.

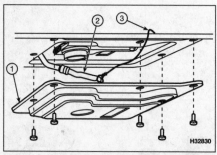

9.2 Drill out the rivets and remove the lower plate (1), release the cable (2), and tie a piece of string to the end (3)

9.5 Unhook the cable end fitting from the release lever

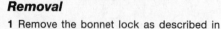

9 Bonnet release cable – removal and refitting

Removal

1 Remove the bonnet lock as described in Section 10.
2 Tie a piece of string to the end of the release cable, and pull the cable out of the front crosspanel. When the cable has been withdrawn, untie the string, and leave it in position for refitting **(see illustration)**.
3 Work back along the cable, releasing it from the cable-ties securing it to the wiring harness, and noting its correct routing.
4 From inside the vehicle, unscrew the retaining bolt securing the bonnet release lever to its mounting bracket **(see illustration)**.
5 Unhook the cable end fitting from the release lever, and remove the lever **(see illustration)**.
6 Returning to the engine compartment, pull away the sound insulation from the bulkhead where the cable passes through. Prise the release cable rubber grommet out of the bulkhead, then pull the cable through into the engine compartment.

Refitting

7 Refitting is a reversal of removal, noting the following points:
a) Feed the cable back through into the vehicle from the engine compartment, and work the rubber grommet into position

9.4 Unscrew the retaining bolt securing the bonnet release lever to its mounting bracket

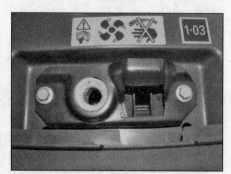

10.5 Undo the two retaining bolts and remove the bonnet lock upper plate

using a small screwdriver (it may also be helpful to lubricate the grommet with a little washing-up liquid, prior to fitting).
b) Use new cable-ties to secure the cable to the wiring harness.
c) Ensure that the cable is routed as noted before removal, with no sharp bends.
d) Attach the cable to the string left in the front crosspanel, and use the string to draw the cable into position for refitting to the bonnet lock.
e) Refit the bonnet lock as described in Section 10.

10 Bonnet lock – removal and refitting

Removal

1 With reference to Chapter 3, remove the radiator.
2 Drill out the rivets and remove the bonnet latch shield.
3 Disconnect the release cable from the lock **(see illustration 9.2)**.
4 Before removing the bonnet lock upper plate, mark around the plate with a marker pen or soft pencil, to indicate its fitted position relative to the crosspanel.
5 Undo the two retaining bolts and remove the bonnet lock upper plate **(see illustration)**.

Refitting

6 Refitting is the reverse of the removal procedure, using the alignment marks made prior to removal. Prior to closing the bonnet, check the operation of the release mechanism while an assistant works the release lever inside the vehicle. Also check that the bonnet striker enters the lock centrally, and adjust if necessary before finally closing the bonnet.

11 Door – removal, refitting and adjustment

Removal

Front door

1 Disconnect the battery negative lead – see Chapter 5A, Section 4.
2 Remove the footwell side trim panel on the side concerned – the trim is secured by one 'scrivet', and five Torx screws.
3 Reach inside past the bonnet release lever and cable, and disconnect the two wiring multiplugs which supply the door.
4 Trace the wiring down from the plugs, and release the harness sheath/grommet from the body. Feed the wiring through towards the door.
5 Using a hammer and suitable punch, carefully tap out the roll-pin securing the check link to the door pillar **(see illustration)**. Discard the roll-pin – a new one should be used on refitting.

11.5 Carefully tap out the roll-pin securing the check link to the door pillar

11.6 Prise off the C-clips from each of the hinge pins

11.18 Slacken the screws to adjust the position of the door lock striker

6 Prise off the C-clips from each of the hinge pins then, with the aid of an assistant, carefully lift the door upwards and away from the vehicle **(see illustration)**. If the C-clips show signs of distortion, renew them.

7 Examine the hinges for signs of wear or damage. If renewal is necessary, mark the outline of the original hinge on the door/pillar, then slacken and remove the retaining bolts and remove the hinge brackets. Note the correct fitted location of the shim(s) and spacer plates which are positioned behind them. Fit the new brackets, making sure that the shim(s) and spacer plates are correctly arranged, and refit the retaining bolts. Align the brackets with the marks made prior to removal, and securely tighten the retaining bolts.

Rear door

8 Disconnect the battery negative lead – see Chapter 5A, Section 4.

9 Prise off the B-pillar trim panel, which is secured by six clips.

10 Disconnect the wiring multiplug at the base of the B-pillar, which supplies the rear door.

11 Trace the wiring from the plug, and release the harness sheath/grommet from the body. Feed the wiring through towards the door.

12 Using a hammer and suitable punch, carefully tap out the roll-pin securing the check link to the door pillar. Discard the roll-pin – a new one should be used on refitting.

13 Prise off the C-clips from each of the hinge pins then, with the aid of an assistant, carefully lift the door upwards and away from the vehicle. If the C-clips show signs of distortion, renew them.

14 Inspect the hinges as described above in paragraph 7.

Refitting

15 Refitting is a reversal of removal, noting the following points:

a) *Apply a smear of multi-purpose grease to the hinge pivots then, with the aid of an assistant, manoeuvre the door back into position. Secure the door in position by fitting a C-clip to each of the hinge pins.*

b) *Align the check link with its mounting bracket, and secure it in position with a new roll-pin.*

c) *Feed the wiring back through the pillar, reconnect the wiring connector(s), and seat the rubber grommet back in the door pillar.*

d) *Once the battery has been reconnected, refer to Chapter 5A, Section 4, for the tailgate glass and alarm resetting procedure following battery disconnection.*

e) *On completion, if necessary, adjust the door position as described below.*

Adjustment

16 Some vertical adjustment of the doors can be achieved by slackening the hinge retaining bolts and repositioning the hinge/door.

17 Some front-to-rear adjustment of the door position can be achieved by adding/removing shims between the door and hinge bracket. To do this, loosen (do not remove) the hinge retaining bolts, then add/remove the relevant number of shims; the shims are slotted to allow them to be adjusted without removing

the door. Once the door is correctly positioned, securely tighten the hinge retaining bolts.

18 Door closure may be adjusted by altering the position of the door lock striker on the body **(see illustrartion)**. Slacken the striker, reposition it as required, then securely retighten it. The striker can also be adjusted by adding/removing shims from behind it.

12 Door inner trim panel
– removal and refitting

HAYNES HINT *It is a good idea to obtain a few trim panel retaining clips before starting, as they are often broken in the course of removal, or will be found to have broken during previous removal attempts.*

Removal

Front door – 3-door models

1 Disconnect the battery negative lead – see Chapter 5A, Section 4.

2 Prise off the triangular trim panel fitted inside the door mirror – this is secured by a central, serrated push-in clip, and is also clipped over a peg on the inside of the door trim panel. Once the mirror trim panel is free, disconnect the speaker wiring plugs inside **(see illustration)**.

3 Carefully prise out the centre section from the door pull handle, then unscrew the two screws underneath and remove the pull handle **(see illustrations)**.

12.2 Disconnect the tweeter speaker wiring inside the mirror trim panel

12.3a Prise out the door pull handle centre section . . .

12.3b . . . then remove the screws . . .

12.3c . . . and take off the pull handle

12.4a Loosen and remove the retaining screw . . .

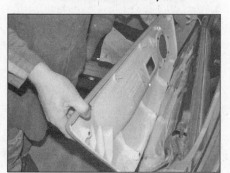

12.4b . . . then unclip and remove the door release handle recess panel

12.5 Remove the Torx screws around the trim panel

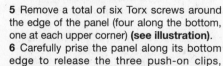

12.6a Lift the door trim panel over the door lock button . . .

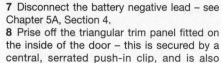

12.6b . . . then remove it from the door

4 Partially pull out the door release handle, and remove the single screw behind which secures the recess panel. Slide the recess panel rearwards initially, to unclip its front edge, then slide it around the release handle, and remove it **(see illustrations)**.

5 Remove a total of six Torx screws around the edge of the panel (four along the bottom, one at each upper corner) **(see illustration)**.

6 Carefully prise the panel along its bottom edge to release the three push-on clips, then lift the panel over the door lock button

and free it from the top of the door **(see illustrations)**.

Front door – 5-door models

7 Disconnect the battery negative lead – see Chapter 5A, Section 4.

8 Prise off the triangular trim panel fitted on the inside of the door – this is secured by a central, serrated push-in clip, and is also clipped over a peg on the inside of the door trim panel. Once the mirror trim panel is free, disconnect the speaker wiring plugs inside **(see illustration 12.2)**.

9 Partially pull out the door release handle, and remove the single screw behind which secures the recess panel **(see illustration)**. Slide the recess panel rearwards initially, to unclip its front edge, then slide it around the release handle, and remove it.

10 Remove two screws from the door pull handle, and a total of five screws from around the door pocket. Note the screw behind the cupholder plastic stud **(see illustrations)**.

11 Carefully prise the panel at the front and rear edges, to release the two push-on clips at each (one half-way up, one at the top corner), then pull the panel away from the door to release three further clips along the top edge **(see illustration)**.

12 Lift the panel over the door lock button and free it from the top of the door window guide.

Rear door

13 Disconnect the battery negative lead – see Chapter 5A, Section 4.

14 On models with manual windows, the winder handle must be removed as follows:

12.9 Remove the single screw which secures the recess panel

12.10a Remove two screws from the door pull handle

12.10b Prise out the cupholder stud . . .

12.10c . . . and undo the trim screw behind it

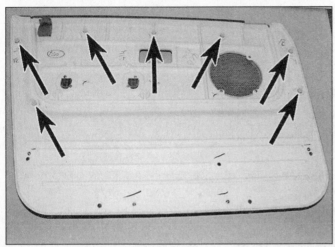

12.11 Front door trim clips (arrowed)

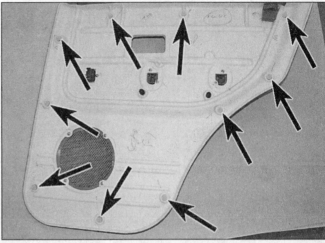

12.17 Rear door trim clips (arrowed)

a) *Prise the winder handle to open a gap between it and the circular disc behind.*

b) *Work the edge of a piece of (clean) cloth/ rag into the gap behind the handle, from below.*

c) *Using a 'sawing' action, work the cloth side-to-side, and also pull the ends of the cloth upwards. It may take some time, but what you're trying to do is snag the ends of the spring clip holding the handle in place – when you do, the sawing action should work the clip up and off, allowing the handle to be pulled from the splines. With patience, it does work – just watch for that spring clip flying off!*

15 Partially pull out the door release handle, and remove the single screw behind which secures the recess panel **(see illustration 12.9)**. Slide the recess panel rearwards initially, to unclip its front edge, then slide it around the release handle, and remove it.

16 Remove two screws from the door pull handle.

17 Carefully prise the panel first at the bottom, then at the front and rear edges, to release a total of ten push-on clips. Pull the panel away from the door, and (where applicable) disconnect the wiring plug from the electric window switch **(see illustration)**.

18 Release the two clips along the top edge of the panel, then lift it over the door lock button and free it from the top of the door window guide.

Refitting

19 Refitting is a reverse of the removal procedure, noting the following points:

a) *Prior to refitting, examine the panel retaining clips for signs of damage – renew any broken clips.*

b) *When refitting, do not forget to align the door lock button with its guide hole in the top of the trim panel.*

c) *To refit the mirror trim panel more easily, loosen the door trim at the top corner nearest the mirror, and fit the mirror trim*

12.19a Pull the door trim front corner away, and clip the mirror trim panel 'feet' into place behind . . .

in behind the door trim, locating its two front 'feet' over the peg on the back of the door trim. Align the mirror trim locating peg with the hole in the door frame, and push it and the door trim panel into place together (see illustrations).

d) *Once the battery has been reconnected, refer to Chapter 5A, Section 4, for the tailgate glass and alarm resetting procedure following battery disconnection.*

13 Door handle and lock components
– removal and refitting

Removal

Front door interior handle

1 Remove the door inner trim panel as described in Section 12. Peel the polythene weathershield away from the door to gain access to the door lock components, noting that the sheet may also be retained by several screw fixings for the door handle or door pocket.

2 Drill out the two rivets securing the door handle to the door **(see illustration)**.

3 Unhook the cable end fitting from the release handle, and remove the handle.

12.19b . . . then line up the trim panel peg with the hole in the door, and push in

4 The release cable is clipped to the door, and a further clip secures it to the lock assembly. Unhooking the other end of the cable from the lock operating lever means removing the lock assembly from the door, as described later in this Section – the cable end is hidden behind a plastic flap.

Front door exterior handle

5 Remove the door inner trim panel as described in Section 12. Peel the polythene weathershield away from the door, to gain access to the door lock components, noting that the sheet may also be retained by several screw fixings for the door handle or door pocket.

13.2 Drill out the two rivets (arrowed) securing the door handle to the door

13.6 Unclip the handle operating rod from the lock assembly

13.7 Remove the three Torx screws securing the lock assembly to the rear edge of the door

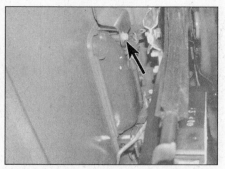

13.8a Exterior door handle bolt (arrowed)

13.8b Prise out the grommet and working through the hole (arrowed), undo the exterior door handle bolt

13.10 On later models, the cylinder is held in place by the exterior handle, and simply pulls out once the handle is removed

6 Working through the door aperture, unclip the handle operating rod from the lock assembly **(see illustration)**.

7 Remove the three Torx screws securing the lock assembly to the rear edge of the door, and lower the lock assembly slightly. If working on the driver's door on early models, unclip the lock barrel operating rod from the lock assembly. On later models the rod from the lock cylinder is a push-fit into the door lock, and is withdrawn when the exterior handle is removed **(see illustration)**.

8 Remove the rubber grommet from the door, then unscrew the two door handle bolts from inside, and recover the handle from outside **(see illustrations)**.

Front lock cylinder

9 Remove the driver's door exterior handle as described above.

10 On early models, the lock cylinder is held on by two screws. Disconnect any link rods

not already removed, then take out the two screws and withdraw the cylinder from the handle. On later models, the cylinder is held in place by the exterior handle, and simply pulls out once the handle is removed **(see illustration)**.

Front door lock

11 Remove the door inner trim panel as described in Section 12. Peel the polythene weathershield away from the door, to gain access to the door lock components, noting that the sheet may also be retained by several screw fixings for the door handle or door pocket.

12 Remove the exterior handle, as described in Paragraphs 5 to 8.

13 Disconnect the multiplug from the base of the lock assembly.

14 Working through the exterior handle aperture, use a small screwdriver to open the plastic flap on the side of the lock, prise

the interior release handle outer cable from the lock and disconnect the inner cable end fitting **(see illustrations)**. Access in limited, and some patience and dexterity will be required.

15 On 5-door models, make sure the door window is fully closed, then remove the two bolts securing the rearmost window glass guide channel, and move the guide towards the outside of the door cavity.

16 Manoeuvre the lock assembly down and out through the door aperture.

Rear door interior handle

17 The procedure is identical to that for the front door interior handle described previously in this Section.

Rear door exterior handle

18 Remove the door inner trim panel as described in Section 12. Peel the polythene weathershield away from the door, to gain access to the door lock components, noting that the sheet is also retained by two screw fixings for the door handle.

19 Working through the door aperture, unclip the handle operating rod from the lock assembly.

20 Remove the large rubber grommet from the door frame, for access to one of the door handle retaining bolts **(see illustration)**.

21 Remove the three Torx screws securing the lock assembly to the rear edge of the door, and lower the lock assembly slightly, for access to the handle retaining bolt. Unscrew both bolts, and remove the handle from outside **(see illustration)**.

13.14a Open the plastic flap on the side of the lock . . .

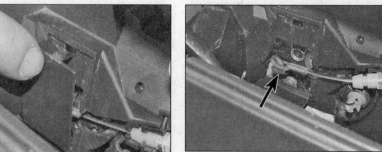

13.14b . . . prise the interior release handle outer cable from the lock and disconnect the inner cable end fitting (arrowed)

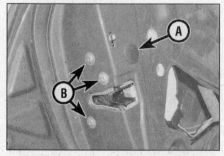

13.20 Remove the grommet (A) to access one of the exterior handle bolts, and undo the lock retaining screws (B)

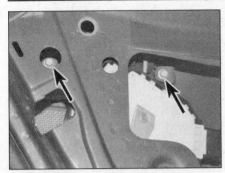

13.21 Undo the retaining bolts (arrowed) and remove the exterior handle

Rear door lock

22 The procedure is identical to that for removing the front door lock, except that there is no lock barrel to disconnect, and the window guide channel does not have to be disturbed.

Refitting

23 Refitting is the reverse of the removal sequence, noting the following points:

a) If a lock cylinder has been removed, check the operation of the lock cylinder before refitting the handle to the door.

b) Ensure that all link rods are securely held in position by their retaining clips.

c) Apply grease to all lock and link rod pivot points.

d) Before installing the relevant trim panel, thoroughly check the operation of all the door lock handles and the central locking system.

14 Door window glass and regulator – removal and refitting

Removal

1 Remove the door inner trim panel as described in Section 12. Peel the polythene weathershield away from the door, noting that the sheet may also be retained by several screw fixings for the door handle or door pocket. Proceed as described under the relevant sub-heading.

Front door window glass

2 Remove the four speaker retaining screws, withdraw the speaker from the door, and disconnect its wiring plug.

3 Lower the door glass until the two clamp bolts are visible in the door lower aperture (see illustration).

4 Loosen the two bolts and release the glass from the regulator. Tilt the glass forwards, and lift it out through the door frame (see illustration).

Rear door window glass

5 Lower the glass until the clamp bolt (nuts, on early models) is/are visible in the door lower aperture. Loosen the nuts or remove the bolt as applicable (see illustration).

6 Carefully prise the window seal from the door frame, and from the guide channel at its rear edge (see illustration).

7 Raise the glass so that it releases from the regulator, then lift it further and release the glass from the rear guide channel.

Rear door quarter-light

8 Remove the rear door window glass as described in Paragraphs 5 to 7.

9 Starting at the lower corner adjacent to the quarter-light, prise the outer seal from the door frame, continuing to the front of the door, up the vertical section, and across to the quarter-light upright (see illustration).

10 At this point, carefully pull the top of the quarter-light, with the seal, towards the front of the door frame and out of the vehicle (see illustration).

11 With the assembly removed from the vehicle, separate the quarter-light and seal. When refitting the quarter-light and seal, use a little soapy water as a lubricant.

Front door window regulator

12 Separate the window glass from the regulator, using the information in paragraphs 1 to 4 above. The glass does not have to be removed (it could be raised and taped up to the top of the frame), but removing it will be helpful.

13 On 3-door models, remove the four Torx screws securing the door brace, then release the regulator cable and remove the brace.

14 Disconnect the multiplug from the base of the window motor.

15 Slacken and remove the five bolts securing the regulator assembly to the door panel, and release the regulator cables from their retaining clips (see illustration).

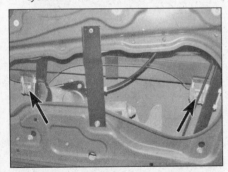

14.3 Front door window glass clamp bolts

14.4 Manoeuvre the window from the door frame

14.5 Slacken the glass clamp bolt (arrowed)

14.6 Carefully prise the window seal from the door frame, and from the guide channel at its rear edge

14.9 Prise the outer seal from the door frame

14.10 Carefully pull the top of the quarter-light, with the seal, towards the front of the door frame and out of the vehicle

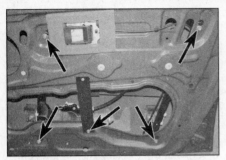

14.15 Undo the five bolts (arrowed) securing the regulator assembly to the door panel

16 Manoeuvre the regulator out through the door aperture **(see illustration)**.

Rear door window regulator

17 Remove the door inner trim panel as described in Section 12. Peel the polythene weathershield away from the door, to gain access to the door lock components, noting that the sheet may also be retained by several screw fixings for the door handle or door pocket.
18 Separate the window glass from the regulator, using the information in paragraphs 5 to 7 above. The glass does not have to be removed (it could be raised and taped up to the top of the frame), but removing it will be helpful.
19 Where applicable, disconnect the multiplug from the base of the window motor.
20 Slacken and remove the three bolts securing the regulator assembly to the door panel **(see illustration)**.
21 Check, where applicable, that the motor wiring and regulator cables have been released from the door frame. Manoeuvre the regulator out through the door aperture.

Refitting

22 Refitting is the reverse of the removal procedure, noting the following points:
a) *Prior to refitting the door trim panel, open and close the window a few times to ensure correct operation. In particular, check that nothing fouls the glass as it moves up and down.*
b) *Refit the plastic sheet, making sure it is securely stuck to the door, then install the trim panel as described in Section 12.*

15.3 Disconnect the three wiring plugs and the rear washer supply tube

14.16 Manoeuvre the regulator out through the door aperture

15 Tailgate and strut – removal and refitting

Removal

Tailgate

1 Disconnect the battery negative lead (see Chapter 5A, Section 4), then remove the spare wheel from the tailgate.
2 Remove the luggage area right-hand side trim panel, as described in Section 27, for access to the tailgate wiring plugs.
3 Disconnect the three wiring plugs which supply the tailgate, and also the rear washer supply tube **(see illustration)**.
4 Remove the two bolts in the rear edge of the luggage sill securing the tailgate check strap, then release the strap and position it to one side **(see illustration)**.
5 Feed the wiring through from the luggage compartment towards the tailgate then, with the tailgate fully open, release the wiring harness sheath and pull the wiring right out of the vehicle body, so that it's just hanging from the tailgate itself.
6 Mark the position of the hinges relative to the body, using a marker pen or soft pencil.
7 Have an assistant ready to take the weight of the tailgate, then loosen the hinge bolts and remove the tailgate from the vehicle.

Strut

8 The tailgate strut damper is located under the interior trim along the lower edge of the tailgate. To remove the strut, using a

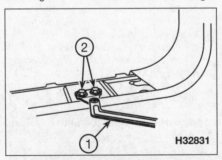

15.4 Remove the two bolts (2) in the rear edge of the luggage sill securing the tailgate check strap (1)

H32831

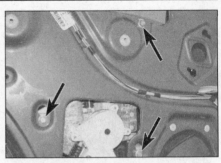

14.20 Slacken and remove the three bolts (arrowed) securing the regulator assembly to the door panel

screwdriver, prise out the retaining clips, and pull the strut from the mounting studs **(see illustration)**.

Refitting

9 Refitting is the reverse of removal, noting the following points:
a) *Locate the tailgate on its hinges, and refit the retaining bolts, tightening them by hand only.*
b) *Fit the tailgate check strap, and tighten the bolts fully.*
c) *Align the hinge marks made prior to removal, then securely tighten the hinge retaining bolts.*
d) *Close the tailgate and check for alignment with the surrounding body panels. Slight adjustments can be made by loosening the hinge bolts and repositioning the tailgate.*

16 Tailgate lock components – removal and refitting

> **HAYNES HiNT** *It is a good idea to obtain a few trim panel retaining clips before starting, as they are often broken in the course of removal, or will be found to have broken during previous removal attempts.*

Removal

1 Disconnect the battery negative lead – see Chapter 5A, Section 4.

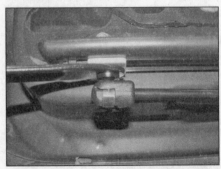

15.8 Using a screwdriver, prise out the retaining clips

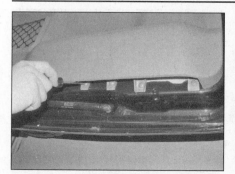

16.2 Remove the four screws at the base of the tailgate trim panel

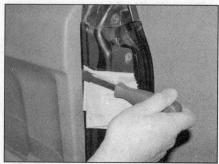

16.3a Release the trim panel clips using a wide-bladed tool . . .

16.3b . . . and pull the trim panel free of the tailgate

16.4 Peel away the plastic sheet from the tailgate

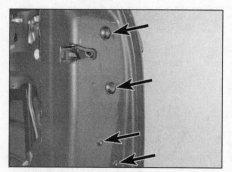

16.5 Remove the four lock assembly retaining screws (arrowed)

16.8 The central locking motor can be separated from the lock assembly after removing the single retaining screw (arrowed)

2 Remove the four screws along the base of the tailgate, below the 'door pocket' **(see illustration)**.

3 The tailgate trim panel is held on by a total of eight push-on clips (three on each side, two at the base). Release the clips using a wide-bladed tool, then pivot the panel out at the base, and lift to release the five further clips along the top of the panel **(see illustrations)**.

4 Very carefully peel away the plastic sheet from the door frame – it's not necessary to remove it completely, but tape it back clear of the working area, so it can be refitted easily later **(see illustration)**. Proceed as described under the relevant sub-heading.

Lock assembly

5 Remove the four lock assembly retaining screws **(see illustration)**.

6 Move the lock assembly slightly out of position, to gain access to the wiring plugs and harness clips.

7 Disconnect the two wiring multiplugs from the lock. Trace the wiring around the lock assembly, and release the two harness clips (one at the top, one half-way down).

8 Manoeuvre the lock assembly out of the tailgate. If required, the central locking motor can be separated from the lock assembly after removing the single retaining screw **(see illustration)**.

Exterior handle

9 Make sure that the tailgate glass is fully raised.

10 Working through the tailgate apertures, remove the three nuts securing the tailgate

handle, and release it from the tailgate **(see illustration)**.

11 Disconnect the two wiring plugs from the number plate light, then disconnect the lock wiring multiplug, and remove the handle completely. Recover the gasket from the door or handle – if its condition is less than perfect, renew the gasket.

Lock cylinder

12 Remove the exterior handle as described above. The lock cylinder appears to be integral with the exterior handle. Consult your Land Rover dealer.

Refitting

13 Refitting is the reverse of the relevant removal procedure, noting the following:
a) *If the lock cylinder has been removed, check the operation of the lock cylinder before refitting the handle.*
b) *Apply grease to all lock and link rod pivot points.*
c) *Once the battery has been reconnected, refer to Chapter 5A, Section 4, for the tailgate glass and alarm resetting procedure following battery disconnection.*
d) *Before installing the tailgate trim panel, thoroughly check the operation of the lock and the window.*

---

17 Central locking system
 – general information

The central locking system fitted to the Freelander is fully integrated with the anti-

theft alarm system, and a whole host of other systems on the vehicle. As such, the central locking comes under the control of a multi-function electronic control unit, called the Central Control Unit (or CCU).

The CCU controls the locking and unlocking functions, when triggered by the microswitch in the driver's door lock barrel, or (on models so equipped) by the remote locking keyfob. The central locking motors are incorporated into the main door lock assemblies (for removal details, see Section 13), and are not available separately. The only exception to this rule is the tailgate motor (see Section 16).

In conjunction with the anti-theft alarm, the CCU enables the vehicle to be locked as normal, or 'superlocked' (deadlocked) – a state in which the doors cannot be opened even using the interior handles, denying a thief entry even if a window has been smashed.

The CCU monitors whether the doors

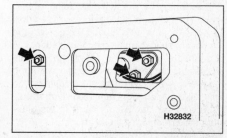

16.10 Remove the three nuts securing the tailgate handle, and release it from the tailgate

18.2 Disconnect the window heating element wiring plugs

18.3 Tailgate glass clamp bolt – note graduations showing glass alignment

18.4 Loosen the clamp bolts, then lift out the tailgate glass

18.7 Tailgate regulator motor securing bolts

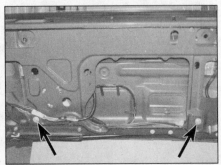

18.9 Slacken the preload adjuster locknuts (arrowed)

and tailgate are open or closed, and uses this information to control a range of other dependent functions, such as interior light delay, door-ajar, headlights-on, seat belt and handbrake-off warnings, and even rear wiper and heated rear window (both inoperative until the tailgate is shut, and the window raised).

The unit is clipped to the rear of the main fusebox, inside the glovebox; any suspected faults should be referred to a Land Rover dealer, for testing with the Testbook diagnostic equipment.

18 Tailgate glass and regulator – removal and refitting

Removal

1 Remove the tailgate trim panel as described in paragraphs 1 to 4 of Section 16.

Glass

2 Starting with the window fully raised, working through the tailgate aperture, disconnect the two wiring plugs for the window heating element **(see illustration)**.
3 Lower the window until the clamp bolts are accessible. Note how the clamps are fitted relative to the glass (there are graduations to indicate the fitted alignment) **(see illustration)**.
4 Loosen the clamp bolts, and lift the glass from the tailgate **(see illustration)**.

Regulator

5 Remove the tailgate glass as described previously.

6 Disconnect the regulator motor wiring plug.
7 Slacken and remove the three motor securing bolts **(see illustration)**, and twist motor to remove it from the door.
8 Loosen four nuts (two each side) securing the top ends of the glass guide channels, and release them from the tailgate.
9 At the base of each guide channel, loosen the preload adjuster locknut, and rotate the adjusters fully clockwise to improve access **(see illustration)**.
10 The regulator can now be manipulated out through the tailgate aperture – as it is removed, release the wiring harness attached to the glass left-hand clamp.

Refitting

11 Refitting is a reversal of removal, noting the following points:
a) *Refit the regulator mounting nuts and adjuster nuts finger-tight only to begin*

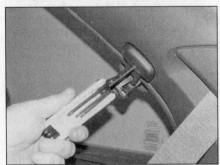

19.3a Remove the rear catch Torx screw . . .

with. Refit the motor, and tighten the nuts securely.
b) *Offer the glass into position, aligning the clamps as noted on removal. Make sure the glass is pushed fully down into the clamp nearest the tailgate hinge, and tighten the clamp bolt securely. Set the glass horizontal alignment using the heater element 'bars' as a guide, then tighten the remaining clamp bolt.*
c) *Close the tailgate, and check the gap either side of the glass, relative to the bodywork. Adjust if necessary after loosening the clamp bolts.*
d) *Raise the glass and connect up the heater element wiring plugs.*
e) *Use the preload adjusters at the base of the guide channels to set the glass preload on the rubber seal. First loosen the adjusters so that a gap exists, then bring them both up into contact with the seal, and finally adjust until a 1 mm preload is placed on the seal. On completion, tighten the adjuster locknuts securely.*
f) *Once the battery has been reconnected, refer to Chapter 5A, Section 4, for the tailgate glass and alarm resetting procedure following battery disconnection.*
g) *Before refitting the tailgate trim panel, raise and lower the window several times to check its operation and alignment. In particular, check that nothing fouls the glass as it moves up and down, and that it seals correctly.*

19 Hinged rear side windows (3-door models) – removal and refitting

Removal

1 Remove the Torx screw from each of the two front hinge covers, and remove the covers.
2 Have an assistant support the window from outside.
3 Remove the single screw from the rear catch, noting its spacer, and release the catch from the C-pillar trim panel **(see illustrations)**.

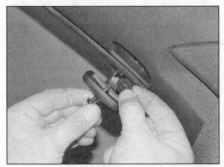

19.3b . . . and release the catch from the C-pillar, recovering the spacer

4 Now have your assistant remove the window from outside. Keeping the glass as flat to the body as possible, remove the window rearwards, easing the front hinges off the window seal from inside **(see illustration)**.

Refitting

5 Refitting is a reversal of removal.

20 Windscreen and fixed windows – general information

These areas of glass are secured by the tight fit of the weatherstrip in the body aperture, and are bonded in position with a special adhesive. The removal and refitting of these areas of fixed glass is difficult, messy and time-consuming task, which is considered beyond the scope of the home mechanic. It is difficult, unless one has plenty of practice, to obtain a secure, waterproof fit. Furthermore, the task carries a high risk of breakage; this applies especially to the laminated glass windscreen. In view of this, owners are strongly advised to have this sort of work carried out by one of the many specialist windscreen fitters.

21 Soft back (3-door models) – general information

The entire soft back roof can be removed as described in the owner's handbook, for fitting the optional hard back roof section. The various hood catches are secured by three

22.3 The sunroof can be opened and closed manually using a suitable screwdriver to turn the motor spindle (arrowed)

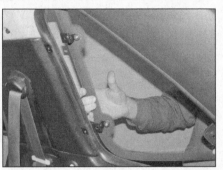

19.4 Pull the hinges off the window seal, and remove it

Torx bolts – mark the positions of the catches before removing. Any operations involving the optional hard back section are fairly self-explanatory – fitting a new primary seal, for instance, involves peeling off the old one and fitting the new one to a cleaned edge. Fitting a new soft back outer cover is not impossible for the DIY mechanic, but would still be better left to a professional – the cover is glued to the front and rear of the hood frame.

22 Sunroof – general information

Three-door models have a simple targa sunroof, with twin removable panels, while five-door models have a more complex electric tilt/slide sunroof.

If the electric roof operates slowly, or the motor appears to be struggling, first ensure that this is not down to a lack of maintenance – all the moving parts and slides should be regularly lubricated with light oil (your Land Rover dealer will be able to advise on a suitable product). The sunroof motor draws quite a heavy current – a battery which is low on charge may struggle to open the roof.

If the sunroof motor fails to operate, first check the relevant fuse. The motor incorporates an automatic cut-out facility, which cuts the motor if the sunroof encounters an obstruction – the motor may therefore cut out if the mechanism is partially seized. An occasional failure to work could also be due to wear in the sunroof switch. If the fault

23.3 Support the mirror assembly, then undo the retaining screws (arrowed)

cannot be traced and rectified, the sunroof can be opened and closed manually using a suitable screwdriver to turn the motor spindle. To gain access to the motor spindle, carefully prise out the trim cover situated at the rear of the sunroof. Insert the screwdriver into the slot in the motor spindle, and rotate to move the sunroof to the required position **(see illustration)**. Due to the complexity of the tilt/slide sunroof mechanism, considerable expertise is needed to repair, renew or adjust the sunroof components successfully. Removal of the roof first requires the headlining to be removed, which is a complex and tedious operation in itself, and not a task to be undertaken lightly (See Section 27). Therefore, any problems with the sunroof should be referred to a Land Rover dealer.

For information on the sunroof switch and sunroof motor, see Chapter 12.

23 Mirrors and associated components – removal and refitting

Exterior mirror

1 Carefully unclip the mirror inner trim panel from the door.
2 Disconnect the two wiring connectors from the tweeter speaker, and the wiring plugs from the mirror.
3 Support the mirror assembly, then undo the retaining screws **(see illustration)**.
4 Remove the mirror assembly from the door, and recover its clamp plate from inside.
5 Refitting is the reverse of removal.

Exterior mirror glass

Caution: If the glass is broken, wear sturdy gloves. Even if the glass is not broken, wearing gloves is a sensible precaution, should the glass break as it is being removed or refitted.

6 Position the glass so its lower edge is fully in, then carefully ease your fingers in behind the upper edge of the glass, and gently pull the glass upwards, and then outwards until it is released from its retaining clips. Take great care when removing the glass; do not use excessive force, as the glass is easily broken **(see illustration)**.

23.6 Gently pull the glass upwards, and then outwards until it is released from its retaining clips

23.13 Press the retaining clips aside, and lift the ECU from the mounting tray

7 Disconnect the wiring connectors from the mirror heating element as they become accessible.

8 On refitting, reconnect the wiring connectors (where necessary). Carefully clip the glass back into position, ensuring that it is securely retained by each of the clips.

Exterior mirror switch

9 Refer to Chapter 12.

Mirror ECU

10 On models equipped with 'Powerfold' exterior mirrors, the function of the mirrors is controlled by an ECU (Electronic Control Unit).

Models up to 2002 model year

11 The ECU is located under the front section of the centre console. Remove the centre console as described in Chapter 12.

12 Disconnect the wiring plug from the side of the ECU.

13 Press the retaining clips aside, and lift the ECU from the mounting tray (see illustration).

14 Refitting is a reversal of removal.

Models from 2002 model year

15 The ECU is located alongside the passenger side A-pillar behind the facia. At the time of writing, no information concerning the removal and refitting of the unit was available.

Interior mirror

16 The interior mirror is released by sliding the mirror arm up and off the mounting plate (see illustration). If the mounting plate needs to be renewed, consult your Land Rover dealer or windscreen specialist.

24 Body exterior fittings
– removal and refitting

Wheel arch liners and body under-panels

1 The various plastic covers fitted to the underside of the vehicle are secured in position by a mixture of screws, nuts and retaining clips. Removal will be fairly obvious on inspection.

2 The front wheel arch liners are held to the wing by five screws at the rear edge, and a total of eight 'scrivets' inside.

3 The underbelly panel and its frame are secured by two screws and a total of ten bolts – the frame bolts are of a different size to the panel bolts, so note their locations.

Roof rails

4 Prise off the covers at the front and rear of the rail, for access to the securing bolts. Note that the covers must be prised off vertically (see illustration).

5 Unscrew the two Allen or Torx bolts front and rear, and lift away the roof rail. Recover the gaskets fitted at either end of the rail, and the seal fitted to each bolt. New gaskets and seals should be fitted on reassembly, if the originals are not in serviceable condition.

Sill finishers

6 Access to the sill finishers is most easily gained with the front of the vehicle jacked up and supported on axle stands (see *Jacking and vehicle support*).

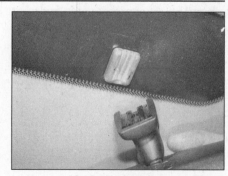

23.16 Interior mirror

7 Remove the covers from both jacking points, then remove the seven 'scrivets' which secure the finisher to the vehicle.

Rear wheel arch mouldings

8 Loosen the relevant rear wheel nuts, chock the front wheels, then jack up the rear of the vehicle and support it on axle stands (see *Jacking and vehicle support*). Remove the rear wheel.

9 On 3-door models, unscrew and remove the six 'scrivets' from inside the wheel arch, then taking care not to damage the paintwork, carefully prise off the extension moulding, which is clipped onto a total of eight studs on the outside.

10 On 5-door models, the procedure is similar to that for 3-door models, but there are only two 'scrivets' and two studs (see illustration).

Radiator grille

11 A separate radiator grille panel is only fitted up to 2001 model year (on models after this date, the grille is part of the front bumper moulding – see Section 6). Remove the four screws along the top edge of the grille, then release the two catches at the base of the grille, and remove it from the front of the vehicle.

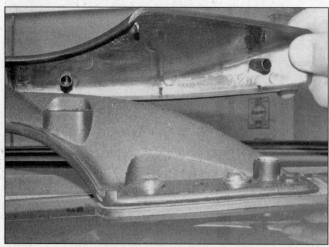

24.4 Prise off the covers at the front and rear of the rail, for access to the securing bolts

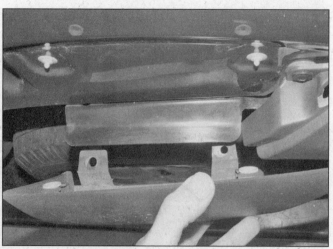

24.10 On 5-door models, the wheel arch extensions are retained by two 'scrivets' and two studs

24.16 Unscrew the six bolts and two nuts, release the wiring loom from the retaining clips, and remove the spare wheel bracket from the tailgate

Body trim strips and badges

12 Most of the various body trim strips and badges are held in position with a special adhesive tape. Removal requires the trim/badge to be heated, to soften the adhesive, and then cut away from the surface. Due to the high risk of damage to the vehicle's paintwork during this operation, it is recommended that this task should be entrusted to a Land Rover dealer.

Spare wheel mounting bracket

13 Lower the tailgate glass using the centre console switch.
14 Undo the three retaining screws, and detach the high-level stop-light unit cover. Disconnect the light unit wiring plug, and remove the light.
15 Unscrew and remove the three nuts securing the spare wheel in position, and remove it from the mounting bracket.
16 The mounting bracket is secured by six bolts and two nuts. Unscrew the various fasteners, release the wiring loom from the retaining clips, and remove the bracket from the tailgate (see illustration).
17 Refitting is a reversal of removal. Tighten the mounting bracket fasteners and the spare wheel nuts to the specified torque.

25 Seats – removal and refitting

Removal

Front seat

1 Remove the ignition key, then disconnect the battery completely (see Chapter 5A, Section 4), and wait at least 10 minutes before proceeding. This is essential, to ensure that the front seat belt pretensioners are not activated when the seat is removed/refitted.
2 Remove the seat cushion side trim panel, which is secured by three screws (two under plastic covers, one accessed inside the rear of the seat). Remove the seat outer trim panel, which is secured by three Torx screws – slide the seat forwards and unclip the hinged cover for access to the third screw (see illustrations).

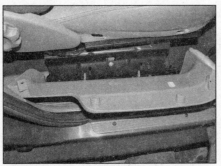

25.2a Remove the seat cushion side trim panel, which is secured by three screws (two under plastic covers, one accessed inside the rear of the seat)

3 Unclip the wiring for the seat belt pretensioner and heated seat elements (where fitted) from the seat frame, then disconnect the wiring plugs. If the passenger front seat is being removed on a vehicle with a CD autochanger, reach under the seat and disconnect the data lead from the CD changer.
4 The seat is secured in position by four Torx bolts, the inner rear one being hidden under a plastic cover. Remove the bolts and take out the seat (see illustration).

Rear seat

5 Three-door models have a one-piece rear seat, while 5-door models have a 60/40 split seat. The only difference for removal and refitting is that the split rear seat is in two sections – it's therefore possible to remove whichever section of seat is required.
6 Working in the rear footwells, fold down the carpet as necessary for access to the two Torx bolts at the base of the seat cushion (see illustration). Remove the two bolts, then fold the seat forwards.
7 With the seat folded forwards, remove the hinge bolts from the floor (see illustration), and take the whole rear seat out through one of the rear doors.

Refitting

8 Refitting is a reversal of removal, noting the following points:
a) When refitting the front seat, ensure that the battery is still disconnected and the ignition key removed. Otherwise,

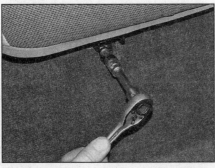

25.6 Working in the rear footwells, remove the Torx bolt below the seat cushion

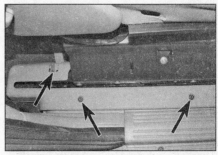

25.2b Remove the seat outer trim panel, which is secured by three Torx screws (arrowed) – slide the seat forwards and unclip the hinged cover for access to the third screw

there is a danger of setting off the seat belt pretensioner when its wiring plug is reconnected. Also make sure that the pretensioner wiring is securely re-attached to the seat, and in no danger of being trapped or damaged.
b) Tighten the seat mounting bolts to the specified torque.

26 Seat belts – removal and refitting

Removal

Front seat belt – 3-door

1 Remove the seat cushion side trim panel, which is secured by three screws (two under

25.4 The inner rear seat mounting bolt is hidden under a plastic cover

25.7 With the rear seat folded forwards, remove the hinge bolts from the floor

26.3 Front seat belt lower mounting rail Torx bolt

26.6 Remove the front seat belt inertia reel bolt

26.10a Remove the seat belt upper mounting nut (arrowed) . . .

26.10b . . . and the inertia reel mounting bolt

26.15 Remove the Torx bolt and washer from the pretensioner

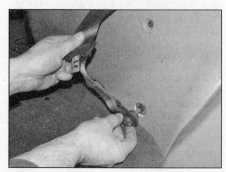

26.17 Unscrew and remove the rear seat belt lower mounting bolt

plastic covers, one accessed under the rear of the seat). Remove the seat outer trim panel, which is secured by three Torx screws – slide the seat forwards and unclip the hinged cover for access to the third screw.
2 Remove the rear side trim panel, as described in Section 27.
3 Unscrew the two Torx bolts securing the seat belt lower mounting rail **(see illustration)**, and unhook the end of the belt from the rail.
4 Unclip the plastic strap/guide which retains the belt to the side of the vehicle.
5 Unclip the trim piece fitted over the seat belt upper mounting, and remove the Torx bolt beneath.
6 Remove the single bolt securing the seat belt inertia reel **(see illustration)**, and remove the seat belt from the vehicle.

Front seat belt – 5-door

7 Remove the seat cushion side trim panel, which is secured by three screws (two under

26.18a Unscrew the seat belt upper mounting bolt . . .

plastic covers, one accessed under the rear of the seat) **(see illustration 25.2a)**. Remove the seat outer trim panel, which is secured by three Torx screws – slide the seat forwards and unclip the hinged cover for access to the third screw **(see illustration 25.2b)**.
8 Remove the B-pillar trim panels, as described in Section 27.
9 Unclip the plastic strap/guide which retains the belt to the B-pillar.
10 Remove the seat belt upper mounting nut **(see illustration)**, and the single bolt securing the seat belt inertia reel **(see illustration)**, and remove the seat belt from the vehicle.
11 If required, the seat belt height adjuster can also be removed, after unscrewing its two Torx bolts.

Front seat belt pretensioner

12 Remove the ignition key, then disconnect the battery completely (see Chapter 5A, Section 4), and wait at least 10 minutes before

26.18b . . . then remove the inertia reel mounting bolt, and remove the seat belt

proceeding. This is essential, to ensure that the pretensioners are not set off accidentally – apart from being inconvenient, this could be highly dangerous if it happened.
13 Remove the rear section of the centre console, as described in Section 28.
14 Unclip the wiring for the pretensioner from the seat frame, then disconnect the wiring plug.
15 Remove the Torx bolt and washer from the pretensioner, and remove the pretensioner from the front seat **(see illustration)**. Remove the pretensioner to a secure storage area – treat it the same way as an airbag unit (Chapter 12).

Rear seat belt

16 Remove either the C-pillar trim panel (3-door models) or the rear window surround (5-door models), as described in Section 27. To access the belt inertia reel, also remove the luggage area side trim panel.
17 Fold the rear seat forwards and remove the seat belt lower mounting bolt **(see illustration)**.
18 Remove the Torx bolt from the seat belt upper mounting, then remove the single bolt securing the seat belt inertia reel, and remove the belt from the vehicle **(see illustrations)**.

Rear seat belt stalk – 3-door models

19 Remove the rear seat as described in Section 25.
20 Unscrew and remove the two screws from the seat hinge cover on the side concerned.
21 Remove the seat centre console, which is secured by a total of four screws (two at the front edge, two at the back).

22 Work around the edges of the seat cushion, and unclip the cushion cover from the seat frame. Remove the cover and padding from the frame.

23 Remove the single Torx bolt which secures the belt stalk, and remove the stalk from the seat.

Rear seat belt stalk – 5-door models

24 Fold the rear seat forwards, and remove the seat hinge cover on the side concerned – the cover is held on by three screws.

25 Remove the four Torx bolts from the seat catch assembly, and remove the assembly from the seat.

26 Unscrew the single Torx bolt which secures the belt stalk, and remove the stalk.

Centre rear seat belt – 5-door models

27 Remove the right-hand section of the rear seat, as described in Section 25.

28 Unscrew the two screws and remove the seat belt reel cover from the centre of the seat **(see illustration)**.

29 Slacken and remove the seat belt reel mounting nut, and release the reel from the seat **(see illustration)**.

30 Remove the hinge cover at either side of the seat – the covers are secured by five screws altogether.

31 Now remove the hinge bolts exposed by removing the covers – there are two Torx bolts one side, and just one on the other. Separate the seat backrest from the cushion.

32 Work along the edges of the cushion and backrest, and unclip the cover and padding from the seat frame, for access to the seat belt components.

33 Remove the Torx bolt which secures the belt lower mounting and belt buckle, and remove the seat belt from the seat.

Refitting

34 Refitting is a reversal of the removal procedure, noting the following points:
a) *When refitting the front seat belt pretensioner, ensure that the battery is still disconnected and the ignition key removed. Otherwise, there is a danger of setting off the pretensioner when its wiring plug is reconnected. Also make sure that the pretensioner wiring is securely re-attached to the seat,*

26.28 Unscrew the two screws and remove the seat belt reel cover from the centre of the seat

and in no danger of being trapped or damaged.
b) *Tighten the seat belt mounting bolts to the specified torque.*

27 Interior trim – removal and refitting

General

1 The interior trim panels are secured using either screws or various types of trim fasteners, usually studs or clips.

2 Check that there are no other panels overlapping the one to be removed; usually there is a sequence to be followed that will become obvious on close inspection.

3 Remove all obvious fasteners, such as screws. If the panel will not come free, it is held by hidden clips or fasteners. These are usually situated around the edge of the panel, and can be prised up to release them. Note, however, that they can break quite easily, so new ones should be available. The best way of releasing such clips in the absence of the correct type of tool, is to use a large flat-bladed screwdriver. Note in many cases that an adjacent sealing strip (such as the rubber door seal) must be prised back to release a panel.

4 When removing a panel, **never** use excessive force, or the panel may be damaged. Always check carefully that all fasteners have been removed or released before attempting to withdraw a panel.

5 Refitting is the reverse of the removal

26.29 Remove the seat belt reel mounting nut

procedure; secure the fasteners by pressing them firmly into place, and ensure that all disturbed components are correctly secured, to prevent rattles.

A-pillar trim panel

6 Peel off the rubber door seal adjoining the trim panel, then carefully prise the panel away from the A-pillar. The panel is held by a total of four push-on clips down the middle of the panel **(see illustrations)**.

Sill inner trim panels

7 The sill trim panels are held by several Torx screws (mainly visible on top, but one or two on the inside edge) **(see illustration)**. The front sill panels may have a further 'scrivet' at the very front inner corner, under the facia. The rear sill panels on 5-door models are held by screws only.

B-pillar trim panels

5-door models

8 Remove the seat cushion side trim panel, which is secured by three screws (two under plastic covers, one accessed inside the rear of the seat) **(see illustration 25.2a)**. Remove the seat outer trim panel, which is secured by three Torx screws – slide the seat forwards and unclip the hinged cover for access to the third screw **(see illustration 25.2b)**.

9 Unscrew and remove the front seat belt lower mounting bolt.

10 The B-pillar trim panel is secured by six push-on clips, arranged in three pairs at the top, middle, and bottom of the panel **(see illustration)**. Prise the panel carefully to

27.6a Peel off the rubber door seal adjoining the trim panel, then carefully prise the panel away from the A-pillar . . .

27.6b . . . the panel is held by a total of four push-on clips down the middle of the panel

27.7 The sill trim panels are held by several Torx screws, some on top, some on the inside

27.10 B-pillar trim panel upper retaining clips

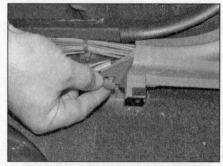

27.11 B-pillar lower trim panel front 'scrivet'

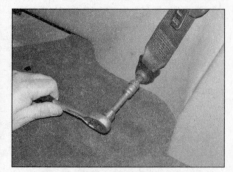

27.14 Unscrew the seat belt lower mounting bolt

27.15 Remove the Torx screws around the edge of the panel

27.16 Carefully prise the panel away, and remove it

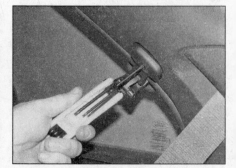

27.18 Remove the rear window catch securing screw

release the clips, then release the seat belt from the panel.

11 To remove the B-pillar lower trim panel, unscrew and remove the 'scrivet' at the front, then remove the single Torx screw at the rear, and take out the panel **(see illustration)**.

12 Refitting is a reversal of removal. Tighten the seat belt mounting bolt to the specified torque.

Rear side trim panel

3-door models

13 Remove the rear seat as described in Section 25.

14 Unscrew and remove the rear seat belt lower mounting bolt, and move the belt clear of the panel **(see illustration)**.

15 Remove a total of five Torx screws from around the edges of the panel **(see illustration)**, noting that the top front corner screw is significantly shorter than the other four.

16 The panel is held in place by two push-on

clips (one top centre, one bottom centre). Prise the panel carefully to release the clips, and remove it from the vehicle **(see illustration)**.

C-pillar trim panel

3-door models

17 Remove the luggage area side trim panel, and the rear side trim panel, as described elsewhere in this Section. It may not, in fact, be absolutely necessary to completely remove these panels, but they should be released where they join the C-pillar trim.

18 Remove the single Torx screw from the hinged rear window rear catch, and release the catch from the panel **(see illustration)**. Recover the spacer washer.

19 Prise out the seat belt access panel from the panel – this is clipped in very tightly.

20 The trim panel is held by a total of four push-on clips down the middle of the panel. Carefully prise the panel away from the

body **(see illustration)**. To remove the panel completely, the rear seat belt lower mounting will have to be removed.

Rear window surround

5-door models

21 Remove the luggage area side trim panel, as described elsewhere in this Section.

22 Loosen and remove the three screws along the bottom of the surround **(see illustration)**.

23 The surround is now held by a total of eight push-on clips along the two sides and top of the panel **(see illustration)**. Carefully prise the panel away from the body. To remove the panel completely, the rear seat belt upper mounting will have to be removed.

Luggage area side trim panel

24 Fold the rear seat forwards. On 5-door models, unscrew the rear seat belt lower Torx bolt.

27.20 Removing the C-pillar trim panel

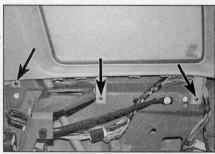

27.22 Loosen and remove the three screws along the bottom of the surround (arrowed)

27.23 The surround is held by a total of eight push-on clips along the two sides and top of the panel

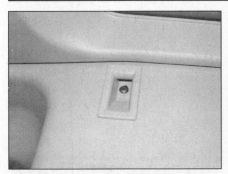

27.25 Remove the screw located in the luggage cover's locating socket

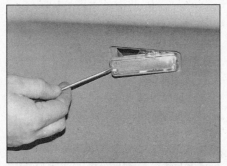

27.26a Prise out the luggage area light . . .

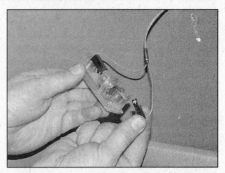

27.26b . . . and disconnect the wiring connectors

27.27 Remove the Torx screws from the carpet retainer trim panel

27.28 Removing a turn-buckle fastener

27.30 Unclip and remove the luggage area side trim panel

25 Where fitted, remove the luggage compartment cover and remove the screw located in the cover's locating socket **(see illustration)**.

26 Prise out the luggage compartment light, then disconnect the two connectors, and remove it from the luggage area side trim panel **(see illustrations)**.

27 Remove the screws securing the carpet retainer at the rear edge of the luggage area **(see illustration)**, and release the retainer and carpet as necessary so that the side trim panel will be free to be removed.

28 Twist and remove the four turn-buckle fasteners securing the side trim panel to release them **(see illustration)**.

29 Where applicable, peel away the weatherstrip fitted to the rear door aperture, adjacent to the trim panel.

30 The side trim panel is held in place by five clips, mainly along the front and top edges. Carefully prise along the edges of the trim

panel to release the clips, and remove it from the vehicle **(see illustration)**.

31 Refitting is a reversal of removal. Where applicable, tighten the seat belt mounting bolt to the specified torque.

Cup holder

32 Open the cup holder, and remove the rubber mats inside, for access to the two retaining screws.

33 Remove the two screws inside the cup holder, and lift the assembly out of the facia.

34 Further dismantling the cup holder is not advisable.

Facia stowage box

35 Remove the rubber mat inside the stowage box, for access to the two securing screws.

36 Remove the two screws, and lift the box out of its location in the facia.

Glovebox (passenger side)

37 Open up the glovebox, and take out its rubber mat.

38 Prise down the glovebox light from the top of the glovebox, and disconnect its wiring connectors. Remove the light completely.

39 Remove the four screws from the glovebox, and withdraw it from the facia **(see illustration)**.

Carpets

40 The passenger compartment floor carpet is in one piece (with a separate piece used in the luggage area), and is secured at its edges by screws or clips, usually the same fasteners used to secure the various adjoining trim panels.

41 Carpet removal and refitting is reasonably

straightforward, but very time-consuming, due to the fact that all adjoining trim panels must be removed first, as must components such as the seats, the centre console and seat belt lower anchorages.

Headlining

42 The rigid headlining is clipped to the roof, and can only be withdrawn once all fittings such as the grab handles, sunvisors, interior light, and related trim panels have been removed, and the door, tailgate and sunroof aperture sealing strips have been prised clear.

43 As with carpet removal, taking out the headlining is not especially difficult, just time-consuming.

Grab handles

44 Prise of the plastic covers either end of the handles, and undo the retaining screws **(see illustration)**.

45 Refitting is a reversal of removal.

27.39 Remove the four screws from the glovebox, and withdraw it from the facia

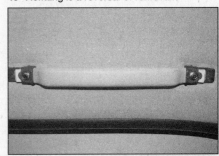

27.44 Prise of the plastic covers either end of the handles, and undo the retaining screws

28.6 Unscrew the heater control panel trim retaining screws (arrowed)

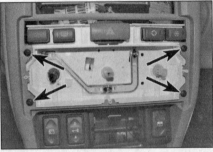

28.9 Unscrew and remove the four screws around the heater control panel location (arrowed)

28.10a The centre console is now held by one screw inside the cubby hole/ashtray below the heater controls (arrowed) . . .

28.10b . . . and one each side at the base of the console

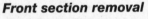

28 Centre console – removal and refitting

Front section removal

1 Disconnect the battery negative lead – see Chapter 5A, Section 4.

2 Remove the rear section of the console, as described later in this Section.

3 Remove the radio/cassette player as described in Chapter 12.

4 On manual gearbox models, remove the hill descent control switch as described in Chapter 9, Section 20.

5 On automatic gearbox models, pull the selector lever knob upwards and out from the selector lever.

6 Pull the outer heater control knobs from the panel, and undo the two retaining screws

28.11 Undo the single screw and remove the mirror ECU holder

located in the knob recesses (see illustration). Lift off the heater control panel trim.

7 Using a small screwdriver, prise up the metal tags inside the radio 'cage' (where fitted), and pull the cage out of its location, for access to two of the centre console retaining screws.

8 Working inside the radio aperture, unscrew and remove the two upper screws.

9 Unscrew and remove the four screws around the heater control panel location (see illustration).

10 The centre console is now held by three remaining screws – one inside the cubby hole/ashtray below the heater controls, and one each side at the base of the console, in line with the gear/selector lever. Remove the ashtray (where fitted), and undo the three screws, and release the console from the facia (see illustrations).

11 On models fitted with electrically-

adjustable mirrors, release the retaining clips and remove the mirror ECU from its holder mounted on the centre tunnel. There is no need to disconnect the wiring plug (see illustration). Undo the single screw and remove the holder.

12 Pull the console back slowly, until the cigar lighter and switch wiring plugs are accessible. Reach in between the console and facia, and disconnect the plugs. On automatic models, disconnect the selector lever and hill descent control switch wiring also. If necessary, identify the wiring plugs for location, to make refitting easier (stick labels or tape on the plugs).

13 Moving the gear/selector lever as necessary, lift the console over the lever and remove it from the vehicle.

Rear section removal

Models without electric rear windows

14 Prise up the cover at the front of the console, then open the ashtray cover at the rear, and remove the ashtray itself (see illustrations).

15 Loosen the four console screws (two front, two rear) by a few turns – it is not necessary to remove them completely (see illustrations).

16 Slide the console rearwards to release it from the four screwheads, then lift it up and unclip the wiring underneath (see illustration).

17 Disconnect the wiring plug from the power socket, then lift the console out over the handbrake lever, and remove it from the vehicle (see illustrations).

28.14a Prise up the cover in front of the handbrake . . .

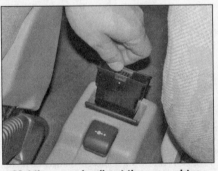

28.14b . . . and pull out the rear ashtray

28.15a Loosen the console screws front and rear . . .

28.15b . . . the console mountings are slotted, so the screws need not be removed

28.16 Unclip the wiring from under the console

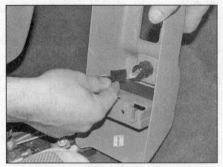

28.17a Disconnect the power socket wiring plug . . .

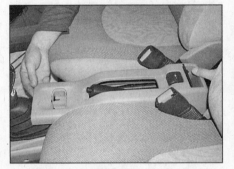

28.17b . . . and lift the console over handbrake lever

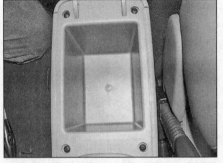

28.20 Undo the four retaining screws and lift out the storage box

28.21a Remove the two screws from the rear of the console . . .

Models with electric rear windows

18 Disconnect the battery negative lead – see Chapter 5A, Section 4.

19 Carefully unclip the rear ashtray panel from the rear of the console. Remove the panel so far, then disconnect the power socket wiring plug and remove it completely.

20 Open the console lid, undo the four retaining screws and lift out the storage box itself **(see illustration)**.

21 Remove the two screws from the rear of the console, then prise up the screw cover at the front, and remove the two screws below that **(see illustrations)**.

22 Reach in through the open lid, and disconnect the wiring plugs from the various console switches. If necessary, identify the wiring plugs for location, to make refitting easier (stick labels or tape on the plugs).

23 Release the switch wiring harness from the clip inside the console, then lift the console out and remove it from the vehicle.

24 To remove the handbrake lever screen assembly, undo the four retaining screws **(see illustration)**.

Refitting

25 Refitting is a reversal of the removal procedure, noting the following:

a) Ensure that all the wiring is correctly routed, and does not become trapped as the console is refitted.

b) On automatic models, ensure the selector lever knob locating tang engages correctly with the corresponding slot in the selector lever.

c) On completion, reconnect the battery, and check the operation of all the switches.

29 Facia panel assembly – removal and refitting

Removal

1 Remove the front and rear sections of the centre console, as described in Section 28.

2 Remove the steering wheel as described in Chapter 10, and the airbag rotary contact unit as described in Chapter 12.

3 Remove the steering column switch assembly as described in Chapter 12.

4 Unscrew the two retaining screws and remove the steering column lower trim panel.

5 Disconnect the wiring plug, and slide the immobiliser 'reader' coil (where fitted) from the ignition switch barrel **(see illustration)**,

28.21b . . . then prise up the screw cover at the front, and remove the two screws below that

28.24 Undo the four retaining screws and remove the handbrake lever screen assembly

29.5 Slide the immobiliser 'reader' coil (where fitted) from the ignition switch barrel

29.6 Disconnect the two wiring multi-plugs (arrowed) from the fusebox

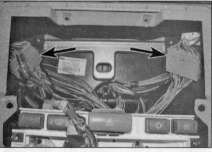

29.10 Disconnect the two main wiring harness plugs located at the centre of the facia panel

29.11a One facia screw each side just inside the two bottom corners of the windscreen (arrowed) . . .

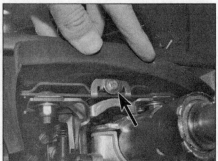

29.11b . . . one above the steering column (arrowed) . . .

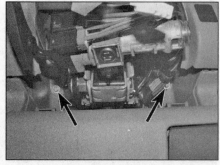
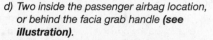

29.11c . . . two either side of the steering column (arrowed) . . .

29.11d . . . two inside the passenger airbag location (arrowed), or behind the facia grab handle . . .

6 Open the driver's glovebox lid and unclip the fusebox cover. Disconnect the two wiring multiplugs from the fusebox, then close the glovebox lid **(see illustration)**.

7 Remove the clock as described in Chapter 12.

8 Take off the A-pillar trim panels and (on models without a passenger airbag) the facia stowage box, as described in Section 27.

9 On models so equipped, remove the passenger airbag as described in Chapter 12.

10 Depress the lower retaining tags, and disconnect the two main wiring harness plugs located at the centre of the facia panel **(see illustration)**.

11 Unscrew and remove the twelve facia mounting bolts – locations as follows:

a) *One each side just inside the two bottom corners of the windscreen (see illustration).*

b) *One inside the clock location.*

c) *Three below the instrument panel (see illustrations).*

d) *Two inside the passenger airbag location, or behind the facia grab handle (see illustration).*

e) *One at each lower outer corner of the facia panel (see illustration).*

f) *Two in the centre, below the centre console location (see illustration).*

12 With the help of an assistant, release the facia from its location, and start to remove it. As the facia panel is removed, it will be necessary to reach in behind it and disconnect the vent grille supply ducts. The facia panel on the Freelander is removed complete with its own wiring loom, so there should be no (standard) wiring to disconnect.

Refitting

13 Refitting is a reversal of the removal procedure, noting the following points:

a) *Manoeuvre the facia into position and reconnect the vent grille supply ducts.*

b) *Refit all the facia mounting bolts and tighten them securely.*

c) *On completion, reconnect the battery and check that all the electrical components and switches function correctly.*

Take great care not to trap any wiring as the facia is installed.

30 Sunvisors – removal and refitting

1 Release the relevant sunvisor from the its retaining clip, undo the two screws, and remove the sunvisor **(see illustration)**. Disconnect the wiring plug as the visor is removed.

2 If necessary, undo and remove the screw securing the sunvisor retaining clip to the roof.

3 Refitting is a reversal of removal.

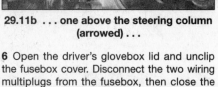

29.11e . . . one at each lower outer corner of the facia panel . . .

29.11f . . . and two in the centre, below the centre console location

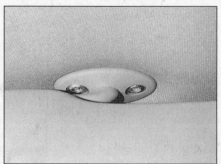
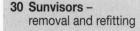

30.1 Undo the two screws, and remove the sunvisor

Chapter 12
Body electrical systems

Contents

Degrees of difficulty

Easy, suitable for novice with little experience	**Fairly easy,** suitable for beginner with some experience	**Fairly difficult,** suitable for competent DIY mechanic	**Difficult,** suitable for experienced DIY mechanic	**Very difficult,** suitable for expert DIY or professional

Specifications

System type . . . . 12 volt negative-earth

Relay locations – typical

Component*	Location
Headlight main/dipped beam relay	No 1 – passenger compartment fusebox
Heated rear window relay.	No 2 – passenger compartment fusebox
Power socket relay.	No 3 – passenger compartment fusebox
Sunroof relay	No 4 – passenger compartment fusebox
Electric window relay	No 5 – passenger compartment fusebox
Flasher unit.	No 6 – passenger compartment fusebox
Fuel pump relay	Engine compartment fusebox
Starter relay	Engine compartment fusebox
Hill Descent Control relay.	Engine compartment fusebox
Main relay	Engine compartment fusebox
Horn relay	Engine compartment fusebox
Air conditioning compressor clutch relay.	Engine compartment fusebox
Rear wash/wipe relay.	Behind luggage area RH side trim panel
Tailgate window relay.	Behind luggage area RH side trim panel

* Not all items fitted to all models

Bulbs

	Wattage
Direction indicator	21
Direction indicator side repeater	5
Front sidelight.	5
Glovebox light	5
Headlight	60/55
High-level brake light	21
Interior lights.	10
Map reading lights	5
Number plate light	5
Rear foglight.	21
Reversing lights	21
Stop/tail-light	21/5

Torque wrench settings

	Nm	lbf ft
Airbag components:		
Driver's airbag unit screws	9	7
Passenger's airbag unit screws	9	7
Airbag module mounting screws	9	7

1 General information and precautions

⚠️ **Warning: Before carrying out any work on the electrical system, read through the precautions given in 'Safety first!' at the beginning of this manual, and in Chapter 5A. This applies particularly to disconnecting the battery – there are various points to be aware of before disconnecting, and when reconnecting, the battery leads.**

The electrical system is of the 12 volt negative-earth type. Power for the lights and all electrical accessories is supplied by a lead-acid type battery, which is charged by the engine-driven alternator.

This Chapter covers repair and service procedures for the various electrical components not associated with engine. Information on the battery, alternator and starter motor can be found in Chapter 5A.

Prior to working on any component in the electrical system, the battery negative terminal should first be disconnected, to prevent the possibility of electrical short-circuits and/or fires – refer to Chapter 5A, Section 4, for details of the precautions to be observed when disconnecting the battery.

2 Electrical fault finding – general information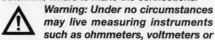

Note: *Refer to the precautions given in 'Safety first!' and in Section 1 of this Chapter before starting work. The following tests relate to testing of the main electrical circuits, and should not be used to test delicate electronic circuits (such as anti-lock braking systems), particularly where an electronic control module is used.*

General

1 A typical electrical circuit consists of an electrical component, any switches, relays, motors, fuses, fusible links or circuit breakers related to that component, and the wiring and connectors which link the component to both the battery and the chassis. To help to pinpoint a problem in an electrical circuit, wiring diagrams are included at the end of this Chapter.

2 Before attempting to diagnose an electrical fault, first study the appropriate wiring diagram to obtain a complete understanding of the components included in the particular circuit concerned. The possible sources of a fault can be narrowed down by noting if other components related to the circuit are operating properly. If several components or circuits fail at one time, the problem is likely to be related to a shared fuse or earth connection.

3 Electrical problems usually stem from simple causes, such as loose or corroded connections, a faulty earth connection, a blown fuse, a melted fusible link, or a faulty relay (refer to Section 3 for details of testing relays). Visually inspect the condition of all fuses, wires and connections in a problem circuit before testing the components. Use the wiring diagrams to determine which terminal connections will need to be checked in order to pinpoint the trouble-spot.

4 The basic tools required for electrical fault finding include a circuit tester or voltmeter (a 12 volt bulb with a set of test leads can also be used for certain tests); a self-powered test light (sometimes known as a continuity tester); an ohmmeter (to measure resistance); a battery and set of test leads; and a jumper wire, preferably with a circuit breaker or fuse incorporated, which can be used to bypass suspect wires or electrical components. Before attempting to locate a problem with test instruments, use the wiring diagram to determine where to make the connections.

⚠️ **Warning: Under no circumstances may live measuring instruments such as ohmmeters, voltmeters or a bulb and test leads be used to test any of the airbag circuitry. Any testing of these components must be left to a Land Rover dealer, as there is a danger of activating the system if the correct procedures are not followed.**

5 To find the source of an intermittent wiring fault (usually due to a poor or dirty connection, or damaged wiring insulation), a 'wiggle' test can be performed on the wiring. This involves wiggling the wiring by hand to see if the fault occurs as the wiring is moved. It should be possible to narrow down the source of the fault to a particular section of wiring. This method of testing can be used in conjunction with any of the tests described in the following sub-Sections.

6 Apart from problems due to poor connections, two basic types of fault can occur in an electrical circuit – open-circuit, or short-circuit.

7 Open-circuit faults are caused by a break somewhere in the circuit, which prevents current from flowing. An open-circuit fault will prevent a component from working, but will not cause the relevant circuit fuse to blow.

8 Short-circuit faults are caused by a 'short' somewhere in the circuit, which allows the current flowing in the circuit to 'escape' along an alternative route, usually to earth. Short-circuit faults are normally caused by a breakdown in wiring insulation, which allows a feed wire to touch either another wire, or an earthed component such as the bodyshell. A short-circuit fault will normally cause the relevant circuit fuse to blow.

Finding an open-circuit

9 To check for an open-circuit, connect one lead of a circuit tester or voltmeter to either the negative battery terminal or a known good earth.

10 Connect the other lead to a connector in the circuit being tested, preferably nearest to the battery or fuse.

11 Switch on the circuit, bearing in mind that some circuits are live only when the ignition switch is moved to a particular position.

12 If voltage is present (indicated either by the tester bulb lighting or a voltmeter reading, as applicable), this means that the section of the circuit between the relevant connector and the battery is problem-free.

13 Continue to check the remainder of the circuit in the same fashion.

14 When a point is reached at which no voltage is present, the problem must lie between that point and the previous test point with voltage. Most problems can be traced to a broken, corroded or loose connection.

Finding a short-circuit

15 To check for a short-circuit, first disconnect the load(s) from the circuit (loads are the components which draw current from a circuit, such as bulbs, motors, heating elements, etc).

16 Remove the relevant fuse from the circuit, and connect a circuit tester or voltmeter to the fuse connections.

17 Switch on the circuit, bearing in mind that some circuits are live only when the ignition switch is moved to a particular position.

18 If voltage is present (indicated either by the tester bulb lighting or a voltmeter reading, as applicable), this means that there is a short-circuit.

19 If no voltage is present, but the fuse still blows with the load(s) connected, this indicates an internal fault in the load(s).

Finding an earth fault

20 The battery negative terminal is connected to 'earth' – the metal of the engine/transmission and the vehicle body – and most systems are wired so that they only receive a positive feed, the current returning via the metal of the vehicle body. This means that the component mounting and the body form part of that circuit.

3.1a The main fusebox is located in the driver's side glovebox

3.1b Engine compartment fusebox

3.4 Pull the fuse out of its terminals, using the plastic 'tweezers' provided in the fusebox

21 Loose or corroded mountings can therefore cause a range of electrical faults, ranging from total failure of a circuit, to a puzzling partial fault. In particular, lights may shine dimly (especially when another circuit sharing the same earth point is in operation), motors (eg, wiper motors or the radiator cooling fan motor) may run slowly, and the operation of one circuit may have an apparently-unrelated effect on another.

22 Note that on many vehicles, earth straps are used between certain components, such as the engine/transmission and the body, usually where there is no metal-to-metal contact between components due to flexible rubber mountings, etc.

23 To check whether a component is properly earthed, disconnect the battery and connect one lead of an ohmmeter to a known good earth point. Connect the other lead to the wire or earth connection being tested. The resistance reading should be zero; if not, check the connection as follows.

24 If an earth connection is thought to be faulty, dismantle the connection and clean back to bare metal both the bodyshell and the wire terminal or the component earth connection mating surface. Be careful to remove all traces of dirt and corrosion, then use a knife to trim away any paint, so that a clean metal-to-metal joint is made.

25 On reassembly, tighten the joint fasteners securely; if a wire terminal is being refitted, use serrated washers between the terminal and the bodyshell to ensure a clean and secure connection. When the connection is remade, prevent the onset of corrosion in the future by applying a coat of petroleum jelly or silicone-based grease. Alternatively, spray on (at regular intervals) a proprietary ignition sealer, or a water-dispersant lubricant.

---

3 Fuses, relays and fusebox – general information

Fuses

1 The main fuses are located inside the driver's glovebox, behind a panel on the right-hand side. In addition, there are a few fuses, and the main fusible links, in the engine compartment fusebox, which is on the left-hand side of the

engine compartment (left as seen from the driver's seat) **(see illustrations)**.

2 To gain access to the main fusebox, open the driver's glovebox and release the fusebox cover by pressing and releasing the two catches. To gain access to those in the engine compartment box, unclip the lid by pressing in the catch at the rear.

3 A label identifying each fuse should be attached to the cover/lid, and a list of the circuits each fuse protects is given with the wiring diagrams.

4 To remove a fuse, first switch off the circuit concerned, and take out the ignition key. Pull the fuse out of its terminals, using the plastic 'tweezers' provided in the fusebox **(see illustration)**. The wire within the fuse is clearly visible; if the fuse is blown, it will be broken or melted.

5 If one of the fusible links has blown, this indicates a serious wiring fault – the links are higher-rated than any fuse, and would not blow without severe provocation. Given that links only protect circuits with a high amp rating, any problem with a link-protected circuit could result in a fire – it is therefore advisable to refer the vehicle to a Land Rover dealer or auto-electrical specialist for testing, rather than just fitting a new link.

6 Always renew a fuse/fusible link with one of an identical rating; never use one with a different rating from the original, nor substitute anything else. Never renew a fuse more than once without tracing the source of the trouble. The rating is stamped on top of the fuse; they are also colour-coded for easy recognition.

7 If a new fuse/fusible link blows immediately, find the cause before renewing it again – a

short to earth as a result of faulty insulation is most likely. Where more than one circuit is protected, try to isolate the defect by switching on each circuit in turn (if possible) until it blows again. Always carry a supply of spare fuses of each relevant rating on the vehicle; a spare of each fuse rating should be clipped into the right-hand side of the fusebox.

Relays

8 The relay locations are given in the Specifications at the start of this Chapter.

9 If a circuit or system controlled by a relay develops a fault and the relay is suspect, operate the system; if the relay is functioning, it should be possible to hear it click as it is energised. If it clicks, the fault lies with the components or wiring of the system. If the relay is not being energised, then either the relay is not receiving a main supply or a switching voltage, or the relay itself is faulty. Testing is by the substitution of a known good unit, but be careful; while some relays are identical in appearance and in operation, others look similar but perform different functions.

10 To renew a relay, first ensure that the ignition switch is off. The relay can then simply be pulled out from the socket, and the new relay pressed in.

11 Some relays are located outside of the main fusebox, closer to the component whose operation they control. On the Freelander, the tailgate glass regulator motor and tailgate wiper motor relays are located next to the right-hand rear suspension turret, behind the luggage area side trim panel **(see illustrations)**.

3.11a Some relays are located outside of the main fusebox

3.11b Tailgate glass regulator motor and wiper motor relays

4.6 Slacken the switch assembly clamp screw

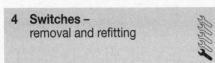

4 Switches –
removal and refitting

Note: *Disconnect the battery negative lead before removing any switch, and reconnect the lead after refitting the switch. Refer to the precautions in Section 1 before proceeding.*

Ignition switch/ steering column lock

1 Refer to Chapter 10.

Direction indicator/ headlight switch

2 Remove the steering column upper and lower shrouds. The upper shroud is clipped to the lower shroud, and there are two clips either side – take care when releasing them to avoid damage. Lift out the upper shroud.

4.13 Undo the screws below the switch 'pods'

4.19 Disconnect the wiring plug from the airbag rotary contact unit

4.7 Remove the two screws, then press in the retaining tab (arrowed) between the screw holes, and withdraw the switch

3 The lower shroud is secured by two screws from below – remove the screws, then lower the steering column tilt lever.
4 Remove the cover from the ignition switch, taking care not to damage the reader coil fitted round the switch.
5 Carefully pull the lower shroud down, releasing it from the clip on the ignition switch, and remove it.
6 Disconnect the two wiring multiplugs from the rear of the switch. **Note:** *The direction indicator/headlight switch and the windscreen wash/wipe switch can be removed from the steering column as an assembly. Disconnect the wiring plugs from the rear of the switches, slacken the clamp screw* **(see illustration)**, *and pull the assembly from the column.*
7 Turn the steering wheel as necessary to gain access to the two switch retaining screws. Remove the two screws, then press in the retaining tab between the screw holes, and

4.14 Disconnect the switch wiring connector, then slide the relevant switch out from the surround

4.21 Disconnect the two connectors from the horn switch

4.11 Press in the retaining tab between the screw holes

withdraw the switch from the steering column **(see illustration)**.
8 Refitting is a reversal of the removal procedure.

Windscreen wash/wipe switch

9 Remove the airbag rotary contact unit as described in Section 23.
10 Disconnect the wiring multiplug from the rear of the switch, and the wiring connector from the centre of the assembly. The connector is difficult to release, it may be prudent to remove the complete switch assembly as follows: Disconnect the wiring plugs from the rear of the switches, slacken the clamp screw **(see illustration 4.6)**, and pull the assembly from the column.
11 Remove the two switch screws, then press in the retaining tab between the screw holes, and withdraw the switch from the steering column **(see illustration)**.
12 Refitting is a reversal of the removal procedure.

Rear wash/wipe switches

13 Slacken and remove the four retaining screws securing the instrument panel surround in position (two in the top of the cowl, one each below the switch 'pods') **(see illustration)**.
14 Move the surround forwards until access can be gained to the required switch wiring connectors. Disconnect the switch wiring connector, then slide the relevant switch out from the surround **(see illustration)**.
15 Refitting is a reversal of the removal procedure.

Rear foglight switch

16 See paragraphs 13 to 15.

Horn switches

Note: *These switches rely on the connection provided through the airbag rotary contact unit – a fault with the contact unit will prevent them from working.*
17 Remove the airbag unit from the steering wheel as described in Section 23.
18 Unclip the horn wiring from the locations inside the wheel.
19 Disconnect the wiring plug from the airbag rotary contact unit **(see illustration)**.
20 Taking care to avoid damage to the steering wheel, prise out the horn switch.

21 Noting their fitted positions, disconnect the two connectors from the horn switch, and remove it **(see illustration)**.

22 Refitting is a reversal of the removal procedure.

Audio system remote control switches

Note: *These switches rely on the connection provided through the airbag rotary contact unit – a fault with the contact unit will prevent them from working.*

23 Remove the airbag unit from the steering wheel as described in Section 23.

24 Unclip the switch wiring from inside the wheel, and disconnect the switch multiplug.

25 Remove the two switch securing screws, and remove the switch from the steering wheel **(see illustration)**.

26 Refitting is a reversal of the removal procedure.

Headlight levelling switch

27 Carefully prise the switch out of its location, taking care not to damage the surrounding facia **(see illustration)**.

28 Disconnect the switch wiring plug, and remove the switch.

29 Refitting is a reversal of the removal procedure.

Glovebox light switch

30 Remove the glovebox as described in Chapter 11.

31 Disconnect the two wiring plugs from the switch, then release the switch retaining lugs and pull the switch out of its location.

32 Refitting is a reversal of the removal procedure.

Heated rear window switch

33 Remove the radio/cassette player as described in Section 19.

34 Pull off the three heater control knobs, then remove the two screws behind securing the heater control panel **(see illustration)**.

35 Remove the panel from the facia, releasing the top row of switches from it as this is done.

36 Disconnect the wiring plug from the switch, and remove it **(see illustration)**.

37 Refitting is a reversal of the removal procedure.

4.25 Undo the two switch securing screws, and remove the switch from the steering wheel

4.34 Pull off the three heater control knobs, then remove the two screws (arrowed)

Air conditioning switch

38 See paragraphs 33 to 37.

Air recirculation switch

39 See paragraphs 33 to 37.

Hazard warning light switch

40 See paragraphs 33 to 37.

Heater blower fan switch

41 Refer to Chapter 3, Section 9.

Mirror switch

42 Carefully prise the switch out of its location, taking care not to damage the surrounding facia **(see illustration)**.

43 Disconnect the switch wiring plug, and remove the switch **(see illustration)**.

44 Refitting is a reversal of the removal procedure.

4.27 Carefully prise the headlamp levelling switch out of its location, taking care not to damage the surrounding facia

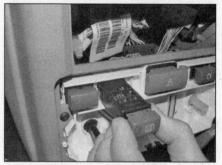

4.36 Disconnect the wiring plug, and then remove the switch

Hill descent control switch

45 See Chapter 9, Section 20 (the descent control is a function of the anti-lock braking system).

Electric window switches

46 On 5-door models with electric rear windows, the window switches (and the rear window isolator switch) are located in the rear section of the centre console, and on the rear door trims. On all other models, the electric window switches are located in the front section of the centre console. Remove the appropriate section of centre console, or door trim as described in Chapter 11.

47 With the console removed, press the relevant switch out from behind to remove it (prising the switch out from the front carries a high risk of damaging the switch, and is not recommended) **(see illustration)**. The rear

4.42 Carefully prise the mirror switch out of its location, taking care not to damage the surrounding facia

4.43 Disconnect the wiring plug and remove the switch

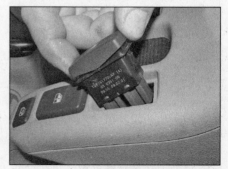

4.47 With the console removed, press the relevant window switch out

4.50 The switches in the centre console push out from behind

4.58 Handbrake-on switch

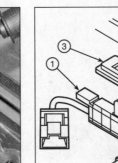

4.61 Remove the hood support bracket bolts (A), and disconnect the microswitch wiring plug (B)

window switches are secured to the door trims by two Torx screws from the inner side of the trim.

48 Refitting is a reversal of the removal procedure.

Central locking switch

49 Remove the front section of the centre console, as described in Chapter 11.
50 With the console removed, press the relevant switch out from behind to remove it (prising the switch out from the front carries a high risk of damaging the switch, and is not recommended) **(see illustration)**.
51 Refitting is a reversal of the removal procedure.

Tailgate glass switch

52 See paragraphs 49 to 51.

Electric sunroof switch

53 See paragraphs 49 to 51.

Heated seat switches

54 See paragraphs 49 to 51.

Cruise control switches

55 To remove the master switch from the centre console, see paragraphs 49 to 51.
56 The steering wheel-mounted switch assembly is removed as described in paragraphs 23 to 26.

Handbrake-on switch

57 Remove the rear section of the centre console, as described in Chapter 11.
58 Disconnect the wiring plug from the

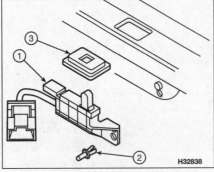

4.62 Hood microswitch (1), securing peg (2), and plunger seal (3)

switch, then unclip the switch from its location, and remove it **(see illustration)**.
59 Refitting is a reversal of the removal procedure.

Soft/hard top sensing switch

60 The purpose of this switch is to detect any attempt to break into the vehicle by removing the soft top or hard top. With the hood or hard top removed, remove the C-pillar trim panel as described in Chapter 11, Section 27.
61 Remove the two bolts securing the hood support bracket, then unclip the microswitch wiring plug from its locating bracket and disconnect the plug **(see illustration)**.
62 The switch is secured to the C-pillar by a plastic peg, which can be prised out. Note the seal fitted to the boss around the switch plunger **(see illustration)**.

5.2 Working in the engine compartment, turn the headlight rear cover slightly anti-clockwise, and remove it

63 Refitting is a reversal of the removal procedure.

Stop-light switch

64 Refer to Chapter 9.

Brake pedal position switch

65 Refer to Chapter 9.

Interior light switches

66 No interior light switches are fitted. The courtesy lights are operated by the ECU based on the signals from the door locks.

Oil pressure warning light switch

67 Refer to Chapter 5A.

5 Bulbs (exterior lights) – renewal

General

1 Whenever a bulb is renewed, note the following points:
a) *Disconnect the battery negative lead before starting work. Refer to the precautions in Section 1 before proceeding.*
b) *Remember that if the light has just been in use, the bulb may be extremely hot.*
c) *Always check the bulb contacts and holder, ensuring that there is clean metal-to-metal contact between the bulb and its live(s) and earth. Clean off any corrosion or dirt before fitting a new bulb.*
d) *Wherever bayonet-type bulbs are fitted, ensure that the live contact(s) bear firmly against the bulb contact.*
e) *Always ensure that the new bulb is of the correct rating and that it is completely clean before fitting it; this applies particularly to headlight/foglight bulbs (see below).*
f) *With quartz halogen bulbs (headlights and similar applications), use a tissue or clean cloth when handling the bulb; do not touch the bulb glass with the fingers. Even small quantities of grease from the fingers will cause blackening and premature failure. If a bulb is accidentally touched, clean it with methylated spirit and a clean rag.*

Headlight

2 Working in the engine compartment, turn the headlight rear cover slightly anti-clockwise, and remove it **(see illustration)**.
3 Pull off the wiring plug from the back of the bulb **(see illustration)**.
4 Unhook and release the bulb retaining clip at the top by pressing it to one side, and lower it for access to the bulb **(see illustration)**.
5 Withdraw the bulb, noting how the three locating tabs sit in the headlight **(see illustration)**.
6 When handling the new bulb, use a tissue or clean cloth to avoid touching the glass with

5.3 Pull off the wiring plug from the back of the bulb

5.4 Unhook and release the retaining clip at the top by pressing it to one side, and lower it for access to the bulb

5.5 Withdraw the bulb from the headlamp

5.10 Pull the bulbholder out for access to the sidelight bulb

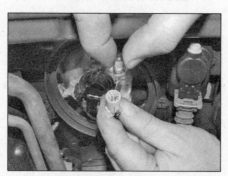

5.11 Sidelight bulb is a push-fit in the bulbholder

5.14 Release the retaining tab at the top by pressing it upwards – the panel then unhooks at the bottom

the fingers; moisture and grease from the skin can cause blackening and rapid failure of this type of bulb.

 HAYNES HiNT *If the headlight bulb glass is accidentally touched, wipe it clean using methylated spirit.*

7 Install the new bulb, ensuring that its locating tabs are correctly located in the light cut-outs, and secure it in position with the retaining clip. Push on the bulb's wiring connector plug.
8 Refit the cover to the rear of the light unit (with the TOP mark uppermost), turning it clockwise to secure.

Front sidelight

9 Working in the engine compartment, turn the headlight rear cover slightly anti-clockwise, and remove it.
10 The sidelight's round bulbholder is located below the headlight bulb wiring plug, and is a push-fit into the back of the headlight. Pull the bulbholder out for access to the bulb **(see illustration)**.
11 The sidelight bulb is of the capless (push-fit) type, and can be removed by simply pulling it out of the bulbholder **(see illustration)**.

 HAYNES HiNT *Sidelight bulbs are notorious for not working, even though they haven't in fact blown – a loose or dirty connection on the bulb or bulbholder contacts is a common reason for apparent failure.*

12 Refitting is the reverse of the removal procedure, ensuring that the headlight rear cover is correctly fitted by turning it clockwise (and with the TOP mark uppermost).

Front direction indicator

13 The direction indicator bulbholders are accessed via a plastic panel inside the front wheel arch – it may be necessary to clean underneath before continuing.
14 The rectangular access panel has a retaining tab at the top, which is released by pressing it upwards – the panel then unhooks at the bottom **(see illustration)**.
15 Reach inside the aperture and twist the bulbholder anti-clockwise to remove it **(see illustration)**.
16 The bulb is a bayonet fit in the holder, and can be removed by pressing it and twisting in an anti-clockwise direction.
17 Refitting is the reverse of removal. When

5.15 Reach inside the aperture and twist the bulbholder anti-clockwise to remove it

refitting the access panel, hook it in at the top edge first, then lower it and clip it in at the bottom.

Direction indicator side repeater

18 Carefully push the light unit towards the front of the vehicle, then unhook it at the rear and withdraw the unit from the wing. Note how the retaining lug at the rear of the unit engages with the hole **(see illustration)**.
19 Turn the bulbholder anti-clockwise to release it from the light unit, then pull the bulb from the bulbholder. Take care while the bulbholder is removed that it doesn't drop back into the hole in the wing **(see illustrations)**.
20 Refitting is a reverse of the removal procedure. Fit the light unit with its retaining lug facing rearwards, as noted on removal – hook it in at the front edge first, then swing the rear end into place, and push the light rearwards to secure.

5.18 Carefully push the light unit towards the front of the car, then unhook it at the rear and withdraw the unit from the wing

5.19a Turn the bulbholder anti-clockwise to release it from the light unit . . .

5.19b . . . then pull the bulb from the bulbholder

5.21 Unscrew and remove the three Torx screws (arrowed) securing the light unit

5.24 Unscrew and remove the two Torx screws (arrowed) securing the light unit

5.25 The bumper-mounted light bulbs are a bayonet fit in the holders

5.28 Undo the three retaining screws (arrowed), and detach the light unit cover

Rear light cluster

21 Unscrew and remove the three Torx (T20) screws securing the light unit, and withdraw it for access to the bulbholders **(see illustration)**.
22 Twist the relevant bulbholder anti-

clockwise, and withdraw it from the rear of the light unit. The bulb is a bayonet fit in the holder, and can be removed by pressing it and twisting in an anti-clockwise direction.
23 Refitting is a reverse of the removal procedure. Check the condition of the foam

seal on the body, and make sure it stays properly aligned as the light is fitted.

Bumper-mounted rear lights

24 Unscrew and remove the two Torx (T20) screws securing the light unit, and withdraw it for access to the bulbholders **(see illustration)**.
25 Twist the relevant bulbholder anti-clockwise, and withdraw it from the rear of the light unit. The bulb is a bayonet fit in the holder, and can be removed by pressing it and twisting in an anti-clockwise direction **(see illustration)**.
26 Refitting is a reverse of the removal procedure.

High-level stop-light

27 Temporarily reconnect the battery, and lower the tailgate glass using the centre console switch.
28 Undo the three retaining screws, and detach the light unit cover **(see illustration)**.
29 Twist the bulbholder anti-clockwise, and withdraw it from the light unit.
30 The bulb is a push-fit type, and can be removed by pulling it from its holder **(see illustration)**.
31 Refitting is a reverse of the removal procedure.

Number plate light

32 Slacken and remove the two retaining screws, then lift out the light unit. It's not essential to disconnect the two wiring connectors from the light, but doing so will make it easier to clean up the bulbholder contacts **(see illustration)**.

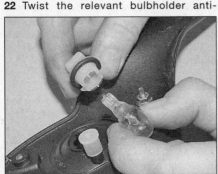

5.30 The high-level brake light bulb is a push-fit type

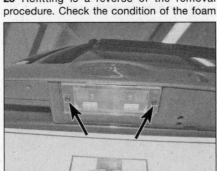

5.32 Slacken and remove the two retaining screws (arrowed), then lift out the light unit

5.33a Twist the relevant bulbholder (there are two) anti-clockwise to remove it from the number plate light unit . . .

5.33b . . . and pull the bulb from the holder

33 Twist the relevant bulbholder (there are two) anti-clockwise to remove it from the light unit. The bulbs are of capless (push-fit) type, and can be pulled from their holders **(see illustrations)**.

34 Refitting is a reverse of the removal procedure.

6 Bulbs (interior lights) – renewal

General

1 Whenever a bulb is renewed, note the following points:
 a) *Disconnect the battery negative lead before starting work. Refer to the precautions in Section 1 before proceeding.*
 b) *Remember that if the light has just been in use, the bulb may be extremely hot.*
 c) *Always check the bulb contacts and holder, ensuring that there is clean metal-to-metal contact between the bulb and its live(s) and earth. Clean off any corrosion or dirt before fitting a new bulb.*
 d) *Wherever bayonet-type bulbs are fitted, ensure that the live contact(s) bear firmly against the bulb contact.*
 e) *Always ensure that the new bulb is of the correct rating and that it is completely clean before fitting it.*

Interior lights

2 Using a suitable screwdriver in the indent provided on the edge of the lens, carefully prise the light unit lens out of position **(see illustration)**.

3 Carefully prise the bulb from the light unit contacts **(see illustration)**.

4 Install the new bulb, ensuring that it is securely held in position by the contacts (bend

6.2 Use a suitable screwdriver in the indent provided, and carefully prise the light unit lens out of position

6.5 Undo the two interior light unit retaining screws (arrowed)

them carefully if necessary), then clip the lens back into position.

Map reading light

5 Using a suitable screwdriver in the indent provided on the edge of the lens, carefully prise the centre interior light unit lens out of position. Undo the two interior light unit retaining screws **(see illustration)**.

6 Using a small screwdriver, carefully prise out the complete interior/map reading light assembly from the roof. If preferred, the wiring plug can be disconnected, and the light unit removed completely, but this is not essential.

7 The map reading light bulbs are located either side of the interior light bulb, and can be pulled from their bulbholders **(see illustration)**.

8 Install the new bulb, ensuring that it is securely held in position, then clip the light back into position.

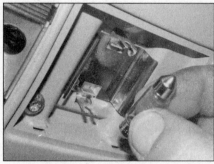

6.3 Prise the bulb from the light unit contacts

6.7 The map reading bulbs are a push-fit in their bulbholders

Glovebox illumination light bulb

9 Open up the glovebox. Using a small flat-bladed screwdriver on the left-hand end of the lens, carefully prise the light unit out of position, then release the bulb from its contacts **(see illustrations)**.

10 Install the new bulb, ensuring that it is securely held in position by the contacts, and clip the light unit back into position.

Vanity mirror light

11 Using a small screwdriver, carefully prise out the vanity light lens from the sunvisor **(see illustration)**.

12 The bulb is held vertically between two spring contacts – carefully prise one to release the bulb.

13 Install the new bulb, ensuring that it is securely held in position, then clip the light and lens back into position.

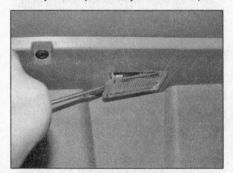

6.9a Carefully prise the light unit out of position . . .

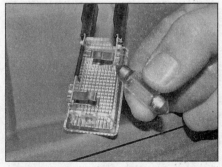

6.9b . . . then release the bulb from its contacts

6.11 Prise out the vanity light lens from the sunvisor

6.15 The luggage compartment light bulb is a bayonet fit in the holder

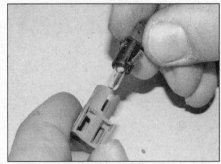

6.19 The lighter bulb is a capless (push-fit) type, and can be pulled out for renewal

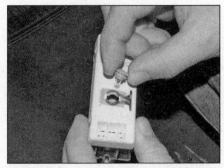

6.21 The clock illumination bulb is integral with the bulbholder

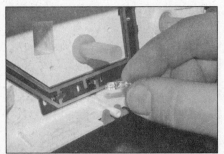

6.26 The heater control illumination bulbs are of the capless type, and can simply be pulled from the bulbholder

6.30 Twist the relevant bulbholder anti-clockwise, and withdraw it from the rear of the panel

6.31 The instrument cluster illumination bulbs are a push-fit in their holders

Luggage compartment light

14 Using a suitable screwdriver on one end of the lens, carefully prise the light unit out of position.

15 Remove the bulb by pressing it and twisting in an anti-clockwise direction (see illustration).

16 Refitting is the reverse of removal.

Cigarette lighter illumination

17 Remove the front section of the centre console, as described in Chapter 11.

18 If not already done, disconnect the main wiring plug from the cigar lighter, to improve access.

19 The grey plastic illuminator assembly is clipped onto the lighter itself, and can be removed by pulling it free; once removed, the bulbholder can be prised from the assembly. The bulb is a capless (push-fit) type, and can be pulled out for renewal (see illustration). Land Rover do not, however, list the bulb as being available separately from the cigar lighter 'socket'.

20 Refitting is the reverse of removal.

Clock illumination

21 Remove the clock as described in Section 11. The bulb and holder assembly is fitted into the rear of the clock – twist and pull to remove (see illustration). Note that the bulb is integral with the bulbholder.

22 Refitting is the reverse of removal.

Switch illumination

23 Most of the switches are fitted with illuminating bulbs; some are also fitted with

a bulb to show when the circuit concerned is operating. These bulbs are an integral part of the switch assembly, and cannot be obtained separately. Bulb renewal will therefore require the renewal of the complete switch assembly.

Heater control panel illumination

24 Pull the control knobs from the panel in the front centre console.

25 Unscrew the two panel retaining screws, located in the control knob recesses (see illustration 4.34).

26 The illumination bulbs are of the capless type, and can simply be pulled from the bulbholder (see illustration).

27 Refitting is a reversal of removal.

Automatic gearbox selector bulb

28 The selector panel is illuminated by integral LEDs. If a fault should develop, the complete panel should be renewed.

7.2 Undo the two upper headlight retaining screws

Instrument panel illumination/ warning lights

29 Remove the instrument panel as described in Section 9.

30 Twist the relevant bulbholder anti-clockwise, and withdraw it from the rear of the panel (see illustration).

31 The bulbs are of the capless (push-fit) type, and can be removed by simply pulling them out of the bulbholder (see illustration). Be very careful to ensure that the new bulbs are of the correct rating, the same as those removed; this is especially important in the case of the airbag and ignition/no-charge warning lights.

32 Refit the bulbholder to the rear of the instrument panel, then refit the instrument panel as described in Section 9.

---

7 Exterior light units – removal and refitting

Note: Disconnect the battery negative lead before removing any light unit, and reconnect the lead after refitting the light. Refer to the precautions in Section 1 before proceeding.

Headlight/ direction indicator light

1 Remove the front bumper as described in Chapter 11.

2 Loosen and remove the two upper retaining screws (see illustration).

3 Loosen the nut underneath the headlight –

there is no need to remove the nut completely **(see illustration)**.

4 Disconnect the two multiplugs from the rear of the headlight, then slide it forwards off its lower mounting and remove it **(see illustration)**. If required, the headlight levelling motor can now be removed – the motor is a bayonet fit in the light; twist the motor to free it.

5 Refitting is a reversal of removal. Have the headlight beam alignment checked by a garage on completion.

Direction indicator side repeater

6 Carefully push the light unit towards the front of the vehicle, then unhook it at the rear and withdraw the unit from the wing **(see illustration 5.18)**. Note how the retaining lug at the front of the unit engages with the hole.

7 Disconnect the wiring plug from the bulbholder. Take care while the wiring plug is disconnected that it doesn't drop back into the hole in the wing – tape it to the outside of the wing as a precaution.

8 Refitting is a reverse of the removal procedure. Fit the light unit with its retaining lug facing rearwards, as noted on removal – hook it in at the front edge first, then swing the rear end into place, and push the light rearwards to secure.

Rear light cluster

9 Unscrew and remove the three Torx (T20) screws securing the light unit, and withdraw it for access to the bulbholders **(see illustration 5.21)**.

10 Twist both bulbholders anti-clockwise, and withdraw them from the rear of the light unit.

11 Refitting is a reverse of the removal procedure. Check the condition of the foam seal on the body, and make sure it stays properly aligned as the light is fitted.

Bumper-mounted rear lights

12 Unscrew and remove the two Torx (T20) screws securing the light unit, and withdraw it **(see illustration 5.24)**.

13 Disconnect the wiring plug from the light unit, and remove it.

14 Refitting is a reverse of the removal procedure.

High-level stop-light

15 Temporarily reconnect the battery, and lower the tailgate glass using the centre console switch.

16 Undo the three retaining screws, and detach the light unit cover **(see illustration 5.28)**.

17 Disconnect the wiring multiplug, and remove the stop-light from the bracket on the spare wheel carrier **(see illustration)**.

18 If required, the light unit lens can be removed by unscrewing the two nuts.

19 Refitting is a reverse of the removal procedure.

7.3 Loosen the nut underneath the headlight

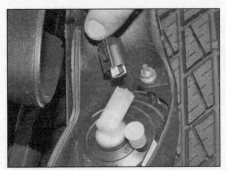

7.17 Disconnect the high-level brake light wiring multiplug

Number plate light

20 Slacken and remove the two retaining screws, then lift out the light unit **(see illustration)**.

21 Disconnect the two wiring connectors from the light, and remove it.

22 Refitting is a reverse of the removal procedure.

---

8 Headlight beam alignment – general information

Accurate adjustment of the headlight beam is only possible using optical beam-setting equipment, and this work should therefore be carried out by a Land Rover dealer or suitably-equipped workshop.

For reference, the headlights can be adjusted using the adjuster assemblies fitted to the rear of each light unit **(see illustration)**.

All models are equipped with an electrically-operated headlight beam adjustment system. To remove the operating motors, the headlights must first be removed as described in Section 7. The recommended switch settings are as follows:

0   *Front seat(s) occupied*
1   *All seats occupied*
2   *All seats occupied and load in luggage compartment*
3   *Driver's seat occupied and load in the luggage compartment*

When adjusting the headlight aim, ensure that the switch is set in position 0.

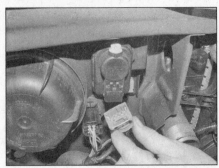

7.4 Disconnect the headlight multiplugs

7.20 Slacken and remove the two retaining screws, then lift out the light unit

---

9 Instrument panel – removal and refitting

Removal

1 Disconnect the battery completely (see Chapter 5A, Section 4), then wait 10 minutes before proceeding, to allow the airbag system time to discharge its stored current.

2 With the steering column in its lowest position, slacken and remove the four retaining screws securing the instrument panel surround in position (two in the top of the cowl, one each below the switch 'pods') **(see illustrations)**.

3 Move the surround rearwards until access can be gained to the switch wiring plugs. Disconnect the plugs, then remove the surround complete with the switches.

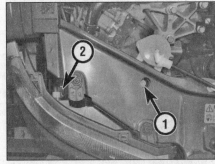

8.2 Headlamp aim adjustment screws

1 Vertical   *2 Horizontal*

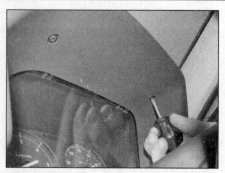

9.2a Undo the two screws in the cowl . . .

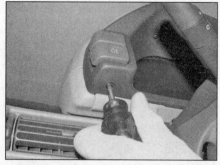

9.2b . . . and the two under the switch 'pods'

9.4 Slacken and remove the retaining screws securing the instrument panel upper cover in position

9.5a Undo the two screws at the back (arrowed) . . .

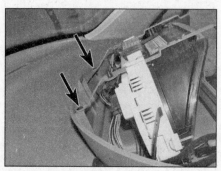

9.5b . . . and the two at the front (arrowed)

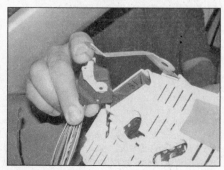

9.6 Disconnect the wiring plugs from the instrument cluster

4 Slacken and remove the retaining screws securing the instrument panel upper cover in position, and lift off the cover **(see illustration)**.
5 Remove the four further screws securing the instrument panel to the facia **(see illustrations)**.
6 Disconnect the wiring plugs from the instrument panel (noting their fitted positions, to make refitting easier) and remove the instrument panel **(see illustration)**.

Refitting

7 Refitting is a reversal of removal. Reconnect the battery, and check the operation of the instrument panel warning lights.

10 Instrument panel components – removal and refitting

Note: *Although it may be possible to dismantle the instrument cluster fitted to vehicles 2001 model year-on, at the time of writing renewal components were only available for vehicles manufactured up to 2001 model year. Consequently, the following procedures only apply to vehicles up to 2001 model year. Check parts availability at your Land Rover dealer prior to dismantling the instrument cluster.*

Removal

1 Remove the instrument panel as described in Section 9, then proceed as described under the relevant sub-heading.
2 The panel lens is secured by six clips around the edges – release the clips and remove the lens from the instrument panel.

3 Release the four clips securing the cowl panel to the instrument panel, and remove the cowl.

Gauges

4 All the gauges are secured to the instrument panel by three screws, from behind. Remove the screws and take out the relevant gauge.

Printed circuit

5 Remove all the gauges as described previously in this Section.
6 Noting the location of each one, remove the twenty-six illumination and warning light bulbholders from the instrument panel.
7 The printed circuit is now secured by one additional screw – remove the screw and carefully take out the printed circuit, releasing it from the location pegs.

Bulbs

8 See Section 6.

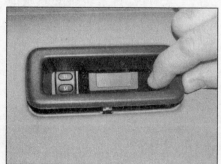

11.1 Prise off the trim panel from around the clock

Refitting

9 Refitting is a reversal of the removal procedure, noting the following points:
a) *Ensure that the printed circuit is correctly located on all the locating pegs.*
b) *Do not overtighten any screws, as the plastic is easily cracked.*

11 Clock – removal and refitting

Removal

1 Carefully prise off the trim panel from around the clock, taking care not to damage it or the facia panel **(see illustration)**.
2 Remove the two clock mounting screws, then withdraw the clock from its location and disconnect the multiplug behind **(see illustration)**. Remove the clock completely.

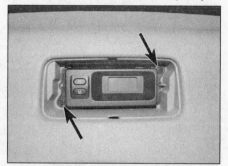

11.2 Undo the two screws (arrowed) and remove the clock

Refitting

3 Refitting is a reversal of removal.

12 Cigarette lighter –
removal and refitting

Removal

1 Remove the cigar lighter element.
2 Remove the front section of the centre console as described in Chapter 11.
3 Unclip the bulbholder from the side of the lighter.
4 Press in the clips above and below the cigar lighter body, and push out the lighter from behind.

Refitting

5 Refitting is a reversal of removal.

13 Horn –
removal and refitting

Removal

1 The horn is located at the front of the engine compartment, at the top on the left-hand side (left as seen from the driver's seat).
2 Where necessary, remove the battery (Chapter 5A) and disconnect the air inlet hose from the inlet elbow (the relevant Part of Chapter 4) to gain access to the horn unit.

15.3a Remove the wiper spindle nut cover . . .

15.3c On the tailgate wiper, disconnect the washer supply hose

3 If not already done, disconnect the battery negative terminal.
4 Disconnect the wiring connector from the horn **(see illustration)**.
5 Slacken and remove the horn bracket mounting bolt, then remove the horn and its bracket from the vehicle. If required, the horn unit itself can be removed from its bracket by unscrewing the mounting nut.

Refitting

6 Refitting is the reverse of removal.

14 Speedometer drive –
general

The Freelander has an electronic speedometer, which receives a speed signal from the vehicle speed sensor fitted to the transmission (non-ABS models) or from the anti-lock braking system ECU, via the wheel sensors. Refer to Chapter 7A for vehicle speed sensor removal and refitting details; for information on the anti-lock braking system, refer to Chapter 9.

15 Wiper arm –
removal and refitting

Removal

1 Operate the wiper motor, then switch it off so that the wiper arm returns to the at-rest ('parked') position.

15.3b . . . and unscrew the spindle nut

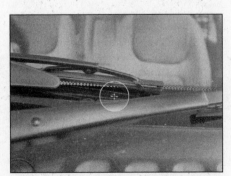

15.6 Align the front wiper blades with the references 'crosses' on the windscreen

13.4 Unplug the wiring connector from the horn

2 If the tailgate wiper arm is being removed, remove the spare wheel mounting bracket as described in Chapter 11, Section 24.
3 Prise out (windscreen) or lift up (tailgate) the wiper arm spindle nut cover, then slacken and remove the spindle nut. On the tailgate wiper arm, pull off the washer supply hose **(see illustrations)**. The windscreen should be marked with reference 'crosses' to aid blade alignment. If these marks are not visible, use insulating tap to mark the position of the parked wiper blade relative to the windscreen **(see illustration 15.6)**.
4 Lift the blade off the glass, and pull the wiper arm off its spindle. If necessary, the arm can be levered off the spindle using a suitable flat-bladed screwdriver.

Refitting

5 Ensure that the wiper arm and spindle splines are clean and dry.
6 Locate the wiper arm on the spindle splines. Aligning the front wiper blades with the references 'crosses' on the windscreen, and the tailgate blade must rest on the rubber weatherstrip at the lower edge of the tailgate window **(see illustration)**.
7 Refit the spindle nut, tightening it securely, and clip the nut cover back in position. On the tailgate wiper arm, reconnect the washer tube and refit the spare wheel mounting bracket as described in Chapter 11, Section 24.

16 Windscreen wiper motor and linkage –
removal and refitting

Removal

1 Remove both windscreen wiper arms as described in Section 15.
2 Disconnect the battery negative lead – see Chapter 5A, Section 4.
3 With the bonnet open, prise out and remove a total of twelve plastic securing studs which hold the windscreen cowl panel in position. To remove the rear row of studs, prise out the centre (using a screw), followed by the outer section. The front row of studs simply pull out. Note that the front row of studs also retain the rubber sealing strip **(see illustrations)**.

16.3a To remove the rear row of studs, prise out the centre (using a screw), followed by the outer section . . .

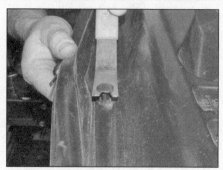

16.3b . . . whilst the front row of studs simply pull out

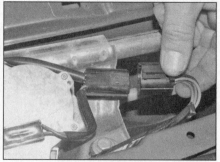

16.5 Disconnect the wiper motor wiring multiplug

Refitting

8 Refitting is a reversal of removal.

17 Tailgate wiper motor
– removal and refitting

Removal

1 Remove the tailgate wiper arm as described in Section 15.
2 Disconnect the battery negative lead – see Chapter 5A, Section 4.
3 Remove the four screws along the base of the tailgate, below the 'door pocket' **(see illustration)**.
4 The tailgate trim panel is held on by a total of eight push-on clips (three on each side, two at the base). Release the clips using a wide-bladed tool, then pivot the panel out at the base to release the five further clips along the top of the panel.
5 Carefully peel away the plastic sheet from the door frame – it's not necessary to remove it completely, but tape it back clear of the working area, so it can be refitted easily later.
6 Unscrew and remove the wiper spindle inner nut, and take off the washer and rubber seal **(see illustration)**.
7 Disconnect the wiper motor wiring multiplug **(see illustration)**.
8 The wiper motor is held in position by two bolts – remove the bolts and withdraw the motor from the tailgate.

16.6 The wiper motor linkage is held in position by three bolts (arrowed)

4 Lift out the panel for access to the wiper motor and linkage.
5 Disconnect the wiper motor wiring multiplug **(see illustration)**.
6 The wiper motor linkage is held in position by three bolts – remove the bolts and

16.7 Separate the linkage by unscrewing the mounting nut, and three mounting bolts and washers

manoeuvre the motor and linkage out from its location **(see illustration)**.
7 If required, the wiper motor can be separated from the linkage by unscrewing the mounting nut, and three mounting bolts and washers, from behind **(see illustration)**.

Refitting

9 Refitting is a reversal of removal.

18 Windscreen/tailgate washer system components
– removal and refitting

Washer system reservoir

1 The single reservoir which supplies both the windscreen and tailgate jets is located under the right-hand front wing.
2 Remove the front bumper as described in Chapter 11.
3 In the engine compartment, undo the two nuts securing the reservoir filler neck to the inner wing **(see illustration)**.

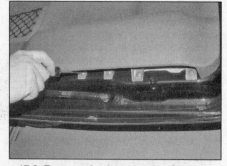

17.3 Remove the four screws along the base of the tailgate

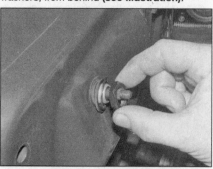

17.6 Remove the wiper spindle inner nut, washer and rubber seal

17.7 Disconnect the wiper motor wiring multiplug

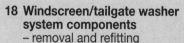

18.3 Undo the two nuts securing the reservoir filler neck to the inner wing

18.7 The washer fluid reservoir is secured by three bolts

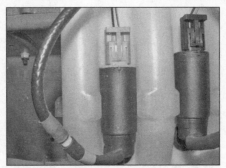

18.11 Disconnect the washer tube from the relevant pump

18.16 Press in the plastic lugs and withdraw the jet from the bonnet

4 Place a container under the reservoir, to catch the washer fluid.

5 Disconnect the washer tubes from each pump, noting the location of each tube, and allow the reservoir contents to drain.

6 Disconnect the pump multiplugs, noting the location of each one.

7 Remove the three reservoir mounting bolts, and withdraw the reservoir from under the wing, complete with the washer pumps **(see illustration)**. If required, the pumps and the filler neck can be prised out of the reservoir, and removed together with their sealing grommets.

8 Refitting is a reversal of removal, noting the following points:
a) If the washer pumps or filler neck were removed, fit new sealing grommets when refitting them.
b) Make sure the washer tubes and wiring plugs are correctly reconnected.
c) Before refitting the bumper, refill the reservoir and check for any leaks from the disturbed connections.

Washer pumps

9 Remove the front bumper as described in Chapter 11.

10 Place a container under the reservoir, to catch the washer fluid.

11 Disconnect the washer tube from the pump, and allow the reservoir contents to drain **(see illustration)**.

12 Disconnect the pump multiplug.

13 Carefully prise the pump out of its sealing grommet in the reservoir. Once the pump is removed, discard the grommet – a new one should be used on refitting.

14 Before assuming that a washer pump has failed, check the following:
a) Is the washer tube (or jet) blocked? Try blowing through it.
b) Is there a poor wiring connection to the pump? The reservoir lives under the wheel arch, so the connector may have corroded.
c) Has the washer pump fuse blown? Fuse number 1 for the rear washer, or number 3 for the windscreen.

15 Refitting is a reversal of removal, noting the following points:
a) Fit a new sealing grommet when refitting the pump.

b) Make sure the pump washer tubes and wiring plugs are correctly reconnected.
c) Before refitting the bumper, refill the reservoir and check for any leaks from the disturbed connections.

Windscreen washer jets

16 Disconnect the washer hose from the base of the jet, then press in the plastic lugs and withdraw the jet from the bonnet **(see illustration)**.

17 Refitting is a reversal of removal.

Tailgate washer jet

18 The tailgate washer jet is clipped into the wiper arm itself, as is its supply tube. First remove the wiper arm as described in Section 15.

19 Unhook and remove the wiper blade for better access to the washer components.

20 Prise out the washer jet from its location in the wiper arm, then pull it out of the supply tube.

21 Refitting is a reversal of removal.

19 Radio/cassette and CD player – removal and refitting

Note: The following procedures apply to the range of radio/cassette units which Land Rover fit as standard equipment; procedures for non-standard units may differ slightly.

Radio/cassette player

1 Some of the radio/cassette players fitted by Land Rover have DIN standard fixings. Two special tools, obtainable from most vehicle accessory shops, are required for removal. Alternatively, suitable tools can be fabricated from 3 mm diameter wire, such as welding rod. Others have one hole either side of the unit, into which an Allen key must inserted.

2 Disconnect the battery negative lead (see Chapter 5A).

Models with DIN fittings

3 Unclip the small access covers (where fitted) from either side of the radio/cassette unit, to reveal the fixing holes.

4 Insert the tools into the holes, and push them until they snap into place – this releases the two tiny catches which lock the sides of

the unit into its mounting 'cage' in the facia aperture.

5 Using the tools for purchase, slide the radio/cassette player out of the facia, then disconnect the aerial lead, and the speaker/power wiring connectors.

6 If required, the mounting 'cage' can be removed by carefully bending up the folded-in metal tabs (above and below, and at the sides) with a small screwdriver. Try not to deform the cage too far as it is being removed, or the radio/cassette will be difficult to refit.

7 Refitting is a reversal of removal. Make sure that the wiring and aerial plugs are properly reconnected, and that the unit is fully located in its cage..

Models without standard DIN fittings

8 Insert an Allen key into the hole either side of the unit, and undo the fixing screws several turns. Repeat this on the remaining fixing screw on the other side of the unit **(see illustration)**.

9 Pull the unit from the console, and lever out the locking element and disconnect the wiring multiplug from the rear of the unit **(see illustrations)**. Disconnect the aerial lead.

10 Refitting is a reversal of removal.

CD autochanger

11 Disconnect the battery negative lead (see Chapter 5A).

12 The autochanger unit is located under the front seat on the passenger side. To gain access to the unit, remove the seat cushion side trim panel, which is secured by three screws (two under plastic covers, one accessed inside the rear of the seat).

13 The unit is mounted in two cradle brackets,

19.8 Insert an Allen key into the hole either side of the unit, and undo the fixing screws several turns

19.9a Lever out the locking element . . .

19.9b . . . and disconnect the wiring multiplug from the rear of the unit

and is secured by four bolts (two at the front, two at the rear). Check that the unit is free to move, then slide it out from the front of the seat.

14 Unplug the main data lead from the autochanger unit.

15 At this stage, the mounting bracket retaining nuts and bolts can also be removed, and the brackets taken out if required.

16 Refitting is a reversal of removal. Make sure that data lead is properly reconnected, and that the unit is securely located in its mounting brackets.

20 Speakers – removal and refitting

Door speakers

1 Remove the relevant door trim panel, with reference to Chapter 11, Section 12.

20.5a Remove the four speaker screws . . .

20.5c . . . and disconnect the wiring connectors

2 Undo the retaining screws, then withdraw the speaker from the door panel, disconnecting its wiring connectors as they become accessible.

3 Refitting is the reverse of removal.

Rear side speakers

4 Remove the rear side trim panel as described in Chapter 11, Section 27.

5 Undo the retaining screws, then withdraw the speaker from the door panel, disconnecting its wiring connectors as they become accessible **(see illustrations)**.

6 Refitting is the reverse of removal.

Tweeter speakers

7 Carefully unclip the mirror inner trim panel from the door.

8 Disconnect the two wiring connectors from the tweeter speaker, then rotate the speaker to release it from the retaining lugs, and remove it from the trim panel **(see illustration)**.

20.5b . . . withdraw the speaker from the side panel . . .

20.8 Disconnect the two wiring connectors from the tweeter speaker

9 Refitting is a reversal of removal. To refit the mirror trim panel more easily, loosen the door trim at the top corner nearest the mirror, and fit the mirror trim in behind the door trim, locating its two front 'feet' over the peg on the back of the door trim. Align the mirror locating clip with the hole in the door frame, and push it and the door trim panel into place together.

21 Radio aerial – removal and refitting

Aerial

3-door models

1 Unclip the sunvisors, then remove the securing screws and lower them from the headlining. Unclip the wiring plug where applicable, and remove the sunvisors completely.

2 Remove the A-pillar trim panels as described in Chapter 11, Section 27.

3 Prise out the interior light lens, then unscrew the two interior light retaining bolts, disconnect the light unit wiring and remove the interior light.

4 Remove the two screws inside the sunglasses pocket.

5 Unclip the headlining trim panel behind the interior light location.

6 Remove the two securing studs from the front corners of the headlining, and lower the front edge down for access to the aerial. If more clearance is required, the rear section of the headlining is secured to the B-pillars by two screws each side.

7 Loosen and remove the two screws securing the alarm sensor bracket, and move it to one side.

8 The aerial is secured to the roof by a single nut from inside, which is also used to connect the aerial co-axial lead. Unscrew the nut and disconnect the lead, then go outside the vehicle and remove the aerial from the roof, together with its rubber seal.

9 Refitting is a reversal of removal. Check the condition of the roof seal, and fit a new one if necessary. After refitting the aerial to the roof and connecting the lead, it would be wise to check its operation before refitting the headlining.

5-door models

10 Prise the interior light and surrounding panel from the headlining, then disconnect the wiring.

11 The aerial mounting nut (which is also used to secure the co-axial lead) is now accessible **(see illustration)**. Unscrew the nut and disconnect the lead, then remove the aerial and its rubber seal from outside.

12 Refitting is a reversal of removal. Check the condition of the roof seal, and fit a new one if necessary. After refitting the aerial to the roof and connecting the lead, check its operation before refitting the interior light.

Aerial lead

13 The original aerial lead cannot be removed, as it is an integral part of the wiring harness. For information, the lead is fed down from the connection at the aerial itself, behind the A-pillar trim, to a further connector located behind the fusebox in the glove compartment.

22 Airbag system –
general information and precautions

A driver's airbag is fitted as standard to all models, and most UK models also came with a passenger airbag. All models also have front seat belt pretensioners, which are linked to the airbag system.

The driver's airbag unit is fitted to the steering wheel, and the passenger's airbag unit is fitted to the top of the facia panel. In addition to the airbag unit(s), there are impact sensors, the control unit, and a warning light in the instrument panel.

The airbag diagnostic control unit (DCU) is fitted to a bracket on the transmission tunnel, directly below the heater, and contains the impact sensors. The airbag system is only triggered in the event of a frontal impact of a predetermined severity – minor bumps will not set the system off, nor will rear impacts or most side impacts. When the system detects that a major front-end impact has occurred, the airbag DCU sends out simultaneous 'fire' signals to the airbag(s) and seat belt tensioners, and the system is deployed.

An airbag is inflated (by a built-in gas generator) within milliseconds, and forms a safety cushion between the driver and steering wheel/passenger and facia. This prevents contact between the driver's/passenger's upper body and wheel/facia, and therefore greatly reduces the risk of injury. The airbag then deflates almost immediately. A rotary contact unit is fitted as part of the driver's airbag system, to provide an interface between the fixed wiring harness and the airbag wiring – note that the same contact unit also provides the connection for other steering-wheel-mounted switches, such as the horn, radio remote controls and cruise control.

The airbag is not intended as a substitute for wearing a properly-adjusted seat belt, and incorporated into the airbag system are the front seat belt pretensioners. In the event of an accident sufficiently severe to set off the airbag(s), the seat belt tensioners are also deployed. The tensioner mechanism uses a cable attached to the seat belt stalk to effectively pull the seat belt tighter in a crash, to stop front seat occupants being thrown forward. The other end of the cable is attached to a piston, at one end of a sealed tube. Using similar technology to airbags, an igniter is triggered by the airbag system, which produces nitrogen gas at high pressure, which in turn drives the piston along the tube and reels in the seat belt.

21.11 Undo the aerial mounting nut (arrowed)

The airbag(s) and seat belt tensioners are classed as explosive devices, and great care must be exercised when working on or around them – this extends to things like removing the steering wheel or front seats, and also to respecting the system wiring (do not, for example, use any airbag wiring as a source for lives or even earths when wiring-in accessories). Once the system has been set off, neither the airbags nor the belt tensioners can be re-used – new components must be fitted. Land Rover specifically warn against using secondhand airbag system components obtained from other vehicles, and against any repair attempts. In addition, Land Rover state that all airbags and seat belt tensioners be renewed regularly, regardless of vehicle mileage (See Chapter 1A or 1B) – their correct operation is presumably not guaranteed beyond this point.

Every time the ignition is switched on, the airbag control unit performs a self-test. The self-test takes between 5 and 8 seconds, and during this time, the airbag warning light in the instrument panel is illuminated. After the self-test has been completed, the warning light should go out. If the warning light fails to come on, remains illuminated after the initial period, or comes on at any time when the vehicle is being driven, there is a fault in the airbag system. The vehicle should be taken to a Land Rover dealer for examination at the earliest possible opportunity.

 Warning: Before carrying out any operations on the airbag system, disconnect the battery positive and negative terminals, and wait

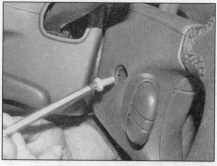

23.3 The airbag is secured to the steering wheel by two Torx screws

AT LEAST 10 minutes, to ensure that the system capacitor has been discharged.
Warning: Note that airbags or seat belt tensioners must not be subjected to temperatures in excess of 85°C. When the airbag is removed, ensure that it is stored the correct way up, to prevent possible inflation. Garages are required to have special 'safes' for storing airbags and tensioners if they are to be left removed for any time – bear in mind the possibility that these devices could go off while removed, and store them safely.

 Warning: Do not use electrical test equipment on the airbag system components or wiring connectors, as this could lead to the system being accidentally triggered. Testing of the airbag system can only be carried out by a Land Rover dealer with access to the special electronic test equipment.

Warning: Do not modify any of the airbag system wiring in any way, as in tapping-off a live feed or an earth (most airbag-related wiring is yellow). Always make sure that the system wiring is securely reconnected, correctly routed and clipped into place following servicing work.

Warning: Do not allow any water, solvents or cleaning agents to contact the airbag unit(s). They must only be cleaned using a damp cloth.

Warning: The airbag(s) and control unit are both sensitive to impact. If either is dropped or shows signs of physical damage or deterioration, they must be renewed.

Warning: Disconnect the airbag(s) and control unit wiring plugs prior to using arc-welding equipment on the vehicle.

23 Airbag system components
– removal and refitting

Note: *Refer to the warnings given in the previous Section before carrying out the following operations.*

1 Disconnect the battery completely (see Chapter 5A, Section 4), and wait at least 10 minutes before proceeding as described under the relevant sub-heading.

Driver's airbag unit

2 The driver's airbag is held in position on the steering wheel by two Torx bolts, accessed from behind the wheel. It may be necessary to turn the wheel for the best access to the bolts.
3 Using a Torx key or socket, loosen and remove the two Torx bolts, then lift the airbag carefully out of its location in the wheel **(see illustration)**.
4 Disconnect the yellow wiring plug from the airbag, and remove it to a safe storage area **(see illustration)**.

23.4 Unplug the airbag connector

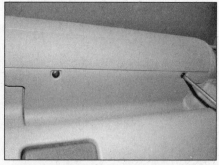

23.8a Remove the two screws from below which secure the airbag lower trim panel . . .

23.8b . . . and remove the panel

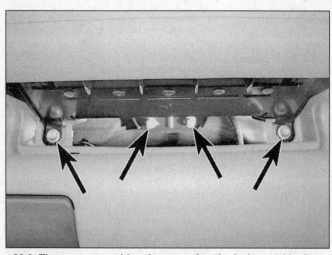

23.9 The passenger airbag is secured to the facia panel by four Torx bolts (arrowed)

23.10 Disconnect the wiring plug from the airbag

5 On refitting, reconnect the wiring connector, then fit the airbag unit to the centre of the steering wheel.

6 Fit the airbag retaining screws, and tighten them to the specified torque setting. **Note:** *If a new airbag has been fitted, the vehicle should be taken to a Land Rover dealer at the earliest possible opportunity, to have the airbag system checked using the special electronic test equipment. This will ensure that the airbag system is fully operational.*

Passenger's airbag unit

7 The passenger's airbag is fitted to the top of the facia panel, directly in front of the front passenger seat.

8 First remove the two screws from below which secure the airbag lower trim panel, and remove the lower and upper panel for access to the airbag mounting bolts **(see illustrations)**.

9 The airbag is secured to the facia panel by four Torx bolts. Remove the bolts, and carefully lift out the airbag **(see illustration)**.

10 Disconnect the wiring plug from the airbag, and remove it to a safe storage area **(see illustration)**.

11 Refitting is the reverse of removal, tightening the airbag retaining screws to the specified torque setting. **Note:** *If a new airbag has been fitted, the vehicle should be taken*

to a Land Rover dealer at the earliest possible opportunity, to have the airbag system checked using the special electronic test equipment. This will ensure that the airbag system is fully operational.

Airbag control unit (ECU)

12 Remove the heater matrix as described in Chapter 3.

13 Disconnect the control unit wiring plug.

14 Unscrew and remove the three Torx retaining bolts, then remove the unit from the vehicle **(see illustration)**.

15 Refitting is the reverse of removal, tightening the retaining screws to the specified

23.14 Unscrew and remove the three Torx retaining bolts, then remove the unit from the car

torque setting. Ensure that the wiring connector is securely reconnected and its retaining clip is correctly seated. **Note:** *The vehicle should be taken to a Land Rover dealer at the earliest possible opportunity, to have the airbag system checked using the special electronic test equipment. This will ensure that the airbag system is fully operational.*

Airbag rotary contact unit

16 Remove the driver's airbag unit as described above.

17 Remove the steering wheel as described in Chapter 10.

18 Remove the steering column upper and lower shrouds. The upper shroud is clipped to the lower shroud, and there are two clips either side – take care when releasing them to avoid damage. Lift out the upper shroud.

19 The lower shroud is secured by two screws from below – remove the screws, then lower the steering column tilt lever.

20 Remove the cover from the ignition switch, taking care not to damage the reader coil fitted round the switch.

21 Carefully pull the lower shroud down, releasing it from the clip on the ignition switch, and remove it.

22 Disconnect the two wiring plugs from the base of the contact unit.

23 Unscrew and remove the four contact

23.23a Unscrew and remove the four contact unit securing screws (arrowed), and remove the contact unit

23.23b Note that the central position of the unit is indicated by a white marking (arrowed) appearing in the indicator window – try and keep the unit in this position for refitting

unit securing screws, and remove the contact unit. Note that the central position of the unit is indicated by a white marking appearing in the indicator window – try and keep the unit in this position for refitting. It is not advisable to turn the contact unit while it is removed (don't let children play with it, for example), or it could be damaged internally. Try using tape to secure the inner part to the outer body **(see illustrations)**.

24 Refitting is a reversal of removal. Ensure that the unit is set to its central position before fitting – if the white mark is not visible in the indicator window, turn the inner part of the unit gently clockwise or anti-clockwise until it appears. The front wheels must be in the straight-ahead position, and the contact unit wiring socket at the top of the unit **(see illustration)**.

Airbag system warning light bulb

25 The warning light bulb can be renewed in the same way as any other instrument panel bulb, as described in Section 6. Make sure, however, that the new bulb is of exactly the same rating as the old one – it could be dangerous to tamper with the airbag wiring, even by fitting a slightly different wattage bulb.

23.24 The contact unit wiring socket must be at the top of the unit

24 Central control unit – general information, removal and refitting

General information

1 The central control unit (CCU) is located in the back of the fusebox below the driver's side facia. If a fault develops, have the systems self-diagnostic facility interrogated by a Land Rover dealer or specialist.

Depending on the market the vehicle was intended for, the CCU is responsible for controlling the following functions:

Transit mode

• In order to minimise battery usage when the vehicle is in storage or transit prior to sale, the CCU can be set by Land Rover into transit mode, where the following functions are disabled:
  a) Remote central locking
  b) Tailgate lock actuator
  c) Tailgate window motor
  d) Interior lamps

Anti-theft alarm system

• The CCU is responsible for controlling the central door locking and alarm/immobilisation functions.

Windscreen wipers

• The CCU controls the intermittent and programmed wash/wipe functions of the windscreen wipers.

Courtesy lamp delay

• The delay function of the courtesy lamp is controlled by the CCU.

Door opening warning lamp

• If any of the doors, tailgate or bonnet are open whilst the ignition switch is on, the CCU illuminates the warning lamp in the instrument cluster.

Key-in alarm

• To prevent the driver inadvertently leaving the key in the ignition, the CCU will sound a continuous alarm if the driver's door is opened with the key in the ignition switch in position 0 or I.

Rear foglamps

• The CCU controls the function of the rear foglamps, only permitting their operation whilst the headlamps are on, and the ignition switch in position II.

Light-on alarm

• To prevent the driver inadvertently leaving the headlamps or sidelights on, the CCU will sound a continuous alarm if the driver's door is opened, whilst the ignition is switched off, and the headlamps or sidelights are switched on.

Seat belt warning

• When the ignition is switched on, the CCU performs a check of the seat belt warning lamp for approximately five seconds, or until the ignition is switched off, or the engine cranks. If the driver attempts to drive away with the seat belt unfastened, the CCU will sound an alarm for approximately five seconds, and illuminate the warning lamp continuously.

Handbrake warning

• With the ignition on, and the handbrake applied, the CCU will illuminate the warning lamp in the instrument cluster.

Rear screen wiper

• The function of the rear screen wiper is controlled by the CCU, via two relays – one 'forward' relay, and one 'reverse' relay. If the window is lowered or not calibrated (see Chapter 5A, Section 4), or on three-door models the roof is down, the CCU will not permit wiper operation.

Tailgate window

• The CCU controls the lowering and raising of the tailgate window. If the tailgate is opened, the CCU lowers the window to the 'clear of seal' position, and raises it fully once the tailgate is closed. On three-door models,

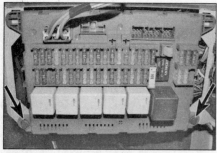

24.5 Slacken and remove the two bolts securing the fusebox to the mounting plate (arrowed)

the CCU lowers the window if the roof is opened/removed.

Heated rear window

• With the ignition on, oil pressure 'sensed', and the tailgate window not lower than the 'clear of seal' position, the CCU will allow heated rear window (HRW) operation for approximately 15 minutes, after which time the CCU will de-energise the HRW relay. The operation of the HRW can be stopped during this period by pressing the HRW switch again.

Heated windscreen

• Power to the heated windscreen relay (located in the electrical box in the passenger side rear corner of the engine compartment), is controlled by the CCU. Operation of the heated elements of the screen is permitted for approximately five minutes, provided the engine is running.

Tailgate lock

• The CCU controls the operation of the tailgate lock motor. If the tailgate handle is operated, the CCU energises the lock motor to approximately 440 milliseconds, provided that the door locking system is in the 'unlocked' state, the alarm system is disarmed, and the vehicle speed is less than 3 mph.

Electric windows

• The power to the electric window relays (located in the main fusebox beneath the facia), is controlled by the CCU. Operation of the windows is permitted whilst the ignition switch is in position II, and for approximately 40 seconds after the ignition is switched off.

Heated seats

• The power to the heated seat relay (located in the main fusebox beneath the facia), is controlled by the CCU. Operation of the heated seat elements is permitted whilst the ignition switch is in position II, and for approximately 40 seconds after the ignition is switched off.

Daytime running lamps

• The CCU illuminates the dipped headlight beams, sidelights, rear lights, number plate

24.7 Separate the Central Control Unit (CCU) from the fusebox

lights, and side marker lights, provided that the engine is running, the selector lever is not in Park, and the headlamps are not switched on.

Removal

2 Disconnect the battery negative lead (see Chapter 5A).
3 Open the driver's side glovebox, and remove the fusebox cover.
4 Undo the three bolts securing the fusebox mounting plate to the steering column support bracket and the vehicle body.
5 Slacken and remove the two bolts securing the fusebox to the mounting plate **(see illustration)**.
6 Disconnect the three wiring plugs in the side of the CCU.
7 Press back the retaining clips, and remove the CCU from the rear of the fusebox **(see illustration)**.

Refitting

8 Refitting is a reversal of removal. Tighten the fusebox mounting plate bolts securely.

25 Anti-theft alarm system – general information

Note: *This information is applicable only to the anti-theft alarm system fitted by Land Rover as standard equipment.*

All models are fitted with an anti-theft alarm system as standard equipment, which is linked to the central control unit (CCU) which controls, among other things, the central locking system. The alarm system has movement-sensing, as well as switches on all the doors (including the tailgate or soft/hard top) and the bonnet. If movement is detected inside the vehicle (volumetric sensing), or if the tailgate, soft/hard top, bonnet or any of the doors are opened (perimetric sensing) whilst the alarm is set, the alarm siren will sound and the hazard warning lights will flash.

The alarm can be activated in either of two ways. The first is by using the remote control

unit; this turns on the movement sensing facility, as well as all the door switches, and also activates the 'superlocking' (or deadlocking) feature, which means that the doors cannot be opened from inside. The second way is to lock the doors using the key in the driver's door lock, this will only turn on the door switches, leaving the movement sensing facility disabled (superlocking can also be key-activated, by turning the key twice in the lock). Land Rover dealers can program the system for 'single-point entry' – this means that, if the vehicle has been superlocked using the key, the first turn of the key will only unlock the driver's door, and the remaining doors will unlock on the second turn of the key.

When the alarm is activated, the hazard lights should flash, and the alarm warning LED will flash rapidly for 10 seconds. After the initial 10-second period, the LED will flash at a slower rate, to indicate that the alarm is active. On disarming the alarm, the hazard warning lights will flash once, and the LED will go out.

The alarm also has an immobiliser function, which makes the engine management and starter relay circuits inoperable whilst the alarm is triggered. The immobiliser has a passive arming feature, meaning that the immobiliser will cut in automatically, even if the vehicle isn't locked. This happens within five seconds of the engine being switched off **and** the driver's door being opened, **or** within five minutes of the ignition being switched off alone.

The immobiliser is disarmed as follows. The alarm handset contains a transponder microchip, and the ignition switch contains a reader coil. When the ignition is switched on with the handset close to the ignition switch, the reader coil recognises the signal from the microchip, and de-activates the immobiliser. For this reason, it is essential that the handset is kept on the same key ring as the rest of the vehicle keys (having two handsets on the key ring will confuse the system, however). It is also essential that the handset battery is renewed when necessary – the need for renewal is first indicated by a buzzer sounding when the driver's door is opened, together with the alarm LED flashing.

One of the most common ways of defeating any alarm system is for the battery to be disconnected. The alarm siren on most models has a battery back-up feature, and will sound the alarm if the vehicle battery is tampered with while the system is armed. The system battery has a life similar to that of the remote handset, however, so it would be wise to have the battery back-up siren checked whenever the remote handset battery is renewed.

Should the alarm system develop a fault, the vehicle should be taken to a Land Rover dealer for examination.

Land Rover Freelander 1997 to 2001 wiring diagrams

Diagram 1

Key to symbols

Bulb	
Switch	
Multiple contact switch (ganged)	
Fuse/fusible link and current rating	F5 30A
Resistor	
Variable resistor	
Connecting wires	
Plug and socket contact	
Item no.	2
Pump/motor	M
Earth point and location	E12
Gauge/meter	
Diode	
Wire splice or soldered joint	
Solenoid actuator	
Light emitting diode (LED)	
Wire colour (brown with black tracer)	Br/Sw
Screened cable	

Dashed outline denotes part of a larger item, containing in this case an electronic or solid state device.
6 - unspecified connector pin 6.
581-1 - Connector 581, pin 1.

Earth points

E1	Earthing strap, battery to body	E9	Engine compartment RH front
E2	Engine compartment RH rear	E10	Engine compartment RH front
E3	Behind RH rear trim panel	E11	Engine compartment LH front
E4	Beneath centre console RH side	E12	Lower drivers side A pillar
E5	Engine compartment LH front	E13	Lower drivers side A pillar
E6	Behind LH rear trim panel	E14	Lower drivers side A pillar
E7	Behind LH rear trim panel	E15	Lower drivers side A pillar
E8	Beneath front console		

Key to circuits

Diagram 1	Information for wiring diagrams
Diagram 2	Front and rear wash/wipe
Diagram 3	Central locking and horn
Diagram 4	Interior lights and instrument lights
Diagram 5	Headlights and levelling, sidelights, tail lights, license plate light cigarette lighter, and accessory socket
Diagram 6	Brake lights, reversing lights, direction indicator lights and hazard warning
Diagram 7	Fog lights, sunroof, door mirrors and airbag
Diagram 8	Electric windows and ABS
Diagram 9	ABS continued, radio, heated rear window and engine cooling (k-series only)
Diagram 10	Heater, cooling fan (l-series) and air conditioning (k-series)
Diagram 11	Air conditioning (l-series), starting and charging (k-series)
Diagram 12	Engine management system (k-series) engine
Diagram 13	Starting and charging (l-series) and engine management system (l-series) engine
Diagram 14	Engine management system (l-series) engine continued and instrument module
Diagram 15	Instrument module continued, starting and charging (Td4)
Diagram 16	Engine management system (Td4) engine
Diagram 17	Engine management system (Td4) engine continued

Fuse table

Engine fuse box

Fusible links	Rating	Circuit protected
FL1	30A	ABS
FL2	60A	Lighting
FL3	60A	Ignition pin 3
FL4	60A	Passenger fuse box
FL5	60A	Ignition pin 1
FL6	120A	Alternator

Fuses	Rating	Circuit protected
F1	30A	Starter - petrol
F2	40A	Condenser fan
F3	20A	Injectors, fuel pump
F4	15A	Hazard warning switch
F6	10A	Horn
F7	40A	Cooling fan

Passenger fuse box

Fuses	Rating	Circuit protected
F1	15A	Rear washer, mirror heaters
F2	15A	Brake, reverse lights
F3	15A	Wash wipe
F4	25A	A/C, heater blower
F5	10A	Starter motor
F6	10A	Engine management
F7	10A	ABS
F8	15A	Direction indicators, hazard warning lights, charging
F10	20A	Cigarette lighter
F11	10A	Radio
F12	10A	Sunroof

Passenger fuse box continued

Fuses	Rating	Circuit protected
F13	25A	Accessory socket
F14	10A	Interior lights, radio, diagnostic socket
F15	20A	Central locking
F16	10A	RH side lights, RH headlight levelling motor, instrument illumination, glovebox light
F17	10A	Electric mirrors
F18	15A	RH main beam, tail lights
F19	10A	Fuel pump, fuel flap
F20	15A	LH main beam
F22	10A	Rear fog lights
F23	20A	Heated rear screen
F24	10A	LH dipped beam
F25	10A	RH dipped beam
F28	10A	LH side lights, LH headlight levelling motor, interior illumination
F30	10A	Rear wiper
F31	20A	Tail door window lift
F32	20A	ABS
F33	20A	LH front window
F34	20A	RH front window
F36	10A	Airbag

H32473

Wire colours

Br	Brown	**Gr**	Gray
Bl	Blue	**Or**	Orange
Ro	Red	**Pk**	Pink
Ge	Yellow	**Pu**	Purple
Gn	Green	**Sw**	Black
LGn	Light Green	**Ws**	White

Key to items

1 Battery
2 Engine fuse box
3 Interior fuse box
4 Ignition switch
5 Central control unit
6 Wash/wipe switch
7 Windscreen wiper motor
8 Washer pump
9 Header joint K109
10 Rear wiper switch
11 Reverse light switch
12 Rear washer switch
13 Rear washer relay
14 Rear washer motor
15 Rear wiper relay
16 Rear wiper motor

Diagram 2

MTS
H32474

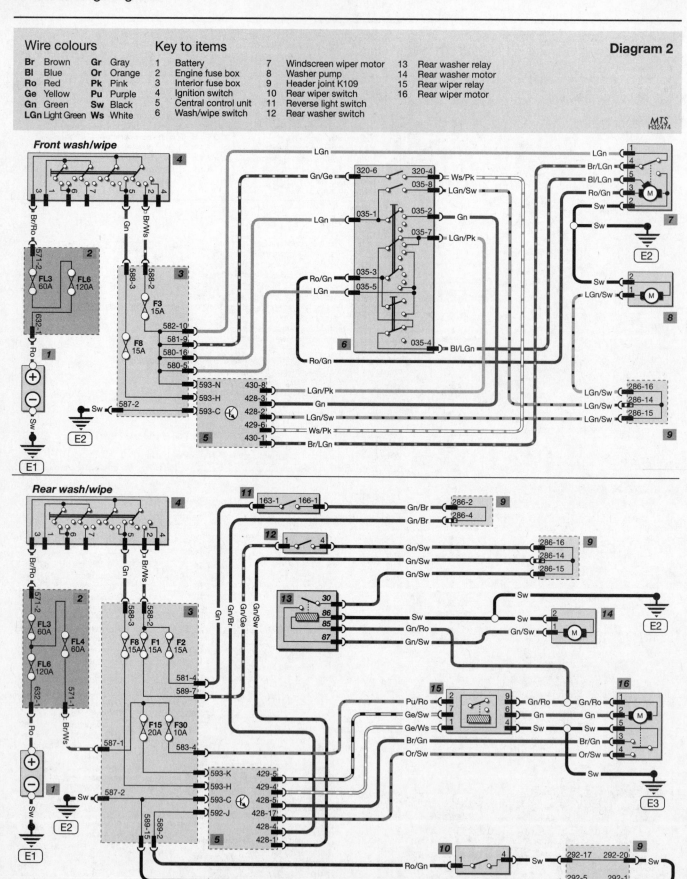

Wire colours

Br	Brown	**Gr**	Gray
Bl	Blue	**Or**	Orange
Ro	Red	**Pk**	Pink
Ge	Yellow	**Pu**	Purple
Gn	Green	**Sw**	Black
LGn	Light Green	**Ws**	White

Key to items

1 Battery
2 Engine fuse box
3 Interior fuse box
5 Central control unit
9 Header joint K109
17 Tailgate locking motor
18 Tailgate switch
19 Central locking switch
20 RH front door lock motor
21 LH front door lock motor
22 RH rear door lock motor
23 LH rear door lock motor
24 Horn relay
25 Horn
26 Horn switch

Diagram 3

★ Five door only MTS
H32475

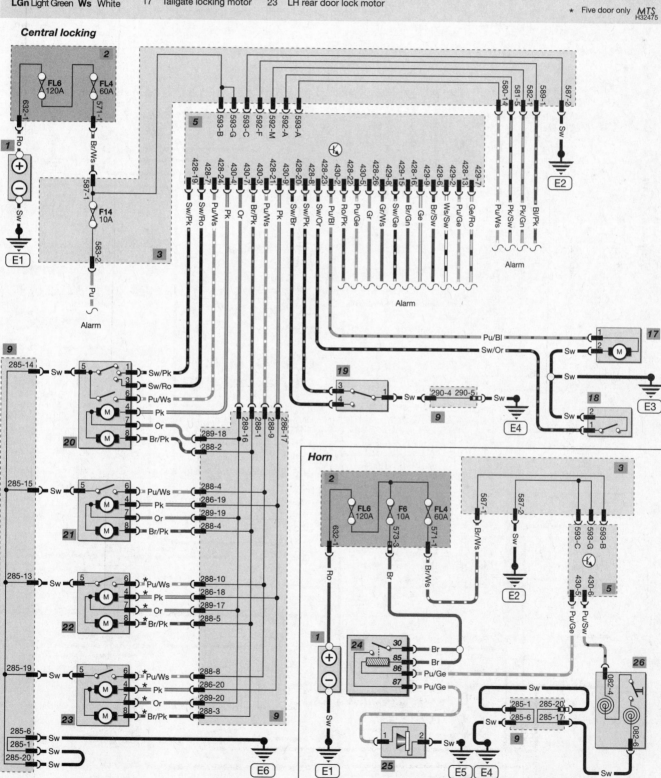

Central locking

Horn

Wire colours

Br	Brown	Gr	Gray
Bl	Blue	Or	Orange
Ro	Red	Pk	Pink
Ge	Yellow	Pu	Purple
Gn	Green	Sw	Black
LGn	Light Green	Ws	White

Key to items

1	Battery	32	LH front door switch	42	Fog light switch illumination	51	RH front window switch illumination
2	Engine fuse box	33	RH rear door switch	43	Rear washer switch illumination	52	Sunroof switch illumination
3	Interior fuse box	34	LH rear door switch	44	Rear wiper switch illumination	53	LH front window switch illumination
5	Central control unit	35	Interior light	45	Central locking switch illumination	54	Hazard warning light switch illumination
9	Header joint K109	36	Load space light	46	Heater control illumination	55	Cigar lighter illumination
27	Light switch	37	Passive coil	47	Air con switch illumination		
28	Glovebox switch	38	5 door rear interior light	48	Air recirculation illumination		
29	Glovebox light	39	5 door front interior light	49	Tailgate window switch		
30	Tailgate switch	40	Instrument illumination	50	Heated rear screen switch illumination		
31	RH front door switch	41	Radio display				

Diagram 4

★ Five door only MTS H32476

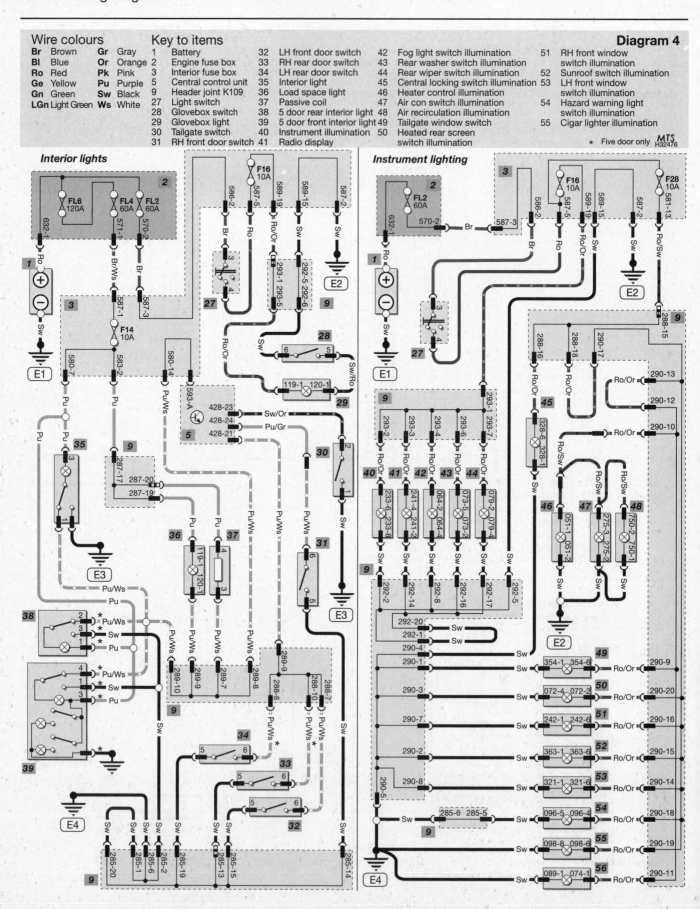

Interior lights

Instrument lighting

Wire colours

Br	Brown	**Gr**	Gray
Bl	Blue	**Or**	Orange
Ro	Red	**Pk**	Pink
Ge	Yellow	**Pu**	Purple
Gn	Green	**Sw**	Black
LGn	Light Green	**Ws**	White

Key to items

1	Battery
2	Engine fuse box
3	Interior fuse box
4	Ignition switch
5	Central control unit
9	Header joint K109
27	Light switch
56	Main beam relay
57	LH headlight cluster
	a) side light
	b) dipped beam
	c) main beam
58	RH headlight cluster (as 57)
59	Headlight levelling switch
60	LH headlight levelling motor
61	RH headlight levelling motor
62	LH rear light cluster
	a) tail light
63	RH rear light cluster (as 63)
64	Licence plate light
65	Trailer connection
66	Cigarette lighter
67	Accessory socket relay
68	Accessory socket

Diagram 5

MTS
H32477

Headlights, headlight levelling, sidelights and tail lights

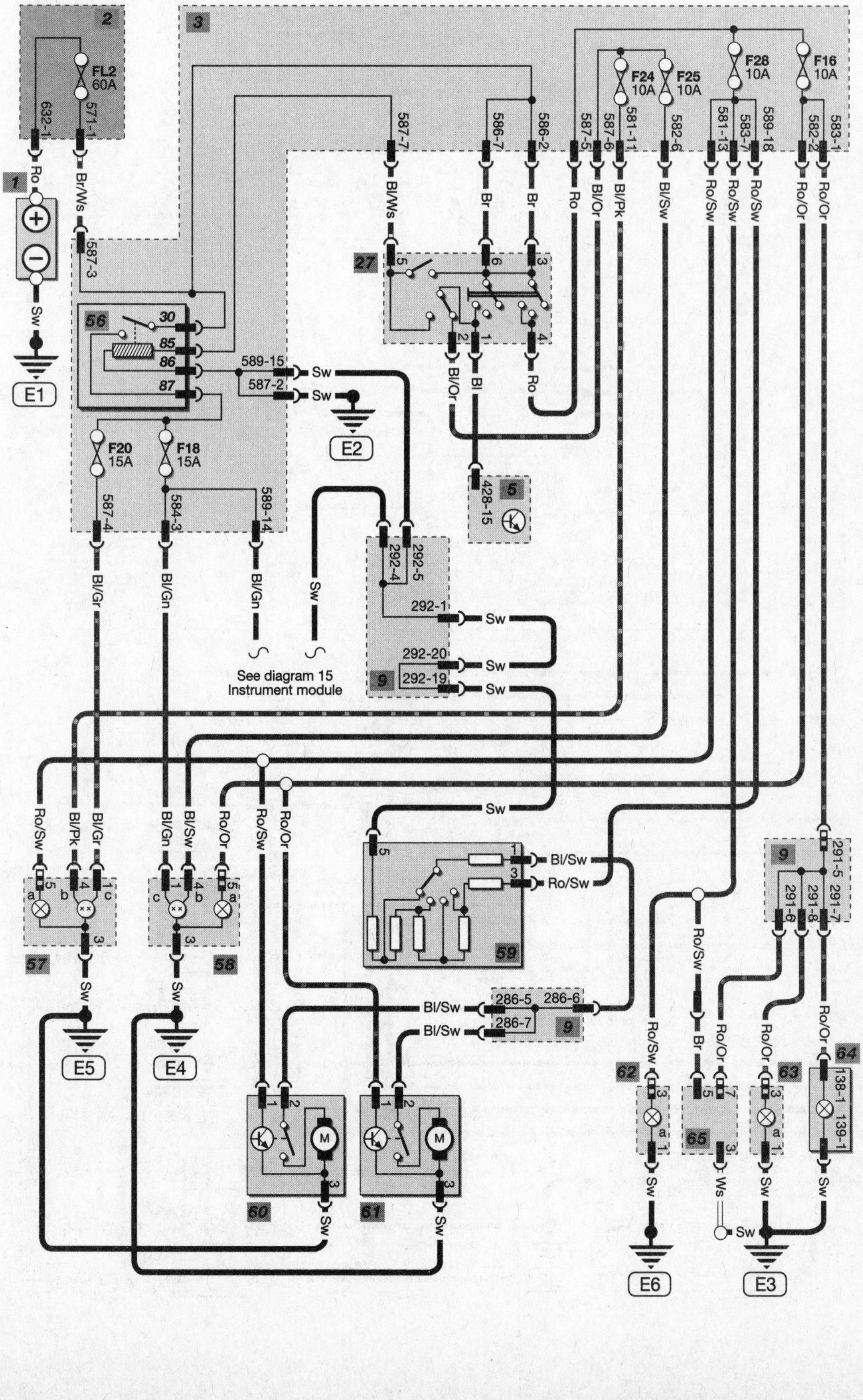

Cigarette lighter

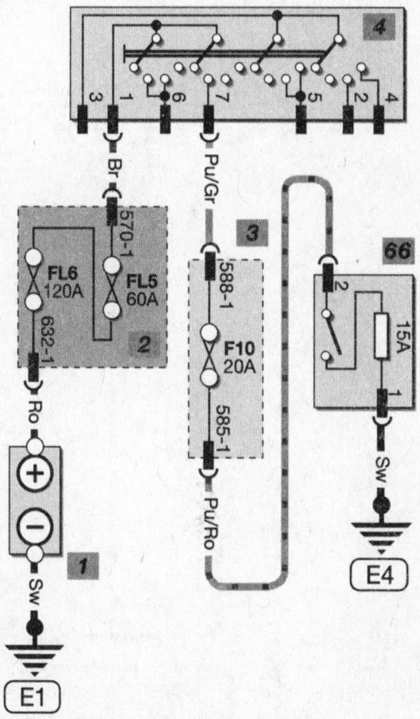

Accessory socket

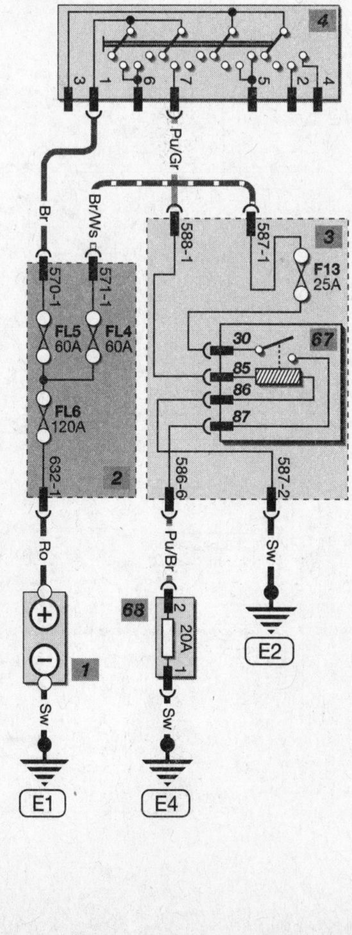

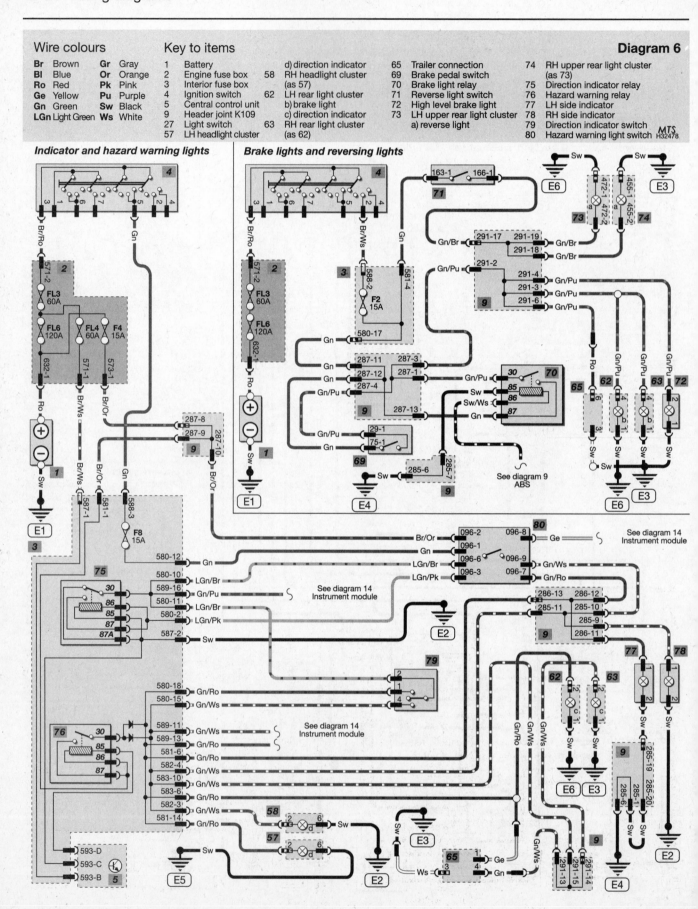

Wire colours

Br	Brown	Gr	Gray
Bl	Blue	Or	Orange
Ro	Red	Pk	Pink
Ge	Yellow	Pu	Purple
Gn	Green	Sw	Black
LGn	Light Green	Ws	White

Key to items

1 Battery
2 Engine fuse box
3 Interior fuse box
4 Ignition switch
5 Central control unit
9 Header joint K109
27 Light switch
57 LH headlight cluster

58 RH headlight cluster (as 57)
62 LH rear light cluster
b) brake light
c) direction indicator
d) direction indicator
63 RH rear light cluster (as 62)

65 Trailer connection
69 Brake pedal switch
70 Brake light relay
71 Reverse light switch
72 High level brake light
73 LH upper rear light cluster
a) reverse light

74 RH upper rear light cluster (as 73)
75 Direction indicator relay
76 Hazard warning relay
77 LH side indicator
78 RH side indicator
79 Direction indicator switch
80 Hazard warning light switch

Diagram 6

MTS H32478

Indicator and hazard warning lights

Brake lights and reversing lights

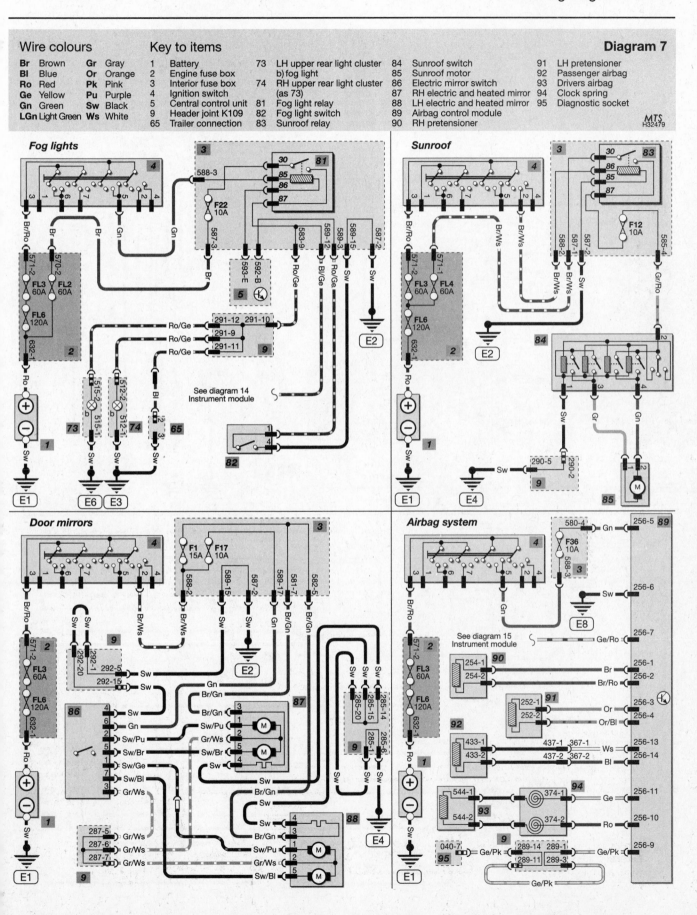

Diagram 7

Wire colours

Br	Brown	**Gr**	Gray
Bl	Blue	**Or**	Orange
Ro	Red	**Pk**	Pink
Ge	Yellow	**Pu**	Purple
Gn	Green	**Sw**	Black
LGn	Light Green	**Ws**	White

Key to items

1 Battery
2 Engine fuse box
3 Interior fuse box
4 Ignition switch
5 Central control unit
9 Header joint K109
65 Trailer connection
73 LH upper rear light cluster
  b) fog light
74 RH upper rear light cluster
  (as 73)
81 Fog light relay
82 Fog light switch
83 Sunroof relay
84 Sunroof switch
85 Sunroof motor
86 Electric mirror switch
87 RH electric and heated mirror
88 LH electric and heated mirror
89 Airbag control module
90 RH pretensioner
91 LH pretensioner
92 Passenger airbag
93 Drivers airbag
94 Clock spring
95 Diagnostic socket

MTS
H32479

Fog lights

Sunroof

Door mirrors

Airbag system

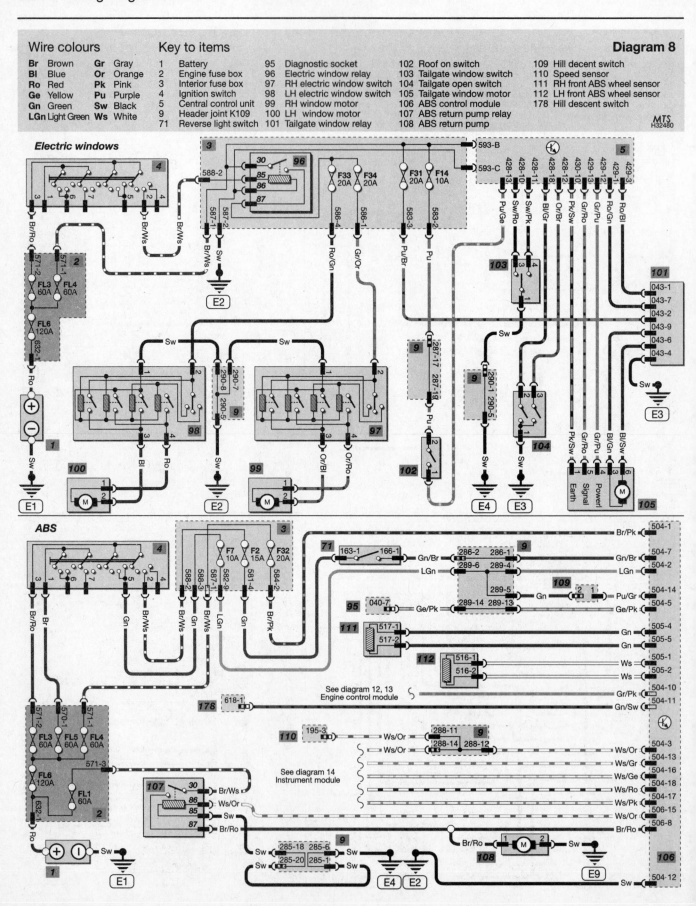

Wire colours

Br	Brown	Gr	Gray
Bl	Blue	Or	Orange
Ro	Red	Pk	Pink
Ge	Yellow	Pu	Purple
Gn	Green	Sw	Black
LGn	Light Green	Ws	White

Key to items

1	Battery	95	Diagnostic socket	102	Roof on switch	109	Hill decent switch
2	Engine fuse box	96	Electric window relay	103	Tailgate window switch	110	Speed sensor
3	Interior fuse box	97	RH electric window switch	104	Tailgate open switch	111	RH front ABS wheel sensor
4	Ignition switch	98	LH electric window switch	105	Tailgate window motor	112	LH front ABS wheel sensor
5	Central control unit	99	RH window motor	106	ABS control module	178	Hill descent switch
9	Header joint K109	100	LH window motor	107	ABS return pump relay		
71	Reverse light switch	101	Tailgate window relay	108	ABS return pump		

Diagram 8

MTS
H32480

Electric windows

ABS

See diagram 12, 13
Engine control module

See diagram 14
Instrument module

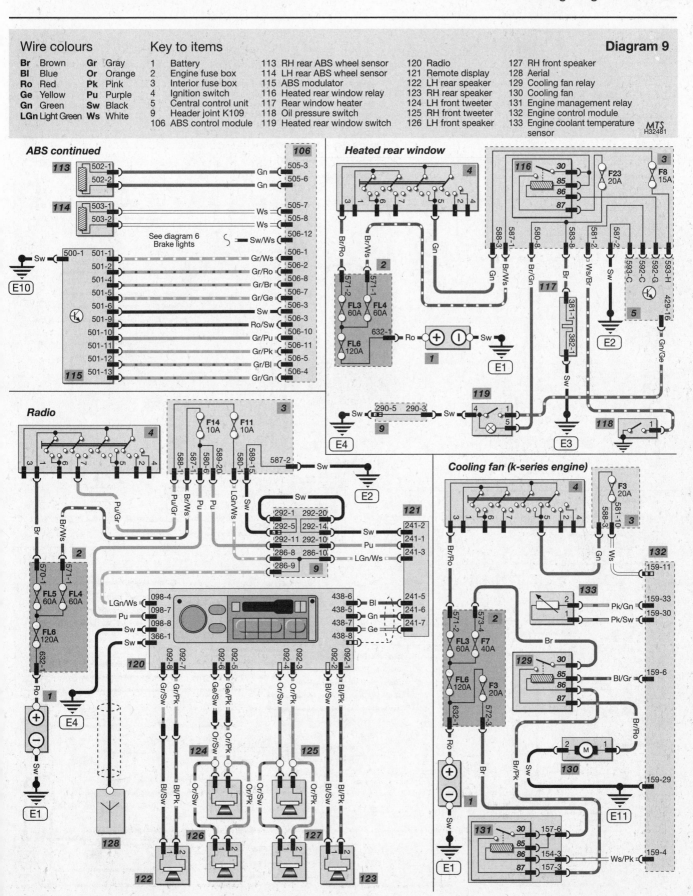

Wire colours

Br	Brown	**Gr**	Gray
Bl	Blue	**Or**	Orange
Ro	Red	**Pk**	Pink
Ge	Yellow	**Pu**	Purple
Gn	Green	**Sw**	Black
LGn	Light Green	**Ws**	White

Key to items

1 Battery
2 Engine fuse box
3 Interior fuse box
4 Ignition switch
5 Central control unit
9 Header joint K109
106 ABS control module

113 RH rear ABS wheel sensor
114 LH rear ABS wheel sensor
115 ABS modulator
116 Heated rear window relay
117 Rear window heater
118 Oil pressure switch
119 Heated rear window switch

120 Radio
121 Remote display
122 LH rear speaker
123 RH rear speaker
124 LH front tweeter
125 RH front tweeter
126 LH front speaker

127 RH front speaker
128 Aerial
129 Cooling fan relay
130 Cooling fan
131 Engine management relay
132 Engine control module
133 Engine coolant temperature sensor

Diagram 9

MTS
H32481

ABS continued

Heated rear window

Radio

Cooling fan (k-series engine)

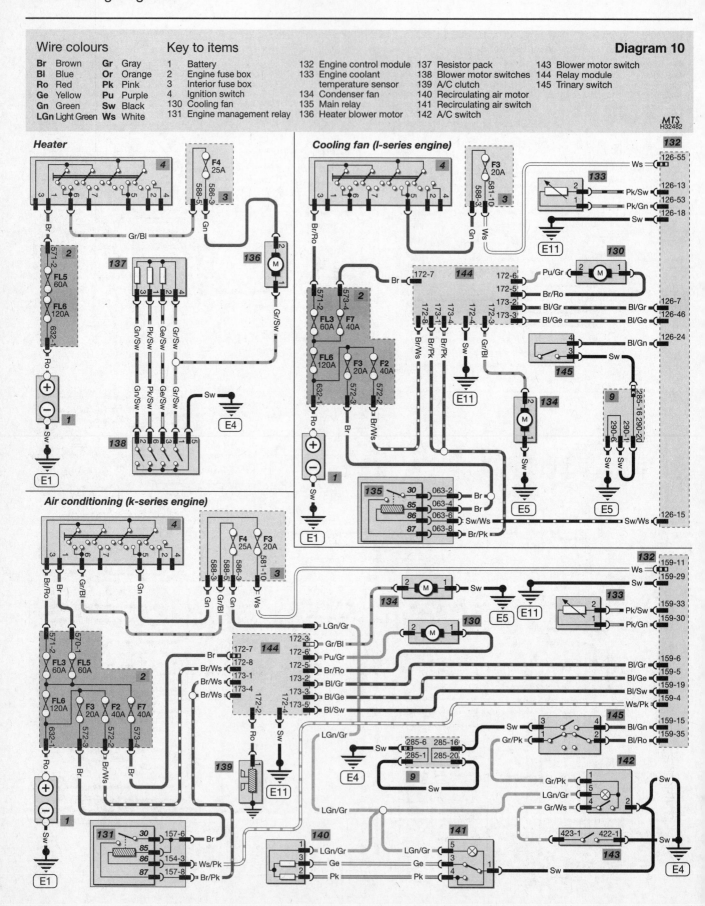

Wire colours

Br Brown	**Gr** Gray
Bl Blue	**Or** Orange
Ro Red	**Pk** Pink
Ge Yellow	**Pu** Purple
Gn Green	**Sw** Black
LGn Light Green	**Ws** White

Key to items

1 Battery
2 Engine fuse box
3 Interior fuse box
4 Ignition switch
130 Cooling fan
131 Engine management relay
132 Engine control module
133 Engine coolant temperature sensor
134 Condenser fan
135 Main relay
136 Heater blower motor
137 Resistor pack
138 Blower motor switches
139 A/C clutch
140 Recirculating air motor
141 Recirculating air switch
142 A/C switch
143 Blower motor switch
144 Relay module
145 Trinary switch

Diagram 10

MTS H32482

Wire colours

Br	Brown	**Gr**	Gray
Bl	Blue	**Or**	Orange
Ro	Red	**Pk**	Pink
Ge	Yellow	**Pu**	Purple
Gn	Green	**Sw**	Black
LGn	Light Green	**Ws**	White

Key to items

1 Battery
2 Engine fuse box
3 Interior fuse box
4 Ignition switch
5 Central control unit
9 Header joint K109
130 Cooling fan

132 Engine control module
134 Condenser fan
135 Main relay
139 A/C clutch
140 Recirculating air motor
141 Recirculating air switch
142 A/C switch

143 Blower motor switch
144 Relay module
145 Trinary switch
146 Inertia switch
147 Starter motor
148 Alternator
149 Fuel pump

Diagram 11

MTS
H32483

Air conditioning (I-series engine)

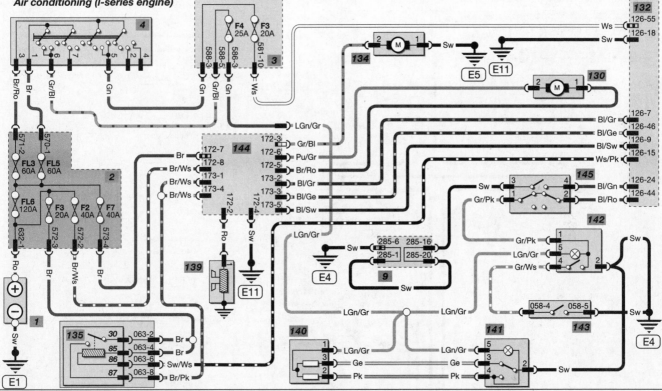

Starting and charging (k-series engine)

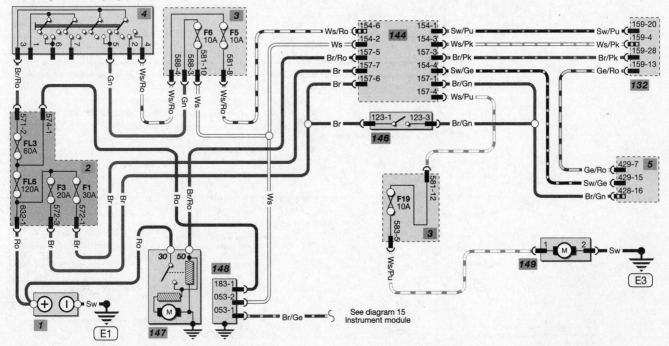

See diagram 15
Instrument module

Wire colours

Br	Brown	**Gr**	Gray
Bl	Blue	**Or**	Orange
Ro	Red	**Pk**	Pink
Ge	Yellow	**Pu**	Purple
Gn	Green	**Sw**	Black
LGn	Light Green	**Ws**	White

Key to items

1	Battery
2	Engine fuse box
3	Interior fuse box
4	Ignition switch
5	Central control unit
9	Header joint K109
95	Diagnostic socket
110	Speed sensor
132	Engine control module
133	Engine coolant temperature sensor
144	Relay module
150	Injector cylinder 1
151	Injector cylinder 2
152	Injector cylinder 3
153	Injector cylinder 4
154	Ignition coil
155	Purge control valve
156	Idle control valve
157	Air inlet temperature sensor
158	Throttle position sensor
159	Throttle pedal switch
160	Oxygen sensor
161	Crankshaft position sensor

Diagram 12

MTS
H32484

Engine management (k-series engine)

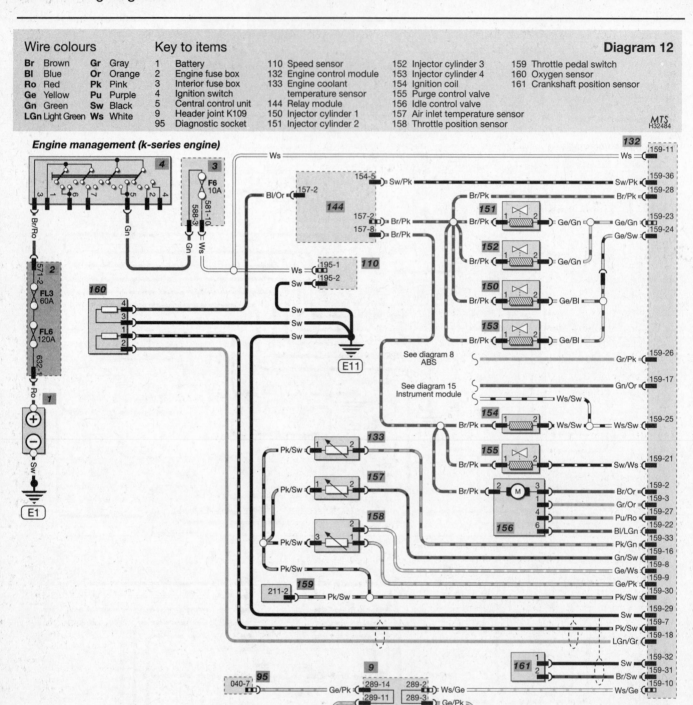

Wire colours

Br	Brown	**Gr**	Gray
Bl	Blue	**Or**	Orange
Ro	Red	**Pk**	Pink
Ge	Yellow	**Pu**	Purple
Gn	Green	**Sw**	Black
LGn	Light Green	**Ws**	White

Key to items

1	Battery	69	Brake pedal switch	147	Starter motor
2	Engine fuse box	132	Engine control module	148	Alternator
3	Interior fuse box	133	Engine coolant	149	Fuel pump
4	Ignition switch		temperature sensor	157	Air inlet temperature
5	Central control unit	135	Main relay		sensor
9	Header joint K109	146	Inertia switch	162	Starter relay

163	Speed sensor
164	EGR valve
165	Mass air flow sensor
166	Glow plug relay
167	Glow plugs
168	Line fuse

Diagram 13

MTS
H32485

Starting and charging (I-series engine)

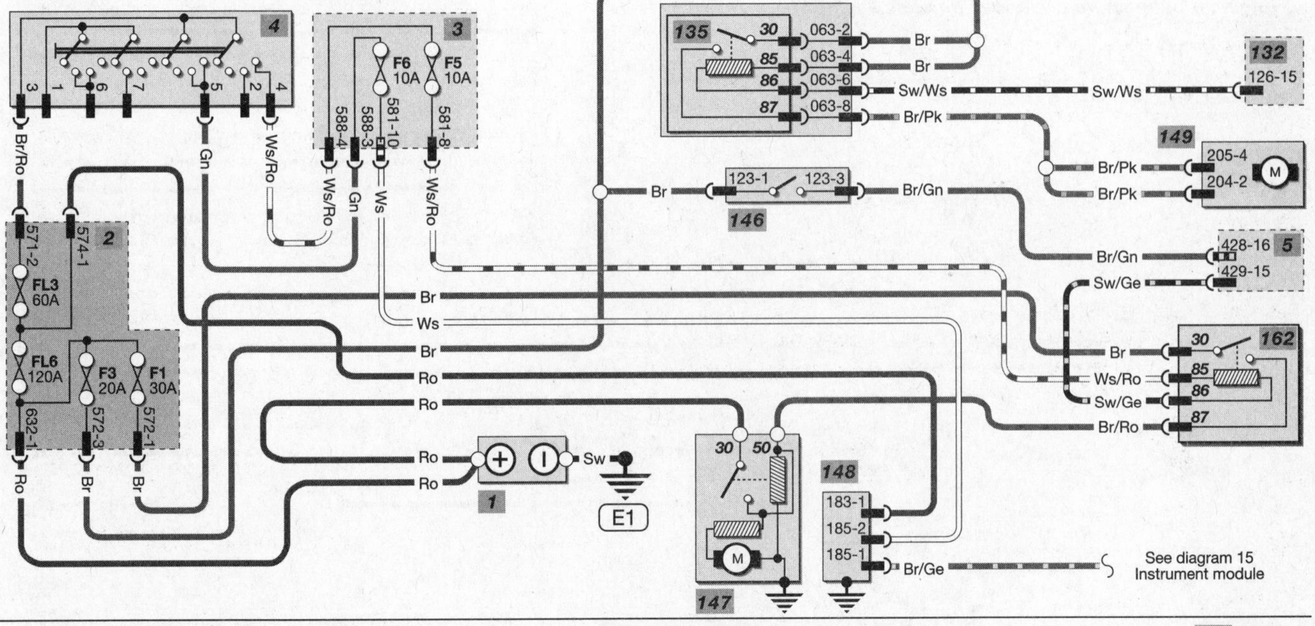

Engine management (I-series engine)

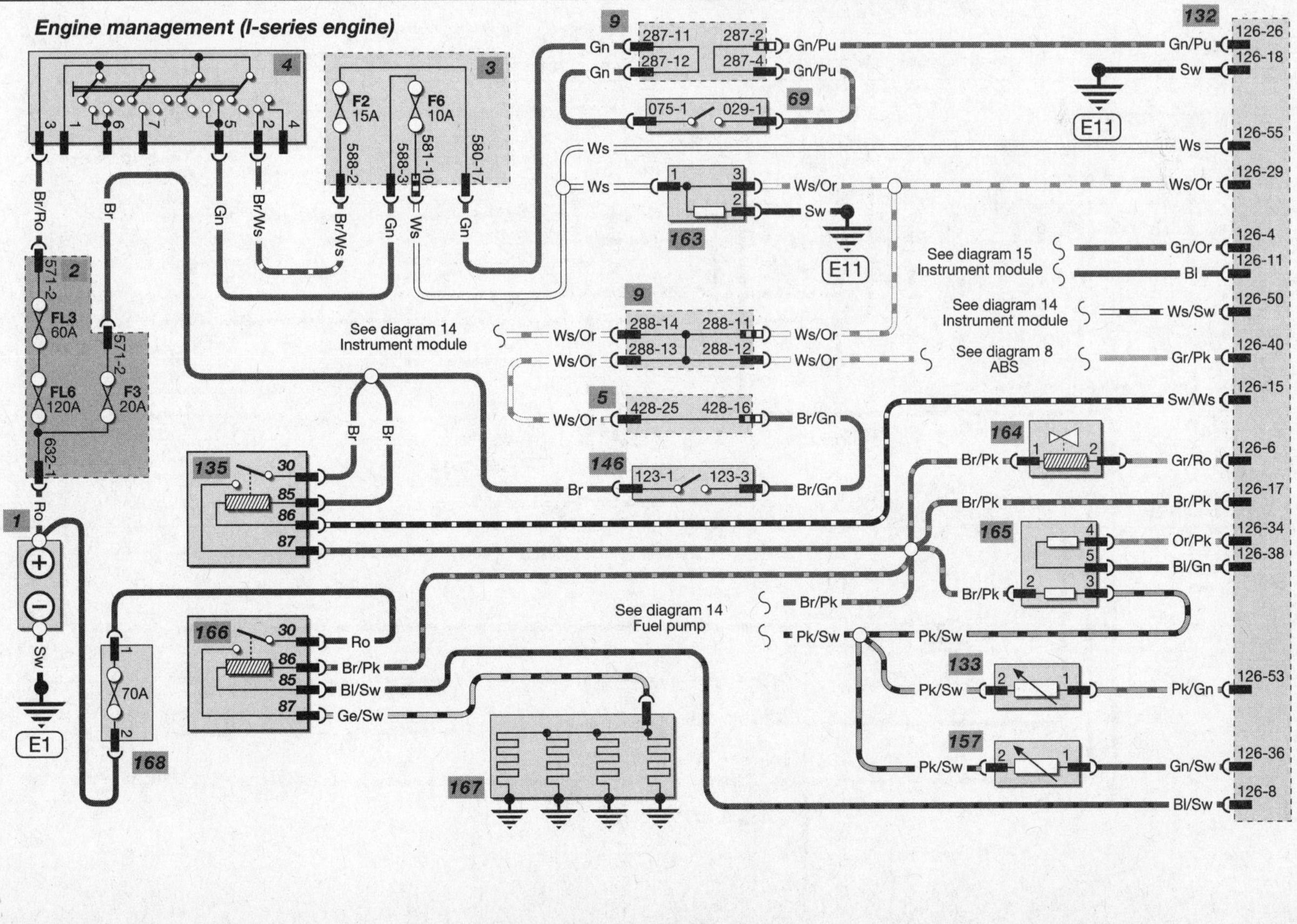

Wire colours

Br	Brown	Gr	Gray
Bl	Blue	Or	Orange
Ro	Red	Pk	Pink
Ge	Yellow	Pu	Purple
Gn	Green	Sw	Black
LGn	Light Green	Ws	White

Key to items

1 Battery
2 Engine fuse box
3 Interior fuse box
4 Ignition switch
5 Central control unit
9 Header joint K109
95 Diagnostic socket
132 Engine control module

144 Relay module
149 Fuel pump
158 Throttle position sensor
161 Crankshaft position sensor
169 Needle lift sensor
170 Boost pressure sensor
171 Coolant temperature
    gauge sensor

172 Fuel gauge sender
173 Instrument module
a) LH direction indicator tell-tail
b) RH direction indicator tell-tail
c) trailer tell-tail
d) fog light tell-tail
e) main beam tell-tail
f) hazard warning light tell-tail

g) speedometer
h) coolant temperature gauge
i) fuel level gauge
j) tachometer
k) dimmer illumination
174 Illumination dimmer switch

Diagram 14

MTS
H32486

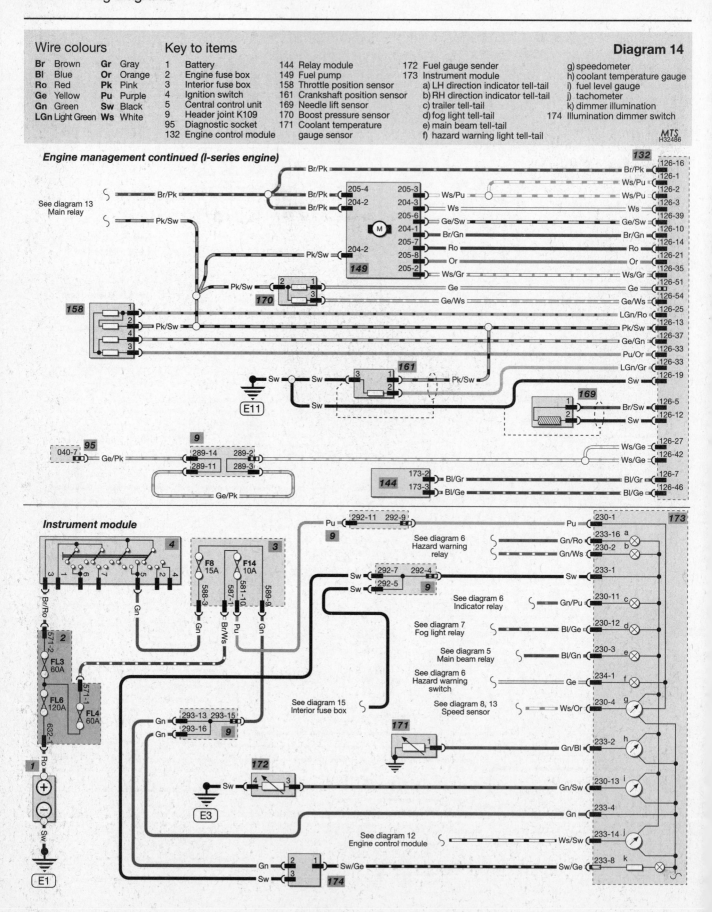

Engine management continued (I-series engine)

Instrument module

Wire colours

Br	Brown	Gr	Gray
Bl	Blue	Or	Orange
Ro	Red	Pk	Pink
Ge	Yellow	Pu	Purple
Gn	Green	Sw	Black
LGn	Light Green	Ws	White

Key to items

1 Battery
2 Engine fuse box
3 Interior fuse box
5 Central control unit
9 Header joint K109
135 Main relay
146 Inertia switch
147 Starter motor
148 Alternator
149 Fuel pump
162 Starter relay
167 Glow plugs
173 Instrument module
 l) seat belt warning light
 m) door open warning light

n) low brake fluid
   level warning light
o) oil pressure warning light
p) charge warning light
q) engine warning light
r) glow plug tell-tail
s) airbag warning light
t) ABS warning light

u) traction control tell-tail
v) hill descent tell-tail
w) hill descent control fault
175 Handbrake switch
176 Brake level switch
177 Oil pressure switch
178 Fuel tank pump unit
179 Fuel pump relay

Diagram 15

MTS
H32487

Instrument module continued

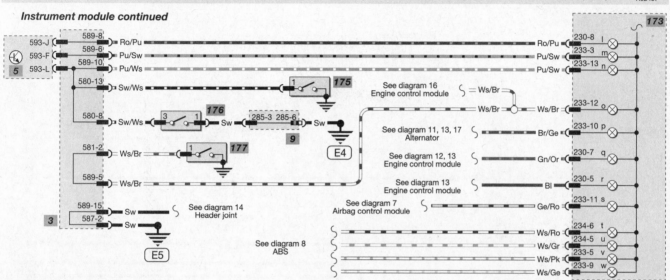

Starting and charging (Td4 engine)

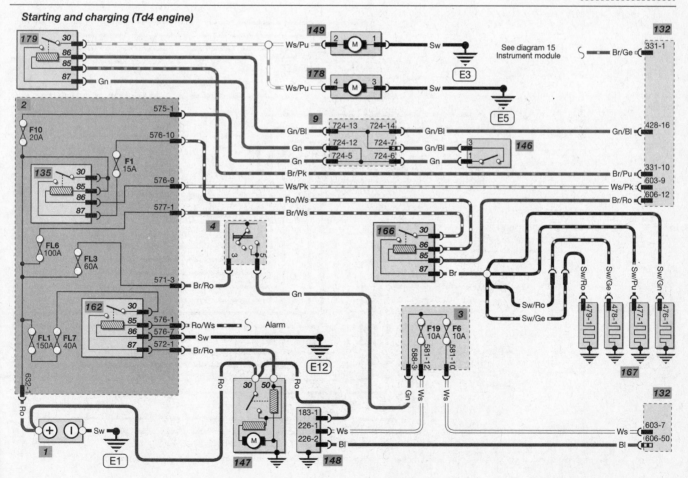

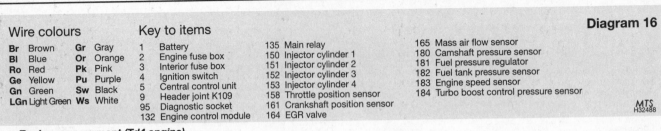

Wire colours

Br	Brown	**Gr**	Gray
Bl	Blue	**Or**	Orange
Ro	Red	**Pk**	Pink
Ge	Yellow	**Pu**	Purple
Gn	Green	**Sw**	Black
LGn	Light Green	**Ws**	White

Key to items

1 Battery
2 Engine fuse box
3 Interior fuse box
4 Ignition switch
5 Central control unit
9 Header joint K109
95 Diagnostic socket
132 Engine control module

135 Main relay
150 Injector cylinder 1
151 Injector cylinder 2
152 Injector cylinder 3
153 Injector cylinder 4
158 Throttle position sensor
161 Crankshaft position sensor
164 EGR valve

165 Mass air flow sensor
180 Camshaft pressure sensor
181 Fuel pressure regulator
182 Fuel tank pressure sensor
183 Engine speed sensor
184 Turbo boost control pressure sensor

Diagram 16

MTS
H32488

Engine management (Td4 engine)

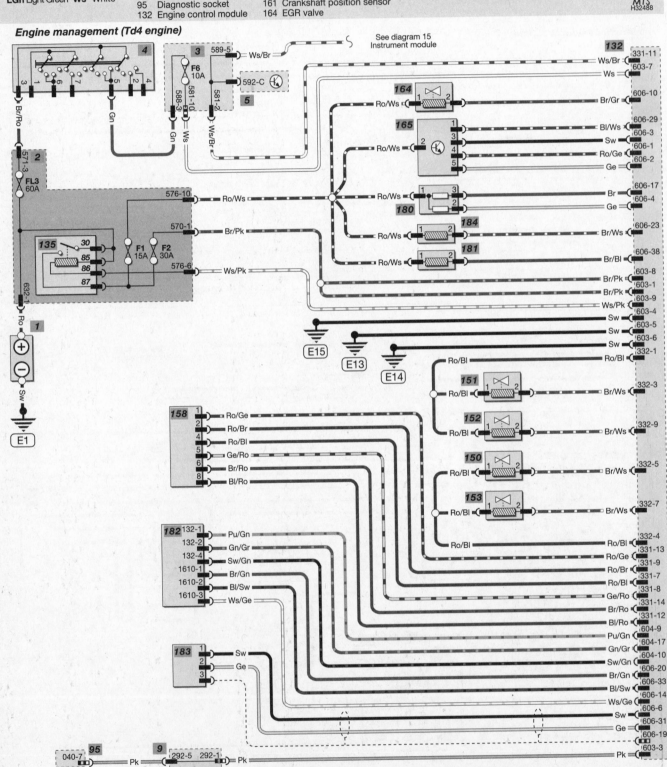

Wire colours

Br	Brown	**Gr**	Gray
Bl	Blue	**Or**	Orange
Ro	Red	**Pk**	Pink
Ge	Yellow	**Pu**	Purple
Gn	Green	**Sw**	Black
LGn	Light Green	**Ws**	White

Key to items

5	Central control unit
9	Header joint K109
69	Brake pedal switch
95	Diagnostic socket
132	Engine control module
133	Engine coolant temperature sensor
158	Throttle position sensor
170	Boost pressure sensor
177	Oil pressure switch

Diagram 17

MTS
H32489

Engine management continued (Td4 engine)

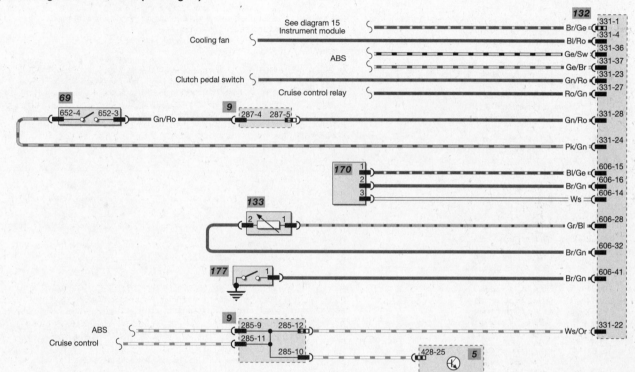

Land Rover Freelander 2001 on wiring diagrams

Diagram 1

Key to symbols

See 1997 to 2001 diagram 1

Earth points

E1	Earthing strap, battery to body
E2	Engine compartment RH rear
E3	Behind RH rear trim panel
E4	Beneath centre console
E5	Engine compartment LH front
E6	Behind LH rear trim panel
E7	Behind LH rear trim panel
E8	Benhind centre console
E9	Engine compartment RH front
E10	Engine compartment RH front
E11	Beneath engine fusebox
E12	Base of drivers side A pillar
E13	Base of passengers side A pillar
E14	Top of engine

Key to circuits

Diagram 1	Information for wiring diagrams
Diagram 2	Front and rear wash/wipe
Diagram 3	Central locking and horn
Diagram 4	Interior lights and instrument lights
Diagram 5	Headlights and leveling, sidelights, tail lights, icense plate light cigarette lighter, and accessory socket
Diagram 6	Brake lights, reversing lights, direction indicator lights and hazzard warning
Diagram 7	Fog lights, sunroof, door mirrors and airbag
Diagram 8	Electric windows and ABS
Diagram 9	ABS continued, radio, heated rear window and heated windscreen
Diagram 10	Heater, cooling fan and air conditioning (k-series)
Diagram 11	Air conditioning (Td4), starting and charging (k-series)
Diagram 12	Engine management system (k-series) engine
Diagram 13	Heated seats, starting and charging (Td4)
Diagram 14	Engine management system (Td4) engine
Diagram 15	Engine management system (Td4) engine continued and instrument module
Diagram 16	Instrument module continued

Fuse table

Engine fuse box

Fusible links	Rating	Circuit protected
FL1	150A	Alternator
FL2	60A	Ignition switch
FL3	50A	Ignition switch
FL4	80A	Passenger fuse box
FL5 (+A/C)	80A	Cooling fan
FL5 (-A/C)	40A	Cooling fan
FL6	100A	Glow plug timer
FL7	40A	Starter relay
FL8	40A	ABS ECM
FL9	40A	Main/dipped beam relay Passenger fuse box
FL11	40A	ABS ECM
FL12	40A	Light switch

Fuses	Rating	Circuit protected
F1 (Td4)	15A	Glow plug, fuel pressure regulator, boost solenoid, EGR solenoid, MAF sensor
F1 (K-series)	15A	Purge control valve, Ho2S
F2	20A	Engine ECM, ignition coils fuel injectors
F3	15A	CMP sensor
F4	15A	A/C, cooling fan, auto transmission cruise control
F5	20A	Heater, engine ECM
F6	15A	Horn
F7	15A	Hazard warning
F8	30A	A/C
F9	10A	A/C clutch relay
F10 (Td4)	20A	Inertia switch, fuel pump
F10 (K-series)	10A	Inertia switch

Passenger fuse box

Fuses	Rating	Circuit protected
F1	15A	Rear washer, power mirrors
F2	15A	Brake, reverse lights, HDC relay
F3	15A	Wash wipe
F4	25A	Heater blower
F5	10A	Instrument module, E-box fan
F6	10A	Engine management
F7	5A	ABS
F8	15A	Hazard warning, instrument module
F9	10A	Radio
F10	15A	Cigarette lighter
F11	10A	Radio, auto transmission inhibit switch
F12	15A	Sunroof switch
F13	20A	Accessory socket
F14	5A	Interior lights, radio, load space light, instrument module diagnostic socket, interior lights
F15	20A	Central locking
F16	10A	RH side lights, RH tail light, licence plates, trailer pick-up, RH headlight levelling motor, interior illumination
F17	10A	Electric mirrors
F18	15A	RH main beam, instrument module
F19	10A	Alternator
F20	15A	LH main beam
F22	10A	Rear fog lights
F23	20A	Heated rear screen
F24	10A	LH dipped beam
F25	10A	RH dipped beam
F26	20A	LH rear electric windows
F27	20A	RH rear electric windows
F28	10A	LH side lights, LH headlight levelling motor, LH tail light, trailer pick-up
F29	25A	Heated seats
F30	10A	Rear wiper
F31	20A	Tail door window lift
F32	5A	Alarm
F33	20A	LH front electric window, electric windows ECM
F34	20A	RH front electric window
F35 (Td4)	10A	Clutch switch, cruise control, main relay, HDC, auto transmission brake pedal switch
F35 (K-series)	10A	Throttle pedal switch, main relay, HDC
F36	10A	Airbag

H32490

Wire colours

Br Brown   **Gr** Gray
Bl Blue   **Or** Orange
Ro Red   **Pk** Pink
Ge Yellow   **Pu** Purple
Gn Green   **Sw** Black
LGn Light Green   **Ws** White

Key to items

1 Battery
2 Engine fuse box
3 Interior fuse box
4 Ignition switch
5 Central control unit
6 Wash/wipe switch
7 Windscreen wiper motor
8 Washer pump
9 Header joint K109
10 Rear wiper switch
11 Rear washer switch
12 Rear washer switch
13 Rear washer relay
14 Rear washer motor
15 Rear wiper relay
16 Rear wiper motor

Diagram 2

MTS
H32491

Front wash/wipe

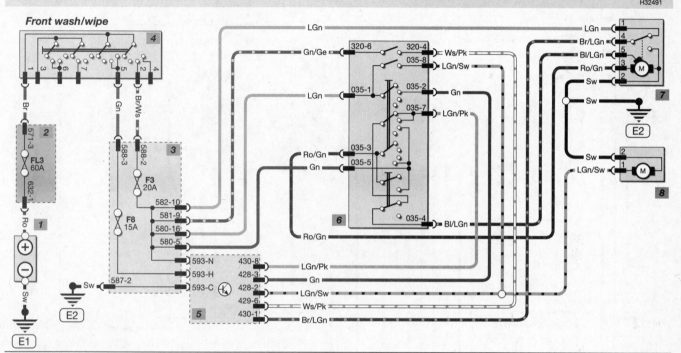

Rear wash/wipe

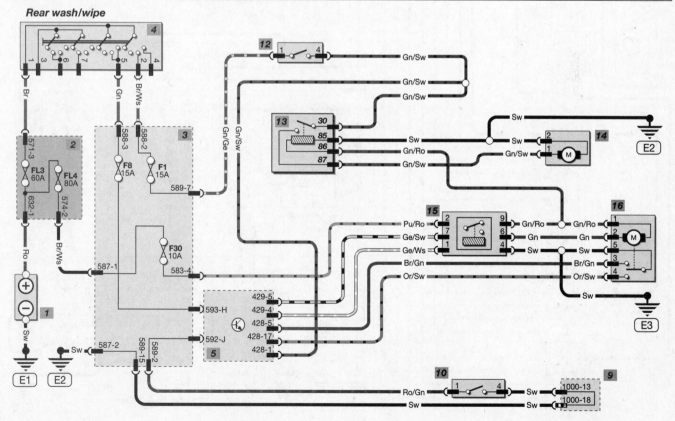

Wire colours

Br	Brown	**Gr**	Gray
Bl	Blue	**Or**	Orange
Ro	Red	**Pk**	Pink
Ge	Yellow	**Pu**	Purple
Gn	Green	**Sw**	Black
LGn	Light Green	**Ws**	White

Key to items

1	Battery	18	Tailgate switch
2	Engine fuse box	19	Central locking switch
3	Interior fuse box	20	RH front door lock motor
5	Central control unit	21	LH front door lock motor
9	Header joint K109	22	RH rear door lock motor
17	Tailgate locking motor	23	LH rear door lock motor

24	Diagnostic socket
25	Inertia switch
26	Radio receiver
27	Roof on switch
28	Horn relay
29	RH horn

30	LH horn
31	Clock spring
32	RH horn switch
33	LH horn switch

Diagram 3

*   Petrol only
**   Diesel only
***   Five door only

MTS
H32492

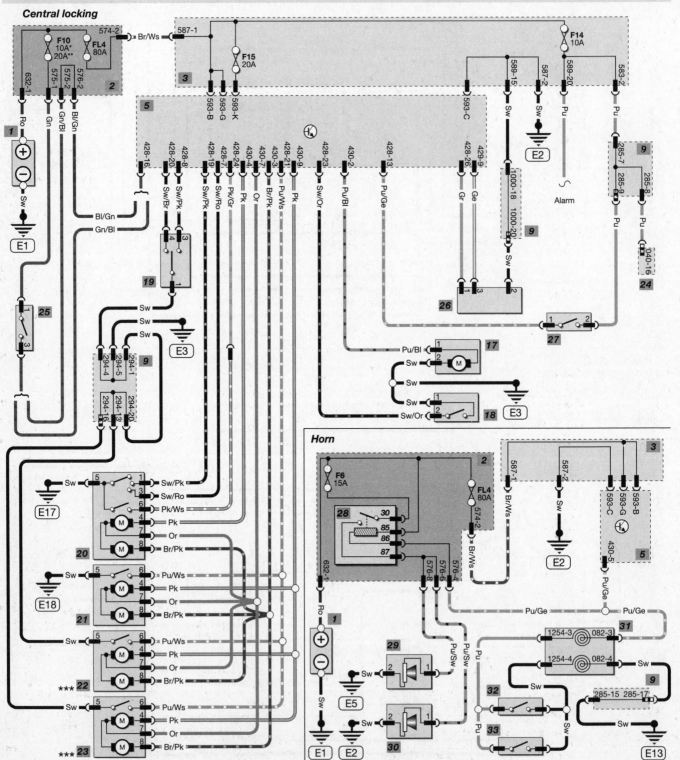

Central locking

Horn

Wire colours

Br	Brown	Gr	Gray
Bl	Blue	Or	Orange
Ro	Red	Pk	Pink
Ge	Yellow	Pu	Purple
Gn	Green	Sw	Black
LGn	Light Green	Ws	White

Key to items

1	Battery	39	LH rear door switch
2	Engine fuse box	40	Tailgate switch
3	Interior fuse box	41	RH front door switch
5	Central control unit	42	Illumination relay
9	Header joint K109	43	Coil transponder
34	Front interior light	44	Glovebox light
35	Rear interior light	45	Glovebox switch
36	Interior light	46	Load space light
37	LH front door switch	47	Light switch
38	RH rear door switch		

Switch Illumination

48	Cruise control switch	58	RH rear window switch
49	Fog light switch	59	LH rear window switch
50	Rear washer switch	60	Heated rear window
51	Rear wiper switch	61	Air con switch pack
52	Instrument module	62	Air recirculation switch
53	Remote radio display	63	Heated windscreen
54	LH front window switch	64	Central door locking
55	RH front window switch	65	LH seat switch pack
56	Radio illumination	66	RH seat switch pack
57	Cigarette lighter	67	Tailgate window switch

Diagram 4

68	Sun roof switch
69	Hazard warning
70	Heater control
71	Hill decent switch

*	Five door only
**	Dimmer only
***	No dimmer

MTS
H32493

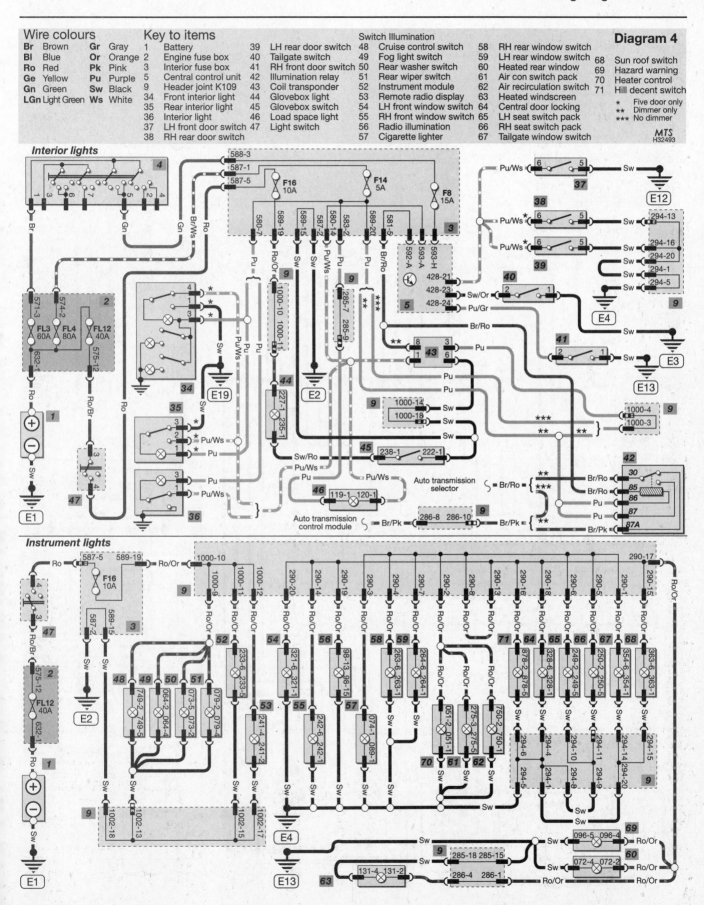

Interior lights

Instrument lights

Auto transmission selector

Auto transmission control module

Wire colours

Br Brown   Gr Gray
Bl Blue   Or Orange
Ro Red   Pk Pink
Ge Yellow   Pu Purple
Gn Green   Sw Black
LGn Light Green   Ws White

Key to items

1 Battery
2 Engine fuse box
3 Interior fuse box
4 Ignition switch
5 Central control unit
9 Header joint K109
47 Light switch
72 Main beam relay
73 LH headlight cluster
  a) side light
  b) dipped beam
  c) main beam
74 RH headlight cluster
  (as 73)
75 Headlight levelling switch
76 LH headlight levelling motor
77 RH headlight levelling motor
78 LH rear light cluster
  a) tail light
79 RH rear light cluster
  (as 78)
80 Licence plate light
81 Trailer connection
82 Cigarette lighter
83 Accessory socket relay
84 Accessory socket

Diagram 5

MTS
H32494

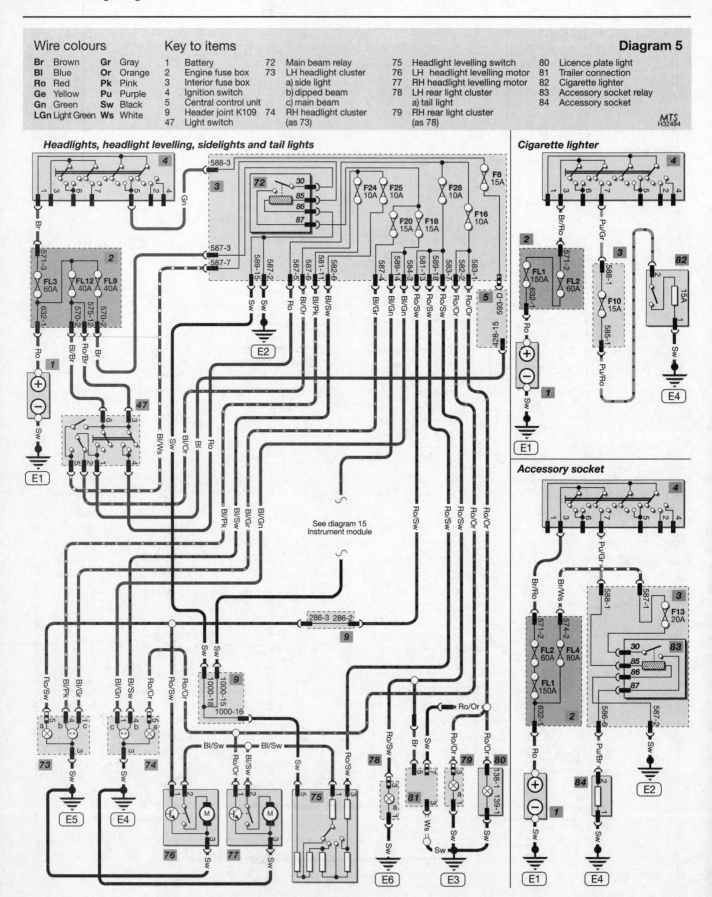

Headlights, headlight levelling, sidelights and tail lights

Cigarette lighter

Accessory socket

See diagram 15
Instrument module

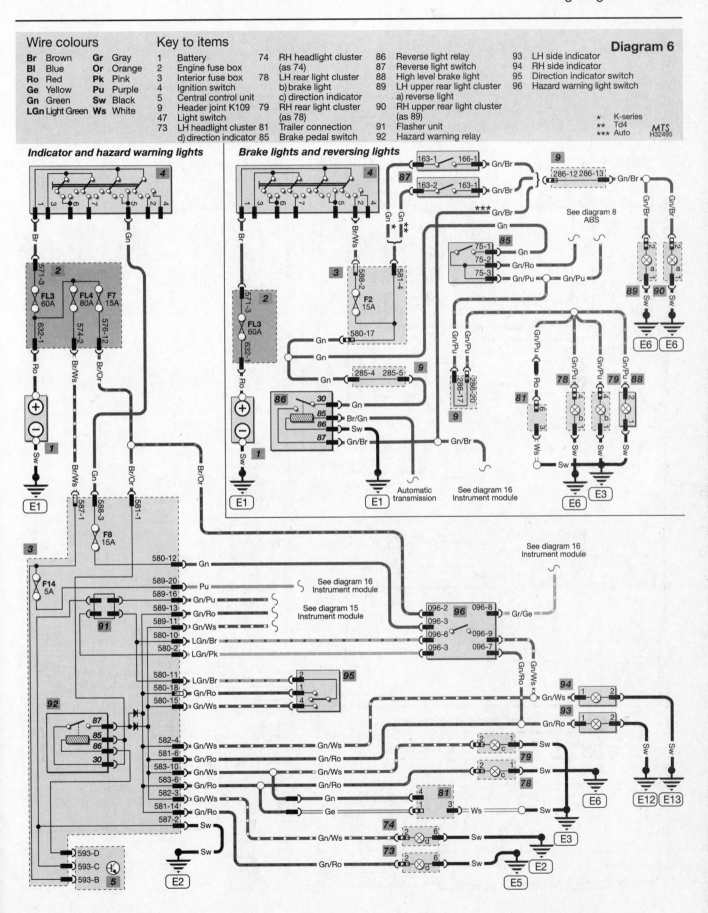

Wire colours

Br	Brown	Gr	Gray
Bl	Blue	Or	Orange
Ro	Red	Pk	Pink
Ge	Yellow	Pu	Purple
Gn	Green	Sw	Black
LGn	Light Green	Ws	White

Key to items

1 Battery
2 Engine fuse box
3 Interior fuse box
4 Ignition switch
5 Central control unit
9 Header joint K109
47 Light switch
73 LH headlight cluster
d) direction indicator

74 RH headlight cluster (as 74)
78 LH rear light cluster
b) brake light
c) direction indicator
79 RH rear light cluster (as 78)
81 Trailer connection
85 Brake pedal switch

86 Reverse light relay
87 Reverse light switch
88 High level brake light
89 LH upper rear light cluster
a) reverse light
90 RH upper rear light cluster (as 89)
91 Flasher unit
92 Hazard warning relay

93 LH side indicator
94 RH side indicator
95 Direction indicator switch
96 Hazard warning light switch

Diagram 6

* K-series
** Td4
*** Auto

MTS
H32495

Indicator and hazard warning lights

Brake lights and reversing lights

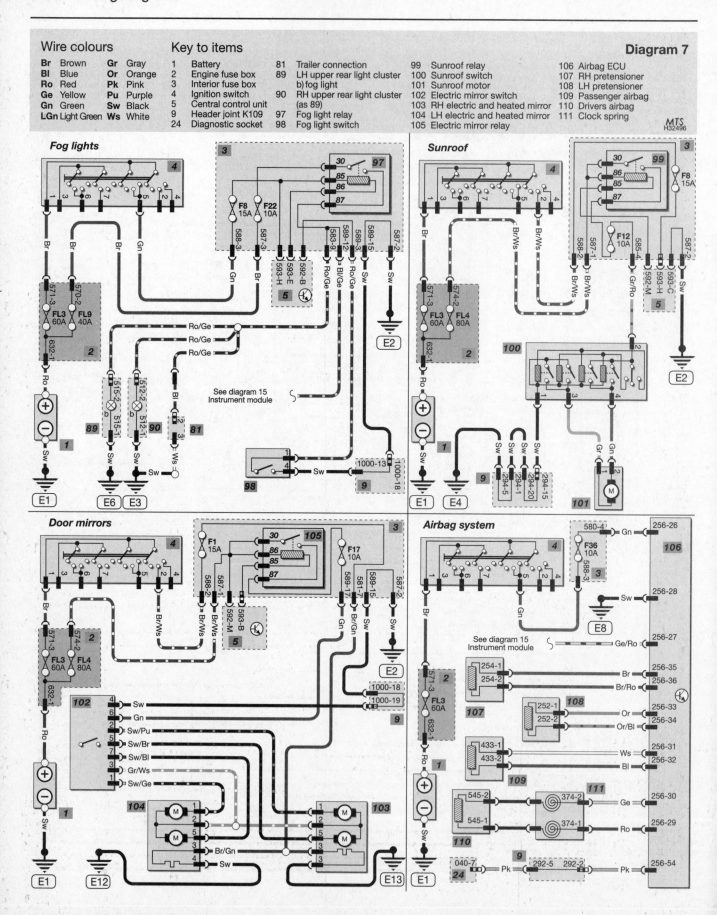

Wire colours

Br	Brown	**Gr**	Gray
Bl	Blue	**Or**	Orange
Ro	Red	**Pk**	Pink
Ge	Yellow	**Pu**	Purple
Gn	Green	**Sw**	Black
LGn	Light Green	**Ws**	White

Key to items

1 Battery
2 Engine fuse box
3 Interior fuse box
4 Ignition switch
5 Central control unit
9 Header joint K109
24 Diagnostic socket

81 Trailer connection
89 LH upper rear light cluster
    b) fog light
90 RH upper rear light cluster
    (as 89)
97 Fog light relay
98 Fog light switch

99 Sunroof relay
100 Sunroof switch
101 Sunroof motor
102 Electric mirror switch
103 RH electric and heated mirror
104 LH electric and heated mirror
105 Electric mirror relay

106 Airbag ECU
107 RH pretensioner
108 LH pretensioner
109 Passenger airbag
110 Drivers airbag
111 Clock spring

Diagram 7

MTS
H32496

Fog lights

Sunroof

Door mirrors

Airbag system

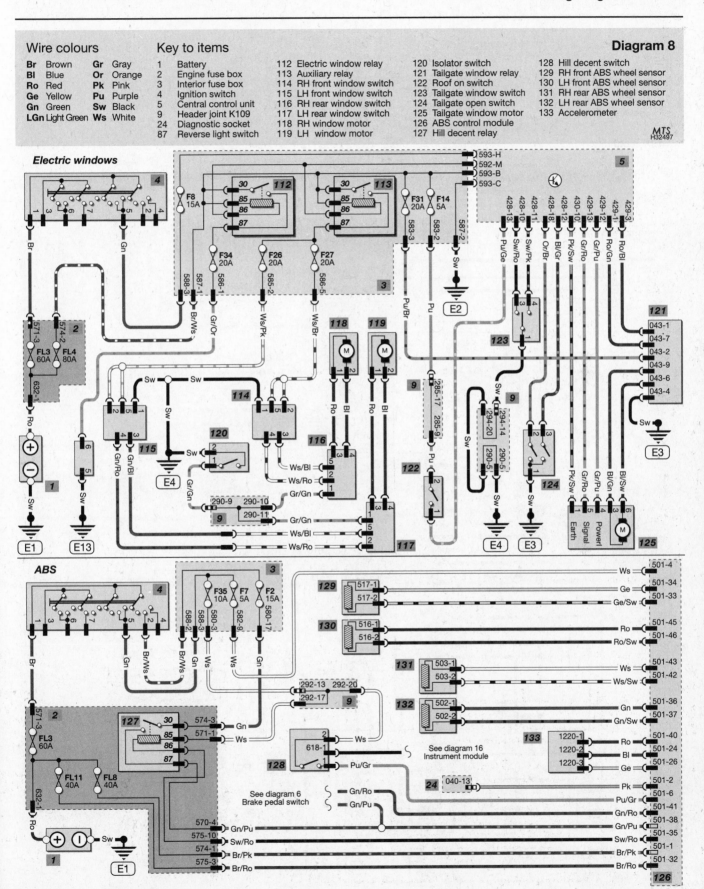

Wire colours

Br	Brown	**Gr**	Gray
Bl	Blue	**Or**	Orange
Ro	Red	**Pk**	Pink
Ge	Yellow	**Pu**	Purple
Gn	Green	**Sw**	Black
LGn	Light Green	**Ws**	White

Key to items

1 Battery
2 Engine fuse box
3 Interior fuse box
4 Ignition switch
5 Central control unit
9 Header joint K109
24 Diagnostic socket
87 Reverse light switch

112 Electric window relay
113 Auxiliary relay
114 RH front window switch
115 LH front window switch
116 RH rear window switch
117 LH rear window switch
118 RH window motor
119 LH window motor

120 Isolator switch
121 Tailgate window relay
122 Roof on switch
123 Tailgate window switch
124 Tailgate open switch
125 Tailgate window motor
126 ABS control module
127 Hill decent relay

128 Hill decent switch
129 RH front ABS wheel sensor
130 LH front ABS wheel sensor
131 RH rear ABS wheel sensor
132 LH rear ABS wheel sensor
133 Accelerometer

Diagram 8

MTS
H32497

Electric windows

ABS

See diagram 16
Instrument module

See diagram 6
Brake pedal switch

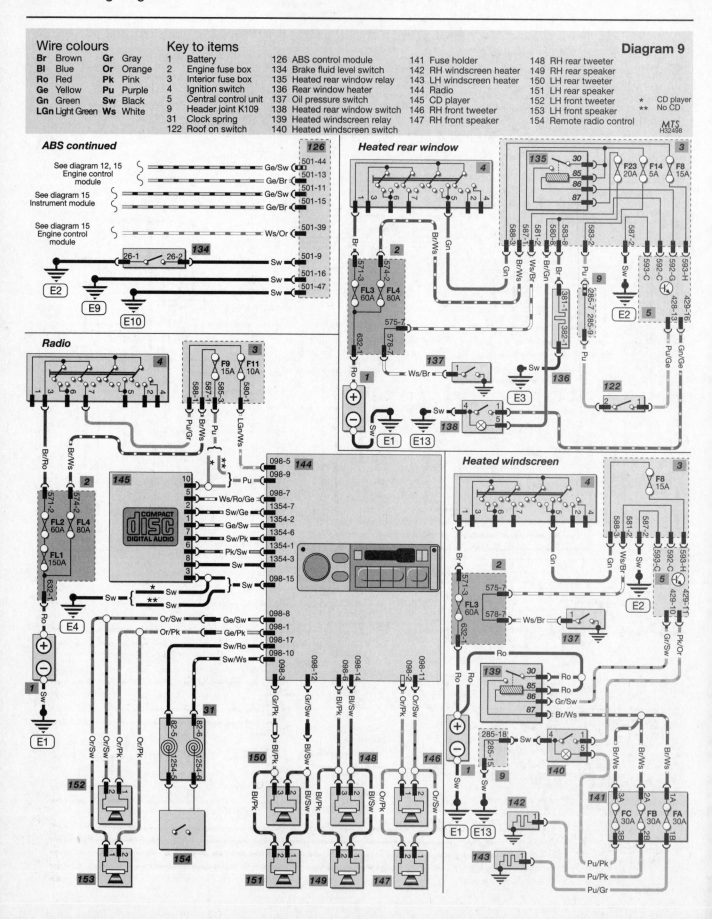

Diagram 9

Wire colours

Br Brown   Gr Gray
Bl Blue   Or Orange
Ro Red   Pk Pink
Ge Yellow   Pu Purple
Gn Green   Sw Black
LGn Light Green   Ws White

Key to items

1 Battery
2 Engine fuse box
3 Interior fuse box
4 Ignition switch
5 Central control unit
9 Header joint K109
31 Clock spring
122 Roof on switch

126 ABS control module
134 Brake fluid level switch
135 Heated rear window relay
136 Rear window heater
137 Oil pressure switch
138 Heated rear window switch
139 Heated windscreen relay
140 Heated windscreen switch

141 Fuse holder
142 RH windscreen heater
143 LH windscreen heater
144 Radio
145 CD player
146 RH front tweeter
147 RH front speaker

148 RH rear tweeter
149 RH rear speaker
150 LH rear tweeter
151 LH rear speaker
152 LH front tweeter
153 LH front speaker
154 Remote radio control

* CD player
** No CD

MTS
H32498

Wire colours

Br	Brown	**Gr**	Gray
Bl	Blue	**Or**	Orange
Ro	Red	**Pk**	Pink
Ge	Yellow	**Pu**	Purple
Gn	Green	**Sw**	Black
LGn	Light Green	**Ws**	White

Key to items

1 Battery
2 Engine fuse box
3 Interior fuse box
4 Ignition switch
155 Blower motor relay
156 Resistor pack
157 Blower motor
158 Blower motor switches
159 Fresh/recirculated air motor
160 Fresh/recirculated air switch
161 Fresh/recirculated air diode
162 Cooling fan relay
163 Cooling fan
164 E-Box temperature sensor
165 Fan-E-Box
166 Starter relay
167 Main relay
168 Coolant temperature sensor
169 Condenser fan
170 A/C clutch
171 A/C switch
172 A/C clutch relay
173 Cooling fan control unit
174 Evaporator sensor
175 A/C pressure sensor
176 Engine control module

* K-series only
** Td4 only
*** Not A/C
**** AC only

Diagram 10

MTS
H32499

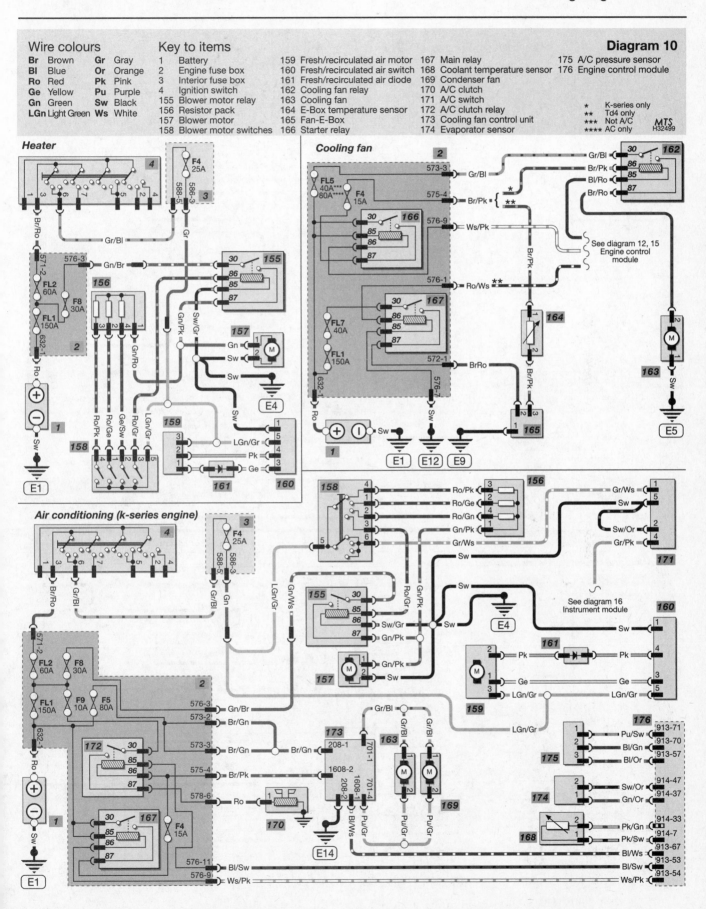

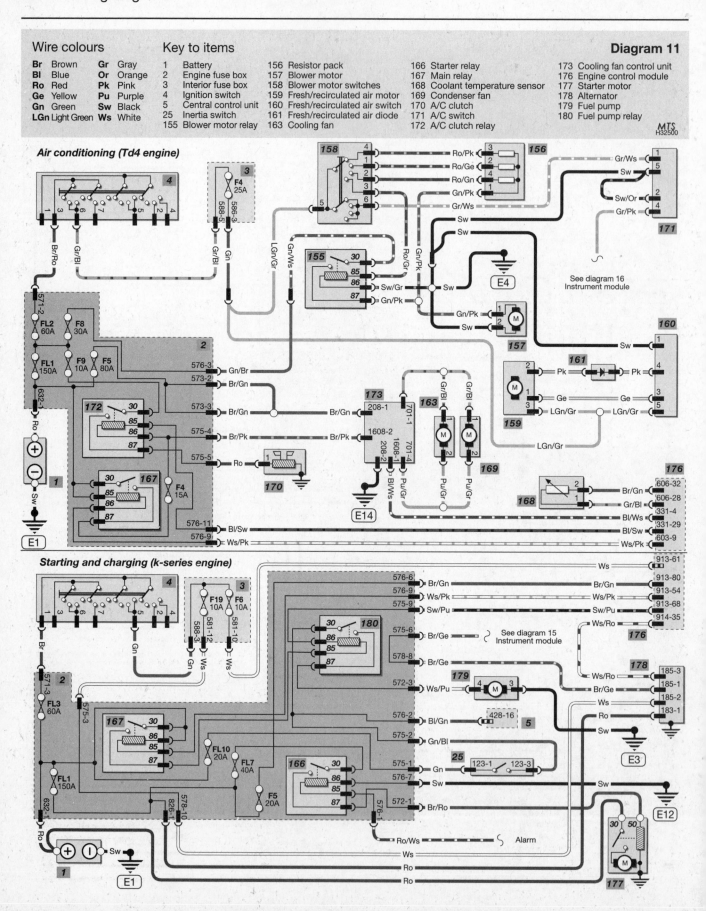

Wire colours

Br	Brown	Gr	Gray
Bl	Blue	Or	Orange
Ro	Red	Pk	Pink
Ge	Yellow	Pu	Purple
Gn	Green	Sw	Black
LGn	Light Green	Ws	White

Key to items

1 Battery
2 Engine fuse box
3 Interior fuse box
4 Ignition switch
5 Central control unit
25 Inertia switch
155 Blower motor relay

156 Resistor pack
157 Blower motor
158 Blower motor switches
159 Fresh/recirculated air motor
160 Fresh/recirculated air switch
161 Fresh/recirculated air diode
163 Cooling fan

166 Starter relay
167 Main relay
168 Coolant temperature sensor
169 Condenser fan
170 A/C clutch
171 A/C switch
172 A/C clutch relay

173 Cooling fan control unit
176 Engine control module
177 Starter motor
178 Alternator
179 Fuel pump
180 Fuel pump relay

Diagram 11

MTS
H32500

Air conditioning (Td4 engine)

Starting and charging (k-series engine)

Wire colours

Br	Brown	**Gr**	Gray
Bl	Blue	**Or**	Orange
Ro	Red	**Pk**	Pink
Ge	Yellow	**Pu**	Purple
Gn	Green	**Sw**	Black
LGn	Light Green	**Ws**	White

Key to items

1	Battery
2	Engine fuse box
3	Interior fuse box
4	Ignition switch
9	Header joint K109
24	Diagnostic socket
167	Main relay
176	Engine control module
182	Rear oxygen sensor
183	Crankshaft position sensor
184	Purge control valve
185	Air inlet temperature sensor
186	Front oxygen sensor
187	Camshaft position sensor
188	Ignition coil 1
189	Ignition coil 2
190	Injector cylinder 1
191	Injector cylinder 2
192	Injector cylinder 3
193	Injector cylinder 4
194	Idle control valve
195	Engine coolant temperature sensor
196	Oil temperature switch
197	Throttle position sensor
198	Dual pressure switch
199	Throttle pedal switch

Diagram 12

MTS
H32501

Engine management (k-series engine)

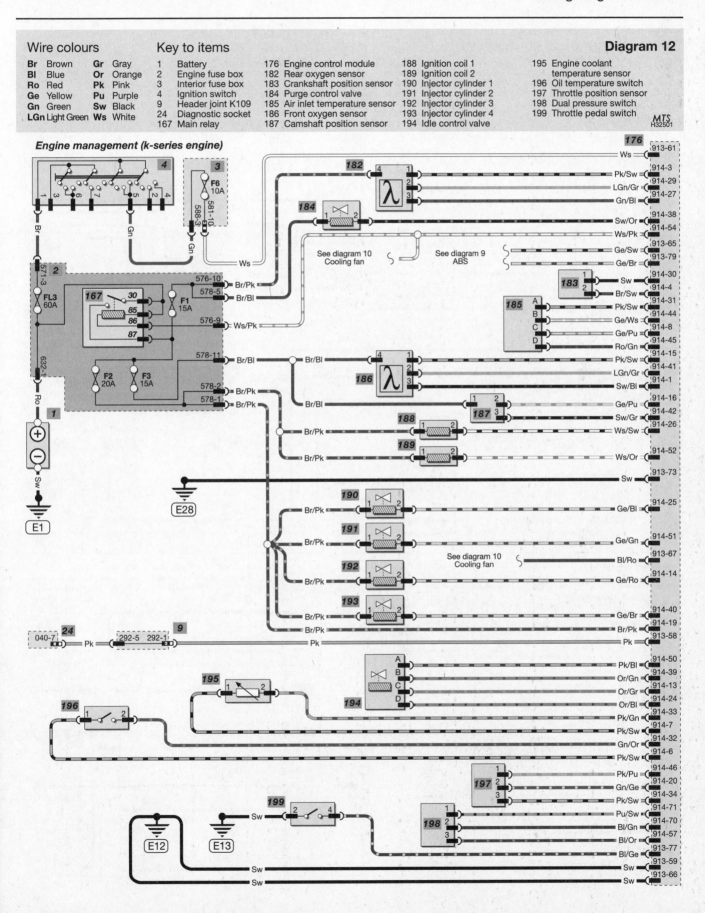

Wire colours

Br	Brown	**Gr**	Gray
Bl	Blue	**Or**	Orange
Ro	Red	**Pk**	Pink
Ge	Yellow	**Pu**	Purple
Gn	Green	**Sw**	Black
LGn	Light Green	**Ws**	White

Key to items

1	Battery	113	Auxiliary relay	180	Fuel pump relay
2	Engine fuse box	166	Starter relay	200	Fuel tank pump unit
3	Interior fuse box	167	Main relay	201	Glow plug relay
4	Ignition switch	176	Engine control module	202	Glow plugs
5	Central control unit	177	Starter motor	203	RH seat heater switch
9	Header joint K109	178	Alternator	204	LH seat heater switch
25	Inertia switch	179	Fuel pump	205	RH seat heater relay

206	RH seat cushion heater
207	RH seat back heater
208	LH seat heater relay
209	LH seat cushion heater
210	LH seat back heater

Diagram 13

MTS H32502

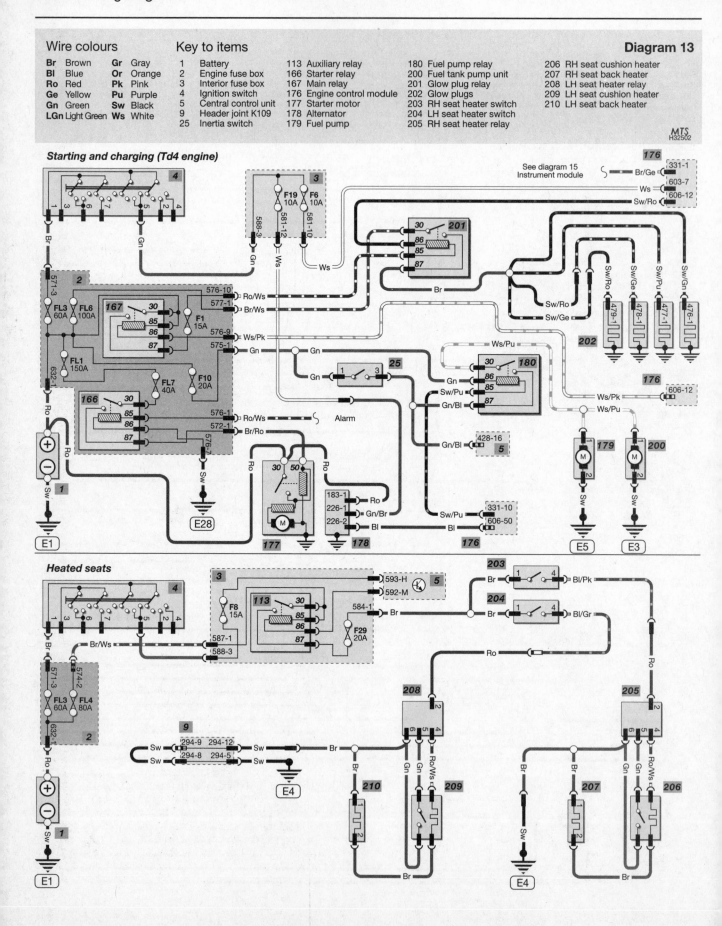

Starting and charging (Td4 engine)

Heated seats

Wire colours

Br	Brown	Gr	Gray
Bl	Blue	Or	Orange
Ro	Red	Pk	Pink
Ge	Yellow	Pu	Purple
Gn	Green	Sw	Black
LGn	Light Green	Ws	White

Key to items

1 Battery
2 Engine fuse box
3 Interior fuse box
4 Ignition switch
5 Central control unit
9 Header joint K109
24 Diagnostic socket
161 Crankshaft position sensor

167 Main relay
176 Engine control module
210 Mass air flow sensor
211 EGR valve
212 Camshaft pressure sensor
213 Fuel pressure regulator
214 Turbo boost control pressure sensor
215 Injector cylinder 1

216 Injector cylinder 2
217 Injector cylinder 3
218 Injector cylinder 4
219 Throttle position sensor
220 Fuel tank pressure sensor
221 Engine speed sensor

Diagram 14

MTS
H32503

Engine management (Td4 engine)

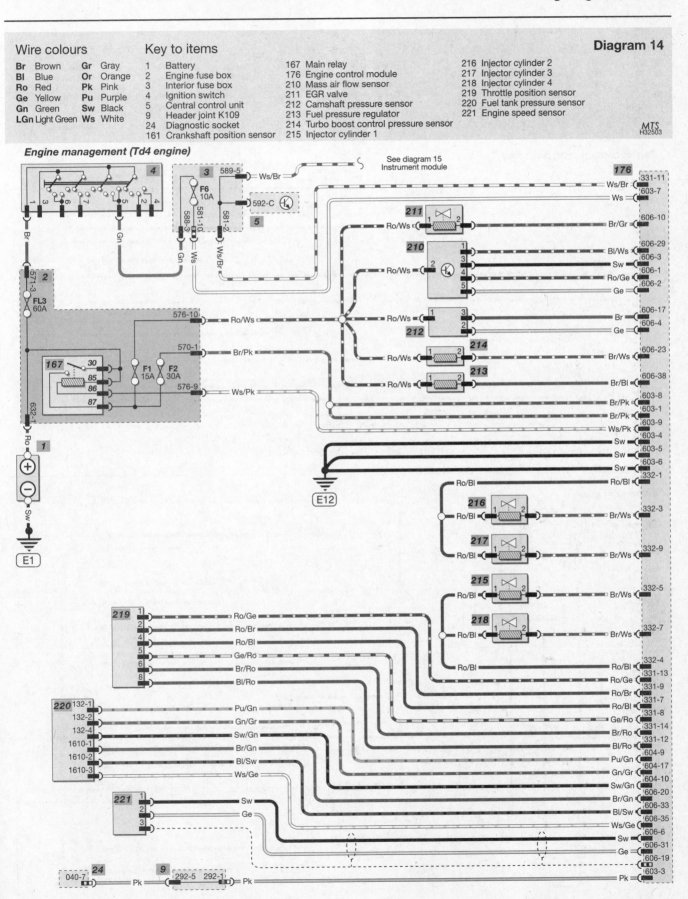

See diagram 15
Instrument module

See diagram 11
Cooling fan

See diagram 9
ABS

Cruise control relay

See diagram 10
Instrument module

See diagram 9
ABS

See diagram 6
Indicators

See diagram 7
Fog lights

See diagram 5
Main beam relay

See diagram 11,13, 15
Alternator

See diagram 7
Airbag

See diagram 9
ABS

Cruise control

See diagram 14
Engine control
module

See diagram 5
Headlights

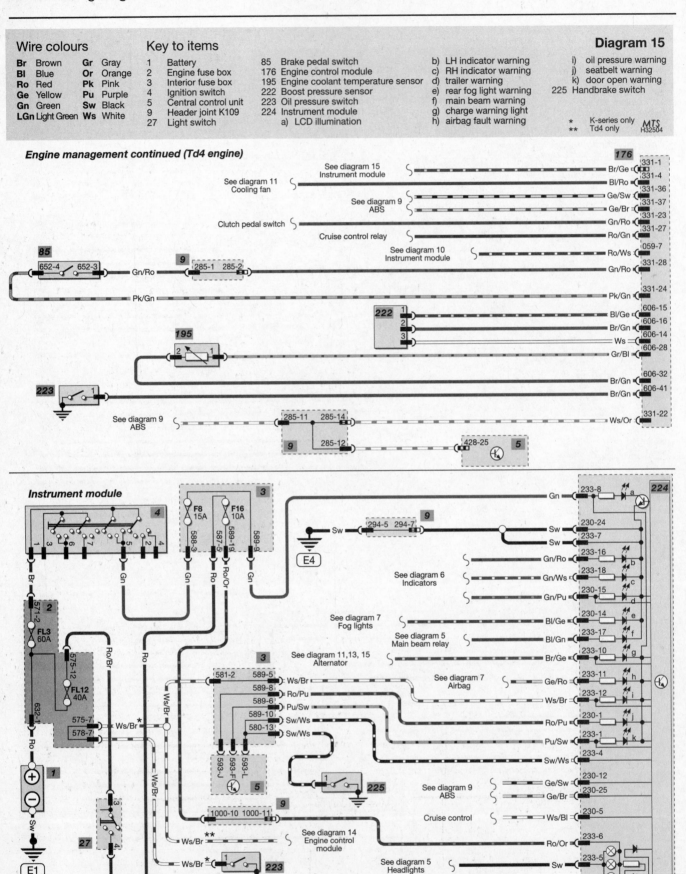

Wire colours

Br	Brown	**Gr**	Gray
Bl	Blue	**Or**	Orange
Ro	Red	**Pk**	Pink
Ge	Yellow	**Pu**	Purple
Gn	Green	**Sw**	Black
LGn	Light Green	**Ws**	White

Key to items

1 Battery
2 Engine fuse box
3 Interior fuse box
4 Ignition switch
5 Central control unit
9 Header joint K109
27 Light switch

85 Brake pedal switch
176 Engine control module
195 Engine coolant temperature sensor
222 Boost pressure sensor
223 Oil pressure switch
224 Instrument module
a) LCD illumination

b) LH indicator warning
c) RH indicator warning
d) trailer warning
e) rear fog light warning
f) main beam warning
g) charge warning light
h) airbag fault warning

i) oil pressure warning
j) seatbelt warning
k) door open warning
225 Handbrake switch

* K-series only
** Td4 only

Diagram 15

MTS
H32504

Engine management continued (Td4 engine)

Instrument module

Wire colours

Br	Brown	**Gr**	Gray
Bl	Blue	**Or**	Orange
Ro	Red	**Pk**	Pink
Ge	Yellow	**Pu**	Purple
Gn	Green	**Sw**	Black
LGn	Light Green	**Ws**	White

Key to items

9	Header joint K109
24	Diagnostic socket
224	Instrument module
l)	hazard light warning
m)	over speed warning
n)	low oil warning
o)	cruise control warning
p)	engine management warning
q)	glow plug warning
r)	traction control warning
s)	ABS warning
t)	hill descent fault warning
u)	handbrake fluid low warning
v)	hill descent warning
w)	engine warning
x)	low fuel warning
y)	speedometer
z)	tachometer
aa)	temperature gauge
ab)	fuel gauge
226	Fuel tank unit
227	A/C pressure sensor
228	Evaporator sensor
*	K-series only
**	Td4 only

Diagram 16

MTS
H32505

Instrument module continued

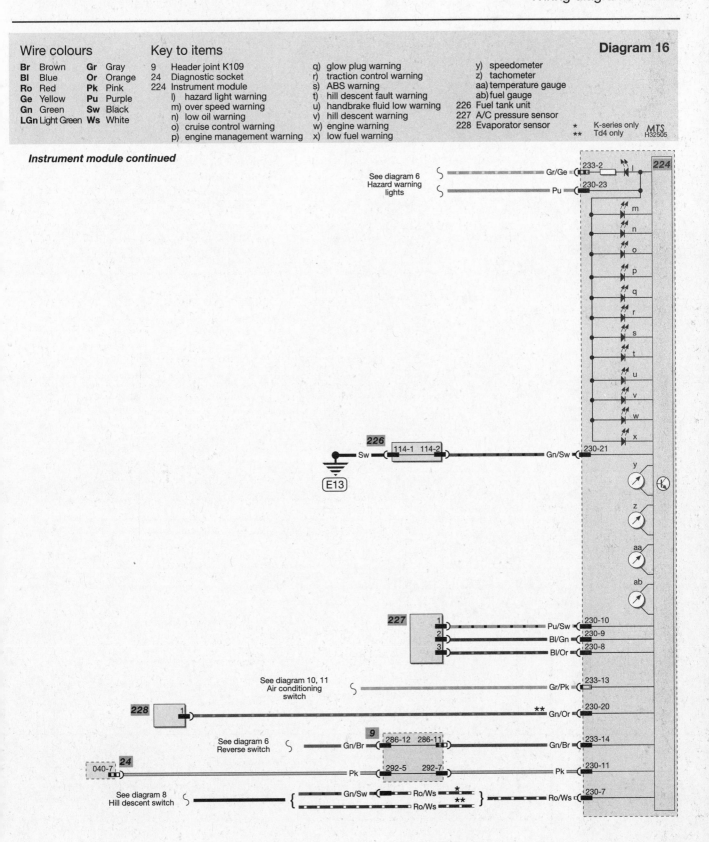

Dimensions and weights

Note: *All figures are approximate, and may vary according to model. Refer to manufacturer's data for exact figures.*

Dimensions

Overall length:	
Including 195/80 spare wheel	4368 mm
Including 215/65 spare wheel	4382 mm
Overall width (including wing mirrors)	2068 mm
Overall height (including roof bars and cross rails):	
3 door	1808 mm
5 door	1828 mm
Wheelbase	2557 mm
Track width:	
Front	1534 mm
Rear	1545 mm

Weights

Unladen (with full fuel tank – excluding options):	
Up to 2001 model year:	
Petrol models	1380 to 1425 kg
Diesel models	1480 to 1525 kg
2001 model year-on:	
Petrol models	1410 to 1620 kg
Diesel models	1540 to 1635 kg
Maximum trailer weight	2000 kg
Maximum roof rack load	75 kg

Conversion factors

Length (distance)

Inches (in)	x 25.4	= Millimetres (mm)	x 0.0394	= Inches (in)
Feet (ft)	x 0.305	= Metres (m)	x 3.281	= Feet (ft)
Miles	x 1.609	= Kilometres (km)	x 0.621	= Miles

Volume (capacity)

Cubic inches (cu in; in³)	x 16.387	= Cubic centimetres (cc; cm³)	x 0.061	= Cubic inches (cu in; in³)
Imperial pints (Imp pt)	x 0.568	= Litres (l)	x 1.76	= Imperial pints (Imp pt)
Imperial quarts (Imp qt)	x 1.137	= Litres (l)	x 0.88	= Imperial quarts (Imp qt)
Imperial quarts (Imp qt)	x 1.201	= US quarts (US qt)	x 0.833	= Imperial quarts (Imp qt)
US quarts (US qt)	x 0.946	= Litres (l)	x 1.057	= US quarts (US qt)
Imperial gallons (Imp gal)	x 4.546	= Litres (l)	x 0.22	= Imperial gallons (Imp gal)
Imperial gallons (Imp gal)	x 1.201	= US gallons (US gal)	x 0.833	= Imperial gallons (Imp gal)
US gallons (US gal)	x 3.785	= Litres (l)	x 0.264	= US gallons (US gal)

Mass (weight)

Ounces (oz)	x 28.35	= Grams (g)	x 0.035	= Ounces (oz)
Pounds (lb)	x 0.454	= Kilograms (kg)	x 2.205	= Pounds (lb)

Force

Ounces-force (ozf; oz)	x 0.278	= Newtons (N)	x 3.6	= Ounces-force (ozf; oz)
Pounds-force (lbf; lb)	x 4.448	= Newtons (N)	x 0.225	= Pounds-force (lbf; lb)
Newtons (N)	x 0.1	= Kilograms-force (kgf; kg)	x 9.81	= Newtons (N)

Pressure

Pounds-force per square inch (psi; lbf/in²; lb/in²)	x 0.070	= Kilograms-force per square centimetre (kgf/cm²; kg/cm²)	x 14.223	= Pounds-force per square inch (psi; lbf/in²; lb/in²)
Pounds-force per square inch (psi; lbf/in²; lb/in²)	x 0.068	= Atmospheres (atm)	x 14.696	= Pounds-force per square inch (psi; lbf/in²; lb/in²)
Pounds-force per square inch (psi; lbf/in²; lb/in²)	x 0.069	= Bars	x 14.5	= Pounds-force per square inch (psi; lbf/in²; lb/in²)
Pounds-force per square inch (psi; lbf/in²; lb/in²)	x 6.895	= Kilopascals (kPa)	x 0.145	= Pounds-force per square inch (psi; lbf/in²; lb/in²)
Kilopascals (kPa)	x 0.01	= Kilograms-force per square centimetre (kgf/cm²; kg/cm²)	x 98.1	= Kilopascals (kPa)
Millibar (mbar)	x 100	= Pascals (Pa)	x 0.01	= Millibar (mbar)
Millibar (mbar)	x 0.0145	= Pounds-force per square inch (psi; lbf/in²; lb/in²)	x 68.947	= Millibar (mbar)
Millibar (mbar)	x 0.75	= Millimetres of mercury (mmHg)	x 1.333	= Millibar (mbar)
Millibar (mbar)	x 0.401	= Inches of water (inH₂O)	x 2.491	= Millibar (mbar)
Millimetres of mercury (mmHg)	x 0.535	= Inches of water (inH₂O)	x 1.868	= Millimetres of mercury (mmHg)
Inches of water (inH₂O)	x 0.036	= Pounds-force per square inch (psi; lbf/in²; lb/in²)	x 27.68	= Inches of water (inH₂O)

Torque (moment of force)

Pounds-force inches (lbf in; lb in)	x 1.152	= Kilograms-force centimetre (kgf cm; kg cm)	x 0.868	= Pounds-force inches (lbf in; lb in)
Pounds-force inches (lbf in; lb in)	x 0.113	= Newton metres (Nm)	x 8.85	= Pounds-force inches (lbf in; lb in)
Pounds-force inches (lbf in; lb in)	x 0.083	= Pounds-force feet (lbf ft; lb ft)	x 12	= Pounds-force inches (lbf in; lb in)
Pounds-force feet (lbf ft; lb ft)	x 0.138	= Kilograms-force metres (kgf m; kg m)	x 7.233	= Pounds-force feet (lbf ft; lb ft)
Pounds-force feet (lbf ft; lb ft)	x 1.356	= Newton metres (Nm)	x 0.738	= Pounds-force feet (lbf ft; lb ft)
Newton metres (Nm)	x 0.102	= Kilograms-force metres (kgf m; kg m)	x 9.804	= Newton metres (Nm)

Power

Horsepower (hp)	x 745.7	= Watts (W)	x 0.0013	= Horsepower (hp)

Velocity (speed)

Miles per hour (miles/hr; mph)	x 1.609	= Kilometres per hour (km/hr; kph)	x 0.621	= Miles per hour (miles/hr; mph)

Fuel consumption*

Miles per gallon, Imperial (mpg)	x 0.354	= Kilometres per litre (km/l)	x 2.825	= Miles per gallon, Imperial (mpg)
Miles per gallon, US (mpg)	x 0.425	= Kilometres per litre (km/l)	x 2.352	= Miles per gallon, US (mpg)

Temperature

Degrees Fahrenheit = (°C x 1.8) + 32

Degrees Celsius (Degrees Centigrade; °C) = (°F - 32) x 0.56

*It is common practice to convert from miles per gallon (mpg) to litres/100 kilometres (l/100km), where mpg x l/100 km = 282

Spare parts are available from many sources, including maker's appointed garages, accessory shops, and motor factors. To be sure of obtaining the correct parts, it will sometimes be necessary to quote the vehicle identification number. If possible, it can also be useful to take the old parts along for positive identification. Items such as starter motors and alternators may be available under a service exchange scheme – any parts returned should be clean.

Our advice regarding spare parts is as follows.

Officially appointed garages

This is the best source of parts which are peculiar to your car, and which are not otherwise generally available (eg, badges, interior trim, certain body panels, etc). It is also the only place at which you should buy parts if the vehicle is still under warranty.

Accessory shops

These are very good places to buy materials and components needed for the maintenance of your car (oil, air and fuel filters, light bulbs, drivebelts, greases, brake pads, tough-up paint, etc). Components of this nature sold by a reputable shop are of the same standard as those used by the car manufacturer.

Besides components, these shops also sell tools and general accessories, usually have convenient opening hours, charge lower prices, and can often be found close to home. Some accessory shops have parts counters where components needed for almost any repair job can be purchased or ordered.

Motor factors

Good factors will stock all the more important components which wear out comparatively quickly, and can sometimes supply individual components needed for the overhaul of a larger assembly (eg, brake seals and hydraulic parts, bearing shells, pistons, valves). They may also handle work such as cylinder block reboring, crankshaft regrinding, etc.

Tyre and exhaust specialists

These outlets may be independent, or members of a local or national chain. They frequently offer competitive prices when compared with a main dealer or local garage, but it will pay to obtain several quotes before making a decision. When researching prices, also ask what 'extras' may be added – for instance fitting a new valve and balancing the wheel are both commonly charged on top of the price of a new tyre.

Other sources

Beware of parts or materials obtained from market stalls, car boot sales or similar outlets. Such items are not invariably sub-standard, but there is little chance of compensation if they do prove unsatisfactory. In the case of safety-critical components such as brake pads, there is the risk not only of financial loss, but also of an accident causing injury or death.

Second-hand components or assemblies obtained from a car breaker can be a good buy in some circumstances, but his sort of purchase is best made by the experienced DIY mechanic.

Vehicle identification

Modifications are a continuing and unpublicised process in vehicle manufacture, quite apart from major model changes. Spare parts manuals and lists are compiled upon a numerical basis, the individual vehicle identification numbers being essential to correct identification of the component concerned.

When ordering spare parts, always give as much information as possible. Quote the car model, year of manufacture, body and engine numbers as appropriate.

The *vehicle identification plate* is situated at the bottom of the left-hand door B-pillar. It gives the VIN (vehicle identification number), vehicle weight information and paint and trim colour codes. The *vehicle identification number* is also repeated in the form of stamped numbers on the centre of the engine compartment bulkhead and on a plate visible through the lower left-hand corner of the windscreen **(see illustrations)**.

The *engine number* is stamped on the front of the cylinder block adjacent to the gearbox on 1.8 litre engines, and on the front of the cylinder block adjacent to the alternator on 2.0 litre diesel engines.

Other identification numbers or codes are stamped on major items such as the gearbox, etc. These numbers are unlikely to be needed by the home mechanic.

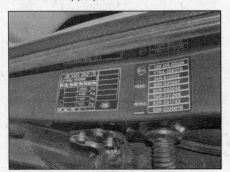

VIN plate on left-hand door pillar

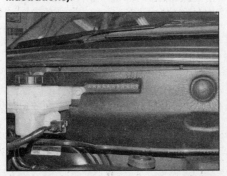

VIN plate on centre of engine compartment bulkhead

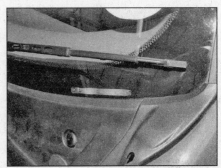

VIN plate seen through windscreen

Whenever servicing, repair or overhaul work is carried out on the car or its components, observe the following procedures and instructions. This will assist in carrying out the operation efficiently and to a professional standard of workmanship.

Joint mating faces and gaskets

When separating components at their mating faces, never insert screwdrivers or similar implements into the joint between the faces in order to prise them apart. This can cause severe damage which results in oil leaks, coolant leaks, etc upon reassembly. Separation is usually achieved by tapping along the joint with a soft-faced hammer in order to break the seal. However, note that this method may not be suitable where dowels are used for component location.

Where a gasket is used between the mating faces of two components, a new one must be fitted on reassembly; fit it dry unless otherwise stated in the repair procedure. Make sure that the mating faces are clean and dry, with all traces of old gasket removed. When cleaning a joint face, use a tool which is unlikely to score or damage the face, and remove any burrs or nicks with an oilstone or fine file.

Make sure that tapped holes are cleaned with a pipe cleaner, and keep them free of jointing compound, if this is being used, unless specifically instructed otherwise.

Ensure that all orifices, channels or pipes are clear, and blow through them, preferably using compressed air.

Oil seals

Oil seals can be removed by levering them out with a wide flat-bladed screwdriver or similar implement. Alternatively, a number of self-tapping screws may be screwed into the seal, and these used as a purchase for pliers or some similar device in order to pull the seal free.

Whenever an oil seal is removed from its working location, either individually or as part of an assembly, it should be renewed.

The very fine sealing lip of the seal is easily damaged, and will not seal if the surface it contacts is not completely clean and free from scratches, nicks or grooves. If the original sealing surface of the component cannot be restored, and the manufacturer has not made provision for slight relocation of the seal relative to the sealing surface, the component should be renewed.

Protect the lips of the seal from any surface which may damage them in the course of fitting. Use tape or a conical sleeve where possible. Lubricate the seal lips with oil before fitting and, on dual-lipped seals, fill the space between the lips with grease.

Unless otherwise stated, oil seals must be fitted with their sealing lips toward the lubricant to be sealed.

Use a tubular drift or block of wood of the appropriate size to install the seal and, if the seal housing is shouldered, drive the seal down to the shoulder. If the seal housing is unshouldered, the seal should be fitted with its face flush with the housing top face (unless otherwise instructed).

Screw threads and fastenings

Seized nuts, bolts and screws are quite a common occurrence where corrosion has set in, and the use of penetrating oil or releasing fluid will often overcome this problem if the offending item is soaked for a while before attempting to release it. The use of an impact driver may also provide a means of releasing such stubborn fastening devices, when used in conjunction with the appropriate screwdriver bit or socket. If none of these methods works, it may be necessary to resort to the careful application of heat, or the use of a hacksaw or nut splitter device.

Studs are usually removed by locking two nuts together on the threaded part, and then using a spanner on the lower nut to unscrew the stud. Studs or bolts which have broken off below the surface of the component in which they are mounted can sometimes be removed using a stud extractor. Always ensure that a blind tapped hole is completely free from oil, grease, water or other fluid before installing the bolt or stud. Failure to do this could cause the housing to crack due to the hydraulic action of the bolt or stud as it is screwed in.

When tightening a castellated nut to accept a split pin, tighten the nut to the specified torque, where applicable, and then tighten further to the next split pin hole. Never slacken the nut to align the split pin hole, unless stated in the repair procedure.

When checking or retightening a nut or bolt to a specified torque setting, slacken the nut or bolt by a quarter of a turn, and then retighten to the specified setting. However, this should not be attempted where angular tightening has been used.

For some screw fastenings, notably cylinder head bolts or nuts, torque wrench settings are no longer specified for the latter stages of tightening, "angle-tightening" being called up instead. Typically, a fairly low torque wrench setting will be applied to the bolts/nuts in the correct sequence, followed by one or more stages of tightening through specified angles.

Locknuts, locktabs and washers

Any fastening which will rotate against a component or housing during tightening should always have a washer between it and the relevant component or housing.

Spring or split washers should always be renewed when they are used to lock a critical component such as a big-end bearing retaining bolt or nut. Locktabs which are folded over to retain a nut or bolt should always be renewed.

Self-locking nuts can be re-used in non-critical areas, providing resistance can be felt when the locking portion passes over the bolt or stud thread. However, it should be noted that self-locking stiffnuts tend to lose their effectiveness after long periods of use, and should then be renewed as a matter of course.

Split pins must always be replaced with new ones of the correct size for the hole.

When thread-locking compound is found on the threads of a fastener which is to be re-used, it should be cleaned off with a wire brush and solvent, and fresh compound applied on reassembly.

Special tools

Some repair procedures in this manual entail the use of special tools such as a press, two or three-legged pullers, spring compressors, etc. Wherever possible, suitable readily-available alternatives to the manufacturer's special tools are described, and are shown in use. In some instances, where no alternative is possible, it has been necessary to resort to the use of a manufacturer's tool, and this has been done for reasons of safety as well as the efficient completion of the repair operation. Unless you are highly-skilled and have a thorough understanding of the procedures described, never attempt to bypass the use of any special tool when the procedure described specifies its use. Not only is there a very great risk of personal injury, but expensive damage could be caused to the components involved.

Environmental considerations

When disposing of used engine oil, brake fluid, antifreeze, etc, give due consideration to any detrimental environmental effects. Do not, for instance, pour any of the above liquids down drains into the general sewage system, or onto the ground to soak away. Many local council refuse tips provide a facility for waste oil disposal, as do some garages. If none of these facilities are available, consult your local Environmental Health Department, or the National Rivers Authority, for further advice.

With the universal tightening-up of legislation regarding the emission of environmentally-harmful substances from motor vehicles, most vehicles have tamperproof devices fitted to the main adjustment points of the fuel system. These devices are primarily designed to prevent unqualified persons from adjusting the fuel/air mixture, with the chance of a consequent increase in toxic emissions. If such devices are found during servicing or overhaul, they should, wherever possible, be renewed or refitted in accordance with the manufacturer's requirements or current legislation.

OIL CARE FOLLOW THE CODE

OIL BANK LINE
0800 66 33 66
www.oilbankline.org.uk

Note: It is antisocial and illegal to dump oil down the drain. To find the location of your local oil recycling bank, call this number free.

The jack supplied with the vehicle tool kit should only be used for changing the roadwheels – see *Wheel changing* at the front of this manual. When carrying out any other kind of work, raise the vehicle using a hydraulic trolley jack, and always supplement the jack with axle stands positioned under the vehicle jacking points.

When using a trolley jack or axle stands, always position the jack head or axle stand head under, or adjacent to one of the relevant wheel changing jacking points under the sills. Use a block of wood between the jack or axle stand and the sill. It is permissible to raise the front or rear of the vehicle with a trolley jack head under the front body crossmember or rear subframe crossmember, providing axle stands are placed under the sill jacking points **(see illustration)**.

Do not attempt to jack the vehicle under the sump, final drive unit, or any of the suspension components.

Never work under, around, or near a raised vehicle, unless it is adequately supported in at least two places.

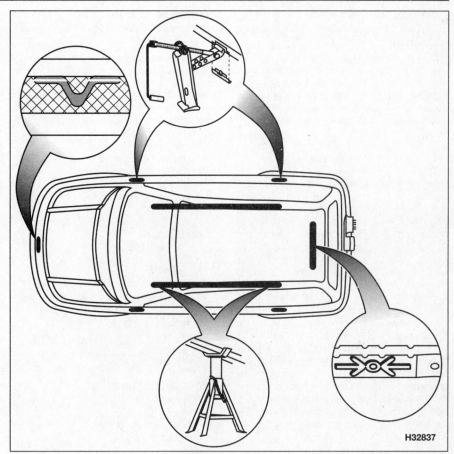

Vehicle jacking points

Radio/cassette/CD unit anti-theft system

The radio/cassette unit fitted as standard equipment by Land Rover is equipped with a built-in security code to deter thieves. If the power source to the unit is cut, the anti-theft system will activate. Even if the power source is immediately reconnected, the radio/cassette unit will not function until the correct security code has been entered. Therefore, if you do not know the correct security code for the unit, do not disconnect the battery negative lead, or remove the radio/cassette unit from the vehicle.

The procedure for reprogramming a unit that has been disconnected from its power supply varies from model to model. Consult the handbook supplied with the unit for specific details or refer to your Land Rover dealer.

Introduction

A selection of good tools is a fundamental requirement for anyone contemplating the maintenance and repair of a motor vehicle. For the owner who does not possess any, their purchase will prove a considerable expense, offsetting some of the savings made by doing-it-yourself. However, provided that the tools purchased meet the relevant national safety standards and are of good quality, they will last for many years and prove an extremely worthwhile investment.

To help the average owner to decide which tools are needed to carry out the various tasks detailed in this manual, we have compiled three lists of tools under the following headings: *Maintenance and minor repair*, *Repair and overhaul*, and *Special*. Newcomers to practical mechanics should start off with the *Maintenance and minor repair* tool kit, and confine themselves to the simpler jobs around the vehicle. Then, as confidence and experience grow, more difficult tasks can be undertaken, with extra tools being purchased as, and when, they are needed. In this way, a *Maintenance and minor repair* tool kit can be built up into a *Repair and overhaul* tool kit over a considerable period of time, without any major cash outlays. The experienced do-it-yourselfer will have a tool kit good enough for most repair and overhaul procedures, and will add tools from the *Special* category when it is felt that the expense is justified by the amount of use to which these tools will be put.

Maintenance and minor repair tool kit

The tools given in this list should be considered as a minimum requirement if routine maintenance, servicing and minor repair operations are to be undertaken. We recommend the purchase of combination spanners (ring one end, open-ended the other); although more expensive than open-ended ones, they do give the advantages of both types of spanner.

- ☐ *Combination spanners:*
  Metric - 8 to 19 mm inclusive
- ☐ *Adjustable spanner - 35 mm jaw (approx.)*
- ☐ *Spark plug spanner (with rubber insert) - petrol models*
- ☐ *Spark plug gap adjustment tool - petrol models*
- ☐ *Set of feeler gauges*
- ☐ *Brake bleed nipple spanner*
- ☐ *Screwdrivers:*
  Flat blade - 100 mm long x 6 mm dia
  Cross blade - 100 mm long x 6 mm dia
  Torx - various sizes (not all vehicles)
- ☐ *Combination pliers*
- ☐ *Hacksaw (junior)*
- ☐ *Tyre pump*
- ☐ *Tyre pressure gauge*
- ☐ *Oil can*
- ☐ *Oil filter removal tool*
- ☐ *Fine emery cloth*
- ☐ *Wire brush (small)*
- ☐ *Funnel (medium size)*
- ☐ *Sump drain plug key (not all vehicles)*

Repair and overhaul tool kit

These tools are virtually essential for anyone undertaking any major repairs to a motor vehicle, and are additional to those given in the *Maintenance and minor repair* list. Included in this list is a comprehensive set of sockets. Although these are expensive, they will be found invaluable as they are so versatile - particularly if various drives are included in the set. We recommend the half-inch square-drive type, as this can be used with most proprietary torque wrenches.

The tools in this list will sometimes need to be supplemented by tools from the *Special* list:

- ☐ *Sockets (or box spanners) to cover range in previous list (including Torx sockets)*
- ☐ *Reversible ratchet drive (for use with sockets)*
- ☐ *Extension piece, 250 mm (for use with sockets)*
- ☐ *Universal joint (for use with sockets)*
- ☐ *Flexible handle or sliding T "breaker bar" (for use with sockets)*
- ☐ *Torque wrench (for use with sockets)*
- ☐ *Self-locking grips*
- ☐ *Ball pein hammer*
- ☐ *Soft-faced mallet (plastic or rubber)*
- ☐ *Screwdrivers:*
  Flat blade - long & sturdy, short (chubby), and narrow (electrician's) types
  Cross blade - long & sturdy, and short (chubby) types
- ☐ *Pliers:*
  Long-nosed
  Side cutters (electrician's)
  Circlip (internal and external)
- ☐ *Cold chisel - 25 mm*
- ☐ *Scriber*
- ☐ *Scraper*
- ☐ *Centre-punch*
- ☐ *Pin punch*
- ☐ *Hacksaw*
- ☐ *Brake hose clamp*
- ☐ *Brake/clutch bleeding kit*
- ☐ *Selection of twist drills*
- ☐ *Steel rule/straight-edge*
- ☐ *Allen keys (inc. splined/Torx type)*
- ☐ *Selection of files*
- ☐ *Wire brush*
- ☐ *Axle stands*
- ☐ *Jack (strong trolley or hydraulic type)*
- ☐ *Light with extension lead*
- ☐ *Universal electrical multi-meter*

Sockets and reversible ratchet drive

Brake bleeding kit

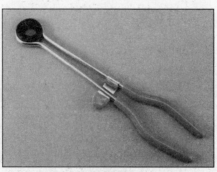

Torx key, socket and bit

Hose clamp

Angular-tightening gauge

Special tools

The tools in this list are those which are not used regularly, are expensive to buy, or which need to be used in accordance with their manufacturers' instructions. Unless relatively difficult mechanical jobs are undertaken frequently, it will not be economic to buy many of these tools. Where this is the case, you could consider clubbing together with friends (or joining a motorists' club) to make a joint purchase, or borrowing the tools against a deposit from a local garage or tool hire specialist. It is worth noting that many of the larger DIY superstores now carry a large range of special tools for hire at modest rates.

The following list contains only those tools and instruments freely available to the public, and not those special tools produced by the vehicle manufacturer specifically for its dealer network. You will find occasional references to these manufacturers' special tools in the text of this manual. Generally, an alternative method of doing the job without the vehicle manufacturers' special tool is given. However, sometimes there is no alternative to using them. Where this is the case and the relevant tool cannot be bought or borrowed, you will have to entrust the work to a dealer.

- ☐ Angular-tightening gauge
- ☐ Valve spring compressor
- ☐ Valve grinding tool
- ☐ Piston ring compressor
- ☐ Piston ring removal/installation tool
- ☐ Cylinder bore hone
- ☐ Balljoint separator
- ☐ Coil spring compressors (where applicable)
- ☐ Two/three-legged hub and bearing puller
- ☐ Impact screwdriver
- ☐ Micrometer and/or vernier calipers
- ☐ Dial gauge
- ☐ Stroboscopic timing light
- ☐ Dwell angle meter/tachometer
- ☐ Fault code reader
- ☐ Cylinder compression gauge
- ☐ Hand-operated vacuum pump and gauge
- ☐ Clutch plate alignment set
- ☐ Brake shoe steady spring cup removal tool
- ☐ Bush and bearing removal/installation set
- ☐ Stud extractors
- ☐ Tap and die set
- ☐ Lifting tackle
- ☐ Trolley jack

Buying tools

Reputable motor accessory shops and superstores often offer excellent quality tools at discount prices, so it pays to shop around.

Remember, you don't have to buy the most expensive items on the shelf, but it is always advisable to steer clear of the very cheap tools. Beware of 'bargains' offered on market stalls or at car boot sales. There are plenty of good tools around at reasonable prices, but always aim to purchase items which meet the relevant national safety standards. If in doubt, ask the proprietor or manager of the shop for advice before making a purchase.

Care and maintenance of tools

Having purchased a reasonable tool kit, it is necessary to keep the tools in a clean and serviceable condition. After use, always wipe off any dirt, grease and metal particles using a clean, dry cloth, before putting the tools away. Never leave them lying around after they have been used. A simple tool rack on the garage or workshop wall for items such as screwdrivers and pliers is a good idea. Store all normal spanners and sockets in a metal box. Any measuring instruments, gauges, meters, etc, must be carefully stored where they cannot be damaged or become rusty.

Take a little care when tools are used. Hammer heads inevitably become marked, and screwdrivers lose the keen edge on their blades from time to time. A little timely attention with emery cloth or a file will soon restore items like this to a good finish.

Working facilities

Not to be forgotten when discussing tools is the workshop itself. If anything more than routine maintenance is to be carried out, a suitable working area becomes essential.

It is appreciated that many an owner-mechanic is forced by circumstances to remove an engine or similar item without the benefit of a garage or workshop. Having done this, any repairs should always be done under the cover of a roof.

Wherever possible, any dismantling should be done on a clean, flat workbench or table at a suitable working height.

Any workbench needs a vice; one with a jaw opening of 100 mm is suitable for most jobs. As mentioned previously, some clean dry storage space is also required for tools, as well as for any lubricants, cleaning fluids, touch-up paints etc, which become necessary.

Another item which may be required, and which has a much more general usage, is an electric drill with a chuck capacity of at least 8 mm. This, together with a good range of twist drills, is virtually essential for fitting accessories.

Last, but not least, always keep a supply of old newspapers and clean, lint-free rags available, and try to keep any working area as clean as possible.

Micrometers

Dial test indicator ("dial gauge")

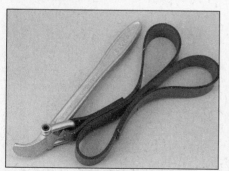

Strap wrench

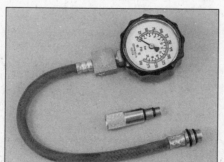

Compression tester

Fault code reader

This is a guide to getting your vehicle through the MOT test. Obviously it will not be possible to examine the vehicle to the same standard as the professional MOT tester. However, working through the following checks will enable you to identify any problem areas before submitting the vehicle for the test.

Where a testable component is in borderline condition, the tester has discretion in deciding whether to pass or fail it. The basis of such discretion is whether the tester would be happy for a close relative or friend to use the vehicle with the component in that condition. If the vehicle presented is clean and evidently well cared for, the tester may be more inclined to pass a borderline component than if the vehicle is scruffy and apparently neglected.

It has only been possible to summarise the test requirements here, based on the regulations in force at the time of printing. Test standards are becoming increasingly stringent, although there are some exemptions for older vehicles.

An assistant will be needed to help carry out some of these checks.

The checks have been sub-divided into four categories, as follows:

1 Checks carried out **FROM THE DRIVER'S SEAT**

2 Checks carried out **WITH THE VEHICLE ON THE GROUND**

3 Checks carried out **WITH THE VEHICLE RAISED AND THE WHEELS FREE TO TURN**

4 Checks carried out on **YOUR VEHICLE'S EXHAUST EMISSION SYSTEM**

---

1 Checks carried out **FROM THE DRIVER'S SEAT**

Handbrake

☐ Test the operation of the handbrake. Excessive travel (too many clicks) indicates incorrect brake or cable adjustment.

☐ Check that the handbrake cannot be released by tapping the lever sideways. Check the security of the lever mountings.

Footbrake

☐ Depress the brake pedal and check that it does not creep down to the floor, indicating a master cylinder fault. Release the pedal, wait a few seconds, then depress it again. If the pedal travels nearly to the floor before firm resistance is felt, brake adjustment or repair is necessary. If the pedal feels spongy, there is air in the hydraulic system which must be removed by bleeding.

☐ Check that the brake pedal is secure and in good condition. Check also for signs of fluid leaks on the pedal, floor or carpets, which would indicate failed seals in the brake master cylinder.

☐ Check the servo unit (when applicable) by operating the brake pedal several times, then keeping the pedal depressed and starting the engine. As the engine starts, the pedal will move down slightly. If not, the vacuum hose or the servo itself may be faulty.

Steering wheel and column

☐ Examine the steering wheel for fractures or looseness of the hub, spokes or rim.

☐ Move the steering wheel from side to side and then up and down. Check that the steering wheel is not loose on the column, indicating wear or a loose retaining nut. Continue moving the steering wheel as before, but also turn it slightly from left to right.

☐ Check that the steering wheel is not loose on the column, and that there is no abnormal

movement of the steering wheel, indicating wear in the column support bearings or couplings.

Windscreen, mirrors and sunvisor

☐ The windscreen must be free of cracks or other significant damage within the driver's field of view. (Small stone chips are acceptable.) Rear view mirrors must be secure, intact, and capable of being adjusted.

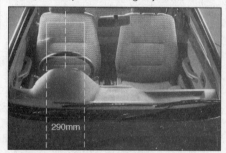

290mm

☐ The driver's sunvisor must be capable of being stored in the "up" position.

Seat belts and seats

Note: *The following checks are applicable to all seat belts, front and rear.*

☐ Examine the webbing of all the belts (including rear belts if fitted) for cuts, serious fraying or deterioration. Fasten and unfasten each belt to check the buckles. If applicable, check the retracting mechanism. Check the security of all seat belt mountings accessible from inside the vehicle.

☐ Seat belts with pre-tensioners, once activated, have a "flag" or similar showing on the seat belt stalk. This, in itself, is not a reason for test failure.

☐ The front seats themselves must be securely attached and the backrests must lock in the upright position.

Doors

☐ Both front doors must be able to be opened and closed from outside and inside, and must latch securely when closed.

2 Checks carried out WITH THE VEHICLE ON THE GROUND

Vehicle identification

☐ Number plates must be in good condition, secure and legible, with letters and numbers correctly spaced – spacing at (A) should be at least twice that at (B).

☐ The VIN plate and/or homologation plate must be legible.

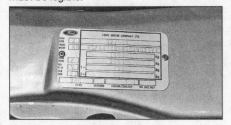

Electrical equipment

☐ Switch on the ignition and check the operation of the horn.

☐ Check the windscreen washers and wipers, examining the wiper blades; renew damaged or perished blades. Also check the operation of the stop-lights.

☐ Check the operation of the sidelights and number plate lights. The lenses and reflectors must be secure, clean and undamaged.

☐ Check the operation and alignment of the headlights. The headlight reflectors must not be tarnished and the lenses must be undamaged.

☐ Switch on the ignition and check the operation of the direction indicators (including the instrument panel tell-tale) and the hazard warning lights. Operation of the sidelights and stop-lights must not affect the indicators - if it does, the cause is usually a bad earth at the rear light cluster.

☐ Check the operation of the rear foglight(s), including the warning light on the instrument panel or in the switch.

☐ The ABS warning light must illuminate in accordance with the manufacturers' design. For most vehicles, the ABS warning light should illuminate when the ignition is switched on, and (if the system is operating properly) extinguish after a few seconds. Refer to the owner's handbook.

Footbrake

☐ Examine the master cylinder, brake pipes and servo unit for leaks, loose mountings, corrosion or other damage.

☐ The fluid reservoir must be secure and the fluid level must be between the upper (A) and lower (B) markings.

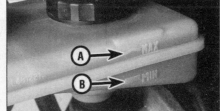

☐ Inspect both front brake flexible hoses for cracks or deterioration of the rubber. Turn the steering from lock to lock, and ensure that the hoses do not contact the wheel, tyre, or any part of the steering or suspension mechanism. With the brake pedal firmly depressed, check the hoses for bulges or leaks under pressure.

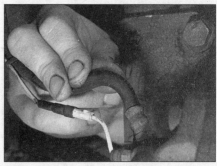

Steering and suspension

☐ Have your assistant turn the steering wheel from side to side slightly, up to the point where the steering gear just begins to transmit this movement to the roadwheels. Check for excessive free play between the steering wheel and the steering gear, indicating wear or insecurity of the steering column joints, the column-to-steering gear coupling, or the steering gear itself.

☐ Have your assistant turn the steering wheel more vigorously in each direction, so that the roadwheels just begin to turn. As this is done, examine all the steering joints, linkages, fittings and attachments. Renew any component that shows signs of wear or damage. On vehicles with power steering, check the security and condition of the steering pump, drivebelt and hoses.

☐ Check that the vehicle is standing level, and at approximately the correct ride height.

Shock absorbers

☐ Depress each corner of the vehicle in turn, then release it. The vehicle should rise and then settle in its normal position. If the vehicle continues to rise and fall, the shock absorber is defective. A shock absorber which has seized will also cause the vehicle to fail.

Exhaust system

☐ Start the engine. With your assistant holding a rag over the tailpipe, check the entire system for leaks. Repair or renew leaking sections.

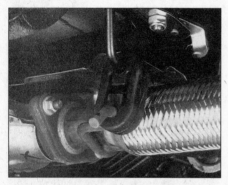

3 Checks carried out **WITH THE VEHICLE RAISED AND THE WHEELS FREE TO TURN**

Jack up the front and rear of the vehicle, and securely support it on axle stands. Position the stands clear of the suspension assemblies. Ensure that the wheels are clear of the ground and that the steering can be turned from lock to lock.

Steering mechanism

☐ Have your assistant turn the steering from lock to lock. Check that the steering turns smoothly, and that no part of the steering mechanism, including a wheel or tyre, fouls any brake hose or pipe or any part of the body structure.

☐ Examine the steering rack rubber gaiters for damage or insecurity of the retaining clips. If power steering is fitted, check for signs of damage or leakage of the fluid hoses, pipes or connections. Also check for excessive stiffness or binding of the steering, a missing split pin or locking device, or severe corrosion of the body structure within 30 cm of any steering component attachment point.

Front and rear suspension and wheel bearings

☐ Starting at the front right-hand side, grasp the roadwheel at the 3 o'clock and 9 o'clock positions and rock gently but firmly. Check for free play or insecurity at the wheel bearings, suspension balljoints, or suspension mountings, pivots and attachments.

☐ Now grasp the wheel at the 12 o'clock and 6 o'clock positions and repeat the previous inspection. Spin the wheel, and check for roughness or tightness of the front wheel bearing.

☐ If excess free play is suspected at a component pivot point, this can be confirmed by using a large screwdriver or similar tool and levering between the mounting and the component attachment. This will confirm whether the wear is in the pivot bush, its retaining bolt, or in the mounting itself (the bolt holes can often become elongated).

☐ Carry out all the above checks at the other front wheel, and then at both rear wheels.

Springs and shock absorbers

☐ Examine the suspension struts (when applicable) for serious fluid leakage, corrosion, or damage to the casing. Also check the security of the mounting points.

☐ If coil springs are fitted, check that the spring ends locate in their seats, and that the spring is not corroded, cracked or broken.

☐ If leaf springs are fitted, check that all leaves are intact, that the axle is securely attached to each spring, and that there is no deterioration of the spring eye mountings, bushes, and shackles.

☐ The same general checks apply to vehicles fitted with other suspension types, such as torsion bars, hydraulic displacer units, etc. Ensure that all mountings and attachments are secure, that there are no signs of excessive wear, corrosion or damage, and (on hydraulic types) that there are no fluid leaks or damaged pipes.

☐ Inspect the shock absorbers for signs of serious fluid leakage. Check for wear of the mounting bushes or attachments, or damage to the body of the unit.

Driveshafts
(fwd vehicles only)

☐ Rotate each front wheel in turn and inspect the constant velocity joint gaiters for splits or damage. Also check that each driveshaft is straight and undamaged.

Braking system

☐ If possible without dismantling, check brake pad wear and disc condition. Ensure that the friction lining material has not worn excessively, (A) and that the discs are not fractured, pitted, scored or badly worn (B).

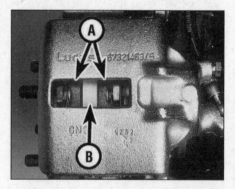

☐ Examine all the rigid brake pipes underneath the vehicle, and the flexible hose(s) at the rear. Look for corrosion, chafing or insecurity of the pipes, and for signs of bulging under pressure, chafing, splits or deterioration of the flexible hoses.

☐ Look for signs of fluid leaks at the brake calipers or on the brake backplates. Repair or renew leaking components.

☐ Slowly spin each wheel, while your assistant depresses and releases the footbrake. Ensure that each brake is operating and does not bind when the pedal is released.

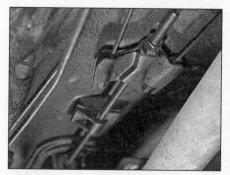

□ Examine the handbrake mechanism, checking for frayed or broken cables, excessive corrosion, or wear or insecurity of the linkage. Check that the mechanism works on each relevant wheel, and releases fully, without binding.

□ It is not possible to test brake efficiency without special equipment, but a road test can be carried out later to check that the vehicle pulls up in a straight line.

Fuel and exhaust systems

□ Inspect the fuel tank (including the filler cap), fuel pipes, hoses and unions. All components must be secure and free from leaks.

□ Examine the exhaust system over its entire length, checking for any damaged, broken or missing mountings, security of the retaining clamps and rust or corrosion.

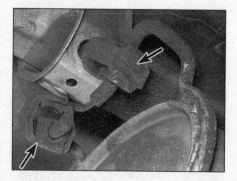

Wheels and tyres

□ Examine the sidewalls and tread area of each tyre in turn. Check for cuts, tears, lumps, bulges, separation of the tread, and exposure of the ply or cord due to wear or damage. Check that the tyre bead is correctly seated on the wheel rim, that the valve is sound and properly seated, and that the wheel is not distorted or damaged.

□ Check that the tyres are of the correct size for the vehicle, that they are of the same size

and type on each axle, and that the pressures are correct.

□ Check the tyre tread depth. The legal minimum at the time of writing is 1.6 mm over at least three-quarters of the tread width. Abnormal tread wear may indicate incorrect front wheel alignment.

Body corrosion

□ Check the condition of the entire vehicle structure for signs of corrosion in load-bearing areas. (These include chassis box sections, side sills, cross-members, pillars, and all suspension, steering, braking system and seat belt mountings and anchorages.) Any corrosion which has seriously reduced the thickness of a load-bearing area is likely to cause the vehicle to fail. In this case professional repairs are likely to be needed.

□ Damage or corrosion which causes sharp or otherwise dangerous edges to be exposed will also cause the vehicle to fail.

4 Checks carried out on YOUR VEHICLE'S EXHAUST EMISSION SYSTEM

Petrol models

□ The engine should be warmed up, and running well (ignition system in good order, air filter element clean, etc).

□ Before testing, run the engine at around 2500 rpm for 20 seconds. Let the engine drop to idle, and watch for smoke from the exhaust. If the idle speed is too high, or if dense blue or black smoke emerges for more than 5 seconds, the vehicle will fail. Typically, blue smoke signifies oil burning (engine wear); black smoke means unburnt fuel (dirty air cleaner element, or other fuel system fault).

□ An exhaust gas analyser for measuring carbon monoxide (CO) and hydrocarbons (HC) is now needed. If one cannot be hired or borrowed, have a local garage perform the check.

CO emissions (mixture)

□ The MOT tester has access to the CO limits for all vehicles. The CO level is measured at idle speed, and at 'fast idle' (2500 to 3000 rpm). The following limits are given as a general guide:

At idle speed – Less than 0.5% CO
At 'fast idle' – Less than 0.3% CO
Lambda reading – 0.97 to 1.03

□ If the CO level is too high, this may point to poor maintenance, a fuel injection system problem, faulty lambda (oxygen) sensor or catalytic converter. Try an injector cleaning treatment, and check the vehicle's ECU for fault codes.

HC emissions

□ The MOT tester has access to HC limits for all vehicles. The HC level is measured at 'fast idle' (2500 to 3000 rpm). The following limits are given as a general guide:

At 'fast idle' – Less then 200 ppm

□ Excessive HC emissions are typically caused by oil being burnt (worn engine), or by a blocked crankcase ventilation system ('breather'). If the engine oil is old and thin, an oil change may help. If the engine is running badly, check the vehicle's ECU for fault codes.

Diesel models

□ The only emission test for diesel engines is measuring exhaust smoke density, using a calibrated smoke meter. The test involves accelerating the engine at least 3 times to its maximum unloaded speed.

Note: *On engines with a timing belt, it is VITAL that the belt is in good condition before the test is carried out.*

□ With the engine warmed up, it is first purged by running at around 2500 rpm for 20 seconds. A governor check is then carried out, by slowly accelerating the engine to its maximum speed. After this, the smoke meter is connected, and the engine is accelerated quickly to maximum speed three times. If the smoke density is less than the limits given below, the vehicle will pass:

Non-turbo vehicles: 2.5m-1
Turbocharged vehicles: 3.0m-1

□ If excess smoke is produced, try fitting a new air cleaner element, or using an injector cleaning treatment. If the engine is running badly, where applicable, check the vehicle's ECU for fault codes. Also check the vehicle's EGR system, where applicable. At high mileages, the injectors may require professional attention.

Engine

- [ ] Engine fails to rotate when attempting to start
- [ ] Engine rotates, but will not start
- [ ] Engine difficult to start when cold
- [ ] Engine difficult to start when hot
- [ ] Starter motor noisy or excessively-rough in engagement
- [ ] Engine starts, but stops immediately
- [ ] Engine idles erratically
- [ ] Engine misfires at idle speed
- [ ] Engine misfires throughout the driving speed range
- [ ] Engine hesitates on acceleration
- [ ] Engine stalls
- [ ] Engine lacks power
- [ ] Engine backfires
- [ ] Oil pressure warning light illuminated with engine running
- [ ] Engine runs-on after switching off
- [ ] Engine noises

Cooling system

- [ ] Overheating
- [ ] Overcooling
- [ ] External coolant leakage
- [ ] Internal coolant leakage
- [ ] Corrosion

Fuel and exhaust systems

- [ ] Excessive fuel consumption
- [ ] Fuel leakage and/or fuel odour
- [ ] Excessive noise or fumes from the exhaust system

Clutch

- [ ] Pedal travels to floor – no pressure or very little resistance
- [ ] Clutch fails to disengage (unable to select gears)
- [ ] Clutch slips (engine speed increases, with no increase in vehicle speed)
- [ ] Judder as clutch is engaged
- [ ] Noise when depressing or releasing clutch pedal

Manual gearbox

- [ ] Noisy in neutral with engine running
- [ ] Noisy in one particular gear
- [ ] Difficulty engaging gears
- [ ] Jumps out of gear
- [ ] Vibration
- [ ] Lubricant leaks

Automatic gearbox

- [ ] Fluid leakage
- [ ] General gear selection problems
- [ ] Transmission will not downshift (kickdown) with accelerator pedal fully depressed
- [ ] Engine will not start in any gear, or starts in gears other than Park or Neutral
- [ ] Transmission slips, shifts roughly, is noisy, or has no drive in forward or reverse gears

Intermediate reduction drive unit

- [ ] Fluid leakage
- [ ] Noisy operation

Final drive

- [ ] Fluid leakage
- [ ] Noisy operation

Driveshafts/Propshaft

- [ ] Vibration when accelerating or decelerating
- [ ] Clicking or knocking noise on turns (at slow speed on full-lock)

Braking system

- [ ] Vehicle pulls to one side under braking
- [ ] Noise (grinding or high-pitched squeal) when brakes applied
- [ ] Excessive brake pedal travel
- [ ] Brake pedal feels spongy when depressed
- [ ] Excessive brake pedal effort required to stop vehicle
- [ ] Judder felt through brake pedal or steering wheel when braking
- [ ] Pedal pulsates when braking hard
- [ ] Brakes binding
- [ ] Rear wheels locking under normal braking

Steering and suspension

- [ ] Vehicle pulls to one side
- [ ] Wheel wobble and vibration
- [ ] Excessive pitching and/or rolling around corners, or during braking
- [ ] Wandering or general instability
- [ ] Excessively-stiff steering
- [ ] Excessive play in steering
- [ ] Lack of power assistance
- [ ] Tyre wear excessive

Electrical system

- [ ] Battery will not hold a charge for more than a few days
- [ ] Ignition/no-charge warning light remains illuminated with engine running
- [ ] Ignition/no-charge warning light fails to come on
- [ ] Lights inoperative
- [ ] Instrument readings inaccurate or erratic
- [ ] Horn inoperative, or unsatisfactory in operation
- [ ] Windscreen/tailgate wipers inoperative, or unsatisfactory in operation
- [ ] Windscreen/tailgate washers inoperative, or unsatisfactory in operation
- [ ] Electric windows inoperative, or unsatisfactory in operation
- [ ] Central locking system inoperative, or unsatisfactory in operation

Introduction

The vehicle owner who does his or her own maintenance according to the recommended service schedules should not have to use this section of the manual very often. Modern component reliability is such that, provided those items subject to wear or deterioration are inspected or renewed at the specified intervals, sudden failure is comparatively rare.

Faults do not usually just happen as a result of sudden failure, but develop over a period of time. Major mechanical failures in particular are usually preceded by characteristic symptoms over hundreds or even thousands of miles. Those components which do occasionally fail without warning are often small and easily carried in the vehicle.

With any fault-finding, the first step is to decide where to begin investigations. Sometimes this is obvious, but on other occasions, a little detective work will be necessary. The owner who makes half a dozen haphazard adjustments or replacements may be successful in curing a fault (or its symptoms), but will be none the wiser if the fault recurs, and ultimately may have spent more time and money than was necessary. A calm and logical approach will be found to be more satisfactory in the long run. Always take into account any warning signs or abnormalities that may have been noticed in the period preceding the fault – power loss, high or low gauge readings, unusual smells, etc – and remember that failure of components such as fuses or spark plugs may only be pointers to some underlying fault.

The pages which follow provide an easy-reference guide to the more common problems which may occur during the operation of the vehicle. These problems and their possible causes are grouped under headings denoting various components or systems, such as Engine, Cooling system, etc. The general Chapter which deals with the problem is also shown in brackets; refer to the relevant part of that Chapter for system-specific information. Whatever the fault, certain basic principles apply. These are as follows:

Verify the fault. This is simply a matter of being sure that you know what the symptoms are before starting work. This is particularly important if you are investigating a fault for someone else, who may not have described it very accurately.

Don't overlook the obvious. For example, if the vehicle won't start, is there fuel in the tank? (Don't take anyone else's word on this particular point, and don't trust the fuel gauge either!) If an electrical fault is indicated, look for loose or broken wires before digging out the test gear.

Cure the disease, not the symptom. Substituting a flat battery with a fully-charged one will get you off the hard shoulder, but if the underlying cause is not attended to, the new battery will go the same way. Similarly, changing oil-fouled spark plugs for a new set will get you moving again, but remember that the reason for the fouling (if it wasn't simply an incorrect grade of plug) will have to be established and corrected.

Don't take anything for granted. Particularly, don't forget that a 'new' component may itself be defective (especially if it's been rattling around in the boot for months), and don't leave components out of a fault diagnosis sequence just because they are new or recently-fitted. When you do finally diagnose a difficult fault, you'll probably realise that all the evidence was there from the start.

Engine

Engine fails to rotate when attempting to start

☐ Battery terminal connections loose or corroded (see *Weekly checks*).
☐ Battery discharged or faulty (Chapter 5A).
☐ Broken, loose or disconnected wiring in the starting circuit (Chapter 5A).
☐ Defective starter solenoid or switch (Chapter 5A).
☐ Defective starter motor (Chapter 5A).
☐ Starter pinion or flywheel ring gear teeth loose or broken (Chapters 2 and 5A).
☐ Engine earth strap broken or disconnected (Chapter 5A).

Engine rotates, but will not start

☐ Fuel tank empty.
☐ Battery discharged (engine rotates slowly) (Chapter 5A).
☐ Battery terminal connections loose or corroded (see *Weekly checks*).
☐ Ignition components damp or damaged – petrol models (Chapters 1A and 5B).
☐ Broken, loose or disconnected wiring in the ignition circuit – petrol models (Chapters 1A and 5B).
☐ Worn, faulty or incorrectly-gapped spark plugs – petrol models (Chapter 1A).
☐ Pre-heating system faulty – diesel models (Chapter 5C).
☐ Fuel injection system faulty (Chapter 4).
☐ Stop solenoid faulty – diesel models (Chapter 4B).
☐ Air in fuel system – diesel models (Chapter 4B).
☐ Major mechanical failure (eg camshaft drive) (Chapter 2).

Engine difficult to start when cold

☐ Battery discharged (Chapter 5A).
☐ Battery terminal connections loose or corroded (see *Weekly checks*).
☐ Worn, faulty or incorrectly-gapped spark plugs – petrol models (Chapter 1A).
☐ Pre-heating system faulty – diesel models (Chapter 5C).
☐ Fuel injection system faulty (Chapter 4).
☐ Other ignition system fault – petrol models (Chapters 1A and 5B).
☐ Low cylinder compressions (Chapter 2).

Engine difficult to start when hot

☐ Air filter element dirty or clogged (Chapter 1).
☐ Fuel injection system faulty – petrol models (Chapter 4A).
☐ Low cylinder compressions (Chapter 2).

Starter motor noisy or excessively-rough in engagement

☐ Starter pinion or flywheel ring gear teeth loose or broken (Chapters 2 and 5A).
☐ Starter motor mounting bolts loose or missing (Chapter 5A).
☐ Starter motor internal components worn or damaged (Chapter 5A).

Engine starts, but stops immediately

☐ Loose or faulty electrical connections in the ignition circuit – petrol models (Chapters 1A and 5B).
☐ Vacuum leak at the throttle body or inlet manifold – petrol models (Chapter 4A).
☐ Blocked injector/fuel injection system fault (Chapter 4).
☐ Immobiliser fault – refer to Land Rover dealer or specialist.

Engine idles erratically

☐ Air filter element clogged (Chapter 1).
☐ Vacuum leak at the throttle body, inlet manifold or associated hoses – petrol models (Chapter 4A).
☐ Worn, faulty or incorrectly-gapped spark plugs – petrol models (Chapter 1A).
☐ Uneven or low cylinder compressions (Chapter 2).
☐ Camshaft lobes worn (Chapter 2).
☐ Timing belt incorrectly fitted (Chapter 2).
☐ Blocked injector/fuel injection system fault – petrol models (Chapter 4A).
☐ Faulty injector(s)/fuel injection system fault – diesel models (Chapter 4B).

Engine misfires at idle speed

☐ Worn, faulty or incorrectly-gapped spark plugs – petrol models (Chapter 1A).
☐ Faulty spark plug HT leads – petrol models (Chapter 1A).
☐ Vacuum leak at the throttle body, inlet manifold or associated hoses – petrol models (Chapter 4A).
☐ Blocked injector/fuel injection system fault – petrol models (Chapter 4A).
☐ Faulty injector(s)/fuel injection system fault – diesel models (Chapter 4B).
☐ Uneven or low cylinder compressions (Chapter 2).

Engine (continued)

Engine misfires throughout the driving speed range

- ☐ Fuel filter choked (Chapter 1).
- ☐ Fuel pump faulty, or delivery pressure low – petrol models (Chapter 4A).
- ☐ Fuel tank vent blocked, or fuel pipes restricted (Chapter 4).
- ☐ Vacuum leak at the throttle body, inlet manifold or associated hoses – petrol models (Chapter 4A).
- ☐ Worn, faulty or incorrectly-gapped spark plugs – petrol models (Chapter 1A).
- ☐ Faulty spark plug HT leads – petrol models (Chapter 1A).
- ☐ Faulty injector(s)/fuel injection system fault – diesel models (Chapter 4B).
- ☐ Faulty ignition coil – petrol models (Chapter 5B).
- ☐ Uneven or low cylinder compressions (Chapter 2).
- ☐ Blocked injector/fuel injection system fault – petrol models (Chapter 4A).

Engine hesitates on acceleration

- ☐ Worn, faulty or incorrectly-gapped spark plugs – petrol models (Chapter 1A).
- ☐ Vacuum leak at the throttle body, inlet manifold or associated hoses – petrol models (Chapter 4A).
- ☐ Blocked injector/fuel injection system fault – petrol models (Chapter 4A).
- ☐ Faulty injector(s)/fuel injection system fault – diesel models (Chapter 4B).

Engine stalls

- ☐ Vacuum leak at the throttle body, inlet manifold or associated hoses – petrol models (Chapter 4A).
- ☐ Fuel filter choked (Chapter 1).
- ☐ Fuel pump faulty, or delivery pressure low – petrol models (Chapter 4A).
- ☐ Fuel tank vent blocked, or fuel pipes restricted (Chapter 4).
- ☐ Blocked injector/fuel injection system fault – petrol models (Chapter 4A).
- ☐ Faulty injector(s)/fuel injection system fault – diesel models (Chapter 4B).

Engine lacks power

- ☐ Timing belt/chain incorrectly fitted or tensioned (Chapter 2).
- ☐ Fuel filter choked (Chapter 1).
- ☐ Fuel pump faulty, or delivery pressure low – petrol models (Chapter 4A).
- ☐ Uneven or low cylinder compressions (Chapter 2).
- ☐ Worn, faulty or incorrectly-gapped spark plugs – petrol models (Chapter 1A).
- ☐ Vacuum leak at the throttle body, inlet manifold or associated hoses – petrol models (Chapter 4A).
- ☐ Blocked injector/fuel injection system fault – petrol models (Chapter 4A).
- ☐ Faulty injector(s)/injection system fault – diesel models (Chapter 4B).
- ☐ Injection pump timing incorrect – L-Series diesel models (Chapter 4B).
- ☐ Brakes binding (Chapters 1 and 9).
- ☐ Clutch slipping (Chapter 6).

Engine backfires

- ☐ Timing belt/chain incorrectly fitted or tensioned (Chapter 2).
- ☐ Vacuum leak at the throttle body, inlet manifold or associated hoses – petrol models (Chapter 4A).
- ☐ Blocked injector/fuel injection system fault (Chapter 4).

Oil pressure warning light illuminated with engine running

- ☐ Low oil level, or incorrect oil grade (see *Weekly checks*).
- ☐ Faulty oil pressure sensor (Chapter 5A).
- ☐ Worn engine bearings and/or oil pump (Chapter 2).
- ☐ High engine operating temperature (Chapter 3).
- ☐ Oil pressure relief valve defective (Chapter 2).
- ☐ Oil pick-up strainer clogged (Chapter 2).

Engine runs-on after switching off

- ☐ Excessive carbon build-up in engine (Chapter 2).
- ☐ High engine operating temperature (Chapter 3).
- ☐ Fuel injection system faulty (Chapter 4).
- ☐ Faulty stop solenoid – L-Series diesel models (Chapter 4B).

Engine noises

Pre-ignition (pinking) or knocking during acceleration or under load

- ☐ Ignition system fault – petrol models (Chapters 1A and 5B).
- ☐ Incorrect grade of spark plug – petrol models (Chapter 1A).
- ☐ Incorrect grade of fuel (Chapter 4).
- ☐ Vacuum leak at the throttle body, inlet manifold or associated hoses – petrol models (Chapter 4A).
- ☐ Excessive carbon build-up in engine (Chapter 2).
- ☐ Blocked injector/fuel injection system fault – petrol models (Chapter 4A).

Whistling or wheezing noises

- ☐ Leaking inlet manifold or throttle body gasket – petrol models (Chapter 4A).
- ☐ Leaking exhaust manifold gasket or pipe-to-manifold joint (Chapter 4).
- ☐ Leaking vacuum hose (Chapters 4 and 9).
- ☐ Blowing cylinder head gasket (Chapter 2).

Tapping or rattling noises

- ☐ Worn valve gear or camshaft (Chapter 2).
- ☐ Ancillary component fault (coolant pump, alternator, etc) (Chapters 3, 5A, etc).

Knocking or thumping noises

- ☐ Worn big-end bearings (regular heavy knocking, perhaps less under load) (Chapter 2).
- ☐ Worn main bearings (rumbling and knocking, perhaps worsening under load) (Chapter 2).
- ☐ Piston slap (most noticeable when cold) (Chapter 2).
- ☐ Ancillary component fault (coolant pump, alternator, etc) (Chapters 3, 5A, etc).

Cooling system

Overheating

☐ Insufficient coolant in system (see *Weekly checks*).
☐ Thermostat faulty (Chapter 3).
☐ Radiator core blocked, or grille restricted (Chapter 3).
☐ Electric cooling fan or thermostatic switch faulty (Chapter 3).
☐ Inaccurate temperature gauge sender unit (Chapter 3).
☐ Airlock in cooling system (Chapter 3).
☐ Expansion tank pressure cap faulty (Chapter 3).

Overcooling

☐ Thermostat faulty (Chapter 3).
☐ Inaccurate temperature gauge sender unit (Chapter 3).

External coolant leakage

☐ Deteriorated or damaged hoses or hose clips (Chapter 1).
☐ Radiator core or heater matrix leaking (Chapter 3).
☐ Pressure cap faulty (Chapter 3).
☐ Coolant pump internal seal leaking (Chapter 3).
☐ Coolant pump-to-housing seal leaking (Chapter 3).
☐ Boiling due to overheating (Chapter 3).
☐ Core plug leaking (Chapter 2).

Internal coolant leakage

☐ Leaking cylinder head gasket (Chapter 2).
☐ Cracked cylinder head or cylinder block (Chapter 2).

Corrosion

☐ Infrequent draining and flushing (Chapter 1).
☐ Incorrect coolant mixture or inappropriate coolant type (see *Weekly checks*).

Fuel and exhaust systems

Excessive fuel consumption

☐ Air filter element dirty or clogged (Chapter 1).
☐ Fuel injection system faulty – petrol models (Chapter 4A).
☐ Faulty injector(s)/fuel injection system faulty – diesel models (Chapter 4B).
☐ Ignition system faulty – petrol models (Chapters 1A and 5B).
☐ Brakes binding (Chapter 9)
☐ Tyres under-inflated (see *Weekly checks*).

Fuel leakage and/or fuel odour

☐ Damaged or corroded fuel tank, pipes or connections (Chapter 4).

Excessive noise or fumes from the exhaust system

☐ Leaking exhaust system or manifold joints (Chapters 1 and 4).
☐ Leaking, corroded or damaged silencers or pipe (Chapters 1 and 4).
☐ Broken mountings causing body or suspension contact (Chapter 1).

Clutch

Pedal travels to floor – no pressure or very little resistance

☐ Faulty master or slave cylinder (Chapter 6).
☐ Faulty hydraulic release system (Chapter 6).
☐ Broken clutch release bearing or arm (Chapter 6).
☐ Broken diaphragm spring in clutch pressure plate (Chapter 6).

Clutch fails to disengage (unable to select gears)

☐ Faulty master or slave cylinder (Chapter 6).
☐ Faulty hydraulic release system (Chapter 6).
☐ Clutch disc sticking on gearbox input shaft splines (Chapter 6).
☐ Clutch disc sticking to flywheel or pressure plate (Chapter 6).
☐ Faulty pressure plate assembly (Chapter 6).
☐ Clutch release mechanism worn or incorrectly assembled (Chapter 6).

Clutch slips (engine speed increases, with no increase in vehicle speed)

☐ Faulty hydraulic release system (Chapter 6).
☐ Clutch disc linings excessively worn (Chapter 6).
☐ Clutch disc linings contaminated with oil or grease (Chapter 6).
☐ Faulty pressure plate or weak diaphragm spring (Chapter 6).

Judder as clutch is engaged

☐ Clutch disc linings contaminated with oil or grease (Chapter 6).
☐ Clutch disc linings excessively worn (Chapter 6).
☐ Faulty or distorted pressure plate or diaphragm spring (Chapter 6).
☐ Worn or loose engine or gearbox mountings (Chapter 2).
☐ Clutch disc hub or gearbox input shaft splines worn (Chapter 6).

Noise when depressing or releasing clutch pedal

☐ Worn clutch release bearing (Chapter 6).
☐ Worn or dry clutch pedal pivot (Chapter 6).
☐ Faulty pressure plate assembly (Chapter 6).
☐ Pressure plate diaphragm spring broken (Chapter 6).
☐ Broken clutch friction plate cushioning springs (Chapter 6).

Manual transmission

Noisy in neutral with engine running

☐ Input shaft bearings worn (noise apparent with clutch pedal released, but not when depressed) (Chapter 7A).*
☐ Clutch release bearing worn (noise apparent with clutch pedal depressed, possibly less when released) (Chapter 6).

Noisy in one particular gear

☐ Worn, damaged or chipped gear teeth (Chapter 7A).*

Difficulty engaging gears

☐ Clutch faulty (Chapter 6).
☐ Worn or damaged gear linkage (Chapter 7A).
☐ Worn synchroniser units (Chapter 7A).*

Jumps out of gear

☐ Worn or damaged gear linkage (Chapter 7A).
☐ Worn synchroniser units (Chapter 7A).*
☐ Worn selector forks (Chapter 7A).*

Vibration

☐ Lack of oil (Chapter 1).
☐ Worn bearings (Chapter 7A).*

Lubricant leaks

☐ Leaking oil seal (Chapter 7A).
☐ Leaking housing joint (Chapter 7A).*
☐ Leaking input shaft oil seal (Chapter 7A).*

*Although the corrective action necessary to remedy the symptoms described is beyond the scope of the home mechanic, the above information should be helpful in isolating the cause of the condition, so that the owner can communicate clearly with a professional mechanic.

Automatic transmission

Note: *Due to the complexity of the automatic transmission, it is difficult for the home mechanic to properly diagnose and service this unit. For problems other than the following, the vehicle should be taken to a dealer service department or automatic transmission specialist. Do not be too hasty in removing the transmission if a fault is suspected, as most of the testing is carried out with the unit still fitted.*

Fluid leakage

☐ Automatic transmission fluid is usually dark in colour. Fluid leaks should not be confused with engine oil, which can easily be blown onto the transmission by airflow.
☐ To determine the source of a leak, first remove all built-up dirt and grime from the transmission housing and surrounding areas using a degreasing agent, or by steam-cleaning. Drive the vehicle at low speed, so airflow will not blow the leak far from its source. Raise and support the vehicle, and determine where the leak is coming from.

General gear selection problems

☐ Chapter 7B deals with checking and adjusting the selector cable on automatic transmissions. The following are common problems which may be caused by a poorly-adjusted cable:
a) Engine starting in gears other than Park or Neutral.
b) Indicator panel indicating a gear other than the one actually being used.

c) Vehicle moves when in Park or Neutral.
d) Poor gear shift quality or erratic gear changes.
☐ Refer to Chapter 7B for the selector cable adjustment procedure.

Transmission will not downshift (kickdown) with accelerator pedal fully depressed

☐ Low transmission fluid level (Chapter 1).
☐ Incorrect selector cable adjustment (Chapter 7B).

Engine will not start in any gear, or starts in gears other than Park or Neutral

☐ Incorrect selector cable adjustment (Chapter 7B).

Transmission slips, shifts roughly, is noisy, or has no drive in forward or reverse gears

☐ There are many probable causes for the above problems, but unless there is a very obvious reason (such as a loose or corroded wiring plug connection on or near the transmission), the car should be taken to a franchise dealer for the fault to be diagnosed. The transmission control unit incorporates a self-diagnosis facility, and any fault codes can quickly be read and interpreted by a dealer or specialist with the proper diagnostic equipment.

Intermediate reduction drive unit

Fluid leakage

☐ Oil seal/O-ring leaking (Chapter 7C).

Noisy operation

☐ Low oil level (Chapter 1).
☐ Worn bearings/differential gears (Chapter 7C).

Final drive

Fluid leakage

☐ Oil seal leaking (Chapter 7C).

Noisy operation

☐ Low oil level (Chapter 8).
☐ Worn bearings/differential gears (Chapter 8).

Driveshafts/Propshaft

Vibration when accelerating or decelerating

☐ Worn inner constant velocity joint (Chapter 8).
☐ Bent or distorted driveshaft (Chapter 8).

Clicking or knocking noise on turns (at slow speed on full-lock)

☐ Worn outer constant velocity joint (Chapter 8).
☐ Lack of constant velocity joint lubricant, possibly due to damaged gaiter (Chapter 8).

Braking system

Note: *Before assuming that a brake problem exists, make sure that the tyres are in good condition and correctly inflated, that the front wheel alignment is correct, and that the vehicle is not loaded with weight in an unequal manner. Apart from checking the condition of all pipe and hose connections, any faults occurring on the anti-lock braking system should be referred to a Land Rover dealer or specialist for diagnosis.*

Vehicle pulls to one side under braking

☐ Worn, defective, damaged or contaminated front or rear brake pads/shoes on one side (Chapters 1 and 9).
☐ Seized or partially-seized front or rear brake caliper/wheel cylinder piston (Chapter 9).
☐ A mixture of brake pad/shoe lining materials fitted between sides (Chapter 9).
☐ Brake caliper or rear brake backplate mounting bolts loose (Chapter 9).
☐ Worn or damaged steering or suspension components (Chapters 1 and 10).

Noise (grinding or high-pitched squeal) when brakes applied

☐ Brake pad/shoe friction lining material worn down to metal backing (Chapters 1 and 9).
☐ Excessive corrosion of brake disc or drum – may be apparent after the vehicle has been standing for some time (Chapters 1 and 9).
☐ Foreign object (stone chipping, etc) trapped between brake disc and shield (Chapters 1 and 9).

Excessive brake pedal travel

☐ Faulty rear drum brake self-adjust mechanism (Chapter 9).
☐ Faulty master cylinder (Chapter 9).
☐ Air in hydraulic system (Chapter 9).
☐ Faulty vacuum servo unit (Chapter 9).
☐ Faulty vacuum pump – diesel models (Chapter 9).

Brake pedal feels spongy when depressed

☐ Air in hydraulic system (Chapter 9).
☐ Deteriorated flexible rubber brake hoses (Chapters 1 and 9).
☐ Master cylinder mountings loose (Chapter 9).
☐ Faulty master cylinder (Chapter 9).

Excessive brake pedal effort required to stop vehicle

☐ Faulty vacuum servo unit (Chapter 9).
☐ Disconnected, damaged or insecure brake servo vacuum hose (Chapters 1 and 9).
☐ Faulty vacuum pump – diesel models (Chapter 9).
☐ Primary or secondary hydraulic circuit failure (Chapter 9).
☐ Seized brake caliper or wheel cylinder piston(s) (Chapter 9).
☐ Brake pads/shoes incorrectly fitted (Chapter 9).
☐ Incorrect grade of brake pads/shoes fitted (Chapter 9).
☐ Brake pads/shoe linings contaminated (Chapter 9).

Judder felt through brake pedal or steering wheel when braking

☐ Excessive run-out or distortion of brake disc(s) or drum(s) (Chapter 9).
☐ Brake pad/shoe linings worn (Chapters 1 and 9).
☐ Brake caliper or rear brake backplate mounting bolts loose (Chapter 9).
☐ Wear in suspension or steering components or mountings (Chapters 1 and 10).

Pedal pulsates when braking hard

☐ Normal feature of ABS (where fitted) – no fault

Brakes binding

☐ Seized brake caliper/wheel cylinder piston(s) (Chapter 9).
☐ Incorrectly-adjusted handbrake mechanism (Chapter 9).
☐ Faulty master cylinder (Chapter 9).

Rear wheels locking under normal braking

☐ Rear brake pad/shoe linings contaminated (Chapters 1 and 9).
☐ Rear brake discs/drums warped (Chapters 1 and 9).

Steering and suspension

Note: *Before diagnosing suspension or steering faults, be sure that the trouble is not due to incorrect tyre pressures, mixtures of tyre types, or binding brakes.*

Vehicle pulls to one side

☐ Defective tyre (see *Weekly checks*).
☐ Excessive wear in suspension or steering components (Chapters 1 and 10).
☐ Incorrect front wheel alignment (Chapter 10).
☐ Accident damage to steering or suspension components (Chapters 1 and 10).

Wheel wobble and vibration

☐ Front roadwheels out of balance (vibration felt mainly through the steering wheel) (Chapter 10).
☐ Rear roadwheels out of balance (vibration felt throughout the vehicle) (Chapter 10).
☐ Roadwheels damaged or distorted (Chapter 10).
☐ Faulty or damaged tyre (see *Weekly checks*).
☐ Worn steering or suspension joints, bushes or components (Chapters 1 and 10).
☐ Wheel nuts loose (Chapter 1 and 10).

Excessive pitching and/or rolling around corners, or during braking

☐ Defective shock absorbers (Chapters 1 and 10).
☐ Broken or weak coil spring and/or suspension component (Chapters 1 and 10).
☐ Worn or damaged anti-roll bar or mountings (Chapter 10).

Wandering or general instability

☐ Incorrect front wheel alignment (Chapter 10).
☐ Worn steering or suspension joints, bushes or components (Chapters 1 and 10).
☐ Roadwheels out of balance (Chapter 10).
☐ Faulty or damaged tyre (see *Weekly checks*).
☐ Wheel nuts loose (Chapter 10).
☐ Defective shock absorbers (Chapters 1 and 10).

Excessively-stiff steering

☐ Seized track rod end balljoint or suspension balljoint (Chapters 1 and 10).
☐ Broken or incorrectly adjusted auxiliary drivebelt (Chapter 1).
☐ Incorrect front wheel alignment (Chapter 10).
☐ Steering gear damaged (Chapter 10).

Steering and suspension (continued)

Excessive play in steering

- ☐ Worn steering column universal joint(s) (Chapter 10).
- ☐ Worn steering track rod end balljoints (Chapters 1 and 10).
- ☐ Worn steering gear (Chapter 10).
- ☐ Worn steering or suspension joints, bushes or components (Chapters 1 and 10).

Lack of power assistance

- ☐ Broken or incorrectly-adjusted auxiliary drivebelt (Chapter 1).
- ☐ Incorrect power steering fluid level (see *Weekly checks*).
- ☐ Restriction in power steering fluid hoses (Chapter 10).
- ☐ Faulty power steering pump (Chapter 10).
- ☐ Faulty steering gear (Chapter 10).

Tyre wear excessive

Tyres worn on inside or outside edges

- ☐ Tyres under-inflated (wear on both edges) (see *Weekly checks*).
- ☐ Incorrect camber or castor angles (wear on one edge only) (Chapter 10).

- ☐ Worn steering or suspension joints, bushes or components (Chapters 1 and 10).
- ☐ Excessively-hard cornering.
- ☐ Accident damage.

Tyre treads exhibit feathered edges

- ☐ Incorrect toe setting (Chapter 10).

Tyres worn in centre of tread

- ☐ Tyres over-inflated (see *Weekly checks*).

Tyres worn on inside and outside edges

- ☐ Tyres under-inflated (see *Weekly checks*).
- ☐ Worn shock absorbers (Chapter 10).

Tyres worn unevenly

- ☐ Tyres/wheels out of balance (see *Weekly checks*).
- ☐ Excessive wheel or tyre run-out (Chapter 10).
- ☐ Worn shock absorbers (Chapters 1 and 10).
- ☐ Faulty tyre (see *Weekly checks*).

Electrical system

Note: *For problems associated with the starting system, refer to the faults listed under 'Engine' earlier in this Section.*

Battery will not hold a charge for more than a few days

- ☐ Battery defective internally (Chapter 5A).
- ☐ Battery electrolyte level low – where applicable (Chapter 5A).
- ☐ Battery terminal connections loose or corroded (see *Weekly checks*).
- ☐ Auxiliary drivebelt worn – or incorrectly adjusted, where applicable (Chapter 1).
- ☐ Alternator not charging at correct output (Chapter 5A).
- ☐ Alternator or voltage regulator faulty (Chapter 5A).
- ☐ Short-circuit causing continual battery drain (Chapters 5 and 12).

Ignition/no-charge warning light remains illuminated with engine running

- ☐ Auxiliary drivebelt broken, worn, or incorrectly adjusted (Chapter 1).
- ☐ Internal fault in alternator or voltage regulator (Chapter 5A).
- ☐ Broken, disconnected, or loose wiring in charging circuit (Chapter 5A).

Ignition/no-charge warning light fails to come on

- ☐ Warning light bulb blown (Chapter 12).
- ☐ Broken, disconnected, or loose wiring in warning light circuit (Chapter 12).
- ☐ Alternator faulty (Chapter 5A).

Lights inoperative

- ☐ Bulb blown (Chapter 12).
- ☐ Corrosion of bulb or bulbholder contacts (Chapter 12).
- ☐ Blown fuse (Chapter 12).
- ☐ Faulty relay (Chapter 12).
- ☐ Broken, loose, or disconnected wiring (Chapter 12).
- ☐ Faulty switch (Chapter 12).

Instrument readings inaccurate or erratic

Instrument readings increase with engine speed

- ☐ Faulty voltage regulator (Chapter 12).

Fuel or temperature gauges give no reading

- ☐ Faulty gauge sender unit (Chapters 3 and 4).
- ☐ Wiring open-circuit (Chapter 12).
- ☐ Faulty gauge (Chapter 12).

Fuel or temperature gauges give continuous maximum reading

- ☐ Faulty gauge sender unit (Chapters 3 and 4).
- ☐ Wiring short-circuit (Chapter 12).
- ☐ Faulty gauge (Chapter 12).

Horn inoperative, or unsatisfactory in operation

Horn operates all the time

- ☐ Horn contacts permanently bridged or horn push stuck down (Chapter 12).

Horn fails to operate

- ☐ Blown fuse (Chapter 12).
- ☐ Cable or cable connections loose, broken or disconnected (Chapter 12).
- ☐ Faulty horn (Chapter 12).

Horn emits intermittent or unsatisfactory sound

- ☐ Cable connections loose (Chapter 12).
- ☐ Horn mountings loose (Chapter 12).
- ☐ Faulty horn (Chapter 12).

Electrical system (continued)

Windscreen/tailgate wipers inoperative, or unsatisfactory in operation

Wipers fail to operate, or operate very slowly

☐ Wiper blades stuck to screen, or linkage seized or binding (see *Weekly checks* and Chapter 12).
☐ Blown fuse (Chapter 12).
☐ Cable or cable connections loose, broken or disconnected (Chapter 12).
☐ Faulty relay (Chapter 12).
☐ Faulty wiper motor (Chapter 12).

Wiper blades sweep over too large or too small an area of the glass

☐ Wiper arms incorrectly positioned on spindles (Chapter 12).
☐ Excessive wear of wiper linkage (Chapter 12).
☐ Wiper motor or linkage mountings loose or insecure (Chapter 12).

Wiper blades fail to clean the glass effectively

☐ Wiper blade rubbers worn or perished (see *Weekly checks*).
☐ Wiper arm tension springs broken, or arm pivots seized (Chapter 12).
☐ Insufficient windscreen washer additive to adequately remove road film (see *Weekly checks*).

Windscreen/tailgate washers inoperative, or unsatisfactory in operation

One or more washer jets inoperative

☐ Blocked washer jet (Chapter 12).
☐ Disconnected, kinked or restricted fluid hose (Chapter 12).
☐ Insufficient fluid in washer reservoir (see *Weekly checks*).

Washer pump fails to operate

☐ Broken or disconnected wiring or connections (Chapter 12).
☐ Blown fuse (Chapter 12).
☐ Faulty washer switch (Chapter 12).
☐ Faulty washer pump (Chapter 12).

Washer pump runs for some time before fluid is emitted from jets

☐ Faulty one-way valve in fluid supply hose (Chapter 12).

Electric windows inoperative, or unsatisfactory in operation

Window glass will only move in one direction

☐ Faulty switch (Chapter 12).

Window glass slow to move

☐ Regulator seized or damaged, or in need of lubrication (Chapter 11).
☐ Door internal components or trim fouling regulator (Chapter 11).
☐ Faulty motor (Chapter 11).

Window glass fails to move

☐ Blown fuse (Chapter 12).
☐ Faulty relay (Chapter 12).
☐ Broken or disconnected wiring or connections (Chapter 12).
☐ Faulty motor (Chapter 12).

Central locking system inoperative, or unsatisfactory in operation

Complete system failure

☐ Blown fuse (Chapter 12).
☐ Faulty relay (Chapter 12).
☐ Broken or disconnected wiring or connections (Chapter 12).
☐ Faulty motor (Chapter 11).

Latch locks but will not unlock, or unlocks but will not lock

☐ Faulty switch (Chapter 12).
☐ Broken or disconnected latch operating rods or levers (Chapter 11).
☐ Faulty relay (Chapter 12).
☐ Faulty motor (Chapter 11).

One solenoid/motor fails to operate

☐ Broken or disconnected wiring or connections (Chapter 12).
☐ Faulty motor (Chapter 11).
☐ Broken, binding or disconnected lock operating rods or levers (Chapter 11).
☐ Fault in door lock (Chapter 11).

A

ABS (Anti-lock brake system) A system, usually electronically controlled, that senses incipient wheel lockup during braking and relieves hydraulic pressure at wheels that are about to skid.

Air bag An inflatable bag hidden in the steering wheel (driver's side) or the dash or glovebox (passenger side). In a head-on collision, the bags inflate, preventing the driver and front passenger from being thrown forward into the steering wheel or windscreen.

Air cleaner A metal or plastic housing, containing a filter element, which removes dust and dirt from the air being drawn into the engine.

Air filter element The actual filter in an air cleaner system, usually manufactured from pleated paper and requiring renewal at regular intervals.

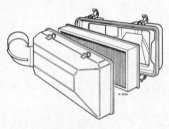

Air filter

Allen key A hexagonal wrench which fits into a recessed hexagonal hole.

Alligator clip A long-nosed spring-loaded metal clip with meshing teeth. Used to make temporary electrical connections.

Alternator A component in the electrical system which converts mechanical energy from a drivebelt into electrical energy to charge the battery and to operate the starting system, ignition system and electrical accessories.

Ampere (amp) A unit of measurement for the flow of electric current. One amp is the amount of current produced by one volt acting through a resistance of one ohm.

Anaerobic sealer A substance used to prevent bolts and screws from loosening. Anaerobic means that it does not require oxygen for activation. The Loctite brand is widely used.

Antifreeze A substance (usually ethylene glycol) mixed with water, and added to a vehicle's cooling system, to prevent freezing of the coolant in winter. Antifreeze also contains chemicals to inhibit corrosion and the formation of rust and other deposits that would tend to clog the radiator and coolant passages and reduce cooling efficiency.

Anti-seize compound A coating that reduces the risk of seizing on fasteners that are subjected to high temperatures, such as exhaust manifold bolts and nuts.

Asbestos A natural fibrous mineral with great heat resistance, commonly used in the composition of brake friction materials.

Asbestos is a health hazard and the dust created by brake systems should never be inhaled or ingested.

Axle A shaft on which a wheel revolves, or which revolves with a wheel. Also, a solid beam that connects the two wheels at one end of the vehicle. An axle which also transmits power to the wheels is known as a live axle.

Axleshaft A single rotating shaft, on either side of the differential, which delivers power from the final drive assembly to the drive wheels. Also called a driveshaft or a halfshaft.

B

Ball bearing An anti-friction bearing consisting of a hardened inner and outer race with hardened steel balls between two races.

Bearing The curved surface on a shaft or in a bore, or the part assembled into either, that permits relative motion between them with minimum wear and friction.

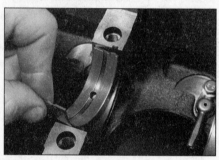

Bearing

Big-end bearing The bearing in the end of the connecting rod that's attached to the crankshaft.

Bleed nipple A valve on a brake wheel cylinder, caliper or other hydraulic component that is opened to purge the hydraulic system of air. Also called a bleed screw.

Brake bleeding Procedure for removing air from lines of a hydraulic brake system.

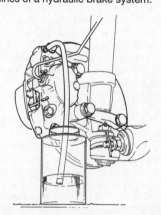

Brake bleeding

Brake disc The component of a disc brake that rotates with the wheels.

Brake drum The component of a drum brake that rotates with the wheels.

Brake linings The friction material which contacts the brake disc or drum to retard the vehicle's speed. The linings are bonded or riveted to the brake pads or shoes.

Brake pads The replaceable friction pads that pinch the brake disc when the brakes are applied. Brake pads consist of a friction material bonded or riveted to a rigid backing plate.

Brake shoe The crescent-shaped carrier to which the brake linings are mounted and which forces the lining against the rotating drum during braking.

Braking systems For more information on braking systems, consult the *Haynes Automotive Brake Manual*.

Breaker bar A long socket wrench handle providing greater leverage.

Bulkhead The insulated partition between the engine and the passenger compartment.

C

Caliper The non-rotating part of a disc-brake assembly that straddles the disc and carries the brake pads. The caliper also contains the hydraulic components that cause the pads to pinch the disc when the brakes are applied. A caliper is also a measuring tool that can be set to measure inside or outside dimensions of an object.

Camshaft A rotating shaft on which a series of cam lobes operate the valve mechanisms. The camshaft may be driven by gears, by sprockets and chain or by sprockets and a belt.

Canister A container in an evaporative emission control system; contains activated charcoal granules to trap vapours from the fuel system.

Canister

Carburettor A device which mixes fuel with air in the proper proportions to provide a desired power output from a spark ignition internal combustion engine.

Castellated Resembling the parapets along the top of a castle wall. For example, a castellated balljoint stud nut.

Castor In wheel alignment, the backward or forward tilt of the steering axis. Castor is positive when the steering axis is inclined rearward at the top.

Catalytic converter A silencer-like device in the exhaust system which converts certain pollutants in the exhaust gases into less harmful substances.

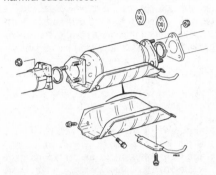

Catalytic converter

Circlip A ring-shaped clip used to prevent endwise movement of cylindrical parts and shafts. An internal circlip is installed in a groove in a housing; an external circlip fits into a groove on the outside of a cylindrical piece such as a shaft.

Clearance The amount of space between two parts. For example, between a piston and a cylinder, between a bearing and a journal, etc.

Coil spring A spiral of elastic steel found in various sizes throughout a vehicle, for example as a springing medium in the suspension and in the valve train.

Compression Reduction in volume, and increase in pressure and temperature, of a gas, caused by squeezing it into a smaller space.

Compression ratio The relationship between cylinder volume when the piston is at top dead centre and cylinder volume when the piston is at bottom dead centre.

Constant velocity (CV) joint A type of universal joint that cancels out vibrations caused by driving power being transmitted through an angle.

Core plug A disc or cup-shaped metal device inserted in a hole in a casting through which core was removed when the casting was formed. Also known as a freeze plug or expansion plug.

Crankcase The lower part of the engine block in which the crankshaft rotates.

Crankshaft The main rotating member, or shaft, running the length of the crankcase, with offset "throws" to which the connecting rods are attached.

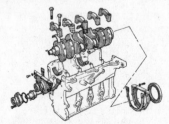

Crankshaft assembly

Crocodile clip See Alligator clip

D

Diagnostic code Code numbers obtained by accessing the diagnostic mode of an engine management computer. This code can be used to determine the area in the system where a malfunction may be located.

Disc brake A brake design incorporating a rotating disc onto which brake pads are squeezed. The resulting friction converts the energy of a moving vehicle into heat.

Double-overhead cam (DOHC) An engine that uses two overhead camshafts, usually one for the intake valves and one for the exhaust valves.

Drivebelt(s) The belt(s) used to drive accessories such as the alternator, water pump, power steering pump, air conditioning compressor, etc. off the crankshaft pulley.

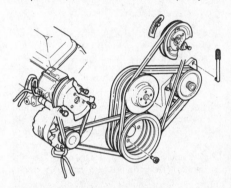

Accessory drivebelts

Driveshaft Any shaft used to transmit motion. Commonly used when referring to the axleshafts on a front wheel drive vehicle.

Drum brake A type of brake using a drum-shaped metal cylinder attached to the inner surface of the wheel. When the brake pedal is pressed, curved brake shoes with friction linings press against the inside of the drum to slow or stop the vehicle.

E

EGR valve A valve used to introduce exhaust gases into the intake air stream.

Electronic control unit (ECU) A computer which controls (for instance) ignition and fuel injection systems, or an anti-lock braking system. For more information refer to the *Haynes Automotive Electrical and Electronic Systems Manual*.

Electronic Fuel Injection (EFI) A computer controlled fuel system that distributes fuel through an injector located in each intake port of the engine.

Emergency brake A braking system, independent of the main hydraulic system, that can be used to slow or stop the vehicle if the primary brakes fail, or to hold the vehicle stationary even though the brake pedal isn't depressed. It usually consists of a hand lever that actuates either front or rear brakes mechanically through a series of cables and linkages. Also known as a handbrake or parking brake.

Endfloat The amount of lengthwise movement between two parts. As applied to a crankshaft, the distance that the crankshaft can move forward and back in the cylinder block.

Engine management system (EMS) A computer controlled system which manages the fuel injection and the ignition systems in an integrated fashion.

Exhaust manifold A part with several passages through which exhaust gases leave the engine combustion chambers and enter the exhaust pipe.

F

Fan clutch A viscous (fluid) drive coupling device which permits variable engine fan speeds in relation to engine speeds.

Feeler blade A thin strip or blade of hardened steel, ground to an exact thickness, used to check or measure clearances between parts.

Feeler blade

Firing order The order in which the engine cylinders fire, or deliver their power strokes, beginning with the number one cylinder.

Flywheel A heavy spinning wheel in which energy is absorbed and stored by means of momentum. On cars, the flywheel is attached to the crankshaft to smooth out firing impulses.

Free play The amount of travel before any action takes place. The "looseness" in a linkage, or an assembly of parts, between the initial application of force and actual movement. For example, the distance the brake pedal moves before the pistons in the master cylinder are actuated.

Fuse An electrical device which protects a circuit against accidental overload. The typical fuse contains a soft piece of metal which is calibrated to melt at a predetermined current flow (expressed as amps) and break the circuit.

Fusible link A circuit protection device consisting of a conductor surrounded by heat-resistant insulation. The conductor is smaller than the wire it protects, so it acts as the weakest link in the circuit. Unlike a blown fuse, a failed fusible link must frequently be cut from the wire for replacement.

G

Gap The distance the spark must travel in jumping from the centre electrode to the side electrode in a spark plug. Also refers to the spacing between the points in a contact breaker assembly in a conventional points-type ignition, or to the distance between the reluctor or rotor and the pickup coil in an electronic ignition.

Adjusting spark plug gap

Gasket Any thin, soft material - usually cork, cardboard, asbestos or soft metal - installed between two metal surfaces to ensure a good seal. For instance, the cylinder head gasket seals the joint between the block and the cylinder head.

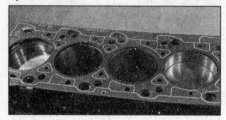
Gasket

Gauge An instrument panel display used to monitor engine conditions. A gauge with a movable pointer on a dial or a fixed scale is an analogue gauge. A gauge with a numerical readout is called a digital gauge.

H

Halfshaft A rotating shaft that transmits power from the final drive unit to a drive wheel, usually when referring to a live rear axle.

Harmonic balancer A device designed to reduce torsion or twisting vibration in the crankshaft. May be incorporated in the crankshaft pulley. Also known as a vibration damper.

Hone An abrasive tool for correcting small irregularities or differences in diameter in an engine cylinder, brake cylinder, etc.

Hydraulic tappet A tappet that utilises hydraulic pressure from the engine's lubrication system to maintain zero clearance (constant contact with both camshaft and valve stem). Automatically adjusts to variation in valve stem length. Hydraulic tappets also reduce valve noise.

I

Ignition timing The moment at which the spark plug fires, usually expressed in the number of crankshaft degrees before the piston reaches the top of its stroke.

Inlet manifold A tube or housing with passages through which flows the air-fuel mixture (carburettor vehicles and vehicles with throttle body injection) or air only (port fuel-injected vehicles) to the port openings in the cylinder head.

J

Jump start Starting the engine of a vehicle with a discharged or weak battery by attaching jump leads from the weak battery to a charged or helper battery.

L

Load Sensing Proportioning Valve (LSPV) A brake hydraulic system control valve that works like a proportioning valve, but also takes into consideration the amount of weight carried by the rear axle.

Locknut A nut used to lock an adjustment nut, or other threaded component, in place. For example, a locknut is employed to keep the adjusting nut on the rocker arm in position.

Lockwasher A form of washer designed to prevent an attaching nut from working loose.

M

MacPherson strut A type of front suspension system devised by Earle MacPherson at Ford of England. In its original form, a simple lateral link with the anti-roll bar creates the lower control arm. A long strut - an integral coil spring and shock absorber - is mounted between the body and the steering knuckle. Many modern so-called MacPherson strut systems use a conventional lower A-arm and don't rely on the anti-roll bar for location.

Multimeter An electrical test instrument with the capability to measure voltage, current and resistance.

N

NOx Oxides of Nitrogen. A common toxic pollutant emitted by petrol and diesel engines at higher temperatures.

O

Ohm The unit of electrical resistance. One volt applied to a resistance of one ohm will produce a current of one amp.

Ohmmeter An instrument for measuring electrical resistance.

O-ring A type of sealing ring made of a special rubber-like material; in use, the O-ring is compressed into a groove to provide the sealing action.

Overhead cam (ohc) engine An engine with the camshaft(s) located on top of the cylinder head(s).

Overhead valve (ohv) engine An engine with the valves located in the cylinder head, but with the camshaft located in the engine block.

Oxygen sensor A device installed in the engine exhaust manifold, which senses the oxygen content in the exhaust and converts this information into an electric current. Also called a Lambda sensor.

P

Phillips screw A type of screw head having a cross instead of a slot for a corresponding type of screwdriver.

Plastigage A thin strip of plastic thread, available in different sizes, used for measuring clearances. For example, a strip of Plastigage is laid across a bearing journal. The parts are assembled and dismantled; the width of the crushed strip indicates the clearance between journal and bearing.

Plastigage

Propeller shaft The long hollow tube with universal joints at both ends that carries power from the transmission to the differential on front-engined rear wheel drive vehicles.

Proportioning valve A hydraulic control valve which limits the amount of pressure to the rear brakes during panic stops to prevent wheel lock-up.

R

Rack-and-pinion steering A steering system with a pinion gear on the end of the steering shaft that mates with a rack (think of a geared wheel opened up and laid flat). When the steering wheel is turned, the pinion turns, moving the rack to the left or right. This movement is transmitted through the track rods to the steering arms at the wheels.

Radiator A liquid-to-air heat transfer device designed to reduce the temperature of the coolant in an internal combustion engine cooling system.

Refrigerant Any substance used as a heat transfer agent in an air-conditioning system. R-12 has been the principle refrigerant for many years; recently, however, manufacturers have begun using R-134a, a non-CFC substance that is considered less harmful to the ozone in the upper atmosphere.

Rocker arm A lever arm that rocks on a shaft or pivots on a stud. In an overhead valve engine, the rocker arm converts the upward movement of the pushrod into a downward movement to open a valve.

Rotor In a distributor, the rotating device inside the cap that connects the centre electrode and the outer terminals as it turns, distributing the high voltage from the coil secondary winding to the proper spark plug. Also, that part of an alternator which rotates inside the stator. Also, the rotating assembly of a turbocharger, including the compressor wheel, shaft and turbine wheel.

Runout The amount of wobble (in-and-out movement) of a gear or wheel as it's rotated. The amount a shaft rotates "out-of-true." The out-of-round condition of a rotating part.

S

Sealant A liquid or paste used to prevent leakage at a joint. Sometimes used in conjunction with a gasket.

Sealed beam lamp An older headlight design which integrates the reflector, lens and filaments into a hermetically-sealed one-piece unit. When a filament burns out or the lens cracks, the entire unit is simply replaced.

Serpentine drivebelt A single, long, wide accessory drivebelt that's used on some newer vehicles to drive all the accessories, instead of a series of smaller, shorter belts. Serpentine drivebelts are usually tensioned by an automatic tensioner.

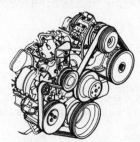

Serpentine drivebelt

Shim Thin spacer, commonly used to adjust the clearance or relative positions between two parts. For example, shims inserted into or under bucket tappets control valve clearances. Clearance is adjusted by changing the thickness of the shim.

Slide hammer A special puller that screws into or hooks onto a component such as a shaft or bearing; a heavy sliding handle on the shaft bottoms against the end of the shaft to knock the component free.

Sprocket A tooth or projection on the periphery of a wheel, shaped to engage with a chain or drivebelt. Commonly used to refer to the sprocket wheel itself.

Starter inhibitor switch On vehicles with an automatic transmission, a switch that prevents starting if the vehicle is not in Neutral or Park.

Strut See MacPherson strut.

T

Tappet A cylindrical component which transmits motion from the cam to the valve stem, either directly or via a pushrod and rocker arm. Also called a cam follower.

Thermostat A heat-controlled valve that regulates the flow of coolant between the cylinder block and the radiator, so maintaining optimum engine operating temperature. A thermostat is also used in some air cleaners in which the temperature is regulated.

Thrust bearing The bearing in the clutch assembly that is moved in to the release levers by clutch pedal action to disengage the clutch. Also referred to as a release bearing.

Timing belt A toothed belt which drives the camshaft. Serious engine damage may result if it breaks in service.

Timing chain A chain which drives the camshaft.

Toe-in The amount the front wheels are closer together at the front than at the rear. On rear wheel drive vehicles, a slight amount of toe-in is usually specified to keep the front wheels running parallel on the road by offsetting other forces that tend to spread the wheels apart.

Toe-out The amount the front wheels are closer together at the rear than at the front. On front wheel drive vehicles, a slight amount of toe-out is usually specified.

Tools For full information on choosing and using tools, refer to the *Haynes Automotive Tools Manual*.

Tracer A stripe of a second colour applied to a wire insulator to distinguish that wire from another one with the same colour insulator.

Tune-up A process of accurate and careful adjustments and parts replacement to obtain the best possible engine performance.

Turbocharger A centrifugal device, driven by exhaust gases, that pressurises the intake air. Normally used to increase the power output from a given engine displacement, but can also be used primarily to reduce exhaust emissions (as on VW's "Umwelt" Diesel engine).

U

Universal joint or U-joint A double-pivoted connection for transmitting power from a driving to a driven shaft through an angle. A U-joint consists of two Y-shaped yokes and a cross-shaped member called the spider.

V

Valve A device through which the flow of liquid, gas, vacuum, or loose material in bulk may be started, stopped, or regulated by a movable part that opens, shuts, or partially obstructs one or more ports or passageways. A valve is also the movable part of such a device.

Valve clearance The clearance between the valve tip (the end of the valve stem) and the rocker arm or tappet. The valve clearance is measured when the valve is closed.

Vernier caliper A precision measuring instrument that measures inside and outside dimensions. Not quite as accurate as a micrometer, but more convenient.

Viscosity The thickness of a liquid or its resistance to flow.

Volt A unit for expressing electrical "pressure" in a circuit. One volt that will produce a current of one ampere through a resistance of one ohm.

W

Welding Various processes used to join metal items by heating the areas to be joined to a molten state and fusing them together. For more information refer to the *Haynes Automotive Welding Manual*.

Wiring diagram A drawing portraying the components and wires in a vehicle's electrical system, using standardised symbols. For more information refer to the *Haynes Automotive Electrical and Electronic Systems Manual*.

Note: *References throughout this index are in the form "***Chapter number***" • "***Page number***". So, for example, 2C•15 refers to page 15 of Chapter 2C.*

Note: *References throughout this index are in the form* "Chapter number" • "Page number". *So, for example, 2C•15 refers to page 15 of Chapter 2C.*

Note: *References throughout this index are in the form* **"Chapter number"** • **"Page number"**. *So, for example, 2C•15 refers to page 15 of Chapter 2C.*

Note: *References throughout this index are in the form* "**Chapter number**" • "**Page number**". *So, for example, 2C•15 refers to page 15 of Chapter 2C.*

Preserving Our Motoring Heritage

< The Model J Duesenberg Derham Tourster. Only eight of these magnificent cars were ever built – this is the only example to be found outside the United States of America

Almost every car you've ever loved, loathed or desired is gathered under one roof at the Haynes Motor Museum. Over 300 immaculately presented cars and motorbikes represent every aspect of our motoring heritage, from elegant reminders of bygone days, such as the superb Model J Duesenberg to curiosities like the bug-eyed BMW Isetta. There are also many old friends and flames. Perhaps you remember the 1959 Ford Popular that you did your courting in? The magnificent 'Red Collection' is a spectacle of classic sports cars including AC, Alfa Romeo, Austin Healey, Ferrari, Lamborghini, Maserati, MG, Riley, Porsche and Triumph.

A Perfect Day Out

Each and every vehicle at the Haynes Motor Museum has played its part in the history and culture of Motoring. Today, they make a wonderful spectacle and a great day out for all the family. Bring the kids, bring Mum and Dad, but above all bring your camera to capture those golden memories for ever. You will also find an impressive array of motoring memorabilia, a comfortable 70 seat video cinema and one of the most extensive transport book shops in Britain. The Pit Stop Cafe serves everything from a cup of tea to wholesome, home-made meals or, if you prefer, you can enjoy the large picnic area nestled in the beautiful rural surroundings of Somerset.

> John Haynes O.B.E., Founder and Chairman of the museum at the wheel of a Haynes Light 12.

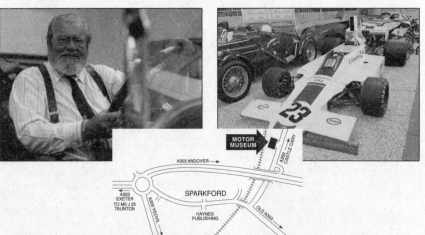

< Graham Hill's Lola Cosworth Formula 1 car next to a 1934 Riley Sports.

The Museum is situated on the A359 Yeovil to Frome road at Sparkford, just off the A303 in Somerset. It is about 40 miles south of Bristol, and 25 minutes drive from the M5 intersection at Taunton.

Open 9.30am - 5.30pm (10.00am - 4.00pm Winter) 7 days a week, *except Christmas Day, Boxing Day and New Years Day*

Special rates available for schools, coach parties and outings Charitable Trust No. 292048